Art of the Royal Court

Treasures in Pietre Dure from the Palaces of Europe

Wolfram Koeppe and Annamaria Giusti

With contributions by Cristina Acidini, Rudolf Distelberger, Detlef Heikamp, Jutta Kappel, Florian Knothe, and Ian Wardropper

EDITED BY WOLFRAM KOEPPE

The Metropolitan Museum of Art, New York

Yale University Press, New Haven and London

This volume has been published in conjunction with the exhibition "Art of the Royal Court: Treasures in Pietre Dure from the Palaces of Europe," held at The Metropolitan Museum of Art, New York, July 1–September 21, 2008.

The exhibition is based on an idea put forward by Annamaria Giusti and was realized with the collaboration of the Opificio delle Pietre Dure, Florence.

The exhibition is made possible by Mercedes and Sid Bass and Frank Richardson and the Honorable Kimba Wood.

Additional support is generously provided by Mr. and Mrs. J. Tomilson Hill III.

The catalogue is made possible by The Andrew W. Mellon Foundation and the Friends of European Sculpture and Decorative Arts.

Additional support is provided by the Mary C. and James W. Fosburgh Publications Fund.

Published by The Metropolitan Museum of Art, New York
John P. O'Neill, Publisher and Editor in Chief
Ruth Lurie Kozodoy, with Ellyn Childs Allison, Carol Fuerstein, and Dale Tucker, Editors
Jayne Kuchna, Bibliographic Editor
Bruce Campbell, Designer
Peter Antony, Douglas J. Malicki, and Christopher Zichello, Production Managers
Robert Weisberg, Assistant Managing Editor
Jane S. Tai, Image Research and Permissions

Texts by Cristina Acidini and Annamaria Giusti translated from the Italian by A. Lawrence Jenkens and Stephen Sartarelli; texts by Rudolf Distelberger and Jutta Kappel translated from the German by Russell M. Stockman
Italian coordination by Linda Carioni
New photography by Mark Morosse, Bruce Schwarz, and Peter Zeray, The Photograph Studio, The Metropolitan Museum of Art

Typeset in Monotype Dante Std; displays in Lanston Type Co. Deepdene OSF and Adobe Trajan Pro
Printed on Cartiere Burgo 130 gsm R-400
Separations by Professional Graphics, Inc., Rockford, Illinois
Printed by Brizzolis Arte en Gráficas, Madrid
Bound by Encuadernación Ramos, S.A., Madrid
Printing and binding coordinated by Ediciones El Viso, S.A., Madrid

Jacket: *Allegory of Sculpture* (detail), design by Giuseppe Zocchi, ca. 1775–80 (cat. no. 110)
Frontispiece: Tabletop depicting flowers (detail), design by Jacopo Ligozzi, 1614–21 (cat. no. 38)

Cataloging-in-Publication data are available from the Library of Congress.
ISBN 978-1-58839-288-6 (hc: The Metropolitan Museum of Art)
ISBN 978-0-300-13672-2 (hc: Yale University Press)

Contents

CATALOGUE

Director's Foreword

Richly colored, imaginatively conceived, and immensely varied, the astonishingly beautiful and exuberant works of art in this exhibition will come as a revelation to many visitors. In this medium, pietre dure—that is, hardstones, or semiprecious stones—are meticulously cut and fitted to create sophisticated decorative patterns, narrative paintings in stone, or extravagantly fashioned luxury objects. Reviving and expanding ancient Greek and Roman techniques, artists of the Italian Renaissance developed pietre dure into an alluring art form. In Florence, the Medici passion for collecting works in hardstone was passed on through generations of the mighty dynasty. Captivated by the extraordinary works when they saw them, royal patrons farther north encouraged Italian artisans to migrate to Prague, Paris, and Spain, and their practice gradually spread through Europe. In the eighteenth and nineteenth centuries lapidary work even became an obsession of the aristocracy in faraway Saint Petersburg.

In an age when science was pursued with excitement and the natural world was being explored, works in pietre dure took on new meaning. Made of natural substances artfully enhanced through human creativity and technical skill, they represented the harmonious interplay of art and nature. Nature as an eternally present force is symbolically embodied, for example, in the lasting forms of flowers that never wilt or fade, thanks to the vivid colors of cut stones. Objects in pietre dure, either alone or in combination with marbles, finely wrought precious metals, or exotic woods, were powerful symbols of wealth and political legitimacy that underlined the authority to rule of the individuals who commissioned them. One of the most illustrious admirers of pietre dure was Holy Roman Emperor Rudolf II; a contemporary viewer of his collection wondered at the way "such small bodies seem to have encapsulated the beauty of the whole world." Several works from Rudolf's legendary *Kunstkammer* are included in this exhibition. Pietre dure's appeal, both visual and tactile, and its sumptuous nature transformed even utilitarian objects into works of intriguing artistic significance. They became status symbols par excellence at the royal and aristocratic courts of Europe. Symbolic meanings and special powers were ascribed to many hardstones that were of exotic origin and shrouded in mystery.

This exhibition, the most comprehensive presentation ever dedicated to the subject of pietre dure, offers an overview of hardstone carved objects and the planar hardstone assemblages known as mosaics. Among these remarkable works are monumental furnishings such as tables and cabinets; vessels made by virtuoso stonecutters and goldsmiths; precious, lavishly decorated small boxes and *objets de vertu*; and breathtaking, forward-looking landscapes composed of subtly variegated stones. Created for the European princely courts, these magnificent works of art were cherished in dynastic treasuries, which in many cases evolved into the preeminent museums of European nations. Others are still esteemed in royal collections. The works are of such importance and value that they have rarely left the palaces or museums in which they are housed. Indeed, several pieces displayed here come from private royal apartments not accessible to the public.

Collaboration is the key to all successful exhibitions, and none more so than an undertaking as ambitious as this one. We thank all the institutions and private individuals who generously agreed to allow their treasures to travel. Without their support, sacrifice, and profound understanding of the importance of this grand project, its realization would not have been possible. Extensive loans from Florentine collections could not have been secured without the generous support of Cristina Acidini, Superintendent of the Florentine museums, who also contributed an essay to the catalogue. It was Annamaria Giusti, former Director of the Opificio delle Pietre Dure in Florence and guest curator of this exhibition, who some years ago broached the idea of an international loan exhibition of pietre dure treasures, focused especially on the seminal works of Florence and Rome. Wolfram Koeppe, Curator in the Metropolitan Museum's Department of European Sculpture and Decorative Arts, in collaboration with Ian Wardropper, Iris and B. Gerald Cantor Chairman of that department, broadened the range of the exhibition to emphasize as well the artistic production of northern and eastern Europe. In this expanded view of the entire subject, the innovative juxtaposition of different kinds of pietre dure work brings out heretofore neglected aesthetic relationships and at the same time illuminates cultural divergences. We thank these organizing curators and all the other trusted experts in their given fields who have harvested the astonishing results we see in this exhibition and its accompanying catalogue. Their effort and scholarship have resulted in a cultural event of significance and éclat.

Our profound thanks are extended to a handful of exemplary individuals who have provided crucial financial support for this endeavor, including Mercedes and Sid Bass, in honor of Jayne Wrightsman's supreme passion for the decorative arts, as well as Frank Richardson and the Honorable Kimba Wood. In addition, the Museum is grateful to Mr. and Mrs. J. Tomilson Hill III and an anonymous donor for their generosity and vision toward ensuring the success of this presentation. With enthusiasm, the Metropolitan also thanks The Andrew W. Mellon Foundation, the Friends of European Sculpture and Decorative Arts, and the Mary C. and James W. Fosburgh Publications Fund for making possible this exceptional catalogue.

Philippe de Montebello
Director, The Metropolitan Museum of Art

Acknowledgments

Hardstone objects were fundamental to princely magnificence and have been the pride of mighty rulers and learned collectors for centuries. However, their important role—and indeed, the works themselves—are unfamiliar to most modern viewers; thus, the aim of this major survey has been to offer a long overdue perspective on the dazzling medium of pietre dure. We hope that the exhibition and its catalogue will serve as the basis for further study of this extraordinarily refined artistic flowering.

This has been an ambitious undertaking, and we would like to express our profound gratitude to all those who helped in its realization. The curators are immensely grateful to Philippe de Montebello, Director of The Metropolitan Museum of Art. His approval and enthusiastic support, in combination with his insistence on excellence, set the standard for our project. His personal support and Mahrukh Tarapor's encouragement helped to shape the comprehensive form in which this exhibition opens to the public. We extend our thanks also to Museum President Emily K. Rafferty and Associate Director for Administration Doralynn Pines for their help and enthusiastic support. Sharon H. Cott, Rebecca L. Murray, and Kirstie Howard worked closely with Herb Moskowitz and the tireless, ever-proficient Aileen Chuk and the staff of the Registrar's Office, all of whom mastered the constantly changing logistical complexities that accompany an international exhibition of this scope. Harold Holzer, Elyse Topalian, Egle Žygas, and Mary Flanagan were instrumental in providing crucial information about the show to our worldwide audience.

Our heartfelt gratitude is extended to all the lenders, named or anonymous. Special thanks are owed to Her Majesty Queen Elizabeth II, The Royal Collection, London; and to the Musée du Louvre, Paris, the Grünes Gewölbe, Staatliche Kunstsammlungen, Dresden, the Museumslandschaft Hessen, Kassel, The J. Paul Getty Museum, Los Angeles, the Museum Gustavianum, Uppsala University, Sweden, and The Gilbert Collection at the Victoria and Albert Museum in London, all of which have been extraordinarily generous with multiple loans. We are grateful to Sabine Haag at the Kunsthistorisches Museum, Vienna, and Sir Hugh Roberts and Jonathan Marsden of The Royal Collection, London, who generously agreed to lend masterpieces without which our presentation would have been much the poorer.

We also wish to single out our coauthor Cristina Acidini, who in her capacity as Superintendent of the Patrimonio Storico Artistico ed Etnoantropologico and of the Polo Museale Fiorentino oversaw the cooperation of the museums of Florence, whose contributions were essential to the success of this endeavor. The directors of the individual museums were especially generous in allowing the loans of these extraordinary works of art, many of which are leaving Florence for the first time in their histories. Our warm thanks go particularly to Serena Padovani, director of the Galleria Palatina and the Appartamenti Monumentali at the Palazzo Pitti; Ornella Casazza, director of the Museo degli Argenti, Palazzo Pitti; Antonio Natali, director of the Galleria degli Uffizi; Monica Bietti, director of the Villa del Poggio Imperiale; and Maria Faietti, director of the Gabinetto Disegni e Stampe at the Uffizi. We are grateful to the Museo dell'Opificio delle Pietre Dure, which has relinquished the most precious pieces of its collections for this exhibition.

We extend profound thanks as well to the numerous other Italian and European museums whose valuable treasures have been included in this exhibition. Private collectors too have been very generous in agreeing to lend the important objects they own.

We are most grateful that the other contributors to this volume, preeminent scholars in their fields—Rudolf Distelberger in Vienna, Detlef Heikamp in Florence, and Jutta Kappel in Dresden—agreed to participate and thus make the book a truly collaborative venture and ensure that this exhibition is accompanied by the publication it deserves.

Florian Knothe, Research Associate, Department of European Sculpture and Decorative Arts at the Metropolitan Museum, who contributed both entries and essays, one jointly written, was an active participant in our research, not only checking details but also making numerous discoveries. His work was indispensable to the organization of the exhibition.

The large and complex catalogue was produced by the Metropolitan Museum's Editorial Department. We thank John P. O'Neill, Publisher and Editor in Chief, for supervising every aspect of its preparation and dispensing constant support. Margaret R. Chace, Managing Editor, saw that editorial activities ran smoothly, and Gwen Roginsky, General Manager

ix

of Publications, made sure that the catalogue will reach its widest natural readership. Without the expertise and competence, encouraging humor, and above all the patience and grace of the team of editors led by Ruth Lurie Kozodoy and also including Carol Fuerstein, Ellyn Allison, and Dale Tucker, who expertly edited manuscripts by the many authors and coordinated the entire catalogue, the publication could not have been realized. Jayne Kuchna served tirelessly as editor of the notes and bibliography, also adding numerous valuable references. Elaine Luthy meticulously prepared the index. Jane S. Tai was assiduous in the pursuit of photographs and permissions. We thank Bruce Campbell for the superb, elegant design. We recognize as well the unstinting efforts of Douglas J. Malicki, Chris Zichello, and especially Peter Antony, who carried out the myriad responsibilities of production and supervised the color correction and printing of the book. Robert Weisberg skillfully oversaw the desktop publishing process. Barbara Bridgers of The Photograph Studio and its photographers Bruce Schwarz, Peter Zeray, and Mark Morasse produced a number of fine photographs for publication. Thanks go as well to Margaret Aspinwall, Cynthia Clark, Mary Gladue, Sarah Jean Dupont, and Richard Gallin, all of whom made important contributions to the publication effort.

The exhibition's creative installation was designed by Daniel Bradley Kershaw; excellent graphics were provided by Sophia Geronimus; and Pamela T. Barr edited the labels. Lighting design was by Clint Ross Coller and Richard Lichte. All aspects of the installation were coordinated by the indefatigable Linda Sylling, assisted by Patricia Gilkison. Kent Lydecker, Joseph Loh, and members of the Education Department contributed to the project by mounting a variety of events. We are most grateful to the staff of the Thomas J. Watson Library at the Museum. Kenneth Soehner, Linda Seckelson, and Robyn Fleming were helpful in many ways.

The curators at the Metropolitan Museum are also grateful to Martha Deese and Emily Vanderpool in the Office of the Director, Nina McN. Diefenbach in the Development Department, Mechthild Baumeister, Linda Borsch, and Jack Soultanian Jr. in the Objects Conservation Department, and Michael Gallagher in Paintings Conservation. Noteworthy special support came from our distinguished curatorial colleagues at the Museum: Carlos A. Picón, Christopher S. Lightfoot, and Matthew A. Noiseux, Greek and Roman Art; Stuart W. Pyhrr, Arms and Armor; Everett Fahy, Keith Christiansen, and Katharine Baetjer, European Paintings; Laurence B. Kanter and Dita Amory, Robert Lehman Collection; Dorothea Arnold, Egyptian Art; Peter Barnet, Barbara Drake Boehm, Helen C. Evans, and Charles T. Little, Medieval Art and The Cloisters; and Stefano Carboni and Navina Haidar Haykel, Islamic Art.

We would like to express special thanks to Alvar González-Palacios, in Rome, whose impressive scholarship has deeply inspired us.

The entire staff of the Metropolitan's Department of European Sculpture and Decorative Arts are to be thanked for the many ways they contributed assistance. We appreciate in particular the help of James David Draper, Clare Vincent, Daniëlle O. Kisluk-Grosheide, Erin E. Pick, Denny Stone, Marina Nudel, Rose Whitehill, Elizabeth Lee Berszinn, and Robert Kaufmann; and Bedel Tiscareño, Juan Stacey, and Jeff Elliott.

Annamaria Giusti writes from Florence: I am especially grateful to friends and colleagues who assisted in the work in a variety of ways. I would like to thank, in addition to the directors of the Florentine museums already mentioned, Patrizio Osticresi, secretary of the Museo dell'Opera di Santa Maria del Fiore; Stefano Casciu and Rosanna Morozzi at the Galleria Palatina; Giorgio Marini and Lucia Monaci at the Gabinetto Disegni e Stampe at the Uffizi; Clarice Innocenti, the new director of the Museo dell'Opificio delle Pietre Dure; and Alessandra Griffo, director of the restoration of mosaics and pietre dure at the Opificio, who also oversaw the restoration and maintenance of the works lent to this exhibition by Florentine museums. I would also like to acknowledge Giancarlo Raddi delle Ruote, head restorer, as well as Luca Rocchi, Chiara Martinelli, Francesca Toso, and Patrizia Castelli. Loriana Campestrelli at the Museo dell'Opificio offered invaluable assistance in management of the many loans from that museum's collection. Lillina Di Mucci was a great help in researching and organizing the material for my contributions to this catalogue. Finally, I would like to offer heartfelt thanks to Linda Carioni, who with her natural efficiency and good nature was the necessary anchor on the Italian side, making it possible to carry out this demanding undertaking.

Last but certainly not least, all the curators would like to thank the many individuals who furnished us with specific information important to this endeavor: Paola d'Agostino, Daniel Alcouffe, Farhan Ali, Pierre Arizzoli-Clémentel, Gillian M. Arthur, Ilsebill Barta-Fiedl, Marc Bascou, Antonia Boström, Michael Brand, Marquis Henri-François de Breteuil, Anthea Brook, Jennie Choi, Alistair Clark, Claudia Clark, Enrico Colle, Brian Considine, Andria Derstine, Prince Jonathan Doria Pamphilj, Renate Eikelmann, Michael Eissenhauer, Karl Graf von und zu Eltz, Godfrey Evans, Helen Costantino Fioratti, Yvonne Fritz, Markus Graf Fugger-Babenhausen, Sarah Gage, Bertrand-Pierre Galey, Louis Godart, Michel Guiraud, Jørgen

Hein, Philip Hewat-Jaboor, William E. Hood, Olga Ilmenkova, Simon Swynfen Jervis, Mark Jones, Franz Kirchweger, Ebba Koch, Olga Kostyuk, Johann Kräftner, Nicolas Kugel, Lars Ljungström, Princess Alexandra Lobkowicz, Jörn Lohmann, Henri Loyrette, Philippe Malgouyres, Lucretia Obolensky Mali, Giorgio Marini, Vladimir Matveyev, Christopher Monkhouse, Ing-Marie Munktell, Tessa Murdoch, Myriam Nechard, Margareta Nisser-Dalman, the Duke of Northumberland, Eva Ottillinger, Princess Maria Camilla Pallavicini, Imerio Palumbo, Sharon F. Patton, Jacques Perot, Mikhail B. Piotrovski, Anna K. Piotrowska, Bertrand Rondot,

Martin Roth, Lord Jacob Rothschild, Sigrid Sangl, Bruno Santi, Annalisa Scarpa, Antje Scherner, Eike D. Schmidt, Margaret H. Schwartz, Wilfried Seipel, Nicola Spinosa, Emmanuel Starcky, Laure Starcky, Timothy Stevens, Lady Cindy Shaw Stewart, Achim Stiegel, William Strafford, Michael Stürmer, Dirk Syndram, Jeffrey Weaver, Stuart Cary Welch, Christopher Wilk, Paul Williamson, Lucy Wood, Henry Wyndham, Rainer Zietz; and especially Michelangelo Lupo.

Annamaria Giusti, Wolfram Koeppe, and Ian Wardropper
Curators of the exhibition

The Role of the Opificio delle Pietre Dure

It is an honor and a source of pride for me to write this brief text. The exhibition "Art of the Royal Court: Treasures in Pietre Dure from the Palaces of Europe" and its accompanying catalogue are in many ways the culmination of a program of research and exhibitions begun when I was Superintendent of the Opificio delle Pietre Dure in Florence and subsequently developed when I became Superintendent of the Polo Museale Fiorentino as well. It was possible to realize the project thanks in great part to the openness of the curators of the Florentine museums, which, joined by other European and American museums, have been the most generous of lenders.

The path to any important international art endeavor is as fascinating as it is full of obstacles, and only with the help of competent and devoted friends can we fully achieve our goal. Such is indeed the case with the present exhibition, which Philippe de Montebello, Director of The Metropolitan Museum of Art, welcomed with a readiness and conviction for which I am deeply grateful. The project was realized by Ian Wardropper and Wolfram Koeppe assisted by Florian Knothe, all of the Metropolitan Museum, in collaboration with Annamaria Giusti of the Museo dell'Opificio delle Pietre Dure.

The Opificio, which grew out of the Medici workshops that produced a great number of the masterworks in this exhibition, has always focused on the vast artistic heritage of Florence and Tuscany. Now it also participates in a variety of international programs of a scholarly and didactic nature, as well as restoration and conservation. Its numerous present-day functions encompass scientific research and applied technology conducted at its in-house scientific laboratory; education carried out at the Scuola di Alta Formazione, which offers a restoration program leading to a degree equivalent to that of a five-year university course; and restoration pursued in twelve different areas: painting on canvas and panel, mural painting, wood sculpture, ceramic and plastic materials, goldwork, bronze and ancient weapons, stone inlay and mosaic, stone-work, tapestry, textiles, paper, and fiber.

The authority granted by Italian law to the Opificio (as to Rome's restoration center, the Istituto Centrale del Restauro di Roma) is nationwide. The Opificio is available for direct intervention and consultation across all of Italy. Recognized both nationally and internationally for its preeminent role in the restoration of pietre dure objects (until recently under the distinguished leadership of Dean Giancarlo Raddi delle Ruote, who continues to share his knowledge as a teacher at the school), the Opificio also participates in international efforts, contributing highly specialized expertise.

Together with my colleagues I recently summarized the present-day mission of the Opificio: "To transpose into current terms the knowledge inherent in works of antiquity and art handed down from ancient traditions to the modern-day

Opificio, thereby ensuring its uninterrupted continuity, its constant updating, and timely, innovative transformation in the light of a vision of the future in order to preserve the heritage of culture, especially of Italy; in particular archaeological, architectural, and artistic culture" (Acidini 2003, p. 11). This mission involves both immediate and long-term courses of action, which, in guiding current projects, will inspire and shape those of the future. Included is the task of publicizing and validating its interventions by exhibiting restored works in Italy and abroad. These exhibitions have excited great interest and disseminated information through accompanying lectures, workshops, conferences, and publications. Their realization has benefited from the crucial contributions of Annamaria Giusti, the author of many specialized studies and an internationally recognized expert in the field of pietre dure, who has given long and invaluable service at the Opificio as director of its museum.

Consistent with the Opificio's goals are the recent important initiatives in partnership with American museums, which have their distant precedent in the 1992–93 Metropolitan Museum exhibition of Verrocchio's bronze sculpture group the *Incredulity of Saint Thomas*. Notable among recent projects of the kind are the show of sculpture from the Florentine Church of Orsanmichele at the National Gallery of Art in Washington, D.C., in 2005–6, on which CASVA (Center for Advanced Study in the Visual Arts) and FIAC (Foundation for Italian Art and Culture) collaborated, and the exhibition of three panels from Lorenzo Ghiberti's bronze doors for the Florence Baptistery, which traveled to the High Museum of Art, Atlanta, the Art Institute of Chicago, and the Metropolitan Museum in 2007 and 2008.

Cristina Acidini
Superintendent, Patrimonio Storico Artistico ed Etnoantropologico and Polo Museale Fiorentino, Florence

Lenders to the Exhibition

AUSTRIA
Vienna, Hofburg, Kaiserliches Hofmobiliendepot: 104, 119
Vienna, Kunsthistorisches Museum, Kunstkammer: 66–69, 72–75, 77

FRANCE
Compiègne, Musée National du Château de Compiègne: 98
Paris, Musée du Louvre: 40, 94, 95, 99, 106
Paris, Muséum National d'Histoire Naturelle: 45
Versailles, Musée National des Châteaux de Versailles et de Trianon: 131

GERMANY
Berlin, Staatliche Museen zu Berlin, Stiftung Preussischer Kulturbesitz, Kunstgewerbemuseum: 21, 52
Burg Eltz, Rhineland-Palatinate, Schatzkammer: 93
Dresden, Staatliche Kunstsammlungen Dresden, Grünes Gewölbe: 85–87, 89, 146
Kassel, Museumslandschaft Hessen Kassel, Sammlung für Kunsthandwerk und Plastik: 76, 81–84
Munich, Bayerisches Nationalmuseum: 47, 48

ITALY
Ferrara, Musei Civici di Arte Antica: 103
Florence, Galleria degli Uffizi: 23, 33, 38, 113
Florence, Museo degli Argenti, Palazzo Pitti: 7, 13, 22, 24, 34, 35, 49, 59, 64, 65, 130
Florence, Museo dell'Opera di Santa Maria del Fiore: 8
Florence, Museo dell'Opificio delle Pietre Dure: 26–32, 39, 44, 50, 58, 71, 108–112, 114, 116–118, 147
Florence, Museo delle Cappelle Medicee, Tesoro di San Lorenzo: 36, 56, 57
Florence, Palazzo Pitti: 37, 46, 55, 105, 107, 115
Florence, Villa del Poggio Imperiale: 12
Naples, Museo Nazionale di Capodimonte: 128
Rome, Palazzo del Quirinale: 11

RUSSIA
Saint Petersburg, The State Hermitage Museum: 141–144

SPAIN
Madrid, Museo Nacional del Prado: 127, 129

SWEDEN
Uppsala, Museum Gustavianum, Uppsala University: 78

UNITED KINGDOM
London, The Rosalinde and Arthur Gilbert Collection: 70, 90–92, 123–125
London, The Royal Collection: 132, 134
London, Victoria and Albert Museum: 43, 136

UNITED STATES
Cleveland, The Cleveland Museum of Art: 17
Los Angeles, The J. Paul Getty Museum: 25, 51, 79, 100, 135
Minneapolis, Minneapolis Institute of Arts: 54, 120
New York, The Metropolitan Museum of Art: 1–4, 6, 10, 15, 18, 41, 62, 63, 80, 88, 96, 97, 101, 102, 121, 126, 137–139
Oberlin, Ohio, Allen Memorial Art Museum, Oberlin College: 20

PRIVATE COLLECTIONS
Banca di Roma—Unicredit Group, Rome: 9
Ambassador Paul and Trudy Cejas: 140
Helen Costantino Fioratti, New York: 14, 61
Philip Hewat-Jaboor: 145
Georg Laue, Munich: 53
Galleria Pallavicini, Rome: 19
Mr. and Mrs. Peter Pritchard: 122
Anonymous lenders: 5, 16, 42, 60, 133

Curators of the Exhibition

ANNAMARIA GIUSTI
Director, Galleria d'Arte Moderna del Polo Museale
Fiorentino, and former Director, Museo dell'Opificio delle
Pietre Dure, Florence

WOLFRAM KOEPPE
Curator, Department of European Sculpture and Decorative
Arts, The Metropolitan Museum of Art, New York

IAN WARDROPPER
Iris and B. Gerald Cantor Chairman, Department of European
Sculpture and Decorative Arts, The Metropolitan Museum of
Art, New York

Contributors to the Catalogue

CRISTINA ACIDINI
Superintendent, Patrimonio Storico Artistico ed
Etnoantropologico and Polo Museale Fiorentino,
Florence

RD   RUDOLF DISTELBERGER
Director Emeritus, Kunstkammer, Weltliche
und Geistliche Schatzkammer, Kunsthistorisches
Museum, Vienna

AG   ANNAMARIA GIUSTI
Director, Galleria d'Arte Moderna del Polo
Museale Fiorentino, and former Director, Museo
dell'Opificio delle Pietre Dure, Florence

DH   DETLEF HEIKAMP
Professor Emeritus, Kunsthistorisches Institut,
Florence

JK   JUTTA KAPPEL
Deputy Director and Chief Curator, Grünes
Gewölbe, Staatliche Kunstsammlungen Dresden

FK   FLORIAN KNOTHE
Research Associate, Department of European
Sculpture and Decorative Arts, The Metropolitan
Museum of Art, New York

WK   WOLFRAM KOEPPE
Curator, Department of European Sculpture and
Decorative Arts, The Metropolitan Museum of
Art, New York

IAN WARDROPPER
Iris and B. Gerald Cantor Chairman, Department
of European Sculpture and Decorative Arts, The
Metropolitan Museum of Art, New York

Note to the Reader

"Pietre dure" means "hardstones." It refers to semiprecious stones themselves and is also a term applied to work principally in semiprecious stone.

A *commesso di pietre dure*, or *commesso*, is an assemblage of flat stone pieces arranged into a decorative or pictorial panel. This type of work was developed in Florence and is often called Florentine mosaic. Thus a pietre dure mosaic is made not of small squares (tesserae) but of cut stone pieces.

Additional terms are defined in the Glossary.

The grand-ducal workshops that produced pietre dure works for the Medici court in Florence were consolidated in 1588 under the name Galleria dei Lavori and housed in the Palazzo degli Uffizi complex. At the end of the eighteenth century the workshops were moved to a different location in Florence, and in the nineteenth century they were given a new name, Opificio delle Pietre Dure.

References to literature are cited in an abbreviated form in the notes. The corresponding full citations are found in the Bibliography.

Unless otherwise noted, dimensions given are in this order: height, width, depth.

Art of the Royal Court

Treasures in Pietre Dure from
the Palaces of Europe

Mysterious and Prized: Hardstones in Human History before the Renaissance

WOLFRAM KOEPPE

From the word "stone" comes the name of an entire period of human evolution. The Stone Age is traditionally divided into the successive but overlapping Paleolithic (literally, Old Stone) Age, which embraces humankind from its earliest use of tools up to the beginnings of agriculture in about 10,000 B.C.; the Mesolithic (Middle Stone) Age; and the Neolithic (New Stone) Age, when, sometime before 8500 B.C., farming and the cultivation of wild cereals appeared. The revolutionary technology based on Neolithic developments made possible the Bronze and Iron Ages, named for the metals that replaced stone as the dominant cutting tool.

Some of the first works of art ever made are of stone, the oldest perhaps being the mesmerizing *Venus of Galgenberg* (fig. 2). A tiny statuette weighing only ten grams, it was carved about 30,000 B.C. out of amphibolite slate with a dark, shiny surface.[1] Of similar size is the famous limestone Venus of Willendorf (Naturhistorisches Museum, Vienna) of about 25,000 B.C.[2] When early Egyptians carved the mysterious Great Sphinx that guards the pyramids on the plateau of Giza, they cut its core out of the limestone bedrock. The tallest of the pyramids, that for the pharaoh Khufu (ca. 2560 B.C.), still shows at its apex some of the polished Tura limestone that once encased the whole. Rising near-white in the desert, it must have created an astonishing effect. The pharaoh's burial chamber within was lined with Aswan granite, a hardstone, which was quarried hundreds of miles upstream, chiseled into blocks weighing up to eighty tons, and conveyed down the Nile.

Objects of stone have been the bearers of enormous religious significance. The Ten Commandments given to Moses were on two "tables . . . of stone, written with the finger of God,"[3] an indication of faith in the material's endurance for generations to come. For Muslims, the Black Stone of Mecca, in the eastern corner of the Kaabah (cube) shrine, has supernatural powers, and tradition associates it with Adam or with Abraham and his son Ishmael. The cube itself, constructed of granite, is a pilgrimage destination for faithful millions each year. The

Spanish Muslim geographer Ibn Jubayr (1145–1217) described the emotion inspired in him by the Black Stone: "The Stone, when kissed, has a softness and moistness which so enchants the mouth that he who puts his lips to it would wish them never to be removed. This is one of the special favours of Divine Providence."[4] Arab culture, in which stone has long been used therapeutically, appears to be the source of our word "talisman" (coming ultimately from the Greek for a consecrated or numious object). An early and important conveyor of Arab lore about the healing value of precious stones was the medical scholar Constantine the African (ca. 1020–1087). Translating Arabic sources into Latin, Constantine compiled a treatise, *De gradibus*, which for the first time made the Oriental medical-lapidary literature available to Western scholars; its influence was widespread.[5]

A special place in the history of the human imagination is occupied by the "philosopher's stone," a legendary substance

Fig. 2. *Venus of Galgenberg*, ca. 30,000 B.C., discovered near Stratzing, Lower Austria. Amphibolite slate, H. 2⅞ in. Weinstadt Museum Krems, Austria

Opposite: Fig. 1. *Gemma Claudia*, Roman, ca. A.D. 49. Onyx with later gold mounts, H. 4¾ in. Kunsthistorisches Museum, Vienna

that supposedly was capable of transforming base metals into gold or silver. Sought after in vain in antiquity, it became an essential part of Western legends and was the principal object of the efforts of alchemists. During the age of the European *Kunstkammer*, or room of art (see "Pietre Dure North of the Alps" by Wolfram Koeppe in this publication), the substance would have been a collector's most prized acquisition. Even today, the idea lives in popular literature.[6] It was thought that a philosopher's stone could be liquefied and would then turn into the *elixir vitae*—or elixir of life—which could prolong life, perhaps forever, and restore a human body to physical perfection.

In human thought, then, stone has embodied everlasting life and eternal beauty. These occupy the opposite end of the spectrum from the characteristics of a living organism, which meets a physiological end and decay. Enlisted as protection against that decay, stones—especially stones of rich colors and varied appearance—dramatize their owners' importance and status, serve as embellishments, and comfort the flaws of the human body. But the symbolic meanings and level of appreciation for different varieties of stones have undergone remarkable transformations throughout history. The reasons include shifts in fashion, fluctuations in a stone's rarity or availability, constraints imposed by sumptuary laws, and changes in customs.[7]

The umbrella term "rock" is used for an aggregate made up of different components, generally stones or minerals. A mineral is a uniform, homogeneous chemical compound (or a single element). A stone is a characteristic mix of one or more minerals and other earth components and has been detached from a rocky mass. Today, stones and minerals can be classified by geologists, gemologists, or crystallographers, who use technical analyses to distinguish their chemical components and determine their physical characteristics.[8] Subtle deviations can then be evaluated and possibly identified as having been caused by the specific conditions of the matrix at the stone's original location. However, until the Age of Enlightenment and the development of modern science, the ability to examine materials and perform accurate chemical tests to identify stones did not exist. Terms were not well defined and were sometimes used interchangeably. Up to the eighteenth century, even red coral,[9] fragile exotic pearls,[10] and amber were counted among the semiprecious stones (see "An Enduring Seductiveness" by Wolfram Koeppe and Florian Knothe in this publication; figs. 85, 94). Even though amber, a fossil resin, could drift over the ferocious waves of the Baltic Sea (making harvesting it rather dangerous) and burn like coal, it still was called a stone.[11]

A good example of the complexity of these characterizations is provided by lapis lazuli, which is not a mineral but an aggregate of various minerals, mainly blue lazurite with calcite, sodalite, pyrite, mica, and other possible constituents. It looks like a precious material out of the *Arabian Nights*, and, indeed, its intense blue color and shimmering bits of pyrite suggest the sparkling constellations of the night sky. A favorite stone for amulets and ornament, it was for millennia mined exclusively in the remote Badakhshan province of Afghanistan. It was not until the mid-eighteenth century that Russian entrepreneurs discovered large

Fig. 3. *Standard of Ur*, detail, ca. 2600–2400 B.C., excavated at the Royal Cemetery of Ur, southern Iraq. Shell, lapis lazuli, and red limestone, wooden core, H. of entire object 7⅞ in. Trustees of the British Museum, London

amounts of this substance in the Ural Mountains, and deposits were later found in Canada and Chile. Confusingly, because sapphire is also blue, its name and that of lapis lazuli were used interchangeably in antiquity and as late as the Middle Ages.[12]

The cradle of cultural evolution, stretching from the life-giving banks of the Nile to the waterways of the Euphrates, has yielded some of the earliest objects incorporating colored stones. At its peak, the Sumerian culture in Mesopotamia (today Iraq) valued lapis lazuli, carnelian, agate, chalcedony, and other hardstones (or semiprecious stones), many of which were incorporated into luxurious artifacts found at the royal cemetery of Ur, in Sumer, of about 2500 B.C. The *Standard of Ur* in the British Museum (fig. 3), with its colored stones inlaid against a ground of lapis lazuli, prefigures the technique that would later be called *commesso di pietre dure*—the assemblage of a mosaic of hardstones (and also softer ones, called *pietre tenere*). In ancient Egypt, lapis lazuli embellished some of the most beautiful works of art ever created—among them the fourteenth-century B.C. gold funerary mask of Tutankhamen (Egyptian Museum, Cairo), inlaid with lapis lazuli and colored glass, and a superb figure of the god Ptah (The Metropolitan Museum of Art, New York)[13]—which demonstrate the capacity of the material to be carved and chiseled with the most minute details. Given this context, it is not astonishing that powdered lapis was used as eye shadow by Cleopatra, who hoped its royal connotations would reinforce her claim to a legitimate right to rule over the lands of the Nile. The affluent society of imperial Rome regarded lapis as an aphrodisiac and dedicated it to Aphrodite.[14] A royal and religious association continued into Christianity, when this stone with seemingly captured stars was thought to reflect the assemblage of all the saints (see entry for cat. no. 18).[15]

The Sumerian civilization of the third millennium B.C. also provides some of the earliest manifestations of the idiosyncratic human desire to encircle the finger with jewelry. Single hardstones of varying colors emerged as the main feature of finger rings; they combined magnificence, value, a show of power, and apotropaic qualities.[16] Rings embellished with signet seals identifying their owners have been found in ancient Egypt. Often a hardstone carved in the form of a scarab carried the signet device engraved on its underside and was strung on a gold wire that constituted the ring, allowing the carved stone to be revolved when the seal was required for use.[17] The symbolic and political significance of such rings is documented in the Bible: when Pharaoh made Joseph vice-ruler of Egypt, he "took off his ring from his hand and put it upon Joseph's hand."[18] The tradition was continued throughout the ancient Roman and Byzantine periods, was passed on to the central European civilizations, and survives in modern times, when these signets in hardstone intaglio still convey the message of ancestry and their bearers' noble roots. In the Anglo-American tradition, similar rings signify the owner's connection to a specific college or uni-

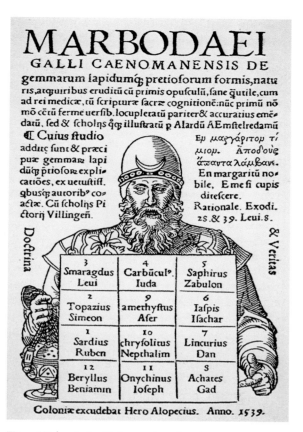

Fig. 4. High priest with breastplate showing gemstones symbolizing the twelve tribes of Israel, title page from Marbodus of Rennes, *De gemmarum* (Cologne, 1539)

versity. Important roles were played by rings for ecclesiastical use. When the pope bestowed them on newly appointed cardinals and bishops, the rings carried certain rights. They were generally set with large, transparent stones—with a natural surface, or step-cut (with a flat top), or as a cabochon (convex)—beneath which was a tiny relic. Unusually large, these rings were worn over liturgical gloves.[19]

The Old Testament is one of the richest sources for descriptions of colored stones. For instance, the prophet Ezekiel reflects on the clothing of the king of Tyros: "Thou has been in Eden, the garden of God; every precious stone was thy covering, the sardius [carnelian], topaz, and the diamond, the beryl, the onyx, and the jasper, the sapphire, the emerald, and the carbuncle, and gold."[20] Among biblical mentions of gemstones, of particular importance is the square breastplate, or *hoshen*, that was worn by the Jewish high priest as recorded in Exodus. It was mounted with twelve precious stones engraved with the names of the twelve tribes of Israel.[21] "And thou shalt set in it settings of stones, even four rows of stones: the first row shall be a sardius, a topaz, and a carbuncle; . . . And the second row shall be an emerald, a sapphire, and a diamond. And the third row a ligure [hyacinth], an agate, and an amethyst. And the fourth row a beryl, and an onyx, and a jasper."[22]

In continuing traditions, the biblical sequence of the stones was often varied (fig. 4),[23] but the number twelve retained an established role, as in John's vision of the Heavenly Jerusalem in the book of Revelation:

[He] . . . shewed me that great city, the holy Jerusalem, descending out of heaven from God. . . . [H]er light was like unto a stone most precious, even like a jasper stone, clear as crystal; . . . the wall it was of jasper; . . . and the foundations of the wall of the city were garnished with all manner of precious stones. The first foundation was jasper; the second, sapphire; the third, a chalcedony; the fourth, an emerald; the fifth, sardonyx; the sixth, sardius; the seventh, chrysolite; the eighth, beryl; the ninth, a topaz; the tenth, a chrysoprasus; the eleventh, a jacinth; the twelfth, an amethyst. And the twelve gates were twelve pearls; every several gate was of one pearl.[24]

Precious stones exist in an astonishing variety of colors and degrees of clarity, which, in addition to weight, are today the

Fig. 5. *Crawford Cup*, Roman, A.D. 1st–2nd century. Fluorspar, H. 3⅞ in. Trustees of the British Museum, London

Fig. 6. Tiger attacking a bullock, A.D. 4th century. Detail of an opus sectile mosaic from the Basilica of Junius Bassus, Rome. Hardstones. Musei Capitolini, Rome

Fig. 7. View in the Palatine Chapel, Aachen Cathedral, Germany, ca. 800. Ancient Roman marble panels reused in the throne, wall decoration, and paving; reused ancient porphyry and granite columns

Fig. 8. *King David*, Upper Rhineland, possibly Constance, ca. 1280, with later portions. Gold, gilded silver, gemstones, hardstones, enamel, gilded wood, and hardstone cameos: Roman period (face) and ca. 1150 northern European (lion). H. 8½ in. Historisches Museum, Basel 1882.80a

main criteria of their value. Hardstones and semiprecious stones have an equally wide color range but also display individual textures. Sometimes flaws have been prized, for they impart special effects to the material. Marble, a metamorphic rock, is susceptible to changes effected by pressure and heat that can give it an unusual color, texture, or grain, and these variations are highly valued. Initially used by the ancient Greeks and later the Romans to adorn their temples and public spaces, in time these materials were fashioned into objects of conspicuous consumption for individual owners and announced their claims to power, wealth, and pedigree.

The term "glyptic" embraces many arts of hardstone carving. It derives from the Greek *glyphein*, "to incise," and, indeed, in the Greek world many of the foundations for the practice were laid.[25] Probably the oldest manifestations of the glyptic art are from the Near East (fourth millennium B.C.) and the Aegean

region; in Cyprus, amalgamating influences from these, the art developed as early as about 2500 B.C.[26] The carving of hardstone reached an unprecedented level of accomplishment in the first century A.D., under the emperor Augustus. Particularly prominent among ancient Roman pieces are cameos, carved in relief on stones such as onyx, sardonyx, or agate, and well described by James David Draper.[27] The stones may have variegated light- and dark-colored strata, or layers, and the carvers often manipulatd the depth of the relief layers so that figures of two or more colors would emerge. One atmospheric example is the *Gemma Claudia* of about A.D. 49, a five-layered onyx cameo, cut with remarkably thin layers (fig. 1), which later became part of the imperial Habsburg collection. Admiration for famous objects like this one, along with the limited availability of such works, ushered in a revival of cameo carving in the Italian Renaissance. Masters of stone carving strove to match the

Fig. 9. Episcopal throne, Church of Santa Balbina, Rome, 12th century. Marble inlaid with Cosmati decoration

Fig. 10. Paving with the signs of the zodiac, San Miniato al Monte, Florence, 13th century. Green and white marble

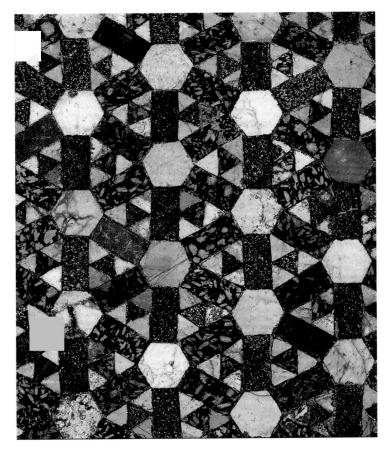

Fig. 11. Detail of paving, Santa Maria in Cosmedin, Rome, 12th century. Polychrome marble

standards of the ancients in order to satisfy the demands of humanist collectors (cat. no. 13).

Pliny the Elder (A.D. 23/4–79) wrote that the emperor Nero, "on receiving tidings that all was lost, in the excess of his fury, dashed two cups of crystal to pieces; this being his last act of vengeance upon his fellow-creatures, preventing any one from ever drinking again from these vessels."[28] Nero was also reputed to have paid more than one million sesterces for a single vessel made of the rare mineral fluorspar (fluorite),[29] a substance that in ancient times could only be obtained in minute quantities and only from Parthia (modern Iran). Costly vessels made from this precious substance, called *vasa murrina* (fig. 5), were said to have special powers. Romans coveted them for their exquisite color layers and the fact that they bestowed a special flavor to the wine drunk from them.[30] Many other varieties of decorative objects and vessels were greatly valued as well (see entry for cat. no. 2).

The ancient Romans also devoted much attention to opus sectile, or inlay work—either floor decoration (*sectilia pavimenta*) or wall incrustations (*incrustationes*)—made from colored stone (fig. 6)[31] or glass (cat. no. 4). Despite the hardness of the materials, artisans were able to transform them into sophisticated

Fig. 12. Vase, Egypt, Fatimid period, late 10th century. Rock crystal. Mounts of gilded silver, pearls, and semiprecious stones added in Venice, mid-13th century. H. with mounts 19¼ in. Procuratoria di San Marco, Venice

patterns; notable examples are the pavement in the Curia of Diocletian in Rome, which includes military motifs such as *peltae* (ancient warrior shields; see cat. no. 10), and the exuberant stone decor applied to the walls of the Baths of Caracalla, which after centuries of burial were excavated in the 1540s. To later ages these stones symbolized the opulence of imperial Rome, the capital of a vanished empire, and their survival must have seemed physical proof that Rome was indeed the Eternal City (see entry for cat. no. 10). Nevertheless, the colorful material in the baths was plundered for reuse in Renaissance and Baroque pietre dure projects.

The harvesting of hardstone spoils was nothing new; it had gone on for centuries after the collapse of the ancient empire.[32] During the Carolingian Renaissance, surviving Roman structures and excavations provided valuable material. Charlemagne's Palatine Chapel in Aachen (ca. 800) incorporated complex ancient stone floor inlays that had been reassembled. The chapel's sumptuous porphyry and exotic granite columns (fig. 7; for the later reuse of an ancient porphyry column, see cat. no. 102) were literally carried over the Alps; according to tradition, they were taken from Rome and Ravenna at the end of the eighth century. They were viewed as having been witness for millennia to the historic activities of great men, and nothing like them had been seen in the North before. So great was the

Fig. 13. Jean Fouquet, *Agnes Sorel as a Madonna with Child*, 1440. Oil on panel, H. 37¼ in. Koninklijk Museum voor Schone Kunsten, Antwerp

fame of these columns that when the French Revolutionary troops occupied the Rhineland in 1794, rather than destroying them they brought them to Paris as trophies. The columns were returned later and in about 1840 were reinstalled and repaired with Egyptian Aswan granite.[33]

Respect for remnants of the past, when combined with an experimental search for a new stylistic language in the making of ecclesiastical objects, sometimes led to fetishlike creations. A prominent example is the jewel-encrusted gold reliquary figure of Saint Faith, or Sainte-Foy, in the abbey church at Conques in southern France. The promise of the relics' healing powers enticed many pilgrims on their way to Santiago de Compostela. During the French Revolution, the image was hidden for safekeeping by devoted locals. Less ostentatious but just as eccentric is the statuette of King David from the treasury of Basel Cathedral (fig. 8). This golden reliquary with a half-length figure, of about 1280, incorporates for the face an ancient Roman cameo representing Medusa, whose snakehead-studded coiffure was slightly altered to create a plausible King David. A second cameo of about 1150, that of a lion, set below the torso, is a reference to David's epithet "Lion of Judah"—a further effort, in this northern work, to distinguish by means of older cameos the identity of the depicted.[34] The Shrine of the Three Kings in Cologne Cathedral represents a high point of this practice. Made of precious metal, enameled, and set with more than one thousand jewels, cameos, and beads, it is a dense compendium of Christological and mystical meanings.[35]

In Italy, Bruno of Segni, who became abbot of the cloister of Monte Cassino in 1107, stressed that a church building is a metaphor for the Holy Church itself, "whose columns are the bishops and scholars, in which each stone sparkles more greatly by how much it is more faithful and better."[36] This analogy was widely subscribed to, and gleaming columns of precious stone were to be found in many churches.[37]

In the stone flooring of the abbey church of Monte Cassino in central Italy, as Annamaria Giusti has pointed out, figured pavements in the ancient Roman style made their reappearance; they were executed by artisans from Byzantium, heir to Roman imperial traditions, who arrived in 1066–71 at the behest of Abbot Desiderius (later Pope Victor III). The floor of Monte Cassino "became the archetype for a tradition of marble inlay that would continue without interruption over ensuing centuries, principally in the shape of those 'Cosmatesque mosaics' of Roman origins but widespread diffusion, and secondly in Tuscan marble inlay."[38] The technique developed by the Roman Cosmati family featured stone disks and bands and simple geometric shapes made up of small triangles and rectangles and set into a stone surface. Two of the most prominent examples of Cosmati work are the twelfth-century episcopal throne in Santa Balbina in Rome (fig. 9)[39] and the pavement of 1268 in front of the high altar in Westminster Abbey. The latter was made by Pietro di Oderisio,

an artisan sent from Rome to London; its intriguing pattern is thought to be a representation of the world according to the Ptolemaic system.[40] Thus, colorful stone inlay was an indivisible part of ecclesiastical decoration. Italian churches from Sicily to Venice were paved with floors of stone inlay, as testified by Santa Maria in Cosmedin, Rome (fig. 11) or Santi Maria e Donato in Murano, Venice.[41] Another source of ideas was the Islamic world; the Cosmatesque technique of geometric stone inlay shows this influence.[42] The stimulus of Arabic textile patterns is obvious in the carpetlike paving of the Florence Baptistery[43] and the nearby church of San Miniato al Monte (fig. 10).[44]

Abbot Suger of Saint-Denis, near Paris, described in a compelling account the cornerstone ceremony held for one part of the church. On July 14, 1140, Suger welcomed to the Saint-Denis construction site an important group of French clerics and King Louis VII, who arrived in solemn possession accompanying the foremost relics of the cloister: "The Most Serene King himself stepped down [into the excavation] and with his own hands laid his [stone]. Also we and many others, both abbots and monks, laid their stones. Certain persons also [deposited] gems out of love and reverence for Jesus Christ, chanting: *Lapides preciosi omnes muri tui* [All thy walls are precious stones]."[45]

Contemporaneously, Islamic North Africa flourished under Fatimid rule (A.D. 909–1171), a period of great commercial and cultural activity.[46] In addition to sponsoring breathtaking achievements of architecture, opulent textile weaving, and fine pottery production, the Fatimids were supporters of an art of hardstone carving of exceptional beauty. Clear eastern African rock crystal (which Pliny the Elder thought was layered ice petrified under pressure)[47] was crafted into imaginatively designed works of art. Later, in Europe, many of these were transformed into translucent receptacles for holy relics (fig. 12).[48]

In the fourth century the bishop Epiphanius wrote, "The onyx is beloved of kings and greatly loved by brides."[49] Throughout the Middle Ages, onyx and agate continued to hold fascination and were the stones particularly of kings and royal consorts. When Agnes Sorel, mistress of Charles VII of France, had herself painted as a *Madonna with Child* by Jean Fouquet in 1440, she was depicted on an elaborate throne of onyx and agate, which greatly enhances the intense drama of the work (fig. 13).[50]

Exquisite pietre dure objects, many discussed in the entries of this catalogue, are composed principally of semiprecious hardstones and marble. However, we should not lose track of these substances' mesmerizing beauty in their own right. They were created by nature, or God, without any human interference. When craftsmen subsequently work these marvelous stones, the resulting creations wonderfully present an interplay of art and nature, *ars et natura* (see cat. nos. 78, 79). Cutting exposes the stones' natural patterns and hidden beauty, while their sparkle and glow imbue the works of art made from them with unsurpassed richness.

1. Neugebauer-Maresch 1990.
2. The height is 4⅜ inches (11 cm). See Angeli 1989.
3. Exodus 31:18. All biblical passages quoted in this essay are from the King James Version.
4. See Ibn Jubayr 1952, p. 85. On the Kaabah, see Faroqhi 1990, pp. 15–43; Graf 2001, pp. 38–39. Ibn Jubayr's travels outside Spain took place in 1183–85.
5. Friess 1980, p. 21; Graf 1999.
6. See, for instance, *Indiana Jones and the Philosopher's Stone* by Max McCoy (1995) and *Harry Potter and the Philosopher's Stone* by J. K. Rowling (1997), later renamed *Harry Potter and the Sorcerer's Stone* for the U.S. edition.
7. Meier-Staubach 1977 (one of the most comprehensive introductions to the subject); Oldershaw 2003.
8. A scale of hardness compiled by the mineralogist Friedrich Mohs in 1812 gives gypsum an absolute hardness of 2 and quartz one of 7; the diamond, the hardest natural mineral, tops the Mohs scale with a hardness of 10. See Pellant 1992, p. 25.
9. Koeppe 2004.
10. See Frerichs 1969, p. 2; Friess 1980, p. 24; Landman et al. 2001.
11. See Seipel 2005, especially the essay by Sabine Haag (Haag 2005); see also Feustel and Heunisch 1992, p. 41.
12. Bowersox and Chamberlin 1995; Oldershaw 2003, "Lapis Lazuli," pp. 184–85; Schumann 2006, "Sapphire," p. 102.
13. MMA 2007.24. See Diana Craig Patch in "Recent Acquisitions" 2007, p. 7, ill.
14. See Friess 1980, p. 150.
15. See Sybille Ebert-Schifferer in *Faszination Edelstein* 1992, p. 193.
16. Scarisbrick 1993, p. 6.
17. Ibid. An example is depicted in *Faszination Edelstein* 1992, p. 95.
18. Genesis 41:42.
19. An example is in the Metropolitan Museum, acc. no. 1989.79. See also Alessandro Della Latta in Castelnuovo 1991, pp. 120–21, no. 20; Scarisbrick 1993, pp. 36–37, 71.
20. Ezekiel 28:13. Frerichs 1969, p. 66.
21. Exodus 28:21. P. Schmidt 1948, pp. 53–57; Friess 1980, pp. 32–33.
22. Exodus 28:17–20. P. Schmidt 1948, p. 53; Friess 1980, pp. 8, 32–33.
23. Graf 2001, ill. p. 22; Rossi (Ferdinando) 2002, p. 89.
24. Revelation 21:10–21. Friess 1980, p. 8; Giusti 2006b, p. 9.
25. Mielsch 1985; De Nuccio and Ungaro 2002; Napoleone 2006.
26. See "Hardstones" 1996, pp. 169–70.
27. See Draper 2008, pp. 5–6, 11–16.
28. Pliny the Elder, *Natural History*, 37:10 (English trans., Pliny the Elder 1855–57, vol. 6, p. 396); Distelberger 2002, p. 15.
29. Pliny the Elder, *Natural History*, 37:7 (English trans., Pliny the Elder 1855–57, vol. 6, p. 393).
30. Pliny the Elder, *Natural History*, 37:8 (English trans., Pliny the Elder 1855–57, vol. 6, pp. 393–94); Martial, *Epigrams*, 14:113 (English trans., Martial 1993, vol. 3, p. 269); see also Loewental, Harden, and Bromehead 1949, pp. 31–32.
31. Rossi (Ferdinando) 2002, p. 8; Guidobaldi 2003, especially p. 47, fig. 53, and p. 64, fig. 78.
32. Napoleone 2006.
33. Braunfels 1968; Belting 1984; Hugot 1986; Binding 1996.
34. Husband 2001, pp. 100–101, no. 35.
35. Schramm and Mütherich 1962, pp. 187–88, fig. 192; Zehnder 1982.
36. "cuius columnae episcopi sunt et doctores, in quo unusquisque lapis tanto amplius rutilat, quanto fidelior et melior est." Bruno of Segni, *Tractatus de sacramentis ecclesiae* 596 (*Patrologiae cursus completus* 1844–65, vol. 165, col. 1092B). See Binding 2002, p. 18, n. 67.
37. Binding 2002, p. 18, n. 67.
38. Giusti 2006b, p. 13.
39. Claussen 1989, pp. 65–80; Morley 1999, p. 64, fig. 107.
40. *Westminster Abbey* 1972, pp. 168–69. I am most grateful to Sir Hugh Roberts and Jonathan Marsden for providing me access to the area of the Westminster Abbey sanctuary containing the royal tombs and the pavement in September 1998.
41. The pavement in Murano is of the twelfth century; see Davanzo Poli 1999, p. 59; Sammartini 2000. The late Alessandro Albrizzi, of Venice and New York, graciously arranged for a special visit to the site in 1992.
42. Wixom 1997, p. 438; Morley 1999, p. 64.
43. Giusti 2006b, pp. 12–13.
44. Rossi (Ferdinando) 2002, p. 71.
45. Abbot Suger, *Libellus alter de consecratione ecclesiae Sancti Dionysii*, chap. 4 (English trans., Suger 1979, pp. 101, 103). See also Speer and Binding 2000, pp. 224–27; Untermann 2003. Ironically, that very day (now called Bastille Day) in 1789 saw the beginning of the French Revolution, during which uncontrolled troops would destroy countless treasures and historic buildings throughout France and, in subsequent years, in continental Europe.
46. Lewis 1958, p. 114.
47. Pliny the Elder, *Natural History*, 37:9 (English trans., Pliny the Elder 1855–57, vol. 6, pp. 394–95); Meier-Staubach in *Faszination Edelstein* 1992, pp. 123–24, no. 7; see also Meier-Staubach 1977, p. 63.
48. Theo Jülich in *Faszination Edelstein* 1992, p. 147, no. 40; Contadini 1998.
49. Epiphanius 1934, p. 165; Meier-Staubach 1977, p. 359.
50. Her hopes were not fulfilled, and she died in childbirth shortly afterward. Herman 2004, pp. 2–3, ill. facing p. 146.

Roman Inlay and Florentine Mosaics: The New Art of Pietre Dure

ANNAMARIA GIUSTI

A new art, or one of the many rebirths the artists of the Italian Renaissance were able to elicit from the inexhaustible reserve of formal models and technical inventions of antiquity? There can be no doubt that the Roman inlay of the Cinquecento was a direct offshoot of the ancient Roman opus sectile.[1] The *Abduction of Hylas* (fig. 15), formerly part of the revetment of the Basilica of Junius Bassus in Rome, is clearly a precedent.[2] Nevertheless, Renaissance hardstone inlay was indeed a new art, and unusually so: very seldom in the history of artistic rebirths do we witness the rapid development of a new form of expression that independently traces an original and long-lived path of its own.

This kind of evolution took place in the case of Florentine mosaics. As early as the later decades of the 1500s, Florentine artists broke away from the ancient model, first by abandoning the various types of marble of archaeological tradition, and then by choosing to treat themes and adopt styles consistent with contemporary developments in painting.

ROMAN POLYCHROME STONEWORK

In Cinquecento Roman inlay the derivation from antiquity remains more in evidence, but it too, even in its initial examples, proved capable of creating, with great élan, a decorative language expressed in original terms. The reemergence of the genre occurred in mid-sixteenth-century Rome, after a series of extraordinary archaeological discoveries made at the start of the century had reignited a passion for antiquity. Artistic taste began to tend toward sophisticated refinement. Although we know well that nothing in history repeats itself in perfectly symmetrical fashion, when we look at the luxurious polychrome inlays that encrusted the walls of Vatican palazzi as early as the middle of the fifteenth century—before they became the preeminent decorative apparatus of Roman church interiors—we cannot help but be reminded of Roman precedents. These ancient artifacts, incidentally, inspired Pliny, conservative in matters of customs and artistic taste, to express his disapproval of the excessive pomp indulged in by the Romans at the end of the Republican era.

The culture and tastes of the later Renaissance were ripe for a reworking of the ancient models that the Quattrocento artists had already looked to with keen attention. We can see such reworking in the drawings that Giuliano da Sangallo (ca. 1445–1516) made after the images he saw in the overlapping layers of the figurative sectile mosaics dating from the third century A.D. that during his day were still largely visible in the palimpsest on the walls of the Basilica of Junius Bassus.[3] And there were still other examples of mosaics—certainly more than have survived down to our time—that the ancient Roman ruins offered to the eyes of artists and lovers of things ancient in the Cinquecento, from floors presenting abstract geometric modules in what seem to be endless variations[4] to wall inlays in which ornamental and or figurative subjects predominate. But the illustrative

Fig. 15. *Abduction of Hylas*, from the Basilica of Junius Bassus, Rome, A.D. 4th century. Opus sectile mosaic and marble. Palazzo Massimo, Rome

Opposite: Fig. 14. Tabletop, Florence, 1570–85. Hardstones. Museo degli Argenti, Palazzo Pitti, Florence

13

Fig. 16. Giovanni Antonio Dosio, Design for a tabletop, Florence. Watercolor. Galleria degli Uffizi, Florence, Gabinetto Disegni e Stampe

mode, concerned with depicting naturalistic figures or landscape or still lifes, that would consistently prevail in Florentine mosaics of the Renaissance was banished or, at most, of marginal importance in Roman inlays. These inlays, at least in the initial phases of their development, most often are attributable to artists who hailed from the ranks of architects. Architects were responsible for designing not only interiors revetted with polychrome inlay but also the inlays when they came down from the walls and onto tabletops and other sumptuous furnishings. These decorations are among the most direct and original products of Renaissance pietre dure.

The *Farnese Table* (cat. no. 10), if not the earliest example of an inlaid table, is surely a fundamental prototype for the decorative style of Roman tabletops. It is based on drawings by the architect Jacopo Barozzi da Vignola (1507–1573). Another architect, like Vignola a designer of many tables, was Giovanni Antonio Dosio (1533–1609), who brought the nonfigurative, classicizing style of Roman inlay to Florence (see fig. 16). It is likely that only works commissioned by particularly illustrious patrons bore signature designs of renowned architects such as Vignola. However, the stone workshops active in Rome in the second half of the sixteenth century followed fashionable prototypes that were probably invented by eminent architects to produce nearly infinite variations on their geometric patterns. They manufactured inlaid tables in great quantities to meet the demands of their socially prominent clients; these tables gradually replaced pietre dure vases as the objects they most sought to collect.

Although produced by different craftsmen and workshops, Roman tables share a common language that derives from architects' designs. The principal elements of this language lie in the expertly used kinds of ancient marble; the focus on a central shape around which the composition is orchestrated; and the predilection for predominantly abstract decorative modules inspired by features of the ancient vocabulary of ornamentation, such as *peltae*, scrolls, and panoplies. There is no doubt that in the mid-sixteenth century a distinct and recognizable Roman

Fig. 17. Tabletop, Rome, 1560s. Marble. Palazzo Farnese, Rome

Fig. 18. Tabletop, Rome, late 16th century. Hardstones and marble. Museo Nacional del Prado, Madrid O-449, O-453

style was born, which developed continuously until the first quarter of the seventeenth century; and that the commonality of language shared by the objects in this geometric style makes it difficult and arduous, if not impossible, to determine the identity of the workshop that produced a particular piece.

The artists who made the inlays were not in the custom of signing their works, even though some of them were famous enough to rise well above the rank of good stonecutter. Take Giovanni Mynardo (Jean Ménard), for instance, the celebrated "Franciosino" (little Frenchman) active from 1552 onward, who frequented Michelangelo's circle in Rome and whose services were fought over by Francesco de' Medici (r. 1576–87) and Catherine de' Medici, wife of King Henry II of France, to whose court the artist finally transferred in 1579.[5] Some years later the Holy Roman emperor Rudolf II (r. 1576–1612) attempted to bring Mynardo to Prague, unaware that he had died in France in 1582.

What qualities made his works so desirable for such illustrious patrons? If it was indeed Mynardo who made the wondrous *Farnese Table*, as has justifiably been proposed,[6] he should be considered the likely creator and skilled craftsman of the typology of tables that feature complex inlaid decorative compositions, which in fact would account for his popularity. The early inventories (the first dates from 1568) of the Palazzo Farnese[7]—which housed one of the first collections of polychrome marble tables—confirm this, describing them as simpler in arrangement of design elements and technique, with most of the patterns disposed around the large central stone

slab. The inventories also make note of a "frieze of various multicolored marble around the perimeters" in listing the earliest of such tabletops, including a number of Cinquecento examples in the initial collections of Cosimo I de' Medici (r. 1537–74),[8] some of which may still be present in the Palazzo Farnese (fig. 17).[9]

The style was inaugurated, or at least magnificently represented, by the *Farnese Table*, the most widely known example of the type. It did not, however, constitute the sole accomplishment of Rome's Cinquecento art of inlay. Indeed, an extraordinary series of works, albeit rather limited in number, includes tables and cabinets, which, in contrast to the omnipresent variations of ancient marble, feature a stunning array of hardstones in sophisticated abstract combinations that exploit the qualities of the medium and its chromatic harmonies to the fullest. This, for example, is what we see in a tabletop in the Prado (fig. 18), which is grandiose, even in terms of size,[10] and the monumental cabinet said to have belonged to Sixtus V (r. 1585–90), now in Stourhead House, Wiltshire, England.[11] The phantasmagorical patterns of stone in these tables express a taste that foreshadows or is contemporary with Francesco I de' Medici's predilection for the shiny siliceous stones that began to appear in Florentine tables commissioned by him or that are simply traceable to his epoch.[12]

The same Roman stone workshops that carved marble often did not work pietre dure, which is a more specialized and complex affair. So difficult is it, in fact, that in Florence, where expertise in artistic techniques was certainly not lacking, at one point

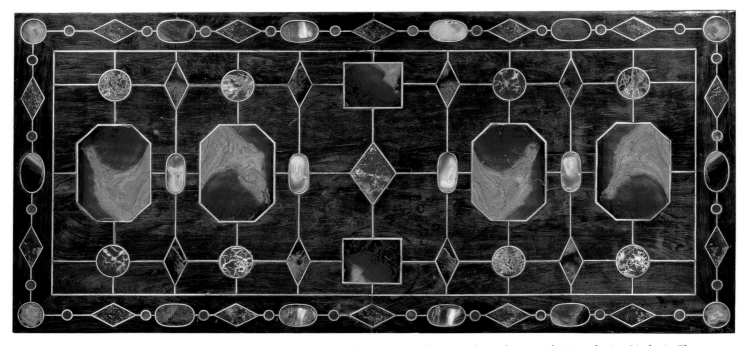

Fig. 19. Tabletop, formerly a pull-out shelf of a cabinet, Florence, late 16th century. Hardstones and wood. Museo di Mineralogia e Litologia, Florence

glyptic specialists were sent for from Milan, to execute in intaglio and even mosaic work the very tasks that shortly thereafter became the pride of the grand duke's workshops. Similarly, in Rome, which had become the principal center of artistic excellence over the course of the sixteenth century, many specialists in the use of precious materials[13] hailed from the north of Italy and may very well have played a part in perfecting the technique of hardstone inlay.

FLORENCE

Opus sectile enjoyed a splendid rebirth in Rome, but Florence was the center for the production of a genre that spread widely and was long-lived, a genre whose very name, "Florentine mosaic," testifies to the city's supremacy in this regard. The principal engine driving the establishment and ascent of Florentine *commessi* was the Medici passion for this technique and the concomitant support the various grand dukes provided to the *manifattura*, or court workshops, founded in 1588 as the Galleria dei Lavori by Ferdinand I de' Medici (r. 1587–1609). Ferdinand gave a "stable organization"[14] to the disparate workshops employed by the Medici and various other clients that Francesco I had brought together in the Vasarian complex of the Uffizi, where they served only the Medici. In this way they became a veritable State works. It was among the first formalized artistic laboratories in the service of a sovereign in Europe, and its example would soon win a widespread and illustrious following.

The institution of the Galleria dei Lavori represented the culmination and formalization of the sort of artistic patronage and collecting practiced by the first grand duke, Cosimo I de' Medici,

and his son Francesco. In their boundless passion for art, a special place was reserved for "le belle pietre," defined by the Dominican monk Agostino del Riccio in his 1597 treatise as utilizing local stones of antique origin and expressing the contemporary passion, impelled by both scientific and artistic motives, for the fantastic forms of Nature.[15] For Cosimo I such stones were, first and foremost, the various kinds of marble used in ancient Rome that were favored by the archaeologizing collectors of the time and brought in great quantity in slabs and fragments to Florence to be reworked. They were acquired as well in Renaissance Rome in the form of inlaid tables[16] and hardstone vases, the latter commissioned by Cosimo I from the famous Milanese workshops of the Saracchi and the Miseroni.[17]

Francesco de' Medici, however, favored the mirrorlike luminosity and seemingly limitless color range of pietre dure, a taste encouraged by his interest in the marvels of *naturalia*, or the products of nature, especially stone, and also, perhaps, by the artistic authority of Giorgio Vasari (1511–1574), who, even before 1557, had already designed a wood tabletop with a Moorish-style inlay of ivory, jasper, and other hardstones (cat. no. 9) for Bindo Altoviti, a Florentine notable residing in Rome. The table is novel for the complexity of its design and the prominence given the hardstones it includes. We should add, however, that the combination of wood and polychrome stone had already appeared, not only in Florence but also in Venice,[18] in the first half of the sixteenth century, the date attributed to an octagonal wood table in the Contini Bonacossi Collection at the Uffizi.[19] Toward the end of the century Francesco and then Ferdinand de' Medici would place in the Tribuna of the Uffizi, in

Fig. 20. *Stipo* (desk cabinet) of Cosimo I de' Medici, 1562–69. Wood, gold, hardstones, various gems, and enamel. Private collection

celebration of the prince's virtue, small architectural cabinets that featured pietre dure inlaid in the doors and in pull-out shelves of fine wood (fig. 19).

Today there remain only a few precious fragments of the grand architectural pieces, housed in the Tribuna, that evolved shortly after the mid-sixteenth century from the little cabinets in the Medici collection.[20] The prototypes are brilliant micro-architectures in which hardstones do not yet play the leading role but remain subordinate to gems and gold chased and shaped by the finest artists of the court.

We can only imagine what Francesco's architectural cabinet looked like, with its gold trimming and miniatures by Bernardo Buontalenti (1531–1608). We must often rely on the literature for information; indeed, it was thanks to the enthusiastic descriptions penned by Francesco's contemporaries Vasari and Vincenzio Borghini that the present author was recently able to identify a *stipo*, or desk cabinet, made between 1562 and 1569 for Cosimo I, which was at the Uffizi until the late eighteenth century. This piece, a magical and nearly intact relic of wonders that was thought to be forever lost, was rediscovered in an English private collection in 1997.[21] It features on its front twenty-eight reliefs in gold over plates of semiprecious stone, illustrating the exploits of Duke Cosimo[22] in three levels separated by pietre dure elements at regular intervals: the top is in agate and gold, the middle is lapis lazuli, and the last, at the bottom, is composed of carnelian half columns. There are also twenty-eight smaller reliefs of symbolic images; seventy-five gems including

Fig. 21. Detail of the *stipo* of Cosimo I de' Medici (fig. 20), showing herms

Fig. 22. Giambologna, *Bernardo Buontalenti Presenting a Model of a Fountain to Francesco I de' Medici in the Gardens of the Villa Medicea di Pratolino*, 1585–87. Gold and amethyst. Museo degli Argenti, Palazzo Pitti, Florence Gemme 1921:822

rubies, emeralds, opals, and turquoise inlaid in enamel cornices; and six modern cameos on the carnelian balustrade of the crown and a seventh of Ganymede on the tympanum over the door (fig. **20**). On the sides, where the rhythm of the herms and pilaster strips in gold and hardstones is echoed, twelve larger cameos, these of Imperial Roman origin, are embedded in the enamels, magnificently completing the cabinet's decoration and at the same time perhaps suggesting its function as a strongbox for Cosimo I's collection of cameos. A treasure enclosing a treasure is the concept that underlies this stunning piece of furniture, in whose golden reliefs we can perceive the hands of two distinct craftsmen (fig. **21**), both clearly from Cellinian circles.[23] Indeed, close examination might allow us to identify one of them, the artist who made the very fine busts on the herms, as Benvenuto Cellini (1500–1571) himself.

Although the authorship of Cosimo's cabinet may be somewhat unclear, it is unquestionable that its golden reliefs set a standard for the artistic milieu of the Florentine court, as witnessed by the plaquettes depicting the deeds of Francesco I (see fig. 22), designed some twenty or more years later to adorn his *studiolo nuovo*.[24] As in other Florentine pieces of the period, the

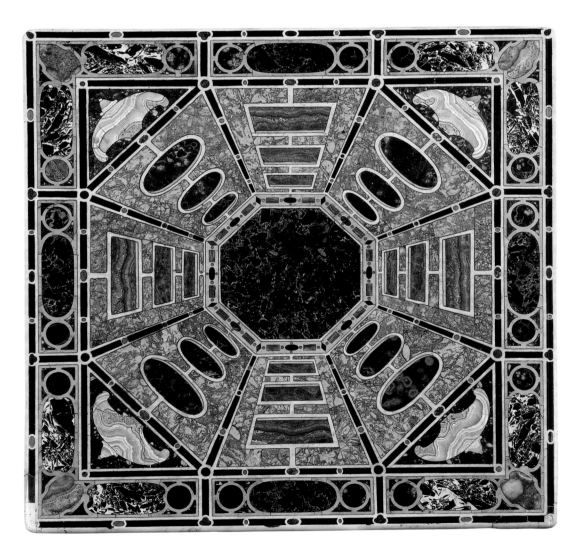

Fig. 23. Tabletop with perspectival geometric decoration, Florence, end of the 16th century. Hardstones. Herzog Anton Ulrich-Museum, Braunschweig, Germany

work of the goldsmith—in this instance the great sculptor Giambologna (1529–1608)—is more important than the stones. However, appreciation of hardstones, as well as their use, was gradually increasing at the Medici court. Vasari recounts that in the 1560s he was already designing tabletops, in which he incorporated such rare stones as chalcedony, carnelian, agate, and rock crystal.[25] Their appearance heralded the supremacy pietre dure would soon enjoy in Florentine works. The skill of local master stonecutters in Cosimo's service[26] alone may not have sufficed to elevate the stature of Florentine works. But the Caroni and Gaffurri families of artisans, who were summoned from Milan by Francesco I, contributed their expertise in the technique of intaglio applied to hardstone vases, an art in which Milan reigned supreme. Their talents together with the skill of local artisans were without doubt decisive in securing Florence's artistic reputation.

At the Casino di San Marco, where Francesco had established workshops specializing in the various artistic techniques he wished to transplant or perfect in Florence, the Milanese masters were to create such works as the celebrated flask designed by Buontalenti (cat. no. 22) and perhaps the astral geometries of the Museo degli Argenti table (fig. 14). Also from their hands may

have come the skilled perspectival schemes of the Birmingham[27] and Braunschweig (fig. 23) tables, which both display a taste for the intrinsic wonder of a broad range of stones, here organized in sophisticated abstract compositions. Under the patronage of Ferdinand I, the Caroni and the Gaffurri clearly enhanced their skill as stonecutters for vases with the craftsmanship of *commessi*, achieving a new level of technical expertise. A single craftsman specialized in but one technique: that of vases or of mosaics. Thus, in the late sixteenth century not even the excellent Ottavio Miseroni, another transplanted Milanese, in his case to the imperial court at Prague, was called upon to make pietre dure mosaics. For that, Rudolf II turned to the Florentine Cosimo Castrucci (see "The Castrucci and the Miseroni" by Rudolf Distelberger in this publication).

Notable among the many fine mosaic works undertaken by the Milanese in Florence was the celebrated table of landscapes, trophies, flowers, and heraldic insignias created for Emperor Rudolf II in the Medici workshops under the direction of Stefano Caroni between 1589 and 1597.[28] Also outstanding is Cristofano Gaffurri's table representing the port of Livorno, completed in 1604 (fig. 24), the extraordinary first attempt at the

Fig. 24. Cristofano Gaffurri, Tabletop with view of the port of Livorno, Galleria dei Lavori, Florence, 1604. Hardstones. Galleria degli Uffizi, Florence

veduta genre in Florentine mosaic. There is no doubt that these pieces mark a technical and formal turning point in the grand-ducal workshops and that they reflect the iron will of Ferdinand I that has left its traces in other spheres of activity as well.

As cardinal, Ferdinand had grown accustomed to the classicizing motifs of Roman inlay (see cat. no. 12);[29] as grand duke he strove to achieve previously unattempted art forms, for example works made of polychrome stone that were not, as he wrote, "in the ordinary form of mosaic"[30] but that could rival painting and, like painting, could treat a nearly limitless array of subjects, ranging from landscape (see cat. no. 27) and portraiture (see cat. no. 25) to themes from the Bible (see cat. nos. 28–30), and still life (see cat. no. 44). Thus out of Ferdinand's will and vision and the extraordinary skill of his craftsmen was born the characteristic, unsurpassed ability of Florentine mosaics to assume the character of paintings in stone. In these works virtuosic precision in the cutting and suture of uneven stone sections and an extreme sensitivity to the shades of the stones together produce the seductive illusion of an image that looks like a painting but is not a painting. Thus does Mannerist *artifizio* seem here to foreshadow and merge with the poetics of Baroque wonder, deceiving the viewers' senses and seducing them with the allure of an endless splendor offered by the inexhaustible chromatic imagination of Nature.

In this way the foundations were laid for the Florentine mosaic style, which changed little over time, despite variations in production and the evolution of taste. The Florentine court workshops epitomized excellence in the field of European decorative arts for more than two centuries, and Ferdinand's taste inspired various sovereigns, beginning with Rudolf II, his contemporary and emulator.

After the death in 1609 of this founder of the Florentine works, the naturalistic themes that had first appeared in the late sixteenth century (see cat. no. 44) came to prevail over other subjects. And in the second decade of the new century, the collaboration of the painter Jacopo Ligozzi (1547–1627)—an analytical, spellbinding draftsman who specialized in depicting the animal and plant worlds—with the Galleria dei Lavori intensified, culminating in the production of magnificent pietre dure mosaics such as that on a tabletop with scattered flowers (cat. no. 38).

Intertwined flowers, fruit-laden branches, and multicolored birds would become the distinctive emblem of Florentine mosaics in the seventeenth century and thereafter. Always recognizable, it was never repetitive, thanks to the inventiveness of the artists responsible for the models and to the perfectionism of the specialized craftsmen. Nor was this the exclusive subject treated in this period, for artists continued to create *vedute* and figurative historical scenes and to experiment with new inventions. The colors and shapes of the stones chosen were imaginatively exploited to create the forms of the images, a Florentine development not seen in contemporary Roman inlay. Among the innovative works one outstanding example is the spectacular ex-voto of Cosimo II (cat. no. 35), a summa of the artistic and material richness of the Florentine *manifattura* in which mosaic and relief in hardstone, enamel, goldsmithy, and jewels coalesce in a single magnificent image.

Over the course of the century, progress on revetting the interior of the Cappella dei Principi—the dazzling Medici mausoleum that must be counted among Ferdinand I's many artistic initiatives[31]—gradually slowed. The work of the Galleria dei Lavori, for its part, however, intensified, producing furnishings of regal magnificence, in which fine, inlaid wood, ivory, tortoiseshell, precious metals, and gilded bronze appear alongside pietre dure. Specialists in aspects of this wide range of luxurious materials, hailing from various places, contributed to the openness and cosmopolitanism of the Medici court. Following the practice instituted by the first grand dukes, the products of the ducal workshops were sent to royal palaces throughout Europe as coveted gifts, bestowed for the purpose of advertising the wealth and refinement of the little Grand Duchy of Tuscany.

During his long reign, lasting from 1670 to 1723, the penultimate grand duke, Cosimo III, was unrivaled in the level of his generosity. This largesse was displayed in a probably doomed attempt to gain favor for his dynasty, by then in decline and without direct heirs. "Certa fulgent sidera" (Surely the stars shine bright) was his reassuring but soon to prove inaccurate motto, taken from Horace; the stars may not have cast their light on Cosimo, but they no doubt smiled on the court's workshops. Beloved and encouraged by Cosimo, these flourished thanks to the presence of brilliant artists such as the sculptor Giovanni Battista Foggini (1652–1725) and Massimiliano Soldani-Benzi (1656–1740), whose bronzework for the Galleria dei Lavori was imitated across Europe.

When Foggini was artistic director of the Galleria dei Lavori, from 1694 until his death in 1725, the workshops produced such masterpieces of Baroque furnishing as a picture frame and a prie-dieu for the electress Palatine (cat. no. 55) and a cabinet for the elector Palatine (cat. no. 59), works that combine grandeur and imagination, material riches and subtle workmanship. These superlative objects were accompanied by other furnishings that were innovative in both form and decoration, such as reliquaries (cat. nos. 56, 57), jewel caskets (cat. no. 54), and clocks (cat. no. 51). In many of these small objects the inky tones of ebony and black marble highlight, by way of contrast, the vivid colors of stones and the luminous brilliance of the mercury-gilded bronze that Foggini molded into fanciful, vibrant forms with inexhaustible creative verve. In some products of the Galleria of this period, for example an octagonal tabletop recently rescued from oblivion (see entry for cat. no. 60), the taste for fashioning a work from numerous types of materials gave way to the exclusive use of hardstones. Magically evocative in their natural state, the stones initially bedazzle the viewer, who

Fig. 25. Tabletop, Galleria dei Lavori, Florence, ca. 1723–37. Hardstones. Staatliche Kunstsammlungen Dresden, Grünes Gewölbe

subsequently comes to explore and enjoy the inventive and consummately crafted details of the piece.

During the reign of the last grand duke, Gian Gastone de' Medici (r. 1723–37), despite the cloud of imminent doom that hung over the court and the grand duchy, the Galleria dei Lavori continued to produce such masterpieces as the medicine box given to Pope Clement XII;[32] the framed pictures and table (fig. 25) sent to Dresden in homage to the elector of Saxony; and especially the spectacular *Badminton Cabinet* (fig. 87),[33] an amazing summa of the Medici workshops' accomplishments in the realm of architectural furniture, as dramatic in structure as it is dazzling in the magnificence of its adornments.

NAPLES: THE REAL LABORATORIO

Surrounded by the splendors of its workshops, the Medici dynasty ended in 1737 with the death of Gian Gastone, who left no immediate heirs. Many contemporaries believed that the decline of the Medici would bring with it the decline of the *manifattura* so closely linked to them. This was surely the fear

of the ten masters who, in the very year of Gian Gastone's death, were invited to transfer to the court of Naples by Charles of Bourbon (1716–1788; ruled Naples 1734–59), who had seen the products of the Medici workshops firsthand in 1732. Thus a third royal laboratory was born of the Florentine matrix, following the first, in Prague, which appeared in the late sixteenth century, and the second, established in 1667 at the Gobelins of Louis XIV (r. 1643–1715) (see "The Castrucci and the Miseroni" by Rudolf Distelberger and *"Pierres fines"* by Florian Knothe in this publication). Installed at San Carlo alle Mortella, the Naples workshop—the Real Laboratorio—remained in existence until the Kingdom of Italy was established, in 1861. As such it was the longest lived of the related shops, although production was erratic, especially as the nineteenth century advanced.[34]

The Naples workshop's most brilliant period was the first decades of its existence, when the Florentine group, supplemented by a small nucleus of local helpers, was headed by Francesco Ghinghi (1689–1766). In Florence, Ghinghi's skills had rivaled those of Giuseppe Antonio Torricelli (1659–1719) (see

cat. nos. 49, 50, 55–59), the most important sculptor of semi-precious stone at the Galleria who was active in the years of Cosimo III's reign (1670–1723). Now, for King Charles, Ghinghi executed works in intaglio as well as mosaic. As we have seen, these were media that appealed to the taste of the last Medici era, when Ghinghi and his hands at the Neapolitan laboratory were learning their skills.

In 1759 Charles departed for Spain, whose monarch he became and where he ruled as Charles III. Many of the works executed or in the process of creation in Naples before that date are known to us only through documentation. The pieces that remain attest to the profound influence of Florentine models on the Neapolitan oeuvre, especially in subject. For instance, a pietre dure relief plaque now in Madrid (fig. 26) that shows the Annunciation[35] was inspired by the celebrated, much venerated Trecento fresco in Florence by a precursor of Giotto that had been the object of numerous translations into stone by the Medici workshops (fig. 27). Similarly, two pairs of tables finished between 1749 and 1763, also now in the Prado, could, if not for the documentary evidence,[36] be mistaken for Florentine works of the last Medici period. (One of the four is in this exhibition:

Fig. 27. *Annunciation*, Galleria dei Lavori, Florence, 1727. Hardstones. Museo dell'Opificio delle Pietre Dure, Florence 466

see cat. no. 127.) The interwoven plant motifs, fluttering birds, and acanthus foliage that give the tabletops their compositional and chromatic lushness closely compare with Florentine models, as do their impeccable workmanship and the broad array of hardstones they use. This last is especially surprising given that

Fig. 28. Console table, after a design by Gennaro Cappella, Naples, third quarter of the 18th century. Hardstones on black marble. Palazzo Reale, Caserta, Italy 1596

the Naples workshop did not have access to the vast reserves of stone that had been accumulated by the Medici.

Neapolitan mosaics show only cautious variations on the familiar themes in the form of the vegetal still life, even after the death of Ghinghi, which might have resulted in a break from the Florentine style. The cabinetmaker Gaspare Donnini, a member of the group that moved from Florence to Naples, succeeded Ghinghi as director of the Naples workshop, a position he held until 1780. He initiated work on two tables for the royal palace in Caserta and a second pair that is now in Palermo,[37] projects that proceeded slowly over the years 1763 to 1768. The single Caserta tabletop still extant (fig. 28) was made after a model by the Neapolitan painter and decorator Gennaro Cappella (active after 1777). Cappella attempted a bit of innovation, using the ultratraditional Florentine floral theme in a garland aflutter with Rococo rhythms and combining the inevitable, typically Florentine device of pearls scattered across the table with the new and fashionable accessory of the fan.[38] The preparatory drawing (also at Caserta) shows that for the background Cappella had originally planned to use a light-colored material along the lines of alabaster. This would have been more in keeping with the contemporary taste for pastel tones than the inexorable black of the final version.

In the last decades of the eighteenth century, Naples began to emerge as one of the liveliest centers of the new Neoclassical taste. At the Real Laboratorio, however, the documented and surviving tabletops strive principally to highlight the stones themselves, which are systematically organized to satisfy the severe aesthetics and the scientific approach of the Enlightenment or are presented as geological curiosities. This approach is apparent in the tabletop of petrified wood trimmed with amethyst created in 1795 and now in Palermo[39] and the table of 1811 featuring a chessboard inscribed within an oval cut from a dramatic fossilized tree trunk (cat. no. 128). This oeuvre does not appear to display the same creative vivacity and richness as the production of the Florentine establishment, which so brilliantly survived the dangerous transition from the Medici to the new stewardship of the house of Lorraine.

FLORENCE AFTER THE MEDICI

The next sovereign, Francis Stephen of Habsburg-Lorraine (1708–1765), chose to absent himself from Florence to fulfill his new role as Emperor Francis I (r. 1745–65) and consort of Maria Theresa of Austria in Vienna. This resulted in a certain provincialization in Florence but did not diminish the excellence of the city's production. In 1748 the workshop was placed in the hands of the enterprising Louis Siriès (ca. 1686–1762).[40] A goldsmith of French origin who specialized in the carving of cameos, Siriès effected a decisive change in Florentine mosaic, abandoning the Baroque style still favored in Naples and at the Vienna court.[41] In 1749 he invited the famous scene painter and high-society portraitist Giuseppe Zocchi (1711/17–1767)[42] to collaborate with the Galleria dei Lavori and design models for its pietre dure mosaics. Thus, two of Zocchi's signature subjects,

Fig. 29. A room in the Hofburg, Vienna

views and scenes of everyday life, became the focus of a series of more than sixty hardstone mosaics the workshop made from 1750 to 1765, destined to make up the extraordinary gallery of the Holy Roman emperor's residence in Vienna (fig. 29). Conceived by Siriès, the series was entirely original; nothing of the kind had ever before been attempted, and under his guidance all the energies of the workshop were focused on its production, winning the astonished admiration of contemporaries.[43]

Thus the Florentine workshops began again to treat the figurative subjects they had abandoned for nearly a century and a half and which had been their pride and glory in the early years under Ferdinand I de' Medici. These mosaics were not subordinate to the art of painting, thanks to their technical virtuosity and, above all, the exquisitely painterly sensibility of the craftsmen of the Galleria dei Lavori, who were able to interpret rather than merely transcribe the model into pietre dure. Their success can probably be attributed in part to Zocchi's direct participation in the choice of the palette of stones, in keeping with a long-established practice in the Galleria: from its very earliest days the workshop had called upon Ludovico Cigoli (1559–1613) and other painters to fulfill the role of "selectors of stones."

By virtue of his leadership in the creation of designs, Zocchi was instrumental in determining the future direction of Florentine mosaics. During his final years at the Galleria, he developed models for a pair of consoles in which the old taste for naturalistic subjects in Florentine mosaics found unusual and fascinating expression. In one it is presented in an airy festoon of flowers enclosing a flight of butterflies (cat. no. 106) and in the other a garland of seashells, pearls, and coral, emerging, as if by miracle, from the blue of a marine background (cat. no. 104). Not long thereafter the Florentine ducal workshops, responding to the current taste for the Neoclassical style, began to produce sober still-life compositions alongside vases in the antique and contemporary style (see cat. no. 115) provided by the new and gifted painter in charge, Antonio Cioci (d. 1792). Nevertheless, the marine themes introduced by Zocchi continued to enjoy favor in Florentine mosaics, presented in tabletops as well as in precious baubles. The Florentine workshops devoted much of their energy to these baubles featuring shells, pearls, and lapis lazuli, especially during the Napoleonic period. It is hardly accidental that the exquisite demi-parure that Élisa Bonaparte, grand duchess of Tuscany, gave to her sister Caroline, queen of Naples (cat. no. 125), is made of such jewels.

BEYOND ITALY: THE BUEN RETIRO
Zocchi's inventions for hardstone mosaics resonated beyond Italy in the workshops of the Buen Retiro, founded in Madrid in 1761 by Charles III of Bourbon after he left the throne of

Naples in 1759 for that of Spain. This sovereign with a passion for the art of pietre dure turned to the Florentine *manifattura*, as he had done twenty years earlier, now to enlist specialists to activate the new laboratory. Originally there were five craftsmen, three of them from Florence; there were nineteen by 1784, and thirty-five by 1808, when the enterprise was destroyed, a victim of the Napoleonic Wars.

In its scarcely more than forty years of life, the Buen Retiro achieved a production that was intense and noteworthy.[44] The series of nine splendid bronze-footed wall tables made between the late 1760s and 1796[45] after preparatory models by the Frenchman Charles-Joseph Flipart (1721–1797) alone validates this judgment. Five of the tabletops feature caprices of ruins, games, and views of ports that recall similar compositions designed by Zocchi for the series executed under Siriès and destined for Vienna. While the consoles' subject matter is often shared by scene painters of more or less the same age who are responding to the latest fashionable themes, this is, rather, a clear instance of Zocchi's influence, proven by the Buen Retiro tabletop with ballplayers (fig. 30), a subject also treated by Zocchi. The tabletop is bordered by a frieze of marine elements set against a lapis lazuli background; it is extremely close in its design and materials as well as the objects represented to a table executed after Zocchi's design in Florence in 1760–61 for the emperor

(cat. no. 104). In fact, they are so close that we can conclude that the Buen Retiro piece must have been directly inspired by Zocchi's table.

Flipart distinguished himself in the originality and imagination of his trompe l'oeil inventions, which present borders of illusionistically rendered objects, sometimes arranged around a central view. In four of the tabletops, one of which is included in this exhibition (cat. no. 129), these objects are the subject of the central composition. Illusionism is an ancient mode in painting as well as in other genres—such as scagliola, which often imitates the nobler art of *commesso*. Hardstone mosaic, however, had not been used to create trompe l'oeil works at the Florentine workshops. We cannot classify the vases in tabletop designs conceived by Cioci (who painted illusionistically in his private practice) as such, because they do not cross the subtle boundary that separates still life from trompe l'oeil deception. But this kind of deception was precisely what Flipart was after; he had, after all, received his artistic training in France, which in the eighteenth century was among the most vital centers of illusionistic painting. His inventions for the Buen Retiro tables were successful ones, magnificently executed by the laboratory's craftsmen and creating an intriguing, two-tiered play between the real-looking objects depicted and the central hardstone mosaic that looks like a painting.

Fig. 30. Console tabletop with ballplayers, workshops of the Buen Retiro, Madrid, after a design by Charles-Joseph Flipart, ca. 1770–80. Hardstones. Museo Nacional del Prado, Madrid O-456

FLORENCE: THE LATER DEVELOPMENT OF THE GALLERIA DEI LAVORI

In Florence, Cioci's successors continued to produce still lifes in his style from the late eighteenth century until the first quarter of the nineteenth century—along with views, which seem to have gone out of fashion after the emperor's stone picture gallery was completed. The grand-ducal workshops were ever eager to adapt their repertory of subject matter to the developments of contemporary artistic tastes. When Giovanni Battista Piranesi's views of ancient Rome enjoyed great success across Europe, for example, the Galleria dei Lavori began a series of six *commesso* frames in the genre (see cat. no. 117), only four of which were realized because of the disruptions of the Napoleonic era.

Unlike its sister workshop in Madrid, the Florentine Galleria survived the political upheavals of the time as well as the later advent of Italian unification (which, however, brought about the closing of the Naples laboratory). Under the new name of Opificio delle Pietre Dure, the old *manifattura* founded by the Medici continued to function into the final years of the nineteenth century,[46] successfully navigating a difficult transition—from serving the pomp of a now-bygone world, to satisfying the taste for luxury of fin-de-siècle bourgeois society. Rather than lowering the exceptional, and extremely costly, level of its production, the Opificio chose to pursue a new course and now works to preserve the magnificent hardstone objects it once created.[47]

1. The first to write of the *lithostrota*, or opus sectile, was Pliny the Elder, in his *Natural History* (36:60, 36:64), in which he states that marble inlay was first used in flooring in the early decades of the first century B.C.

2. What remains of the revetments in opus sectile in the Basilica of Junius Bassus, which date from the fourth century A.D., is today divided between the Musei Capitolini and the Palazzo Massimo, both in Rome. While side-by-side examination would confirm that the *Abduction* was an important example of opus sectile with a figurative theme, unfortunately it was not possible to include the prototype in this exhibition. Essential references on these and other *sectilia* are De Nuccio and Ungaro 2002, pp. 161–78, 465–81; Guidobaldi 2003.

3. See preceding note.

4. For full documentation of opus sectile floors, see Guidobaldi 2003.

5. For the rediscovery of this forgotten craftsman who played such an important role in the development of sixteenth-century Roman inlay, we are indebted to Tuena 1988.

6. Koeppe in Kisluk-Grosheide, Koeppe, and Rieder 2006, pp. 23–25, no. 7.

7. See Jestaz 1981.

8. Published in Conti 1893.

9. Datable to the third quarter of the Cinquecento, they were published in part in Giusti 1992, pp. 11–12, figs. 4–7.

10. González-Palacios 2001, pp. 59–64, no. 2.

11. Dated about 1585–90, the cabinet is cited several times in the literature but has not yet been the object of a monographic study; it was first published in González-Palacios 1982a, p. 17.

12. A fine example of Francesco I's taste is a square tabletop in white marble with geometric hardstone inlays in the Museo degli Argenti in Florence. Giusti in Baldini, Giusti, and Pampaloni Martelli 1979, p. 255, no. 1, pl. 1.

13. We need only recall that in the first half of the sixteenth century, stone-cutters on the level of Valerio Belli of Vincenza and Giovanni Bernardi of Castelbolognese were working in Rome, and that the renowned cameo master Giovanni Antonio de' Rossi moved there from Milan in 1560.

14. The Galleria dei Lavori, which brought together the disparate workshops of the grand-ducal court and artistic activities undertaken in them, was founded by Ferdinand I, with a letter patent, dated September 3, 1588; published in Zobi 1853, pp. 162–65.

15. Del Riccio 1597 (1996 ed.).

16. On the close connections between Roman inlay and Florentine *commessi* in the early period, see Giusti 2003b.

17. There still exists no systematic, comprehensive study of the vase collections of Cosimo, Francesco, and Ferdinand. Nevertheless, important research has been carried out, and we are greatly indebted to that of Aschengreen Piacenti 1967; Heikamp 1971; and especially Fock 1988 (with bibliography). More recently, on Milanese-made vases in the

Museo degli Argenti, see Mosco in *Magnificenza alla corte dei Medici* 1997, pp. 168–78, nos. 129–39; McCrory in Acidini et al. 2002, pp. 254–56, nos. 110–12.

18. See, for example, the lacquered wood tabletop studded with rare marble from Venice now in the Kunsthistoriches Museum, Vienna, first published in González-Palacios 1982a, p. 7.

19. The table was already listed in Cosimo I's 1553 inventory. See Maddelena Trionfi Honorati, who first published the piece in *Palazzo Vecchio* 1980, p. 208, no. 388.

20. Florentine museums have three surviving wood elements studded with semiprecious stones arranged in geometric patterns with metal trim from the cabinets of Francesco I and Ferdinand I; see Heikamp in *Magnificenza alla corte dei Medici* 1997, pp. 80–81, 83, nos. 41, 42, 44.

21. Giusti 1997c.

22. The iconography of Cosimo I's exploits is inspired by medals of the time: there is a striking recurrence of subjects borrowed from famous medals by Cellini, but the closest similarities are seen in the series of medals celebrating Duke Cosimo coined by Pietro Paolo Galeotti, an engraver at the Medici mint from 1555.

23. The sculptor Domenico Poggini worked at the Medici mint at the same time as Galeotti. Like Galeotti, Poggini was associated with Cellini. While the exquisite gold reliefs of the cabinet might be attributed to either of these craftsmen, those more strictly Cellinian in appearance, marked by refinement of modeling and developed sculptural approach, are more likely to be by Poggini.

24. The seven reliefs in gold leaf in this series are among the most celebrated pieces in the Museo degli Argenti, Florence. They depict the exploits of Grand Duke Francesco I in four lunettes set against a background of bloodstone and three rectangular panels set against a background of amethystine quartz. The most exhaustive studies on the reliefs are Heikamp in Giusti 1988, pp. 96–100, no. 12. I–VII; Amelio Fara in *Magnificenza alla corte dei Medici* 1997, pp. 74–77, nos. 33–39.

25. Vasari 1568 (1962–66 ed.), vol. 8, p. 37. In 1568, Vasari mentions a table made from one of his drawings for Cosimo I as already finished, calling it a "rare thing, all inlaid in Oriental alabaster, with the large pieces [being] of jasper, heliotrope [bloodstone], carnelian, lapis, and agate, with other stones and gems of value worth twenty thousand scudi." Just begun, on the other hand, was a "small table richly adorned with gems," also based on a design by Vasari, for the heir apparent, Francesco de' Medici.

26. The names of masters that emerge from the documents of the time are Bernardino di Porfirio of Leccio, mentioned by Vasari (see preceding note) as the author of two tables for Cosimo and Francesco de' Medici and the table for Bindo Altoviti in the present exhibition; and Domenico di Polo. Both worked in a laboratory equipped for their activities in the

Palazzo Vecchio, in which the prized marble specimens collected by Cosimo I were stored.

27. Giusti 1992, fig. 11.

28. After he received a table with rock crystals as a gift from Ferdinand I, Rudolf II secured permission from the grand duke to have a tabletop made by the Florentine laboratory at his own expense. This tabletop featured Bohemian jasper sent to Prague expressly for use in the table. Work on the table was carried out from 1589 to 1597 under the direction of Caroni, who accompanied it to Prague so he could present it to the emperor in person. Long since lost, the tabletop won the admiration of contemporaries, among them Agostino del Riccio (see note 15) and the Venetian ambassadors to the imperial court, who left behind partial descriptions of it.

29. Concerning Ferdinand's activities as a patron and collector when he was a cardinal in Rome, see Hochmann 1999.

30. The passage is from the letter Ferdinand I wrote accompanying the gift of the *commesso* portrait of Pope Clement VIII (cat. no. 25); published in Zobi 1853, p. 187.

31. Construction of the Cappella dei Principi, which was in its planning stages in the early years of Ferdinand I's rule, began in 1604, at which time part of the inlay designed for the dado and the altar-ciborium were ready or in the process of being made.

32. See Giusti in Giusti 2006a, pp. 73–74, no. 13.

33. See, in this connection, and also for its bibliography, Kräftner 2007.

34. I am indebted to Alvar González-Palacios for his reconstruction of the activities of the Naples laboratory in a series of studies published from 1977 to 1984. See also Valeriani 1988; Giusti 1992, pp. 223–47.

35. González-Palacios 2001, pp. 152–55, no. 26. It was González-Palacios who plausibly suggested dating the plaque now in Madrid to the first years of the Neapolitan laboratory's activity, identifying it with the work that Francesco Ghinghi wrote about in an autobiographical letter, taking credit for the execution of the two reliefs of the Virgin and the annunciating angel.

36. Ibid., pp. 149–51.

37. The tops of the two Palermo tables, made between 1763 and 1768, retain the naturalistic decoration against a black background but organize it into a more monumental and open composition bristling with plant shoots and conch shells in an orchestration of Rococo rhythms. Giusti 1992, pl. 117.

38. See Valeriani in Giusti 1988, p. 254, no. 75.

39. Giusti 1992, pl. 120.

40. This subject was recently explored in the exhibition "Arte e manifattura di corte a Firenze dal tramonto dei Medici all'Impero (1732–1815)," held at the Palazzo Pitti, Florence; see Giusti 2006a, in particular in the introductory essay (Giusti 2006c).

41. Flowers, feathery foliage, and pearl necklaces on black grounds are still the decorative motifs on a tray from about 1745 in the Schatzkammer, Kunsthistorisches Museum, Vienna (Valeriani in Giusti 1988, p. 194, no. 53), and on a table also made about midcentury, also in the Kunsthistorisches Museum, Vienna (Giusti in Giusti 2006a, pp. 104–5, no. 39).

42. For a reconstruction of Zocchi's career as a painter, see Tosi 1997.

43. The publication of the relevant documents and the study of the Vienna picture series was initiated by Giusti in Giusti, Mazzoni, and Pampaloni Martelli 1978, pp. 319–25, nos. 459–526. For a bibliographical update, see the more recent Giusti 2006a.

44. For the history and activity of the Madrid laboratory, see González-Palacios 2001. Indeed it is to González-Palacios that we are indebted for a good deal of what we know about the Madrid works.

45. Eight tables are in the Museo Nacional del Prado, Madrid, and the ninth is at the Palácio Nacional da Ajuda, Lisbon. Ibid., pp. 170–87, nos. 27–31.

46. The Opificio continued to function as a laboratory devoted to working with pietre dure until the end of the 1890s, yielding artistically felicitous results that had little commercial success. This was due to the high cost of its products, compared to those of the many private workshops active at the time in Florence. These competing workshops often imitated the designs of the Opificio but executed them without the perfectionism of the Florentine techniques. For a sense of the Opificio's activities in the period from 1860 to 1890, which are still awaiting exhaustive study, see Giusti, Mazzoni, and Pampaloni Martelli 1978, pp. 277–81; Giusti in Giusti 1988, pp. 222–23, no. 66; Massinelli in Giusti 1988, pp. 228–29, no. 69; Pampaloni Martelli in Giusti 1988, pp. 224–27, nos. 67–68; Giusti 2006b, pp. 237–48.

47. On this subject, see "The Opificio delle Pietre Dure" by Cristina Acidini in this publication.

The Castrucci and the Miseroni: Prague, Florence, Milan

RUDOLF DISTELBERGER

By about 1600, Prague had developed into Europe's third major center of glyptic art, after Milan and Florence, thanks almost solely to Holy Roman Emperor Rudolf II (r. 1576–1612), who had moved the imperial residence there from Vienna in 1583. The fashioning of decorative objects from hard or semiprecious stones (pietre dure) had become the rage among the elite of Europe. Because the value of vessels made of rock crystal or jasper far exceeded that of paintings by even the most famous masters, works of pietre dure were ideal vehicles for the ostentatious expression of princely wealth, and they began to fill the *Kunstkammern* (art rooms) that were just then coming into fashion.

As a young man Rudolf II had spent several years (1563–71) at the court of Philip II in Spain, where his eye was schooled on the very finest works of art. His standards were, accordingly, demanding. As emperor he sought to avoid the onerous rivalries among Europe's princes and to acquire his own sources of glyptic art. Rudolf was no doubt aware of the wealth of ornamental stones in Bohemia: the walls of the Wenceslas Chapel in Prague Cathedral as well as the Chapel of Saint Catherine (fig. 63) and the Holy Cross Chapel at Karlstein Castle had been covered with agates and jaspers during the reign of Charles IV (r. 1355–78), and there were a few surviving fourteenth-century vessels in the imperial collections and elsewhere (see, e.g., cat. no. 6). Where these stones had originated was no longer known, however, and thus the emperor dispatched stone hunters to relocate the sources of such treasures. In the fourteenth century the primary source for jasper and agate had been Ciboušov, a town in the Erzgebirge (literally, Ore Mountains), but since by the end of the sixteenth century this site had been forgotten, the majority of colored stones from Bohemia in the period beginning with Rudolf's reign would come instead from Kosakov, a mountain near Turnov, northeast of Prague. Certain varieties also came from the region around Freiburg, in so-called Further Austria (the scattered Hapsburg territories in Swabia, southern Alsace, and the Breisgau).

Before the establishment of the Prague workshop, Rudolf sent the most beautiful Bohemian stones to be worked in Milan, as is demonstrated by the fact that when the jeweler Jacomo Cyinich presented his wares in Prague in the spring of 1586, the emperor showed him "many types of stones and vases that he'd had made in Milan, and the stones were from Bohemia" ("molte sorte di pietre e vasi, che fa eseguire in Milano e quelle pietre sono di Boemia").[1] Scholars have heretofore paid scant attention to the origins of stones used in works of pietre dure, and as a result a number of errors have persisted. In general, it appears that the Prague workshops did not use stones from Sicily or the Apennines; on the other hand, Bohemian stones were certainly employed in Florence.

While in Spain, the young Rudolf had seen Roman tabletops decorated with marble intarsia, which is why, when he first set about to commission works of pietre dure, he attempted (in 1585) to lure a Roman master to Prague through his ambassador.[2] Although his efforts were unsuccessful, in 1589 Grand Duke Ferdinand I de' Medici (r. 1587–1609) sent the emperor an inlaid tabletop, which has now been lost. According to contemporary descriptions of it by the Venetian ambassador, Francesco Vendramin, as well as the 1619 inventory of the imperial collections at Prague, the tabletop was made of marble inlaid with alabaster, rock crystal, lapis lazuli, and other stones.[3] This would indicate that it had been executed in the Roman tradition, like early Florentine tabletops, and therefore that, like the Roman models, it had an abstract design (see, e.g., cat. nos. 10, 15).

That same year, Rudolf II ordered a table from the Medici court workshops, for which he sent stones from Bohemia and assumed all expenses. A team of *segatori* (stone sawyers) began cutting the first stones as early as November 1589, and the *gioiellieri* (jewelers) Ambrogio and Stefano Caroni (both d. 1611) and Giorgio di Cristofano Gaffurri (d. 1591) are said to have begun with the *commessi di pietre dure* in August 1590, working on them with a series of assistants until the end of February 1597.[4] (One marvels that it was possible for the most skilled artisans from the Florentine court workshop to devote themselves to an

Opposite: Fig. 31. Dionysio Miseroni, Vase with flowers, 1647. Citrine, gold, and hardstones. Kunsthistorisches Museum, Vienna, Kunstkammer

outside commission for six and a half years, although it is true that at the time the Cappella dei Principi, with its rich cladding of marble and pietre dure, had not yet been begun.) The painter Daniel Fröschl (1563–1613) created a colored drawing of the tabletop (now lost) for the Guardaroba (ducal furnishings) in 1597, before its chief master, Ambrogio Caroni, delivered the piece to Prague. According to Vendramin's report the tabletop cost an astonishing 20,000 scudi.[5] The sculptor Adriaen de Vries (ca. 1545–1626) created a bronze base for it in the form of a kneeling Ganymede with an eagle. In 1609 the Flemish naturalist and mineralogist Anselmus Boetius de Boodt immoderately praised the tabletop in his *Gemmarum et Lapidum Historia* as the seeming eighth wonder of the world.[6]

THE LANDSCAPE ISSUE

Although the tabletop Rudolf II commissioned from the Medici workshop has been lost, it plays a major role in the literature on pietre dure, especially with regard to the relationship between the artistic productions of Florence and Prague, and it is necessary to form some idea of what it looked like. We know that the table was roughly 4 feet (2 bracci) square, and that it was executed on a bronze backing.[7] The supervisor of the work was Jacques Bijlivert (1550–1603); according to his description of the table, a wide frieze ran around its edge, and within it were narrower, concentric friezes. Bijlivert complained in March 1592 that he had only just then received the design and the description (perhaps meaning the description of a section); he also noted that a crate of stones had arrived earlier, but without any instructions, and that this had caused delays.[8] Was he referring to instructions from Prague? From somewhere else? In 1593 the painter Lodovico Buti, a specialist in decorative designs, finally delivered drawings for the table's surrounding frieze, for three coats of arms, and for the three narrower friezes.[9]

A crucial question is whether or not the table included landscape *commessi*; although it has generally been maintained in the literature that it did, what has been written and often repeated is not necessarily true. The best description of the lost tabletop is by the Florentine Dominican monk Agostino del Riccio, who in his 1597 book on stones wrote, "it appears all of a piece, and not assembled in marble . . . the way they make tables in Florence and Rome" ("apparisce tutto d'un pezzo e non commessa in marmo . . . come si fanno i tavolini in Firenze ed in Roma").[10] This implies that a new technique had been employed to make the tabletop, one that corresponded to marquetry in wood. The many colors and the richly varied markings of the Bohemian stones were wholly new to the Florentine workshop. Del Riccio marvels at the agates: "they were in various colors and patterns, which were made of said stones" ("avevano varii colori e scherzi, che erono in dette pietre"), as well as the jaspers and carnelians "that vary in the color and patterns

that mother nature gives them" ("che variano di colori e scherzi che fa la madre natura in esse"). He also describes birds and weapons (trophies), among other things, depicted in the tabletop, but he makes no mention of any landscapes, even though these, if present, would have been the most sensational aspect of the piece, since they had not been previously produced in Florence.

It was the Fleming De Boodt, appointed personal physician to Rudolf II, who in his 1609 *Gemmarum* mentions seeing "landscapes" in the table. Yet his comments must be interpreted with caution. In his chapter on agates, for example, he writes—with no reference to Rudolf's tabletop—that in the stones' patterns one can make out woods, rivers, trees, animals, fruits, flowers, plants, and clouds: almost anything imaginable.[11] He repeats much of that in his chapter on jasper, relating how in the emperor's collection he has seen jaspers in which woods, trees, clouds, and rivers could be seen so clearly that they could almost be taken for pictures instead of stones. He goes on to say that the emperor had commissioned a tabletop of such stones, and that it had been ornamented with stones picturing villages, rivers, trees, mountains, cities, and clouds precisely as though in imitation of painting, so much so that one could not adequately praise the artistry of nature as well as the diligence and industry of the artist.[12] He particularly mentions how the artist had managed to fit the pieces together so that no lines were visible.

At that time, nature, as the work of God, outranked the works of humankind. The artist's selection of stones must have been such that one could *imagine* seeing in them landscapes, or portions of landscapes. Del Riccio described them succinctly: "patterns that mother nature gives them" ("scherzi che fa la madre natura"). Thus the stones themselves were what fascinated De Boodt, who had nothing to say about flowers, birds, or trophies: the products of human hands. Nothing by either writer provides any sure indication that Rudolf's table featured landscape *commessi*; they only mention agates and jaspers that *looked* like landscapes. Indeed, the Galleria dei Lavori, the grand-ducal workshop in Florence, was not producing landscape *commessi* either in the years before, or immediately after, the execution of Rudolf's table. The earliest surviving Florentine pietre dure landscape—a small family altar with a depiction of Christ and the Samaritan woman at Jacob's well (Kunsthistorisches Museum, Vienna)—dates from 1600.[13]

The center of Rudolf's table was ornamented with his monogram, *IRI*, made of gold bands with inset rows of garnets.[14] The monogram appears in the same unusual form on the large bloodstone bowl by the Prague stonecutter Ottavio Miseroni, dating from 1608, in the Louvre.[15] Rows of garnets, used to decorate vessel mountings made in Prague, are characteristic of the emperor's court workshop. This decorative motif alone could be an indication that someone in Prague helped to determine the tabletop's design.

THE CASTRUCCI FAMILY

During the time that work on Rudolf II's tabletop was under way in Florence, the so-called Castrucci workshop was producing its first works in Prague. The workshop's typical output is illustrated by four *commessi* in this exhibition (cat. nos. 66–69). The emperor had managed to attract the Florentine *gioielliere* Cosimo Castrucci to his court. Just when this occurred is unclear, but it very likely had something to do with the construction of the lavish table, whose materials and design necessitated frequent communication between Prague and Florence. Almost from the very beginning, the interlocutor in that exchange was Cosimo Castrucci, who in 1592 was provided by the emperor with a passport to Italy in which he was called "Ir. May. Edelsteinschneider" (His Majesty's gemcutter).[16] Who was Cosimo? No document has yet come to light in Florence that would indicate any connection between Cosimo and the Galleria dei Lavori. Two stone-grinding wheels purchased in Prague in 1593 for the grinding shop in nearby Bubentsch, presumably for Castrucci's use, were doubtless more useful for the creation of *commessi* than for the gem cutting of works in the style of Ottavio Miseroni (whose career is discussed later in the essay). The sources have little to say about Cosimo; they tell us only that in April 1600 he sent Bohemian stones to Florence.[17]

The key work in reconstructing Cosimo Castrucci's oeuvre is *Landscape with a Chapel and a Bridge*, which the artist signed on the back and dated 1596 (cat. no. 66; fig. 32). It is the earliest surviving landscape *commesso*, and it was executed not in Florence but in Prague.[18] The composition is based on Pieter Bruegel the Elder's painting *Hunters in the Snow* (Kunsthistorisches Museum, Vienna), which in 1595 had found its way to Prague. In Cosimo's small work, one can readily appreciate the characteristic features of his style. Both its compositional scheme and the way the artist employed stones to create forms as well as the illusion of space are repeated in the magnificent panorama in *Landscape with the Sacrifice of Isaac* (cat. no. 67; fig. 33). Once we have become familiar with Cosimo's hand from these two pieces, it is possible to recognize it once again in the lovely octagonal *commesso* in the center of a table in the Schatzkammer of the Residenz in Munich, into which it was inserted by the Augsburg craftsmen Hans Georg Hertel and Lucas Kilian in 1626.[19]

From historical sources, we can surmise that Cosimo Castrucci died in 1602. We know that his son Giovanni was in Prague by 1598 at the latest and by 1599 was selling to Florence smoky quartz, amethysts, and garnet rosettes from Prague.[20] In Florence it was probably suspected after Cosimo's death that the workshop would be dissolved and accordingly proposed that Giovanni Castrucci be summoned back from Prague. It was not Giovanni's artistic abilities that were needed, however, but his technical, craftsmanly skills. Indeed, Jacques Bijlivert wrote in a letter to the secretary of state, Belisario Vinta, that he did not

Fig. 32. Detail of Cosimo Castrucci, *Landscape with a Chapel and a Bridge* (cat. no. 66)

Fig. 33. Detail of Cosimo Castrucci, *Landscape with the Sacrifice of Isaac* (cat. no. 67)

need any more masters but good apprentices, since they tended to get more work done.[21] The small altar Rudolf II presented to Zdenek Adalbert von Lobkowicz and Polyxena von Pernštejn on the occasion of their marriage, in November 1603, bears almost no trace of Cosimo's superior mastery (see fig. 115).[22] And in a letter dated October 5, 1604, the director of the Florentine manufactory, Costantino de' Servi, wrote to Vinta from Prague that, as for *commessi*, there were no other masters in Prague but "Castruccio" and that he did not especially admire his works.[23] The Castruccio mentioned by de' Servi can only have been Giovanni, since Cosimo's artistic stature was beyond question.

In 1602 the Prague workshop set about renovating the grinding shop in Bubentsch. From a sketch by Friedrich Metzger, from Waldkirch (near Freiburg), we learn that slices for *commessi* were cut there.[24] This source, along with the Lobkowitz altar noted above, would indicate that the Bubentsch grinding shop was restored so that the *commessi* workshop could carry on. In sources from Florence and Prague the name Cosimo no longer appears after 1602, but in 1605 Giovanni Castrucci was paid 3,871 guilders for works he had made in Prague, and in 1609 he received another 9,270. Had his father still been active, these payments would have been made to him, as the workshop's director. These sizable sums, which suggest an active operation employing several hands, doubtless covered the costs of more than the seven panels of Giovanni's listed in the 1607–11 inventory of Rudolf II's *Kunstkammer*. Chief among these is the relatively large *Landscape with an Obelisk* (cat. no. 68). In this panel it is easy to make out Giovanni's personal style, which clearly diverges from that of his father. The composition is flat—a succession of zones parallel to the picture plane—and both the three-dimensionality of the scene and the sense of space are considerably reduced in comparison to Cosimo's works. Overall, one can say that Giovanni's works are notable for their decorative effect rather than for their illusionism.

Giovanni made himself popular in Florence by selling large quantities of stones at very reasonable prices. In June 1610, during a stay in Milan, he received 535 scudi and 5 lire for stones, and the following September he was paid 2,042 scudi, 2 lire, and 10 soldi for 1,033 pounds of Bohemian jasper that he had sent to the Florentines by way of Milan.[25] (Rudolf II's suspicion that the stone hunters he dispatched in Bohemia sold some of their findings for their own profit, referred to in a letter from the Bohemian court in 1608, was thus probably altogether justified.[26]) The Florentine court showed its gratitude to Giovanni by entering him in the grand duke's *ruolo* on August 22, 1610—without pay, however, but with all the associated privileges. On April 1 that year the emperor had appointed him gem cutter to the court, with a fixed stipend of 20 guilders a month.[27] From 1611 to 1612, Giovanni (or his associates) furnished stones, once again at a favorable price, for the Cappella dei Principi. In 1613 Ottavio

Miseroni sent four barrels of the highest-quality "diaspro di Boemia" (Bohemian jasper) to Florence, and Castrucci was once again on the move in Italy, about to leave for Prague to search for specific pieces of jasper for a work in Milan.[28] All this indicates that Giovanni Castrucci was highly active as an entrepreneur, which would have prevented him from being very personally engaged in the workshop. It is unsurprising, therefore, that earlier motifs were often repeated, and that works of uneven quality were allowed to leave the atelier.

Sources indicate indirectly that Giovanni Castrucci died in 1615, for in that year Grand Duke Cosimo II commissioned Giovanni's son, Cosimo di Giovanni, to finish as quickly as possible *Abraham and the Three Angels*, a *commesso* after a design by the painter Bernardino Poccetti (1548–1612).[29] Giovanni had apparently found the job beyond his abilities and had left it unfinished for many years. The younger Cosimo, a gifted artist who created the wonderful allegory of *Fame* in Florence (cat. no. 71)—which we assume is also based on a design by Poccetti[30]—died shortly thereafter, however, in 1619. The *Abraham commesso* was instead completed by Giovanni Castrucci's son-in-law, Giuliano di Piero Pandolfini, who delivered it himself to Florence in 1622.[31] These two figural *commessi* were as atypical for Prague as Prague's landscapes were a novelty for Florence. The *Landscape with Penitent Magdalen* and *Landscape with a Flaming Sky* (cat. no. 69), both of which reveal a new approach, can be dated to this late period in the Castrucci workshop. Especially characteristic of these two panels, now in Vienna, is the dramatically roiling sky, which had been prefigured in Giovanni's *Landscape with a Seated Peasant*[32] but that is otherwise unprecedented. It must remain undecided whether both pieces are the work of the younger Cosimo or represent the earliest of Pandolfini's *commessi*; arguments could be made for both possibilities.

In the Castrucci workshop's final years virtually nothing more was produced for the imperial court, now back in Vienna. Religious conflicts were raging, and after the victory of the Catholic League in the Battle of White Mountain on November 7, 1620, the wealthy and ambitious Prince Karl von Liechtenstein (1569–1627) entered Prague, armed with all the authority of a vice-regent and free to engage the atelier to create works for himself. At that time the workshop's director was Ottavio Miseroni, but it was Giuliano Pandolfini who set the artistic tone. The workshop executed a tabletop (fig. 34) and chest (fig. 35) for Prince Karl between 1621 and 1623.[33] Only in 1627, however, after the prince's death, did Pandolfini receive an additional 449 guilders for his work on the chest, while a certain Hans Bartzels was paid the balance of 25 guilders for his collaboration on the tabletop.[34] These late payments should not be taken as evidence that the Castrucci workshop was still in existence in 1627; indeed, since Pandolfini had resettled in Florence in either 1622 or 1624, it is much more probable that the

Fig. 34. Tabletop, Castrucci workshop, Prague, 1621–23. Hardstones, gilded bronze frame. Liechtenstein Museum, Vienna

workshop was dissolved, at the latest, following the death of Ottavio Miseroni in 1624.

THE CASTRUCCI AND FLORENCE

The independence of the Prague Castrucci workshop from the Galleria dei Lavori in Florence is demonstrated by differences in the technical execution of their respective *commessi*. In Prague, the individual slices of stone were not cut to a uniform thickness;

their undersides were ground with a series of irregular waves, and their edges were beveled. This required a considerable amount of extra work, although that could, of course, be delegated to assistants. To compensate for the varying thicknesses, the Prague workshop applied a layer of adhesive between the stones and the supporting slate thicker than that used in Florence. Another difference is that the adhesive used in Prague had a reddish tone (its composition has not yet been analyzed).

Fig. 35. Chest, Castrucci workshop, Prague, 1621–23. Gilded bronze and hardstones. Liechtenstein Museum, Vienna

Holes were drilled at regular intervals in the slate support, probably to facilitate the drying of the thick adhesive layer.

With Giuliano Pandolfini's move to Florence, the artistic presence and importance of the Castrucci family in that city becomes visible for the first time. The master had taken with him at least a portion of the Prague workshop's pattern material. Probably the first pieces he created there, about 1625, were three landscape *commessi* for Prince Karl von Liechtenstein (all Collection of the Reigning Prince of Liechtenstein, Vaduz)[35] composed of more Italian than Bohemian stones. *Landscape with a City on a River* was based on the same pattern as a Prague panel, now in Vienna, from the time of Giovanni Castrucci.[36] Clare Vincent has identified an engraving by Johann Sadeler I, dated 1593, as the pattern for *Landscape with a Tower and Houses on a Rock*.[37]

At roughly the same time these panels were being made, a cabinet chest with pietre dure inlays was produced in Florence.[38] The front was adorned with a beautiful landscape in the style of the Liechtenstein panels (that is to say, in Pandolfini's style), scattered flowers in the Florentine manner, geometric figures,

and slices of agate that look like landscapes. On each side of the chest is a bouquet of flowers following the same pattern as two bouquets on a Florentine tabletop dated by Alvar González-Palacios to about 1625–26.[39] The flowers are made of Italian stones. The ornamental panels above and below the side bouquets are repeated, in exactly the same form, on a Florentine cabinet now in the National Gallery of Canada, Ottawa.[40] The preponderance of Florentine elements on the Vienna cabinet clearly demonstrates that it was executed in Florence. Nevertheless the landscape—a Bohemian motif, although done for the most part without Bohemian stones—has led to the assumption that it was created in Prague.

An additional work of Pandolfini's, made while he was in Florence, is the slightly raised floral panel on the lid of the chest commissioned by Liechtenstein, which must have been inserted into it somewhat later.[41] It could be that the payment to Pandolfini in 1627, noted above, was in some way related to this piece. The panel comprises mainly Italian stones, and its individual sprays of flowers are based on the same pattern used for a second table that was made for Liechtenstein in about 1636.[42] These examples indicate that Pandolfini, under the influence of the Galleria dei Lavori, gradually abandoned the depiction of landscape in favor of the decorative, floral style of Florence, with its birds and butterflies. And with this shift, the dominance of the Castrucci workshop in the genre of landscape *commesso* was broken, even though isolated landscapes in the Prague style continued to be produced in Florence in the seventeenth century.

Landscape *commesso* had been a unique child born of Prague artists and Prague imperial direction. Its interplay between art and nature appealed directly to Rudolf II's pansophical world-view, which held that all things are permeated by a single spirit. This belief is more strikingly revealed in the depiction of land-scape in *commessi* than anywhere else: in the patterning and beauty of the stones themselves, derived from the macrocosm of nature, and in the work of the artist, who belongs to the microcosm.

THE MISERONI FAMILY

Among the artists surrounding Rudolf II, the Miseroni work-shop developed a style of its own. The so-called Prague school of stonecutting had begun in January 1588 with the appoint-ment to the court of the twenty-year-old Ottavio Miseroni (ca. 1568–1624), who had received his training in the workshop of his father, Girolamo, in Milan.[43] Ottavio's brothers, Aurelio and Alessandro, came to Prague with him, and his older step-brother, Giovanni Ambrogio (ca. 1551/52–1616), often spent time in Prague as well. From January 1598 on, the last was also engaged by the court; although he became *capo della casa* in Milan in early 1600, he continued to receive a stipend in Prague.[44] Since Giovanni was a specialist in *arte minuta* (gem cutting), one can probably detect his hand in the figural works from the Prague atelier. They are closely related in style to that of the Milan Miseroni workshop, and they are clearly distinguished from Ottavio's works by their sure treatment of human anatomy and sharper lines (see, e.g., cat. no. 72). Alessandro Miseroni was per-manently appointed to the court on December 1, 1605, although a passport from 1600 already identifies him as the emperor's gem cutter.[45] Aurelio, some three years older, was probably Ottavio's most important assistant in the beginning, but by 1610 he was once again living in Milan. With a proclamation dated September 2, 1608, the emperor elevated Ottavio and his brothers to the hereditary nobility, noting that all the brothers (not just Ottavio) had loyally served the emperor for more than twenty years at the imperial court in Prague, where they were at the time and would doubtless continue to be in future.[46]

Ottavio Miseroni's artistic development can by divided into three periods. In his works from the first period (1588–1600), he closely followed the Milanese tradition,[47] a prime example being his six-lobed jasper bowl (cat. no. 74). Chief among the works from this time is a large chalcedony pitcher, whose rim Paulus van Vianen (ca. 1570–1613) clad in gold in 1608 in a manner that accentuates the dragon's head on the handle, a later addition

(fig. 36).[48] Because the jar's round base originally required no mounting, Vianen sensitively placed the jar on a broad gold cir-clet that complements the Nereid figure on the lid.

During Ottavio's middle period, which lasted roughly until the death of Rudolf II in 1612, he developed, under the influence of Prague stonecutting, a new, unmistakable style approaching the Auricular (or lobed) style and which is unparalleled in glyptic art. By that time Ottavio had become established in the circle of court artists and was familiar with their works, distinguished by their soft, sensual surface treatments in this style. He, too, began to cut hardstone almost as if it were pliant and could be laid into folds. Characteristic of this mode—and an early exam-ple of the Auricular style—is his oval bowl made of variegated jasper (fig. 37), whose longer sides are decorated with grotesque masks seemingly made of some flowing substance.[49] Ottavio's most assured work, and certainly the masterpiece of his middle period, is a large bloodstone basin of 1608, now in the Louvre.[50]

Fig. 36. Ottavio Miseroni and Paulus van Vianen, Pitcher, ca. 1588–1600, 1608. Chalcedony and gold. Kunsthistorisches Museum, Vienna, Kunstkammer

Fig. 37. Ottavio Miseroni, Oval bowl, Prague, ca. 1600–1612. Jasper, enameled gold mounts. Kunsthistorisches Museum, Vienna, Kunstkammer

Ottavio Miseroni was particularly inspired during this time by his collaboration with the goldsmith and jeweler Jan Vermeyen (before 1559–1608) and his workshop,[51] resulting in *Kunstkammer* pieces of extraordinary beauty, such as a chalcedony bowl, the famous prasem (green quartz) bowl, and a bowl with a youthful Bacchus (fig. 38).[52] The Prague school distinguished itself by the variety and brilliance of the stones it employed, as it cultivated a new interest in the aesthetics of the materials themselves. In addition to vessels, the Miseroni workshop created cameos and relief *commessi*, a genre invented by Ottavio. With the latter, it was possible to achieve completely new, painterly effects, as

seen, for example, in his signed *Saint Mary Magdalen* (cat. no. 73). The workshop's style was now unique: that is to say, it had forged an artistic direction independent of both Milan and Florence, one that can appropriately be referred to as "Rudolfine."[53]

Interest in Ottavio's art declined after the death of Rudolf II. The court withheld payment from him, and the master's works became more rigid and increasingly lacking in their earlier verve. In 1622 Ottavio delivered a number of unmounted works to Vienna himself.[54] Part of that delivery was a large nephrite bowl probably conceived in his middle period (cat. no. 75). The most important works from his late years are two monstrances

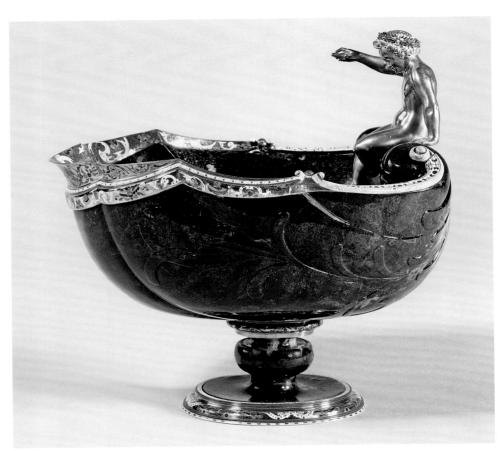

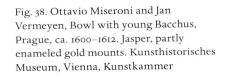

Fig. 38. Ottavio Miseroni and Jan Vermeyen, Bowl with young Bacchus, Prague, ca. 1600–1612. Jasper, partly enameled gold mounts. Kunsthistorisches Museum, Vienna, Kunstkammer

with depictions of the Madonna and Saint Anne in relief *commesso* and six large candelabra of Bohemian jasper.[55] Ottavio managed to get his son Dionysio (ca. 1607–1661), then only about sixteen, appointed to the court in 1623, but after Ottavio's death in 1624 the young artist was not yet experienced enough to be able to fill his father's shoes.

The late period of the Prague school begins with Dionysio Miseroni and comes to an end with the death of his son Ferdinand Eusebio (1639–1684).[56] In 1633 Dionysio was requested by the imperial court to deliver his father's unfinished vessels.[57] An imperial document from January 24, 1650, in which a large bonus payment is announced, refers to the fact that Dionysio had faithfully served for twenty-two years,[58] so it would appear that his service to the court had actually begun in 1628. The emperor later assigned him a variety of tasks; he became treasurer, was awarded the rank of groom of the chamber, and was appointed supervisor of building activities at Prague Castle. Dionysio owned two houses in the Malá Strana (Lesser Quarter) of Prague, below the castle, but he nevertheless kept his workshop and residence in the castle complex. The master's first

documented work, and thus the key piece in reconstructing his early years, is a large quartz vase (Collection of the Reigning Prince of Liechtenstein, Vaduz) from 1638 made for Prince Karl Eusebius von Liechtenstein (1611–1684).[59] The heavy, blocklike vase is shaped like a six-sided quartz crystal, a new form that would remain one of Dionysio's hallmarks. A system of ridges and fluting covers the vase's surface, producing a rich play of light. In 1642 Dionysio became highly celebrated for having turned a very large emerald from the mines at Muzo, Colombia, into a vase weighing 2,680 carats.[60] Another of his major works is the monolithic citrine vase from 1647, with its dense sculptural decoration and spectacular floral array (fig. 31).[61] In the 1650s Dionysio produced his major rock crystal pieces, most notably the famous pyramid (fig. 39),[62] whose upper cylinders he carved of crystal taken from inside the largest one on the bottom.[63] Work on eight very large crystal works in this relatively brief span of years required a sizable workshop; we know from documents that his shop, accordingly, employed fourteen people, among them specialists in *arte minuta*, who made intaglios.[64] Dionysio now stood at the height of his fame and fortune. He

Fig. 39. Dionysio Miseroni, "Pyramid" vase, Prague, 1650s. Rock crystal, gilded silver and enameled gold mounts. Kunsthistorisches Museum, Vienna, Kunstkammer

Fig. 40. Karel Škréta, *Dionysio Miseroni and His Family*, 1650s. Oil on canvas. Národní Galerie, Prague

even commissioned the Bohemian painter Karel Škréta (ca. 1610–1674) to paint a large portrait of himself and his family in the shop (fig. 40).[65]

The accession of Emperor Leopold I (r. 1658–1705) coincided with the end of Dionysio Miseroni's precipitous rise. By the time of his death in 1661, the genre of hardstone cutting had reached such heights of perfection that a considerable degree of creativity would have been required of his son, Ferdinand Eusebio, for him to continue in, or improve upon, the Miseroni tradition. But Ferdinand was not very gifted; his activity consti-

tutes a mere footnote to the Prague school, in which hardly any new ideas would be explored. Milanese gem cutters had in the meantime established themselves closer to the court in Vienna, and they thought little of Ferdinand's works. When Ferdinand died, in 1684, the Viennese court declined his widow's request to have his unfinished vessels completed with the help of an apprentice. Whereas the Castrucci workshop had exerted considerable influence on further developments in pietre dure in Florence, the long-standing Miseroni workshop simply died of old age.

1. Bertolotti 1889, pp. 52–53; Kris 1929, vol. 1, p. 104, n. 19.
2. Neumann 1957, pp. 166–67.
3. Ibid., pp. 167–68. Rebellious Protestants began an inventory of the imperial collections, complete with estimated values, in 1619, in preparation for the sale of the objects to help finance their troops. Morávek 1937, p. 12.
4. Fock 1974, pp. 107, 145–46; Fock 1988, p. 53. This early start is surprising, for as yet there was no overall design for the tabletop; see below.
5. Neumann 1957, p. 169.
6. Ibid., pp. 171–73.
7. Fock 1974, p. 145, n. 259. Accounting from May 1591.
8. Fock 1988, p. 54.
9. Ibid., p. 53.
10. Del Riccio 1597 (1996 ed.), pp. 183–84.
11. De Boodt 1609, chap. 95, pp. 245–46.
12. Ibid., chap. 103, pp. 255–56.
13. Fock 1974, p. 147; Distelberger 2002, pp. 174–76, no. 91. The oval panel with the depiction of the Piazza Signoria and the equestrian statue of Cosimo I of 1599–1600 (cat. no. 34) is not a landscape in the sense the term is being used here.
14. Bauer and Haupt 1976, p. 62, no. 1155.
15. Alcouffe 2001, pp. 343–44, no. 168; Distelberger 2002, pp. 272–74, no. 155.
16. I am extremely grateful to Manfred Staudinger for this information. Latin passport for Italy for Cosimo Castruccio, 1r. May: Stainschneid[er], tax gratis. Österreichisches Staatsarchiv, Vienna, Haus-, Hof- und Staatsarchiv, Reichshofkanzlei, Taxbücher, vol. 72 (1592), fol. 42r.
17. Przyborowski 1982, p. 401, doc. no. XIII.1 from June 16, 1600.
18. Cosimo could hardly have proven himself "a master of the 'pictorial' technique perfected by the Medici manufacture," as Annamaria Giusti says, because he never belonged to that manufactory in Florence; Giusti 2006b, p. 117. Rather, he proved to be the inventor of the landscape commesso in the spirit of Prague's court workshops.
19. Brunner 1970, no. 519; Seelig 1987, p. 34, and fig. 6; Langer in Langer and Württemberg 1996, pp. 62–67, no. 5; Giusti 2006b, ill. no. 103.
20. Przyborowski 1982, pp. 276, 528, doc. no. XVIII.3 from November 12, 1599.
21. The letter is reprinted in Fock 1974, p. 123, n. 146; Przyborowski 1982, p. 180, n. 179. From this same letter we learn that there was also thought of securing assistants from the workshop of Ottavio Miseroni. "It is interesting to point out that at this point Florence was already turning to the imperial court atelier for the recruitment of new hands and not to the traditional gem cutting center Milan"; Fock 1974, p. 123.
22. Nelahozeves Castle; Prag Mittelböhmische Galerie, inv. XI Ea1; 25¼ × 18⅛ inches. Bukovinská 1988, p. 166, and fig. 131; Hagemann 1988, p. 86.
23. Krčálcová and Aschengreen Piacenti 1979, p. 251; Giusti 1992, p. 140.
24. Bukovinská 1988, p. 161.
25. Fock 1974, p. 146, n. 266; Fock 1988, p. 52.
26. Köpl 1911–12, p. xx, doc. no. 20214.
27. Boeheim 1889, p. XVIII, doc. no. 5685; Neumann 1957, p. 180; Fock 1988, p. 52.
28. Przyborowski 1982, pp. 409ff., doc. nos. XXV.1 from February 1611, XXVI.1 from August 1612, XVII.1 from May 4, 1613.
29. Przyborowski 1982, pp. 276–77, 579–80, doc. no. LXXVII.3 from June 2, 1610, pp. 593–94, doc. no. XCVI.3 from May 12, 1622.
30. Museo dell'Opificio delle Pietre Dure, inv. 465; Giusti in Giusti, Mazzoni, and Pampaloni Martelli 1978, pp. 290–91, no. 81, pl. 67; Giusti 2006b, ill. no. 97.
31. Przyborowski 1982, pp. 276–77, no. 23. The panel is now in the Museo dell'Opificio delle Pietre Dure in Florence (inv. 460); Giusti in Giusti, Mazzoni, and Pampaloni Martelli 1978, p. 290, no. 75, pl. 79; Giusti 2006b, pp. 126, 128, ill. no. 100. In the document from May 12, 1622 (see note 29), the work is praised as having been executed "con bellissime macchie et al naturale di finissimi diaspri."
32. Distelberger 2002, p. 292, no. 176.
33. Vincent 1987; Distelberger 2002, pp. 296–300, nos. 180, 181.
34. Haupt 1983, p. 287, nos. 738, 739.
35. Distelberger 2002, pp. 333–34, nos. 206–8.
36. Kunsthistorisches Museum, Vienna, Kunstkammer, inv. 3000. Neumann 1957, p. 200, no. 25, fig. 212.
37. Vincent 1987, pp. 170–71.
38. Kunsthistorisches Museum, Vienna, Kunstkammer, inv. 3392. Distelberger 1998; Distelberger 2002, pp. 334–38, no. 209. Annamaria Giusti's claim that the work was executed in Prague is untenable; see Giusti 2006b, pp. 120 (caption to ill. no. 98), 128.
39. Whereabouts unknown. González-Palacios 1986, vol. 2, fig. 170; González-Palacios 2001, ill. p. 95. See also the flowers on the Florentine tabletop from 1624 in the Museo Nacional del Prado, Madrid: González-Palacios 2001, pp. 93–96, no. 12. An additional Florentine tabletop with very similar bouquets of flowers is in Vienna's Schönbrunn Palace. Giusti 2006b, ill. no. 73.
40. Giusti 2006b, ill. no. 99.
41. Today in the Liechtenstein Museum, Vienna; illustrated in Distelberger 2002, p. 251, fig. 37.
42. Giusti 2006b, ill. no. 108.
43. Distelberger 1999.
44. Kris 1929, vol. 1, p. 133; Distelberger 1999, p. 313.
45. Boeheim 1889, p. xv, doc. no. 5647; Distelberger 1999, p. 313.
46. Paraphrase of the proclamation in the Österreichisches Staatsarchiv, Vienna, Haus-, Hof- und Staatsarchiv, Verwaltungsarchiv, Reichsakten; attached to the proclamation is the new coat of arms for the Miseroni family painted on paper.
47. See Distelberger 1978; Distelberger 2003.
48. Distelberger 2002, pp. 259–61, no. 143.

49. Ibid., p. 270, no. 152.
50. Alcouffe 2001, pp. 343–44, no. 168; Distelberger 2002, pp. 272–74, no. 155.
51. Vermeyen, the son of the painter Jan Cornelisz. Vermeyen, had come to Prague by way of Frankfurt, where he worked between 1589 and 1597. He was appointed goldsmith to the court in Prague on October 1, 1597. Staudinger 1995.
52. Distelberger 2002, pp. 264–68, nos. 147–49.
53. See Distelberger 1997.
54. Bodenstein 1916, pp. CXV–CXVII, doc. no. 20608; Distelberger 1978, pp. 141–52.
55. Distelberger 2002, pp. 284–87, nos. 169–71.
56. For Dionysio and Ferdinand Eusebio Miseroni, see Klapsia 1979.
57. Bodenstein 1916, p. CXVI, doc. no. 20608, app. 6; Zimmermann 1905, p. LVII, doc. no. 19435, p. LXIX, doc. no. 19440, under JJ.

58. Distelberger 1979, p. 114.
59. Distelberger 2002, pp. 300–301, no. 182.
60. Kunsthistorisches Museum, Vienna, Kunstkammer, inv. 2048; 4⅜ × 2⅞ × 3⅜ inches; Distelberger 1979, pp. 126–31; Distelberger 2002, pp. 253–54. Displayed in the Schatzkammer.
61. Distelberger 2002, pp. 302–4, no. 184.
62. Ibid., pp. 310–13, no. 194.
63. Mineralogists maintain that one of the cylinders is not from the same block of crystal. Dancker Danckerts, who in 1655 produced an etching of the pyramid with a detailed legend, believed that the piece's creation out of a single block was its most amazing aspect.
64. Klapsia 1944, pp. 350–51, no. 154.
65. Národní Galerie, Prague, inv. O 560; Distelberger 2002, pp. 309–10, no. 193.

Pierres fines: *The Manufacture of Hardstone Works at the Gobelins under Louis XIV*

FLORIAN KNOTHE

Decorative arts produced in seventeenth-century France display much foreign influence, both direct and indirect. The direct impact of foreign artists is documented in objects made by artisans invited to work in France, such as Flemish tapestry weavers and Florentine lapidaries, as well as in those by artists who found their own way to the capital of the *industrie de luxe*, among them the cabinetmaker Domenico Cucci and the sculptor Philippe Caffieri. Less direct was the influence of works produced in manufactories outside France. The glassworks in Murano (est. 1291), the Galleria dei Lavori in Florence (est. 1588), tapestries workshops in Flanders (act. mainly fifteenth and sixteenth centuries), and, later, the Meissen porcelain manufactory near Dresden (est. 1710) are but a few European workshops that invited French emulation. In addition, from the early seventeenth century onward, the importing of Asian objects, most significantly Chinese porcelain and Japanese lacquer, enriched the domestic French market and inspired French artists to make adaptations of them.[1]

The fashion for foreign works of art was spread by connections between royal and aristocratic families both in France and outside the country. Italian products were first introduced to the French court by the Medici in the sixteenth century, becoming increasingly desirable after Henry II married Catherine de' Medici in 1533 and again when Henry IV wedded Maria de' Medici in 1600.[2] That interest was continued during the reign of Louis XIII (r. 1610–43) by the cardinals Armand-Jean du Plessis, duc de Richelieu, and Jules Mazarin, who collected Italian art seriously and invited foreign artists to work in France.[3]

The idea of organizing the arts and funding a royal workshop to support outstanding artists and artisans, both French and foreign, originated with Henry IV (r. 1589–1610). Workshops were established in 1602 in the Galerie d'Eau of the Louvre, a new wing that connected to the recently constructed Palais des Tuileries.[4] However, the main purpose of this initiative was, by a material show of force, to establish and strengthen the newly installed Bourbon family as kings of France.[5]

Opposite: Fig. 41. Detail of cat. no. 98, tabletop with landscapes, birds, and the goddess Diana, 1670–80

THE ROYAL GOBELINS WORKSHOPS

The hegemonial ambition of Louis XIV (r. 1643–1715) led to the foundation of numerous highly specialized royal manufactories that produced visual evidence of the king's *gloire*. The acumen and organizational skill of his controller general of finance, Jean-Baptiste Colbert, made it possible for the Crown to invest enormous amounts in these undertakings. From 1662, the Manufacture Royale des Meubles de la Couronne aux Gobelins was built up in Paris by bringing together existing local tapestry workshops and offering additional workspace and royal funding to the draftsmen, painters, engravers, and dyers involved in the production of new designs for tapestries, as well as to embroiderers, sculptors, cabinetmakers, and lapidaries (fig. 42). Colbert, Surintendent des Bâtiments du Roi from 1664 to 1683, was the manufactory's administrative director, while Charles Le Brun—who had organized a similar but smaller enterprise in Maincy, south of Paris, for the former finance minister Nicolas Fouquet, and had been named First Painter to the King in 1661—became the artistic director, overseeing the production of furnishings for the royal palaces. Following Colbert's economic directives, Le Brun collaborated with foreign artists and adapted their techniques to French production rather than importing costly objets d'art, especially Flemish tapestries and Italian hardstone panels, from abroad.

While the production of tapestries in France followed the Flemish tradition, the design of wooden furniture at the Gobelins owed much to earlier Italian examples: by Roman *ebanisti* (cabinetmakers) and *scultori*, such as Cucci, Caffieri, and Jean-Baptiste Tuby, and by the Florentine lapidaries known in France as Horace and Ferdinand Megliorini (Orazio and Ferdinando Migliorini), Philippe Branchi (Filippo Branchi), and Jean Ambrosio Gachetti (Gian Ambrogio Giacchetti).[6] The number of immigrant master craftsmen involved was substantial; indeed, throughout the seventeenth century the practices of *ébénisterie* (cabinetmaking) and *menuiserie* (carpentry) were dominated by furniture-making traditions from outside France. Although he directed the efforts of the workshops at the royal manufactory, Le Brun recognized the creativity and skill of his foreign collaborators and exerted minimal control over their work.

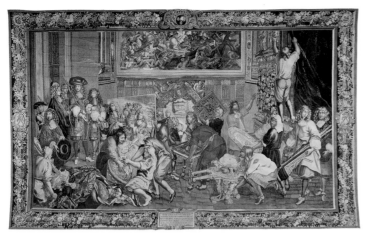

Fig. 42. Jean Jans after a design by Charles Le Brun, *The King Visits the Gobelins,* from the tapestry series *History of the King,* Manufacture Royale des Gobelins, Paris, 1665–80. Wool, silk, and gilt-metal-wrapped thread, 15 ft. 9 in. × 22 ft. 6⅞ in. Mobilier National, Paris GMTT 95/10

The manufacture of stone mosaic panels, completely new to the local industry, was one of the arts supported under Colbert's reorganization of French industry and trade according to mercantilist policies. In 1668, a workshop for *pierres fines*—precious stones—was established at the Gobelins. Here, four Italian masters—Branchi, Gachetti, and the brothers Megliorini—together with, at various times, French journeymen and apprentices, including Antoine Barré, François Chefdeville, André and Jean Dubois, Jean Le Tellier, and Claude Louette, as well as the workers Cheron and Cullot, produced marble panels

in the Florentine technique perfected at the Galleria dei Lavori, although in a somewhat different style.[7] These polychrome mosaic panels, executed both flat and in relief, served as tabletops and decorated cabinets made by Cucci. Their influence on the type of furniture produced at the royal manufactory was significant and continued unchanged until about 1699.

In his description of "the most remarkable sites in Paris," first published in 1684, the topographer Germain Brice wrote of the hardstone workshops at the royal manufactory,

> The works in inlaid stone were made in a workshop that was previously run by BRANQUIER and *Ferdinand* de MELIORI, who had come from Florence expressly for that type of work, which was still unknown in these regions. The entire composition was of precious stones, of different agates, of carnelians, jade, jasper, lapis lazuli, and other sorts, with which they fashioned landscapes, birds, flowers, and fruit, and which were used to decorate cabinets or tabletops. LE TELLIER, the student of the Italian masters of whom we have just spoken, continued that uncommon work, which required a very particular patience, but he stopped some time ago.[8]

Although Brice cites the production of pietre dure objects as a novelty in France, at the time that he wrote the royal workshops had been cutting stone and assembling decorative mosaic panels for fifteen years.

Fig. 43. Tabletop, probably Manufacture Royale des Gobelins, Paris, ca. 1670. Hardstones, 52⅞ × 40⅛ in. Musée du Louvre, Paris MR 406

Fig. 44. Tabletop, Manufacture Royale des Gobelins, Paris, ca. 1670–80. Hardstones, 68¼ × 52⅜ in. Musée du Louvre, Paris OA 5508

TABLETOPS MANUFACTURED AT THE GOBELINS

Under Louis XIV, the Garde-Meuble, or furniture repository, conducted inventories between 1663 and 1715 that altogether list twelve tables with hardstone mosaic tops. Four of these are known to be in public collections today.[9] One of them (fig. 43), from the collection of the Musée du Louvre, may be the earliest of the group and is related in design to early seventeenth-century Roman panels. It seems to represent an intermediary stage in the development of an independent style for "French" furniture manufactured by Italian master craftsmen. Its overall composition of spread-out flower garlands and ornament is traditional and foreign (see cat. no. 14), but it also includes golden fleurs-de-lis, the French royal insignia and an element found on many pieces of furniture commissioned for the royal households. Here, on a ground of lapis lazuli, the fleurs-de-lis surmount lyres, alluding to a symbolic relationship between Louis XIV and Apollo, the Greek god of music and light identified with the sun. Manifest in this early piece of Gobelins lapidary work is the visual program fabricated around the Sun King to proclaim the glory of his reign, which was greatly expanded, especially in the years 1661–89, to find expression in numerous artistic media.

In contrast to this piece, a second table at the Louvre (fig. 44) and its near companion at the Château de Compiègne (cat. no. 98; figs. 41, 46) exemplify the qualities of developed Gobelins hardstone manufacture, which departs from earlier

Fig. 45. Drawing for a hardstone tabletop, ca. 1670. Ink and watercolor on paper, 12½ × 16½ in. Bibliothèque Nationale de France, Paris, Cabinet des Estampes, Fonds Robert de Cotte, Ha 18 76C77040

Italian examples. While the decoration typical of Florentine and Roman panels is evenly distributed across the entire surface, each of these two Gobelins tabletops is partitioned into separate fields, creating the impression of being composed of several smaller panels. The depictions of flora and fauna, especially the isolated, rather precise ornithological representations of domestic birds, executed in a wide variety of hardstones with a range of colors, give these French works a less stylized, more natural appearance than their Italian models.[10] The Louvre table (fig. 44),

Fig. 46. Tabletop, cat. no. 98, with landscapes, birds, and the goddess Diana, ca. 1670–80

Fig. 47. Drawing for a hardstone tabletop, ca. 1670. Ink and watercolor on paper, 12⅝ × 16½ in. Bibliothèque Nationale de France, Paris, Cabinet des Estampes, Fonds Robert de Cotte, Ha 18 F000282

explicitly described in the royal inventory as "fait aux Gobelins" contains six tableaux depicting birds and four corner panels each with a large crowned intertwined *L*. In the central field, reserved for the French royal emblem, a large crowned cartouche displays three fleurs-de-lis on a lapis lazuli ground and is surrounded by spreading laurel branches like a victor's wreath. On the companion table (fig. 46) are a total of seventeen individual panels, the central one depicting Diana, goddess of the hunt, but no royal emblem. Of the four large rectangular panels, two show hunting scenes and the other two a duck and a woodcock; they refer to the royal hunt and, by extension, the Château de Versailles, which was conceived of as a hunting lodge for the French kings. The birds represented in the four corner panels are, however, more stylized and exotic than those in the larger ornithological depictions and are reminiscent of Florentine manufacture.

Both tabletops relate closely to a set of four watercolor drawings preserved today in the Cabinet des Estampes in Paris (figs. 45, 47–49). These finely executed designs display particularly un-Italian compositions and seem to have been drawn especially for the Gobelins pietre dure manufactory by Le Brun or members of his workshop.[11] The similarities of these drawings to the hardstone works make it obvious that, like cartoons for the tapestries, these were precise models, to be followed for layout and design as well as for color.[12]

A fourth surviving hardstone tabletop, which probably also originated in the royal manufactory, is completely different in composition (cat. no. 99).[13] It presents a polychrome map of France in the year 1684—including newly annexed regions to the north and east—all cut out of variously colored stones and inlaid into white marble. This work is an excellent example of

Fig. 48. Drawing for a hardstone tabletop, ca. 1670. Ink and watercolor on paper, 10⅜ × 13⅝ in. Bibliothèque Nationale de France, Paris, Cabinet des Estampes, Fonds Robert de Cotte, Ha 18 F000283

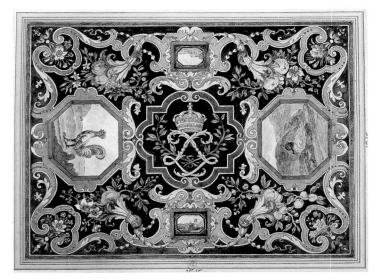

Fig. 49. Drawing for a hardstone tabletop, ca. 1670. Ink and watercolor on paper, 10⅜ × 13⅝ in. Bibliothèque Nationale de France, Paris, Cabinet des Estampes, Fonds Robert de Cotte, Ha 18 F000284

the use of art to project Louis XIV's royal propaganda. The political import of this piece is emphasized by an inlaid tribute taken from the *Aeneid*, "Hae tibi erunt artes," glorifying the Sun King's military campaigns. Virgil's phrase, "These are your arts," refers to the Roman "arts" of conquest and rule.[14] Other parts of the inscription state that the table was presented to the king by Claude-Antoine Couplet, a founding member at the Académie des Sciences in Paris, where he was professor of mathematics, and a page of the royal music ensemble the Grande Écurie. Clearly this gift also served to promote the young scientist and, he hoped, to advance his career.[15]

Custom-made tables of this kind were often designed for a specific location in the royal household. The table with ornithological depictions was commissioned for the Ménagerie palace in the gardens at Versailles.[16] This one with a map of an enlarged France is likely to have occupied a public place in Versailles, possibly in the state apartment or the Grand Trianon. These pieces of furniture importantly extend the range of objects produced at the Gobelins and of the imagery they disseminate, being both unique treasures in the royal collection and propagandistic expressions of the pervasive theme of royal grandeur.

Neither the royal inventory nor the royal account book provides sufficiently detailed information to support the attribution of objects to individual makers.[17] However, rare signatures are found in two seventeenth-century Gobelins relief plaques that were mounted on Parisian eighteenth-century commodes and cabinets (their reuse testifies to the revived interest in hardstone mosaics under Louis XVI; see "An Enduring Seductiveness" by Wolfram Koeppe and Florian Knothe in this publication). The signature is that of Jean Ambrosio Gachetti, whose service at the royal manufactory has been recorded in payments from 1670 to 1675.[18] It seems likely that he collaborated with the Megliorini and Branchi, who were also proficient in both relief and flat technique, since *artisans du roi* at the manufactory were often matched in teams and received collective payments from the royal accounts.[19]

Other insights into the lapidaries' working methods and information on their suppliers and the sources of their raw materials are provided by the lapidary Ferdinand Megliorini's detailed probate inventory (December 17, 1683); it contains evidence about his personal wealth, the size of his pietre dure workshop, and the objects and materials that were in stock at the height of its activity (fig. 50). Megliorini amassed jewelry as well as fine and decorative arts, many executed in hardstone, that indicate his social standing as a privileged *artisan du roi*.[20] The inventory, which was initiated by the royal administration, also lists numerous cut and polished stones ready to be assembled into relief panels as well as completed landscape and animal mosaics, all clearly stated to belong to the Crown, not the master craftsman. They were therefore to be transferred to Branchi, by then head of the royal manufactory's hardstone workshop.[21]

Other surviving documents include bills received by Branchi's workshop during the period after the deaths of Gachetti and Megliorini (May 18, 1688–July 2, 1693).[22] Branchi's "Memoires de menues dépenses faites pour le service du Roy" present his expenses for raw materials and tools and note payments the lapidary advanced to his helpers. Two documents concern the delivery of lapis lazuli, for which the price rose from 9 to 11.5 livres per pound over the five years documented, and another that of corals, for which a merchant, Pierre Balliot, was paid 35 sols per ounce.[23] Further papers refer to the employment of Jean Le Tellier, Antoine Barré, and Cullot, who were each paid a daily wage of 25 sols for polishing stones. They received their income directly from the Bâtiments du Roi, as did the apprentices at the royal manufactory, and seem to have been working exclusively for Branchi—the only lapidary recorded to have had this kind of support.[24]

Tabletops of *pierres fines* were displayed on gilded wood console stands, many of which (together with some of the matching gueridons) were probably the work of Philippe Caffieri and Paul Goujon La Baronnière.[25] Caffieri, a highly talented Neapolitan sculptor in wood, joined the Manufacture Royale des Gobelins in 1664 and, sometimes in collaboration with Domenico Cucci, was responsible for much of the sculptural furniture. In Caffieri's workshop delicate console tables were carved, many of them painted or gilded by La Baronnière, a French varnisher and gilder who had joined the Parisian art association the Academy of Saint Luke in 1651 and also worked at the royal manufactory.

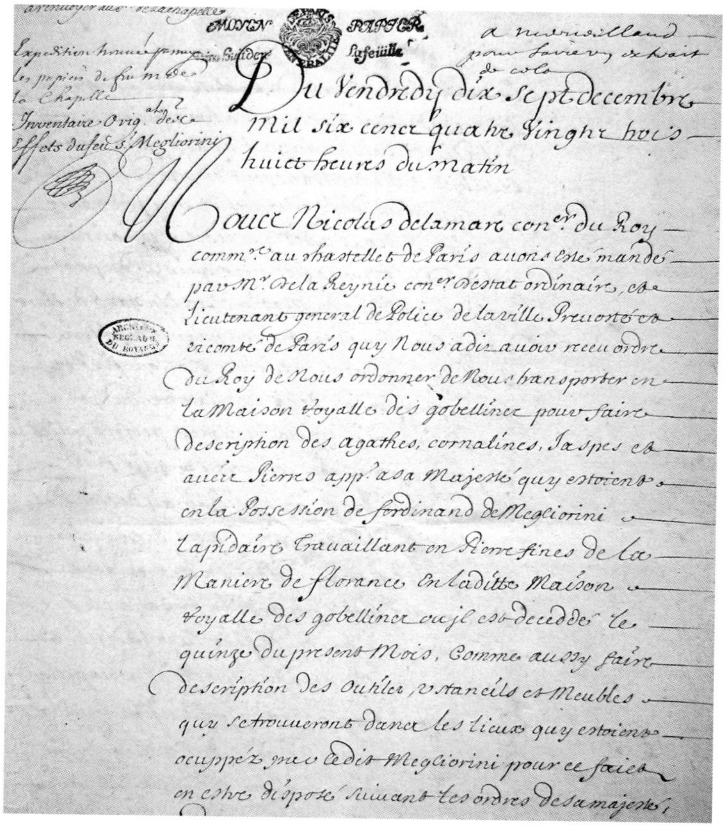
Du Vendredy dix sept decembre mil six cent quatre vingt trois huict heures du matin
Nous Nicolas delamare con.er du Roy commis.re au chastellet de Paris avons este mandez par Mr. de la Reynie con.er d'estat ordinaire, lieutenant general de Police de la ville Prevosté et vicomté de Paris quy nous a dit avoir receu ordre du Roy de nous ordonner de nous transporter en la Maison royalle des gobellins pour faire description des agathes, cornalines, Jaspes et autre Pierres app.t a sa Majesté quy estoient en la Possession de ferdinand de Megliorini lapidaire travaillant en Pierre fines de la Maniere de florence en laditte Maison royalle des gobellins ou il est decedde le quinze du present Mois, Comme aussy faire description des outilz, ustancils et Meubles quy se trouveront dans les lieux quy estoient occuppez par led. Megliorini pour ce faict en estre disposé suivant les ordres de sa majesté

Fig. 50. Page from the probate inventory of Ferdinand Megliorini, December 17, 1683. Archives Nationales, Paris O[1] 2040[B]

Fig. 51. Domenico Cucci, one of a pair of cabinets, 1679–83. Ebony, oak carcass, gilded bronze mounts, marble slabs, and hardstone mosaic panels; 83⅝ × 63 × 17 ¾ in. Collection of the Duke of Northumberland, Alnwick Castle, Northumberland, England

Fig. 52. Domenico Cucci, one of a pair of cabinets, 1679–83. Ebony, oak carcass, gilded bronze mounts, marble slabs, and hardstone mosaic panels; 83⅝ × 63 × 17¾ in. Collection of the Duke of Northumberland, Alnwick Castle, Northumberland, England

Fig. 54. Plaque depicting a dog, detail of fig. 51. Hardstones

Fig. 53. Plaque depicting a cockerel, detail of fig. 52. Hardstones

COLLABORATIVE PRODUCTION OF CABINETS

In addition to tables, a number of cabinets decorated with hardstone plaques are listed in the Inventaire Général du Mobilier de la Couronne, or royal inventory (1663–1715). Two of these are described as "faite aux Gobelins"; but all of them, in materials employed and style of decoration, are linked to the production of the royal manufactory.[26]

The best known and most celebrated of all the Gobelins furniture makers was Cucci, whose manufacture of monumental cabinets mounted with hardstone panels deserves detailed analysis. He produced very traditional cabinets of a type deriving from the Italian *stipo*, a large ornamental cupboard, and decorated them with inlaid hardstone mosaic panels in a rich, conservative style known from earlier workshops such as the Galleria dei Lavori in Pietre Dure in Florence.[27] Cucci's training in Naples and continued practice following Italian traditions made possible the reproduction in France of goods that had formerly been imported, and he became a very successful supplier of decorative cabinets to royal châteaux. The Comptes des Bâtiments records fifteen pieces of furniture Cucci was paid for; the Inventaire du Mobilier lists two cabinets (nos. 10, 11) explicitly named as by Cucci and describes another eighteen objects of similar Baroque architectural style, materials, and techniques and associated with the late sixteenth and early seventeenth centuries, suggesting that other woodworkers also contributed to the undertaking.[28]

Cucci's artistic versatility as a sculptor, cabinetmaker, and bronze founder, together with the royal privileges he enjoyed as an *artisan du roi*, guaranteed him close control over a kind of production that, outside the royal workshops, would have been the work of professional craftsmen belonging to three different guilds.[29] From his woodwork and metalwork shops emerged pieces of furniture that, in both their combinations of materials and their perfection of detail, were novelties in France; and, by collaborating with Branchi, Gachetti, and the Megliorini, he was able to decorate his finely worked wooden, bronze-mounted carcasses with both flat and relief panels in pietre dure.

A pair of cabinets produced at Cucci's workshop between 1679 and 1683, now in Alnwick Castle in England, demonstrate the sculptural qualities that distinguish French royal furniture of the late seventeenth century; they also incorporate a variety of materials that would have been possible to finance and politically permissible only for a royal workshop (figs. 51, 52).[30] In the Inventaire du Mobilier, where they are listed as numbers 372 and 373, the pieces are said to have been made at the Gobelins (a rare instance of objects being assigned to a specific workshop) and are described as large cabinets with relief stone plaques in the Florentine manner; the gilded bronze decorations are enumerated at length.[31]

The structure of the cabinets is unusual. Each has an additional lower register with three lockable fall fronts mounted

Fig. 55. Engraving of the cabinet shown in fig. 52, annotated in black ink. Private collection

with pietre dure panels; above this is a more traditional upper cabinet with three doors, also mounted with stone panels, in a highly architectural setting. The top frieze contains gilded bronze mounts over hardstone plaques, which flank a round central medallion displaying Louis's monogram of intertwined *L*s and a crown. The stand is low in comparison to those of other seventeenth-century cabinets and is decorated with richly carved swags of flowers and shell motifs just above the "pieds de boeuf" feet.[32] Cucci employed ebony discreetly, as a veneer in narrow strips rather than as full panels. It provides a contrast to the brightly gilded bronze term figures and architectural details and the colorful hardstone plaques.

Since the chests were especially commissioned by the Crown, it is surprising that their pietre dure panels seem not to have been custom-made for their specific placements but rather selected on the basis of size to fit into the bronze-framed doors and fall fronts. They are flat mosaic depictions of animals and landscapes, and relief panels of fruits and flowers (figs. 53, 54). The upper doors are each composed of two or three different plaques, and the lower fall fronts are mounted with one or two hardstone panels each, arrangements that seem dictated by the

Fig. 56. Mme de Montespan's *appartement des bains*, Versailles, ca. 1675. Painting on the leaf of a fan, gouache on paper. Victoria and Albert Museum, London

sizes of the plaques, not their iconographies. The individual plaques are separated and framed in wide gilded bronze mounts to make them large enough to cover the door panels. The small landscape scenes seem too small for the spaces they decorate, and for the viewer to appreciate. Furthermore, the overall pictorial scheme is incoherent. While royal symbolism typically adorns Louis XIV furniture, there is none in the stonework, and neither the landscapes nor the flora and fauna refer to anything specifically French.[33] The cabinets are clearly described as having been made entirely at the Gobelins, yet the nature and arrangement of the pietre dure panels make them more closely resemble pieces of furniture mounted with plaques that had been collected as souvenirs than they do more thoughtfully designed cabinets—or, indeed, the iconographically superior (if at times equally incoherent) *pierres fines* tabletops assembled at the Gobelins.[34]

Of great importance to an evaluation of the Alnwick cabinets and of production at the royal manufactory in general are two engravings representing the cabinets, hitherto unknown to the scholarly community, that survive in a private collection in France (fig. 55).[35] Engraved in meticulous detail, the prints show the fine quality and design of the mosaic panels and include handwritten notes in ink indicating the colors of the pilaster and frieze panels; these seem to be precise annotations made on

the spot by a visitor to the royal palaces or workshops and showing a keen interest in the style, materials, and color scheme of these monumental pieces. (Unlike the watercolor drawings of tabletop designs used in their manufacture, these prints do not provide any measurements.)

Possibly of even greater importance at the time than these two cabinets were another six similar ones celebrating Apollo and Diana, Glory and Virtue, and War and Peace, for which Cucci was paid by the Crown from 1665 to 1673.[36] None of them are known to survive today. At a cost of 35,500 livres the pair, the cabinets representing the temples of "la Gloire" and "la Vertu" were the most richly decorated and expensive pieces of furniture ever made for the king. Alexandre Pradère notes that one such cabinet is depicted on a fan leaf in what is believed to be an imaginary representation of Mme de Montespan's *appartement des bains* at Versailles (fig. 56).[37] If the cabinet did indeed belong to Mme de Montespan, it is noteworthy that it relates closely to those at Alnwick: its upper part seems to contain a central door flanked on each side by three smaller doors or drawers, all faced with pietre dure plaques, and its central panel is separated from the side panels by gilded bronze statues. Caryatids also flank the outer corners at the front and back of the upper cabinet, intensifying the architectural quality of the design, which evokes the facades and interior wall paneling of

Fig. 57. *Louis XIV Receives the Ambassadors of the King of Siam, September 1, 1686.* Published in the *Almanach Royale,* 1686. Musée du Louvre, Paris, Département des Arts Graphiques

low relief representing the principal motif of Le Brun's painting *Battle of the Granicus,* which depicts Alexander the Great's first victory against the Persians. The inclusion of this image here alludes not only to the painting but also to the Gobelins tapestries and engravings by Sébastien Le Clerc, the principal engraver at the Gobelins, on the same subject, as well as to subsequent prints produced to propagate the *Histoire d'Alexandre,* a five-piece set of images by Le Brun depicting scenes from the classical hero's life that metaphorically praises the king's own virtues and military achievements.[42]

This tapestry representation of a cabinet, and further images of cabinets or other decorative furniture in pictorial sources such as the fan leaf described above, do not prove the existence of the pictured items or their exact appearance. However, since nearly identical objects in a coherent style appear repeatedly on canvas, in tapestries, on silver plate, and in textual descriptions, it seems possible that these works known today exclusively from visual representations did exist in much the way they are shown. Like decorative tables of *pierres fines,* the cabinets served primarily as showpieces rather than utilitarian objects; the furnishing of Louis XIV's palaces provided for both everyday necessities and artistic display.

FOREIGN VISITORS AND CHANGING PRACTICES

From its foundation, the royal Gobelins manufactory was regularly visited by not only Louis XIV but also foreign dignitaries and ambassadors, who were led, often by Le Brun himself, on guided tours through the workshops to acquaint them with the costly artifacts produced for the French court. These minutely planned official visits, along with others to the richly decorated royal châteaux, were part of a larger program to impress visitors with the sophistication of France's artistic production and to establish the Bourbon king as a generous patron of the arts.

One magnificent diplomatic visit was that from the ambassadors of the king of Siam (modern Thailand) in 1686 (fig. 57).[43] As European powers became increasingly interested in establishing contacts with East Asian countries during the second half of the seventeenth century, Siam received visits from a French ecclesiastical mission in 1673 and from diplomatic and commercial envoys in 1684.[44] Two years later a delegation from the Siamese king arrived in France in response to the French visit, and its lengthy sojourn caused something of a sensation.[45] The royal audiences, receptions, and visits held in its honor were avidly described in the *Mercure galant,* a fashionable society magazine. Among the royal institutions visited by the ambassadors from Siam were the Académie Royale de Peinture et de Sculpture and the Manufacture Royale des Gobelins, where Le Brun explained the various types of artworks and crafting techniques. At the Gobelins, he first led his visitors to his atelier and apartment, next passed a courtyard in which tapestries were

Renaissance and Mannerist buildings.[38] As with the two surviving cabinets, here gilded bronze mounts frame the hardstone plaques; natural stone panels, in this case of lapis lazuli, are used as pilasters and for the frieze; and ebony, employed economically, creates an effective contrast to the gilded bronze mounts and figures and the colorful stones.[39]

Three other cabinets, possibly related to the production of Cucci's workshop, were decorated with busts of the kings of France, miniature paintings representing the combats fought and towns captured during the reign of Louis XIV, portraits of the king of Spain and of Louis XIV and his ministers, and small paintings of their games and diversions—all extending the iconography of a set of fourteen tapestries entitled *Histoire du roi* (History of the King) that presents a visual history of Louis XIV's life.[40] A fourth piece, similarly decorated, is depicted in the Gobelins tapestry commemorating the audience given by Louis XIV to the papal nuncio Cardinal Chigi at Fontainebleau on July 28, 1664.[41] At the center it shows an oval bronze plaque in

displayed, and then entered "the place where they work on inlaid stone pieces, which cost more than a thousand écus per square foot, according to what [Le Brun] told the ambassador, who asked about it." As the *Mercure galant* went on to explain, "All the stones that become part of this work are precious stones, and they cut such small ones that it is almost impossible to see them before they have been set in place. The work is lengthy because of the hardness of the material, and it takes several years to complete a single square. The ambassador not only looked at the stones used for this work, he also examined all the small pieces drawn from them and all the tools that the workers used."[46] By reporting on Le Brun's explanations and the ambassadors' keen interest in the work of the lapidaries, the *Mercure* introduced its entire readership to the *pierres fines* workshops at the Gobelins and brought an awareness of the value and status of their meticulously assembled mosaic panels.

In 1687, following this visit, the king of Siam was presented with twelve "marble tables with sculpted and gilded stands," eight from Louis XIV and four from his son, called Monseigneur, according to an account in the *Mercure*, "Presens qui sont partis pour Siam."[47] Although there is no further explanation of the marble tabletops or the carved stands, it seems more than likely that these now-lost pieces originated at the Gobelins, since it was customary to offer visiting court dignitaries objets d'art of the kind and value they observed during visits to the royal palaces and workshops.[48] Payments to the lapidary Branchi and sculptor Caffieri from the royal account in 1686 suggest that they made these precious objects.[49] Constantin Phaulkon, a Greek Christian who served Phra Narai, king of Siam, as prime minister and had organized and led the embassy to France, received similar gifts from François-Michel Le Tellier, marquis de Louvois, and Jean-Baptiste Colbert, marquis de Seignelay and Louis XIV's controller general: "six large tables in oval jaspé marble," "a very rich Savonnerie carpet," and "four large marble tables, with their frames and sculpture stands entirely gilded," among other works of art, luxury objects that also likely originated in the royal workshops.[50]

Testimony of a different foreign visitor to the Gobelins sheds additional light on the manufactory. Between 1675 and 1702, Ehrenfried Walther von Tschirnhaus, a German scientist and mathematician, made four research trips to major European cities, including Paris, to engage in an exchange of knowledge and conduct industrial espionage. He was in Paris in 1675–76, 1679, 1682, and 1701–2.[51] In 1702 Tschirnhaus described a previous visit to the Gobelins manufactory, where he seems to have been especially interested in, and impressed by, the pietre dure workshops: "In addition I have been at the Gobelins, where tables and panels are created *à la mosaica*, of a beauty and richness seen nowhere else. They use a great deal of our Saxon jasper in these, and when I showed them the samples I had brought with me they were very interested in it, but only

lamented that at the moment the king showed so little desire for more such work."[52]

While the lapidaries at the Gobelins complained to Tschirnhaus about a dwindling number of commissions of pieces with jasper decoration, he himself observed over time an increasing production of wooden furniture with marquetry veneer. The making of silver furniture, an art so cherished by Louis and his contemporaries at home and abroad, had stopped somewhat abruptly, for monetary reasons, in 1689. And the manufacture of pietre dure mosaic panels at the Gobelins diminished considerably after Branchi died in 1698 and the last of the three original workshops came under the direction of Jean Le Tellier, who had been in Branchi's employ.[53] Le Tellier continued to be paid as a journeyman by his master's daughter, Catherine-Charlotte Branchi, until at least 1699; thereafter he ran the workshop as the principal master, with one apprentice, his son Louis, until 1727.[54] Thus Colbert's original plan had succeeded. Foreign workers, invited to France to produce there masterpieces of a kind hitherto imported from abroad, had transferred their artistic skill and expertise to a younger, French generation.[55]

Tschirnhaus witnessed a change in the style of royal furniture and decoration, which took place about the turn of the century. To some extent, this reflected the desire of French courtly society to distance itself from stiff court etiquette and its most opulent and monumental expressions in art. In fact, only two hardstone-mounted cabinets were inventoried in the royal collection after 1684, and they were of Italian origin; they came to the French court as diplomatic gifts from the papal nuncio Cardinal Antonio Pignatelli.[56] After this time, it seems that mosaic tabletops were the only objects in pietre dure that continued to be manufactured for the royal collection.

Altogether, the Sun King's need for art presenting royal iconography probably diminished with his increasing age; nevertheless, methods of royal propaganda remained intact, and fashions changed more rapidly outside the palaces than inside. In this period, some courtiers moved from Versailles to Paris, and that move in itself brought certain social changes. But there were other, more significant forces at work at the turn of the century. The French economy had been weakened by international warfare and national upheaval, necessitating a reduction in royal spending for the arts. The first *arrêt du conseil*, in 1691, limited the employment of precious raw materials like gold and silver; following that, a royal edict issued in 1700 forbade the gilding of bronze mounts and wood for application on furniture.[57] Contemporary with these economic changes and financial restrictions was a generational change at the Gobelins manufactory. The overall result was that after the 1699 appointment of Jules Hardouin-Mansart, the king's chief architect, as superintendent of royal buildings, the Gobelins workshops entered a new phase in which production was almost exclusively focused on tapestry weaving. Painters and engravers remained on staff to produce cartoons for the tapestries and engravings after them and continued to be funded by the Crown. But from then on, furniture for royal use was either bought from independent makers and dealers or produced at the Louvre workshops, where André-Charles Boulle became the most celebrated *ébéniste* of the early eighteenth century.[58]

An analysis of the descriptions in the royal inventory suggests that the large pietre dure cabinets designed by Cucci in a homogeneous, opulent style had been favored items for the decoration of large interiors in the Louvre and at Versailles. But when production by the royal workshops was reduced in the mid–1690s the manufacture of those monumental works ended, and from then on smaller pieces, often veneered with marquetry of wood, tortoiseshell, brass and pewter, or colored horn, were favored.[59] In 1702 Tschirnhaus wrote of this technique being the latest thing: "I have also carefully studied the kind of work that is now the great fashion in France, called marquetry,

from which they produce writing tables, cabinets, and many other things. Have brought along an example of it."[60] The stylistic advances in French furniture making had been achieved by incorporating and then further refining long-practiced techniques introduced to France by immigrant *ébénistes*, such as Cucci, in the mid-seventeenth century. However, the loss of creative leadership at the Gobelins after the death of Le Brun in 1690, together with the aging of the manufactory's entire founding generation, ultimately resulted in a shift of artistic dominance from the Gobelins to the Louvre. There a younger generation of highly skilled furniture makers, such as Boulle and Alexandre-Jean Oppenordt, carried out work based on designs by Jean Bérain, an outstanding practitioner of the Rococo style that was taking shape in France in the early 1700s. These artists developed the new types of furniture and surface decoration by which French furniture making rose to dominate European taste in the eighteenth century.[61]

1. Huth 1971, pp. 86–89; Wolvesperges 2000, pp. 13–15, 89–95.

2. Jean Ménard (ca. 1525–1582), a French lapidary, operated a highly regarded workshop in Rome (see cat. no. 10), from which he exported hardstone mosaic panels to Catherine de' Medici, among other patrons. He returned to France in 1579. See Ronfort 1991–92, pp. 140–42.

3. A pietre dure table in the Musée du Louvre, Paris (MR 405), was made in Italy during the last quarter of the sixteenth century and was part of Cardinal Richelieu's collection in the Château de Richelieu. See Alcouffe, Dion-Tenenbaum, and Lefébure 1993, vol. 1, pp. 332–33; Goldfarb 2002. Although less than half the size, it resembles a hardstone table attributed to Jean Ménard that was made for Alessandro Farnese about 1568–73 (cat. no. 10).

   Cardinal Mazarin owned a large collection of objects imported from his native Italy, including twenty-one Florentine cabinets, seven of which were decorated with hardstone panels. See "Inventaire des meubles, cabinets, joyaux, médailles, vaisselle, tableaux, statues, tapisseries et argent du cardinal Jules Mazarin," March 31, 1661, Bibliothèque Nationale de France, Paris, MS, Mélanges Colbert, no. 75. For Mazarin's collecting, see Aumale 1861; Alcouffe 1974; Michel 1999; Laurain-Portemer 1975, pp. 65–100; Conihout and Michel 2006.

4. A royal edict protecting the Louvre workshops was released by Henri IV on December 22, 1608; see Archives Nationales, Paris, MS, O¹ 1672.

5. The religious and civil unrest that accompanied Henry IV's accession to power was not overcome, and the political and economic situation was not stabilized, until after the Thirty Years' War (1618–48) and the resolution of the Fronde, or civil disturbances, that followed (1648–53).

6. Furniture made at the Louvre workshops, in contrast, utilized techniques brought in by German and Flemish makers. This development to some extent paralleled the success of German and Flemish émigré artists in Florence, where their techniques were adapted by local manufacturers. See Bohr 1993, pp. 63–65. See also entry for cat. no. 41.

7. Mosaic panels of the quality presented here were described in Italy as "commessi in pietra dura" or "pietre dure" and in France today are called "pierre dure." However, in French seventeenth-century sources we find the terms "pierre de rapport" (inlaid stone) and "pierre fine" and "pierre de Florence," references to the subtle (*fine*) and difficult technique and to its foreignness.

8. "Les ouvrages de pierre de rapport se faisoient dans un attelier, qui a été autrefois conduit par BRANQUIER & par *Ferdinand* de MELIORI, venus exprès de Florence pour cette espece de travail qui étoit encore inconnu

en ces pays ci. Toute la composition en étoit de pierres précieuses, d'Agates différentes, de Cornalines, de Jade, de Jaspe, de Lapis Lazuli, & d'autres sortes, desquelles ils formoient des payïsages, des oiseaux, des fleurs & des fruits, qui servoient à embellir des cabinets, ou des dessus de table. Le TELLIER éleve des maîtres Italiens dont on vient de parler, a continué ce rare travail qui demande une patience toute particuliere, mais il a cessé depuis quelque tems." Brice 1725, vol. 2, pp. 397–98. In fact, it was Branchi who resumed direction of the hardstone atelier in 1683. He continued to practice until his death in 1698.

9. Two tables are in the Musée du Louvre, one is at the Château de Versailles, and one is at the Château de Compiègne. Also listed are tabletops made from single sheets of stone, such as porphyry. Guiffrey 1885–86, vol. 2, pp. 131–32, 136–40, 147, 151, 155, 156, 159, nos. 12, 13, 53–56, 60–72, 74, 164, 234–36, 279, 304, 339–41.

10. The closest comparison to these Gobelins tabletops is perhaps the panels made by Cosimo Castrucci the Elder and Younger in Prague; see "The Castrucci and the Miseroni" by Rudolf Distelberger in this publication.

11. Bertrand Jestaz' argument linking this design to number 279 in the royal inventory is interesting, but although it clearly shows the "chiffres du Roy couronnez," it does not have "quatre bouquet de fleurs" in the corners, suggesting rather that the Gobelins produced a range of very similar objects. See Jestaz in *Collections de Louis XIV* 1977, p. 283, no. 294.

12. It might be argued that the unusual character of these drawings and the fact that they were part of Robert de Cotte's collection of graphic works are indications that the four drawings were made after completed tabletops as a record of works produced at the Gobelins during Cotte's superintendence. But such a practice is otherwise unknown, and Cotte became superintendent only in 1699.

13. See D. Meyer 2002, vol. 1, pp. 194–95.

14. Virgil, *Aeneid*, 6:851–53. See Griffin 1979, pp. 65–66.

15. For Couplet's involvement at the academy, see Briggs 1991.

16. See A. Marie and J. Marie 1976, p. 221. The royal artisans also produced for the same Ménagerie palace a table varnished to imitate jasper. See ibid., p. 224.

17. Typically the lapidaries were paid in a lump sum, for their appointment. For example, the payment of 1,920 livres to Branchi year after year suggests that he received a stipend for his services to the Crown, like other royal artisans, and was not reimbursed for valuable materials he obtained, despite the declaration of his expenses. Nor was he paid for the individual works he made. See Guiffrey 1881–1901, vols. 1–4.

18. Two commodes, one in the English and one in the Swedish royal collection, are decorated with Gobelins *pierres fines* panels signed by Gachetti. See Setterwall 1959, p. 433, figs. 8, 13; Watson 1960.

19. See Guiffrey 1881–1901, vol. 1, cols. 445, 559, 708, 777, 852.

20. The furniture, tools, machines, rings, silver plate, and some of the stones and other personal goods (including snuffboxes presented by the grand dukes of Tuscany), inventoried as nos. 50–55, 129, 131–39, were passed on to the abbé Zipoli, the executor of Megliorini's last will. Some of the tools, nos. 41 and 42, were given to Branchi. See "Inventaire orig. ᵃᵖdeces. Effets dufeu sʳ Megliorini," December 17, 1683, Archives Nationales, Paris, MS, Oᴵ 2040ᴮ.

21. Ibid. All agates, jaspers, chalcedonic stones, and other hardstones listed in the inventory as nos. 1–37, the tools nos. 38, 39, 46–48, and a Florentine mosaic panel depicting ruins, no. 130, belonged to the Crown and were transferred to Branchi's workshop.

22. "Diverses memoires de menues dépenses faites pour le service du Roy par Philippes Branky lapidaire aux Gobelins depuis et compris le 18 may 1688 jusqu' et compris le 2 juillet 1693," Archives Nationales, Paris, MS, Oᴵ 2040ᴬ; and "Inventaire orig. ᵃᵖdeces. Effets dufeu sʳ Megliorini."

23. Deliveries to the lapidaries seem to have been separate from the large orders of marble brought in for building and decorating the royal châteaux. For the latter enterprise, one of the suppliers who delivered large quantities of Italian marble was Haudiquer de Blancourt et Comp—which was paid enormous sums, for example, 151,200 livres for an individual delivery in 1686. See Guiffrey 1881–1901, vol. 2, col. 860.

24. Ibid., vol. 4, cols. 344, 487. These *garçons lapidaires* were apparently only paid in the summers of 1698 (Culot) and 1699 (Barré and Le Tellier). Since it seems unlikely that all three were first employed only after Branchi's death, and the production of hardstone panels had been no smaller previously, it is possible that helpers had been paid before by the masters they worked for, and that only the death of Édouard Colbert, marquis de Villacerf, in 1699, and the subsequent installation of Jules Hardouin-Mansart as Surintendant des Bâtiments, Arts et Manufactures brought this change in the system of administration.

25. Guiffrey 1885–86, vol. 2, pp. 165–66, 169–71, nos. 420–22, 450–56, 459, 460, 464, 466–68.

26. See ibid., pp. 155, 160–62, nos. 279, 372, 373.

27. The Galleria dei Lavori in Pietre Dure had been established in Florence in 1588 by the Medici family, grand dukes of Tuscany, to produce furniture and hardstone objects for their residences and for diplomatic gifts. See "Roman Inlay and Florentine Mosaics" by Annamaria Giusti in this publication. When the Gobelins was established, Cucci began making cabinets similar in overall composition to those made earlier at the Galleria. See Guiffrey 1881–1901, vol. 1, cols. 46 and 98, for "cabinets d'Appollon et de Diane" and "cabinets qui représentent le Temple de la Gloire et le Temple de Vertu."

28. The royal account lists payments to Cucci from 1664 through 1706 but without detailed descriptions of the objects commissioned; see Guiffrey 1881–1901, vols. 1–5, in particular, vol. 1, col. 735, "29 novembre [1673]: à Cuccy, pour parfait payement de 27568 livres pour deux grands cabinets d'ébène enrichis de divers ornemens, 6568 livres." The royal inventory, on the other hand, lists and describes 21 cabinets, 29 tables, and 39 consoles for marble tops, some of which had matching gueridons, that are likely to have originated with Cucci and Caffieri (together with La Baronnière). See Guiffrey 1885–86, vol. 2, pp. 129–32, 136–40, 147, 149–51, 155, 156, 159–62, 165–66, 169–71, nos. 3–4, 6, 7, 10–14, 16, 53–72, 74, 164, 219–26, 234–36, 279, 304, 339–41, 372, 373, 420–22, 450–56, 459, 460, 464, 466–68.

29. As an *artisan du roi*, Cucci was exempt from the guild rules and allowed to work in wood and metal. See Loats 1997; Epstein 1998.

30. The *Mercure galant*'s description of the furnishings at Versailles repeatedly characterized objects as being made from gold. See "Description de la galerie" 1682.

31. "Deux très grands cabinets d'ébeine, ornés dans le milieu d'un portique enrichy de deux tableaux de pierres de relief manière de Florence, entre deux Termes de cuivre doré, dont les chapiteaux sont d'ordre corinthe; aux costez dudit portique, de quatre pilastres de marbre dont les bases et chapiteaux sont pareillement de cuivre doré d'ordre corinthe; au-dessus, d'une attique au milieu de laquelle sont les chiffres du Roy de cuivre doré dans une bordure ronde aussy de cuivre doré, cizelée de fueüilles de laurier, sur la corniche, de trophées d'armes et de six vazes de cuivre doré, et sur toutte la face, de douze autres tableaux de pierres de rapport, aussy manière de Florence, faits aux Gobelins, représentans des paysages, fleurs et oyseaux et animaux enfermez dans des moulures et ornemens de cuivre doré, portés sur un pied de bois doré, sculpé de pieds de boeuf et de festons; lesdits cabinets haults, avec leur pied, de 7 pieds 5 pouces, larges de 5 pieds 4 pouces, sur 1 pieds ½ de profondeur." (Two large ebony cabinets, adorned in the middle with a portico embellished with two stone pictures in relief in the Florence manner, between two terms of gilt copper, whose capitals are of the Corinthian order; on the sides of that portico, four marble pilasters whose bases and capitals are similarly in gilt copper of the Corinthian order; above, an attic with, in the middle, the king's monogram in gilt copper inside a round border, also of gilt copper, carved on the cornice with laurel leaves, military trophies, and six vases in gilt copper, and over the entire face, with twelve other pictures in inlaid stone, also in the Florence manner, made at the Gobelins, representing landscapes, flowers, and birds, and animals enclosed in moldings and ornaments of gilt copper, supported by a base of gilt wood sculpted with ox feet and festoons; these cabinets, with their bases, are about 7 feet 5 inches tall by 5 feet 4 inches wide by 1½ feet deep.) Guiffrey 1885–86, vol. 2, pp. 160–62 (registered in Paris on March 20, 1684).

32. Although the cabinet depicted in the tapestry entitled *The King Visits the Gobelins* (fig. 42) seems taller than the Alnwick cabinets, it, too, has a high waistline and a stand similar to a *bureau brisé*, suggesting an identical arrangement. The unusual term "pieds de boeuf" occurs in the description of the cabinets in the royal inventory, March 20, 1684. See Guiffrey 1885–86, vol. 2, p. 161.

33. The right-hand door panel of one of the cabinets depicts a cockerel (fig. 53). Although this animal was often used as a symbol of France, it seems oddly out of context here, and no scheme is recognizable.

34. Åke Setterwall notes that two of the flat mosaic panels might correspond to those listed in Megliorini's probate inventory as "une canne entrant dans l'eau" and "une canne sortant de l'eau." See Setterwall 1959, p. 429. See also "Inventaire orig. ᵃᵖdeces. Effets dufeu sʳ Megliorini."

35. I am grateful to Alexis Kugel for sharing this information with me.

36. For an account of the payments, see Guiffrey 1881–1901, vol. 1, cols. 46, 98, 151, 216–17, 735. For a description of the cabinets, see Guiffrey 1885–86, vol. 2, pp. 131, 149, nos. 10, 11, 219, 220. The "cabinets d'Appollon" and "de Diane," ten other cabinets, and one Florentine pietre dure table (see cat. no. 45) were among the numerous hardstone objects, including seventy cabinets, stored at the Louvre until the late 1740s; they were transferred in 1748 to the Cabinet Royal d'Histoire Naturelle upon the request of the naturalist Georges-Louis Leclerc, comte de Buffon, keeper of the Jardin du Roi from 1739, and the consequent order of Louis XV, to make possible the study of their stones. See Hamy 1896, p. 311; Setterwall 1959, p. 429. Other objects considered old-fashioned were sold at auctions of items from the French royal collection that took place at the Palais des Tuileries in 1741, 1751, and 1752. See Archives Nationales, Paris, MSS, Oᴵ 3659, Oᴵ 3660, and Oᴵ 3664. See also "An Enduring Seductiveness" by Wolfram Koeppe and Florian Knothe in this publication.

37. Pradère 1989, p. 59, and fig. 8; see also Cowen 2003, p. 84.

38. Exemplary facades and interior paneling with inlaid marble decoration may be seen at the churches of San Miniato al Monte and Santa Maria Novella, and the Cappella dei Principi in San Lorenzo, all in Florence. See also cat. no. 48.

39. A similar contrast in colors, with turned columns veneered in lapis lazuli and with gilded bronze mounts against a dark ground of ebony veneer, is achieved on the cabinet depicted in the tapestry commemorating the king's visit to the Gobelins (fig. 42).

40. For the cabinets, see Guiffrey 1885–86, vol. 2, pp. 138–39, nos. 57–59. In addition to the fourteen Gobelins tapestries (see Fenaille 1903–23, vol. 2, pp. 99–127), prints after them by Sébastien Le Clerc and other works elaborated the theme of the "histoire du roi." The thematic idea was developed by the Petite Académie (est. 1663), a small group of literary scholars drawn from the Académie Française and commissioned to

invent and organize the production of royal propaganda, both through texts and through the iconography of artworks.

41. Yves Bottineau identified this piece as no. 5 in the royal inventory; see D. Meyer 1980, p. 74, and ill. pp. 72–73. However, that inventory description does not mention the cabinet's most individual characteristic, the oval plaque, and gives measurements (116¼ × 108½ in.) for a larger object; see Guiffrey 1885–86, vol. 2, p. 130, no. 5.

42. See Knothe in Campbell 2007, pp. 365–73, no. 40.

43. See "Voyage des ambassadeurs de Siam en France" 1686, pp. 339–75; "Description de la galerie de Versailles" 1686.

44. In 1684 Alexandre de Chaumont, the French ambassador, was joined by priests and Jesuits interested in the arts and sciences, who tried to strengthen the political alliance between the two countries and to convert Phra Narai, king of Siam, and his closest followers to Catholicism. See Mosheim 1863, vol. 3, p. 190; Love 1996.

45. The Siamese embassy stayed in France from June 18, 1686, through March 1, 1687.

46. "Voyage des ambassadeurs de Siam en France" 1686, p. 366.

47. See "Presens qui sont partis pour Siam" 1687, pp. 60, 65.

48. See Knothe forthcoming a, chap. IV-2.

49. The discrepancy between the number of pietre dure tables paid for by the Crown and the number inventoried by its Garde-Meuble further implies that objects from the Gobelins were purchased as gifts.

50. "Presens qui sont partis pour Siam" 1687, pp. 97, 104.

51. *Allgemeine deutsche Biographie*, ed. Königliche Akademie der Wissenschaften, s.v. Tschirnhaus, Ehrenfried Walther v. (entry by O. Liebmann). In Paris, besides the Gobelins, Tschirnhaus visited the porcelain manufactory at Saint-Cloud, the Savonnerie carpet manufactory at Chaillot, and the mirror manufactory in the faubourg Saint-Antoine, among other workshops. See Cassidy-Geiger 1999, pp. 97–98. I am grateful to Maureen Cassidy-Geiger for sharing her essay with me and informing me about Ehrenfried Walther von Tschirnhaus's journeys to Paris.

52. "Weiter bin ich auch gewesen aux Gobelins, allwo Tische und Tafeln à la Mosaica verfertiget werden, Dergleichen anderswo von solcher Schönheit und Kostbarkeit nicht zu sehen. Sie brauchen viel von unserm Sächsischen Jaspis hierzu, und wie ich ihnen meine mitgebrachte Proben zeigete, waren sie sehr begierig darzu, beklageten nur, dass iezo

der König so schlechte Lust mehr zu dergleichen bezeigete." Ehrenfried Walther von Tschirnhaus, "Allerhand Project . . . ," 1702, Sächsisches Hauptstaatsarchive Dresden, MS, Loc. 489; quoted in Cassidy-Geiger 1999, p. 108, n. 13.

53. All four Italian lapidaries had joined the Gobelins in 1668. Branchi died sometime between May 17 and June 7, 1698; his daughter maintained the workshop at least until the end of May 1699. Gachetti, the last to survive, was recorded as late as 1709 as unemployed and poor. See Guiffrey 1881–1901, vol. 4, col. 486.

54. Ibid., cols. 486, 487, 623, vol. 5, cols. 344, 421, 436, 516, 617, 702, 795, 881; González-Palacios 1982b, p. 49.

55. No objects by Le Tellier were recorded in the royal inventory during the lifetime of Louis XIV. See Guiffrey 1885–86, vol. 2.

56. The two ebony cabinets given to the French Crown by Pignatelli (who became Pope Innocent XII in 1691) and recorded in the royal inventory on April 22, 1697, seem old-fashioned compared to the furniture being produced in the royal workshops at this time. Ibid., p. 174, nos. 510, 511.

57. La Mare 1722, vol. 1, p. 454. In the meantime, silver and gold objects belonging to the Crown were melted down: on January 13, 1700, and February 18, 1701. See Archives Nationales, Paris, MS, O¹ 3664.

58. Even Boulle would have been greatly limited, if not completely prohibited, in his use of precious materials, such as bronze for mounts. See Knothe 2006, p. 57.

59. Surface decoration using red tortoiseshell and colored (most commonly blue, green, or red) horn imitated the color scheme that had been introduced to France with hardstone panels mounted on furniture, even though the technique and materials were vastly different.

60. "Auch habe ich die Arbeit wohl in Acht genommen, so iezo in Franckreich grand Mode ist, die Marqueterie genannt, woraus sie Schreibe-Tische, Schräncke, und viele andere Sachen fabriciren, Darvon eine Probe mit genommen." Tschirnhaus, "Allerhand Project"; quoted in Cassidy-Geiger 1999, p. 108, n. 13.

61. See Knothe forthcoming b. Objects in the collection of The Metropolitan Museum of Art attributed to Oppenordt and Boulle include a *bureau brisé* (1986.365.3), an armoire (59.108), and a commode (1982.60.82). See Koeppe in Kisluk-Grosheide, Koeppe, and Rieder 2006, pp. 50–53, no. 17, pp. 66–68, no. 23, pp. 85–87, no. 31.

Pietre Dure North of the Alps

WOLFRAM KOEPPE

From the Mediterranean the art of pietre dure spread across northern Europe, undergoing a complicated dissemination. While throughout the Renaissance and Baroque periods northern craftsmen continued to be inspired by objects created in Florence, Milan, and other Italian centers, they were working in locales very different from Italy and with limited technical means. In their efforts to satisfy their patrons, they developed various innovative approaches. The diversity of this northern production reflected the geographic and political range of the aristocratic and princely courts beyond the Alps, extending toward Scandinavia and the Baltic Sea. Yet all, whether large or small, were part of the loose agglomeration of states known as the Holy Roman Empire.

INSPIRATION FROM ANTIQUITY

The rich and sophisticated art of Byzantium had been an admired model for many European developments. For instance, during the eleventh century Byzantium's hardstone artistry influenced work at the Abbey of Monte Cassino in central Italy, from which the fame of these techniques spread. Throughout Italy—in the north of Italy (part of the Holy Roman Empire), in the southern part of the peninsula, and in Sicily—this stimulus worked in concert with the progressive art patronage of the Hohenstaufen dynasty, which originated in Swabia and in the twelfth and thirteenth centuries provided several emperors who lived in Italy or traveled there frequently (see cat. no. 5).[1] In northern Europe, curiosity was evoked by merchants' and travelers' accounts of the refinements of Byzantine aristocratic life on the banks of the Bosporus, where the opulent display of the ancient Roman legacy continued.

This fabled splendor was embodied by the powerful Byzantine princess Theophano (960–991).[2] In 972 she journeyed from Constantinople to the West to marry Holy Roman Emperor Otto II, a union that sealed a concordat between the two empires.

Opposite: Fig. 58. *Saint George*, designed by Friedrich Sustris, Munich, ca. 1586–97; base added 1638–41. Chalcedony, rock crystal, rubies, pearls, emeralds, various other hardstones, gold, and enamel, H. 20½ in. Munich Residenz, Schatzkammer, Bayerische Verwaltung der Staatlichen Schlösser, Gärten und Seen

Theophano arrived attended by a lavishly costumed retinue and with a magnificent dowry. Part of her treasure was a sizable quantity of holy relics housed in valuable reliquaries that were crafted with great virtuosity out of precious metals, enameled, and ornately set with prized stones and cameos. When her husband died in 983, Theophano quickly had her three-year-old son crowned Emperor Otto III at Saint Peter's in Rome. As regent she ruled the Ottonian dominions, which also included much of present-day Italy, until her death in 991.

Although later described as overbearing, the illustrious empress had added a new dimension to northern courtly life through her political ambitions and by introducing luxurious ways into Germany: daily bathing, cosmetic procedures, ostentatious clothing, and the love of jewels and precious stones. Many of her devotional possessions entered church treasuries, especially those in her beloved Cologne, and inspired a remarkable artistic legacy. One part of this legacy, the golden ambo of Holy Roman Emperor Henry II (r. 1014–24) in the cathedral at Aachen (fig. 59), unites the skill of northern goldsmithing with the mystique of ancient and exotic carved precious substances. It is covered with adornments: sixth-century Alexandrian ivories, Roman cameos of semiprecious stone, chess figures, a Fatimid rock crystal cup and cover, an ancient agate bowl, and large polished stones of many colors. Many of these lapidary items had been part of Theophano's dowry.[3] Later arriving to enrich the ambo was the *Eagle Cameo*, an ancient state treasure presented to Augustus in 27 B.C. and symbolizing the mighty Imperium Romanum. Brought to Byzantium in about the fifth century, it was taken as a spoil by Crusaders in 1204 and immediately afterward given to the Aachen cathedral, where it was set into the ambo to proclaim its new owners' succession to the holy throne of Constantinople. This magnificent hardstone carving, more than eight inches in diameter, fascinated generations of northern artisans. In about 1750 it was transferred again, this time to become a highlight of the Habsburg treasury in Vienna, where it remains (Kunsthistorisches Museum, Vienna).

The *Eagle Cameo* was only one of the thousands of art objects of ancient pedigree to be relocated. In 1198 Pope Innocent III (r. 1198–1216) called for a Fourth Crusade to free the Holy Land

Fig. 59. Ambo (pulpit) made for Emperor Henry II, 1002–14. Gilded copper, incorporating earlier objects made of rock crystal, jade, sardonyx, hardstones, and sixth-century Alexandrian ivory reliefs. Cathedral, Aachen

from Muslim domination. The Venetians, who agreed to provide sea transportation for the nobles and troops gathering from all parts of Europe, also persuaded them to plunder towns along the eastern side of the Adriatic, weakening those longtime economic competitors of La Serenissima, as Venice was known. The enriched crusading hordes finally turned to Constantinople, and for three days in March 1204, the Eastern capital was subject to unprecedented devastation and massacre by Christians supposedly intent on freeing Jerusalem—leaving Constantinople so vulnerable that it would eventually succumb to Ottoman rule (1453). Countless prized objects and materials were looted, especially holy relics and stones of symbolic importance.

These events of the Fourth Crusade had an enormous impact on regions beyond the Alps, with the avalanche-like transfer of religious and cultural property from the East amounting to a vast artistic infusion. In particular, the acquisition of holy relics, which subsequently became the destination of a steadily growing number of pilgrimages, initiated a financial upswing for the clergy. This in turn encouraged ecclesiastical building in the Gothic style, as well as a modernizing of the *vasa sacra* and other liturgical objects.[4] Appropriate architecture had to be created as a setting for the relics. An outstanding example is

Amiens Cathedral, which benefited from the relics brought home from the Crusade by the canon Wallon de Sarton, most importantly an alleged fragment of the head of Saint John the Baptist.[5]

Above all, the plunder of Constantinople benefited Venice. The basilica of Saint Mark was showered with spoils—its famous four bronze horses as well as quantities of marbles, columns, capitals, and figural reliefs. This influx of riches from the capital of the Eastern Roman Empire emboldened Venetians to think that they could compete in glory with the pagan past.

The four porphyry tetrarchs that now stare in different directions from a corner of Saint Mark's seem to search for their original location, the Philadelphion, or "place of friendship," in Constantinople.[6] Because of its royal purple color, porphyry had been reserved for the imperial dynasties since Roman times (see entry for cat. no. 121). A round porphyry slab of the fourth century A.D. lay in Saint Peter's basilica in Rome, built by Constantine, where for centuries it indicated the spot at which every heir apparent was anointed by the pope during the ceremony of his coronation as the Holy Roman Emperor. (By the time the slab had been transferred to the new Saint Peter's, built in Rome in 1506–1615, the pope no longer crowned the empire's northern rulers, but the stone retained its symbolic importance.)[7] Constantine the Great and many of his successors in the East and, later, in the West, among them the Holy Roman emperors Henry VI (r. 1191–97), with his empress Constance, and Frederick II (r. 1220–50) of the Hohenstaufen dynasty, had themselves interred in sarcophagi of porphyry.[8] When Otto II, Theophano's husband, died in Rome in 983, his tomb was sealed with an ancient porphyry lid.[9] One late continuation—or revival—at the dawn of the Renaissance is the marker designed by Andrea del Verrocchio for the tomb of Cosimo de' Medici, memorialized after his death in 1464 as Pater Patriae, in San Lorenzo in Florence (fig. 60).[10]

The stone of emperors, porphyry, or its green variant, was further interpreted as the stone of the Savior, and in portable altars a rectangular tablet of it was generally used as the miniature mensa placed above the relics (fig. 61), a practice that had been specified for such items since the ninth century. As early as 517, the Council of Epaon in Gaul had established that only stone should be employed for altars.[11]

All these developments constituted a foundation for the ecclesiastical use of hardstones in the twelfth century in the German-speaking cultural area that constituted large parts of the Holy Roman Empire. Theophilus Presbyter, a transmitter between ancient traditions and their later renaissance, in his treatise *De diversis artibus* of about 1110–40, gives careful instructions on the proper treatment of precious and semiprecious stones and methods of enhancing them with a suitable setting.[12] Theophilus has traditionally been identified with the artisan and Benedictine monk Roger of Helmarshausen, although that

hypothesis is now debated.[13] A theoretician who sketched his design inventions, he was also the head of a highly skilled monastic workshop (exempt from the regulations that worldly goldsmiths were required to observe, such as ensuring that the precious metals used were tested to verify their purity). A small number of portable altars are associated with "Roger Theophilus" and the Helmarshausen school.[14]

FRANCE AND BOHEMIA

An extraordinarily high level of craftsmanship was achieved by court artisans working for the dukes of Burgundy in the fourteenth and fifteenth centuries. Records of the abundant contents

of treasuries and of courtly gifts and church donations evoke a luxury that can be vaguely glimpsed from manuscript illuminations and tapestries of the period. The inventory conducted for Charles the Bold (r. 1467–77), the last of Burgundy's great dukes, lists no less than forty-eight objects of cut hardstone. The most important of the surviving pieces is the so-called *Burgundian Court Cup* of about 1453–67 (fig. 62).[15]

Burgundian stonecutters are likely to have been influenced by Parisian artists. In 1259 the Cristalliers et Pierriers de Pierres Natureus of Paris had already received their first guild statutes. This was an epoch of vital architectural innovation; barely a decade earlier, the towers of Notre Dame Cathedral had been

Fig. 61. Top of a portable altar, Rhenish, ca. 1207–18. Gilded silver and porphyry, wooden core, 12⅝ × 7¼ × 1⅝ in. Museo Diocesano Tridentino, Trento

completed and Saint-Chapelle, with its airy, light-filled sanctuary, had been consecrated (1248). Those landmark monuments set a standard for the other arts. Rudolf Distelberger points to the confidence of the Parisian hardstone cutters, who described themselves as serving "for the glory of the Holy Church and high-ranking men."[16] This energy was intensified by the growing intellectual supremacy of the French in the thirteenth century, in which the king played an encouraging role. When Pope John XXII (r. 1316–34) took up permanent residency in Avignon, becoming the first pontiff based outside Italy, France's political and cultural standing was further enhanced.

Extravagant items of furniture incorporating hardstones are known from paintings of this period (see fig. 13), but virtually no actual examples survive, leaving much room for speculation about the real nature of the designs. Domestic furnishings with stone decoration, but far less ornate, do survive from the Île-de-France region. During the early Renaissance (sixteenth century), marble and hardstone were used to beautify walnut armoires and cabinets meant for display.[17] Often, fashions were revived after some generations; thus another wave of lapidary work, initiated by the Gobelins workshop, swept over Paris in the second half of the seventeenth century. And one hundred years later the enthusiasm for semiprecious stone embellishment was revived again in France, when late-eighteenth-century Parisian *ébénistes* produced furniture of high artistry that spread their makers' fame from Lisbon to Saint Petersburg (on these developments, see *"Pierres fines"* by Florian Knothe and *"An Enduring Seductiveness"* by Wolfram Koeppe and Florian Knothe in this publication).

Farther east, Charles IV, Holy Roman emperor and king of Bohemia (r. 1347–78), was deeply committed to the enrichment of royal churches in his capital, Prague, and of his favorite residence, Karlstein Castle. When a specific type of agate containing large inclusions of amethyst was discovered in Ciboušov (formerly Zibisch) in Bohemia, the emperor reserved most of the material for his court and his ambitious building plans. At the time, amethyst was very rare and was counted among the precious stones, equal in value to diamonds, sapphires, rubies, and emeralds. (Only when substantial deposits of amethyst were discovered in Brazil in the nineteenth century did its rank fall to "semiprecious.")[18] The emperor decided to clad the walls of his beloved Saint Wenceslas Chapel in the Prague Cathedral and his private chapel at Karlstein with hundreds of hardstone tablets, reflecting the preciousness of the holy relics and valuables sheltered in the chapels.[19] The interiors he created were truly jewels that could be walked into (fig. 63). From what land the stonecutting specialists who had migrated to Bohemia came is not known. The thin hardstone plates they were able to produce are cut in a technique very similar to the one that would later be used to create inlays and mosaics—*commessi di pietre dure*.[20] Prague was to assume an even more important role as a leading cultural center under Emperor Rudolf II, in the decades around 1600 (see "The Castrucci and the Miseroni" by Rudolf Distelberger in this publication).

MUNICH

Munich, at the crosspoint of the centuries-old trade roads linking imperial Vienna with royal Paris and the electorate of Saxony in Dresden with grand-ducal Florence, was itself the seat of the Bavarian ducal court. The Munich palace known as the Residenz on several occasions hosted a Habsburg ruler on the way to his coronation as emperor in Frankfurt or traveling to the imperial city of Augsburg.[21]

Fig. 62. *Burgundian Court Cup*, with cover, Burgundian-Netherlandish, ca. 1453–67. Rock crystal, gold, enamel, precious stones, and pearls, H. 18⅛ in. Kunsthistorisches Museum, Vienna, Schatzkammer 27

It was obligatory during state visits to Munich for dignitaries to be taken on a tour through the *Kunst- und Wunderkammern* (rooms of curiosities and marvels), which were housed in a separate structure, the town's first Renaissance edifice, built between 1553 and 1567. A 1565 description mentions its arcaded courtyard and a "formation of cloisterlike ambulatories, with four wings comprising several floors" to house nearly 3,500 items. The costly project had been realized by Duke Albrecht V of Bavaria (r. 1550–79) on the suggestion of his artistic adviser Samuel van Quiccheberg, who called the building "a theater of the world."[22]

Although collecting the extraordinary and mysterious had been a human activity since time immemorial, the passion for it was not cultivated to an extreme degree until the Renaissance. In this era a natural substance that was grotesque or of striking beauty was frequently ascribed multiple symbolic meanings.

Such objects, called *naturalia* and harvested or unearthed under dangerous circumstances or from exotic lands, had a material value equal to that of the most intricate luxury items crafted of precious metals. One purpose of the *Kunstkammer* was to demonstrate the owner's encyclopedic interests and broad humanistic knowledge. But in Munich and other northern seats of rule, an even more important function may have been to project social status. A ruler's *virtus*, or worth, was reflected by such an elaborate and comprehensive display, and thus these art collections celebrated the glory and rank of his dynasty (in Munich, the Wittelsbach dynasty). Like a collection of holy relics, a *Kunstkammer* was arranged in such a way as to bring out the beauty of its objects and demonstrate their value. Both displays glorified not just the Almighty but also his foremost worldly servant, the princely sovereign.

The Munich *Kunstkammer* contained one of the largest collections of hardstones and lapidary work ever assembled. The stones were part of the *naturalia*, extravagant products made by nature and thus ultimately by God. These constituted, along with *artificialia*—artworks made by man—and *scientifica*—scientific instruments invented to measure and affect the world in this age of exploration—the essential contents of these curiosity chambers. The strength of the *Kunstkammer* was largely one of accumulation, bringing together in one space much that was apparently dissimilar, especially if it was spectacular or exotic. And diverse hardstones, in addition to being *naturalia*, were often the predominate ingredients of the *artificialia*.[23] Carved lapis lazuli from Afghanistan, Oriental alabaster and amethyst (cat. no. 21), or rock crystal from Milan (cat. no. 62), as well as hardstones combined with colorful enamel and gold (cat. nos. 22, 76) joined the jewelry, sculpted ivories, and many other recondite items suitable for a *Schatzkammer* (treasury) that captivated the viewer.

There were *Kunstkammer* collections similar to the Munich one at Ambras Castle near Innsbruck and in Vienna, Prague, Kassel (cat. nos. 76, 81–84), Berlin, and Copenhagen, to name a few. The Dresden *Kunstkammer*, one of the first documented, was founded in about 1560 by Elector August of Saxony. It was called a "working collection," and its purpose was didactic: to improve the professional skills of local artisans and stimulate the cultural interests of the visiting public.[24] A late example was established by Czar Peter I (Peter the Great; r. 1682–1725) in 1714 in Saint Petersburg, where, in conjunction with a far-reaching collection of natural specimens, it was opened to the public in 1719. Many objects from these curiosity chambers are preserved today in European museums.[25]

Some private *Kunstkammern* also existed; they were assembled by affluent patricians, intellectuals, and entrepreneurs with humanist interests. One of these was the Augsburg connoisseur and art agent Philipp Hainhofer (1578–1647), whose correspondence and documents, which survive in part, are a treasure

Fig. 63. Saint Catherine's Chapel, Karlstein Castle, Prague, before 1365

trove of descriptions of the marvels he collected, commissioned, and admired on his travels. When he visited the Munich Residenz in 1611, Hainhofer wrote about two display tables he saw: "a table inlaid with various Bohemian and other stones, as if it were painted" and "a large table with one piece of agate surrounded by lapis lazuli, onyx, and chalcedony, inlaid."[26] Very likely these tables were made in Prague, in Bohemia (cat. nos. 66–69), or were of local manufacture or at least of northern origin. Stonecutters from the area included the talented Valentin Drausch, who was employed by the Wittelsbachs at the courts of Landshut (1570–79) and Munich (1580–82) before moving on to become "chamber-goldsmith" at the court of Emperor Rudolf II in Prague.[27] Hainhofer also mentions an octagonal table "with various beautiful precious stones . . . inlaid in a black marble stone, as if painted, made in Florence." Its shape echoed that of its location, the octagon garden pavilion, and it had a top of Florentine *commesso di pietre dure*.[28] The 1627–30 inventory of the Kammergalerie in the Munich Residenz under Maximilian I lists three *commessi*, one depicting Prague. Each had its own ebony frame with a protective sliding lid, indicating that these were prized artifacts requiring the same sort of setting-off and protection as paintings.[29]

One of the most prized objects in the Munich collection was a reliquary representing Saint George (fig. 58). The object is a tour de force of hardstone cutting. Seated on his proud stallion, the knight Saint George grasps in his right hand a sword of flawless rock crystal whose purity symbolizes his own. His horse is carved of chalcedony with eyes of inlaid opals. (Chalcedony was already regarded by the scholars Bede [d. 735] and Haymo of Auxerre [d. 865] as symbolic of the unity of all saints, of their strength and spiritual invincibility, and of the thirsting of the faithful after paradise.)[30] The vanquished dragon, of gold and enamel, bleeds rubies from wounds all over its body. The statuette contains a relic of Saint George that Ernst of Wittelsbach, archbishop and elector of Cologne, sent to his brother Duke Wilhelm V in 1586. Their father, Duke Albrecht, had stipulated in his will of 1565 that the family's particularly valuable hereditary and dynastic jewels should stay together as a united, undividable heirloom.[31] Wilhelm V had enlarged his father's collection and commissioned from the court artist Friedrich Sustris the design for a statuette in the form of a miniature equestrian monument *à l'antique*. The work is an expression of the Wittelsbach family's religious devotion and loyalty to the patron saint of chivalry, Saint George. The high base with dynastic arms was added between 1638 and 1641 by the goldsmith Stephan Hoetzer. Sapphires (known as a symbol of fidelity) on the oval shield signified the Bavarian Wittelsbachs' loyalty to the Catholic faith[32]—a matter of particular urgency during the Thirty Years' War (1618–48) waged largely between Catholics and Protestants.

Although often most appreciated for its goldsmithing and enamel artistry, the reliquary should above all be counted among the great examples of northern hardstone carving.[33] It was displayed on high church feast days and the saint's day (April 23) on the altar of an equally richly decorated chapel, called the Schöne Kapelle or Reiche Kapelle (Magnificent Chapel, Ornate Chapel), at the Munich Residenz (fig. 64). This chapel, consecrated in 1607, was built for Elector Maximilian I and his immediate family as a place of private worship and also a treasure house for the elector's collection of sacred relics, which were then regarded as far more valuable than profane gold, precious stones, or *Kunstkammer* objects. The idea of a *Kunstschrank,* or miniature *Kunstkammer* (see cat. nos. 78, 79), has its analogue in Hainhofer's description of what he saw in the Reiche Kapelle: "On the left side of the altar is again an altar, filled with drawers, like a writing desk, and in each of them a reliquary sanctorum."[34] The fact that the Reiche Kapelle was created to be the religious center of the residence complex gave it a specific character. It was not meant to be a burial site, like the Medici Capella dei Principi at San Lorenzo in Florence (fig. 102),[35] or even to combine a royal necropolis with a place for worship before a relic altar, like the chapel at the center of the Escorial Palace in Spain.[36]

The name Philipp Hainhofer is a recurring one in any cultural account of this period. After law studies in Siena and Padua and wide-ranging travels, he worked as a merchant and banker and was entrusted with diplomatic missions by his native city of Augsburg. He was an acute observer and essential disseminator of information about creative developments in the decorative and fine arts in central Europe, particularly in southern Germany, during the first half of the seventeenth century. After visiting the Reiche Kapelle complex in 1611, Hainhofer wrote: "The vault and wall are beautiful . . . white with various colors of cast and polished plaster, so that [even] the emperor's stone-cutters were apparently deceived, thinking it was beautifully inlaid with natural precious stones; the pavement, however, is a design of jasper, agate, and similar stones."[37] The walls were surfaced with scagliola, a less expensive, time-saving alternative to pietre dure developed in the sixteenth century. In this process, gypsum is pulverized and colored, then applied to a gesso ground in patterns that imitate stone inlay; when the resulting surface is highly polished, the effect is very similar to that of hardstone (see cat. no. 61). The artist Blasius Fistulator and his workshop in Munich, who were largely responsible for the Reiche Kapelle, achieved an extraordinary level of refinement with this technique.[38]

A few years after the completion of the Reiche Kapelle, the duke embarked on the building program for the Steinzimmer (Stone Rooms), the most extensive suite of display rooms added to the Munich Residenz in this era. Its subtly chosen stone, marble, and scagliola decoration constitutes a monumental testimony to the appreciation for those materials in the early seventeenth century (fig. 65). The decorative scheme, reflecting a Mannerist sensibility, owes its attraction to the contrast inherent in *ars et natura*—the beauty of natural substances, enhanced and transformed by human artistry. The trompe l'oeil effects on the suite's walls were complemented by furniture of colored hardstone and marble that had been transferred from the *Kunstkammer* to the Steinzimmer and adjacent Kammergalerie, an annex to the elector's private rooms.[39] The ensemble was of such splendor that in 1644 the Italian musician Baldassare Pistorini described it as "imperial rather than ducal."[40] The Munich collections also incorporated Florentine and Italian pietre dure works and objects of cut stone, most spectacularly an assemblage of rock crystal artifacts that was rivaled only by the Habsburg dynasty's holdings.

AUGSBURG

The Munich Residenz, described here at length, is an outstanding example of a major court, one of the many capitals of German independent noble dominions and principalities within the divided map of northern Europe. The city of Munich depended on the ducal court. In contrast, Augsburg, also in southern Germany, was an imperial city, whose town council answered to no feudal lord except the Holy Roman emperor. Its special role as a center for the production of goldsmiths' works and collector's cabinets set Augsburg apart; other cities tried but were not fully able to match its success. The city's monuments expressed its artistic leadership. The earliest Italianizing structure is the Fugger Chapel (1509–12; consecrated 1518), adjacent to the Church of Saint Anna, often called the first example of Renaissance architecture in Germany. The chapel's interior presents an imaginative arrangement of diverse stones, mostly marbles and honestone, integrated into a subtly colored, harmonious space. A religious sanctuary with a classically inspired design of colored stones, creating an aura of serenity, was until then unknown in northern architecture; it was in imperial residences that, since antiquity, such color juxtapositions had traditionally been found. By constructing the chapel and financing the election of Charles V as Holy Roman emperor in 1519, the Fugger family demonstrated that they were loyal servants of the Habsburgs and furthered their political ambitions through this show of financial power, which could be witnessed by the German princes when they met in assembly in Augsburg. The chapel's innovative conception was a source of inspiration for northern visitors, princely patrons and artisans alike.[41]

Among his other accomplishments, Hainhofer was a key figure for the development of artistic furniture in Augsburg. His own *Kunstkammer* was a magnet for learned visitors to Augsburg, among them the duke of Mantua and Duke Wilhelm V of Bavaria.[42] Hainhofer acted as an artistic adviser and with his network of workshops prefigured the eighteenth-century French

marchand-mercier, who was both a designer-contractor and a shopkeeper.[43] Between 1619 and 1626 his brother Christian lived in Florence, where he bought pietre dure panels and other carved and uncarved stones for the Augsburg firm. Those were sold individually or incorporated into furniture. During the first third of the seventeenth century Hainhofer established a monopoly on such artifacts in Augsburg (see cat. nos. 78, 79). Hainhofer also developed the furniture type known as a *Schreibtisch* or *Kunstschrank* (a collector's cabinet) and also a variety of multipurpose traveling furniture[44] executed in rare and costly materials that were held in the highest regard by connoisseurs all over Europe.

Hainhofer's indefatigable cultural and intellectual ambition transformed the collector's cabinet into an art form in its own right. Not merely a piece of furniture in which to secure valuable items, it became an encyclopedic *Gesamtkunstwerk* intended to mirror all of humanistic knowledge, the arts, explorers' discoveries, and achievements of contemporary European science. His innovations built on ideas from the late medieval academic tradition and the early Renaissance concept of the *studiolo*, a private study often housing valued possessions.[45] Familiar with Italy and its cultural landmarks, Hainhofer especially admired the concept of the Tribuna, a "temple of arts" in the Uffizi in Florence, which was a gallery filled with the most outstanding paintings, antiquities, and natural objects.[46]

"Here [in Augsburg] very beautiful *Schreibtische* are made of ebony, ivory, and other woods, with secrets [compartments] or without, which are bought as far afield as Prague, France, Italy, and Spain," wrote Hainhofer in 1610.[47] In craftsmanship and design, desks of German origin were unrivaled in Europe at the time, and royal and princely inventories testify that they were widely valued. The list of possessions of King Philip II of Spain, made after his death in 1598, prominently includes several "escritorio[s] de Alemania,"[48] and estate lists for Catherine de' Medici (1589) and Gabrielle d' Estrées (1599) contain the classification "cabinets d'Allemagne."[49] Such terms indicate the widespread appreciation of southern Germany as an artistic center[50] and the close ties among European courts. Hainhofer's masterpieces were three monumental cabinets; one is the *Collector's Cabinet of Gustavus Adolphus* in Uppsala (cat. no. 78).

While for most of the sixteenth century Nuremberg was the center of goldsmiths' and metalwork production in central Europe, toward the end of the century Augsburg surpassed Nuremberg as chief producer of luxury goods in that region. Although it is obvious from the early cabinets with hardstone decoration and related artifacts that cutters of hardstone wares resided in Augsburg before the time of Hainhofer,[51] no actual documents offer evidence of their activity before 1641, when a little-known Augsburg artisan, Caspar Renz, made an agate bowl for the court in Vienna.[52] The ornate items in a painting of an arrangement of *Kunstkammer* objects, dated 1666, include a bejeweled, enameled casket in its protective leather case and a

Fig. 64. Reiche Kapelle (Ornate Chapel), Munich Residenz, consecrated 1607. Bayerische Verwaltung der Staatlichen Schlösser, Gärten und Seen

hardstone cup and cover, all with precious metal mounts that in style reflect Augsburg goldsmithing of the period (fig. 66).[53]

In the years about 1700 and the first quarter of the eighteenth century, consumption of the exotic beverages tea, chocolate, and coffee called for ostentatious tableware in the latest fashion. Chinese porcelain, lacquer, and silver vessels were available, but, as in previous centuries, the European courts searched for ever more unusual showpieces of the utmost delicacy. Among the specialists catering to this demand were the Augsburg goldsmiths Tobias Baur and Elias Adam. In their workshops, thin-walled vessels of grained agate and other semiprecious stones were mounted with gilded silver or even gold (see cat. no. 84). Skilled Augsburg artisans transmitted this great tradition well into the eighteenth century.[54]

A few hardstone objects made in Augsburg that were in the *Kunstkammer* of the dukes of Württemberg survive.[55] Other

Fig. 65. Steinzimmer (Stone Rooms), Munich Residenz, early 17th century. Bayerische Verwaltung der Staatlichen Schlösser, Gärten und Seen

examples in the collection are by the very talented goldsmith and stonecutter Hans Kobenhaupt, who in about the years 1609–23 served at the Württemberg court in Stuttgart.[56] This master, who worked with the goldsmith François Guichard, created some of the most intriguing semiprecious stone objects north of the Alps. Kobenhaupt's exquisite works may have entered the Grünes Gewölbe (Green Vault) in Dresden (see cat. no. 85) and other princely collections as diplomatic gifts. A cup in Rosenborg Castle, Copenhagen, cut from veined agate of unusually rich color, proudly displays the master's monogram *HK* on its stem.[57]

OTHER CENTERS

Lapidary work depended on huge amounts of water: to turn the grinding stones of the mills and drive other machinery, to cool the saws, and to polish (fig. 67). Only certain regions could support this activity.

In the seventeenth century the town of Freiburg im Breisgau, which belonged to the Habsburg dominions, was, after Milan, the most productive center for the refined carving of rock crystal and to a lesser degree of agate and other hardstones (see cat. no. 80). Most hardstones were obtained in the nearby Black Forest and the Saarland. Spurred by concerns that huge, flawless blocks of rock crystal capable of being transformed into rich vessels might instead be broken up to make rosaries and small devotional items, government officials imposed increasingly severe taxes and restrictions on the practice of crystal cutting during the seventeenth and eighteenth centuries. Selected members of the guild were sent to acquire rock

Fig. 66. Georg Hinz, *Still Life with Kunstkammer Objects*, 1666. Oil on canvas, 45⅛ × 36¾ in. Hamburger Kunsthalle

crystal, amethyst, chalcedony, and jasper from merchants in Switzerland or stone traders at the fairs in Frankfurt am Main, Nuremberg, and Strasbourg.[58] Stagnation and decline set in, and it was not until the reign of Empress Maria Theresa (r. 1740–80) that guild regulations were modernized and the craft revived. The grinding and cutting of semiprecious stone was supported as one component of the feudal mercantilism of European courts, and also to demonstrate the courts' artistic refinement.[59] In 1753 no fewer than 1,400 workers were directly or indirectly connected to the Freiburg region's lapidary industry.[60]

Innsbruck, in the Tirolean Alps, was also a locale for work in hardstone, although relatively little is known about it. As early as 1498 the emperor Maximilian I was furnishing a workshop for the "court crystal-cutter Caspar" to produce "chess figures and boards . . . beakers, spoons, saltcellar[s] [for] kings, princes [and] counts."[61] Archduke Ferdinand II ordered a considerable quantity of natural rock crystal from Freiburg to be refined—for what purpose is unknown—by Innsbruck stonecutters. One artisan stands out: Hans Tannenberg, a cutter-engraver of rock crystal and glass documented as working in 1619–30.[62] In 1625 he sent an order to Freiburg for cut rock-crystal items without decoration, accompanied by a drawing specifying the design (fig. 68). This working sheet, a rare survival, suggests that Tannenberg only exercised his engraving art for the decorative embellishment of vessels that had already been shaped and polished.[63]

In the adjacent province, in the city of Salzburg, a powerful ecclesiastical seat, the prince-archbishop Guidobaldo established his own rock crystal mill in competition with Prague's. Begun about 1662, the enterprise was recorded as still operating in 1746. In Lucerne, Switzerland, an entrepreneur set up a hardstone mill and employed two crystal cutters whom he lured away from Freiburg; whether the mill was successful is not known.[64] There were numerous quarries of rock crystal in the Swiss Alps.

After the imperial court relocated from Prague to Vienna in the seventeenth century, this city on the Danube became the pulsing heart of the Holy Roman Empire, and the demand for luxury objects grew correspondingly. Early in the eighteenth century, two brothers named Palm were employed as court jewelers and hardstone cutters; a gold pacificale (house altar-reliquary) in the Geistliche Schatzkammer (Sacred Treasury) bears their signature and its date, "von gebrüder Palm 1704." The object, designed as a miniature version of a monumental reliquary altar, is among the most important masterpieces of goldsmithing work produced in imperial Vienna.[65] A rather substantial collection of hardstone objects, some of petrified wood, was owned by Empress Maria Theresa and bequeathed to her daughter Marie Antoinette, queen of France. Some of the works carried high-quality gilded bronze mounts made by the Viennese court goldsmith Joseph Wuerth.[66]

ACTIVITY IN THE EIGHTEENTH CENTURY

The heraldic devices on an extraordinary nephrite coronation cup of about 1700 (cat. no. 88) reflect the complicated legal structure of the Holy Roman Empire in the eighteenth century. As diverse as the map of central Europe was the array of locations north of the Alps where hardstones were crafted. In some of the smaller centers, remarkable objects were being produced by

Fig. 67. *Lapidary Workshop with Stone Sawyers and Abraders*, engraving from Francesco Carradori, *Istruzione elementale per gli studiosi della scultura* (Florence, 1802)

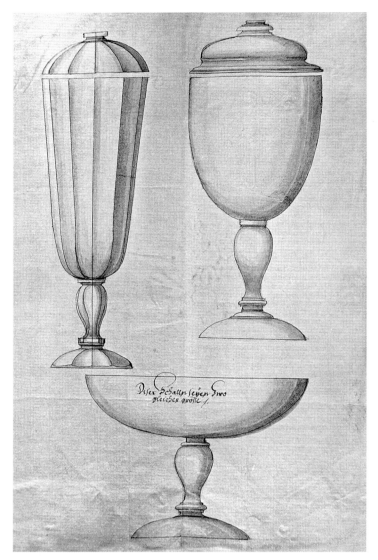

Fig. 68. Hans Tannenberg, Innsbruck, design for three rock-crystal vessels, 1625. Ink and wash (?) on paper. Landesregierungsarchiv, Innsbruck

remarkable artisans. One of them was Christoph Labhardt (see cat. no. 81), born in 1641 in Steckborn in the canton of Thurgau, Switzerland, and trained as a wax modeler in the Bavarian town of Regensburg. In about 1671 he moved to the small court of Count Johannes zu Saarbrücken of the Idstein-Nassau dynasty, in Idstein, in the Hesse region in southwest Germany. There he created an enormous allegorical hardstone relief later bought by Frederick Augustus I, elector of Saxony (Augustus the Strong); it is now in Dresden.[67] Labhardt next won an appointment to the larger court in nearby Kassel, where he was in the employ of the landgrave Karl I of Hesse (1654–1730) (fig. 69).[68]

A design for a minature facade, perhaps hardstone embellished and probably for a coin collector's cabinet, by Labhardt's student Johann Albrecht Lavilette (fig. 70) demonstrates the breadth of northern lapidary workers' ambition. The cabinet's flat top is crowned by an equestrian figure, most likely Landgrave Karl, whose name is inscribed in the frieze below the tympanum. Lavilette or his patron may have been inspired by the

famous ivory and lapis lazuli coin cabinet made in 1618–24 by Christoph Angermeier that is crowned by an ancient Roman emperor on horseback (Bayerisches Nationalmuseum, Munich).[69] On the other hand, both the idea of stone decoration and the design of the Baroque facade partly recalling Saint Peter's in Rome could have been suggested by the landgrave after his three months' grand tour of Italy in 1699–1700. He spent only three days in Florence but surely used the time to become familiar with the Medici collection. The design's half- or three-quarter-round columns and cabochon-shaped "windows" strongly suggest that it was intended to be executed in hardstone. The plan may have called for the incorporation of earlier stone carvings, such as a treasured bust of a woman made by Labhardt in about 1690, possibly a mythological figure to whom the little "temple" was to be dedicated (see cat. no. 81).

Other aspects of Kassel's lapidary tradition—which has a complex history and is of great artistic importance (see cat. nos. 81–84)—cannot be dealt with here, but the subject merits its own comprehensive study, as do those of many other centers. Much research remains to be done on smaller hardstone workshops off the mainstream, such as those of Idar-Oberstein and Frankfurt, both not far from Idstein (see cat. nos. 88, 89).[70] On the other hand, the court of Dresden, where stonecutting was first documented in about 1600,[71] has long been the object of study. The abundance of diplomatic gifts of pietre dure from Italy may well have influenced its production.[72] Celebrated artisans included the ingenious designer Johann Melchior Dinglinger (1664–1731)[73] and Johann Christian Neuber (see cat. no. 92).[74] Neuber's so-called *Teschen Table* of 1779, finely crafted for the marquis de Breteuil, is, with its restrained shape, an icon of early Neoclassicism (fig. 71).[75]

On the edge of his capital city, Berlin, Frederick II of Prussia (the Great; r. 1740–86) built his palace, Sanssouci. In this private place atop a hill in Potsdam, where the motto "Without a care" could be found entwined with a vineyard motif based on his beloved garden, Frederick sought contemplation while forcefully invading his neighbors.[76] Vineyard symbolism, an obsession of Frederick's, was also incorporated in the furnishings and decor. He initiated a specific type of Rococo decoration, called "Friderizianisches Rokoko," whose dominant elements were twisted trelliswork and leaves, floral stone relief carvings, *pinnate-rocailles* (feathery motifs), and other playful elements (see cat. no. 90)—even though by that time the reigning style was early Neoclassicism.

Frederick's fondness for pietre dure work is evident from a description of the important artistic objects in Sanssouci written in 1773 by Matthias Oesterreich, "Inspektor" of paintings. Of the Marble Gallery he wrote, "There are also in this gallery three beautiful 'antique' tables in mosaic work, with real stones and oriental agates. These tables were discovered in 1745 in the ruins of the pleasure residence of Emperor Hadrian, between Rome and Tivoli." He marveled over Frederick's state bedroom: "There is an ostentatious cabinet here, in [hardstone] mosaic, from Florence, all composed of precious stones and oriental agates. The stand on which it rests is tortoiseshell and, like the cabinet itself, abundantly decorated with gilded bronze. All this was made by Melchior Kambly [the court cabinetmaker] in Potsdam."[77]

Outside the Holy Roman Empire, decorative stonecutting was practiced as far away as the British Isles (cat. nos. 138, 139), Denmark, and Sweden (cat. no. 140) and became an important art form in imperial Russia. Especially in these kingdoms far from the center of the art's principal development, particularly fine lapidary works were often used as diplomatic gifts, serving to show off the country's refined taste as well as its possession of skilled craftsmen and valuable natural resources. Only a few years ago a number of Scandinavian stone works were added to the body of knowledge; they include two extraordinary pedestals that are preserved with the Danish crown jewels in Copenhagen (fig. 72). Of opaque calcite, quarried at Hegustadir in Iceland and mounted with gilded silver, they display an extremely forward-looking, geometric design of great elegance. A related bowl of Norwegian smoky rock crystal was made for the Copenhagen court in 1696 by Denis Piengart.[78] Beyond their magnificent artistic qualities, such pieces symbolized the claims of their royal owners to the far northern territories where the hardstones were found.

In imperial Russia, an interest in exploration and mineralogy had developed during the eighteenth century into what Empress Catherine the Great called "a common disease."[79] The discovery of large deposits of various semiprecious stones led to the establishment of several lapidary manufactories, both imperial and private. The first Russian stonecutting mill was at Peterhof, founded in 1721 by Peter the Great. The imperial Kolyvan Lapidary Works in Siberia were established in 1786 and soon supplied works that rivaled the best lapidary objects from France. These two important factories and also one founded in 1726 in Yekaterinburg were placed under the administration not of a manufacturer but of a distinguished connoisseur, Count Aleksandr Stroganov, who himself possessed one of the most important mineral collections in the country. The Demidov family, leaders of Russian industry as well as art collectors, were among the first privately to explore the new field of decorative stone, expanding their holdings to include precious metal and stone mines and numerous stonecutting factories (see cat. no. 126).

During the Renaissance and early Baroque periods, the pietre dure objects created in Italy and Prague displayed an ingenuity of design and quality of craftsmanship unrivaled in Europe. In the age of mercantilism that followed in the seventeenth and eighteenth centuries, a large number of innovative approaches emerged north of the Alps, through which this impressive

Fig. 69. Attributed to Christoph Labhardt, *Karl I, Landgrave of Hesse*, Kassel, ca. 1692–95. Face and visor possibly by Johann Albrecht Lavilette. Shell and hardstones on slate, brass frame, H. without frame 10⅜ in. The Royal Danish Collections, Rosenborg Castle, Copenhagen

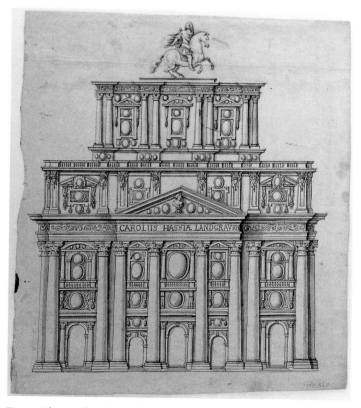

Fig. 70. Johann Albrecht Lavilette, Design for a miniature facade, probably of a coin cabinet, late 17th century. Ink and wash (?) on paper. Museum für Kunst und Gewerbe, Hamburg

Fig. 71. Workshop of Johann Christian Neuber, Dresden, *Teschen Table*, 1779. Gilded bronze, enamel, and hardstones, W. 27½ in. Collection of the Marquis de Breteuil, Chevreuse, France

tradition of luxury-object manufacture was adapted to local needs. The variety of cultures that characterized the widely diverse northern courts was mirrored in the even wider spectrum of hardstone products introduced. But only in a few centers of vigorous artistic activity did the seeds of southern Europe fall on truly fertile ground. First came Paris, gleaming in the rays of the Sun King, Louis XIV. Dresden, with extraordinary artisans like Dinglinger and later Neuber working under royal patronage, saw the production of many objects of unsurpassed ingenuity. In Augsburg, additional valuable and exotic materials were incorporated into a distinctive variant of the artistic legacy. In Berlin under the reign of Frederick the Great, an original interpretation of the Rococo style was developed that resulted in some of Europe's most sumptuous hardstone objects, such as the king's famous snuffboxes. This northern onrush of invention culminated in the lapidary work carried out in Russia in the second half of the eighteenth and early nineteenth centuries, which not only could compete with the best that France or Italy had to offer at the time but indeed surpassed the Western models, taking the art of cutting hardstones and skillfully embellishing them with precious mounts to unprecedented levels.

1. Wentzel 1972; Wolf 1991; Westermann-Angerhausen 1995.
2. Davids 1995.
3. See Georg Minkenberg in Kramp 2000, vol. 1, p. 341, no. 3.34. On Saint Pantaleon in Cologne, Theophano's favorite church, see Ciggaar 1995, p. 59; Lafontaine-Dosogne 1995, p. 212.
4. Legner 1985.
5. Durand 1901–3, vol. 2, p. 619.
6. Graf 2001, p. 30, ill. p. 31; Malgouyres 2003, figs. 11, 12.
7. Butters 1996, pp. 140–41, fig. 66. From 1562 on, the emperor was elected and crowned in Frankfurt am Main, Germany; see cat. no. 88.
8. Schramm and Mütherich 1962, vol. 1, pp. 185–86, nos. 186, 187, p. 197, no. 215.
9. It was later removed and became the giant Baroque baptismal font today still in use in Saint Peter's, Rome; see ibid., pp. 145–46, no. 78.
10. See Del Riccio 1597 (1996 ed.), pl. VII; Butters 1996, pl. XVI, and pp. 541–92 (bibliography on porphyry).
11. Hassett 1907, p. 362.
12. See Braun 1924, vol. 1, p. 70; Schramm and Mütherich 1962, vol. 1, p. 32; Butters 1996, pp. 197, 500.
13. Steinberg 1938; Stiegemann and Wemhoff 2006.
14. A simpler Rhenish example of a portable altar survived in the cathedral of Trent; see Cinzia Piglione in Castelnuovo 1991, pp. 70–73, no. 6. A piece of about 1200 from the Helmarshausen workshop (British Museum, London) still contains relics, among them semiprecious stones associated with Saint Christopher. Recent research has shown that the red "porphyry" slab of this small altar is actually "Purbeck marble," a crystalline limestone quarried on the English Isle of Purbeck, a peninsula in the English Channel. How this material came to be available in medieval Hildesheim in Lower Saxony in about 1200 remains a mystery. The object might have been a courtly commission of Duke Henry of Saxony, who had married Matilda, daughter of Henry II of England, in 1168. See Steinberg 1932, p. 512; Steinberg 1938, p. 72. Was the rare Purbeck marble slab part of her dowry?
15. Hahnloser and Brugger-Koch 1985, pp. 27, 179, no. 335, pl. 285; Distelberger 2002, pp. 30–31, fig. 9. See also Brugger-Koch 1985.
16. "à la honorance de sainte Eglise et des hauts hommes." See Distelberger 2002, p. 29.
17. Koeppe 1992, pp. 81–84, nos. M15, M16; *Parures d'or et de poupre* 2002, pp. 130–33, nos. 27, 28 (painted imitation of hardstone), p. 137, no. 30.
18. Friess 1980, pp. 84–91.
19. Legner 1978; Boehm and Fajt 2005, p. 80 and fig. 6.1; Fajit 2006, ill. p. 9 and fig. 11.46.
20. Distelberger 2002, pp. 54–56.
21. Charles V enjoyed the hospitality of the Wittelsbach court in Munich in 1530, as did Ferdinand II (r. 1619–37). Janowitz 2002, p. 51.
22. Quiccheberg 1565. See Kaufmann 1978, pp. 25, 28, n. 15; Seelig 1985b; Fickler 2004; Warren 2005.
23. Koeppe 2002a; Koeppe 2004.
24. Syndram 2004a.

Fig. 72. Two pedestals, Copenhagen, ca. 1668–69. Icelandic calcite and gilded silver, H. 4 in. and 3½ in. The Royal Danish Collections, Rosenborg Castle, Copenhagen

25. *Treasury in the Residenz Munich* 1988; González-Palacios 1982a; Habsburg 1997.

26. "ain tisch mit allerley Böhmischen vnd andern stainen, als wann er gemahlet were, eingelegt"; "ain grosser tisch von einem stuckh Agat umbhero mit lapis lasoli, onichel vnd Chalcedon eingelegt." Hainhofer, quoted in Langer 1996, p. 21.

27. In the spring of 1585 Rudolf sent Drausch and Ferdinand Krug to Silesia to search for precious stones and hardstones. Lietzmann 1998, p. 152.

28. Hainhofer, quoted in Langer 1996, p. 21. The *commesso* was perhaps Roman; see entry for cat. no. 11.

29. Seelig 1987, p. 34.

30. Friess 1980, p. 105. The German word *chalzedon* derived from Calchedon (or Chalkedon), a Greek port town near Istanbul that hosted one of the more important councils of the early Christian church; see Oldershaw 2003, p. 162; Korzeniewski 2005, p. 70. House altars were often of chalcedony. A holy water stoup with chalcedony columns is in the collection of the counts of Schönborn in Pommersfelden Castle, Germany. See Sybille Ebert-Schifferer in *Faszination Edelstein* 1992, p. 193, no. 103.

31. Seelig 1985b, p. 76.

32. Graf 2001, pp. 92–93.

33. For an attribution of the statuette to Valentin Drausch, which needs further investigation, see Lietzmann 1998, pp. 49–53.

34. Hainhofer, quoted in Haeutle 1881, pp. 67ff.; Alfter 1986, p. 41.

35. Przyborowski 1982.

36. *El Escorial* 1967, esp. pls. 66, 123. On reliquary chapels, see Koeppe and Lupo 1991.

37. Seelig 1985a, p. 29.

38. Klein 1969; Seelig 1987, pp. 28–31.

39. Langer 1996, pp. 21–22; Langer in Langer and Württemberg 1996, pp. 52–56, no. 3; Janowitz 2002, pp. 53–57.

40. See Janowitz 2002, p. 51. Pistorini further noted that the rooms were "inlaid with rare and precious marble" ("incrostati di rari, e pregiate marmi"); Pistorini, quoted in ibid., p. 54.

41. See Bischoff 1999; Koeppe 2002b, p. 43, fig. 5.

42. Alfter 1986, p. 47.

43. Since the *marchand-mercier* operated outside the guild system, he was permitted to combine the work of different craftsmen, such as cabinetry, stone mosaic panels, and gilded bronze mounts.

44. Heikamp 1966; Alfter 1986, p. 97, nos. 11–15, figs. 32–35, 37–43; André van der Goes in *Princely Splendor* 2004, pp. 298–301, no. 161.

45. Even in the eighteenth century, David Roentgen (1743–1807), the most important cabinetmaker in Europe in that era, would pay homage to Hainhofer's encyclopedic idea with his three major masterpieces, monumental cabinets embellished with depictions of the seven Liberal Arts.

46. Heikamp 1963.

47. Hainhofer, quoted in Doering 1894, p. 5; Alfter 1986, p. 10.

48. See Alfter 1986, pp. 42, 107, n. 190.

49. Havard 1887–90, vol. 1, col. 483.

50. Alfter 1986, p. 42.

51. See ibid., p. 96, no. 2, fig. 11.

52. See Schwarzacher 1984, p. 64; see also Baumgärtner 1995. For another Augsburg piece in Vienna, see Paulus Rainer in *Hauptwerke der Geistlichen Schatzkammer* 2007, p. 100, no. 39.

53. Painting by Georg Hinz, Kunsthalle Hamburg, inv. 435. See Heinrich 1996, pp. 9, 52. For similarly decorated objects, see Ralf Schürer in Baumstark and Seling 1994, pp. 253–54, nos. 57, 58.

54. Seelig in Baumstark and Seling 1994, pp. 420–23, no. 110, pp. 428–29, no. 114; Marina Lopato in ibid., pp. 423–27, nos. 111–13.

55. Fleischhauer 1976, figs. 19, 39; for other examples, see Kappel 1998, p. 146, and no. 49.

56. Fleischhauer 1976, figs. 19, 39; Kappel 1998, p. 54.

57. Reinhard Sänger in *Die Renaissance im Deutschen Südwesten* 1986, vol. 2, pp. 617–21, nos. L1–L12; Hein 2003, fig. 5.

58. Irmscher 1997, p. 43. Irmscher describes the struggle over material between top-level carvers and less skillful workers.

59. Ibid., p. 37.

60. Ibid., pp. 43–44.

61. "Hof-Krystall-schneider": see Egg 1959, p. 56; "Schachzagel, pret, . . . pecher, lefel, salzfass . . . kinig, fürsten, graufen": Irmscher 1997, p. 32.

62. See Irmscher 1997, p. 98, no. 12.

63. Egg 1959, p. 56; Irmscher 1997, p. 32.

64. Irmscher 1997, pp. 33, 46, n. 48; Ebner 2002.

65. Paulus Rainer in *Hauptwerke der Geistlichen Schatzkammer* 2007, pp. 118–19, no. 47. For more on Viennese work, see *Die lasterhafte Panazee* 1992, pp. 91, 100, 116; Distelberger 2002, pp. 323–25, 326–29, nos. 203–5.

66. Baulez 2003, p. 81.

67. In the Grünes Gewölbe (Green Vault) of the Staatliche Kunstsammlungen Dresden. Schnackenburg-Praël 1999. Meinolf Siemer in Schmidberger and Richter 2001, pp. 298–99. See the summary of related publications for stonecutting in the Idar-Oberstein region in Fischer 1979.

68. For the portrait of Karl I of Hesse illustrated here, see Hein 2008, no. 575.

69. Eikelmann 2000, p. 148.

70. A full understanding can only be achieved through collaborative efforts in art history, archival work, and mineralogy.

71. Syndram 2004b, p. 47.

72. Cassidy-Geiger 2007a, app., pp. 323–48; Cassidy-Geiger 2007b, p. 223.

73. Watzdorf 1962; Syndram 1998; Syndram 2004b.

74. On Dresden as a lapidary center, see Kappel 1998, pp. 59–72.

75. Briat 1973, p. 4, figs. 8, 9.

76. The king's desire was to live there "in close proximity to his own crypt symbolizing the end of human life. . . . Sanssouci was a microcosm, a place of personal seclusion." Streidt and Frahm 1996, p. 27. See also Hohenzollern 1992.

77. Oesterreich 1773, pp. 7, 26. I am most grateful to Professor Michael Stürmer, Berlin, who pointed out to me this little-known reference (fax, January 17, 2008). For the furniture at Sanssouci, see Nicht 1980, esp. pp. 64–66, no. 115, cabinet by Kambly.

78. Hein 2003, fig. 14; Hein 2008, nos. 268, 269 (pedestals), 306 (bowl). Not until 1690 does one find Piengart paid in the court rolls—at 200 rigsdaler a year—but in 1685–90 the royal accounts list a number of payments to "the French lapidary," including 10 rigsdaler "for outlay on transport of the stones he brought from Norway" in October 1688. In November 1692 Piengart was paid, "as per account for some stone bowls," 100 rigsdaler—a relatively large sum, since he also received his regular salary. I am grateful to Jørgen Hein for this archival information.

79. See Mavrodina 2000, p. 163. See also *St. Petersburg um 1800* 1990, pp. 407–11; *Ice for Ever* 2006; Kuchumov 1981, p. 319.

Sculpture and Mosaic in Pietre Dure

IAN WARDROPPER

Pietre dure, or work in hardstones, is predominantly associated with architecture and the decorative arts. The impressive revetments of church interiors, such as the Cappella dei Principi in San Lorenzo, Florence (fig. 102), and the embellishment of tabletops, for example the *Farnese Table* (cat. no. 10), and grand case furniture, epitomized by the *Badminton Cabinet* (fig. 87), convey pictorial imagery through design in color. Numerous pieces in this exhibition illustrate the power of pietre dure to rival painting and to render the transitory charms of pigment permanent in stone surface decoration.

The relationship of sculpture with pietre dure is complex. Hardstone carving found varied expressions in three dimensions. Shaping rock crystal or lapis lazuli into vases or other decorative objects frequently occupied artisans in Italy and northern Europe. Furthermore, the technique of fitting cut pieces of stone into flat mosaic developed into the assembly of pieces carved in relief as well as fully three-dimensional sculpture. The artisans depicted by Giuseppe Zocchi in the pietre dure plaque *Allegory of Sculpture* (fig. 73; cat. no. 110) work in a sculptor's yard, modeling and carving that most classical material, white marble.[1] In so doing they ignore the chromatic range offered by various stones and, ironically, reject the palette suggested by the very material that Zocchi's design utilized. Zocchi and other painters often furnished designs for manufacture in colored stone, yet sculptors such as Giovanni Battista Foggini were responsible for some of the most elaborate of these creations, whether high-relief pietre dure or objects carved from hardstones or mixtures of materials. This essay explores some of the connections between sculpture, especially at small or medium scale, and pietre dure: the influence of antiquity; the different characters of relief and freestanding statuary; the role of artistic media associated with the sculptor's atelier, such as cameos, wax, and metal; and sculpture's function as accessory to hardstone carving or pietre dure mosaic in mixed-media objects.

Ancient cameos and hardstone carvings garnered enormous respect in the Renaissance. Lorenzo de' Medici's cameo collection was one of his most prized possessions and was passionately studied by artists.[2] Small cameos provided compositions for contemporary artists, including Michelangelo, to follow, models for artists to emulate, and lessons on ancient history for collectors. Large ones, such as the magnificent Hellenistic sardonyx agate *Farnese Cup* (Museo Nazionale, Naples), or the *Gemma Augustea* (Kunsthistorisches Museum, Vienna), inspired the Medici to associate themselves with ancient emperors and to emulate them.[3] In one example, the overlapping profiles of Cosimo I de' Medici and his family (cat. no. 13) follow models of this kind from antiquity, while the extravagantly large chunk of chalcedony from which they are carved testifies to the family's wealth. A drawing by Giorgio Vasari (Christ Church College, Oxford) from about 1559 for the work is a rare graphic model for a Renaissance cameo and permits us to imagine the frame intended for this unfinished carving. Displayed in the Tribuna of the Uffizi by 1589, this cameo was paired with an ancient one, *Antonius Pius Sacrificing to Spes*, a clear demonstration that Renaissance artists sought comparison with the artists of antiquity.[4]

Cameos continued to celebrate dynastic achievement through generations of the Medici family: the chalcedony depicting Cosimo III and Tuscany in front of the Temple of Peace (cat. no. 50) substitutes Baroque allegorical conventions for the classically inspired profiles of the earlier works. Unlike the Cosimo I cameo, it is not based on a fresh invention designed specifically for the final piece. Rather, it depends on the reverse of a bronze medal by Florentine sculptor Massimiliano Soldani-Benzi, cast in 1684, a few years before the cameo was executed.[5]

In these two Medici commissions, neither Giovanni Antonio de' Rossi nor Giuseppe Antonio Torricelli, working, respectively, in the mid-sixteenth century and at the end of the seventeenth, exploited the striations of the stone in the manner of true cameos. The brown streak down Eleonora de Toledo's sleeve in the earlier piece is not incorporated in the design. In the later work, Cosimo III emerges from the creamy part of the chalcedony that contrasts with the more reddish orange of Tuscany. Although this carver manipulated the stone's properties to create atmospheric effects and spatial zones, he did not strictly delimit from

Opposite: Fig. 73. Detail of cat. no. 110, *Allegory of Sculpture*, ca. 1775–80. Hardstones

with color. It is the beauty of stone as material for carving that inspired both works.

Statuettes carved from a single hardstone challenge the dexterity of the craftsman to overcome the difficulties associated with a particular material. Purple or red porphyry, prized for its ancient imperial associations, is an especially dense material that lends itself best to repeated smoothing into rounded shapes such as those of vases or basins; sumptuous examples from eighteenth-century France and Sweden testify to the taste for using this material for decorative arts (cat. nos. 102, 140). Carving a stone that is harder than the conventional steel tools used to shape it was an exercise in virtuosity; limitations in rendering details in porphyry were accepted as the price of working in this prized material. Matthias Ferrucci was famed for his skill in tempering his steel tools and for his patience through the months, and sometimes years, each of his sculptures required for completion. Maria Maddalena of Austria acknowledged the degree of difficulty Ferrucci encountered in making the bust of her husband, Grand Duke Cosimo II (Palazzo Pitti, Florence), even though she was disappointed in the result, calling it "a rare thing but not very much like him."[6]

Sculptures in porphyry were so prized that the Medici used them as diplomatic gifts. In 1565 Francesco de' Medici sent a porphyry relief, the *Head of Christ* (now Národní Galerie, Prague), to Emperor Maximilian II, providing evidence of the value of this material for diplomatic gifts of sculpture.[7] Romolo di Francesco Ferrucci del Tadda's *Virgin and Child*, copied from Donatello's *Pazzi Madonna*, was sent to King Philip II before 1582.[8] Still in the Escorial in Spain, this relief earned the intermediary, Gonzalo de Liaño, praise from the sovereign, who was eagerly awaiting "our Lady in porphyry."

Creating a small porphyry statue particularly tests the limits of the material, as the blocky forms and generalized details of Pier Maria Sebaldi's *Venus and Cupid* (fig. 74) make clear. Wood, or even the denser ivory, would have permitted a finer and more detailed composition at this scale; the mere fact that it was attempted in porphyry reveals that it was an exercise in luxury, showing the artist working against the properties of an expensive stone.[9]

The tendency of another hardstone, lapis lazuli, to splinter or fracture in the working encouraged its use in sheets that could be sawed rather than chiseled. These sheets were featured as inserts for cabinets (see cat. no. 21) or brilliantly hued backgrounds against which gold relief-work was set off. Exceptionally, lapis lazuli was carved into a vessel, such as the flask (cat. no. 22) after Bernardo Buontalenti's design in which fantastic winged creatures swell out of the receptacle's hip to form handles. Jacques Bijlivert's enameled gold mounts complete the creatures' heads and exuberantly delineate the junctures and edges of the flask, forming a glittering foil to the flecked stone. The artists' ability to master the stone, to coax complex yet graceful forms from

Fig. 74. Pier Maria Serbaldi, *Venus and Cupid*, early 16th century. Porphyry. H. 10¼ in. Museo degli Argenti, Palazzo Pitti, Florence 1914:1067

the otherwise smooth surface, triumphs in this object. Like porphyry, lapis was seldom used for small sculpture: a Medici cameo in the Metropolitan Museum (fig. 75) shows the habitual tendency of lapis carvers to simplify the image. This portrait of Duke Cosimo I de' Medici is based on a bronze medal by Pietro Paola Galeotti dating about 1567.[10] Like the porphyry relief after Donatello, this cameo was prized not for the originality of its invention—for its composition was copied from that of another artist—but for its expensive stone and the skill exhibited in working it. A number of vases and other decorative objects were produced in the Medici workshop at the Casino di San Marco during this period, yet the difficulty of carving the demanding stone at a small scale was such that only one other comparable Renaissance lapis cameo is known.[11]

In a final flourish of virtuosity, exceptionally accomplished hardstone carvers were able to create statuettes in which they incorporated the stone's striations into a three-dimensional composition; difficult to achieve in relief, this task taxes the limits of an artisan's skill in a freestanding work. In Prague, Ottavio and Giovanni Ambrogio Miseroni, both talented members of a Milanese artistic dynasty, advanced their careers by astounding Rudolf II with their technical feats. From a chunk of chalcedony worked by Giovanni Ambrogio emerge the naked Venus and Cupid (cat. no. 72), the creamy white of their bodies set against the dark red ground. A darker section of the stone is turned into the vase behind them and extends through Venus's auburn hair, fading to a light color in tresses that trail down her shoulder. As in the most brilliant cameo work, the artist's exploitation of the natural material here seems effortless and inevitable.

In relief sculpture a transition from flat mosaic work to three-dimensional inlay was becoming increasingly evident about 1600. Hardstone decoration on one plane continued to dominate seventeenth- and eighteenth-century furniture and objects, but artisans were becoming more ambitious and expanding the range of their works by employing three-dimensional carving raised above the plane to create sumptuous relief. Two examples illustrate this evolution clearly. One oval plaque of 1599–1600 depicting the Piazza Granducale in Florence (cat. no. 34) successfully projects a sense of depth but does so using pictorial means. Bernardino Gaffurri's checkerboard paving stones and gold strings marking parapets of the Palazzo della Signoria and Loggia dei Lanzi adhere strictly to one-point perspective. Bijlivert's images of the famed sculptures on the piazza are miniature reliefs; however, they act essentially as furniture mounts on the hardstone surface, diminishing in size according to per-

spective rather than establishing their positions in space by projecting from the relief plane at different heights.

Comparison to another plaque commissioned by the Medici but created about two decades later, an ex-voto of Cosimo II de' Medici (cat. no. 35), makes evident the advantages of relief. As in the earlier plaque, hardstone mosaic defines the architectural setting through perspectival rendering of the floor and wall panels, but the kneeling figure of Cosimo II is given prominence, literally and artistically, by means of inlays of pietre dure and enameled metal. Adroitly chosen colored stones clarify the space of the composition and represent the rich stuffs of the duke's clothing, while carving enhances his three-dimensional amplitude. His bent left leg and left arm protrude in front of his head and right arm farther into our space; the folds of the drapery of his mantle are carved in depth rather than pictorially incised. Had it been framed within the altar frontal for which it was intended, the image of the duke would have been the focus of attention in the chapel, echoing the patron's pose when he knelt in prayer before it.

Fully three-dimensional sculpture of the sixteenth century and later that is composed of varied hardstones also had precedents in antiquity. Numerous examples of ancient porphyry, alabaster, or basalt torsos completed by marble heads—original or not—survived and served as inspiration for these works.[12] Paul Heermann's violet amethyst bust of a woman overlaid with Johann Christoph Hübner's gilded bronze robe (cat. no. 87) clearly reflects ancient Roman canons of beauty and bears witness to the continuation of this taste into the eighteenth century. Heermann, who was a restorer of antique sculpture and a collaborator with court jeweler Johann Melchior Dinglinger as well as a sculptor, carved most of the head from a single large chunk of amethyst and laid segments of the semiprecious stone comprising the torso into the gilded bronze robe. Quarried in the Erzgebirge mountain range near Dresden, the amethyst brings this tour de force of hardstone carving into the realm of gem cutting on an unusually large scale.[13]

Busts that combine various hardstones—as well as those that use both marble and bronze—were meant to surpass those carved from a single material. One approach to combining materials uses the marble bust as a matrix for inserts of colored stones, as exemplified by Guglielmo della Porta's bust of Pope Paul III (fig. 76). Into the capacious alabaster cappa magna the sculptor set marble tablets of allegorical figures worked in high relief and overlaid it with an elaborate brooch in darker stone. The daring nature of the admixture of the inset panels is apparent when the piece is compared with della Porta's less exuberant albeit still powerful bust of Paul III executed in the same materials but lacking such inserts.[14] Della Porta emphasized vibrant contrasts and high relief to represent the pope's gloriously embroidered cape and to create an indelible image that publicly pronounced Paul's power. Taking a cue from Leone

Fig. 75. *Duke Cosimo I de' Medici*, ca. 1567–88. Cameo, lapis lazuli, 2¼ × 1⅞ × ⅜ in. The Metropolitan Museum of Art, New York, The Milton Weil Collection, 1938 38.150.13

Fig. 76. Guglielmo della Porta, *Pope Paul III*, ca. 1546. Alabaster and marble. Museo di Capodimonte, Naples

Leoni's mixed-media portrait busts of Charles V and his own knowledge of ancient precedents gained as a restorer of antiquities unearthed in the Campo dei Fiori in Rome, della Porta successfully synthesized various media. His complex portrait of Paul likely depends on a small wax model that was widely distributed as a bronze. The sculptor enriched his original concept of a bust in a single medium—successively in a wax model, bronze cast from the original model, and carved white marble—and gave it more potency by adding marble reliefs and placing the marble portrait of the pope within a vibrant alabaster setting.

Giuseppe Antonio Torricelli's almost frighteningly polychromed portrait bust of Grand Duchess Vittoria della Rovere, of about 1697 (cat. no. 49), like the bust of the pope, is a sculpture extended beyond the single medium in which it was conceived. However, the bust of the duchess is composed entirely of pieces of stone that are interlocked rather than inset into a master stone or combined with bronze. In the *Bust of Olimpia Maidalchini*, of about 1646 (Galleria Doria Pamphilj, Rome), the influential Roman Baroque sculptor Alessandro Algardi created

the prototype of a forbidding matriarch's visage set against a billowing hood.[15] Florentine master sculptor Giovanni Battista Foggini followed Algardi's initiative when he created a white marble bust of Vittoria della Rovere shown as a younger woman in the Galleria degli Uffizi (probably early 1680s) and an elaborate white marble bust framed by an enormous colored marble wall monument to her memory in the chapel at La Quiete (fig. 77). In turn, Foggini's work was the model for Torricelli's elaborate version.[16]

It is interesting that the realistic aspects of the later bust—the flesh-colored skin, rose lips, brown eyes, and black robes (the garments of an oblate of the Congregazione di Montalve, of which della Rovere was patron)—do not necessarily make her more lifelike than the woman shown in the earlier, single-medium versions. While there is some sense of a wax sculpture, the colored stones—an Egyptian stone for the flesh, Volterra chalcedony for the black cloth—fix the bust as a decorative object, while the white marble more successfully captures her personality. The soft surface of wax sculpture, for example, a

Fig. 77. Giovanni Battista Foggini, monument to the memory of Vittoria della Rovere, begun 1694, installed 1698. White and colored marble. Conservatorio delle Montalve, Villa La Quiete, Florence

Fig. 78. Bust of the future king Frederick VI of Denmark, ca. 1771. Wax. The Royal Danish Collections, Rosenborg Castle, Copenhagen

polychrome bust of the future king Frederick VI (fig. 78), has a morbid resemblance to human flesh, while the hardstone of portraits nearly always lends the image a decorative and abstract quality. Torricelli was one of the best sculptors of pietre dure statuary and was proud of his self-proclaimed skill in creating lifesize figures entirely in hardstone, a notably difficult task. About this bust he boasted: "I believe that this is the first lifesize portrait created in hardstone, and I made it with great diligence, knowing that it could only be made with much labor by a man."[17]

Rare surviving models for pietre dure reliefs and statuettes are often made of wax, and written accounts document the relationship of soft modeling material and hardstone sculpture. That wax models were used is perhaps not surprising, since this medium could be tinted to simulate the colors of the stones. Furthermore, it was possible to convert the wax models into other media, as cast-bronze statuettes and reliefs testify. The connection between hardstone and wax is underlined by the nature of the training of some of the masters who worked in pietre dure: for example, Torricelli apprenticed to Dom Gaetano

Zumbo, among the most famous and accomplished specialists in wax sculpture who worked at the Florentine court.[18]

A bronze relief group of the *Flagellation of Christ* in the Metropolitan Museum (fig. 79) in which each figure is cast separately in high relief and the figures are meant to be mounted together on stone or wood was the model for a pietre dure panel in a console (fig. 80).[19] James David Draper attributes them to a follower of Giambologna.[20] On the basis of style we can conclude that the bronzes are likely to be Florentine and date to the beginning of the seventeenth century. The pose of Christ bound to the column and the executioner at the right in the bronze *Flagellation* (he appears at left in the hardstone panel) and the heights in relation to the height of the panels correspond closely. That the detailing of the bronzes is more precise than that of the hardstone versions implies that any wax models that might have been used for them predate the hardstone pieces. The carver used only two of the three wax models, adding a third from a different source or a missing figure from the bronze group, suggesting that these wax models were not

Fig. 79. *Flagellation of Christ*, early 17th century. Bronze relief figures, maximum H. 9 in. The Metropolitan Museum of Art, New York, The Friedsam Collection, Bequest of Michael Friedsam, 1931 32.100.196a–c

Fig. 80. *Flagellation of Christ*, early 17th century. Hardstones. Private collection, Florence

originally intended for the use of hardstone carvers but were repurposed to that end.[21] Alvar González-Palacios, unaware of the Metropolitan Museum bronzes, attributes the carvings to Francesco Mochi, who, along with his father, Orazio, is known to have worked in hardstone relief in this era. He also proposes that Ludovico Cigoli, who is documented to have created colored wax models for statues of the altar of the Cappella dei Principi in Florence about 1605, designed the composition of the hardstone *Flagellation* as well. While the identity of the artists involved in this production is uncertain, the project's development indicates the role of wax models for pietre dure and works in other media as well.

Artists in Florence continued to make wax models in preparation for hardstone carvings over the next two centuries. In the mid-eighteenth century, for example, the Baroque artist Antonio Francesco Selvi was accustomed to making low-relief monochrome waxes on flat backgrounds of slate as models for bronzes.[22] Selvi, a medalist responsible for a famous series of portraits of the Medici, prepared a model in red wax on wood, *Leopards Attacking a Deer in a Grotto* (fig. 81), for a hardstone relief (fig. 82) that was executed in the grand-ducal workshops.[23] The impressionistic sketches of foliage of the wax model do not translate well into hardstone carving, but the simplified contours of the animals and blocky formations of the grotto are well suited to carved stone and reveal that they were designed deliberately for ease of adaptation to it.

The discovery and collecting of ancient sculptures, and, in particular, their restoration that took place during the Renaissance were important factors in renewing the taste for free-standing statuary in stones of varied colors. Replacement of missing heads and limbs became so prevalent and expert by the seventeenth and eighteenth centuries that it is difficult now to distinguish the original parts from later modifications of works from this era.[24] Whether or not they are partially restored, the *Diana Borghese* (Musée du Louvre, Paris) and the *Old Fisherman* (called *Dying Seneca*; also Musée du Louvre) testify to the ancient taste for sculpture composed of variegated marble and onyx.[25] However, Renaissance artists found full-length standing statues of variously colored hardstones were difficult to assemble. Furthermore, the bright hues acceptable for statuettes were often considered inappropriate for full-length statues, which it was believed should be dignified.[26]

Nicolas Cordier was one of the few artists who occasionally did use hardstones in full-length statues, as epitomized in his *Moor*, of 1600 (Musée National du Château de Versailles), in which bronze limbs are deliberately substituted for marble ones to create a rich and exotic mix of surfaces and textures that suits its subject.[27] More typically, Cordier completed damaged ancient sculpture with contrasting marble: *The Gypsy Woman* (fig. 83) combined an ancient marble fragment in *marmo bigio* with Cordier's own white marble and bronze.[28] Goldsmiths also repaired and augmented the remains of broken antique statues

Fig. 81. Antonio Francesco Selvi, *Leopards Attacking a Deer in a Grotto*, 1750. Wax on wood. Private collection, Italy

Fig. 82. *Leopards Attacking a Deer in a Grotto*, Galleria degli Lavori, Florence, ca. 1750. Hardstones. Hofburg, Vienna

Fig. 83. Nicolas Cordier, *The Gypsy Woman (La Zingarella)*, 1607–12. Marble and bronze additions to an ancient marble torso. Galleria Borghese, Rome

Fig. 84. *Charity*, 1600–1650. Hardstones. Cappella Palatina, Basilica di San Lorenzo, Florence

Fig. 85. Christoph Labhardt, Bust of a young woman, ca. 1680. Amber, H. 7½ in. Museumslandschaft Hessen Kassel

Fig. 86. Simon Troger, *Old Beggar Carrying a Child*, ca. 1725–50. Ivory, fruitwood, glass, and leather, H. 21 in. The Art Institute of Chicago, Jane B. Tripp Endowment, 1991.641

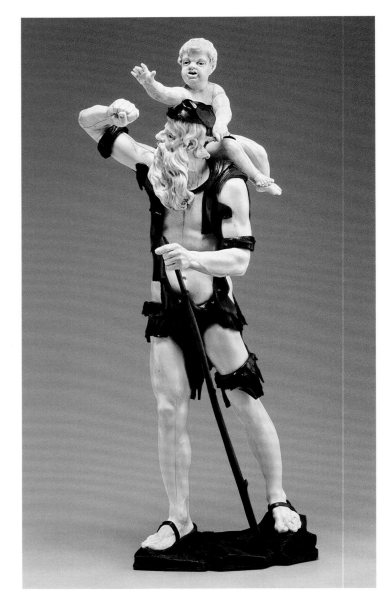

in this manner. In the second half of the sixteenth century an ancient torso of cipolin marble in the Ludovisi collection was transformed into an image of Saint Peter by a Roman artisan, possibly Sebastiano Torrigiano, by adding a gold head, hands, feet, and attributes.[29]

Pietre dure statues, although they piece together elements of restored ancient statues, are essentially three-dimensional extensions of high relief. Annamaria Giusti, Umberto Baldini, and Annapaula Pampaloni Martelli have signaled the critical role of the Cappella dei Principi in Florence in the history of hardstone work, particularly relief and three-dimensional carving.[30] The elaborate but ultimately unrealized altar for this chapel was the focus of sculptural work in the Galleria dei Lavori through the first half of the century. It is not surprising that some of the original models for the pietre dure statues in the Galleria dei Lavori are documented to be by Antonio Susini, one of the inheritors of the Giambologna workshop, which had dominated Florentine sculpture in the second half of the sixteenth century. Susini provided two wax models for the *Evangelists*,

while a third was colored by the painter Ludovico Cigoli. These were furnished to Orazio Mochi, perhaps best known for marble and stone statues of genre subjects in the Boboli Gardens. Following conventional apprenticeship in sculpture, Mochi trained later in his career under Stefano Caroni (before 1572–1611), a Milanese active in the production of pietre dure inlay in Florence. Orazio's sons Stefano and Francesco continued this project through the 1630s and into the next decade, when they were paid, in 1644. The long-term nature of the work is reflected in the project's divergent styles, ranging from the tightly controlled composition of Susini, still working in the Giambologna tradition, to the exuberant, linear Baroque of Mochi.

High-relief figures, at long last assembled at the altar of the Cappella Palatina in the Palazzo Pitti in 1785, had been intended for the altar when they were carved in the early seventeenth century. Like the flat compositions in the same commission—decorative vases, for example—each is limited to five or six stones in a relatively simple arrangement. In *Charity* (fig. 84), for instance, different pieces fit together as in mosaic; however,

Fig. 87. *Badminton Cabinet*, Galleria dei Lavori, Florence, 1726. Ebony, hardstones, and gilded-bronze mounts, 152 × 91½ × 37 in. Liechtenstein Museum, Vienna

they protrude unevenly—elements such as the figure's raised knee give a sense of the figure's recession in space.[31] Details are kept to a minimum: the folds on Charity's red cloak are the most actively worked, and the facial features are the most precisely rendered. Some decorative carving seems superfluous, such as the foliate designs carved into the tawny stone, which are meant to indicate the embroidered lining of her blue outer mantle. The sumptuous colors, sheen, and textures of the stones are more than sufficient to portray this allegorical subject; the additional carving tends to make the figures too busy visually, not to mention more difficult to fabricate.

These criteria apply as well to the fully three-dimensional figures, such as *Saint Mark the Evangelist* (cat. no. 24) and also the reliefs executed at the beginning of the seventeenth century and meant for the Cappella dei Principi. The palette is restricted to a range of sober hues similar to that seen in the reliefs—dark blue, red, and orange-brown—set against light flesh tones and the figure's white collar. Decorative carving, retained on Charity's cloak, is eliminated altogether in favor of a broad sweep of

drapery. Though it is composed of pieces of stone ingeniously fitted together, the statue reads as a single unified image rather than as the sum of its disparate parts. By carefully selecting the stones, the artist balanced them so that no single element dominates another; rather, all combine to create a focus on the saint's impassive, noble face.

A rare variation of Italian pietre dure work features small statuettes in *commessi di pietre dure* placed before pietre dure landscapes to form small tableaux: the most famous and accomplished in this genre is the *Christ and the Samaritan Woman at the Well of Jacob*, of 1600, by Cristofano Gaffurri in a rock crystal frame with enameled mounts by Ambrogio Caroni and Jacques Bijlivert (Kunsthistorisches Museum, Vienna).[32]

The quality of German statuettes in hardstone reached its apogee in the eighteenth century, with pieces that increasingly resemble jewels. The workshop of Johann Bernhard Schwarzenburger used stone from Idar and Oberstein, long centers for cameo carving, to produce a series of Roman emperors about 1730.[33] In their use of varied colored stones Schwarzenburger's statuettes

Fig. 88. Giuseppe Antonio Torricelli and Giovanni Battista Foggini, *Elector Johann Wilhelm*, 1709. Chalcedony and gilded bronze. Detail of cat. no. 59, a cabinet made for the elector Palatine. Museo degli Argenti, Palazzo Pitti, Florence

(cat. no. 89) clearly were influenced by Florentine examples such as Mochi's *Evangelists*.[34] Whereas the solid color stones in the Italian examples neatly separate one from the other, the chalcedony, agate, and jasper in the German statuettes are variegated so that the individual parts blur and appear to merge. Many of their surfaces are carved with patterns. Accessories such as swords, sashes, and epaulettes are encrusted with jewels to emphasize their costly and precious nature.

The strong figural composition of the luxurious Italian examples has been sacrificed for an increased focus on material wealth. This attitude can be said to characterize German work in general in Dresden at the court of Augustus the Strong (1670–1733)—where jeweled figurines and toys by Johann Melchior Dinglinger and others were beloved. Nonetheless, such gold and enameled accessories appear on early seventeenth-century Italian allegorical figures of Virtues worked in low relief in jasper, lapis lazuli, and agates by the grand-ducal workshop for the Cappella Palatina but never installed.[35] As a courtly art form, pietre dure works were subject to embellishment

throughout Europe, even if the most powerful Italian examples eschew excessive adornment.

The practice of combining various pietre dure with gold, jewels, and the like was paralleled in other media. For example, amber was considered a precious stone during the Renaissance and Baroque periods, and dark woods such as ebony and walnut were worked together with ivory. Thus, in Kassel about 1680 the artisan Christoph Labhardt (1644–1695) produced a bust of a young woman (fig. 85), fitting a golden amber portrait head into a reddish brown amber bust. Usually, however, amber was cut into decorative objects, such as caskets or beads. Because it could be shaped more precisely, ivory was frequently substituted for amber, especially for small elements.[36] Both ivory and ebony were prized and were admired when used together in cabinetry for the sharply drawn contrast of black and white they produced. The inherent drama of these materials, like that of pietre dure, was first exploited by sculptors, primary among them Austrian Simon Troger (1683–1768). Troger developed a complex method of fashioning and interlocking the parts of his composition, utilizing an even more restricted palette than in pietre dure objects, to represent flesh with ivory and cloth with ebony or other dark woods (see fig. 86).[37] These so-called Troger Figures were completed by leather sandals, glass eyes, and other accessories, finishing touches that played the same role as the gold and silver additions to Schwarzenberger and Dinglinger statuettes. Virtuoso technique and luxurious materials together create images in a style that approaches realism but remains abstract because of the decorative patterning of black ebony and white ivory. The natural colors of hardstone and of woods used in mosaic reliefs produced in Eger (see cat. no. 53) would seem to allow a more realistic expression in a work of art than when the palette is limited to black and white; yet hardstone sculpture shares with Troger Figures a decorative aspect in their emphasis of material richness over purely realistic representation.

Sculptors often provided gilded bronze statuettes as mounts to complete furniture featuring pietre dure mosaic and carvings. A brilliant example is a Florentine cabinet (cat. no. 47) on which bronze figures of a child and monkey contest a basket of fruit. The child is trying to frighten away the monkey that is stealing carved hardstone fruit from a basket, whose latticework is gilded bronze. Harmoniously arranged gilded bronze mounts and hardstone carvings cover the surface of the ebony cabinet so that the sculptural figures are fully integrated into the decoration of the whole.

On a grander scale than the monkey and the child are the statuettes of the Four Seasons by Girolamo Ticciati that crown the *Badminton Cabinet* (fig. 87) in a composition that echoes the effect of architectural models with marble statues supported by church facades.[38] Ticciati's statuettes are fully independent of the cabinet and could be used on a different piece of furniture

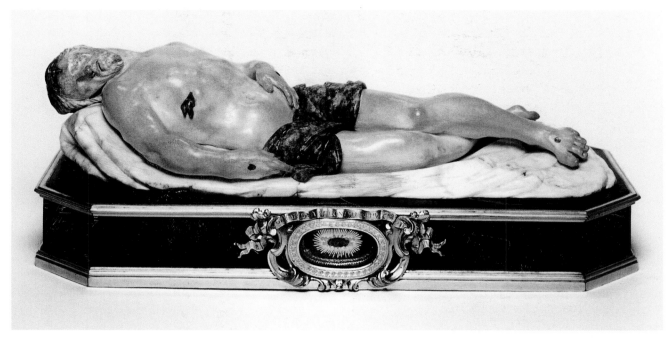

Fig. 89. Giuseppe Antonio Torricelli, *Reliquary of the Holy Sepulchre (Christo Morto)*, ca. 1714. Ebony, hardstones, rock crystal, and gilded bronze, 4⅛ × 14 in. Private collection, London

Fig. 90. Pierre Legros the Younger, *The Blessed Stanislas Kostka on His Deathbed*, 1702–3. Carrara and Belgian marble, *giallo antico*, and banded calcite, figure lifesize. Sant'Andrea al Quirinale, Rome

or stand alone on the shelves of a collector's display room. Although they are part of a composition completed by the carved hardstone fruit basket, even the child and monkey could exist apart from the Florentine cabinet, which is, in a sense, a pedestal for them. However, the sculptures are necessary to complete both cabinets, flourishes whose gilding and forms bring the overall compositions to their culmination and act as foils to the colored, largely flat decoration beneath them.

The most brilliant examples of hardstone sculptures seamlessly integrated into decorative furnishings issued from the fertile imagination of Giovanni Battista Foggini and the inspired execution of Giuseppe Antonio Torricelli. Accomplished in working in bronze and marble, Foggini was fully capable of conceiving sculptures as part of larger wholes, a particularly popular practice in the early eighteenth century, when the integration of all the arts was encouraged. The design genius of Foggini and the collaborative talents of Torricelli and furniture maker Adam Suster are agreeably combined in the kneeling stool of the electress Palatine (cat. no. 55). The carved hardstone cherub heads seem to grow from the ebony volutes, so perfectly interdependent are the prie-dieu's parts. The craftsmen sensitively depicted the cherubims' hair in the stone's darker striations and dexterously bound the hardstone fruit swags across the furniture's surface with gilded bronze mounts.

One of the greatest of their collaborative efforts is the cabinet of the elector Palatine (cat. no. 59). The furniture and the decorative elements celebrate the central image of Elector Johann Wilhelm. At the top of the cabinet, Wilhelm's coat of arms and other emblems, all executed in pietre dure, are accompanied by bronze allegorical figures of the Virtues Magnanimity and Strength. The statuette of the elector (fig. 88) in the central niche shows him seated on a trophy of armor and weapons. The elector's torso and drapery as well as the pile of armor beneath him were designed and cast by Foggini in bronze, but his limbs and bewigged head were fashioned by Torricelli in chalcedony. While we perceive the stone and wood in the kneeling stool of the electress as fundamentally separate, bronze and hardstone seem to fuse in the central figure of the elector's cabinet.

The expression of Torricelli's personal touch in hardstone statuettes and relief reached its height in reliquaries he made for San Lorenzo. Foggini's hand clearly remains evident in one of these, the reliquary of Saint Ambrose (cat. no. 56), in the fluttering silhouette and the gilded bronze angels supporting the vase, and, moreover, to his role in their creation. But the lively multicolored stone high-relief carving of the prophet Daniel surrounded by lions in his cave showcases Torricelli's own abilities as a sculptor; although he may have followed another artist's design, the realization of that design through his selection and shaping the materials in colored stones affirms his personal genius. Executed twelve years later than the reliquary of Saint Ambrose, the reliquary of Saint Emeric (cat. no. 57) is predominantly a display of the art of the hardstone carver, bronze and wood elements being relegated to supporting roles. The ebony base and gilded bronze rays of light are the armature for Volterra chalcedony clouds supporting the Virgin with the dead Christ, ringed by angels carrying symbols of the Passion. Saint Emeric kneels reverently below the group. Torricelli chose carefully the material of the attributes: delicate lances and banderoles in bronze, column and Veronica's veil in hardstone. The saint's yellow Sicilian agate cloak worn over a red Bohemian agate tunic and belted with lapis lazuli displays the period's taste for mottled stones and decorative richness and already reveals a sensibility conveyed by the Schwarzenberger figures made a decade later in Dresden. The Christ, carved from a single piece of Volterra jasper and overlaid with a white marble loincloth, testifies to Torricelli's acumen as carver. The tawny stone of the Christ figure eloquently suggests flesh, while the convincing realization of the compressed legs and slack arms poignantly expresses death.

Torricelli's sensitive treatment of the *Christo Morto*, as part of a larger group in the reliquary of Saint Emeric, is seen again in a single, separate sculpture carved to crown a reliquary that was registered in the Guardaroba of Cosimo III in 1713 (fig. 89).[39] With great care the sculptor carved the stone to represent Christ's brown hair, while the flecked chalcedony is eerily realistic in approximating the freckled appearance of his body. A lapis lazuli loincloth, white marble shroud, and red jasper wound accent the body. In a time when much decorative work was collaborative, Torricelli effortlessly allowed his talents to merge with those of others in multimedia pieces. However, efforts pursued alone, such as the reliquary from the Guardaroba of Cosimo III, remind us of his own artistic powers.

Most of the examples cited here are refined, small-scale hardstone sculptures of or depending on the Florentine tradition. It is worth comparing this oeuvre with a near-contemporary life-size sculpture of colored marbles in Rome, which reflects a grander, architecturally oriented approach. Pierre Legros the Younger's *Blessed Stanislas Kostka on His Deathbed* (fig. 90) was commissioned by the Jesuits in 1702 to mark the chamber in Sant'Andrea al Quirinale where the eighteen-year-old Polish novice died.[40] The youth's head is sensitively carved in white Carrara marble that contrasts with black Belgian marble robes. To reduce cost, veneers of other stones, such as *giallo antico* marble, were used for Kostka's mattress and bedcover. Comparison with Torricelli's *Christo Morto* makes it clear that in the Roman monument Legros was more concerned with creating broad blocks of color and overall theatrical effect than with suggesting details such as hair. In this, Legros followed the Baroque innovations of Gianlorenzo Bernini, who created stunning and quite pictorial contrasts of colored stones with white marble portraits in his great papal tombs in Saint Peter's and the *Ecstasy of Saint Teresa* in the Cappella Cornaro.[41] On the grand stage that is Rome such sculptures had to hold their own within the vast, charged interiors in which they were integrated. Although the works of Torricelli and Legros appear to be linked by their use of colored stone and type of composition, they in fact represent distinct sculptural attitudes.

Sculpture intersects with pietre dure in various ways. The cameo carver's exploitation of the properties of particular minerals influenced many sculptures in hardstone. A jeweler's virtuosity in mastering technically demanding material is often on show in hardstone sculpture. Composite stone statuettes and busts developed from the mosaic relief tradition, at the same time reflecting the inspiration of ancient mixed-media work. Wax models often served as the basis of sculpture in pietre dure, although the illusionism of wax portraits was less important than the fashioning of a precious object. Finally, sculptors such as Foggini often provided models for statues and reliefs in hardstone and created bronze accessories for them, and the carvers tended to follow those models rather than inventing their own compositions. Compositional originality is not the point. Novel combinations of precious materials and the high levels of skill and ingenuity exercised in their creation have made these pietre dure works prized and continuously fascinating.

1. Giusti in Giusti 1988, p. 198, no. 55. This is one of four *Allegories of the Arts* designed by Zocchi in 1752 and executed as pietre dure work for Grand Duke Peter Leopold in 1776–80. Pietre dure work not only represents marble but also masquerades as wood and contributes a three-dimensional flourish in the trompe l'oeil frame.

2. For Lorenzo de' Medici's cameo collection, see Beschi 1983.

3. For the *Farnese Cup*, see Tuena 1992b, pp. 23–26, 31–33; De Caro 1996, pp. 340–41. The *Gemma Augustea* is reproduced in Giusti 2006b, ill. no. 3.

4. See McCrory in Acidini et al. 2002, pp. 252–53, nos. 107, 108; Maria Sframeli in Giusti 1988, p. 76, no. 2.

5. Maria Sframeli in Giusti 1988, p. 176, no. 45, retains the attribution to Torricelli over one proposed to Francesco Ghinghi in González-Palacios 1977b, p. 280, n. 16. See Langedijk 1981–87, vol. 1, p. 642, no. 121, for the medal that is the basis of the hardstone carving.

6. Cesare Tinghi, "Diario di Ferdinando I e Cosimo II fra Duca di Toscana scritto da Cesare Tinghi da '22 luglio 1600 sino a' 12 settembre 1615," Biblioteca Nazionale Centrale di Firenze, Fondo Gino Capponi, fol. 261, quoted by Butters in Acidini et al. 2002, p. 202, no. 65. Butters 1996, vol. 1, p. 293, gives an account of Ferrucci's work for the Medici.

7. Butters in Acidini et al. 2002, pp. 202–3, no. 66; Salort and Kubersky-Piredda 2007, p. 224.

8. Salort and Kubersky-Piredda 2007, p. 228, fig. 7.

9. See Giusti 1989, pp. 10–11, fig. 2.

10. It is quite likely the one mentioned in an inventory of the possessions of Cosimo's son Don Antonio de' Medici, drawn up at the Casino di San Marco. See McCrory in Acidini et al. 2002, pp. 253–54, no. 109. See also Langedijk 1978, who notes that patrons in the Renaissance would have been pleased that their contemporaries had succeeded in a material that artists of antiquity found challenging. Pliny the Elder, *Natural History* (37:39), wrote that lapis lazuli was useless for sculpture because of its hard cores.

11. For the cameo of Admiral Andrea Doria (1466–1560; Bibliothèque Nationale, Paris; 2 × 1⅝ in.), see Babelon 1897, no. 965.

12. See, for example, the bust of Septimius Severus of about A.D. 200–210, with a white marble head and an alabaster torso, and the bust of Caracalla of A.D. 212–217, a marble head in a porphyry bust (both Museo Capitolino, Rome). Both belonged to Cardinal Albani; for their prior provenance, see Marina Mattei in De Nuccio and Ungaro 2002, pp. 328–29, nos. 26, 27.

13. See Kappel 1998, p. 172, no. 71; Kappel in *Glory of Baroque Dresden* 2004, pp. 170–72, no. 4.28.

14. *Tiziano* 2006, pp. 221–22, no. C26b, and for the bronze bust, Gramberg 1959.

15. See Montagu 1985, vol. 2, p. 437, no. 165, fig. 170.

16. Langedijk 1979; Giusti in Giusti 1988, p. 174, no. 44.

17. "Credo che sia il primo ritratto grande, quanto al naturale che sia stato fatto di duro, e lo feci per impegno, conoscendo non esser fatica per un uomo." Giuseppe Antonio Torricelli, "Trattato delle gioie e pietre dure e tenere che s'adoperano nella Real Galleria e nella Cappella di San Lorenzo . . . ," Biblioteca Nazionale Centrale di Firenze, MS, II, I, Misc. Palagi, 478, quoted by Giusti in Giusti 1988, p. 174, no. 44.

18. For Torricelli's training with Zumbo, see González-Palacios 2003b. For Zumbo, see Giansiracusa 1991.

19. The bronze relief group in the Metropolitan Museum has the accession number 32.100.196a–c. For the pietre dure panel, see González-Palacios 2003b, fig. 2.

20. Unpublished note in the files of the Department of European Sculpture and Decorative Arts, Metropolitan Museum.

21. The position of the figure to the left of Christ is correct in the pietre dure plaque, implying that it also stood at the left in the bronze and that there are figures missing from the right side of the bronze group.

22. See Toderi 1993. I discuss a set of Selvi's portrait medals in Naeve and Roberts 1986, p. 31, no. 19. Selvi's medals are most commonly bronze, but the set under discussion is executed in lead with wax corrections.

23. First published in González-Palacios 1986, vol. 1, p. 111, vol. 2, fig. 287.

24. For discussion and bibliography of Baroque sculptors as restorers, see Montagu 1989, chap. 7, "The Influence of the Baroque on Classical Antiquity" (pp. 151–72).

25. For a discussion of the influence of ancient sculpture on later sculptors, see Papet in Margerie and Papet 2004, pp. 53–54, figs. 20a, b.

26. The historical bias against using color in sculpture is discussed in Blühm 1996.

27. Pressouyre 1984; Napoleone 2003, p. 180.

28. Pressouyre 1984, pp. 415–17, no. 22. See also Pratesi 1993, p. 473.

29. See Palma 1983, pp. 6–7.

30. Baldini, Giusti, and Pampaloni Martelli 1979.

31. Ibid., pp. 302–3, no. 123.3, pl. 190.

32. See Distelberger 2002, pp. 174–76, no. 91.

33. On Schwarzenburger, see Kappel 1998, pp. 160–61.

34. Ibid.

35. González-Palacios 1982a, p. 28, fig. 1.

36. See, for example, Aschengreen Piacenti 1981.

37. For Troger, see Philippovich 1961; Theuerkauff 1986, pp. 267–73. For the example illustrated in fig. 13, see Wardropper 2001, pp. 7–8, fig. 7.

38. Christie's 1990; Christie's 2004; Kräftner 2007.

39. In the latter work, the *Reliquary of the Holy Sepulchre*, the pietre dure body of Christ lies on a base veneered in ebony and fitted with gilded bronze mounts; a rock crystal cover for the relic is inscribed on its mount: *De Lapide Unctiones in Sepulcrum*. (The piece measures 4½ × 14 × 6⅞ inches; private collection.) See *Die Pracht der Medici* 1998, vol. 2, p. 69, fig. B48; see also Lankheit 1962, p. 312, doc. no. 612, and p. 324; González-Palacios 1977e, p. 59, fig. 16; Pratesi 1993, vol. 3, fig. 696.

40. Bissell 1997, pp. 73–79. See also the discussion in Penny 1993, pp. 96–98, and color ill., fig. 90.

41. See Wittkower 1966, no. 77, pl. 122, for the tomb of Pope Alexander VII, 1671–78, and no. 48, pls. 71–75, for the altar of Saint Teresa, 1645–52, in the Cappella Cornaro of Santa Maria della Vittoria, Rome. Effective color reproductions by David Finn can be found in Avery 1997, pp. 135, 147.

An Enduring Seductiveness: The Reclaiming of Pietre Dure in the Eighteenth Century

WOLFRAM KOEPPE AND FLORIAN KNOTHE

Hardstones can . . . best preserve antiquity and memory as one has seen [of work] in porphyry, jasper, and in cameos and in other types of very hard stones which . . . endure the pounding of water and wind and other mishaps of chance and time and that can be said as well of our Duke who, because of the constancy and virtue of his soul, can endure opposition to his governing and resolve with temperance all dangerous misfortunes.[1]

So wrote Giorgio Vasari in his *Ragionamenti*, begun in 1558, in an imaginary conversation with the young Francesco de' Medici. Vasari's deeply felt appreciation of hardstones and of their longevity and metaphysical association with princely virtues offers an insight into the attitudes of Cinquecento artists toward fashionable artistic culture in Florence.[2] His remarks regarding the enduring qualities of pietre dure have proved accurate and prescient, for this sophisticated medium long continued to occupy an essential place in aristocratic European life. In an age of rapidly expanding mercantilism and technological advances, a class of influential merchants and entrepreneurs as well as local princes would look to this medium to celebrate their status. They would admire hardstone work and be concerned with its safekeeping, interpretation, and reuse. Its place was firmly assured by the grand-ducal workshops in Florence and the legendary Italian craftsmen who worked in Prague, at the court of Rudolf II, and in Paris in the sixteenth and seventeenth centuries—and was further assured by its continuing importance throughout the eighteenth and nineteenth centuries.[3]

Beginning in the mid-1700s, two centuries after Vasari decorated the Palazzo Vecchio and wrote his *Ragionamenti*, in which he discusses the Renaissance in general and decorative stones, especially hardstones, in particular, his work contributed decisively to the formation of the Neoclassical style.[4] Widely published and discussed archaeological excavations of ancient settlements in Herculaneum (begun in 1738) and Pompeii

(carried out initially from 1748 to 1763) also encouraged the development of Neoclassicism and the adoption of classicizing motifs. The Medici's patronage of lapidaries and their reevaluation of antique stones were crucial in this context. Crucial as well was the continuing commitment to the medium at the Habsburg and Bourbon courts in the seventeenth century, which resulted in idealizing works closer to the culture of Louis XVI and George III's courts than to antique precedents.[5]

As the uninterrupted production of hardstone mosaic objects and panels in Florence and their often prominent placement in palatial interiors and princely *Kunstkammern* demonstrate, the manufacture and appreciation of pietre dure flourished throughout the eighteenth century. While the extensive collecting of scientific instruments, shells, and coral during the Renaissance testifies to that era's new awareness of scientific advances (see cat. nos. 78, 79), in the eighteenth century further references to advances in humanist education appeared, along with a new cultural consciousness. Decorative schemes and the depictions of classical statuary expressed a heightened interest in antiquity and reflected contemporary academic debate (see cat. no. 139). Alongside the ornamentation that issued from the well-documented antique and Renaissance revivals, the illusionistic qualities of some contemporary painting powerfully influenced the development of pictorial, sometimes trompe l'oeil effects in mosaic stone surfaces.

The materials and techniques of eighteenth-century hardstone works were much admired. In some objects, they attained a level of virtuosity and beauty that rivaled the pietre dure precedents that inspired them.[6] From the sixteenth century onward, with the most variety in the seventeenth and eighteenth centuries, some three-dimensional objects, tabletops, and pictorial wall panels were made from scagliola, in imitation of pietre dure.[7] Scagliola is composed of pulverized selenite mixed with glue, which is heated and applied to a wet gesso foundation. Reverse-painted glass, or *verre églomisé*, in which the paint is applied to the back of the glass, was also explored, as was the double-walled glass vessel, a product of ancient Roman origin that reached its zenith in early eighteenth-century *Zwischenglas*. Specialists in *verre églomisé* achieved a remarkable level of visual

Opposite: Fig. 91. Pietre dure room, Schloss Favorite, near Rastatt, Germany, 1710–30

Fig. 92. Cabinet, Rome, ca. 1600. Ebony, oak carcass, pietre dure mosaic panels. Kunsthistorisches Museum, Vienna 3410

deception with imitations of pietre dure, visible in some of their precious collector's objects.[8] A telling comparison is that of an ebony cabinet with drawer fronts in pietre dure made in Rome at the end of the sixteenth century (fig. 92) and a cabinet with reverse-painted glass (*verre églomisé*) panels, attributed to the workshop of Hans Jakob Sprüngli in Zürich about 1600 to 1620 (fig. 93), in which the reverse-painted elements are sophisticated imitations of agate panels.[9] Amber, traditionally consid-

ered a strange mystical stone that drifted on the waves of the Baltic Sea, was regarded as a kind of semiprecious stone throughout the seventeenth and eighteenth centuries and was often employed for the manufacture and embellishment of objects such as caskets (fig. 94) intended as princely gifts or destined for *Kunstkammer* displays (see "Pietre Dure North of the Alps" by Wolfram Koeppe in this publication). The translucency of this fossil resin resembles that of finely carved stones (see

Fig. 93. Cabinet, attributed to the workshop of Hans Jakob Sprüngli, Zürich, ca. 1600–1620. Ebony, oak carcass, reverse-painted glass panels, 16⅜ × 29¾ × 12⅞ in. Ryser Collection, Romont, Switzerland M 50

Fig. 94. Detail of a casket by Michel Redlin, Gdańsk, Poland, ca. 1680. Amber, gold foil, gilded brass, and wood, 11⅞ × 13 × 8¼ in. The Metropolitan Museum of Art, New York, Walter and Leonore Annenberg Acquisitions Endowment Fund, 2006 2006.452a–c

materials. In Berlin in 1786 Friedrich Nicolai observed that some of Frederick the Great's snuffboxes (see cat. nos. 90, 91) were not decorated with natural stones but were perfected by the application of colored glass developed specifically by a "painter [named] Busse" as a substitute for precious stones. Nicolai also remarked that "various skillful chemists are engaged in this subject."[14] Colored wax was another medium used as a substitute for hardstones (see fig. 78 and "Sculpture and Mosaics in Pietre Dure" by Ian Wardropper in this publication). That there was so much interest in substitutes for pietre dure indicates, by extension, that pietre dure itself was still of enormous interest. In addition, the development of new materials resulted in flourishing new forms of decoration that were influential, albeit less so than pietre dure, and testifies to the existence of a creative and highly talented workshop.

The undiminished importance of precious and semiprecious stones led to a complicated and pervasive reuse of jewels, stone panels, and other objects that is a constant in the history of decorative arts. Study of this reuse not only celebrates the works themselves but also illuminates their cultural and social context. Certain pearls and precious stones in royal collections have been mounted and remounted for successive rulers over

cat. nos. 96, 97, 142). Decorative patterns composed of light, dark, translucent, and milky varieties of amber call to mind colorful hardstone pavements and panels.[10]

The portable altar with a painting by Jacopo Ligozzi in this exhibition, dated 1608 (cat. no. 20), is an outstanding example of this artist's work. The case bears Christological symbols and floral arrangements that relate to the contemporary pietre dure style of Florence (see cat. nos. 38, 39) and to painted decoration exemplified by the dado in the Tribuna at the Uffizi, which shows birds, fish, shells, plants, and stones that follow a design by Ligozzi.[11] Northern collectors were surely familiar with the trompe l'oeil effect involved in painted representations of marble, porphyry, and hardstone mosaics. The intricately painted decoration of the impressive coin cabinet of Archduke Ferdinand II of Tirol in Ambras Castle near Innsbruck is among the most spectacular examples of the trompe l'oeil technique (fig. 95). Wood, like hardstone, is a natural material with countless variations in color and grain that can be enhanced with stains or paint. In the form of veneer it is universally employed to create a wide variety of effects.[12] Seventeenth- and eighteenth-century artists relied on colorful stained-wood Eger marquetry and straw-relief marquetry as alternatives to and imitations of pietre dure mosaic.[13]

In an age of technological and scientific progress, craftsmen experimented with chemicals to change the look of certain

Fig. 95. Coin cabinet of Archduke Ferdinand II of Tirol, ca. 1590. Pine and oil paint, 53⅛ × 34⅞ × 32⅛ in. Ambras Castle, near Innsbruck, Austria 34534

Fig. 96. Ewer, France (?), 14th century, with mounts made in Paris after a design by Juste-Aurèle Meissonnier, 1734–35. Jasper, gold mounts, H. 13¼ in. Museu Calouste Gulbenkian, Lisbon 2379

long periods, adapted to embellish the ever-changing necklines and crowns dictated by the vagaries of fashion.[15] Thus, original pieces and objects with reused stones were accorded equal value. Similarly, eighteenth-century furniture with remounted pietre dure panels was highly admired. However, the pietre dure panels on furniture reached a much wider audience than the pearls and precious gemstones—diamonds, emeralds, rubies, and sapphires—of crown jewels, which were passed down in one royal family, at least for as long as the dynasty prevailed, changing hands only rarely, when included in a dowry.

An enormous quantity of semiprecious-stone panels and furniture from Louis XIV's collection swept through the Paris art market in the mid-eighteenth century and was acquired by eager furniture dealers, or marchands-merciers. In fact, at this moment much royal furniture entered the public domain and, whether for their provenance, style, or materials, found favor among the local and foreign aristocracy as well as the prosperous Parisian bourgeoisie. Four consecutive auctions of "old and

useless" furniture held at the Palais des Tuileries in Paris between 1741 and 1752 dispersed much of the king's opulent Baroque furniture, unpopular after lighter forms evolved during the Regency and Rococo periods.[16] Among the famous pieces of furniture were five pierres fines–mounted cabinets. Two large cabinets, the only ones surviving from the Gobelins workshops, have been in the collection of the dukes of Northumberland since 1824. The three others, now lost, were dispersed from the royal collection on February 25, 1751, and bought by Parisian dealers.[17] The growing role of the marchands-merciers signaled the emergence of a wealthy and ambitious merchant class that would gain much authority over the production of decorative artifacts—in particular, furniture—during the following four decades that ended in 1789 with the French Revolution.

Visionaries and tastemakers, the marchands-merciers purchased pieces of furniture mounted with lacquer and hardstone panels and veneered with Boulle marquetry; those they could not pass on intact they dismantled to harvest their costly materials for reuse. Recognizing the artistic and material value of the largely dismissed treasures of an earlier era, they supplied cabinetmakers with pieces that were inserted either singly or in novel combinations in new pieces. To be sure, through the eighteenth century there lingered an interest in the production and restoration of Boulle marquetry, the technique popularized by André-Charles Boulle (1642–1732), master cabinetmaker to the French court, wherein thin veneers of materials such as ebony, tortoiseshell, brass, pewter, and mother-of-pearl create certain characteristic patterns. The sons of Boulle and especially Étienne Levasseur (master 1767) continued to refine and adapt this seventeenth-century technique of veneering and to restore previously made pieces.[18] For the most part, however, craftsmen focused on the skillfully made exterior panels they found on carcasses then considered oversized and overdecorated. Many Asian lacquer panels were cut down and thinned for use on curvaceous Rococo commodes and cupboards, a practice that became a specialty of Bernard II van Risenburgh (master 1730), Mathieu Criard (master 1738), Jacques Dubois (master 1742), Adrien Delorme (master 1748), and Adam Weisweiler (master 1778). These craftsmen either acted as dealers themselves, if they had sufficient financial backing, or relied on merchants.[19] Hardstone panels enjoyed renewed popularity in the 1770s and especially throughout the 1780s, when their rigid flat surfaces harmonized with the straight lines, sharp angles, and severe forms of the Neoclassical furniture of the Louis XVI style.[20]

Thomas-Joachim Hébert (d. 1773) sold numerous objects decorated with reused Asian lacquer, some of which may have come from Japanese screens or boxes formerly in the French royal collection.[21] A specialist in decorative items and furniture he made in collaboration with the master craftsmen Van Risenburgh and Criard in Paris, Hébert was among the pioneers who opened elegant shops in the rue Saint-Honoré and thereby provided the first opportunity for out-of-house shopping rather than through visits by the dealer to his clients' homes. Hébert's former apprentice and successor, Lazard Duvaux (ca. 1703–1758), was one of the most successful and best-documented *marchands-merciers* in mid-eighteenth-century Paris. His account books for the years 1748 through 1758 are preserved and offer a wealth of information about his daily sales to prominent clients.[22] The period recorded by his surviving sales books is particularly interesting as it falls within the few years of the Tuileries auctions. However, his books do not list objects dispersed from the royal collection. Rather they record the sales of numerous stylish contemporary objects and pieces of furniture by Joseph Baumhauer (*ébéniste privilégié du roi*, or priviledged cabinetmaker to the king, ca. 1749) to Louis XV and, especially, to Madame de Pompadour, testimony to the fashionableness of *marchands-merciers* and their wares.[23]

A medieval ewer decorated with a Rococo mount (fig. 96) is a rare example of a hardstone object in the taste of the *marchands-merciers*.[24] The vessel is made from a jasper dominantly red and green with some yellow and is likely to have been cut in the fourteenth century, whereas its mounts were made of pure gold in Paris between 1734 and 1735 after a design by the fashionable architect, painter, and goldsmith Juste-Aurèle Meissonnier.[25] The highly inventive ornamental language of the contemporary gold mounts reveals the virtuosity of the craftsmen who made them and suggests that the best material was remounted by only the most talented artisans. Objets d'art of this caliber formed the core of the collections of Marie Antoinette and Louis Marie Augustin, duc d'Aumont, and of that of the lesser-known Baron de Hoorn de Vlooswyck.[26] Together with furniture of the same level of quality, such rare artifacts were offered

in the *marchands-merciers'* shops and appeared in probate sales appraised and executed by those dealers.

Among the Parisian dealers, Simon-Philippe Poirier (ca. 1720–1785) was, as early as 1759, the principal client for contemporary Sèvres porcelain plaques, which he had mounted—mostly by Martin Carlin (master 1766)—into elaborate pieces of furniture. Poirier worked independently in his shop until 1771 and with Dominique Daguerre (ca. 1740–1796) from 1771 until 1776. Daguerre took over the business in 1776 and worked in partnership with a merchant called Francotais from 1777 to 1781 and from 1789 with Martin Eloi Lignereux (1750–1809).[27] In 1793 Lignereux enlarged the scope of his stock, which now, famously, includes furniture refurbished with pietre dure panels.[28] After Daguerre's death in 1796, Lignereux continued by himself; on his own retirement in 1804 he sold the shop to the renowned bronze caster Pierre-Philippe Thomire.

Another respected member of the dynasty of merchants was Claude François Julliot (1727–1794), a well-known dealer in old Boulle furniture (especially from 1769 to 1789) and new pieces mounted with previously employed pietre dure panels.[29] A set of pen-and-ink and watercolor drawings (fig. 97), dated September 7, 1784, and attributed to Julliot depicts a newly designed cabinet, whose overall composition and applied bronzes are closely related to objects by Weisweiler. The center panel as shown in the watercolors is the same as the center panel mounted in a commode in the Swedish royal collection (fig. 98), suggesting that Julliot was largely responsible for the design of the architectural form of the carcass and bronzes that embellish furniture typically ascribed to Weisweiler's workshop.[30]

In 1782 Daguerre initiated a close business relationship with clients in England. He lived in London in 1792, supplying local

Fig. 97. Claude François Julliot, Drawings of a cabinet, dated September 7, 1784. Ink and watercolor on paper, overall 9⅞ × 22⅞ in. Musée des Arts Décoratifs, Paris 25180

Fig. 98. Commode, Adam Weisweiler, Paris, 1770s. Ebony, oak carcass, inlaid with brass, pewter, and porphyry, with 17th-century hardstone panel by Jean Ambrosio Gachetti, 40⅛ × 56¼ × 23¼ in. Royal Palace, Stockholm

patrons from a shop in Piccadilly and exporting English furniture and Wedgwood porcelain plaques to France.[31] He was appointed sole agent in Paris for Wedgwood by Josiah Wedgwood in 1787. Lignereux never settled in London, but as a furniture designer and dealer he traded with English clients as well.[32] The pieces known to have been made in and for his shop are representative of the early Empire style that had evolved from the Neoclassical mode deeply rooted in tradition. Empire works retained an audience into the very early nineteenth century; one piece is documented as sold by Lignereux as late as 1803.[33] As suppliers to the French court, Daguerre and Lignereux sold to Marie Antoinette seventeenth-century hardstone vessels, which complemented objects that had been in the royal collection since the reign of Louis XIV, as well as contemporary vases, goblets, and cups that were more suited to the tastes of the young queen.[34]

The cabinetmakers who collaborated with the marchands-merciers during the ancien régime often were immigrants of German or Dutch descent. They began their careers and frequently continued to work in the faubourg Saint Antoine, a suburb east of Paris. The Church, which owned the land, for the most part rented to craftsmen and offered them tax breaks, thereby creating a labor force that developed rapidly in the eighteenth century.[35] Excluded from the privileges enjoyed by guild members located within the city, but also free of the restrictions that bound Parisian artisans, the foreigners were employed in woodworking shops where German and Dutch were spoken. They worked for the Parisian dealers, who supplied them with so-called exotic materials and designs.[36] Joseph Baumhauer, Carlin, Weisweiler, and Guillaume Benneman (master 1785)

were foreign craftsmen who established their careers through their relationships with the marchands-merciers, who sold their fashionable pieces within the city walls. The influence of the marchands-merciers was enormous: close to their prosperous clients and knowledgeable about their tastes and needs, the dealers were able to respond to individual desires and set trends.[37] Moreover, they had the financial means to purchase lacquer, pietre dure, and porcelain panels, to order skillfully executed gilded bronze mounts, and to collaborate with technically advanced and highly talented woodworkers.

Daguerre must have had an important stock of hardstone panels and appears to have played a role in designing some of the most celebrated eighteenth-century pieces of furniture. The probate inventory taken after his death mentions "26 small and medium sized pietre dure plaques of Florentine origin and 10 larger panels of the same genre" (priced at 108 francs the lot) showing fruits and birds resembling those in the drawing attributed to Julliot and found in cabinets and tables by Weisweiler.[38] As Daguerre would have been too young to buy pieces from the Tuileries auction sales of 1741 to 1752, we can probably conclude that the inventory he took over from Poirier, or possibly purchased at Julliot's sale in 1777, included pietre dure examples, many of which were made in the Gobelins workshops of Horace and Ferdinand Megliorini, Philippe Branchi, and Jean Ambrosio Gachetti in the 1670s and 1680s.

The signing of furniture, or elements thereof, was highly unusual, especially in the royal workshops, during the seventeenth and eighteenth centuries. To date, only three signed panels of this era have been found. One is on a commode made by

Fig. 99. Cabinet, Adam Weisweiler, Paris, ca. 1785. Ebony and mahogany, oak and pine carcass, Japanese lacquer panels, gilded-bronze mounts, 51⅞ × 31⅝ × 16½ in. The Huntington Library, Art Collections, and Botanical Gardens, San Marino, California 27.21

Fig. 100. Cabinet, Adam Weisweiler, Paris, ca. 1785. Ebony and mahogany, oak and pine carcass, pietre dure mosaic panels; gilded-bronze mounts, 52 × 31 × 16 in. Dalva Brothers Inc., New York

Weisweiler in the 1770s and today preserved in the Swedish royal collection (fig. 98). It bears a relief mosaic panel depicting a vase of flowers that is signed on the reverse by Gachetti. The others are two similarly executed smaller panels mounted on a commode by Carlin in the English royal collection, both of which bear the name of Gachetti in incised script (cat. no. 132).[39] Numerous pieces by Carlin, Weisweiler, and Benneman include hardstone panels of either French or Italian origin that follow no particular decorative scheme, although seascapes and depictions of flora and fauna predominate. This testifies to the fact that the dealers valued the medium itself rather than the theme portrayed. Thus, they appointed cabinetmakers to focus on the *pierres fines* and not on specific iconographic programs. This argument is strengthened by the observation that the *marchands-merciers* commissioned fine, sometimes identical pieces with reused panels of exotic lacquer and Boulle marquetry salvaged from earlier pieces. Under the supervision of Daguerre,

Weisweiler incorporated panels supplied by Daguerre to execute a pair of display cabinets of identical form and bronze mount-decoration, one of which is embellished with Japanese lacquer panels (fig. 99) while the other bears Italian hardstone plaques (figs. 100, 101).[40] Each design emphasizes the material mounted into the door panels, which had been rescued or harvested from outmoded furniture sold at public auction in the Palais des Tuileries and elsewhere.[41]

The appreciation of semiprecious hardstone panels of both past and contemporary manufacture was not restricted to Paris, or to the tastemaking French merchants and luxury-oriented courts engaged in conspicuous consumption, but spread to the wealthy bourgeoisie throughout Europe. Indeed, the taste for pietre dure sometimes approached frenzy. The collectors in its grip purchased pietre dure not only in panels integrated into single objects but also as elements that make up entire chambers made of the material. One such room exists in Schloss

Fig. 101. Pietre dure panels, detail of cabinet shown in fig. 100

Favorite near Rastatt, Germany, belonging to Marchioness Franziska Sibylla Augusta of Baden (1675–1733) (fig. 91).[42] Built as her *maison de plaisance* between 1710 and 1730, the castle houses, in addition to an outstanding group of porcelains, a room that was especially conceived for the display of an enormous pietre dure panel collection. The visitor who enters this ostentatious room is struck by the fact that although it is unusual in its ambitious size and scope, it displays the familiar eighteenth-century taste for mirrored cabinets, abundantly decorated Oriental porcelain, and lacquer chambers.[43]

In England the interest in traveling and studying foreign cultures and the history of art and architecture was much stimulated by the excavations that took place in Herculaneum and Pompeii in the mid-eighteenth century. Aristocratic English travelers went on grand tours of Europe, especially to the Italian peninsula, where they admired ancient stones and purchased contemporary ones to complete their distinguished educations. They bought souvenir plaques of hardstones that would later be incorporated in decorative schemes and furniture and expressing explicitly Neoclassical taste as advanced by Robert Adam (1728–1792) (cat. nos. 136, 138, 139). A curious example is an ebony casket mounted with early eighteenth-century pietre dure panels placed on a Neoclassical stand by Adam in 1777 and thereby modernized.[44]

In England, as in France, the newer fashion was not limited to stone but also embraced a renewed appreciation of Asian lacquer and inlaid brass and tortoiseshell in Boulle marquetry.[45] As the latest fashions crossed the Channel, so did several of the finest pieces of French furniture, following the upheaval of the Revolution.[46] An abundance of French objects became available that were eagerly sought by English connoisseurs and art collectors and also by notable Russians, including Empress Catherine the Great (r. 1762–96). Catherine enriched her legendary collection with the spoils of the French Revolution, and, inspired by the beauty of imported hardstones, patronized the domestic lapidary production established by Peter I in Peterhof in 1721.[47] Eastern European aristocrats such as Prince Aleksandr Andreyevich Bezborodko (1747–1799), Count Aleksandr Sergeievich Stroganov, and other members of Russia's cosmopolitan elite lived in new palaces built in the Neoclassical style along the shores of the Neva in booming Saint Petersburg. They bought only the best from the *décor de la vie* of the fading French aristocracy.[48] The French luxury trade and the Parisian art market progressively deteriorated, and their products gradually became bargains beginning about 1790 and lasting until the Restoration of the Bourbon dynasty in 1814.

1. Vasari 1588 (1906 ed.), p. 39; translated in Fusco and Hess 1994, p. 68.

2. For the propagandistic purpose of Vasari's *Ragionamenti*, see Tinagli 2001.

3. In France the magnificence of lapis lazuli, jasper, and porphyry, along with that of gold and silver, was mentioned in a description of the newly decorated royal apartments at the Château de Versailles. See "Sur la beauté des apartemens du Roy à Versailles" 1682, p. 365.

4. Vasari 1762.

5. Numerous contemporary publications explained and illustrated surviving elements of Roman architecture and ornamentation. See, for example, Caylus 1752–67.

6. See Knothe 2008.

7. Seelig 1985a; Bremer-David 1993, p. 252, no. 446; Synge 1999, pp. 28, 31, fig. 19.

8. Lanz and Seelig 1999 (with bibliography).

9. Agate panels with the "eye" motif are also inserted at the base and top of the niche in cat. no. 16, a seventeenth-century tabernacle for displaying the Eucharist. For a comprehensive entry on Sprüngli's cabinet, see Ryser and Salmen 1995, pp. 136–37, no. G19.

10. For an important amber casket, see Koeppe in "Recent Acquisitions" 2007, p. 26, and ill. p. 5.

11. Heikamp 1963, p. 201.

12. Michaelsen and Buchholz 2006, pp. 473–74, fig. 527, and many other examples that fall outside the scope of this essay.

13. For Eger marquetry, see ibid., pp. 87–88, fig. 115. For straw-relief marquetry, see ibid., pp. 135–36, figs. 198–201, and a casket in the collection of the Metropolitan Museum (acc. no. 30.64; see Draper in *Arts under Napoleon* 1978, no. 66).

14. Quoted in Baer 1993, p. 7.

15. For the remounting of jewels, see, among other works, Field 1987, pp. 82–87; Koeppe and Michelangelo Lupo in Dal Prà 1993, pp. 383–84, no. 128; Landman et al. 2001, pp. 13–21.

16. Archives Nationales, Paris, MSS, O¹ 3659, O¹ 3660, O¹ 3664.

17. Also see ibid.; Guiffrey 1885–86, vol. 2, pp. 129, 150, nos. 3, 225, 226; Setterwall 1959, pp. 426, 429.

18. Pradère 1988.

19. Pradère 1989; Wolvesperges 2000, esp. pp. 69–74.

20. In 1774 André Jacob Roubo (1739–1791), the acclaimed author of the encyclopedic *L'Art du menuisier ébéniste*, deemed the incorporation of hardstone panels in fine cabinetry "out of fashion." He was proven wrong by the enormous success throughout the late 1770s and 1780s of the merchants who sold furniture in which such panels were inserted. See Roubo 1769–72, vol. 3, pt. 3, chap. 14, pp. 982–83; Setterwall 1959, p. 429.

21. See Pradère 1989, pp. 30–33.

22. Duvaux 1965.

23. None of the merchants dealt in objects explicitly identified as made of hardstone. No fewer than 490 entries refer to sales of decorative objects and jewelry to Madame de Pompadour during this period. Ibid., vol. 2, passim.

24. See Isabel Pereira Coutinho in Baetjer and Draper 1999, p. 113, no. 52.

25. Hahnloser and Brugger-Koch 1985, p. 225, no. 472; Fuhring 1999, vol. 2, p. 220, no. 51. The mounts were made by Thomas Germain.

26. For examples of hardstone objects mounted in gilded bronze and collected at Versailles, see Baulez 2007. For the duc d'Aumont's outstanding collection of prized hardstone objects, see *Catalogue des vases* 1782; Malgouyres 2003, pp. 172, 173–77, nos. 65–68; Pradère 2007, pp. 209–10, 219.

27. See Guillemé-Brulon 1983, p. 36. Poirier bought porcelain at Sèvres from the last quarter of 1759 until the last quarter of 1775. Daguerre's name appears in the lists from "année 1772" until August 1791 and that of Lignereux, together with Daguerre's, from August 1790 until August 1791. See Manufacture National de Sèvres, Archives, Registres des ventes, Vy I–X, October 1, 1752–September 23, 1801.

28. See Metropolitan Museum 1964, p. 115; De Bellaigue 1968, p. 283; De Bellaigue 1974, pp. 858–59; Sargentson 1996, p. 27.

29. Claude François Julliot's father, Claude Antoine Julliot, also stocked increasing numbers of marble vases, rock crystal vessels, and gilded bronze mounts. See *Catalogue des marbres* 1777; Setterwall 1959, pp. 430, 433; Sargentson 1996, pp. 23–25.

30. Other panels depicted in the drawing show the friezes of two cabinets in the Swedish royal collection and one side table in the English royal collection, all made by Weisweiler. This suggests that the furniture in the drawing was not executed but that Julliot's cabinetmaker used the hardstone plaques he delivered on several different pieces. See Setterwall 1959, pp. 433–34. Two more pietre dure panels, with swags of fruit, related to those known to be of Gobelins origin and recorded in Julliot's drawing, decorate a pair of cabinets by Weisweiler in the Wallace Collection, London (F395, F396); see Hughes 1996, vol. 2, pp. 599–606, no. 129. Another pair of cabinets, formerly in the collection of Charles de Pauw, is mounted with two panels in the same style. Both pairs are decorated with bronze plaques of a type that was also recorded in Daguerre's probate inventory (entry no. LXVI; see also note 38); see Sotheby's, Monaco, June 22, 1986, sale cat., lot 640; Hughes 1996, vol. 2, p. 604. The upper and lower center plaques on a cabinet made by Robert Hume in 1824 relate very closely to those made at the Gobelins and depicted in Julliot's drawing; see Massinelli 2000, pp. 49–50, no. 9.

31. De Bellaigue 1974, p. 859; De Bellaigue 1995; Wolvesperges 2000, p. 209.

32. De Bellaigue 1968, p. 283.

33. Ibid., p. 290.

34. See Alcouffe 1999.

35. Prat 1963; Minnaert 1998; Knothe 2007a.

36. Kaplan 1988; Thillay 2002.

37. For Weisweiler's affiliation with Daguerre and the "English" influence of the merchant on the artist, see Lemonnier 1983, pp. 37–49.

38. See "Inventaire après décès du citoyen Daguerre," 15 Frimaire an V (December 5, 1796), Archives Nationales, Paris, Minutier Central, XXXVI-633, entry no. LVII. Most of the hardstone panels in Daguerre's shop seem to have been of French (Gobelins) origin. Daguerre is not known to have imported pietre dure mosaics from Italy, where, beginning in 1790, he had extensive business relations with Ferdinand IV, king of Naples, to whom he sold Japanese and French lacquer–mounted cabinets by Weisweiler, three of which are at the Metropolitan Museum (acc. nos. 1977.1.12–14). For Daguerre's dealings in Naples, see González-Palacios 2003a.

39. Watson 1960.

40. See Knothe in Bennett and Sargentson 2008, pp. 109–13.

41. The size of the reused hardstone plaques determined the layout of the cabinets' doors and their gilded bronze framing. The Japanese lacquer panels were cut to conform to the size of the hardstone plaques so that the two cabinets were true counterparts, with one door opening to the left and the other to the right, an important detail that emphasizes their purpose. See ibid., p. 112.

42. Przyborowski 1998.

43. Kisluk-Grosheide 2003.

44. See Jervis 2007, fig. 8. In Germany the taste is exemplified in furniture by Johann Gottlob Fiedler. See *Johann Gottlob Fiedler* 1992.

45. Alongside high-quality pieces in his own style, Thomas Chippendale (1718–1779) is known to have dealt in Boulle marquetry furniture and to have catered to the developing eighteenth-century British taste for French furniture. In 1759, for example, he supplied to Dumfries House, Ayrshire, Scotland, an early eighteenth-century Boulle marquetry-veneered writing desk in the style of Jean Bérain (1638–1711) but mounted on mid-eighteenth-century cabriole legs. See Christopher Gilbert's entry in Christie's, London, July 12–13, 2007, sale cat., vol. 1, pp. 186–88, lot 53.

46. Among the beneficiaries of the dispersal of French luxury goods that followed the Revolution were the Prince Regent (see entry for cat. no. 134), William Beckford (1760–1844), and Alexander Hamilton, tenth duke of Hamilton (1767–1852), all of whom amassed important collections of pietre dure furniture. See Turpin 2001, pp. 186–87.

47. Kagan 1996; Koeppe forthcoming.

48. See Asvarishch 1993, p. 3. For Count Stroganov, see cat. no. 144.

The Opificio delle Pietre Dure: Half a Millennium

CRISTINA ACIDINI

The Opificio delle Pietre Dure is located and rooted in Florence. It originated in 1588, when Grand Duke Ferdinand I de' Medici (fig. 103) decreed that the artistic workshops in the service of the Medici and the court be reorganized and grouped together as the Galleria dei Lavori in the recently constructed Uffizi complex. Foremost among the precious objects produced in the Galleria were works in hardstone and soft stone known as *commessi di pietre dure*, or Florentine mosaics. These were designed to be incorporated in tables, cabinets, and other household furnishings. They were meant as well for objects of monumental proportions, such as the polychrome marble revetment of the Cappella dei Principi (fig. 102) at the Church of San Lorenzo, which housed the funerary monuments of the grand dukes of Tuscany beginning in the sixteenth century in the era of Cosimo I. Although the quality of these works reached its peak in the eighteenth century, about the time the Medici dynasty began to decline, production continued at a level of excellence under the subsequent Habsburg-Lorraine dynasty, and under the Savoy kings of a united Italy, when Florence was the capital of the new realm, from 1865 to 1870.

Throughout this history, the Galleria dei Lavori was able to survive the kind of political crises that destroyed similar artistic laboratories created by ancien-régime European monarchs in Naples, Madrid, Paris, and Peterhof (Saint Petersburg). At the beginning of the nineteenth century, the Galleria dei Lavori moved from Giorgio Vasari's Uffizi complex, where the growing demands of the Galleria degli Uffizi were encroaching, to its present location, a former monastery in the historic heart of Florence on a block of the Via degli Alfani between the cathedral (the Duomo) and the Church of San Marco. Renamed the Opificio delle Pietre Dure and thanks to the enlightened strategy of the house of Habsburg-Lorraine, it became part of a genuine citadel of theoretical and practical knowledge that would come to include the Accademia di Belle Arti, the Galleria dell'Accademia (today famous above all as the location of Michelangelo's *David*), and the Conservatorio di Musica Luigi Cherubini. All were a stone's throw away from the Studio Fiorentino, which would become the Università degli Studi di Firenze in 1860 (officially, in 1923). To its new venue the Opificio brought its old workbenches and tools, not to mention a veritable Fort Knox of stone reserves: all the shards, slabs, and fragments of marble and other stones ancient and modern, exotic and local, that the Galleria dei Lavori had accumulated over the centuries. Catalogued by mineral content (jasper, porphyry, granite, and so on), these historic stone materials are on exhibit today in the Opificio courtyard (fig. 104).

However, when Rome became the capital of Italy in 1870, Florence faced a crisis that threatened the Opificio's survival, as commissions and clients suddenly evaporated. Thanks to

Fig. 103. Pietro Tacca, *Ferdinand I de' Medici*, first half of the 17th century. Bronze. Museo Nazionale del Bargello, Florence

Opposite: Fig. 102. Cappella dei Principi, San Lorenzo, Florence, begun 1604

Fig. 104. Archival stone materials in the courtyard of the Opificio delle Pietre Dure, Florence

the wise and courageous decisions of Edoardo Marchionni, the Opificio's director during the late nineteenth century, the institute's mission and that of its craftsmen, machinery, and materials were transformed: henceforth, the goal would no longer be the production of artworks but their restoration (figs. 105, 106). Marchionni's farsighted resolution saved the Opificio and allowed it to continue functioning without interruption into its fifth century of existence.

A second turning point, which led the Opificio to assume its present form as a conservation institute of nationwide stature, occurred in 1975, with the birth of what was then known as the Ministero per i Beni Culturali e Ambientali. The complex of workshops, by then almost entirely dedicated to restoration, drew upon its own experience throughout World War II, the postwar period, and especially during and after the tragic flood of 1966 in Florence. From the earliest stages of the Florence emergency, under the guidance of Umberto Baldini, the Opificio led the efforts to rescue the city's endangered artistic treasures—its technicians having gained valuable expertise in the restoration of paintings on canvas and wood panel beginning in 1932, at the Gabinetto di Restauro in the "Vecchia Posta," or Old Post Office, in the Uffizi building.

On the long road from the Medicean Galleria dei Lavori to the Opificio of the Lorraine and Savoy Crowns, and to the present-day Opificio, the core identity of the institute has remained firmly under the control of the Settore di Restauro di Commesso Lapideo e Mosaico, which more than any other

Fig. 105. Recovery of Roman-period mosaics unearthed in the Piazza San Giovanni, Florence, by rolling on a drum, 1895

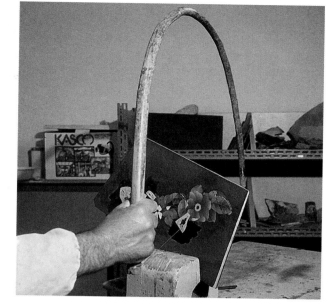

Fig. 106. Restoration of a Roman-period mosaic from the island of Kos that had been used to decorate a floor in the castle of the Knights of Saint John, Rhodes. Photograph 1920s

Fig. 107. Wire bow saw being used to cut stone at the Opificio delle Pietre Dure

department is concerned with continuity from early times to the present. The proper planning and realization of all conservation and restoration projects presume a thorough knowledge of the original materials and techniques on the part of experts and technicians. This knowledge is of particular importance for the restorer of pietre dure objects, who is called upon to recreate the missing elements with great care and fidelity. To do so, these restorers use the same equipment and techniques as their predecessors: *deschi* (worktables and cutting blocks), wire bow saws (fig. 107), vices, drills, traditional materials variously mixed and applied—components of a sort of archaeology of labor (see cat. no. 147). Because of this peculiarity, the restoration of pietre dure objects, and of certain decorative arts in other materials, is subject to exceptions to the basic modern principles of art restoration known and applied by adepts in the field. In Italy these tenets derive from the theories of Cesare Brandi, founder and longtime director of the Istituto Centrale del Restauro di Roma.[1] As numerous authorities have pointedly remarked, critical reflection on restoration in the decorative arts has not given rise to passionate and burning debates of the sort that has characterized other areas of restoration.[2]

The exceptional status of the decorative arts, including those with stone inlay, becomes poignantly clear in the case of a damaged object that, having lost materials, is disfigured by lacunae. Many masterpieces of pietre dure have been handed down to us in near-perfect condition thanks to the durability of their materials and techniques. But these are untouched, indeed painstakingly preserved objects. When, however, the microclimate is unfavorable to the glues employed or a piece is vandalized or damaged accidentally, even this art, created for eternity, can sustain devastating losses.

Restoration theory, above all when applied to painting (whose strength lies in its maker's autograph), prescribes that the restoration of lacunae should not only be reversible but also recognizable close-up. Therefore the missing colors should be integrated in a manner distinct from those of the original, not supplied in imitation of the original. These are the tenets of Umberto Baldini, who developed and elaborated Brandi's theories regarding the use of differentiated methods of mixing and applying color, methods he defined as "abstraction" and "selection."[3]

Florentine works in pietre dure are a different matter altogether. They are not born as autograph works of art: "They are born as transcriptions, often executed by several different artisans, of the work of the artist who created the model. In restoration, therefore, we do not place ourselves in the irreplaceable role of the artist, but instead repeat the work of transcription performed at the start."[4] Here the material is the medium of transmission for the image's creation, not an irreplaceable constituent part of it. Other important statements that constitute specific, innovative contributions to restoration theory were made at sessions of a conference held in 2002 and 2003 at the Salone del Restauro in Ferrara under the auspices of the Opificio:[5] "When integrating the missing areas, it seems essential to respect the object's nature as a sophisticated, precious furnishing and the eloquence of the design and materials peculiar to these works. Since these articles represent the translation of a plan conceived by an artist other than the one executing the inlay, who himself was hardly ever the sole craftsman, their exact recreation should be taken not as an improper substitution but rather as a work of maintenance. Such a procedure becomes all the more acceptable and indeed desirable if the original materials and techniques are used."[6]

Fig. 108. Detail of a Roman tabletop, 17th century, sent from the Palazzo Ducale, Mantua, to the Opificio for restoration

At the Ferrara conference it was decided to bring to public attention case histories and reflections on the treatment of lacunae in the various arts. With pietre dure, in order to imitate missing parts and to distinguish the reconstruction from its original context in marble and stone, restorers have returned to the ancient technique that uses scagliola, a durable plasterlike mixture.[7] The participants in the first session in Ferrara, however, declared that authentic stone materials of the same nature

as the originals should be employed: "It does not seem appropriate to use imitative materials that cannot help but alter the impact of these objects, whose materially precious nature is fundamental to what they are."[8] Quite successful alternatives were devised in the extremely rare instances when the proper stone for filling in the lacunae was not found—either because it was not available on the market or because the Opificio had reservations about it. This was the case with a seventeenth-century Roman tabletop sent to the Opificio by the Palazzo Ducale of Mantua. Lost areas—little strips originally made of a Greek breccia stone known as *seme santo* (holy seed)—were re-created with colored resins mixed with marble fragments, using those still in place as models (fig. 108).[9]

A continuity of vision and technique has existed from the time of the Opificio's founders and early protagonists to the practice of present-day artisans—all trained at the school of the institute—constituting an unbroken chain of learning that puts long-standing skills and knowledge in the service of conservation. A few examples will illustrate the fidelity of techniques used in restorations performed in recent decades, all carried out by expert restorers of the Opificio under the direction of Annamaria Giusti.

A circular tabletop with flowers made in the last quarter of the nineteenth century in Florence was sent to us in 1991 by the Gilbert Collection, then in Los Angeles. The table had fallen and

Fig. 109. Florentine tabletop, last quarter of the 19th century, sent from the Gilbert Collection to the Opificio for restoration, with original pieces arranged in place

parts had shattered: one area of the background of black Belgian marble, featuring an exquisite bouquet of roses and morning glories in its middle, had broken into many pieces. The reusable fragments of the flowers were put back in place (fig. 109), but reassembling the existing large and small pieces of black marble would have created an intolerable spiderweb effect. This would have contradicted the essence of pietre dure art, as achieved by virtuoso craftsmen who assembled individual pieces so that they appear to form a single sheet, without visible lines of abutment. It was thus decided to replace the shattered parts with new, whole pieces of stone. The greatest difficulty was finding Belgian marble of the correct tone, and after many searches with foreign suppliers, a slab was chosen from the Opificio's own stocks that most resembled the material used in the nineteenth century. Reassembled down to its finest details (fig. 110), the tabletop was lined with a single support of slate to ensure maximum stability and very carefully polished with diamond-tipped swabs.[10]

Another Florentine-made tabletop, this from the early seventeenth century, was found in the storage area of the Museo Nacional del Prado in Madrid. It had belonged to the noble Don Rodrigo Calderón and, when he fell into disfavor, had become the property of the Spanish Crown. The tabletop was beautifully inlaid with representations of plants and birds against a white background, its original lively polychromy achieved with intensely colored alabaster, breccia, coral, and lapis lazuli. The coral and lapis lazuli, which are particularly valuable, had been removed with sharp instruments, and many of the adjacent strips had been damaged in the process. The tabletop's poor state of conservation necessitated a long period of restoration in the Opificio's laboratories, during which the many lacunae were filled. By agreement with the Prado, this was accomplished by reconstructing the missing parts (including those of precious stone) in imitation of the remaining complete motifs. One motif was a pair of small birds that were almost entirely missing yet still defined by their silhouettes in the casing, the hollow into which they had been inserted. After lengthy study of other bird motifs in the tabletop and in contemporary objects, it was decided to reconstruct the plumage of their heads and backs of marbles in harmony with the examples that had been considered, basing the reconstructed birds on the design and arrangement of their companions on the table. Because the reconstruction was arbitrary, it was made so that it would be reversible and, therefore, removable on request. Thus, the new little birds were created on a slate support with two small magnets on its back that were attached to other magnets fixed in the cavities of the tabletop (figs. 111, 112). The resulting element, called "extractable casing," had been used in other pietre dure objects for reconstructing missing parts.[11]

Fig. 110. Tabletop in fig. 109 after restoration

Fig. 111. Detail of a Florentine tabletop, early 17th century, sent from the Museo Nacional del Prado, Madrid, during restoration at the Opificio. A replacement bird is ready to be set into its cavity, where two magnets for attaching it are visible.

Fig. 112. Detail of the tabletop in fig. 111 after restoration

A third Florentine table in pietre dure[12] is in the collection of the Kunsthistorisches Museum in Vienna and dates from the mid-eighteenth century, when Louis Siriès was director of the Galleria dei Lavori. The rich decoration of the top—flowers and birds on a black background embellished by a trompe l'oeil string of pearls at the center—was intact except for two missing pearls. However, the legs were damaged, having lost fruits made of semiprecious stone and gilded copper leaves. The Opificio had ample experience with such fruits, which were fully in the round and composed of a variety of stones, for they were so common in its Baroque-era production[13] that a category of craftsmen, the *fruttanti*, was created for them. At the Opificio, the table's missing parts were replaced. New leaves were made from small copper slabs worked with chisels and pushers to create veins and then gilded. The little fruits were fashioned from rough pebbles according to the ancient techniques: "using rotating points and abrasive flinty powders, they proceeded first to outline and then gradually to shape each fruit. Then the surfaces were polished with finer and finer abrasives, rubbed with rotating swabs. Finally, the arrangement was harmoniously completed when the fruits were fixed to the festoons with the original metal pins."[14]

For the sake of brevity, I have touched lightly in this essay on subjects deserving much further development. My intention, however, has been to give an idea of the antiquity of pietre dure craftsmanship, which is on splendid display in this exhibition and catalogue, and to outline its role in the formation of the old and the present-day Opificio; I also wished to highlight particular practices of the Opificio's restorers, which are poised between the imitation of traditional techniques and the introduction of new stratagems that conform to fundamental modern principles of restoration theory such as recognizability and reversibility. Judicious successful application and testing of Brandi's theories have made it possible to restore objects in pietre dure without falling short of the unified approach to restoration in general that he recommended, while at the same time recovering the triumphant beauty born of the marriage of the aesthetic value of natural materials and the sublime skill of craftsmen, a beauty that with informed attentiveness we can fully appreciate.

1. Brought together in the form of a treatise in 1963, the writings of Cesare Brandi were recently translated into English as *Theory of Restoration*; see Brandi 2005.

2. Examples are the controversy over the cleaning of paintings that arose in London in the 1960s, initiated by Humphrey Brooke (see Brooke 1962); or the polemics that accompanied the restoration of Michelangelo's frescoes on the vault of the Sistine Chapel in the 1990s.

3. Baldini 1978–81.

4. "Piano di tavolo con fiori" 1993, pp. 169–70.

5. The proceedings of the conference are published in *Lacuna* 2004.

6. Ciatti, Giusti, and Innocenti 2004, p. 65.

7. Scagliola is obtained from a mineral, selenite, which in its pure state takes the form of thin sheets or scales (hence the name). It is heated, ground into a fine powder, and then mixed with colored soils and animal glues. The original design is transferred onto a slab, traced with a hammer and chisel and then carved deep into the stone. The furrows of the carved drawing are filled with the colored mixtures. After these harden, they are leveled with water and pumice stone. The plane is now etched with a burin and ready to receive more shades of color. Following the procedures established in the nineteenth century, the shadings in the particularly well-defined motifs are retouched with distempered scagliola applied with a paintbrush. Finally, the design is polished with "stones" of wax and lacquer. For a description of the restoration in the 1980s of a chest with pietre dure decoration using scagliola, among other materials, see Giusti and Frizzi 1986.

8. Ciatti, Giusti, and Innocenti 2004, p. 65.

9. Giusti et al. 1986.

10. "Piano di tavolo con fiori" 1993, pp. 169–70.

11. Giusti et al. 2002.

12. Giusti in Giusti 2006a, pp. 104–5, no. 39.

13. Examples are furniture and fittings of the time of Cosimo III de' Medici (r. 1670–1723), Gian Gastone de' Medici (r. 1723–37), and Anna Maria Luisa de'Medici (1667–1743), electress Palatine, the last representative of her family.

14. "Il restauro di un tavolo in pietre dure" 2007.

CATALOGUE

Origins

I. Sphinx of Senwosret III

Egypt, 2nd millennium B.C.
Anorthosite gneiss; 16¾ × 11⅝ ×
28¾ in. (42.5 × 29.3 × 73 cm)
The Metropolitan Museum of Art,
New York, Gift of Edward S.
Harkness, 1917 17.9.2

PROVENANCE: Possibly from
the Temple of Amon at Karnak;
purchased from Nahman, Cairo,
1917; given by Edward S. Harkness
to the Metropolitan Museum, 1917

REFERENCES: Habachi 1984–85;
Egypt and the Ancient Near East
1987, pp. 9, 42–43, pl. 27

With its clever exploitation of the natural markings in the stone to emphasize the musculature, this statue is an ancient example demonstrating an appreciation of hardstone—the most durable of media and the most difficult to work. The sculpture represents a sphinx, a lion with a human head. The face is a portrait of Senwosret III (r. 1878–1841 B.C.), the fifth monarch of the Twelfth Dynasty of the Middle Kingdom in Egypt.[1] A hieroglyphic inscription in sunken relief gives the Horus name and prenomen of the pharaoh. He is wearing a *nemes* headcloth and a cobra, indicators of his royal status. Comparison with a nearly identical, slightly larger, and much more poorly preserved sphinx at the Temple of Amon at Karnak suggests that both were cut from the same block of anorthosite gneiss excavated at the quarry at Khufwy in Nubia, and that they were sculpted, and possibly displayed on pedestals flanking the temple's doorway, to commemorate the great pharaoh Senwosret.[2]

By reputation the most powerful Egyptian ruler of his dynasty, Senwosret expanded Egyptian territory by leading successful military campaigns against Nubia (modern-day northern Sudan), Palestine, and Syria and by erecting strongholds to fortify his country. He was worshiped as a god, and a pyramid in his honor was constructed from local red limestone at Dahshur, twenty-five miles south of Cairo. Smaller dedicatory sculptures were also carved, such as this elegant depiction in gneiss, and placed in the temples of Amon at Karnak and of Mentuhotep at Deir el-Bahri.[3]

The statue's preservation through nearly four millennia testifies to a continuous interest in stone portraiture and to the importance of the image as political or royal propaganda. The ancient tradition this sphinx exemplifies survived alongside the creation of contemporary portrait imagery (see cat. nos. 50, 87).
F K

1. Lions have been associated with kingship since prehistoric times, and in Egypt the body of a lion was depicted with the recognizable face of a ruling king in order to immortalize the represented ruler and affirm his relationship with the rising sun.
2. Habachi 1984–85.
3. Ibid., p. 15. Gneiss was often used in the predynastic period for stone vessels. In the Old and Middle Kingdoms (ca. 2650–1650 B.C.), statues were produced in the material, before it became rare. A related kind of gneiss has been mined in Maryland since the early 1800s. Architects, builders, and homeowners select the quarry's gneiss for its warm and distinctive silver-gray-brown appearance.

2. Perfume bottle

Rome, 1st century B.C.–
A.D. 1st century
Banded agate; H. 3¼ in. (8 cm)
The Metropolitan Museum of Art,
New York, Purchase, Mr. and
Mrs. Sid R. Bass Gift, in honor
of Annette de la Renta, and Rogers
Fund, 2001 2001.253

PROVENANCE: Purchased
from R. Symes, London, by the
Metropolitan Museum, 2001

REFERENCES: Christopher S.
Lightfoot in "Recent Acquisitions"
2001, p. 11; Picón et al. 2007, pp. 338,
483, no. 393

This small, finely carved perfume bottle (an *amphoriskos,* in Greek) was made from white- and dark-banded agate, a kind of chalcedony. This semiprecious stone, commonly used for cameos and vessels in antiquity, is rarely found in Europe; it was imported, mostly from India.[1] The material, quality, and purpose of this bottle indicate that it was a luxury object carved for the personal use of a member of the Roman aristocracy. It is an early masterpiece, exemplifying the long-lasting tradition in the highly developed centers of pre-Christian Europe of fine decorative and domestic objects being carved from agate.[2] There were no lapidary workshops in Italy before the first century B.C., when gem cutters from the Near East, Egypt, and Greece emigrated to Rome to work there; subsequently they spread out to other Italian towns, including Pompeii, Aquileia, and Tarentum.[3] The numerous Roman carved gems and vessels that survived formed the nucleus of European princely collections throughout the centuries. They were treasured for their beauty and rarity as well as for their artistic, material, and political value, since they carried associations to the mighty political power of the Roman Empire.[4]

FK

1. Bühler 1973, pp. 4–5. Due to the scarcity of banded agate in Europe, it was regularly imitated in objects made of glass from as early as the Augustan period (27 B.C.–A.D. 14); see ibid., pp. 12–13.
2. See cat. no. 96, a somewhat comparable object made later in Byzantium.
3. Bühler 1973, pp. 30–31.
4. Wells 2004.

3. Bowl

Rome, 1st century B.C.–
A.D. 1st century
Granodiorite; Diam. 7⅞ in. (20 cm)
The Metropolitan Museum of Art,
New York, Gift of the Aboutaam
Family, 1995 1995.83

PROVENANCE: Gift from
the Aboutaam family to the
Metropolitan Museum, 1995

This bowl is an artifact of delicacy and fine quality, one of a very few objects made by Roman lapidaries working in granodiorite—a hardstone that is difficult to carve and was most commonly used for columns and foundation or paving stones in buildings.[1] As is the obelisk of Ramesses II (r. ca. 1279–1213 B.C.),[2] this vessel is made from stone that is likely to have been quarried at Aswan, in southern Egypt, the source of most granodiorite.

The bowl's survival strongly suggests that it was always treated as a precious belonging and was never used as domestic tableware. Like a contemporary perfume bottle (cat. no. 2), it exemplifies qualities that inspired wonder in the princes of the Renaissance and Baroque periods who assembled *Kunst-* and *Wunderkammern* (collectors' cabinets). To them such a work represented both the beauty and variousness of nature, by its material, and the power of humankind over nature, by its skillfully carved, thin-walled shape.[3] In the seventeenth and eighteenth centuries, ancient objects were collected along with modern lapidary works and gems, and sometimes mounted, engraved, or otherwise decorated according to their collector's taste.[4]

FK

1. Dodge 1988.
2. Ägyptisches Museum und Papyrussammlung, Berlin, no. 12800.
3. T. Richter 2005; Evans and Marr 2006.
4. Two among several notable collections of this type were those of the Gonzagas in Italy and of Louis XIV in France. See Morselli 2002; Alcouffe 2001.

4. Panel with plant scroll

Rome, ca. A.D. 1st century
Glass; 10 × 17 in. (25.4 × 43.2 cm)
The Metropolitan Museum of Art,
New York, Rogers Fund, 1913
13.231.4

PROVENANCE: Purchased
from E. Jandolo, Rome, by the
Metropolitan Museum, 1913

REFERENCES: G. M. A. Richter
1915, p. 212, fig. 7; McClees 1925,
p. 22; McClees 1933, p. 26; Zahn
1933, p. 71

Colorful leafy branches shown in lively motion within a rectangular frame are a typical decorative motif in the art of imperial Rome. This panel's original location may have been on the Palatine Hill. *Palatium* is the etymological origin of "palace"; since antiquity there has been a continuum of the settings for such objects. The Palatine overlooks the Forum Romanum and is the centermost of the seven hills of Rome, housing its most ancient structures.

The Metropolitan's panel was made in the mosaic technique called opus sectile (a Latin term meaning "cut work." Such panels were used to embellish not only floors but also walls, and the fragile material of which this one is made suggests it found its place on a wall. Unlike the more familiar mosaic technique in which uniformly sized squares of stone, known as tesserae, are assembled to make a pattern (see cat. no. 130), opus sectile mosaics are made with pieces of different sizes and materials of different types, such as hardstones, marble, ivory, and mother-of-pearl—or glass, as in

the present case. The usually polychrome materials were inlaid in walls and floors, where they formed an ornamental or figural picture. The technique is similar to that used to construct *commessi di pietre dure*. Indeed, after disappearing from the Italian peninsula after the fall of the Western Roman Empire, the opus sectile technique survived in Byzantium in the East—until in medieval times Greek artisans brought it back to Italy, where it became a major influence on the evolution of hardstone mosaic.[1] The lavish floral decorations on ancient panels like this one were obviously the inspiration for opulent pietre dure compositions such as a tabletop in the collection of the Metropolitan Museum (cat. no. 15). A sophisticated variant of the opus sectile technique was practiced in the Orient, where glass artisans learned to imitate the look of jewels, creating the shimmer of pearls and the flash and color of semiprecious stones.

W K

1. James 2001.

5. Jug

Unknown Norman court workshop, southern Italy or Sicily, ca. 12th century
Rock crystal; H. 11 in. (27.8 cm), Diam. 6⅜ in. (16.2 cm)
Private collection, on loan to The Metropolitan Museum of Art, New York L.2005.45a,b

PROVENANCE: Sale, Christie's, London, December 13, 1994, lot 56; purchased at that sale by a private collector

REFERENCE: Distelberger 2002, pp. 40–41, no. 3

An unusually large block of nearly flawless rock crystal was used to create this astonishing vessel, the second-largest known of its type.[1] In the perfection of its execution and the beauty and fragility of the material, the jug is an embodiment of what the culture that produced it must have considered the ultimate prestige item. The raw material—itself worth a fortune—was surely entrusted to the most superior and experienced workshop to minimize the possibility of an accident during the manufacturing process. The pear-shaped, twelve-lobed body, skillfully hollowed out, stands on a relatively small, faceted foot. The form of the foot and the profile of the lip indicate that mounts of precious metal were formerly applied in these places. Such mounts not only would have enhanced its rich appearance but also would have served to balance the vessel, whose shape is slightly distorted. The unusual thickness and the Saracenic shape of the stepped handle set this object apart from rock crystal vessels made in Venice during the fourteenth century.[2]

Closely related seems a jug with later gilded-silver mounts in the Topkapi Sarayi Museum in Istanbul.[3] Its provenance is also unknown, and it is still attributed by that museum to Burgundy and dated to the first half of the fifteenth century. There is no conclusive argument, however, for not dating both vessels much earlier.[4] A date in the twelfth century is supported by the flowing lines and smooth-edged softness (if that word can be used in connection with rock crystal) of this handle. Later Italian and Parisian examples in rock crystal[5] and other hardstones—for example, a ewer, in the Gulbenkian collection (fig. 96), remounted in the eighteenth century by Thomas Germain[6]—have sharp-edged handles that are totally different in style. The present jug is a rare survival from a region that served as threshold between the cultures of the Orient and of the Occident.

WK

1. Distelberger 2002, p. 41.
2. See, for example, Hahnloser and Brugger-Koch 1985, p. 233, no. 494.
3. Inv. 2/472. See *Turchia* 2006, pp. 100–101. The rock crystal lid of the Topkapi Sarayi jug has a different cut that does not match the style of the body; it was likely added at the time its mount was attached. I am grateful to Michelangelo Lupo for bringing this object to my attention during the June 2007 exhibition "Turchia: 7,000 anni di storia" at the Palazzo Quirinale, Rome.
4. Hahnloser and Brugger-Koch 1985, p. 227, no. 477, dates the Topkapi Sarayi jug in the fourteenth century.
5. Distelberger 2002, pp. 46–54, nos. 6–11.
6. See Baetjer and Draper 1999, pp. 112–13, no. 52.

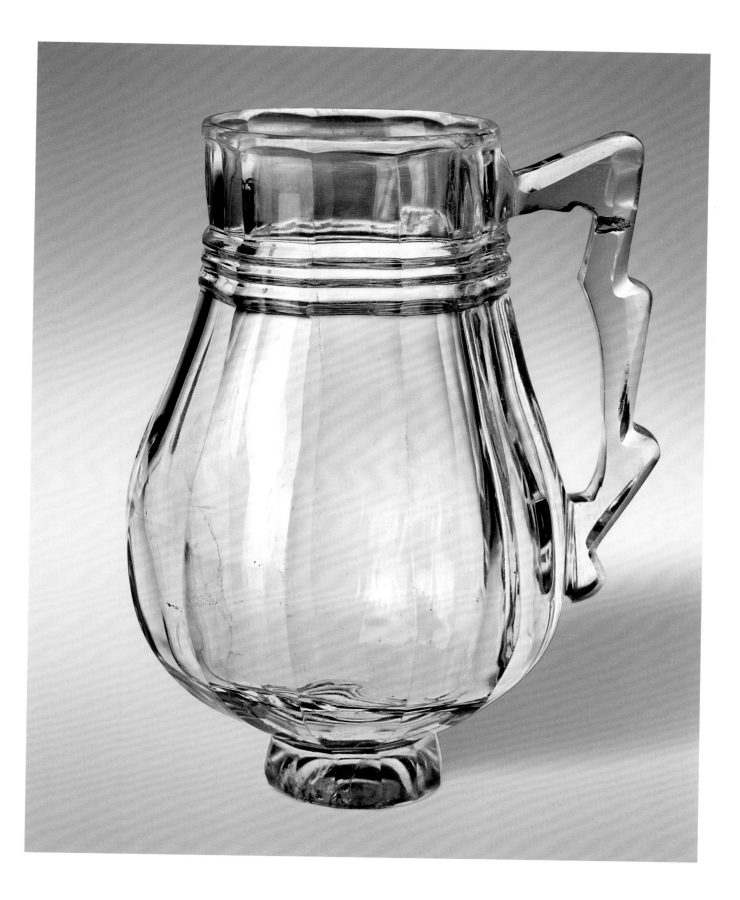

6. Flagon

Prague, third quarter of the
14th century
Bohemian jasper; H. 13¾ in. (35 cm)
Mounts: late 14th or first quarter
of the 15th century
Gilded silver
The Metropolitan Museum of Art,
New York, Gift of J. Pierpont
Morgan, 1917 17.190.610

PROVENANCE: Parish church,
Reinkenhagen, Mecklenburg-
Vorpommern (Pomerania,
Germany); acquired by J. Pierpont
Morgan (1837–1913), ca. 1876;
his gift to the Metropolitan
Museum, 1917

REFERENCES: Lamm 1929–30,
vol. 1, p. 225, pl. 81, 2; Wentzel
1972, pp. 79–80, fig. 82; Fritz 1982,
p. 236, no. 362; Hahnloser and
Brugger-Koch 1985, p. 226, no. 475,
colorpl. XXVII; Boehm in Boehm
and Fajt 2005, pp. 166–70, no. 36, a;
Boehm in Fajt 2006, pp. 256–60,
no. 93, a

This sumptuous vessel conjures up the refined etiquette and way of life at the court of Holy Roman Emperor Charles IV (r. 1355–78), who lived most of each year in Prague and at his favorite residence, Karlstein (Karlštejn) Castle, twelve miles southwest of the city. The beauty of the hardstone is complemented by the precious silver mounts and the superb gilding that harmonize with the purple-red jasper. In some areas the stone looks like Oriental porphyry, which since antiquity had an imperial association. The source of this Bohemian hardstone is near Ciboušov (formerly Zibisch).[1] A mystery still to be explored is why these deposits were forgotten after Charles's death and not rediscovered until the twentieth century.

The flagon belongs in a small group of secular parade objects, most with lavish mounts and nearly all in major museum collections throughout Europe. Some years ago the Metropolitan Museum was able to acquire a footed cup with a trefoil handle that perfectly complements the flagon.[2] The flagon's shaped silver foot is reminiscent of the forms of contemporary Gothic architecture, and through its dramatic elevation of the heavy stone body and domed lid it imparts a well-proportioned and elegant look to the vessel. The entire design reflects the wealth and imperial status of its first owner. A canted handle appears often on European hardstone objects of this period; the handle's raised double ridges may have helped ensure safe handling and a tight grip during festive banquets.[3] The two acorns with crossed stems that serve as a thumbpiece are a traditional symbol of strength and continuity and may have been intended to flatter the recipient of this piece.[4]

Charles IV chose irregular slabs of Bohemian jasper to sheathe the walls of some of the chapels that he commissioned or embellished (see fig. 63). The large amethyst inclusions frequently found in this type of jasper may have influenced his choice, for amethyst was counted at that time among the precious gems. The lid of this flagon has a translucent crystal inclusion, which, as Barbara Boehm has observed, would be seen and appreciated each time the vessel was used.[5]   W K

1. Boehm in Boehm and Fajt 2005, p. 167.
2. MMA 2000.504; Boehm in ibid., pp. 169–70, no. 36, g; Boehm in Fajt 2006, pp. 256–60, no. 93, g.
3. See Hahnloser and Brugger-Koch 1985, p. 226, no. 475.
4. Perhaps the most famous noble family to use crossed oak branches with acorns as its emblem was the Italian Della Rovere family.
5. Boehm in Boehm and Fajt 2005, p. 168.

Italy through the Seventeenth Century

7. Two-handled vase with lid

Attributed to Venetian craftsmen,
late 14th century
Red jasper; H. 15⅞ in. (40.2 cm)
Mounts: attributed to a Venetian
goldsmith, 15th century
Gilded silver and enamel
Museo degli Argenti, Palazzo Pitti,
Florence Gemme 1921:772

PROVENANCE: Piero de' Medici,
before 1456; Lorenzo de' Medici;
Basilica di San Lorenzo, Florence,
from 1532; Palazzo degli Uffizi,
Florence, from 1785; Museo degli
Argenti, from 1921

REFERENCES: Kris 1929, vol. 1,
p. 178, no. 431; Morassi 1964, pl. 17;
Aschengreen Piacenti 1967, p. 141,
no. 240; Heikamp in Heikamp
and Grote 1974, pp. 125–27, no. 25,
figs. 46, 47 (with bibliography);
Tuena 1992b, p. 42; Mosco 2004b,
pp. 35–36, fig. 2

Of the sixteen vases in the Museo degli Argenti bearing the inscription "LAU.R.MED," this splendid specimen best communicates the importance and rarity of the collection of pietre dure vases amassed in the Quattrocento by Piero de' Medici and his son, Lorenzo the Magnificent, whose name the initials represent. Piero (1416–1469), known as Il Gottoso ("the Gouty"), was the son of Cosimo the Elder and an active participant in the humanist culture of Florence, which greatly venerated the artistic forms of the ancient world. Among the ancient Roman treasures collected by Piero and his contemporaries in pursuing their antiquarian passion, a special place was reserved for *la glittica* (glyptics)—or works of hardstone carved in the form of cameos and vases. Piero's extraordinary collection, inherited and expanded by Lorenzo, included vases that, as recent art historians have recognized, actually originated in a variety of epochs and geographic areas, some of which cannot be identified. Such uncertainties of attribution are not infrequent for hardstone vases, especially those in stylized, simple forms, which do not lend themselves to definitive stylistic interpretations. Such is the case with this two-handled vase, for which a variety of conflicting attributions[1] were made before it was ascribed most recently, with the approbation of the majority of art historians, to Venetian craftsmen of the late Trecento.

Before the blossoming of the glyptic arts in the sixteenth century, by which time there were several specialized pietre dure centers on the Italian peninsula, this difficult craft was practiced in few places in Europe. Two such places were France and Venice—where, we know from existing carved rock crystal liturgical objects from the thirteenth century, an early tradition of hardstone carving must have been established. The gray-speckled red jasper that forms the body of this vase, a rare material, is found in a small number of such objects; these include a cross at the Museo dell'Opera del Duomo di Siena that is considered a typically Venetian work,[2] and another cross, now in the Victoria and Albert Museum, London, for which a French origin has been hypothesized.[3]

The mounts of gilded silver and enamel, like the mounts of other Medici vases, date from the time when the vase was in the Medici collections. A 1456 inventory of the Medici holdings and its 1463 supplements mention only simple mountings in silver; they were probably in place when Piero acquired the vases. In Piero's *Ricordi* (Memoirs) of 1465, he describes the current, richly enameled mounts of several works, which must have been made sometime in the intervening two years, quite likely in Florence. But they were not necessarily the work of Florentine goldsmiths. In the case of this vase, the morphology of the foot, with its sculpted seedpod motif, and especially the enamels, characterized by subtle arabesques and plant forms, have recently led scholars to attribute it to an unknown Venetian goldsmith working at that time in Florence.[4]

Upon Piero's death the vase passed to Lorenzo, who was perhaps responsible for the addition of the ferrule rising up from the crown on the lid. The silver sphere, enclosed by a diamond-pointed ring with three ostrich feathers, displays the seven red balls of the Medici coat of arms. After being inherited by Pope Clement VII (Giulio de' Medici), along with the other vases formerly in the collection of Piero and Lorenzo, this vase was donated by Clement in 1532 to the Basilica of San Lorenzo, the Medici family church in Florence, where it was transformed into a reliquary. In 1785 Grand Duke Peter Leopold of Habsburg-Lorraine removed the relics from the vases and exhibited the latter in the Gabinetto delle Gemme of the Palazzo degli Uffizi.

AG

1. For a complete examination of the different critical opinions on the vase, see Heikamp in Heikamp and Grote 1974, pp. 125–27, no. 25.
2. Hahnloser 1973.
3. Heikamp in Heikamp and Grote 1974, p. 127.
4. This mounting and other examples had previously been attributed to Giusto da Firenze (see Heikamp in Heikamp and Grote 1974, pp. 125–27, no. 25), but Dora Liscia Bemporad has persuasively rejected this hypothesis on the basis of morphological and stylistic differences between the Medici mountings and documented works by Giusto. See Liscia Bemporad 1996.

8. Reliquary casket

Workshop of Andrea del
Verrocchio, Florence, 1480s
or 1490s
Silver, gilded silver, and hardstones
on a wood carcass; 13 × 10¼ × 6 in.
(33 × 26 × 15 cm)
Museo dell'Opera di Santa Maria
del Fiore, Florence
O.P. A. 90.87.1264

PROVENANCE: Baptistery,
Florence; Opera di Santa Maria
del Fiore, Florence; Museo
dell'Opera di Santa Maria del
Fiore, from 1954

REFERENCES: Gori 1748–53, vol. 3
(1749), pp. 89ff.; Steingräber 1955,
pp. 92ff., fig. 9; Brunetti in
Becherucci and Brunetti 1969,
pp. 249–50, vol. 2, no. 20, pl. 129;
Liscia Bemporad 1993, vol. 1,
fig. 16; Cantelli 1996, pp. 96–97,
142, fig. 61; Elisabetta Nardinocchi
in *Il Rinascimento in Italia* 2001,
p. 80, no. 33

Even among the richly varied goldsmith work produced in fifteenth-century Florence, this casket is remarkable for the multicolored pietre dure decorating its wooden structure. The reliquary has the form of a sarcophagus; it is closed by a tall lid with four sloping sides that are framed by bands of partially gilded silver and crowned by a pair of acanthus volutes made of gilded silver. There are four more large, silver and gilded silver acanthus volutes at the corners. The casket is supported by four lion's paws, and it has a band of gilded silver decorated with appliqués of stylized silver corollas along its bottom edge. The seductive array of jasper and agate adorning the casket's lid is arranged in parallel rows to form a revetment of scalelike tiles. The stones on the short sides of the body are arranged in vertical and horizontal rows; on the long sides they form a pattern of diamond-shaped lozenges.

A document dated 1749 tells us that this casket was at the time among the treasures of the Florentine Baptistery, together with a pendant piece that has since been lost.[1] Ignored in the literature until it was put on display in the Museo dell'Opera di Santa Maria del Fiore in the mid-twentieth century, the casket was then connected to a payment made to Lorenzo Ghiberti's son, Vittorio, for a "stone chest,"[2] although the chest mentioned in the document is most likely to have actually been carved from stone.[3] Still, the hypothesis that Vittorio made this casket is not necessarily to be abandoned, since he was a goldsmith and expert metalworker.

Recently it has been suggested that this unique object may instead have been designed by an artist in Andrea del Verrocchio's circle.[4] The piece does seem to have been influenced by Verrocchio's sarcophagus for Giovanni and Piero de' Medici in the Old Sacristy at San Lorenzo, dated 1472–73. The sarcophagus, too, has lion's-paw feet and the acanthus leaves that on the casket wrap softly around the corners; in addition, the pairs of vines on the casket are a slender, elegant reduction of the sumptuous crowning bronze element on the Medici tomb. No doubt the transition from a monumental scale to such small dimensions could

have been accomplished only by someone, like Verrocchio, who possessed the skills of an expert sculptor-goldsmith but, more important, the vision of an artist. Of course there are other works that might also have influenced the design of the reliquary. The tall lid, for example, with its four sloped sides, is reminiscent of Roman sarcophagi, and the scalelike pattern of the tiles closely resembles that on the lid of a stone casket now in the Museo dell'Opera but originally easily seen, along with many others, in the area around the Baptistery.[5] A scalelike arrangement is also used for majolica tiles in objects produced by the Della Robbia workshop both before and contemporary with the making of this reliquary casket.

But this casket is extraordinary in that it appears to represent the first use of hardstones as a revetment. Their geometric arrangement also seems to foreshadow a fascination with intricate patterns of stone inlay, something that would be skillfully expressed in the pietre dure works made in Florence some three centuries later. In the late fifteenth century, although working in pietre dure was at its very beginnings in Florence, the artistic possibilities for such resplendent stone materials had already been demonstrated by Piero and Lorenzo de' Medici's collection of antique vases (see cat. no. 7). Perhaps these ancient pieces were what inspired the Medici craftsmen to perfect the difficult art of cutting hardstones. Andrea del Verrocchio was certainly capable of meeting the challenge, as he had already demonstrated in the Medici sarcophagus by working porphyry into a large-scale, three-dimensional sculpture.

A G

1. Gori 1748–53, vol. 3 (1749), pp. 89ff. A similar but not identical piece is illustrated in Collareta 1991, fig. 14.
2. Steingräber 1955, pp. 92ff.
3. Giulia Brunetti was the first to make this logical objection to Steingräber's hypothesis, in Becherucci and Brunetti 1969, vol. 2, pp. 249–50, no. 20.
4. This suggestion, first made by Dora Liscia Bemporad in a verbal communication, has largely been accepted by Giuseppe Cantelli (1996, pp. 96–97) and Elisabetta Nardinocchi (in *Il Rinascimento in Italia* 2001, p. 80, no. 33).
5. I am grateful to Patrizio Osticresi of the Museo dell'Opera di Santa Maria del Fiore for information about this sarcophagus.

9. Tabletop with Moorish-style decoration

By Bernardino di Porfirio da
Leccio, Florence, before 1557;
design by Giorgio Vasari
Ebony, ivory, and jasper;
Diam. 60⅜ in. (153.5 cm)
Collection of the Banca di
Roma—Unicredit Group 89

PROVENANCE: Bindo Altoviti;
private collection, France; art
market, Paris, after 1945; W.
Appolloni, Rome; Aldo Pannuzzi,
Rome, in 1970; Banca di Roma,
from 1972

REFERENCES: González-Palacios
1982a, p. 5; González-Palacios 1988a,
p. 43, fig. 1; Giusti 1988a, p. 22,
n. 13; González-Palacios 1991,
pp. 145–46, no. 62; Giusti 1992,
pp. 26–27, pl. 2; González-Palacios
1993, vol. 1, pp. 380–81, vol. 2,
fig. 688; González-Palacios in
Chong, Pegazzano, and Zikos 2003,
pp. 432–34, no. 34; Giusti 2006b,
p. 28, ill. no. 20

This tabletop is a very early demonstration of the taste and high standard of workmanship that would make Florence a center of excellence in the production of pietre dure. The extraordinary piece can be dated and identified because of direct evidence provided by the illustrious biographer Giorgio Vasari, who was also the artist responsible for its design. In the second edition of his *Lives,* published in 1568, Vasari, referring to a pietre dure table then being made from his design for Francesco de' Medici, notes that the gem carver executing it, Bernardino di Porfirio da Leccio, who was from "the area around Florence," had already made a table for him that was "likewise of jasper, an octagon inlaid with ebony and ivory."[1] That table was created for Bindo Altoviti, a distinguished member of the Florentine mercantile and banking class who lived for some time in Rome, where he died in 1557. This date becomes a terminus ante quem for dating Vasari's octagonal tabletop, which I have argued should be identified with the present work.[2]

The two tabletops Vasari designed for Cosimo and Francesco de' Medici have been lost, making this example unique both for its singular design and because it provides tangible evidence that the versatile Vasari also made designs for inlaid stone pieces. A Moorish-style pattern radiates from the center of the smaller octagon inscribed within the tabletop. The multilateral shape at its center, made of jasper, generates complex concentric and interlacing designs that are, nevertheless, easy to follow visually because of the strong contrasts between the velvety ebony ground, the whiteness of the ivory, and the warm tones of the Sicilian jasper. A band around the edge of the table completes the design; it has interlocking cartouches and medallions that seem to suggest the classical motifs that inspired sixteenth-century Roman intarsia masters, here given an imaginative, orientalizing twist. The arabesque motif was popular throughout sixteenth-century Europe and was widely disseminated in the form of prints, including those found in the collection of the so-called Accademia Vinciana, which Vasari almost certainly would have known.[3] The fact that this Moresque tabletop was executed with ivory inlaid in wood also suggests the direct inspiration of Islamic furniture, in which this is a common pairing of materials. Apparently this was not the only work of its kind Altoviti owned. Among his

possessions were "two octagonal jasper pietre dure tables with ivory inlaid in ebony and another square one, all with their bases," which were given, years after his death, to the royal House of Savoy.[4]

The question of whether these rare sixteenth-century tables combining pietre dure with ebony and ivory reflect a Roman or a Florentine taste is impossible to answer with any confidence, given how little we know of the subject. Florentine works with a certain affinity to them include an octagonal table, in the Contini Bonacossi collection and now at the Uffizi, that was made in Florence about 1550 and has a walnut top inlaid with briarwood that simulates stone; its decoration is in a halo of rays alternating with eight pieces of pietre dure.[5] There is also a drawer in a cabinet made for Ferdinand I de' Medici in 1593 that has eight pietre dure panels set into ebony, although they are bordered with gilded bronze rather than ivory.[6]

A wooden tabletop in the State Hermitage Museum, Saint Petersburg, with a crowded but classicizing composition includes pietre dure and panels of lapis lazuli surrounded by inlaid ivory.[7] It is tempting to identify this mid-sixteenth-century tabletop, which I have suggested was made in Florence, with a "table . . . of ebony set with many pieces of lapis lazuli, fine cornelian, jasper, and agate and edged with ivory and made in the same way and of the same wood" listed in the 1682 inventory of the storerooms of the Palazzo di Magnanapoli, Rome.[8] Here, again, we are faced with the complicated and intertwined relationship between Rome and Florence that contributed so much to the vitality of the early history of pietre dure mosaics.

A G

1. Vasari 1568 (1962–66 ed.), vol. 8, p. 37.
2. Giusti 1988a, p. 22, n. 13; the table was first published by González-Palacios (1982a, p. 5), who suggested it was a German work from the first quarter of the seventeenth century. Taking my opinion into account, however, he has since 1988 also indicated that there could be a relationship between Vasari and this tabletop. See González-Palacios 1988a, p. 43.
3. This consists of six engravings on copper now in the Biblioteca Ambrosiana, Milan. See Pedretti 1978, pp. 296–308, "L'ornato e gli emblemi."
4. According to a ca. 1612 inventory of furnishings sold to the duke of Savoy, published in Chong, Pegazzano, and Zikos 2003, pp. 361–62, and in González-Palacios 1993, vol. 1, p. 381. González-Palacios wrote there that sometime in the past the tabletop had been cut into two equal pieces to make two console tables. As evidence for this assertion he published an old photograph (vol. 2, fig. 689) of half of the cut tabletop supported by a base (a later addition). The present

table belonging to the Banca di Roma is intact, however, and shows no evidence of ever having been cut in two or of having been reassembled. That raises the question of whether the cut table might have been the second octagonal tabletop Altoviti owned, perhaps made as a pendant to this one and now in some unknown collection.

5. The Contini Bonacossi table was first published and attributed by Maddalena Trionfi Honorati; see *Palazzo Vecchio* 1980, p. 208, no. 388.
6. Identified by Massinelli in Giusti 1988, p. 106, no. 12.x.
7. Giusti 2006b, p. 28, ill. no. 21.
8. The inventory is quoted in González-Palacios 1993, vol. 1, p. 381.

10. *Farnese Table*

Farnese Palace workshop, Rome,
ca. 1568–73
Design by Jacopo Barozzi da
Vignola; piers by Guglielmo della
Porta; top attributed to Giovanni
Mynardo (Jean Ménard)
Marbles, hardstones, and Egyptian
alabaster; 37½ × 149¼ × 66¼ in.
(95.3 × 379.1 × 168.3 cm)
The Metropolitan Museum of Art,
New York, Harris Brisbane Dick
Fund, 1958 58.57a–d

PROVENANCE: Commissioned
by Cardinal Alessandro Farnese
(d. 1589); Farnese collection,
Palazzo Farnese, Rome (listed in
palace inventories from 1653 to
1796, but not in one of 1834); by
tradition, a convent in Verona,
Italy; acquired from that convent
by Alexander Hamilton, tenth
duke of Hamilton (d. 1852),
for Hamilton Palace, South
Lanarkshire, Scotland (recorded
as in the palace in 1844 [in a fire
insurance document], 1852, and
1876 [inventories]); descended in
the Hamilton family until 1919,
when it was sold at auction from
Hamilton Palace; purchased at
that sale by Viscount Leverhulme
(d. 1925), London; art market,
London; purchased by the
Metropolitan Museum, 1958

REFERENCES: Raggio 1960;
González-Palacios 2001, pp. 50–51,
ill.; Koeppe in Kisluk-Grosheide,
Koeppe, and Rieder 2006,
pp. 23–25, no. 7

The *Farnese Table,* one of the most superbly executed and evocative pietre dure objects in existence, became a key piece in the encyclopedic collection of the Metropolitan Museum when it was acquired in 1958.[1] Since the table's reevaluation in an essay published in 2006,[2] some new archival information regarding its provenance has come to light. An 1852 inventory of the fabled collection at Hamilton Palace, Scotland, indicates that "the magnificent large and massive antique Pietre Dura Altar Table inlaid with various precious stones" departed the Farnese collection in Rome sometime after 1796. An annotation, which was made on an inserted page and in a different hand, indicates that the table subsequently entered the collection of a "convent in Verona," where the duke of Hamilton was able to acquire it, "on condition of [the] Duke's repairing [the] Convent which cost him between £ 4,000 and £ 5,000. The freight to Greenock [seaport] amounted to £ 800."[3] The fact that the 1852 inventory describes the table as an altar would seem to give weight to the assertion in the annotation that it previously belonged to a convent. The sums that the duke allegedly had to pay to add this trophy to his collection seem exorbitant. By comparison, in 1811 the Prince Regent (later King George IV) paid a mere 5,250 pounds for *The Shipbuilder Jan Rijcksen and His Wife, Griet Jans,* by Rembrandt, and in July 1812 he acquired a highly desirable Boulle secretaire for

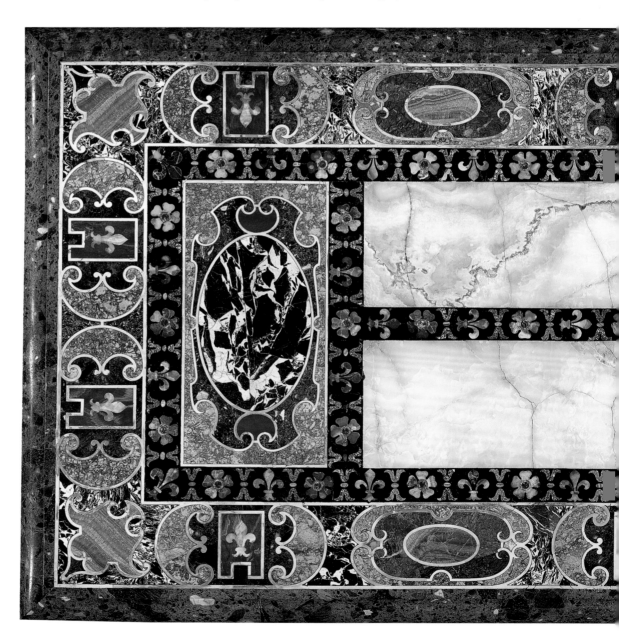

367 pounds.[4] But this table, a monumental *objet de vertu* with unsurpassed work in pietre dure, must have struck the duke as unique and fascinating in a way that still holds true today.

The table's design, by the architect Jacopo Barozzi da Vignola (1507–1573), recalls ancient Roman prototypes that can be seen in frescoes.[5] The top is a slab of white marble richly inlaid with marbles of many different colors and with semiprecious stones. The inlay fills most of the white marble background, which is visible only in the lines around certain borders and the medallions, cartouches, rectangles, and ovals. The center is inlaid with two rectangular panels of Egyptian alabaster.[6] The geometrical pattern of the tabletop also includes some of Vignola's favorite decorative motifs—for example, the confronted *peltae* (which are based on the shape of a Roman shield) and the broken rectangles enclosing the Farnese lilies. He may have discovered the motifs in ancient Roman pavements executed in opus sectile.[7]

The coats of arms on the three supporting marble piers, which are the work of the sculptor Guglielmo della Porta (d. 1577), are embellished with six stylized fleurs-de-lis. This heraldic symbol, which recurs on the tabletop, refers to Cardinal Alessandro Farnese, who commissioned the table to complement his collection of ancient sculpture and required that it be made from hardstones. In 1547, shortly after Vignola began to work for Farnese, the cardinal's architects went to Roman ruins "to get colored marbles for the Palace." All the stones used for the table are of ancient origin, and many of them were taken from the Baths of Caracalla, where excavations had begun in the 1540s under the supervision of Farnese himself.[8]

When the owner of the Farnese Palace was away, the "large table . . . supported by three marble feet in the shape of harpies with the arms of the Lord Cardinal" was protected "in a wooden box [with] a chain [that] loops to close it and in the middle a small mattress full of wool, covered with a quilted checkered cloth." There was also "a cover for this table, made of tooled and gilded leather with four fringes, decorated borders, and fleur-de-lis."[9] Cardinal Alessandro adopted the coat of arms carved on the table's supports in 1566, so Vignola's design must date from that year or later. There are references to other inlaid tables—two

of alabaster, two of porphyry, and one inlaid with many types of stone—in Farnese Palace inventories dating from 1566 and 1568. It is therefore likely that the Museum's table was under construction in the late 1560s—certainly by 1573, when Vignola died.[10] The hardstone and soft stone mosaic inlay is believed to have been created by a French master, until recently little known, named Jean Ménard, who in Italy was called Giovanni Mynardo (ca. 1525–1582). He was considered one of the finest craftsmen in stone intarsia and mosaic decoration working in Rome during the 1560s.[11]

W K

I am very grateful to Olga Raggio and Daniëlle Kisluk-Grosheide, curators in the Department of European Sculpture and Decorative Arts, and to Jack Soultanian Jr., conservator in the Objects Conservation and Scientific Research Department, all, Metropolitan Museum, for discussing various subjects related to the *Farnese Table* with me.

1. Two years later Olga Raggio presented it as a "rediscovered work by Vignola" in an article that has remained a model for subsequent studies in the history of furniture; see Raggio 1960.
2. See Koeppe in Kisluk-Grosheide, Koeppe, and Rieder 2006, pp. 23–25, no. 7.
3. I am most grateful to Daniëlle Kisluk-Grosheide for sharing the results of her archival research with me, as follows: The inventory of 1852 is in vol. 1228, NRAS 2177, in the National Register of Archives for Scotland, Edinburgh, and the description of the table is on pp. 98–99; the separate sheet with the annotation is inserted after p. 99. The quotation from the inventory of 1876 is on the first page of the original document, which is now in the Hamilton Town Hall Library, South Lanarkshire. My thanks are also due to Godfrey Evans, Principal Curator of European Applied Art, National Museum of Scotland, Edinburgh, who will publish more information on the tenth duke of Hamilton and the *Farnese Table* in a doctoral dissertation.
4. *Carlton House* 1991, pp. 66–67, no. 17, pp. 80–81, no. 32; in 1791 a commode by Adam Weisweiler (see cat. no. 134) cost 110 guineas (115.5 pounds; one guinea was equal to 21 shillings, or 1.05 pounds, with slight variations during the following decades until 1816).
5. Morley 1999, p. 24 and fig. 36.
6. The brittle alabaster slabs have been repaired several times. The beautiful (later ?) *antico verde* marble border, with a convex profile and stepped design, finds no match in other Renaissance examples (compare cat. no. 11).
7. For example, one in the Curia of Diocletian in Rome (see Koeppe in Kisluk-Grosheide, Koeppe, and Rieder 2006, p. 25, n. 14) and another, of the fourth century A.D. from Ostia, now in the Museo Ostiense (see Napoleone 2003, fig. 1).
8. Raggio 1960, p. 219 (including the quotation).
9. Farnese Palace inventory of 1653, quoted in ibid., p. 215. Leather covers for furniture have rarely survived. For some English examples, see Wilson 2007.
10. Koeppe in Kisluk-Grosheide, Koeppe, and Rieder 2006, p. 24.
11. Ronfort 1991–92, p. 139; Raggio 1994, p. 8. For a similar tabletop, see Sotheby's, London, June 8, 2005, sale cat., lot 4 (catalogue entry by González-Palacios).

11. Octagonal tabletop on a dolphin stand

Tabletop: Rome, late 16th century
Alabastro a tartaruga, *bianco* and
nero di Aquitania marbles, and
various hardstones; Diam. 46⅞ in.
(119 cm)
Stand: workshop of Filippo Parodi,
Genoa, ca. 1665–80
Gilded wood; H. ca. 31 in. (78.7 cm)
Palazzo del Quirinale, Rome

PROVENANCE: House of Savoy,
Alcove Room of the Palazzo Reale,
Turin, until 1898; Palazzo del
Quirinale, Rome, 1898–June 1946;
Presidential Apartments, Palazzo
del Quirinale

REFERENCES: González-Palacios
1996b, pp. 350–52, no. 140;
González-Palacios 2007b, fig. 3

The tabletop has at its center a piece of vividly veined cloudy *alabastro a tartaruga* (the name is a reference to tortoiseshell); this is framed by a sixteen-spike band of *nero di Aquitania* marble in a design that resembles a jewelry chain. Surrounding these elements are eight stylized *peltae* with attached S-shaped volutes. In the corners between the *peltae*, on a black ground, acanthus blossoms spouting seeds shown as strings of pearls of diminishing size alternate with stylized palmette motifs. The cornucopia-like plant with sprays of seeds is a typical Roman motif that appears in related form on various tabletops originating in Roman workshops (see cat. no. 15). A broad octagonal frieze incorporating scrollwork cartouches and stylized fleurs-de-lis completes the composition. The whole is framed by a concave border made up of angled pieces that recalls gadrooning.

The table's octagonal form may be based on examples similar to one made of wood and inlaid with hardstone that was designed by Giorgio Vasari (cat. no. 9).[1] It is known that on January 8, 1585, Cardinal Ferdinand de' Medici sent a hardstone-inlaid octagonal table from Rome to Naples.[2] Only five known examples of tables of this shape from the period survive today, all of Roman origin. They were recently published together and insightfully discussed by the doyen of Roman pietre dure studies, Alvar González-Palacios, in a catalogue note devoted to one of them, then in the London art market.[3] The tables, in addition to the present example in the Quirinale, are in Arundel Castle, West Sussex; the Victoria and Albert Museum,

11, top view

London; and the Sacromonte Abbey, Granada. The last-named offers the closest comparison to our example. González-Palacios also identified a drawing in the Biblioteca Nacional de España, Madrid, attributed to the Florentine friar Giovanni Vincenzo Casale (1540–1593), that is an early preparatory draft with two proposed designs, one clearly for the Quirinale table and the other possibly for the Granada table (fig. 114).[4] In addition, an octagonal table with an alabaster center is represented in a minature of about 1601–3 portraying the Genoese doge Agostino Doria surrounded by his family and court members.[5]

The present tabletop is one of the rare pietre dure examples in which the colored pieces are inlaid in a white marble matrix (see cat. nos. 10, 45). The border that alludes to metal gadrooning has a parallel on a rectangular Roman tabletop honoring the Battle of Lepanto (fig. 18).[6]

The table's flamboyant stand can be attributed to the workshop of the Genoese sculptor Filippo Parodi (1630–1702). His designs were widely

Fig. 113. Drawing from a design book of an octagonal table with stand, mid-16th century. Ink and wash on paper. The Metropolitan Museum of Art, New York, Rogers Fund, 1966 66.621.2

Fig. 114. Giovanni Vincenzo Casale, Design for an octagonal tabletop, late 16th century. Ink on paper. Biblioteca Nacional de España, Madrid

admired, and he received commissions from the Liechtenstein family in Austria and important patrons in northern Italy.[7] The spiral eyes of the dolphins are typical features in his ornamental oeuvre.[8] The canted base molding echoes the octagonal shape of the table's top, and the complex

composition, in which abundantly arranged grapes, leaves, and vines harmonize with the intertwined bodies of the two animals, creates a sense of movement, inviting appreciation of this sculptural work from all angles. There are two shades of gilding, with the vine leaves a naturalistic greenish gold. A console table with a closely related stand was on the Roman art market in 2006.

The present table exemplifies par excellence the frequently occurring situation in which a pietre dure top of the sixteenth or seventeenth century is placed on a stand of later manufacture. The virtuosity of the artistic hardstone work was the table's most important quality, treasured over generations, while the support could be subject to changing fashions and was regularly replaced.[9] A leaf in a mid-sixteenth-century design book in the Metropolitan Museum showing an octagonal table with stand (fig. 113) gives an idea how the original support for this table may have looked. The pattern of the tabletop in the drawing is similar in arrangement to that on a rectangular wooden tabletop with hardstone inlay in the Museo di Mineralogia e Litologia, Florence (fig. 19).[10] The base drawn by the artist shows two extremely heavy volute legs—very different from the present stand's decorative sculpture with a zoomorphic theme, which is in a fully developed Baroque style. The massiveness of the support in the drawing indicates that the top was intended to be completely of pietre dure or at least unusually weighty in its construction.[11]

W K

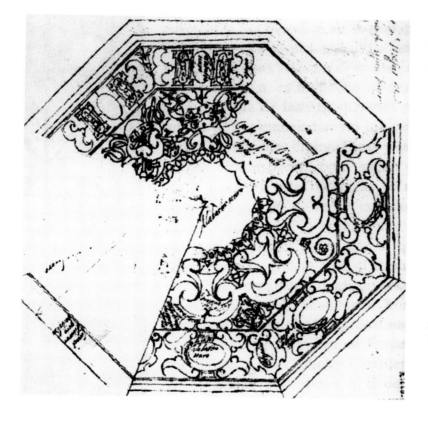

I thank Michelangelo Lupo, who arranged for the examination of the table at the Palazzo del Quirinale in June 2006 and gave invaluable advice.

1. For an earlier example of an octagonal-format table, see Sigrid Sangl in Langer and Würtemberg 1996, pp. 261–62, no. 73.
2. Bertolotti 1877; González-Palacios 2007b, pp. 48, 54, n. 2.
3. González-Palacios 2007b.
4. Ibid., fig. 8; on Casale, see also Kubler 1978.
5. González-Palacios 1982a, p. 8; González-Palacios 1996a, fig. 60.
6. Giusti 2006b, pp. 40–41, ill. no. 29.
7. Raggio in *Liechtenstein* 1985, pp. 25–26, nos. 15, 16; Rotondo Briasco 1962; Oreste Ferrari, "Filippo Parodi," in *Dictionary of Art* 1996, vol. 24, pp. 202–3; González-Palacios 1996a, pp. 77–96.
8. For other examples, see González-Palacios 1996a, figs. 110a, 112.
9. An octagonal top of about 1550 with its original matching canted baluster support is in the J. Paul Getty Museum, Los Angeles (Bremer-David 1993, p. 317, no. 316). See the example on a carved eagle support in González-Palacios 1982a, p. 8, and also González-Palacios 1996a, figs. 88–111.
10. Giusti 2006b, ill. no. 39.
11. Byrne 1981, p. 110, no. 141. For other works owned by the Savoy family, see Castelnuovo 2007.

12. Tabletop with mythological subjects and grotesques

Rome, after 1560
Marble, alabaster, mother-of-pearl, and engravings on paper; 53 ½ × 53 ½ in. (136 × 136 cm)
Villa del Poggio Imperiale, near Florence Mobili Poggio Imperiale 1872:1345

PROVENANCE: Villa Medici, Rome, until 1789; Villa del Poggio Imperiale, after 1789

REFERENCES: Giusti in Baldini, Giusti, and Pampaloni Martelli 1979, pp. 293–94, no. 105, pls. 157–61; Giusti in *Palazzo Vecchio* 1980, p. 244, no. 470; González-Palacios 1982a, p. 14; González-Palacios in Giusti 1988, p. 86, no. 7; Tuena 1988, p. 60, fig. 5; Hochmann in Hochmann 1999, p. 230, no. 50; Giusti 2003b, p. 209, fig. 11; Fioratti 2004, ill. no. 437; Giusti 2006b, p. 43, ill. no. 31

The ancient art of opus sectile, or stone inlay, was revived in Rome in the middle of the sixteenth century, albeit in a new form. Pieces of ancient marble were recut and assembled into sophisticated, nonfigural designs used to decorate wall revetments and tabletops (see cat. nos. 10, 11). The present example, one of the oldest and most unusual objects of stone inlay in the Medici collection, was for many years hidden away at the Villa del Poggio Imperiale, near Florence.[1] The tabletop came to Florence in 1789 as part of the collection of the grand dukes of the Habsburg-Lorraine dynasty. It had been among the furnishings at the Villa Medici in Rome—Ferdinand I de' Medici's residence near the Church of Trinità dei Monti and a repository for his collection of treasures of ancient and contemporary art. The table is itemized in the villa's 1588 inventory as "in the third room of the apartment toward the [Piazza del] Popolo" and is described as being supported by "two wooden goat kids that served as legs."[2] Ferdinand, an extremely refined patron of the arts and also a cardinal, came to appreciate these novel tabletops during his long Roman sojourn (1564–87). Such works also influenced the earliest hardstone mosaics made in Florence in the last decades of the sixteenth century.

This tabletop is unique even within the varied and sophisticated context of Roman production in the second half of the sixteenth century. As Alvar González-Palacios has pointed out, the composition is conceived as a set of elevations in which one sees the four decorated walls of a room.[3] Within its geometric scheme it includes four classicizing structures, two small temples and two *tempietti*, aediculae housing statues of Mercury, Venus, Minerva, and Apollo. Between them is a frieze with Nereids, Tritons, and aquatic animals, which borders the alabaster diamond at the center. There are four sea gods at the corners of the diamond, and pairs of small, grotesque female heads appear in the eight panels of Spanish *brocatello* marble that run around the tabletop, which has an outer border of *rosso antico* marble. Another novel element is the technique used to execute the figural images.

They were engraved and printed on paper, which was then inserted beneath transparent alabaster, giving the panels an evocative, illusionistic effect of depth.[4]

An assortment of rare stones reused from antiquity enhances the sophisticated elegance of this work, including the transparent alabaster as well as the rare alabaster in the center square, of a type called "marine" alabaster; only a few examples of it are known. The brown breccia in the four panels at the center of each side was discovered during excavations undertaken at Tivoli between 1559 and 1565. The fluorite in the four corners, better known as Spanish *smeraldina*, has iridescent veins of color that shift from violet to green. It could very well have been this stone that attracted Ferdinand's eye, since it was also used for the center panel of a large tabletop that, like this example, was once in the Villa Medici.[5] The cardinal apparently also liked mother-of-pearl, used here for the garlands that connect the aediculae with the herms flanking them. Mother-of-pearl was used extensively in Florentine mosaics executed during the reign of Ferdinand I.

This is a work of refined and cerebral taste, and its decoration conceals an as-yet-unidentified meaning. In subject matter and style the engravings incorporated can be associated with the brilliant circle of artists who worked in Rome in the wake of Raphael, Baldassare Peruzzi, and Polidoro da Caravaggio, as Alvar González-Palacios has already suggested; he attributed the engravings to the circle of Michele Lucchesi, who was active from 1553.[6]

A G

1. It had been largely ignored there until discussed by Giusti in Baldini, Giusti, and Pampaloni Martelli 1979, pp. 293–94, no. 105.
2. Quoted by Hochmann in Hochmann 1999, p. 230, no. 50.
3. González-Palacios in Giusti 1988, p. 86, no. 7.
4. The 1588 inventory mentions the "printed paper" of the tabletop. The use of this technique was verified by the Opificio delle Pietre Dure, Florence, during the restoration of this tabletop in the early 1980s.
5. It is now in the Galleria Palatina of the Palazzo Pitti, Florence. See Giusti 2006b, p. 42, ill. no. 30.
6. González-Palacios in Giusti 1988, p. 86, no. 7.

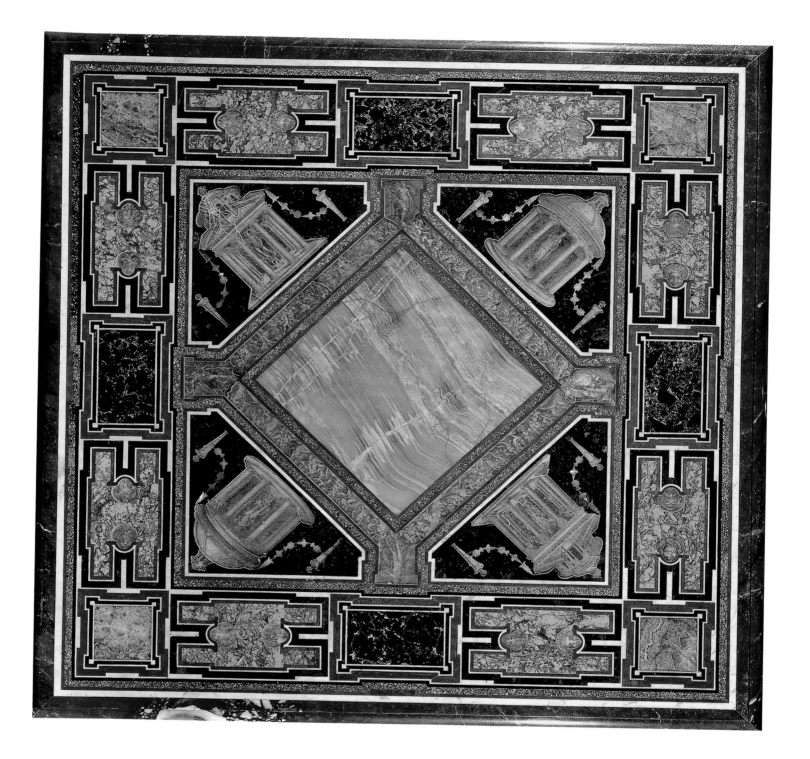

13. Cameo depicting Cosimo I de' Medici and his family

By Giovanni Antonio de' Rossi,
Florence and Rome, ca. 1559–62
Chalcedony; 7⅜ × 6½ in. (18.5 ×
16.5 cm)
Museo degli Argenti, Palazzo
Pitti, Florence, 1917 Bargello 1917
(VII), n.1

PROVENANCE: Medici collections,
Palazzo Vecchio, Florence, 1562;
Tribuna, Palazzo degli Uffizi,
Florence, from 1589; transferred to
the Museo del Bargello, Florence,
in 1907 and to the Museo degli
Argenti after 1917

REFERENCES: Vasari 1568 (1878–85
ed.), vol. 5, p. 387; Gori 1767, vol. 2,
p. CLVI, n. 2; Zobi 1853, p. 59, no. 1853;
Poggi 1916, ill. facing p. 42; Kris 1929,
vol. 1, pp. 79–80, 171, no. 309; Morassi
1964, p. 22, pl. 25; Aschengreen
Piacenti 1967, p. 144, no. 306, fig. XVI;
Pampaloni Martelli 1975, pp. 68–69,
no. 33; Langedijk 1978, pp. 77–78;
McCrory 1979, p. 512, fig. 47;
McCrory in *Palazzo Vecchio* 1980,
pp. 147–48, no. 277; Langedijk
1981–87, vol. 1, pp. 504–5, no. 175;
Maria Sframeli in Giusti 1988, p. 76,
no. 2; Giusti 1995, p. 43, ill. no. 15;
McCrory 1998, pp. 48–49, fig. 13;
McCrory in Acidini et al. 2002,
pp. 252–53, no. 107

Duke Cosimo I de' Medici and his wife, Eleo-nora de Toledo, are depicted here beneath the flying figure of Fame blowing her trumpet. They are accompanied by their five sons—Francesco, Giovanni, Garzia, Pietro, and Ferdinand—all represented as children or young men. In describing this cameo, however, Giorgio Vasari wrote that the couple's two daughters, Isabella and Lucrezia, were also included. The discrepancy between his description and the object itself was originally explained as a mistake on Vasari's part.[1] More recently it has been proposed that the parts of the cameo showing the daughters have broken off, and in fact the edges of the stone do appear to be chipped.[2] It seems unlikely that Vasari would make an error about a piece he knew well, having made a drawing for a frame in which to mount the carved gem.[3] But the depiction of the cameo in the drawing shows only the figures visible today, so the problem remains unsolved.

As was common practice at the time, Vasari's drawing offers two designs for the frame, both to be made from precious metals, leaving it to the patron to decide which one he wanted. It also shows a collar of the Order of the Golden Fleece, which was given to Cosimo, surrounding the blank circular cartouche Cosimo and Eleonora hold. We know from archival documents and inventories that the cameo was never mounted and that the cavity at its center was never filled. The recess was intended to hold a medal or perhaps a second cameo representing Florence or Tuscany; the uncertainty about this comes from the contradictions between descriptions of the piece offered by Vasari and Donato Minali, Cosimo's ambassador in Rome.

The Milanese craftsman Giovanni Antonio de' Rossi (1517–after 1574) began carving this stone in Florence in 1559 and continued the work in Rome, where he moved permanently in 1560. Two years later the unfinished gem was in Florence, in what were the storerooms of the Palazzo Vecchio during the Medici era.

Duke Cosimo I commissioned the cameo from de' Rossi, one of the greatest gem carvers of his day. He had been trained in Milan, which was at that time an important center of pietre dure production. Cosimo wanted to celebrate the power of his dynasty with a work that recalled the great cameos of imperial Rome (see fig. 1) in both size and skill of execution. The size of this piece is unusual—even given the resurgent popularity of carved cameos in the sixteenth century—and its dimensions may have created a problem for de' Rossi. Despite the extreme refinement of the carving, the brown veins of the stone running across the faces of the ducal couple create a disfiguring effect, especially on the duchess's countenance.

AG

1. Maria Sframeli in Giusti 1988, p. 76, no. 2.
2. See McCrory in Acidini et al. 2002, pp. 252–53, no. 107. McCrory concludes that the two missing areas on the sides probably contained the images of the daughters, although only of their heads.
3. This drawing is in the collection of Christ Church College, Oxford. See McCrory in Acidini et al. 2002, p. 253, no. 108.

14. Tabletop with comb and mirror motifs

Attributed to a Roman workshop, first quarter of the 17th century
Marble and colored stones; 35⅜ × 23⅝ in. (90 × 60 cm)
Helen Costantino Fioratti, New York

REFERENCES: Walker in Walker and Hammond 1999, p. 193, no. 60; Fioratti 2004, ill. no. 439

The slab of white marble from which this tabletop is made is visible only in the raised borders outlining the inlay work and the mosaics of colored stones. The rest of the table's surface is covered with dense decoration that surrounds a large oval of *breccia di Quintilina,* also referred to as *breccia di Tivoli,* a rare marble recovered from archaeological sites and much sought after at the end of the sixteenth century. It takes its name from the village of Quintiliolo, near Tivoli, where small, unworked blocks of this stone were discovered about 1550.

The central oval is framed by a large stylized cartouche that connects to the four smaller cartouches at the corners of the tabletop. In the outer field between the cartouches, frames made of abstract decorative forms and curvilinear white marble outlines contain naturalistic images of birds and flowers set against a black ground. These motifs were common in stone inlay work in the early seventeenth century. In contrast, the double-sided comb and the mirror—on the long sides of the table, facing each other diagonally—are extremely unusual. The comb, made from *giallo antico* marble, is set against, and surrounded by, curling ribbons of lapis lazuli and other stones. The mirror is flanked by two owls; what would be its reflective surface is made of Corsican green jasper, the only real hardstone among the various calcareous stones used here, which for the most part were recycled from classical sites. These include *verde antico, lumachella, giallo antico, rosso antico* (most of these are types of marble), and an array of flamboyant and striped alabasters that are used mostly in the center frame and corner cartouches. These materials, too, were very popular in imperial Rome.

The comb and mirror, the latter of which is decorated with corollas at its corners and tiny discs of mother-of-pearl along its sides, make it likely that the tabletop was intended for a woman. The two owls, signifying wisdom, would seem to suggest that the decoration held some symbolic meaning—perhaps extolling the patron's feminine grace while also implying her possession of the "ornaments" of intellect. Or perhaps it was a reminder to the patron to use her beauty wisely, an appropriate exhortation in the context of the Counter-Reformation refrain that all is vanity.

The unusual decoration raises some questions about where this work might have been produced, although in my opinion its Roman origins are clear. Among other considerations, it would have been difficult, if not impossible, to find such a large piece of *breccia di Quintilina* anywhere but Rome. The predominance of reused colored stone from archaeological sites also suggests proximity to Rome. Furthermore, the general style of the decoration, whose dense variety of themes constitutes a kind of horror vacui, can be found in other Roman intarsia work of the early seventeenth century. The same is true of the bird and flower motifs. These were inspired by Florentine mosaics—in their ascendancy in this period—but here are more subdued, making use of contrasting colors but without the nearly obsessive subtle shadings that Florentine craftsmen brought to these subjects.

A number of other small but significant details underscore the Roman provenance of the tabletop. They include the border of quadrilateral corollas around the center oval, a motif that recurs in the same form and position on many Roman tables, and the twisting red and yellow frame, a simplified but effective version of the "tongues" that can be found on Roman tabletops and architectural intarsia in the last quarter of the sixteenth century. It is worth noting that the comb and mirror, made to appear as though they are actual objects set on a woman's table, are an early attempt at trompe l'oeil. This type of representation later found more mature expression in a few rare Florentine works but especially in mosaics produced in the royal workshop of Madrid in the eighteenth century (see cat. no. 129).   AG

15. Tabletop

Rome, late 16th or early
17th century
Hardstones, alabaster, and marble;
54⅜ × 94⅞ in. (138 × 241 cm)
The Metropolitan Museum of Art,
New York, Gift of Mr. and Mrs.
Francis J. Trecker, 1962 62.259

PROVENANCE: Mr. and Mrs.
Francis J. Trecker; their gift to the
Metropolitan Museum, 1962

REFERENCES: Giusti 1992, p. 30,
fig. 15; González-Palacios in
Sotheby's, London, July 3, 2007, sale
cat., pp. 20, 21, fig. 4 (under lot 6)

The geometrical design of this tabletop is characteristic of works made at pietre dure shops in Rome at the turn of the seventeenth century. The feature that distinguishes this example from contemporary Florentine or Neapolitan versions is the central oval of alabaster and the two roundels of a marble called *breccia di Tivoli*. These stones, probably excavated from the ruins of an ancient Roman building, are framed by a wide band that resembles a goldsmith's mounting for a precious gem. The oval panel is surrounded by *brocatello* marble scrolls and four bold strapwork cartouches that are particularly lavish and restless in their expression. This arrangement recalls iron strapwork, and to strengthen the allusion, it is held in place by four imitation bolts in lapis lazuli. Unusual is the extensive use of *bianco* and *nero antico* marble, which heightens the prominence of the strapwork ornament. The bold center panel is surrounded by a playfully designed border containing floral sprays, blossoms emitting seeds like strings of pearls, leafy scrollwork that ultimately derives from ancient Roman mosaics (see cat. no. 4), wild animals, snails, and birds on fruit-bearing branches. A border embodying abundance enframing antique marbles in a jewel-like

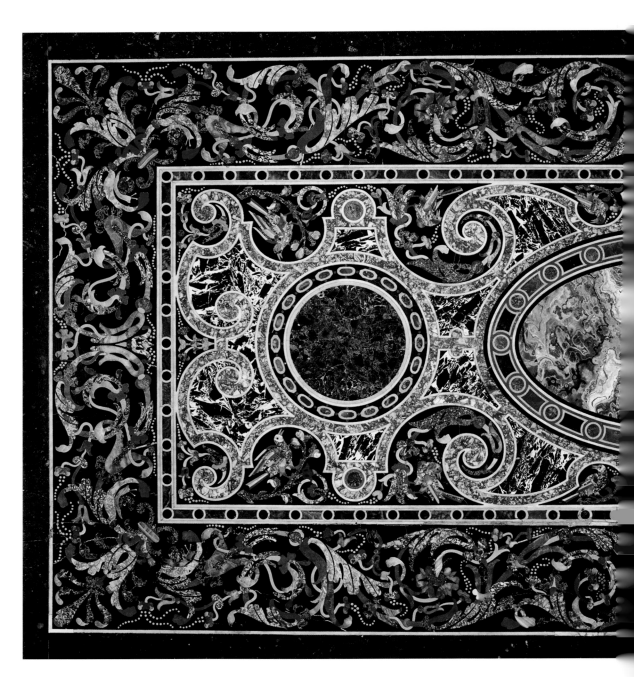

setting—was the designer alluding to Mannerist Rome's ambition to take the place of the vanished empire?

Competition for commissions was intense during this period, and the various workshops must have been under great pressure to formulate a fresh ornamental language. But given the large number of tabletops with decorative schemes like this one, it must have been extremely difficult to come up with something both new and successful. A Roman table of the 1570s that was formerly in the collection of that discerning connoisseur Cardinal Richelieu also combines a geometric border with a detailed leaf decoration and a gigantic jewel-like setting in the center.[1] A tabletop in the J. Paul Getty Museum, Los Angeles, has a border of bold scrolls and strapwork framing an alabaster central oval and windblown leaves, while another tabletop, in the Galleria Borghese in Rome, shows an analogous configuration.[2] All three may ultimately derive from the most important example, the *Farnese Table* in the Metropolitan Museum (cat. no. 10).

We know that this furniture type was held in high esteem by generations of later owners because it has survived in relatively large numbers.[3] Such

works were among the prestigious souvenirs that English noblemen acquired for their estates while traveling in Italy on a grand tour (see entries for cat. nos. 10, 139).　　　　　　　　　　　　W K

1. Giusti 1992, p. 25, fig. 9.
2. Wilson 1983, pp. 30–31, no. 15; Giusti 1992, p. 30, fig. 14.
3. Similar tabletops are in collections at Charlecote Park, Warwickshire, England (González-Palacios 2001, ill. p. 73); the Museo Nacional del Prado, Madrid (Giusti 1992, p. 31, fig. 16; González-Palacios 2001, pp. 59–64, no. 2); the Palazzo Ducale, Mantua (Sotheby's, London, July 3, 2007, sale cat., p. 21, fig. 5); and the Museu Nacional di Arte Antiga, Lisbon (González-Palacios 1988a, fig. 3). Another example was sold at auction at Sotheby's, London, July 3, 2007, lot 6 (cat. entry by González-Palacios).

16. Eucharistic throne of exposition

Rome, ca. 1690
By Domenico Trionfi, after a design by Antonio Maria Ricci
Wood, lapis lazuli, and other hardstones, colored marbles, and gilded bronze, gilded yellow-metal mounts; 64⅝ × 39¾ × 20⅞ in. (164 × 101 × 53 cm)
Inscribed on reverse: *Antonio / Maria / Ricci Luchese / Inventor Domenico / Trionfi / Romano / Construx*
Private collection

PROVENANCE: Château de Sauvage, Rambouillet; acquired by Barbara Piasecka Johnson, 1981; the present owner

REFERENCE: Konstanty Kalinowski in Grabski 1990, pp. 376–78, no. 77

Hardstone mosaic was considered eminently suitable for decorating ecclesiastical buildings, furniture, and furnishings. It was applied to altars, floors, and walls—even spread across the whole interior of a structure. The most famous example of such lavish use is the interior of the Cappella dei Principi in the Basilica of San Lorenzo in Florence (fig. 102).[1] In eighteenth-century Venice, the use of stone inlay to achieve trompe l'oeil effects reached new extremes in the church of Santa Maria Assunta dei Gesuiti, where even altar steps, a baldachin (inspired by Gianlorenzo Bernini), and an elaborate pulpit canopy are covered with a mosaic pattern that imitates the look of silk-cut velvet or brocade—thus commemorating the products of the silk weavers' and tailors' guilds—the church's main patrons—for all eternity (it was hoped) in stone.[2]

One of the most striking and original contributions of the Roman Baroque was to tabernacle design. Architects and designers competed to create the most extravagant and theatrical forms for these receptacles for the Eucharist. Some took the shape of *tempietti;* others—in response to the meaning of the word "tabernacle" in the Old Testament—that of a securely closed case. The elaborate structure was placed in the center of an altar to protect and draw attention to the Host within.[3]

In contrast to the lockable variety, this niche-like type of tabernacle is called a little throne (*tronetto*), or throne of exposition.[4] Set high on an altar, it could be opened through a small door in the back when the Eucharist, in a monstrance, was to be placed in the niche for public adoration. The *tronetto* was used only during liturgical ceremonies such as a specific mass or for the veneration of the Blessed Sacrament by a congregation.

The present example is unusual in its elaborate decoration. The vaulted niche with coffered ceiling is surmounted by a tympanum, which is crowned with gilded bronze figures. In the center is Fortitude (with a lion and Samson's broken pillar), one of the three cardinal virtues, which derive from the Eucharist.[5] The theological virtues Charity and Faith are seated to the right and left, respectively. The disposition of canted sections, contracting and expanding spaces, pilasters on the outside, and columns to support the recessed inner vault all echo the complex architectural inventions of the Roman architect Francesco Borromini.

An inscription on the wooden back of the throne documents the fruitful collaboration of the designer-architect, Antonio Maria Ricci, from Lucca, and the maker, Domenico Trionfi, from Rome. So far, neither name has been found elsewhere. Such an inscription, including not only the names but the hometowns of the artists, is extremely rare on ecclesiastical furnishings. Stylistically, the canted base and the careful placement of the colorful hardstones are typically Roman, as are the brass stringing between the strips of Sicilian jasper on the columns and the agate plates with irregular "eyes" surrounded by lapis lazuli (compare fig. 92).[6] Although the throne's early history remains a mystery, its size and quality point to a patron at the highest princely level.　　　　　　　W K

1. On the Cappella, see Baldini, Giusti, and Pampaloni Martelli 1979; Przyborowski 1982.
2. Davanzo Poli 1999, pp. 48–51.
3. For various tabernacle forms, see Massinelli 2000, pp. 121–22, no. 39.
4. I thank Michelangelo Lupo for bringing this to my attention; see Montevecchi and Vasco Rocca 1987, pp. 94–95 (with bibliography).
5. Hall 1979, pp. 127, 336.
6. Compare the columns and volute-shaped bronze feet of a Roman clock in Walker in Walker and Hammond 1999, pp. 196–98, no. 62.

17. Marriage casket

Rome, 1731
Possibly by Antonio Arrighi
Lapis lazuli, malachite, enamel,
silver, and partly gilded silver,
on a wood carcass; 7½ × 16 × 9 in.
(19.1 × 40.6 × 22.9 cm)
Inscribed on the lid's central
cartouche: *AMOR / GIGNIT
AMOREM / ROMAE MDCCXXXI*
The Cleveland Museum of Art,
Bequest of John L. Severance Fund,
1974 1974.86

This chest, the Boncompagni-Ludovisi–
Ottoboni casket, documents in several ways
the complicated social structure of Roman society
during the Baroque period. Until recently, scholars
were mainly interested in the inscription on top of
the lid and the iconographic program of the gilded
silver plaquettes on the four sides. The text "AMOR
GIGNIT AMOREM" (Love begets love) and the lateral
scenes of the mythological story of the maiden
Psyche and the god of love, Cupid (in Latin, Amor),
allude to a "union with desire," which in the case
of an arranged aristocratic marriage meant the
task of producing a male heir.[1] In relation to the
wedding of Maria Francesca Ottoboni and Pier
Boncompagni-Ludovisi on January 6, 1731, such a

happy event would have been especially crucial.
The bride was the niece of Cardinal Pietro
Ottoboni, who entered the priesthood in 1724 and
could not marry. He was the last male heir to the
family's fortune, part of which would revert to the
Holy See (the cardinal's great-uncle was Pope
Alexander VIII) after his death, under the Roman
law of primogeniture. With a special dispensation,
the cardinal arranged that the future husband,
Pier, would adopt the Ottoboni name, thus guar-
anteeing the continuation of the line. The casket
was likely commissioned as a precious container
for the papal exemption document or the wedding
contract and possibly also jewels for the bride. The
casket thus stands in the tradition of the cassone,

PROVENANCE: Commissioned by Cardinal Pietro Ottoboni (1667–1740); his niece Maria Francesca Ottoboni and her husband, Pier Gregorio Boncompagni-Ludovisi, in 1731; acquired by The Cleveland Museum of Art, 1974

REFERENCES: Hawley 1975; Olszewski 1999, pp. 105, 110, n. 76; Walker in Walker and Hammond 1999, pp. 146–47, no. 25; Olszewski 2003, pp. 97, 109–13, figs. 1, 17–20

the Italian Renaissance bridal chest, as a significant part of the wedding ceremony.[2]

The color scheme of the hardstones and the other materials used to cover the box's wooden carcass has been neglected by art historians. The use of malachite (see cat. no. 144) as embellishment for decorative objects was rather uncommon in eighteenth-century Rome. Furthermore, its color, a bold green, does not harmonize with the blue of the lapis lazuli, with its look of a partly cloudy sky. The key to the choice is the symbolic meaning of the hardstones. The heraldic colors of the Ottoboni family include gold, silver (some of the silver mounts were not gilded), green, and blue. In addition, the lapis symbolizes the company of saints in heaven (see cat. no. 18), praying in unison for a blessed and fruitful marriage. The color red, which appears in the enamel under the cherub volutes on the corners of the casket, refers to the dragon emblem of the Boncompagni-Ludovisi family, which is cut in half,

spilling forth blood. (Because the focus here is on the Ottoboni dynasty, red is restricted to the corners.) Stylized shields with the engraved coats of arms of both families flank the lid's center cartouche. It has been suggested that the goldsmith Antonio Arrighi (1687–1776) made the casket. He is documented as having executed several commissions for Cardinal Ottoboni.[3] By including the hardstones in the overall program of the casket, the artisan has created a masterpiece of High Baroque style, in which all parts are decorative and at the same time gracefully serve to fulfill the propagandistic purpose of the object.   WK

I thank Prince Virgilio Ottoboni, Orbetello (near Rome), and Michelangelo Lupo, Rome, for explaining the Ottoboni heraldry to me in detail and for their patience in answering my questions.
1. Walker in Walker and Hammond 1999, pp. 146–47, no. 25.
2. On this subject, see Koeppe 1995; Koeppe in Kisluk-Grosheide, Koeppe, and Rieder 2006, p. 21, no. 6.
3. Olszewski 1999, p. 110, n. 76; Walker in Walker and Hammond 1999, p. 147.

18. Holy-water stoup

Rome, ca. 1702
By Giovanni Giardini
Lapis lazuli, silver, and gilded bronze; 23¾ × 14⅜ in. (60.3 × 36.5 cm)
Inscribed: in red chalk, MT / 1427; in ink, St. E.3762; branded: "T&T" below a crown
The Metropolitan Museum of Art, New York, Wrightsman Fund, 1995
1995.110

PROVENANCE: Commissioned by Pope Clement XI; his gift to Giovanni Battista Borghese, King Philip V of Spain's ambassador to the Holy See; princes of Thurn und Taxis, Schloss Sankt Emmeram, Regensburg (inv. StE.3762); sale, Sotheby's, Regensburg, October 12–15, 1993, lot 1022; acquired by the Metropolitan Museum, 1995

REFERENCES: González-Palacios 1995a, pp. 367–69, fig. 16; Raggio in "Recent Acquisitions" 1995, p. 38; Bowron 2002, p. 49, fig. 5; González-Palacios 2004a, p. 131, ill. p. 133

Giovanni Giardini (1646–1721) was the leading goldsmith in Rome during the pontificate of Clement XI (r. 1700–1721). The ecclesiastical objects he created for private use or for small, intimate chapels are of such technical perfection that they outshine many other fine works of a similar nature made in Rome during the same period. His major legacy, however, may be his engraved designs illustrating much of his oeuvre, published in 1714, which had great influence throughout Europe.[1] This holy-water stoup for private use had long been forgotten when it appeared in 1993 in the sale of objects from the Thurn und Taxis collection in Regensburg and was identified afterwards by Alvar González-Palacios as a papal commission and diplomatic gift. The scroll ornamentation on the gilded bronze frame provides the powerful movement within a bold yet simple architectural design that distinguishes the finest secular and ecclesiastical works of the High Roman Baroque. The daring juxtaposition of polished gilded metal and lapis lazuli flecked with myriad specks of sparkling golden pyrites has a mesmerizing effect. For obvious reasons, lapis lazuli symbolizes the choir of saints in heaven, and the attention of the person using this stoup would have been directed toward heaven, a treasury

of everlasting joy. Set around the central image of Mary of Egypt in ecstasy, the lapis plaques also suggest that the saint is part of the company of heaven.[2]

In its multidirectional interaction of concave and convex surfaces and the contrasting colors and textures of its media, the architectonic frame complements the inwardly curved repoussé silver relief, which is an exquisite translation of a painting by the Roman artist Benedetto Luti (1666–1724). His composition survives in several versions, the best most likely being the one from the Crozat collection, today at the State Hermitage Museum in Saint Petersburg.[3] Giardini's silver relief has a painterliness that reflects his command of the precious metal. Nuances include a delicate sfumato of light rays in the back and the near three-dimensionality of the skull in the saint's hand.[4]

Several similar frames embellished with hardstones by Giardini's workshop are known. The most complete is in the Schatzkammer of the Residenz in Munich.[5] When the present frame is compared with a much more ornamental pietre dure example in Florence (cat. no. 58), the compact, architectural power of Giardini's creation is experienced with particular intensity.

WK

18

1. Montagu 1996, pp. 118–54.
2. See Sybille Ebert-Schifferer in *Faszination Edelstein* 1992, p. 193, no. 103.
3. Bowron 2002, p. 48, fig. 3.

4. First observed by Olga Raggio in 1995; see her note in the files of the Department of European Sculpture and Decorative Arts, Metropolitan Museum.
5. González-Palacios 2004a, pp. 131–35. Another related frame was with Di Castro, Rome, some years ago.

19. Portable altar

Rome, first half of the 17th century
Ebony, hardstones, and oil paint on
amethyst, gilded silver and silver
mounts; 24½ × 13⅞ × 3⅝ in. (62 ×
35 × 9 cm)
Galleria Pallavicini, Rome
12-00961337

PROVENANCE: Pallavicini
collection, Rome

REFERENCES: González-Palacios
1971, p. 73, fig. 19; González-Palacios
in Giusti 1988, p. 144, no. 29;
González-Palacios 1991, p. 150,
no. 72; González-Palacios 1993,
vol. 1, p. 387, vol. 2, fig. 709;
González-Palacios 2004a, p. 62,
ill. p. 63

Dating from the second half of the seventeenth century, this house altar consists of a devotional painting on stone set in a sumptuous frame that is veneered in ebony and decorated with small agate, jasper, and lapis lazuli plaques, red jasper columns, and finely sculpted silver mounts.[1] The painting is executed in oil on amethyst, a stone at the time considered precious.[2] It shows an Adoration of the Magi below a pair of putti; they float above the holy scene in a cloudy sky that is suggested simply by the natural, unpainted grain of the stone substrate.

The Pallavicini altar belongs to a group of a dozen surviving altarpieces that were employed in the sixteenth and seventeenth centuries for devotion in the chapel of a private house or by members of the aristocracy when traveling.[3] The design of these pieces clearly derives from Roman Baroque architecture and relies on the classical orders, proportions, even materials found in contemporary facade design. The altars all differ in the style of their frames, however, as well as in the subject and technique of the central painting, which is executed (possibly varying according to the workshop of origin) in oil on wood, hardstone, or copper (see cat. no. 20); or in pietre dure mosaic (fig. 115). The present example is particularly elaborate. The gilded silver ornaments and capitals are meticulously chased, and silver figures such as the caryatids on either side are rarely seen in this genre. Even the subject of the painting suggests the wealth and high social standing of the Pallavicini family, since the worshiper praying in private in front of the altar is in close proximity to the iconic image of the three kings, as if in the company of that adoring group. Although the artist remains anonymous, it is worth noting that a very similar,

Fig. 115. Portable altar with pietre dure mosaics, depicting Mary Magdalen and, in cartouches, the Lobkowicz and Pernštejn coats of arms, Castrucci workshop, Prague, before 1603. Ebony and hardstones, 25⅝ × 17¾ × 4 in. Lobkowicz Collections, Prague LR5272

though slightly less elaborate and smaller, altar is recorded as having been made by Ermanno Fiammingo in Rome in 1623.[4]   FK

1. González-Palacios in Giusti 1988, p. 144, no. 29.
2. Until the nineteenth century, when large deposits were found in Brazil, amethyst was classified as one of five precious stones.
3. Pieces similar in design and size include two altars in the Courtauld Institute of Art Gallery and the Victoria and Albert Museum, both London, as well as a number of night clocks that are decorated with religious scenes. See González-Palacios 2004a, pp. 62–67, 104–9.
4. Now in the Victoria and Albert Museum, London. González-Palacios 1991, p. 150, under no. 72; González-Palacios 2004a, ill. p. 62.

20. Portable altar in a carrying case

By Jacopo Ligozzi, Florence, 1608
Ebony, ebonized wood, hardstones, and oil paint on copper, silver mounts; 21⅝ × 13⅜ × 3¼ in. (54.9 × 34 × 8 cm)
Case: Painted wood, metal fittings; 29⅛ × 16¼ × 5½ in. (74 × 41.3 × 13.8 cm)
Signed and dated on painting at lower left: *Jacopo / Ligozzi. F. 1608*
Allen Memorial Art Museum, Oberlin College, Oberlin, Ohio, R. T. Miller Jr. Fund, 1958

PROVENANCE: Bauer, Vienna; [F. Kleinberger & Co., New York]; Allen Memorial Art Museum, Oberlin College, 1958

REFERENCES: Bacci 1963b; González-Palacios 1986, vol. 1, p. 65, n. 5, vol. 2, fig. 173; González-Palacios in Giusti 1988, p. 144, under no. 29

This small house altar is the creation of the painter Jacopo Ligozzi (1547–1627). If he made it at the Galleria dei Lavori in Florence, it is one of a very few religious pieces produced at the grand-ducal workshops for the Medici family.[1] Ligozzi was personally responsible for the finely composed central painting, *Christ on the Mount of Olives*, which he executed in oil on copper and signed and dated at lower left. Below it is a small oval depiction on lapis lazuli of the sacrifice of Isaac—an event described in the Hebrew scriptures that is said to prefigure the sacrifice of Jesus Christ on the cross and that is also found in the Koran.

Ligozzi's role in the creation of the elaborate tabernacle frame for his painting and of the carrying case (an accessory that only rarely survives) was probably that of designer. A comparison between the naturalistic motifs executed at the Galleria in the early seventeenth century and Ligozzi's own scientific drawings for Cosimo I de' Medici reveals many similarities (see entry for cat. no. 39).[2] Both the inlaid pietre dure decoration in the panel below the main picture and the painted design imitating stonework on the soft wood case closely resemble the arabesque ornamentation of pietre dure panels produced for the Medici.[3] The case's doors display a large oval cartouche framing the letters IHS (the Latin abbreviation for Jesus), a cross, and a pierced heart—a concentration of Christian symbolism. The small oval beneath the cartouche echoes in size, shape, and position the oval stone plaque on the altar itself. The painted ovals on the case and the arabesque floral motifs surrounding them, all executed in oil paint, closely imitate *commessi di pietre dure* in design and color.[4]   FK

case

1. Ligozzi worked for the Florentine court from the late 1580s until his death, in 1627. However, the lack of archival evidence for this piece may indicate that it was made for a patron outside the Medici court, or that it was a gift and therefore never entered the Medici collection. See Bacci 1963b.
2. Bacci and Forlani Tempesti 1961.
3. I am grateful to Andria Derstine, Curator of Western Art, Allen Memorial Art Museum, for granting me unrestricted access to the altar and its case.
4. *Frieze of Cupids, Satyrs, and Monsters with Acanthus Tendrils* (Chatsworth, Collection of the Duke of Devonshire), a drawing now attributed to Ligozzi (by Michael Jaffé; Jaffé 1994, pp. 29, 65, no. 32), includes scrollwork like that on the present case. For this entry I have drawn on notes by Marjorie E. Wieseman in the file for this object in the Allen Memorial Art Museum.

21. Collector's cabinet

Venice, 1565–80
Painted fruitwood (possibly pear)
on a carcass of coniferous wood
(possibly fir), poplar, and alder,
amethyst, alabaster, lapis lazuli,
and other hardstones, partly
gilded and painted mother-of-
pearl, yellow-metal and iron hard-
ware; 31⅞ × 44¼ × 19¼ in. (81 ×
112.2 × 48.8 cm), H. of fall front
30¾ in. (78 cm)
Staatliche Museen zu Berlin,
Stiftung Preussischer Kulturbesitz,
Kunstgewerbemuseum 1933.26

PROVENANCE: Dr. Stephan
Kekule von Stradonitz, Berlin;
bought from his estate by the
Kunstgewerbemuseum, 1933

REFERENCES: Hellbing 2005;
Koeppe in Carboni 2007, p. 338,
no. 146

Because for centuries Venice was the main European port of entry for exotic hardstones from the Orient, it is not surprising that La Serenissima—the Republic of Venice—has a long history of hardstone cutting. The hardstone carvers' guild was established there in 1284, only slightly later than the one in Paris. Regulations for the craft followed in 1318 and were enforced.[1] Venetian luxury goods flooded into the northern states of Italy and encouraged the growth of the industry, not only there but also in much of Europe (see "Pietre Dure North of the Alps" by Wolfram Koeppe in this publication and cat. nos. 63, 64). Albrecht Dürer was only one of many Northern artists who profited from the cultural magnetism of the prosperous city on the Adriatic. There he was inspired by Venetian Renaissance art, whose style he introduced into his prints, influencing generations of Northern artisans.

The Northern taste for curiosity rooms found no echo among the urban patricians of Venice, however. They preferred elaborate cabinets furnished with many drawers and secret compartments to hold their collections of rare and beautiful objects both natural and man-made. The appearance of these cabinets frequently reflects the style of contemporary palatial architecture; the miniature format offered an opportunity to "build" these small imitation palaces using the most precious and costly materials. The present cabinet may have been inspired by the Palazzo Corner, a splendid residence designed by Jacopo Sansovino and begun about 1545 on the Grand Canal.[2]

Like most collector's cabinets, this one has no lower support structure and was probably placed on a table or a modest trestle-stand that had been covered with an exotic-looking carpet or length of precious fabric. One unusual feature is the fall front that forms an apronlike extension of the facade when opened. Its inner surface is beautifully decorated with a striking pattern of marquetry strapwork and shaped hardstone inserts. The fall front was undoubtedly included in order to heighten the excitement of "exploring" a complex structure with many cunningly devised compartments.[3]

This piece is the finest example in a group of about a dozen similar, but for the most part smaller, collector's cabinets.[4] It was probably one of a pair, of which the other is preserved in Bebenhausen Castle in southwestern Germany.[5] The carefully chosen semiprecious stones and alabaster tablets with beautiful veining (*naturalia*) and the elegant design and fine craftsmanship of the wooden structure, decorated with sparkling gold paint and arabesques (*artificialia*), make this a curiosity cabinet par excellence.[6] The Oriental alabaster and lapis lazuli from Afghanistan were either brought west along Ottoman trade routes that ended in Venice or were spoils from Byzantium.

W K

1. Hahnloser and Brugger-Koch 1985, pp. 27–28. Much of this entry is based on Koeppe in Carboni 2007, p. 338, no. 146.
2. Brown 2004, p. 39, fig. 44. Other Venetian buildings that inspired the cabinet design are Jacopo Sansovino's Biblioteca Marciana and Vincenzo Scamozzi's Procuratie Nuove on the Piazza San Marco; Brown 2004, fig. 219, and Hellbing 2005, pp. 20–24.
3. Hellbing 2005 is the most detailed study of this collector's cabinet. Achim Stiegel is currently preparing a catalogue of the Renaissance furniture in the Kunstgewerbemuseum, Berlin, including the present object. Related decoration appears on a cabinet in Vienna (see Windisch-Graetz 1983, pl. IV and p. 244, figs. 94, 95).
4. Windisch-Graetz 1983, figs. 92, 93, illustrates a fully documented Venetian lacquered piece of great importance, a small dressing cabinet from the *Kunstkammer* of Archduke Ferdinand II of Tirol at Ambras Castle, near Innsbruck. It is listed in the 1596 inventory of the castle and since then seems not to have left the imperial Habsburg collection; for the lacquering technique, see Grube 2007.
5. Hellbing 2005, pp. 20–24.
6. Koeppe in Carboni 2007, p. 338, no. 146. A lacquered wooden tabletop from the second half of the sixteenth century with related hardstone inlays is in the collection of the Kunsthistorisches Museum in Vienna. González-Palacios 1982a, ill. p. 7.

22. Flask

Grand-ducal workshop, Florence, 1583–84
Design by Bernardo Buontalenti; mounts by Jacques Bijlivert
Lapis lazuli, gold, enamel, and gilded copper; H. 16 in. (40.5 cm)
Inscribed on foot: *FM*; dated under foot: *1583*
Museo degli Argenti, Palazzo Pitti, Florence Gemme 1921:802

PROVENANCE: Francesco I de' Medici; Palazzo degli Uffizi, Florence, 1589–1921; Museo degli Argenti, Palazzo Pitti, from 1921

REFERENCES: Poggi 1920; Holzhausen 1929, p. 16, fig. 1; Kris 1929, vol. 1, pp. 131, 187, nos. 577, 578; Morassi 1964, p. 25, pl. 26; Aschengreen Piacenti 1967, p. 141, no. 259, pl. 27; Hayward 1976, pp. 153, 333, pl. IV; Fock 1980, pp. 323–24; Fock in *Palazzo Vecchio* 1980, p. 226, no. 430; Fock in Giusti 1988, p. 82, no. 5; Barocchi and Gaeta Bertelà 1990, pp. 562–63, pl. CXLII; Tuena 1992b, pp. 78, 79; Corsini 1993, p. 62, fig. 34; Cantelli 1996, pp. 168–69, 194, fig. 20; Mario Scalini in *Magnificenza alla corte dei Medici* 1997, p. 164, no. 125; Aschengreen Piacenti 2003, p. 41, fig. 10; Mosco 2004c, pp. 76–78, fig. 18

In the sixteenth century this flask was one of the most famous objects in the Medici collection of vases, justly admired for its fantastic and elegant design as well as for its refined carving and goldsmith work. Although documents concerning the Medici collection of carved gemstones often neglect to mention the names of the artists who made such pieces, or when they made them, this flask is an exception.

The grand-ducal crest is engraved on the foot with the letters FM, referring to Francesco I de' Medici, who often had the vases he commissioned marked this way. Engraved under the foot is the date 1583, which must refer to the completion of the work of carving the monolithic block of lapis lazuli, since the flask's exquisite gold and enamel fittings, made by the Flemish goldsmith Jacques Bijlivert (1550–1603), were not finished until 1584.[1]

The design for the flask's shape and decoration (cat. no. 23) was provided by Bernardo Buontalenti and then rather liberally interpreted by the anonymous but extraordinarily talented master who carved the vase. No doubt he was one of the gem-cutting experts Francesco de' Medici had brought in from Milan specifically so that he could compete with the Milanese workshops for supremacy in this art, so admired and sought after by sixteenth-century collectors. The brothers Ambrogio and Stefano Caroni arrived at the grand duke's court from Milan in 1572, followed three years later by Giorgio di Cristofano Gaffurri.[2] All of them were lodged at the Casino di San Marco, Francesco's private residence, in which he gathered together the various artisans' shops working for him. This was the nucleus of what would later become the Galleria dei Lavori, officially founded by his brother, Ferdinand I, in 1588.

Before establishing his own workshop, Francesco, like his father, Cosimo I, had turned to the famous craftsmen of Milan when he wished to add to his already vast collection of pietre dure vases, most notably to the Saracchi and Miseroni workshops (see cat. nos. 64, 65). The young prince's considerable resources, however, and his interest in the technical aspects of creating these objects, soon led him to bring in specialists to Florence, where he could watch their creations come to life before his very eyes. The skillful organization of artistic production that for centuries guaranteed the excellence of objects made in the grand-ducal workshops was already evident at the Casino di San Marco. The high quality of the work depended on a collaboration among specialists in different media, and this flask is a paradigmatic example of the practice. Buontalenti, the "creative" artist to whom the design was entrusted, was responsible for the vase's harmonious oval form and the handles, which are fashioned like the bodies of harpies, an expression of the Florentine Mannerist's taste for the metaphoric and the grotesque. The anonymous carver then shaped the lapis lazuli, the preferred material for vases in the sixteenth century, almost as if it were malleable wax, giving the harpies a sculptural energy. The creatures' long, serpentine necks are a masterwork by Bijlivert. Decorated with enamels, they terminate in the sinuous curves of the two small heads.

Although the Medici collection overflowed at the time with marvelous works of art, the extraordinary quality of Buontalenti's flask was underscored by its exhibition, beginning in 1589, among the treasures gathered in the Tribuna at the Palazzo degli Uffizi. And there it stayed until it was stolen (and damaged) about 1768 by the gallery's first keeper, Giuseppe Bianchi. Although Bianchi was eventually arrested and tried, Bijlivert's original gold chain was never recovered; it was replaced by the rather second-rate copy, made of gilded copper, we still see today.

A G

1. Bijlivert was at work on the commission by December 1581, when he received his first delivery of gold. In December 1583 more gold arrived, from which he made the flask's chain. On March 16, 1584, Bijlivert delivered the fittings to the Guardaroba, the administrative unit that managed the Medici's household furnishings.
2. Mosco (2004c, pp. 76–78) suggests that Stefano Caroni made this vase, but there is neither documentation nor any stylistic evidence that would allow us to assign it to one brother or the other, both of whom were described as "i maestri rarissimi di Milano" (most exceptional Milanese masters) by Agostino del Riccio, their contemporary (Del Riccio 1597 [1996 ed.], p. 159).

23. Study for a lapis lazuli flask

Grand-ducal workshop, Florence,
ca. 1580
By Bernardo Buontalenti
Pen and ink with traces of black
chalk on paper; 15⅞ × 11⅝ in.
(40.3 × 29.5 cm)
Galleria degli Uffizi, Florence,
Gabinetto Disegni e Stampe 694Orn

PROVENANCE: Medici collections;
Palazzo degli Uffizi, Florence,
then Galleria degli Uffizi

REFERENCES: Poggi 1920, p. 7,
ill. p. 6; Botto 1968, pp. 38–39,
no. 30 (with bibliography); and
see References for cat. no. 22

Although Bernardo Buontalenti (1531–1608) made other drawings for vases and household furnishings, this study is the only one that can be associated with a known work:[1] a lapis lazuli flask (see cat. no. 22) that was among the most famous pieces in the Medici collection of pietre dure vases. An artist of diverse talents, Buontalenti, who also worked as an architect and sculptor and designed furniture and theatrical sets and costumes, was for more than fifty years a kind of versatile genius loci at the Medici court.[2] Working under the first three grand dukes, he confronted the various challenges of their patronage with an inexhaustible well of invention.

It is not surprising that Francesco I de' Medici, who considered Buontalenti one of his most trusted artists, chose him to design the vase, which was to be carved by master gemstone carvers he had imported from Milan. Although it was not unusual to give rock crystal and pietre dure vases fantastical animal forms, thus conforming to the Mannerist taste for sophistication as well as polymorphism and eccentricity, here Buontalenti followed that tradition in a very idiosyncratic way. The powerful oval shape of the body of the flask, its size, and its sense of formal harmony are almost architectonic. He borrowed the acanthus leaves at the base from the repertoire of classical motifs; the same is true of the harpies, who have the bodies of women, the wings of birds, and mermaids' tails. Buontalenti further transformed these already hybrid mythical creatures by using them as handles, elongating their necks so that their heads flank the neck of the vase.

The soft modeling of the harpies' bodies in the actual carving attenuates some of the plastic, dynamic tension found in Buontalenti's drawing. Likewise, while the heads in the drawing seem to have been intended to buttress the neck of the vase, some of their strength has been diffused in the small, slender heads Jacques Bijlivert worked in gold.[3] These changes could be considered simply the craftsman's interpretation of the design. There is one true variation between the object and the drawing to be noted, however: the thin moldings, which create a simple band around the body of the flask, were envisioned by Buontalenti as a decorated band.   A G

1. Another drawing by Buontalenti now in the Gabinetto Disegni e Stampe at the Palazzo degli Uffizi (672Orn) shows detailed studies for a pitcher, a cup, and an urn, although they cannot be directly associated with any surviving object belonging to the Medici family. See Heikamp in *Magnificenza alla corte dei Medici* 1997, p. 263, no. 209.
2. Especially remarkable are Buontalenti's costume designs for a production of *La Pellegrina* at the Medici Theater at the Palazzo degli Uffizi. See *Magnificenza alla corte dei Medici* 1997, pp. 265–68, nos. 211–14 (entries by Elvira Garbero Zorzi), p. 269, no. 215 (entry by Amelia Fara).
3. These observations were first made in Botto 1968, pp. 38–39, no. 30.

24. *Saint Matthew* and *Saint Mark*

Galleria dei Lavori, Florence,
second quarter of the 17th century
Probably after a design by
Francesco Mochi
Hardstones; H. 12⅝ in. (32 cm)
Museo degli Argenti, Palazzo Pitti,
Florence Gemme 1921:765, 510

PROVENANCE: Galleria dei Lavori,
Florence; Palazzo degli Uffizi,
Florence, from 1782; Museo degli
Argenti, Palazzo Pitti, from 1921

REFERENCES: Giulanelli 1753,
pp. 139ff.; Zobi 1853, pp. 203–4;
Weigelt 1931, p. 171; Lankheit 1962,
p. 321, doc. no. 598; Aschengreen
Piacenti 1967, p. 134, no. 83, p. 140,
no. 236, pl. 34; Fock 1974, p. 149,
fig. 110 (*Saint Mark*); Giusti in
Baldini, Giusti, and Pampaloni
Martelli 1979, p. 263, no. 43, pl. 47
(*Saint Mark*), no. 46, pl. 40 (*Saint
Matthew*); Przyborowski in Giusti
1988, p. 134, no. 25; Giusti 1992,
p. 79, pl. 31 (*Saint Mark*); Casazza
2004b, pp. 85–86, figs. 5 (*Saint
Matthew*), 6 (*Saint Mark*)

These two statues were originally part of a group representing the four Evangelists that was intended, along with other pietre dure sculptures and reliefs, to decorate the monumental altar-*tempietto,* or ciborium, that Ferdinand I de' Medici commissioned in the early seventeenth century for the center of the octagonal Cappella dei Principi in San Lorenzo, Florence.[1] Work on the sumptuous hardstone elements was both time-consuming and delayed by frequent changes in the altar's decorative program, however, prolonging the execution of the project (the altar itself was never finished). The group of the four Evangelists, for example, was begun in 1602–3, immediately after the model for the ciborium was completed for Giovanni de' Medici, but was not finished until 1659.

Surviving documents do not allow us to reconstruct in full the planning and execution of these figures. It is likely, though, that Orazio Mochi (d. 1625), a sculptor who worked in marble and pietre dure, played a major role in their creation, assisted by Giovanni Battista Caccini (1556–1613).[2] Writing at the end of the seventeenth century, the Florentine historian Filippo Baldinucci noted that Mochi was normally employed "in the grand duke's workshops to design and sometimes carve pietre dure statues for the grand-ducal chapel in San Lorenzo [the Cappella dei Principi]."[3] Mochi was already in his fifties in 1605 when it was observed that "the two niches with Evangelists are both by one hand, and that is the sculptor Orazio Mochi, and really one can see that they are well and carefully made and being that he is close to Maestro Stefano one would think it would go well."[4] The documents thus seem to suggest that although Mochi had begun carving pietre dure relatively recently, he had an excellent teacher in "Maestro" Stefano Caroni, the skilled Milanese craftsman.

The 1638 inventory of work completed for the ciborium lists only two Evangelists, both

unfinished at the time. The following year, Orazio's son Francesco presented an invoice for the wax model of an Evangelist and for a second wax model he made with his brother Stefano. In the absence of specific documentation, we can only speculate that the two present figures (Saint Matthew on the left, Saint Mark on the right) date from the second phase of the project, when Francesco Mochi was involved. Their confident, complex poses and expressive gravitas make them more "modern" than the figures of Saint John the Evangelist and Saint Luke and reflect a seventeenth-century sense of naturalism. This is especially true of Saint Mark's intense features and bald head, which pointedly refer to Donatello's figure of Habakkuk carved for the Florence Campanile, one of the most important examples of fifteenth-century naturalism.

The series of pietre dure sculptures and reliefs for the ciborium of the Cappella dei Principi were made in the Galleria dei Lavori, the grand-ducal workshop in Florence. The principal art form there was the *commesso*, a type of mosaic made from separately cut pieces of stone assembled into a single image, and the sculptures represent a new type of hard-stone art for the workshop—one that would continue for some time. Cristofano Gaffurri's figures-in-the-round group of Christ and the Samaritan Woman, from about 1599–1600, was the first pietre dure sculpture made in the Florentine workshops.[5] Although Giovanni Ambrogio and Ottavio Miseroni's marvelous reliefs (see cat. nos. 72, 73), carved in the shop founded in Prague by Emperor Rudolf II, echo this novel carving technique, pietre dure sculpture took root principally in Florence, where it reached levels of exceptional virtuosity.

A G

1. The figures of Saint John the Evangelist and Saint Luke are also in the Museo degli Argenti (nos. 513, 621).
2. Some of these documents were published by Giusti in Baldini, Giusti, and Pampaloni Martelli 1979, pp. 263–65, supplemented by Przyborowski in Giusti 1988, p. 134, no. 25.
3. Baldinucci 1681–1728 (1845–47 ed.), vol. 4, pp. 423–25.
4. Quoted by Giusti in Baldini, Giusti, and Pampaloni Martelli 1979, p. 263.
5. The sculpture was placed in an aedicula made from rock crystal, now in the Kunsthistorisches Museum, Vienna.

25. Pope Clement VIII

Galleria dei Lavori, Florence, 1601
By Romolo di Francesco Ferrucci del Tadda, after a work by an unknown painter and a design by Jacopo Ligozzi
Hardstones, marble, and mother-of-pearl, gilded bronze frame;
40 × 29⅝ in. (101.7 × 75.2 cm)
The J. Paul Getty Museum, Los Angeles 92.SE.67

PROVENANCE: Pope Clement VIII, from 1601; Aldobrandini collection; Palazzo Corsini, Rome, ca. 1853; Getty Museum, from 1922

REFERENCES: Lastri 1799, p. 39; Zobi 1853, pp. 186–88; Gotti 1872, p. 67; Marchionni 1891, pp. 99–100; Pastor 1952, p. 32, n. 2; Bacci 1963a, p. 75, n. 5; Giusti in Giusti, Mazzoni, and Pampaloni Martelli 1978, p. 282, under no. 39; Giusti in *Palazzo Vecchio* 1980, p. 239, under no. 456; Giusti 1992, p. 143; "Acquisitions" 1993, p. 144, no. 69; González-Palacios 1993, vol. 1, pp. 393–96, pl. LXVII; Fusco and Hess 1994; J. Paul Getty Museum 1997, p. 34, no. 25; Giusti 1997b, p. 122; Wilson and Hess 2001, pp. 252–53, no. 522; Giusti 2006b, p. 68, ill. no. 52

This bust-length portrait of Pope Clement VIII (Ippolito Aldobrandini; r. 1592–1605) was meant to hang on the wall and still has its original simple bronze frame.[1] The image of the pope, who is dressed in full papal regalia, is of inlaid marble and pietre dure set against a ground of black Belgian marble. His triple tiara is made largely of translucent chalcedony interspersed with single pieces of hardstone of various colors meant to suggest the effect of gemstones set into the crown. The pope's face and beard are made of colored marble, as are parts of his cope, which has mother-of-pearl and arabesques of porphyry set into the white marble on the shoulders. Small luminous pieces of mother-of-pearl, a material used frequently in Florentine mosaics after the reign of Ferdinand I de' Medici (d. 1609), dot the tiara and the cope's stole.

The Medici registers in the Guardaroba Medicea, which so often reveal little or no information about objects produced in the workshops, tell us in this instance that the portrait was made by Romolo di Francesco Ferrucci del Tadda, called Francesco Ferrucci, one of the first Florentine craftsmen to specialize in the then-new art of hardstone mosaic (see cat. no. 45). The painter Jacopo Ligozzi (1547–1627) is also recorded in the registers as having been paid in February 1601 for "a colored design on paper for the vestments."[2] Ligozzi, who at the time had begun to work more frequently with the pietre dure workshop, thus seems to have been responsible only for the design of the pope's clothing. The actual portrait on which the mosaic is based had come from Rome, where it was the work of an unknown painter at the papal court. There is a precedent for this working method in the Medici documents concerning a now-lost pietre dure portrait of King Henry IV of France that was sent to him as a gift on the occasion of his marriage to Maria de' Medici in 1601. The Opificio delle Pietre Dure, Florence, still has an oil portrait of the king, sent from France, that was the source from which Santi di Tito worked to make his design for the mosaic and in which Henry appeared in royal regalia.[3]

When founded in 1588, the Medici pietre dure workshop, the Galleria dei Lavori, experimented with these stone portraits, almost certainly at the request of Grand Duke Ferdinand I. Perhaps one reason why Ferdinand so highly esteemed pietre dure portraiture is that he relished the potent symbolism inherent in an image of a ruler made

of such splendid but durable materials. In a letter he wrote to his ambassador in Rome, announcing that he was sending Clement the portait as a gift, he described as "our invention of this new way of representing, in inlaid marble and not in the ordinary manner of mosaics but with another and more ingenious skill, the effigies and portraits of people with natural colors and in all parts of the face."[4] The first fruit of this "invention" was the 1597 portrait of Cosimo I de' Medici now in the Museo dell'Opificio delle Pietre Dure.[5] Like the portrait of Clement VIII, it was made by Francesco Ferrucci; it is based on an oil painting by Domenico Passignano (1559–1638) and is composed entirely of Tuscan marble. In 1601, the same year the papal portrait was made, Ferdinand, following his father's example, sent a portrait of himself to the workshop for Ferrucci to translate into pietre dure; there is no record, however, of whether it was ever realized.

The portrait of the pope was sent to Rome in November 1601. The grand duke, proud of the bold, novel piece produced by his workshops, urged his ambassador to use it to impress its august recipient: "Have the pope see it in natural light, placed up high and at a distance."[6] Indeed, neither this portrait nor that of Cosimo I was designed to be scrutinized at close range, and neither benefits from the refined color shifts found in other contemporary Florentine mosaics. For this reason, they can seem rather cold and static up close. Perhaps this is also why Ferdinand's successors abandoned hardstone portraiture even though it had been so dear to the heart of the workshop's founder.

AG

1. We owe much of our knowledge of this unique work, including its dating and subject matter, to Alvar González-Palacios. It was noted among the works in the Palazzo Corsini, Rome, in the mid-nineteenth century by Antonio Zobi, the first historian of the grand-ducal workshop in Florence; see Zobi 1853, pp. 186–88. After that time, however, and until recently, its location was unknown.
2. Document published in González-Palacios 1993, vol. 1, p. 394.
3. See Giusti in Giusti, Mazzoni, and Pampaloni Martelli 1978, p. 333, no. 570, pl. 500, and p. 317, no. 456, pl. 386; Giusti 1992, fig. 67; Giusti 2003b, fig. 26.
4. ". . . nostra inventione un nuovo modo di rappresentare in marmi commessi insieme non in foggia ordinaria di musaico, ma con altro e più ingegnoso artificio, l' effigie et i ritratti delle persone con i colori naturali, et propri in tutte le parti della faccia." Zobi 1853, p. 187.
5. Giusti in Giusti, Mazzoni, and Pampaloni Martelli 1978, pp. 282–83, no. 39, pl. 43.
6. Zobi 1853, pp. 187–88.

26. Pair of bedpost finials

Galleria dei Lavori, Florence, first half of the 17th century
Lapis lazuli and jasper, gilded bronze mounts; each 15¾ × 7⅞ in. (40 × 20 cm)
Museo dell'Opificio delle Pietre Dure, Florence 1905:2705a-b

PROVENANCE: Medici collections; deposited in the Galleria dei Lavori (subsequently Opificio delle Pietre Dure), Florence, probably 18th century; Museo dell'Opificio, from 1995

REFERENCES: Giusti 1995, pp. 44, 46, ill. nos. 17, 18; Giusti 2003b, p. 226, fig. 28; Giusti 2007, p. 27

As the direct descendant of the grand-ducal workshops in Florence, the Opificio delle Pietre Dure inherited many major works in hardstone mosaic from the Medici, and these have been the core of the Opificio's museum collection since the end of the nineteenth century. In addition the Opificio has a group of fragments, some not considered particularly important. Several years ago, among the heterogeneous material that had accumulated in the storerooms, four poorly preserved polyhedrons came to light. They had lost many of the triangular pieces of stone that were once part of their surface decoration as well as some of their interior fill. The structural integrity of two of the finials had remained intact, and a decision was made to restore them, using stones from the other two to replace missing pieces. The result is this pair of finials, which have been catalogued as part of the collection of the Museo dell'Opificio delle Pietre Dure since 1995. They give the modern museum visitor a sense of the fascinating quality of even the small objects created at the Medici workshops.

These powerful geometric finials, with their diaper pattern of blue lapis lazuli and yellow and red jasper framed in gilded bronze, are possibly the only surviving remains of the magnificent and fantastical furniture created by the Florentine workshops. Seventeenth-century Florentine palace inventories list beds made of pietre dure and precious metal, and as late as 1739 an observant visitor, the French man of letters Charles de Brosses,

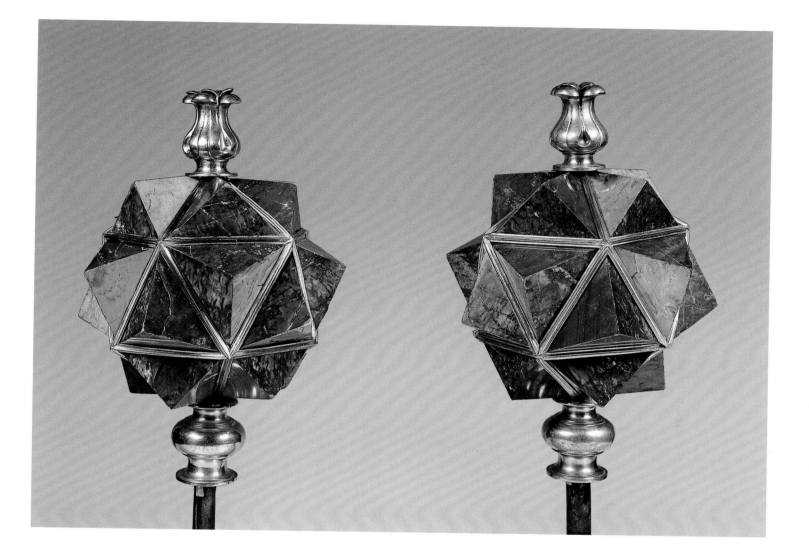

saw "a four-poster bed all of lapis lazuli, jasper, and agate mounted in nickel silver" in the storehouse of the Palazzo Pitti. Even more valuable must have been a bed listed in a Palazzo Pitti inventory of 1689 that had silver posts decorated with grapevines bearing clusters of amethyst fruit. The Medici used such furniture to express the grandeur of the dynasty as well as to indulge their taste for the marvelous. Their Habsburg-Lorraine successors, however, had no sympathy for the Mannerist and Baroque impulses of the previous era. Out of fashion, much of the Medici's furniture was dispersed or destroyed, and the precious metals it contained were reused.

Pietre dure beds were first made during the reign of Ferdinand I de' Medici (r. 1587–1609), who was untiring in his efforts to use pietre dure in as many ways as possible. A 1606 document notes that two craftsmen, named Marchionne and Tommaso, both from Germany, were working in that year on the wooden framework of a bed that was to be covered in pietre dure.[1] It is tempting to connect the present finials with that document. The unusual polyhedrons remind us, furthermore, of the representations of the three-dimensional geometric shapes that appear in the contemporary hardstone mosaics made in Prague under the auspices of Emperor Rudolf II, who had close ties to Florence (see entry for cat. no. 48).

AG

1. Published in Giusti 2003b, p. 226.

27. Tuscan landscapes

Galleria dei Lavori, Florence, 1608
Design by Bernardino Poccetti
Hardstones; 6¼ × 20⅛ in.
(16 × 51 cm)
Museo dell'Opificio delle Pietre
Dure, Florence 1905:463, 464

PROVENANCE: Intended for a
ciborium in the Cappella dei
Principi, Basilica di San Lorenzo,
Florence; Medici collections;
deposited in the Galleria dei Lavori
(subsequently Opificio delle Pietre
Dure), Florence, probably 18th
century; Museo dell'Opificio,
by 1905

REFERENCES: Bartoli and Maser
1953, pp. 6, 24; Rossi (Ferdinando)
1967, p. 93, pl. VII; Pampaloni
Martelli 1975, p. 30, no. 11; Giusti in
Giusti, Mazzoni, and Pampaloni
Martelli 1978, pp. 288–89, nos. 68,
69, pls. 70, 71; Przyborowski 1982,
pp. 279–83, nos. 25, 26, figs. 134,135;
Przyborowski in Giusti 1988,
p. 120, no. 19; Giusti 1997b, p. 130,
ill. p. 131; Giusti in Dolcini and
Zanettin 1999, pp. 57–59; Giusti in
Giusti et al. 2004, p. 160; Giusti
2006, p. 68, ill. no. 51

Two landscape panels (only one shown here) are part of a group of three now in the Museo dell'Opificio delle Pietre Dure, Florence. As is true of many surviving hardstone mosaics with biblical or symbolic subject matter, these panels were meant to embellish the jewel-like altar-ciborium Ferdinand I de' Medici (r. 1587–1609) intended to make the centerpiece of the Cappella dei Principi, the Medici mausoleum in Florence. Work on this brilliant altar in the form of a *tempietto*, which was to be fashioned of pietre dure and precious metals, started in 1599, before the chapel itself was begun. In the mid-seventeenth century the altar was assembled in the grand-ducal workshop and work on it was proceeding apace. Yet despite the valiant efforts of Ferdinand I and his successors, it was never completed, and it remained in the Galleria dei Lavori until about 1780, when it was disassembled by order of the grand dukes of Habsburg-Lorraine. Many of its panels are now widely dispersed (see also cat. nos. 28, 29, 37).[1]

A few extant documents and drawings record the altar's appearance; although the description they provide is incomplete, they suggest a work that was exceptional for its elegance, the magnificence of its materials, and the virtuosic skill of the craftsmen who labored over it. These documents also record the surviving pietre dure panels, including the three small Tuscan *vedute* that stand out for their particularly innovative subjects. Indeed, they are precocious examples from early-seventeenth-century Florence of landscapes without narrative

subject matter—which at that time still dominated Florentine murals and easel painting.

From documents dated to 1607–8, we know that the painter Bernardino Poccetti (1548–1612) delivered three designs for the panels to the stonecutters Francesco di Gaspero Salina and Camillo di Ottaviano. Although Poccetti was no longer young when he made these designs, he nevertheless challenged himself with this new, plein air view of the Tuscan countryside, which includes such picturesque details as the white facade of a small church flanked by cypress trees and a heavily loaded little donkey, which help make the scene believable. These ingenious compositions were skillfully adapted to the medium of hardstone mosaic. The representations of the architecture and figures are simplified and somewhat naive to facilitate legibility, while the craftsman's sophisticated use of his material enables him to evoke the landscape terrain solely through the natural shading of the stone. Sicilian jasper was selected for the rolling hills, some of which are depicted in full sun and others in partial shade. Variegated lapis lazuli was used to represent the changeable spring sky.

AG

1. Two altars in Florence incorporate mosaics originally made for the unfinished altar in the Cappella dei Principi: the high altar in San Lorenzo, and the altar in the Palatine Chapel in the Palazzo Pitti, both of which were assembled in the last quarter of the eighteenth century for Grand Duke Peter Leopold of Habsburg-Lorraine. See Giusti in Baldini, Giusti, and Pampaloni Martelli 1979, pp. 300–306, nos. 123, 124, pls. 178–202.

28. Melchizedek and the Menorah

Galleria dei Lavori, Florence,
ca. 1600–1620
Hardstones; 11 × 21⅝ in.
(28 × 55 cm)
Museo dell'Opificio delle Pietre
Dure, Florence 1905:457

PROVENANCE: Intended for a cibo-
rium in the Cappella dei Principi,
Basilica di San Lorenzo, Florence;
Medici collections; chapel, Villa
del Poggio Imperiale, near
Florence, 1782–1820; Galleria dei
Lavori (subsequently Opificio delle
Pietre Dure), Florence, from 1820;
Museo dell'Opificio delle Pietre
Dure, by 1905

REFERENCES: Weigelt 1931, p. 171,
fig. 102; Bartoli and Maser 1953,
pp. 6, 24, ill. p. 40; Neumann 1957,
p. 164; Rossi (Ferdinando) 1967,
pl. IX; Pampaloni Martelli 1975,
p. 28, no. 8; Giusti in Giusti,
Mazzoni, and Pampaloni Martelli
1978, pp. 289–90, no. 73, pl. 74;
Przyborowski 1982, pp. 305–9,
no. 35, fig. 143, a; Przyborowski in
Giusti 1988, p. 114, no. 16; Giusti
1992, p. 78; Giusti 1995, p. 31,
ill. no. 8

This panel is one of six hardstone mosaics, each representing an important story from the Old Testament, made for the base of a triumphal arch that was part of the extraordinary altar-ciborium complex Grand Duke Ferdinand I de' Medici envisioned for the Cappella dei Principi at San Lorenzo, Florence (see cat. nos. 27, 37; fig. 102). The altar was intended to contain both narrative and decorative panels of pietre dure. Claudia Przyborowski has demonstrated[1] that the panels were part of a complex iconographic and symbolic program juxtaposing the heroes of the faith in the Old Testament, as seen here, with rock crystal niches containing reliquaries with the remains of Christian martyrs—that is, the heroic witnesses to the truth of the Gospels.[2] The present panel contains references to both the Old and New Testaments. In it we see Melchizedek, king of Salem (Jerusalem), awaiting Abraham's victorious return from his battle against the four kings. He will offer Abraham bread and wine, regarded by Christians as a prefiguration of the eucharistic sacrifice. As both king and high priest, Melchizedek himself was also seen as a foreshadowing of Christ.

It seems likely that some gifted prelate at Ferdinand's court conceived of the iconographic program for the altar. It is also possible that the grand duke, an exemplary Counter-Reformation ruler, was himself responsible for the choice of material, since pietre dure is an eloquent and durable medium that, he perhaps reasoned, could convincingly proclaim the truths of the faith in a language at once alluring and immutable.

The panel depicting Jonah after escaping from the whale (cat. no. 30) must have been intended as the pendant to this one. The two have identical dimensions, and each contains a similar panoramic landscape that opens on to the left behind a naturalistic, gnarled tree. I am not suggesting, however, that the two were designed by the same artist.[3] The Jonah panel was designed by a little-known artist referred to as "Emanuele Tedesco."[4] Probably Flemish, he was evidently interested in landscape as a subject in its own right, even though in that panel the landscape is subordinated to the narrative. In the Melchizedek panel, on the other hand, the figure of the priest and the menorah and other liturgical objects in the foreground dominate the composition, while the landscape occupies a strictly secondary place in the background. The image is constructed using a telescopic perspective that suggests a Tuscan sense of clarity and proportion. Indeed, the classicizing architecture, whose compact volumes are meant to suggest the

city of Salem, puts this work squarely in the context of Florentine painting in the first two decades of the seventeenth century.

The panel is one of several that in 1782 Grand Duke Peter Leopold of the Habsburg-Lorraine dynasty ordered reused in a pietre dure altar for a chapel at the Villa del Poggio Imperiale. That altar was disassembled during renovations in 1820, when the chapel was furnished with a new marble altar by Bertel Thorvaldsen that remains there today.

AG

1. Przyborowski in Giusti 1988, p. 114, no. 16.
2. See cat. no. 37, a tabletop made in the eighteenth century by combining two panels originally intended for the altar in the Cappella dei Principi.
3. Przyborowski in Giusti 1988, p. 116, no. 17.
4. Document published by Przyborowski in ibid.

29. Elijah and the Angel

Galleria dei Lavori, Florence, first decade of the 17th century
Hardstones; 5⅞ × 21⅝ in.
(15 × 55 cm)
Museo dell'Opificio delle Pietre Dure, Florence 1905:462

PROVENANCE: Intended for a ciborium in the Cappella dei Principi, Basilica di San Lorenzo, Florence; Medici collections; chapel, Villa del Poggio Imperiale, near Florence, 1782–1820; Galleria dei Lavori (subsequently Opificio delle Pietre Dure), Florence, from 1820; Museo dell'Opificio, by 1905

REFERENCES: Weigelt 1931, p. 173; Bartoli and Maser 1953, pp. 6, 24; Neumann 1957, p. 164; Pampaloni Martelli 1975, p. 26, no. 7; Giusti in Giusti, Mazzoni, and Pampaloni Martelli 1978, p. 289, no. 72, pl. 77, and p. 289, under no. 73; Przyborowski 1982, pp. 293–96, no. 29, fig. 139; Przyborowski in Giusti 1988, p. 112, no. 15; Giusti 1992, p. 78, pl. 27

This panel was one of a series of hardstone mosaics intended for the altar in the Cappella dei Principi, Florence (see cat. nos. 27, 28). The altar was begun at the end of the sixteenth century, and although work on it continued until the middle of the following century, it was never completed. As originally conceived, it was to be surmounted by a triumphal arch whose base would be embellished with six pietre dure panels with representations of heroes from the Old Testament who are regarded as prefigurations of Christ. Although only a few components of this extraordinary ensemble survive, they suggest some of the magnificence of the altar as a whole and the sumptuousness of its constituent parts—from the fluted columns of rock crystal with jewel-studded lapis lazuli capitals to the hardstone altar frontal, which was later transformed into a tabletop (cat. no. 37). The exquisite renderings in stone of landscapes and sacred stories intended for the altar were dispersed and are now either incorporated into other Florentine altars or in the Museo dell'Opificio delle Pietre Dure.

This scene of the angel reviving and giving succor to the prophet Elijah in the desert is not mentioned in documents related to the altar's construction, but its execution and color scheme are close enough to the panel of *Samson and the Lion* (Museo dell'Opificio delle Pietre Dure, Florence) that it can probably be attributed to the same craftsman, Gualtieri Cecchi. Cecchi made the Samson panel in 1612 after a design by a little-known artist referred to as "Emanuele Tedesco."[1] The Galleria dei Lavori, the Florentine pietre dure workshop, employed northern European artists who worked alongside local ones such as Jacopo Ligozzi and Ludovico Cigoli to make the painted designs for the mosaics and then translate them into hardstone mosaics. The international character of the workshop at this time foretells the cosmopolitan nature of the Medici court and its artistic taste throughout the seventeenth century.

The Elijah panel stands out as one of the best of these early, extraordinary mosaics. In a letter dated 1601, Grand Duke Ferdinand I de' Medici—a great promoter of this new style of pietre dure—

29, detail

wrote that one might "find in these stone pictures an image as alive as any one would see in a painted picture."[2] This was the moment when the geometric style of stone inlay favored by Francesco I, Ferdinand's brother and predecessor, was abandoned in favor of images that imitated paintings of both decorative and figural subjects. They were intended not simply to imitate painting, however, but to create a wholly new pictorial genre that would exploit the natural palette of the stones to interpret a compositional idea and create a sense of fantasy.

A G

1. Giusti, Mazzoni, and Pampaloni Martelli 1978, p. 289, no. 71, pl. 78.
2. Zobi 1853, p. 188. This passage comes from a letter written to Pope Clement VIII that accompanied the gift of his portrait executed in hard and soft stone (cat. no. 25).

30. *Jonah after Escaping from the Whale*

Galleria dei Lavori, Florence, 1612
By Fabiano Tedesco, after a design
by Emanuele Tedesco
Hardstones; 11 × 21⅝ in.
(28 × 55 cm)
Museo dell'Opificio delle Pietre
Dure, Florence 1905:456

PROVENANCE: Intended for a cibo-
rium in the Cappella dei Principi,
Basilica di San Lorenzo, Florence;
Medici collections; chapel, Villa
del Poggio Imperiale, near
Florence, 1782–1820; Galleria dei
Lavori (subsequently Opificio delle
Pietre Dure), Florence, from 1820;
Museo dell'Opificio, by 1905

REFERENCES: Bartoli and Maser
1953, pp. 6, 24; Neumann 1957,
p. 164; Pampaloni Martelli 1975,
p. 28, no. 9; Giusti in Giusti,
Mazzoni, and Pampaloni Martelli
1978, p. 290, no. 74, pl. 75;
Przyborowski 1982, pp. 302–5,
no. 34, fig. 142, a; Przyborowski in
Giusti 1988, p. 116, no. 17; Giusti
1992, p. 78, pl. 28; Giusti 1995, pp. 31,
34, ill. no. 9; Giusti in Chiarini and
Acidini 2000, p. 60, under no. 8

Among the pietre dure mosaics depicting biblical subjects that were created for the altar-*tempietto* in the Cappella dei Principi, Florence (see cat. nos. 28, 29), this one stands apart for the predominance of its landscape component.[1] The panel's central narrative, which conflates several events from the story of Jonah,[2] shows the prophet after his escape from the sea monster, which lingers among the waves and watches him menacingly as he kneels in prayer on a rocky shore. The small figure of Jonah at bottom center—although carefully rendered, displaying both suppleness of pose and chromatic refinement in its whitish pink flesh tones—is so tiny that it almost disappears within the picturesque setting of trees, shore rocks, city ruins, and seascape.

The Jonah panel was intended as a pendant to the panel *Melchizedek and the Menorah* (cat. no. 28), which has the same dimensions but a different pictorial style and rendering. As had been the custom since the early days of the Galleria dei Lavori (the semiprecious-stone workshops founded in 1588 by Ferdinand I de' Medici), a painter was assigned the task of creating a model for the mosaic, and a craftsman skilled in sectional mosaic inlay, what the Florentines call *commesso,* would then execute the work. In this case, the registers of the Galleria dei Lavori show that in 1612, one "Emanuele Tedesco" submitted a color drawing of the story of Jonah "when he comes out of the fish," which was to be executed by the hand of "Fabiano Tedesco."[3] It is somewhat unusual for both men involved in the creation of a mosaic to have been *tedeschi,* or "Germans," a term applied at the time to people from anywhere in north-central Europe.

Although little information has emerged on the mysterious Emanuele—who that same year also made the model for an image of *Samson Triumphing over the Lion,* and who the previous year had provided several drawings of "villages"[4]—we can assume that he was trained in the landscape tradition made popular through Flemish painting. It is possible that at some point he was active at the court of Prague, which had engaged in an intense exchange of ideas and artists with Florence, thanks to the presence of the pietre dure workshop established there by Holy Roman Emperor Rudolf II. Cosimo II de' Medici, who acceded to the grand-ducal throne of Tuscany in 1609, assiduously cultivated his own cosmopolitan circle of artists while also maintaining the cordial relations his father had established with the imperial court. Indeed, it is likely that the master stonecutter "Fabiano the German" was apprenticed in stone inlay in Prague, for in his magisterial execution he displays a predilection for Bohemian and Alsatian jasper, stones typical of Prague mosaics. In addition, certain elements of his compositional style—for example, the gnarled tree trunk in the foreground and the broad expanse of sky, with its clouds of pinkish gray chalcedony—echo the works of the Castrucci family, the Florentine dynasty of *commesso* specialists who had moved to Prague in the late 1500s at the invitation of Rudolf II and remained active there until the 1630s (see cat. nos. 66–69). Whatever the quality of Emanuele's lost model, the version Fabiano has left us remains one of the most sensitive and creative manifestations of the painterly possibilities of pietre dure.   AG

1. See the interpretation by Przyborowski in Giusti 1988, p. 116, no. 17.
2. As noted elsewhere in this volume, the unfinished altar was dismantled about 1778 and its parts were reused elsewhere; a few were appropriated for the new altars of the Basilica of San Lorenzo and the Palatine Chapel of the Palazzo Pitti, where they still are today, and a number of others found their way to the Opificio delle Pietre Dure.
3. Quoted by Przyborowski in Giusti 1988, p. 116.
4. Two landscapes with rivers and northern European-style villages now at the Museo dell'Opificio (inv. 468, 459) could possibly be attributed to Emanuele; the picture of the story of Samson (inv. 461) is also at the Museo dell'Opificio.

31. *Jonah and the Whale*

Galleria dei Lavori, Florence,
ca. 1620
Painting by Filippo Napoletano
or a member of his circle
Soft stones, hardstones, and oil on
stone, painted and gilded wood
frame; without frame 10¼ × 31⅛ in.
(26 × 79 cm), with frame 14⅝ × 37 in.
(37 × 94 cm)
Museo dell'Opificio delle Pietre
Dure, Florence OA 1911:784

PROVENANCE: Medici collections;
deposited in Galleria dei Lavori
(subsequently Opificio delle Pietre
Dure), Florence, 1878; Museo
dell'Opificio, by 1905

REFERENCES: Bartoli and Maser
1953, pp. 6, 24; Pampaloni Martelli
in *Pittura su pietra* 1970, no. 8;
Pampaloni Martelli in Giusti,
Mazzoni, and Pampaloni Martelli
1978, p. 345, no. 621, pl. 546; Giusti
1992, p. 80, fig. 25; González-
Palacios 1993, vol. 1, p. 466, n. 30;
Giusti 1995, p. 99; Giusti in Chiarini
and Acidini 2000, p. 60, no. 8;
Giusti 2006b, p. 35, ill. no. 26

This panel offers examples of two types of pietre dure work that were popular at the Medici court, especially during the first quarter of the seventeenth century. The first is seen in the scroll that frames the scene and the second in the painting, executed in oil on a stone slab, which shows the biblical story of the prophet Jonah, who has been thrown from his ship and is about to be torn apart by a large sea monster (for a similar treatment, see cat. no. 78).

Both the Late Mannerist design of the scroll and the palette of the calcareous stones from which it is made (lapis lazuli and *verde antico, rosso antico, giallo di Siena*, Belgian black, and *verde d'Arno* marbles) are characteristic of the mosaics that issued from the Medici workshops in the early 1600s. They can be compared with a pair of early seventeenth-century panels of *pietra paesina* inlaid with images of fish and swans, now also in the Museo dell'Opificio delle Pietre Dure, which were incorporated into the wall decoration of a chapel in the Medici villa at Poggio Imperiale in 1691.[1] (On *pietra paesina*, see entry for cat. no. 32.) Like most paintings on stone,[2] the *Jonah* panel was likely to have been intended as an independent picture to be hung on a wall, and the presence of the painted and gilded wooden frame seems to confirm this hypothesis. The deli-

cately wrought scrolling vines that decorate it appear to be contemporary with the painting; similar tracery can also be found in several seascapes painted on Albarese marble in the Museo dell'Opificio delle Pietre Dure.[3]

The painting can be linked to the seascapes not only by its style but also by the fact that both are executed on *lineato d'Arno*, a type of rock that comes from the bed of the Arno River. Its undulating patterns suggest a seething expanse of sea, which in this case tips Jonah's ship and drives the prophet inexorably toward the open jaws of the whale. The identity of the artist who so skillfully exploited the possibilities offered him by nature is not known, but he may well have been Filippo Napoletano (ca. 1587–1629). A specialist in painting on stone, Napoletano was active at the court of Grand Duke Cosimo II de' Medici from 1618 to 1621. Cosimo was a passionate collector of evocative artistic creations that pair geological peculiarity with pictorial inventiveness.

A G

1. Pampaloni Martelli in Giusti, Mazzoni, and Pampaloni Martelli 1978, p. 345, nos. 619, 620, pls. 545, 550.
2. Colle 1993, p. 21.
3. Pampaloni Martelli in Giusti, Mazzoni, and Pampaloni Martelli 1978, p. 345, nos. 622–24, pls. 552–54.

32. Pair of *pietra d'Arno* panels

Galleria dei Lavori, Florence,
17th century
Albarese marble, painted and
gilded wood frame; each panel
17 × 16⅛ in. (43 × 41 cm)
Museo dell'Opificio delle Pietre
Dure, Florence OA 1911:1935, 1936

PROVENANCE: Medici collections,
Convent of San Marco, Florence,
then Galleria delle Statue, Palazzo
Pitti, Florence; Museo dell'Opificio
delle Pietre Dure, from 1882

REFERENCES: Bartoli and Maser
1953, pp. 11, 29; Pampaloni Martelli
in *Pittura su pietra* 1970, no. 3;
Pampaloni Martelli in Giusti,
Mazzoni, and Pampaloni Martelli
1978, p. 344, nos. 614, 615, pls. 544,
547; Giusti in Chiarini and Acidini
2000, p. 100, no. 28

Although this kind of Albarese marble, noted for its fantastical veining, is not found exclusively in Tuscany, it has long been most warmly appreciated in Florence. Indeed, as early as 1597, in his history of marble, the *Istoria delle pietre*, Agostino del Riccio described the Florentines as lovers of these beautiful stones.[1] He wrote at a time when an enduring passion for precious stones was growing in Florence and at the Medici court, extending from the imperial marbles then being excavated in Rome to exotic pietre dure and even to modest local stones, all of which appealed to the curiosity and artistic sensibilities of the late sixteenth century.

Pietra paesina—"landscape rock," so called for the effect of its bands of color—and *lineato d'Arno* (see entry for cat. no. 31) are the two most common and most striking types of Albarese marble. During the seventeenth century, Florentine craftsmen often employed Albarese as a support for paintings (see cat. nos. 31, 78), but it was also admired in its natural state. Unadorned, it was used for some of the cut pieces in Florentine mosaic plaques that decorated cabinets. Slabs with exceptional markings, like the present pair, were framed and hung on the wall. These two panels, in which the natural patterns in the stone are mirror images, were evidently cut from a single block. Certain areas of the exposed face suggest a view in three dimensions, and it is this specific characteristic of the stone that was often referred to in older documents and inventories as *paesina*. The parallel, undulating bands in the upper area of the panels exemplify what was usually described as *lineato d'Arno*.

A wooden frame (partially shown here), painted white and gilded, can be dated to the seventeenth century.

A G

1. Del Riccio 1597 (1996 ed.), pp. 122–23.

33. The Inferno

By Vincenzo Mannozzi, Florence,
ca. 1634
Oil on black marble (paragone),
ebony frame inlaid with hardstones;
23¼ × 29⅜ in. (59 × 74.5 cm)
Galleria degli Uffizi, Florence
1890:4974

PROVENANCE: Villa della Petraia,
near Florence, 1649; Villa del
Poggio Imperiale, near Florence,
1760; Palazzo degli Uffizi, Florence,
1861; storerooms of Chamber of
Deputies, Rome, 1925; Galleria
degli Uffizi, from 1977

REFERENCES: Chiarini 1970, p. 36,
fig. 7; Chiarini in *Pittura su pietra*
1970, n.p. (introduction); Borea
1975, pp. 26, 28, 37, n. 27, fig. 3;
Borea 1977, pp. 25, 53, no. 27;
Galleria degli Uffizi 1979, p. 364;
González-Palacios 1986, vol. 1,
p. 61, vol. 2, fig. 158

The seventeenth-century historian Filippo Baldinucci mentioned that Vincenzo Mannozzi was a disciple of the great Florentine painter Francesco Furini,[1] but no paintings by Mannozzi (1600–1657) were known until an analysis[2] of the 1649 inventory of Lorenzo de' Medici's collection of pictures allowed us to attribute this work to him, along with two others on canvas.[3] Lorenzo, a son of Grand Duke Ferdinand I, was, like all members of his family, a sophisticated collector. This picture was paired in his collection with Stefano della Bella's *Burning of Troy* (also in the Uffizi), which has been dated to about 1634.[4] Both paintings are nocturnal scenes illuminated by flashes of fire, and the two have similar, attractive frames made from ebony with guilloche moldings and Florentine mosaics in the corners. The mosaics represent flowers and are set into touchstone.

The decision to use a support of paragone (black marble) for the painting was probably dictated by the patron himself and reflects the widespread taste for paintings on stone that endured throughout the seventeenth century, especially in Florence. The practice of painting on stone was rooted in technical experiments conducted by Sebastiano del Piombo, but it evolved quickly from ensuring that the support was stable and would not warp—the original reason for trying it—into a medium appreciated for the intrinsic pictorial qualities of the stone background. The genre became popular in Florence in the first decade of the seventeenth century in the circles of Cosimo II de' Medici. The preferred support at that time was *pietra d'Arno* or *paesina*, which was ideal for suggesting rugged rocky landscapes or undulating seascapes.[5] In some instances the eccentric, naturally occurring patterns and colorations of the stone were so admired that a piece of it was framed and made into a picture without the addition of paint (see cat. no. 32).

In the second quarter of the seventeenth century, during the reign of Ferdinand II de' Medici,

the preference in this kind of work shifted to a uniformly colored background (which had been the original choice when pictures of this type were first being made). In the ongoing debate about the relative predominance of art and nature, a plainer backdrop, it was once again believed, allowed a greater emphasis on the art. In Mannozzi's picture, the polished midnight black of the paragone is a perfect ground for the firelight, which casts a flickering glow over the many scenes brought together in the small oval field. Depicted in the upper part of the work is the abduction of Persephone, with Pluto riding in a golden carriage accompanied by devils as green as lizards. In the lower center of the painting, the nude body of Prometheus appears chained to a rock as an eagle gnaws on his liver. To the right, Cerberus chases after a group of nude sinners, herding them toward a blazing cave. Charon's barge navigates the waters of the river Styx on the left.

Mannozzi apparently was most at ease working on large narrative pictures, as attested by the great numbers of them recorded in various Medici archives. Even on a smaller scale, however, as seen here, he handled the drama of his events in a spirited style, placing them in theatrical settings that recall contemporary stage sets. In particular, there are echoes in Mannozzi's *Inferno* of Giulio Parigi's designs for the sets of *Nozze degli Dei*, a melodrama staged at the Palazzo Pitti for the wedding of Ferdinand II. Although Parigi's design drawings were ephemera that have not survived, the designs are known through engravings of them made by Stefano della Bella.[6]   A G

1. Baldinucci 1681–1728 (1845–47 ed.), vol. 4, p. 643.
2. Borea 1975.
3. These three pictures have survived; a fourth mentioned in the inventory is lost. Borea 1977, pp. 52, 54–55, nos. 26, 28.
4. Ibid., pp. 38–39, no. 11a.
5. A recent and complete discussion of this genre can be found in Chiarini and Acidini 2000.
6. Borea 1977, p. 53, no. 27.

34. *View of the Piazza Granducale, Florence*

Galleria dei Lavori, Florence,
1599–1600
By Bernardino Gaffurri and
Jacques Bijlivert
Hardstones and gold, gilded
bronze frame; 7⅛ × 9⅞ in.
(18 × 25 cm)
Museo degli Argenti, Palazzo
Pitti, Florence Gemme 1921:823

PROVENANCE: Attached to
a cabinet commissioned by
Ferdinand I de' Medici, Tribuna,
Palazzo degli Uffizi, Florence;
transferred in 1776 to the Gabinetto
di Fisica e di Storia Naturale and in
the mid-19th century to the
Gabinetto delle Gemme, Palazzo
degli Uffizi; entered the Museo
degli Argenti, Palazzo Pitti, 1921

REFERENCES: Zobi 1853, pp. 197ff;
Heikamp 1963, pp. 226, 251–52, doc.
no. 46, p. 254, doc. no. 57, fig. 47;
Heikamp 1964, p. 18, fig. 30; Morassi
1964, p. 30, pl. 34; Aschengreen
Piacenti 1967, p. 142, no. 271, pl. 24;
Berti 1967, p. 137, pl. XVII; Casarosa
1973, p. 294, no. 441; Fock 1974,
pp. 134–35, 176; Spini 1976, pp. 66–67,
fig. 21; Fock in *Palazzo Vecchio* 1980,
p. 236, no. 449; Langedijk 1981–87,
vol. 1, p. 504, no. 174; Heikamp
1988; Heikamp in Giusti 1988,
p. 104, no. 12.IX; Massinelli 1990,
p. 118, fig. 14; Silvia Blasio in
Magnificenza alla corte dei Medici
1997, pp. 78–79, no. 40; McCrory in
Acidini et al. 2002, p. 257, no. 114;
Aschengreen Piacenti 2003, p. 42,
fig. 12; Giusti 2003b, p. 220, fig. 21;
Casazza 2004b, pp. 83–84, fig. 1, and
ill. p. 82; Giusti 2006b, p. 47, ill. no. 34

Commissioned in 1599, this plaque is one of the masterpieces produced by the grand-ducal workshops during the reign of Ferdinand I de' Medici. It was made for a large cabinet (called the *Studiolo Grande*) that Ferdinand ordered in 1593 but that took several years to complete. Bernardino Gaffurri (d. 1606) and Jacques Bijlivert (1550–1603), two of the best craftsmen in the Medici workshops at the end of the sixteenth century, collaborated to make the plaque. Gaffurri came from a family of well-known and accomplished lapidaries in Milan, whence Francesco I de' Medici had brought him to Florence some twenty years earlier.[1] Bijlivert was a Flemish craftsman whom Ferdinand put at the head of the court workshop, the Galleria dei Lavori, which was founded in 1588.

Gaffurri's mosaic shows the Piazza della Signoria (at the time known as the Piazza Granducale) in a remarkable perspective view that is both realistic and magical. The buildings on the square are fashioned from rock crystal that has been painted on the reverse; they stand under a sky of lapis lazuli—the natural white markings in the stone suggest that it is dotted with gauzy clouds—and around a piazza paved with bloodstone and carnelian. The transparency of the crystal allows the architecture to be defined monochromatically with ground silver, while gold paint, also applied behind the crystal, was used to represent the people in the Palazzo della Signoria as well as the statues in the Loggia dei Lanzi. Golden stringcourses enrich the buildings and at the same time enhance their three-dimensionality. The same is true of the gold borders around the paving stones, which increase the perspectival effect of the scene.

It seems likely that Bijlivert was responsible for these additions in gold, since he executed the gilded reliefs representing the statues in the piazza and on the raised pavement along the Palazzo, work for which he was paid on December 1, 1600. The inspiration for these gold reliefs as well as the technique used to execute them came from the bas-reliefs that Giambologna and his shop made for Francesco I de' Medici—representing scenes from his reign—in 1585–87.[2] The thin gold sheet was pressed from behind with a bronze die made for that purpose. In the present oval, however, the relief ground is not a neutral field but this extraordinary mosaic of the piazza, which was modeled on an anonymous woodcut made in 1583. The pietre dure version adds a gold relief of the equestrian monument of Cosimo I that his son Ferdinand I erected in the square in 1594.

This plaque was placed on the *Studiolo Grande* in the niche under the central cornice. For nearly two centuries this cabinet was one of the most admired masterpieces in the Tribuna at the Uffizi. It was moved in 1776 to the new Gabinetto di Fisica e di Storia Naturale. Shortly afterward the cabinet was disassembled and its parts dispersed, having become the victim of a modern, Neoclassical taste that no longer appreciated the fanciful and magnificent furniture of the Medici period.

A G

1. The brothers and pietre dure specialists Angelo and Stefano Caroni moved from Milan to Florence in 1572. They were followed in 1575 by Bernardino and Giorgio Gaffurri, also from Milan. The latter were described in *Istoria delle pietre* of 1597 by the Dominican friar Agostino del Riccio as "exceptionally skilled in carving crystal."
2. See Heikamp in Giusti 1988, pp. 96–100, no. 12.I–VI.

35. Ex-voto of Cosimo II de' Medici

Galleria dei Lavori, Florence, 1617–24
Design by Giulio Parigi and perhaps Giovanni Bilivert; mosaic inlay and relief by Michele Castrucci and Gualtieri Cecchi; gem setting and enamel reliefs by Jonas Falk
Hardstones and enamel, gilded bronze frame; 21½ × 25⅜ in. (54.5 × 64.5 cm)
Museo degli Argenti, Palazzo Pitti, Florence Gemme 1921:489

PROVENANCE: Commissioned by Cosimo II de' Medici, by 1617; Guardaroba Medicea, Florence, 1624–1789; Palazzo degli Uffizi, Florence, from 1791; Museo degli Argenti, Palazzo Pitti, from 1921

REFERENCES: Zobi 1853, pp. 266–68; Berti 1951–52, p. 94, n. 9; Bartoli and Maser 1953, pp. 14, 32; Lankheit 1962, p. 96; Morassi 1964, p. 32, pl. 35; Aschengreen Piacenti 1965; Aschengreen Piacenti 1967, p. 133, no. 64, pl. 37; Rossi (Ferdinando) 1967, p. 108, pl. XXXIV; Aschengreen Piacenti in *Artisti alla corte granducale* 1969, p. 150, no. 146, fig. 115; Pampaloni Martelli 1975, p. 58, no. 28; Giusti in Baldini, Giusti, and Pampaloni Martelli 1979, pp. 265–66, no. 51, pl. 48; Maria Sframeli in Giusti 1988, pp. 158–60, no. 36; Nardinocchi 1993, p. 102, fig. 62; Giusti 1997b, p. 138, ill. p. 139; Giusti in Acidini et al. 2002, pp. 258–60, no. 116; Giusti 2003a, p. 239, fig. 9; Casazza 2004b, p. 89, fig. 10

Among the most important commissions given by Cosimo II de' Medici, grand duke of Tuscany, to his court workshops was one for a small but sumptuous altar that he intended to install in the chapel of Charles Borromeo in Milan Cathedral. Canonized in 1610, Charles had immediately become the focus of widespread veneration because of his curative powers, and Cosimo was among those who prayed to the saint for relief from ill health. This devotion found expression in a work befitting the munificence of the Medici. The solid gold altar, now lost, had a finely wrought gold frontal, with this image of its illustrious donor mounted in the center.

The scene on the panel, one of the great masterpieces of European hardstone sculpture, conveys a political message in the language of art. The grand duke is shown with all the solemn symbols of his authority, from his bejeweled ermine robes to the crown and scepter placed in front of him. The unmistakable view of Florence through the window suggests the supplicant's identity, which is confirmed by the Medici coat of arms included on the golden altar.[1] The conspicuous value of the altar's materials, the seductive preciousness of the central panel combining the two demanding techniques of mosaic relief carving and inlay, and the magnificence of the work as a whole would have proclaimed the Florentine court's splendor and artistic refinement to both Milanese and foreign visitors to the chapel.

The project did not proceed as anticipated, however. Work began in 1617, but Cosimo died in 1621, and the altar was not finished until 1624. Among the highly specialized and skilled craftsmen who participated were the Italian goldsmith Cosimo Merlini, who fashioned the altar and set its inscription with rubies. On the ex-voto, the Scandinavian goldsmith Jonas Falk executed the enamel reliefs on the grand duke's robes and set the dozens of diamonds in his clothing. The cutters of semiprecious stones Michele Castrucci and Gualtieri Cecchi—described as *pietristi*, or stonecutters, in a contemporary document[2]—created the inlay, the relief figure of the grand duke, and the mosaic in the background. The architect Giulio Parigi (1571–1635) was responsible for the overall design of the altar, although the painter Giovanni Bilivert (1585–1644) likely assisted him by designing the central scene.

Once it was finished, the ex-voto stayed in Florence. The gold altar was melted down in 1789 at the order of Grand Duke Peter Leopold of the Habsburg-Lorraine dynasty, who consigned most of the precious-metal objects made for the Medici to a similar fate. The central panel, however, was enclosed in the frame it has today, transforming it into a picture meant to hang on a wall.

A G

1. There is a detailed description of the lost altar in a Medici inventory of 1783. See Giusti in Baldini, Giusti, and Pampaloni Martelli 1979, p. 265.
2. The word is used in the inventory cited in n. 1, which quotes an earlier *Giornale dei manifattori*, dated 1624. See Baldini, Giusti, and Pampaloni Martelli 1979, p. 265.

36. Reliquary with a representation of the Flagellation

Rome (?), early 17th century
Silver, partly gilded silver,
chalcedony, agate, and rock
crystal; H. 21 in. (53.5 cm)
Museo delle Cappelle Medicee,
Florence, Tesoro di San Lorenzo
1945:139

PROVENANCE: Christina of
Lorraine, Palazzo Pitti, Florence,
by 1621; Palazzo degli Uffizi,
Florence, 1624; Basilica di San
Lorenzo, Florence, from 1785;
Tesoro della Basilica di San
Lorenzo, from 1945

REFERENCES: Zobi 1853, p. 262;
Palazzo Vecchio 1980, pp. 238–39,
no. 454; Massinelli 1992, pp. 118,
119; Nardinocchi in Bertani and
Nardinocchi 1995, p. 46, no. 11;
Mario Scalini in Acidini et al.
2002, p. 272, no. 131

This reliquary was made to hold several relics, among them a fragment believed to be from the column to which Christ was bound when he was flagellated. It is that relic that determined the design of the vessel, which is shaped like a hexagonal *tempietto*; inside it is a scene of the Flagellation set atop a stepped podium of gilded silver. The small figure of Christ is carved in the round from a rare, rose-colored agate, and the drum of the column he is tied to is cut from plasma, a slightly translucent green quartz. The two tormentors flanking Christ, cast in silver, are posed to create rhythmic counterpoints in the composition. The *tempietto* stands directly on a hexagonal silver base that has six small drawers openable by means of tiny knobs. The drawers contain three more relics, each labeled on a card with a gilded border.[1]

The vertical structure of the *tempietto* is made from silver and is supported by chalcedony Corinthian columns placed on high plinths with rock crystals set on their outer faces. Rock crystal is also used to create a luminous sheathing over the cupola, whose harmonious curve emerges from the balustrade set over the columns and terminates in a lantern. The dome is divided into eighteen segments by a framework of silver ribs, each decorated with seven table-cut pieces of rock crystal set in gilded silver mounts. The effect of these 126 crystals was echoed in the six rock crystal obelisks, of which only two survive, standing on the corners of the hexagonal balustrade.

Although today the *tempietto* rests on a platform of molded and gilded wood, originally it had a hexagonal base made of carved ebony, with small drawers that stood about 4 inches high. The original base is documented in a detailed, full-scale rendering of the reliquary now in the Uffizi; on the side of the sheet is a list of the materials used to make it as well as its measurements, expressed in *palmi* and *oncie*.[2] These terms refer to the standard set of measures used in Rome and suggest that the piece was made there. Its size and architectural style reflect, as has been noted, the style of Giovanni Antonio Dosio, who was born in Florence but received his artistic education in a Roman milieu.[3]

We also know that this reliquary was not produced in the grand-ducal workshops in Florence, because the Uffizi drawing is of the type that was executed after the object itself had been made in order to show it to potential patrons—a relatively widespread practice at the time. The reliquary was likely not intended for the Medici, but it ended up in their collections and is mentioned in the 1621 inventory of Christina of Lorraine's chapel in the Palazzo Pitti. In the first decades of the seventeenth century, the Medici workshop was working on the altar-*tempietto* for the Cappella dei Principi (see entries for cat. nos. 27–30), whose cupola, like that seen here, was to have a revetment of rock crystal. The similarity is an indication of the syntony that existed between the art centers of Florence and Rome, both of which were marked by a taste for refined, precious objects decorated with forms borrowed from the language of classical antiquity.

AG

1. The labels are inscribed: "Columna Flagellationis D.N. Jesu Christi quae extat Romae in Templio S. Praxedis"; "Ex altera Columna ad quam Christus Dom. Ligatus et caesus fuit, quae colitur Hiersolymi"; "Ex Petra Hostii Monumenti Domini N/ Jesu Christi."
2. Reproduced in *Palazzo Vecchio* 1980, p. 239.
3. This is suggested in *Palazzo Vecchio* 1980, p. 239, although Mario Scalini in Acidini et al. 2002, p. 272, argues that it was made in Florence.

detail

37. Tabletop depicting Eucharistic symbols

Galleria dei Lavori, Florence,
ca. 1603–10
Design by Bernardino Poccetti
and Jacopo Ligozzi; originally
assembled by Francesco and
Giovanni Battista Sassi and Jacopo
Autelli (called Monnicca) in the
workshop of Cristoforo Gaffurri;
gold inlay by Angelo Serani
Hardstones, gold, and silver with
petrified wood frame; 73¼ × 38¼ in.
(186 × 97 cm)
Palazzo Pitti, Florence, Galleria
Palatina OA 1911:1512

PROVENANCE: Part of the altar
in the Cappella dei Principi,
Basilica di San Lorenzo, Florence
(dismantled in 1779 and the panels
reassembled as a tabletop); documented in 1789 in the Palazzo Pitti,
Florence; taken by Napoleon's
troops to Paris, 1799; returned
to Florence, 1816; documented in
the Palazzo Pitti in 1911

REFERENCES: Zobi 1853, pp. 210–11;
Weigelt 1931, pp. 174–75, pl. 103, 2;
González-Palacios 1977c, pp. 51, 65,
n. 54, pl. 51; Giusti in Baldini,
Giusti, and Pampaloni Martelli
1979, pp. 268–69, no. 57, pls. 59, 60;
González-Palacios 1982a, p. 27,
ill. p. 26, fig. 2; Przyborowski 1982,
p. 226, no. 2; Przyborowski in
Giusti 1988, p. 108, no. 13; Giusti
2006b, p. 68, ill. no. 56

Between 1604 and 1610, the fresco painter Bernardino Poccetti (1548–1612), who had been entrusted with the creation of the altarpiece of the Cappella dei Principi in Florence, made drawings for the altar's antependium, incorporating designs commissioned the previous year from Jacopo Ligozzi (1547–1627), an artist famous for his beautiful and very accurate studies of flowers, plants, and birds (fig. 116).[1] The final design called for five mosaic panels, all reflecting the iconographic program of the monumental altar itself, which was dedicated to the seven Sacraments, with special emphasis on the Eucharist.

The hardstones were assembled into the panels between 1605 and 1610 in the workshop of Cristoforo Gaffurri.[2] The gold inlay around the images of vases and among the wheat stalks and leaves had been prepared in 1603, before the panels were assembled, by the goldsmith Angelo Serani, who was associated with the Galleria dei Lavori and who also made the bronze framework for the monumental ciborium in the Cappella dei Principi.[3] Nearly two centuries later the altar was dismantled, and these two panels and another pair were joined to make two tabletops, each with a bilaterally symmetrical design framed in petrified wood.

Grand Duke Ferdinand I de' Medici, who with his wife, Christina of Lorraine, commissioned the altar, had a passion for translucent stones, especially chalcedony—thought to symbolize, among other things, the triumph of Christ the Redeemer—and ordered a large amount of it to be incorporated

into the mosaics. However, before the project was completed Ferdinand died, and the original concept was subsequently changed. Silver foil was placed behind the translucent stones to increase the trompe l'oeil effects,[4] and yellowish jasper was substituted for the planned gold relief mounts glorifying the patrons. The foil behind the translucent amethysts and Oriental chalcedony, which is the background stone, has oxidized, marring some splendid effects. But the technical virtuosity of the execution is astonishing. This and the sophisticated iconography place the five panels among the finest works in pietre dure ever made in Florence.

The two panels that now constitute this tabletop were originally positioned on the altar's antependium on either side of a center panel (today on the high altar in San Lorenzo, Florence) that illustrates two Old Testament passages foretelling

God's gift of the bread and wine of the Eucharist: the falling of manna from heaven and the finding of water in the desert. Symbols of the eucharistic bread and wine are also found in these panels, in the form of stalks of wheat and twisting vines heavy with grapes surrounding a large two-handled jug. Two other panels from the antependium now form a second tabletop on which are represented smaller vases filled with passionflowers, emblematic of Christ's suffering.[5]

The vases depicted here, of unusual form, stand on volute pedestals. They resemble a type of display vessel, usually of gilded silver and mounted with agate and colorful gems in such a way that the wall of the vessel seems to be bulging through a gilded, glittering net. This idea was possibly inspired by Mexican *bucaros* vases, which had begun to enter Europe in the early seventeenth century.[6] Each vase contains spring flowers—an imposing crown-imperial fritillary and two Florentine irises (see cat. no. 45). Caterpillars, butterflies, and bees—all extremely lifelike, thanks to the deft hand of Ligozzi—can be discovered crawling on the ground around the flowers. The first two creatures allude to death and resurrection, and the bees, on account of the sweetness of their honey, were often compared to Christ's goodness.[7] The garden itself surely alludes to Paradise and the immortality of believers, implicit in the beauty of stone flowers that will not waste away, while the observer is in contrast a perishable human being. The nearly-white original color of the chalcedony background symbolizes the strength and endurance of the heavenly saints, who maintain a "burning faith."[8]

The splendid birds in the vines are special species; shown in the upper area are the red American cardinal (*Cardinalis cardinalis*) and a stylized species of rock thrush (*Monticola saxatilis*) that breeds from southern Europe to northern China, while sitting on branches below are the orange and black Paradise Whydah (family Viduinae) and the black and white Pin-tailed Whydah (*Vidua macroura*), both exotic birds living south of the Sahara Desert and recognizable by their long tails.[9] Although Ligozzi was a precise draftsman, artistic freedom and stylization play a part here. The Medici dukes may have kept those specimens in their Florentine palaces more or less as living *Kunstkammer* objects. Birds conventionally represent the souls of the blessed, but the presence of these types in this mosaic suggests a reference to the ambitions of the Catholic Church in the Americas and other distant lands. The cardinal may also allude to

Fig. 116. Jacopo Ligozzi, *Fig Branch with a Bird of Paradise and Exotic Finches,* ca. 1603. Gouache on paper, 26⅜ × 17¾ in. Galeria degli Uffizi, Florence, Gabinetto Disegni e Stampe Orn 1958

who admired the splendor of the Medici dynasty, which was—especially after the marriage of Maria de' Medici to King Henry IV of France in 1600—about to be recognized as a European power as significant as the Habsburgs.

In 1779 the altar in the Cappella dei Medici was dismantled, and ten years later this tabletop made from some of its parts had found its way into the Palazzo Pitti in Florence. A decade later it was carried off to Paris by Napoleon's soldiers, together with its mate, the second tabletop made from pieces of the altar. In 1816 this tabletop was returned to its original home in Florence, but the other remained in France, in the Palais des Tuileries and then the Louvre, where it is today. [12]

W K

the fact that in the sixteenth century four Medici family members had served the pope as cardinals at the Holy See.[10]

Crown imperials (*Fritillaria imperialis*)[11] were associated with the Holy Roman emperors and the Habsburg dynasty, which ruled not only in central Europe and parts of Italy but also, through its Spanish branch, large areas of the Americas— where, it was widely supposed, was located the fabulous land of Eldorado, a paradisiacal place where gold and gems lay scattered about in abundance. The Habsburgs and the Medici dukes were considered the defenders of the Catholic faith, and these panels were intended to celebrate the leading role of Habsburg monarchs in bringing their religion to the four continents, symbolized by the exotic birds. The Medici were deeply indebted to the Habsburgs, who had made Cosimo a duke. In the many years between the Council of Trent (1545–63) and the end of the Thirty Years' War (1648), Florence was full of northern visitors

1. For details on the commission and the progress of the work, see Przyborowski 1982, p. 226, no. 2; Przyborowski in Giusti 1988, p. 108, no. 13. On Poccetti, see the entry by Paul C. Hamilton in *Dictionary of Art* 1996, vol. 25, pp. 58–59.
2. Information on the assembly is given by Przyborowski in Giusti 1988, p. 108.
3. He was allowed by the court to work in different media. Przyborowski 1982, p. 129.
4. Visible in Giusti 2006b, ill no. 56.
5. Exodus 16:14, 15:22–27. On the symbolism of the objects in the five panels, see González-Palacios 1982a, pp. 26–27.
6. On *bucaros* vases, see Mosco 2004d, pp. 173–74, fig. 8; Francesco Morena in Casciu 2006, p. 267, nos. 134, 135. See also Margaret E. Connors McQuade in *Arts in Latin America* 2006, pp. 115–21, nos. I-1–I-11.
7. Impelluso 2005, p. 334.
8. See Sybille Ebert-Schifferer in *Faszination Edelstein* 1992, p. 193, no. 103; see also Friess 1980, "Chalzedon," pp. 102–6.
9. I am grateful to Lucrecia Obolensky Mali, New York, and Paul Sweet, Department of Ornithology, Division of Vertebrate Zoology, American Museum of Natural History, New York, for suggesting the identifications of the various bird species.
   Decades later, the motifs of the cardinal and rock thrush were used in the decoration of another tabletop, although with many details changed; see Giusti 2006b, ill. no. 73.
10. See González-Palacios 2001, p. 23. I thank Johanna Hecht, Associate Curator in the Department of European Sculpture and Decorative Arts, Metropolitan Museum, for discussing this subject with me.
11. In April 1576 a plant of this exotic species from the high plains of the Himalayas blossomed for the first time in the gardens of Emperor Maximilian II in Vienna. Krausch 2007, pp. 267–69 (all the flowers listed were sought after and prized by European gardeners by the end of the seventeenth century.)
12. Przyborowski in Giusti 1988, p. 108, no. 13.

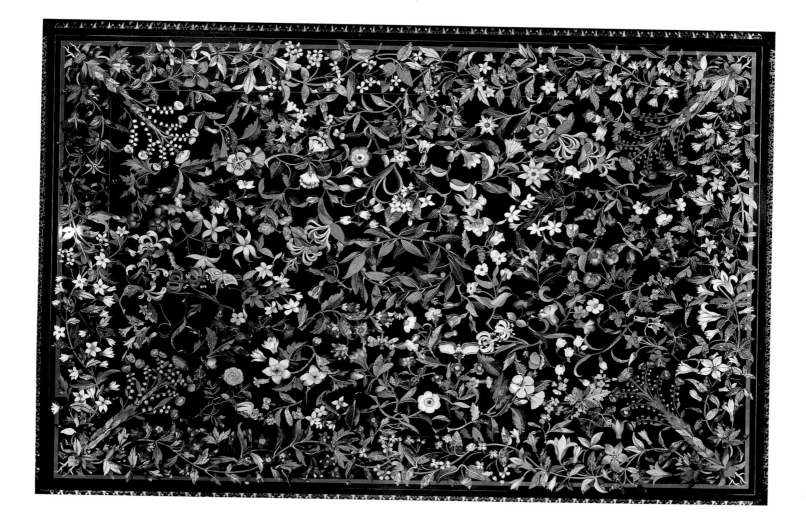

38. Table with top depicting flowers

Galleria dei Lavori, Florence, 1614–21
Design by Jacopo Ligozzi;
assembled by Jacopo Autelli
(called Monnicca)
Hardstones and gold; 37 × 44⅛ ×
63¾ in. (94 × 112 × 162 cm)
Base: carved and gilded wood,
made later
Galleria degli Uffizi, Florence
OA 7

PROVENANCE: Palazzo degli Uffizi,
Florence, from 1635

REFERENCES: Zobi 1853, pp. 232–33;
Weigelt 1931, pl. 104, 2; Neumann
1957, p. 158, n. 5, fig. 192; Aschengreen Piacenti 1974, p. 45, fig. 3;
Giusti in Baldini, Giusti, and
Pampaloni Martelli 1979, pp. 286–
87, no. 95, pls. 124, 125; González-
Palacios 1982a, p. 30; Giusti 1992,
p. 79, pl. 32; González-Palacios
1993, vol. 1, pp. 391–92, pl. LXVIII;
Giusti 2006b, p. 83, ill. no. 60

The creation of this splendid floral tabletop, which was initiated in 1614 and finished in 1621, is well documented in the archives of the Guardaroba Medicea (Archivio di Stato, Florence). In a letter of 1618, when work on the tabletop was well under way, Vincenzo Giugni, head of the Guardaroba, wrote that Grand Duke Cosimo II had asked the painter Jacopo Ligozzi (1547–1627) for a "full-size and partly colored" design for it in 1614.[1] Once this model, made on a 1:1 scale, had been approved, Ligozzi was charged with doing "what he must do to see it made into mosaic by Maestro Jacopo Monica [*sic*] in the Galleria [dei Lavori]"—that is, he was to finish the design and make tracings of it.[2]

Work on the tabletop began in 1615, when Ligozzi was asked by the chief of the Guardaroba to "select the stones to make the flowers and foliage." It was not unheard of to trust the painter, with his heightened sense of color, to choose which stones from among the vast assortment available

in the Medici collection would be used. As early as the beginning of the seventeenth century, for example, Ludovico Cigoli was given the task of overseeing the creation of the mosaics for the Cappella dei Principi, to ensure the craftsmen would "paint pictures not with pigment and brushes but with compositions in a variety of semiprecious stones."[3] By selecting those with the perfect nuances of color, Ligozzi could guarantee the surreal and alluring qualities of these "paintings in stone," which evidently were so important to Ferdinand I de' Medici, founder of the Florentine workshop, and to his successors (see, e.g., cat. no. 25).

Giugni's letter suggests that this tabletop, replete with flowers and alive with color, was nearly finished in 1618. The following year Ligozzi received an additional payment for full-size colored drawings for the frame of a table with scattered flowers, or *sparti*, as they are generally called in documents of the period. Thus, even the table-top's unusual and jewel-like frame is a product of the painter's imagination. It has pearl-shaped drops of chalcedony that hang from small lapis lazuli and chalcedony escutcheons outlined in gold and set into the tabletop's beveled edge, which is made of Flemish black marble. The master who made it, Camillo di Ottaviano Profili, is documented as working on "the black marble frame for a mosaic of pietre dure and gold" in 1620 and 1621.

It seems likely that this table was always intended for the gallery within the Palazzo degli Uffizi that was originally housed in the Tribuna and then expanded, along with the selection of furniture and works from the Medici collection that were to be exhibited. It was listed among the works in the gallery in the inventory of 1635, when it was one of the few examples of pietre dure; others included the famous collector's cabinets of Francesco I and Ferdinand I and a "collector's cabinet from Germany" that occupied the same space as the table.[4]

The floral motif, which had been common in Florentine hardstone mosaics since the end of the sixteenth century, reaches its apogee in this work, where it becomes the sole subject of the composition. Here Late Mannerist stylization is abandoned in favor of an aesthetic of horror vacui, and the richly hued flowers covering the surface show a

precise fidelity to nature. Even as an old man, Ligozzi remained faithful to the naturalistic vision that had characterized the botanical drawings he had made forty years earlier for Francesco de' Medici, and he used it to guide the translation of his painterly vision into stone, taking full advantage of the medium's unique effects of color and light.

The table's original base, of wood inlaid with ivory, is now lost, as is its successor. The present base (not shown) is of gilded wood, with carved decoration in a sober Neoclassical style.

A G

1. See Giusti in Baldini, Giusti, and Pampaloni Martelli 1979, p. 286, no. 95.
2. "quello che vi avea bisogno per farsi di comeso da M. Iacopo Monica in Galeria." Ibid. This practice is still in use today at the Opificio delle Pietre Dure. From traced copies of a painted design, the mosaic master determines which pieces of hardstone he intends to fit together, cutting out sections of the design and using them as guides to shape the sections of stone.
3. The credible source of this information is Cigoli's nephew, who in 1628 wrote a biography of his uncle that was eventually published in 1913. See Giusti in Baldini, Giusti, and Pampaloni Martelli 1979, p. 301, under no. 123.1.
4. The cabinet, the *Stipo Tedesco*, made in 1619–26 in the workshop in Augsburg, is now in the Museo degli Argenti, Florence. It was acquired by Archduke Leopold V of Austria in 1628 and given, two years later, as a gift to his wife's nephew, Ferdinand II de' Medici; see Alfter 1986.

39. Design for a tabletop depicting flowers

Galleria dei Lavori, Florence, ca. 1610–20
By Jacopo Ligozzi
Oil on paper; 30¾ × 34⅝ in. (78 × 88 cm)
Museo dell'Opificio delle Pietre Dure, Florence 1905:2703

PROVENANCE: Galleria dei Lavori, Florence (subsequently Opificio delle Pietre Dure); Museo dell'Opificio, by 1905

REFERENCES: Giusti in Giusti, Mazzoni, and Pampaloni Martelli 1978, p. 328, no. 548, pl. 476; Giusti 1995, p. 51, ill. no. 21; Giusti in Gregori and Hohenzollern 2002, p. 256

This is a rare surviving example of a full-scale design for a piece of furniture to be executed in pietre dure in the Medici workshops in Florence. From the time the earliest Florentine mosaics were made in the mid-sixteenth century (see cat. no. 9), it was the usual practice in the workshop to engage an artist who would furnish the craftsmen with a design, generally in the form of a "disegno colorito su carta," or painting on paper. These painted designs—another is a sixteenth-century example by Giovanni Antonio Dosio now in the Galleria degli Uffizi (see fig. 16)—were then presumably translated into working drawings by the mosaic craftsmen so that they could be used in making the *commessi*.[1] The late sixteenth-century, lifesize oil portraits of Cosimo I de' Medici and Henry IV of France, which were themselves conceived as models (and see also the portrait of Pope

Clement VIII, cat. no. 25), are an exception to this practice, as is this design for a tabletop, made some twenty years later.[2] Although undocumented, the drawing can be attributed to Jacopo Ligozzi (1547–1627) on the basis of its style.

Ligozzi moved from his native Verona to Florence early in his life, and by the 1570s, in addition to making large paintings mostly of sacred subjects, he was producing detailed drawings of plants and animals to satisfy Francesco de' Medici's taste for the natural sciences.[3] An intimate of the Medici, Ligozzi became a pivotal figure in the design of the mosaics executed in the grand-ducal workshop in the 1610s for the new grand duke, Cosimo II, who preferred landscapes and, especially, still lifes with fruits, flowers, and birds to the figural subjects that interested his predecessor, Ferdinand I. Ligozzi proved to be the ideal artist

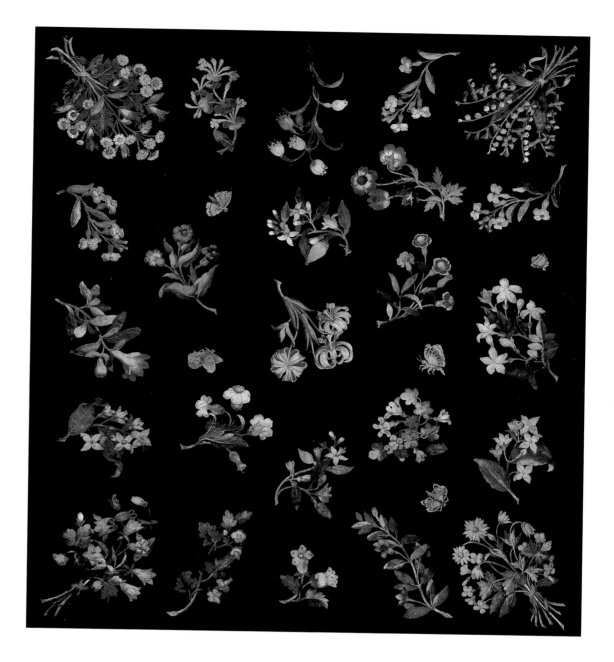

for this subject matter, uniting in his designs a careful naturalism and a tantalizing sense of the decorative. An early example of this is his superb tabletop with flowers (cat. no. 38), made between 1614 and 1621, which led to the creation of other floral works. These include a chessboard now in the Museo degli Argenti, Florence, and a lost "table with flowers for Madama Serenissima"—that is, for Grand Duchess Christina of Lorraine—for which Ligozzi made "a full-size, colored design" that he was paid for in 1618.[4] The same year, Giovanni Battista Sassi, one of the most highly skilled craftsmen in the Medici workshop, executed a small table "with many flowers in pietre dure" that was delivered to the "chamber of Madama Serenissima."[5] The black background of the present design by Ligozzi, its floral motif, and the

precise rendering of the flowering branches suggest that this was perhaps the design for the grand duchess's lost table.

A G

1. See González-Palacios 1993, vol. 1, p. 357, vol. 2, fig. 697.
2. The source painting for the portrait of Cosimo I was made by Domenico Passignano in 1597, and the pietre dure mosaic, made from Tuscan marble, was finished the following year. Both works are now in the Museo dell'Opificio delle Pietre Dure, Florence, as is the portrait of Henry IV, painted by Santi di Tito in 1600 (its translation into mosaic has been lost).
3. See Tongiorgi Tomasi 1993.
4. For the chessboard, see Casazza 2004b, p. 91, fig. 12. The chessboard was made by G. B. Sassi from a design by Ligozzi and finished in 1619. The document mentioning the tabletop was published by Giusti in Baldini, Giusti, and Pampaloni Martelli 1979, p. 258.
5. Document published by Giusti in Baldini, Giusti, and Pampaloni Martelli 1979, p. 287.

40. *Pearl Fishing in the West Indies*

Florence, ca. 1600–1620
By Antonio Tempesta
Oil on lapis lazuli, frame
(not shown) of gilded copper,
enameled silver, and crystal;
11⅞ × 19¾ in. (30 × 50 cm)
Musée du Louvre, Paris
MR supl. 243

Not in exhibition

PROVENANCE: Gift from Pietro
Strozzi to Cosimo II de' Medici;
Tribuna, Palazzo degli Uffizi,
Florence, 1635; Guardaroba
Medicea, Florence, 1769; Palazzo
degli Uffizi, 1783; Guardaroba
Medicea, 1796; Musée du Louvre,
from 1832

REFERENCES: Cecchi 1986; Giusti
1992, pp. 79–80, fig. 24 (as by
Cristofano Allori)

The 1635 inventory of the Uffizi Tribuna provides a detailed description of both this painting, which it attributes to Antonio Tempesta (1555–1630), and its precious-metal frame.[1] The inventory also records that the picture was given as a gift to Grand Duke Cosimo II de' Medici by Pietro Strozzi, member of a noble Florentine banking family that had previously been at odds with the Medici. Tempesta had died only five years before the inventory was drawn up, so the attribution is credible. Moreover, both the painter and Strozzi were living in Rome at the beginning of the seventeenth century, lending further weight to this attribution. Strozzi, a well-known theologian, was called to the papal court in 1595, where, as a collector and connoisseur, he oversaw the pope's artistic commissions. By his own account, Tempesta was often in Rome after he finished his training in Giovanni Stradano's workshop in Florence, as early as the beginning of the 1580s. Strozzi may have commissioned the painting in Rome before returning permanently to Florence in 1617 and giving it to the grand duke.

Cosimo must have been particularly pleased by this gift. He had a passion for paintings on stone, a genre that first became fashionable at the end of the sixteenth century and remained popular thereafter, especially in Florence. The circle of cosmopolitan artists active at Cosimo's court achieved an especially high level of artistry in this medium.[2] Tempesta, whose oeuvre of prints and paintings was relatively large, likely made paintings on stone because their small size and refined execution appealed to him personally and to those who collected his work.[3]

Until 1769 this picture hung in the Tribuna, a sure sign of the esteem in which it was held. Indeed, this is one of Tempesta's most successful works, appreciated for its exotic subject presented in an expressive and elegant Mannerist style, which recalls a similar work Alessandro Allori made for Francesco I's *studiolo*. The fluidity of the brushwork defines the crowded composition quickly but precisely, and the enameled colors match the luminosity of the stones. Tempesta achieved an amazing harmony between the painting itself and the natural patterns in the lapis lazuli—one of the greatest challenges of painting on stone. He made particularly successful use of the white veins in the lapis to evoke disjointed clouds, rocky riverbanks, and the foam on choppy water.

The precious-metal frame (not seen in the photograph), like the painting of exquisite execution, consists of gilded-copper fillets flanking a center band of silver worked with enamel. The silver band was once set, as the inventory tells us, with "four large garnets, two large emeralds and four small ones, and four hyacinths [a blue stone]." This small trove of gemstones disappeared at some unknown time and was replaced by colored crystals.

AG

1. Alessandro Cecchi, who researched this work and published a detailed study of it, was responsible for identifying the painting in the inventories of the Medici collections.
2. See Chiarini and Acidini 2000 (with bibliography).
3. For works on stone by Tempesta, including the *Death of Adam* in the Galleria Sabauda, Turin, which has a metal frame almost as fine as the present example, see Cecchi 1986.

41. *Barberini Cabinet*

Galleria dei Lavori, Florence, ca. 1606–23
Ebony and other exotic woods on an oak and poplar carcass, marbles and hardstones; 23¼ × 38⅛ × 14⅛ in. (59.1 × 96.8 × 35.9 cm)
The Metropolitan Museum of Art, New York, Wrightsman Fund, 1988 1988.19

PROVENANCE: Made for Cardinal Maffeo Barberini (later Pope Urban VIII; 1568–1644); acquired by the Metropolitan Museum, 1988

REFERENCES: Vincent in Metropolitan Museum 1988, pp. 28–29; Bohr 1993, pp. 200–203, no. III, fig. 19 (dated 1665–75); Ramond 1994, pp. 63–66; Riccardi-Cubitt 1992, pp. 76–77, 174–75, pl. 20; Koeppe in Dal Prà 1993, pp. 399, 400, ill. p. 398; Massinelli 1993, fig. 90; Koeppe in Kisluk-Grosheide, Koeppe, and Rieder 2006, pp. 28–30, no. 9 (with additional ills. on CD-ROM)

Fig. 117. Detail of alcove wall in the throne chamber, Divan-i 'Am (Hall of Public Audience), Red Fort, Delhi, ca. 1631–40. Marble and hardstones. In the arched panel is Orpheus with a *lira da braccio*, surrounded by animals.

The *Barberini Cabinet* is named after the bearer of the coat of arms that is set like a colorful jewel in the center of the broken pediment on this cabinet. The stylized armorial cartouche displays, on an azure ground, three golden bees, and is surmounted by a *galero*, the scarlet wide-brimmed hat of a cardinal.[1] These refer to Maffeo Barberini, who was appointed to the College of Cardinals in 1606. Maffeo was one of the six sons of Antonio Barberini, a Florentine merchant. This abundance of male offspring would be a great advantage to the Barberini during the seventeenth century. Some sons entered the Church, a rich source of power and wealth, and others made advantageous marriages, benefiting the family as a whole.[2] Maffeo left Florence for Rome in 1584 to pursue an ecclesiastical career. There he became a protégé of his uncle Monsignor Francesco Barberini, the Vatican's protonotary.[3]

When the young churchman became papal nuncio in 1604 at the Parisian court of Henry IV and his consort, Maria de' Medici, the stimulating cultural environment of the French capital may have kindled Maffeo's love of art and enjoyment of the luxuries of life. Back in Rome in 1607, he made steady progress within the Vatican, emerging after the white smoke of the conclave on August 6, 1623, as pope, at which time he adopted the name Urban VIII. During his pontificate he became one of the most energetic art patrons of his age. He commissioned many churches and other buildings in Rome and was responsible for a

host of new projects at Saint Peter's, including Gianlorenzo Bernini's baldachin above the high altar. He also has gone down in history as a nepotist on the grand scale by appointing his brother and three of his nephews cardinals. As princes of the Church, they received a guaranteed income that would form the basis of their dynasty's huge and long-lasting fortune.[4]

Probably made between 1606, when Maffeo became a cardinal and added the *galero* to his coat of arms, and 1623, when he became pope, the cabinet may have been a gift to him—as a true son of Florence—from the grand-ducal court or from his family on the occasion of his appointment to the College of Cardinals.[5] It may also have been commissioned at any time during those years by Maffeo himself. As for its manufacture, the beautiful pietre dure plaques reflect the high artistic standards of the Galleria dei Lavori in Florence.[6] The large panels on the sides and top were probably executed after designs by Jacopo Ligozzi (1547–1627). They show flowering branches and birds. The scenes on some of the drawers are based on woodcuts in Francesco del Tuppo's edition of Aesop's *Fables* (Naples, 1485).[7] The subjects include the dog that loses the piece of meat he has got in his jaws when trying to grab the one he sees reflected in the water (the reflection is cleverly executed on rock crystal painted on the back). Two plaques show mythical creatures: on the left side of the cabinet is a salamander (emblem of Francis I of France, a celebrated patron of the arts, like Maffeo himself), and on the right is a phoenix (emblem of Pope Clement VIII, who had appointed Maffeo to the French court). Along the base are scenes of men and animals hunting. These plaques and others surround a larger one on the door of the central compartment, which shows Orpheus, the legendary Thracian poet, playing his *lira da braccio* to charm the animals and beasts with his music.

The Orpheus theme was a popular one at the Galleria dei Lavori: at least twenty-two hardstone mosaic Orpheus plaques, most with slight variations, are now documented,[8] and other plaques with a different subject, such as the mythological centaur, are handled in a stylistically similar way.[9] Exciting finds emerge from Ebba Koch's study of the program of the hardstone mosaic paneling surrounding the throne in the Hall of Public Audience at the Red Fort in Delhi. There, at the

top of the alcove, is an almost identical panel depicting Orpheus (fig. 117).[10] This significant piece, which is surrounded by other panels from Florence, must have impressed the Indian Mughal rulers in the same way that artifacts imported from the East have impressed Western monarchs and left their legacy in Europe (see cat. no. 42).　　　　W K

1. The changing heraldry of Maffeo Barberini is discussed by Koeppe in Kisluk-Grosheide, Koeppe, and Rieder 2006, pp. 28–29, no. 9.
2. Waddy 1990, p. 128.
3. On Maffeo Barberini's career, see John Beldon Scott in *Dictionary of Art* 1996, vol. 3, pp. 205–7; Schütze 2007.
4. Waddy 1990, p. 130.
5. See Koeppe in Kisluk-Grosheide, Koeppe, and Rieder 2006, p. 30.
6. The cabinetry may have been executed by German woodworkers, known to have settled in Florence and been employed at the grand-ducal workshop; see ibid.
7. Vincent in Metropolitan Museum 1988, pp. 28–29; Del Tuppo 1485, *fabulea* 2, 6, 18, 23, 35.
8. Archival note, Department of European Sculpture and Decorative Arts, Metropolitan Museum. See also E. Koch 1987; E. Koch 1988, pls. 15, 17, 19, 26.
9. See, for example, Przyborowski 1998, figs. 26, 28.
10. E. Koch 1988, pls. 15, 19.

42. Frieze panel

Agra, India, second quarter of
the 17th century
Marble and hardstones; 5½ ×
25 × 1 in. (13.9 × 63.3 × 2.5 cm)
Private collection

PROVENANCE: Art market,
London; private collection

This white marble panel is inlaid, in an Indian
version of the hardstone mosaic technique,
with a very abstract pattern of floral tendrils,
pomegranate motifs, and quatrefoil rosettes made
up of black, brown, and ocher stones. Continuous
repetition of the short pattern of scrolling polychrome flowers and vines on the white ground
achieves an astonishing effect of serene beauty. A
thick black border emphasizes and seems to support this highly individual ribbon of ornament.

The panel must have formed part of an architectural scheme in a tomb for a member of the
Mughal imperial family, perhaps the tomb of
Itimad al-Daula at Agra.[1] The title Itimad al-Daula
(Emperor's Pillar) was bestowed on Mirza Ghiyas
Beg—the wazir, or prime minister—by the
emperor Jahāngir (r. 1605–27). In 1611 Jahāngir
married Mirza Ghiyas Beg's daughter Nūr Jahān,
and when her father died in 1622, she commissioned

an ornate mausoleum to honor him. Completed
in 1628, it was the first Mughal structure made
entirely of marble. Its extensive hardstone mosaic
ornamentation is of a type associated with the Taj
Mahal (begun in 1630) and the throne room at the
Red Fort in Delhi (built in 1639; see entry for
cat. no. 41).[2] Stone friezes with stylized floral
motifs from all these grand Mughal structures call
to mind "the swagging vegetation of Gandharan
and Mauryan art, Caesar Augustus's Ara Pacis,
and Enea Vico's engravings of acanthus ornament
(published in Rome about 1590)—all of which
contributed to the Mughal artistic synthesis."[3]

WK

1. See Okada 2003.
2. I am most grateful to Navina Haidar, Associate Curator,
   Department of Islamic Art, Metropolitan Museum, for her
   advice and help with this entry.
3. Welch 1985, p. 251. For another panel with a similar design,
   see Leoshko 1989, p. 66, fig. 56.

43. Panel depicting a blossoming orange tree

Galleria dei Lavori, Florence,
early 17th century
Hardstones, marble, and alabaster;
52⅜ × 30⅜ in. (133 × 77 cm)
Victoria and Albert Museum,
London 810–1869

PROVENANCE: Medici collections;
Villa del Poggio Imperiale, near
Florence, from 1691; deposited in
Galleria dei Lavori (subsequently
Opificio delle Pietre Dure),
Florence, 1789; Victoria and Albert
Museum, from 1867

This panel is one of a pair at the Victoria and
Albert Museum, London; the other shows a
vase of flowers. They come from the same set as
a pair of floral panels in the Museo dell'Opificio
delle Pietre Dure in Florence (see cat. no. 44). It
seems likely that the wall decoration that included
these four panels consisted of alternating representations of a vase of flowers and an orange tree,
although this is the only extant example of the latter. The decoration was made in the early years of
the seventeenth century, and it is described in the
1789 inventory of the Opificio delle Pietre Dure

as consisting of eleven panels intended for the
walls of an oratory in the Medici villa at Poggio
Imperiale, south of Florence, where they were
seen and mentioned in 1691.[1]

To members of the Medici family praying in
the oratory, these lovely views of nature must
have seemed like openings in the walls revealing
the real garden that surrounded the villa. This
enchanting secular embellishment also included a
decorated socle, two sections of which are preserved
in the Museo dell'Opificio. There is a cartouche in
each with inlaid aquatic scenes—alternating swans

REFERENCES: Giusti, Mazzoni, and Pampaloni Martelli 1978, pp. 287–88; González-Palacios 1982a, p. 23, ill. p. 22; Giusti in Giusti 1988, p. 138; Giusti in Acidini et al. 2002, pp. 264–65, no. 122

and fish—that are made of pieces of painted alabaster fitted into a ground of Albarese marble from the Arno River valley.

The oratory was dismantled when the villa was renovated in the Neoclassical taste, and the panels were put in storage. We cannot be sure, however, if all of them were sent to the Opificio, since the 1789 inventory lists only eleven, which seems too few for a decoration that ran around at least three of the chapel walls. The Galleria dei Lavori suffered a financial crisis after the proclamation of the Kingdom of Italy in 1861 and was forced to sell off its collections, including part of this series of panels. The two now at the Victoria and Albert Museum were purchased in 1867 at the Exposition Universelle in Paris. An additional seven were sold shortly afterward to private buyers.

A panel representing a vase of flowers was recently acquired on the London market by the Fine Arts Museums of San Francisco, and there is a similar one in the collection of the Museum of Fine Arts, Saint Petersburg, Florida. Probably these both belonged to the set from Poggio Imperiale and were sold in the second half of the nineteenth century. The varying levels of quality in the extant panels, especially in the choice and juxtaposition of the colored stones, may reflect the different abilities of the craftsmen in the workshops. Surely many people were involved, as this commission probably was executed over a period of several decades.

AG

1. See Giusti, Mazzoni, and Pampaloni Martelli 1978, pp. 287–88.

44. Panel depicting a vase of flowers

Galleria dei Lavori, Florence, early 17th century
Probably by Romolo di Francesco Ferrucci del Tadda, after a design by Matteo Nigetti
Hardstones and marble; 52⅜ × 30⅜ in. (133 × 77 cm)
Museo dell'Opificio delle Pietre Dure, Florence 1905:576

PROVENANCE: Medici collections; Villa del Poggio Imperiale, near Florence, from 1691; deposited in Galleria dei Lavori (subsequently Opificio delle Pietre Dure), Florence, 1789; Museo dell'Opificio delle Pietre Dure, from 1887

REFERENCES: Marchionni 1891, pp. 123–24; Bartoli and Maser 1953, pp. 6, 24; Giusti, Mazzoni, and Pampaloni Martelli 1978, pp. 287–88, nos. 66, 67, pl. 68; Giusti in Giusti 1988, p. 138, no. 26; Giusti 1995, p. 26, ill. no. 3; Giusti in Acidini et al. 2002, p. 262, no. 121; Giusti in *Splendour of the Medici* 2008, p. 331, no. 209

A vase of flowers, one of the earliest and most common motifs in Florentine mosaics, appears in this large panel in a refined and elegant composition that would become very popular. The large-scale naturalistic motif is enclosed in an architectonic frame of cartouches and other abstract ornament. It was customary in the grandducal workshops to entrust the overall design for a mosaic to an artist in the Medici circle, and in this case the artist chosen was perhaps Matteo Nigetti (1560–1649). Nigetti, Grand Duke Ferdinand de' Medici's favorite architect, designed vessels for the altar of the Chapel of the Annunciation in the Florentine Church of the Santissima Annunziata that, in their silhouette and forms, are similar to the vase in this mosaic.[1]

The panel is one of the first examples in which black Belgian marble is used for a mosaic ground. This stone would become the obligatory background for dazzling colored-stone inlays of flowers, fruit, and birds—the principal subject matter of Florentine mosaics—throughout the seventeenth century and later. The unexpected but effective juxtaposition of semiprecious and calcareous stones seen here is most characteristic of mosaics made early in the history of the grand-ducal workshops' production. In this panel, for example, siliceous stones with evocative patterns, such as agate

and Sicilian jasper, are found in the frame, and jaspers from Barga and Corsica define the surface on which the vase stands, whereas the background is made from Apuan *bardiglio*, a rather common marble. *Verde antico* marble, salvaged from archaeological sources, is used for the rectilinear cartouches, while the lapis lazuli of the vase, though full of impurities, was carefully chosen to create an effect of pulsating color across its convex body. The large lily that dominates the array of flowers was created from a piece of rare and transparent Oriental chalcedony placed over colored metallic foil to give it effects of light and depth.

The extraordinary refinement in the execution of this piece and its use of color may point to the hand of Romolo di Francesco Ferrucci del Tadda (d. 1621), one of the first masters to specialize in Florentine mosaic (see cat. no. 25). His workshop produced other inlaid views of vases set in a black background in the first years of the seventeenth century.[2] The Museo dell'Opificio has a second panel identical to this one; the pair survive from a set in which representations of a vase with flowers alternated with depictions of an orange tree in bloom (see cat. no. 43).

AG

1. Berti 1951–52, fig. 3.
2. See Giusti in Giusti 1988, p. 138, no. 26.

43

44

45. Table celebrating the sea victory at Lepanto

Tabletop: Galleria dei Lavori,
Florence, ca. 1602
Attributed to Romolo di Francesco
Ferrucci del Tadda
Marbles, lapis lazuli, and hard-
stones; 37 × 104 × 54 in. (94 × 264 ×
137 cm)
Piers: French, mid-17th century
Cast and patinated bronze
Muséum National d'Histoire
Naturelle, Paris MNHN A96

PROVENANCE: Cardinal Jules
Mazarin (1602–1661); by inheritance,
Armand de la Porte (1631–1713), duc
de Mazarin–La Meilleraye; purchased for the French royal collection under Louis XIV, before 1681;
transferred to the Cabinet Royal
d'Histoire Naturelle (now Muséum
National d'Histoire Naturelle),
Paris, 1748

REFERENCES: Guiffrey 1885–86,
vol. 2, p. 138, no. 54; Hamy 1896;
Schubnel 1977, no. A.96; González-
Palacios 1982b, p. 42, ill. p. 36;
Saule 1982; Giusti 1992, pp. 197, 263,
nn. 6, 8, pl. 103; Giusti 2006b, p. 150,
ill. no. 118

On October 7, 1571, navies of a coalition of Catholic maritime states called the Holy League defeated, against heavy odds, 260 war vessels of the Ottoman Turks off western Greece. The victory of the Christians at Lepanto was commemorated in European art for many generations thereafter.

While this table was long thought to have been made at the Manufacture Royale des Gobelins in Paris,[1] the top was correctly identified as Florentine in 1977.[2] More recently, Annamaria Giusti has been able to associate the tabletop with a document of 1602 in the Archivio di Stato in Florence referring to Francesco Ferrucci's workshop.[3] This craftsman must be Romolo di Francesco Ferrucci del Tadda (d. 1621), who worked in the Galleria dei Lavori in Florence and about 1600–1601 executed a *commesso di pietre dure* portrait of Pope Clement VIII, which is also in this exhibition (cat. no. 25).[4] As that portrait was a diplomatic gift from Ferdinand I de' Medici to the pope, this tabletop may likewise have left Tuscany as an ambassadorial present. It is interesting to note that the same artist also made a lost hardstone portrait of Henry IV, the first Bourbon king of France, who married Maria de' Medici, the niece of Ferdinand I, in 1600.[5]

Sometime before 1661 this table entered the great art collection of Cardinal Jules Mazarin,

detail showing pier

chief minister to the French king, who was Italian by birth.[6] Whether the skillfully sculpted and cast bronze dolphin piers were added at that time or earlier is not known. The expressive style of these bronzes is distinctively French; they represent an extremely rare survival of French metalwork from the mid-seventeenth century. The next owner was Armand de la Porte, duc de Mazarin–La Meilleraye, who inherited the table from Mazarin and sold it to Jean-Baptiste Colbert. A former financial adviser to Mazarin, Colbert had advanced his career and become one of the most important men at the French court (see *"Pierres fines"* by Florian Knothe in this publication). Probably he remembered the regal table and purchased it for the king because it would express the grandeur and superior power of France in Europe. It remained in the French royal collection and was among the seventy pietre dure objects stored at the Palais du Louvre in the mid-1740s. These objects and twelve hardstone-mounted cabinets were transferred in 1748 to the Cabinet Royal d'Histoire Naturelle upon the request of Georges-Louis Leclerc, comte de Buffon, who wished to make a study of the stones. Today these pieces are in the Musée National d'Histoire Naturelle.[7]

The tabletop is in the virtuoso Late Mannerist style of the Florentine grand-ducal ateliers at the turn of the seventeenth century. The high quality of its manufacture easily supports the complexity of the iconography. The four animals in cartouches in the border represent the four Elements, although the salamander—seen here immersed in its element, fire—may also symbolize France.[8] The dolphin, on one of the short ends of the table, signifies water, and the chameleon, across the table from the salamander, symbolizes air (according to Pliny, the reptile ate and drank nothing, but lived on air). The snake represents earth and is usually shown with a cornucopia, symbol of Ceres, the goddess of agriculture; her presence here is alluded to with equal effectiveness by the abundance of inlaid flowers.[9] A snake of very similar form occupies the center of a Roman hardstone table in the Doria Pamphilj collection in Genoa.[10]

The central field of the tabletop offers a breathtaking display of birds and flowers. Corner bouquets include the Turk's-cap lily (*Lilium martagon*) and the turban lily (*Lilium pomponium*).[11] The stylized iris growing out of the suspended vase seen in the center of the table is encircled by a ducal

crown. It may represent the Florentine iris (*Iris florentina*),[12] which is the emblem of Florence and also—since Maria de' Medici had just married the French king—of the French Bourbon dynasty. Myriad swallows (with divided tails) and songbirds fly around it carrying flower stems or olive and berry branches in their beaks. A reference to the dove that was sent out from the ark by Noah and returned carrying an olive branch seems obvious here. The dove has long been a symbol of good tidings and peace.[13]

Military trophies (canons, torches, weapons, and flags) alternate in the border with peace symbols, such as olive and palm branches. The flags showing the Ottoman crescent are similar to those flown on the Turkish ships in the famous battle. Like a Roman hardstone mosaic table in the Museo Nacional del Prado (fig. 18), this more sophisticated example memorializes the victory at Lepanto and serves also as a reminder of the continuing threat posed by the Turkish empire—since only in peaceful times can prosperity and abundance be sustained.

W K

1. Hamy 1896.
2. Schubnel 1977, no. A.96; see also González-Palacios 1982b, p. 42.
3. Giusti 1992, p. 263, n. 8. Confusingly, Giusti mentions in her later book (Giusti 2006b, p. 68), a "Francesco Ferrucci (1489–1530)," who was a famous Italian mercenary, and in Giusti 1992, p. 36, a "Francesco Ferrucci del Tadda" (the father of our artist, who may have been a sculptor) without any reference to Romolo di Francesco Ferrucci del Tadda.
4. See Fusco and Hess 1994 (with documents and bibliography).
5. The oil sketch for the French king's portrait is still preserved in the Opificio delle Pietre Dure in Florence. Giusti 1992, fig. 67.
6. Goyau 1911.
7. Hamy 1896. The distinguished naturalist Buffon had been appointed keeper of the Jardin du Roi (today the Jardin des Plantes) in Paris in 1739; during his tenure he made this royal garden into a study center and museum.
8. The salamander was the emblem of King Francis I (1494–1547), but eventually it became a more generalized symbol of France itself. It appears on the facade of San Luigi dei Francesi, the French national church in Rome, completed in 1589, where it guards the entrance. See Hall 1979, pp. 270–71; Koeppe in Kisluk-Grosheide, Koeppe, and Rieder 2006, p. 30, n. 7.
9. On the four Elements, see Hall 1979, p. 128.
10. For this Roman hardstone table, see González-Palacios 1982a, ill. p. 16. I thank Prince Doria Pamphilj for providing me with valuable information. I am extremely grateful to Michelangelo Lupo for generously discussing the fruits of his research with me.
11. Krausch 2007, pp. 267–69.
12. Ibid., p. 231. The species is still cultivated on Florentine farms for its rhizome, which is used for cosmetics and potpourris.
13. Hall 1979, p. 109.

46. Octagonal frame for a *Madonna and Child* by Carlo Dolci

Frame: Galleria dei Lavori, Florence, 1697
By Giovanni Battista Foggini, gilding by Cosimo Merlini
Ebony, gilded bronze, and hardstones; 46⅛ × 39 × 12¼ in. (117 × 99.1 × 31.1 cm)
Painting: by Carlo Dolci, 1675
Oil
Palazzo Pitti, Florence, Appartamenti Reali OA 1911:751

PROVENANCE: Galleria dei Lavori, Florence; Residenz, Düsseldorf, 1697; Palazzo Pitti, Florence, from 1717

REFERENCES: Zobi 1853, p. 276; Lankheit 1962, pp. 64–65, 317, 318, doc. nos. 554, 556, 558, fig. 247; Aschengreen Piacenti and

This extraordinary frame was the first of many magnificent gifts Cosimo III de' Medici sent to his daughter, Anna Maria Luisa, who had married Johann Wilhelm, the elector Palatine, in 1691. It was made in 1697 to complement the oil painting seen here, a *Madonna and Child* of 1675 by Carlo Dolci (1616–1687). Especially renowned for his devotional images, Dolci had been a favorite painter of Cosimo's mother, Vittoria della Rovere. She bequeathed this work to her son in 1694. The idea of sending the picture to his daughter as a memento of her grandmother may have represented a purely paternal sentiment on Cosimo's part, but the frame he ordered for it was certainly intended to express the magnificence of the Medici court.

The frame's decorative exuberance and the sensual handling of the precious materials are charac-teristic of the style of Giovanni Battista Foggini (1652–1725), who had been appointed director of the Galleria dei Lavori in 1694. Its large octagonal format amplifies these qualities but without sacrificing their refinement. It seems likely that the frame is one of the first objects made at the grand-ducal workshops from a design of Foggini. His authorship is supported not only by the sculptural handling of the red jasper mounted in gilded bronze—its swollen plasticity seems only barely contained—but also by the verve of the unusually large hanging bracket that caps the frame's play of red and black with a dramatic flash of golden light. The exquisite bronze garlands with bunches of hardstone fruit draped over the broad ebony band are also in the manner of Foggini. This is one of the earliest examples of a motif that the grand-

González-Palacios in *Twilight of the Medici* 1974, p. 356, no. 199; González-Palacios 1977e, p. 60; Giusti in Baldini, Giusti, and Pampaloni Martelli 1979, pp. 277–78, no. 78, pls. 98, 99; González-Palacios 1986, vol. 1, p. 43; Colle and Livi Bacci 1997, p. 290; Colle, Griseri, and Valeriani 2001, p. 70, no. 21; Giusti 2003a, pp. 253–54, fig. 22; Giusti in Casciu 2006, p. 272, no. 140; Giusti 2006b, pp. 95, 98, ill. no. 79

ducal workshops would develop and use successfully throughout the first half of the eighteenth century (see cat. nos. 55, 58).

The published documents do not reveal the names of the masters responsible for this work with the exception of the goldsmith Cosimo Merlini, who was paid for gilding the bronze elements of the frame. We do know, however, from the correspondence of a Florentine visitor to the Palatine court in Düsseldorf that while Johann Wilhelm expressed the greatest admiration for the paintings by Andrea del Sarto and Raphael his father-in-law had sent him, Anna Maria Luisa preferred the gift she had received from her father. She took it back to Florence with her in 1717 after she was widowed.[1]

A G

1. Archivio di Stato, Florence, Mediceo del Principato 2669. This document was brought to light by Stefano Casciu.

47. Della Rovere Jewelry Cabinet

Galleria dei Lavori, Florence,
ca. 1669
Cabinetry by Cosimo Maures;
statuettes by Damiano Cappelli,
ca. 1667
Ebony and hardstones, gilded
bronze statuettes and mounts;
29⅛ × 21⅝ × 20 in. (74 × 54.7 ×
50.7 cm)
Bayerisches Nationalmuseum,
Munich R2094

PROVENANCE: Vittoria della
Rovere, grand duchess of Tuscany
(1622–1694); possibly acquired by
Maximilian II Emanuel, elector
of Bavaria (1662–1726); mentioned
as in the Residenz, Munich, in 1778
and 1807; Bayerische Akademie der
Wissenschaften, Munich, and later
the Königliches Münzkabinett
[medal cabinet], Munich; transferred to the Bayerisches
Nationalmuseum, ca. 1855

REFERENCES: González-Palacios
1977e, fig. 8 (as by "G. B. Foggini?");
González-Palacios 1982a, p. 41,
ill. p. 39 (as by "G. B. Foggini?,"
and "before 1693"); Sigrid Sangl
in Langer and Württemberg 1996,
pp. 261, n. 2, ill. ("1667"); Giusti
2006b, p. 95, ill. no. 78 ("before
1694"); Jervis 2007, pp. 246, 253 n. 17

"On 20th September, 1667 Cappelli submitted a bill for 28 *scudi* to the office of the Galleria [dei Lavori] for two bronze statuettes of an infant eight *soldi* (23.3 cm) in height and a monkey, together with their wax models, which were designed to be combined with a basket of fruit in *pietre dure* above a cabinet to be executed for Vittoria della Rovere."[1] This summary of information from an archival document concerns a commission executed by the Florentine sculptor Damiano Cappelli (d. 1688) for the grand-ducal workshops in Florence. The cabinet mentioned is certainly the present one, as Cappelli's style is evident in the corporeality of both figures and in the boy's coiffure.[2] Cappelli's work was inspected by the Florentine court sculptor Ferdinando Tacca on October 15, 1667, and he "revised the bill to 20 *scudi*. In March 1669, the statuettes were consigned to the cabinet maker Cosimo Maures."[3] On this occasion, the monkey was described as a "*gatto mammone*," a fairy-tale monster.[4] This change in the description may reflect a new understanding of the themes in the cabinet's decoration, which would have been chosen by the patroness, Grand Duchess Vittoria della Rovere, wife of Ferdinand II de' Medici.

Vittoria della Rovere loved pearls. She esteemed them and their luster as symbols of purity, and she had herself depicted again and again wearing extremely ornate pearl jewelry.[5] One of Vittoria's favorite patron saints was the virgin saint Margaret of Antioch; the name Margaret comes from the Greek word for pearl. The duchess's motto, "The gift of purity" ("Dos in candore / La dote è nel candore"), appears on her memorial monument, near the bottom (fig. 77). Purity is represented on her cabinet by "shells" and "pearls" made of semiprecious stones. On either side is represented a half shell that encloses one pearl;[6] on the front, two half shells are depicted, each containing three pearls—an allusion to the six balls (*palle*) in the armorial bearings of her husband. One of these pearls is darker than the others, as is true also of the crowning ball in the Medici arms.[7] Suspended above the shells on the front are a cluster of grapes and a ripe pomegranate, a fruit that symbolizes chastity and the Resurrection.[8] Its rather tough skin breaks open only when the many seeds within—which here are shaped like and glisten like tiny pearls—are fully ripe.[9]

Colorful hardstone fruits and flowers fill the gilded bronze basket atop the cabinet. A vanitas theme is suggested by the dark spots and changing colors that mark the fruits, suggesting the inevitability of decay; these effects are created by the beautiful veining and mottling of some of the hardstones chosen for the carving. Cappelli's "infant"—a putto, possibly the one who accompanies Erato, muse of love and lyric poetry—faces the monkey-monster across the basket, gesturing so forcefully that his drapery swings in agitated folds. His passionate gesture is clearly aimed at keeping the creature from touching the fruit. The scene may represent innocent purity in conflict with temptation, an unending drama that engages every Christian throughout life, as is suggested by the temporality of the fruit.

In its form, this cabinet with drawers (some pulls are missing) recalls earlier Northern Renaissance caskets with a similar boxlike superstructure on the lid.[10] Large, unadorned areas, dominated by the velvety sheen of ebony veneer, and the boldly curving, spatially dynamic profiles at the corners of the superstructure command attention. The casket seem to bulge from the pressure of the owner's valuables within—a kind of sculptural expressiveness that is rarely seen in furniture.[11]

The production at the Galleria dei Lavori of objects like this one required the technical expertise of various pietre dure artisans. The *maestri in piano* were responsible for *commesso* panels with a flat surface. The *maestri in rilievo* and the *fruttisti* (fruit carvers) cut three-dimensional hardstone arrangements.[12]

This cabinet was displayed in the palace of the Wittelsbach rulers of Bavaria in Munich on an octagonal table with a hardstone-inlaid wooden top made about 1590 in Florence.[13] As one of the first objects from the Royal Bavarian collections, the cabinet became part of the newly founded Bayerisches Nationalmuseum about 1855.[14]

W K

I thank in particular Sigrid Sangl, Curator, Bayerisches Nationalmuseum, Munich, who provided invaluable information. She
suggested that Elector Maximilian II Emanuel, who loved pietre
dure, acquired this object. Michelangelo Lupo, Rome, gave further
advice. I am also grateful to Paola d'Agostino, Sylvan C. Coleman
and Pamela Coleman Memorial Fund Fellow, Metropolitan
Museum, for her advice on the subject of Vittoria della Rovere.

1. Letter of January 30, 1996, from Dr. Anthea Brook, London, to Dr. Peter Volk, Bayerisches Nationalmuseum (object file, Bayerisches Nationalmuseum), describing the results of her archival research in Florence. Sigrid Sangl provided information from Dr. Brook's letter in a fax communication of January 8, 2008, to the present author. Hereafter cited as Brook to Volk.

2. Pratesi 1993, pp. 38–39, and see figs. 57–60.
3. Brook to Volk.
4. Ibid.
5. Langedijk 1981–87, vol. 1, p. 195, n. 49, vol. 2, pp. 1476–77, nos. 110,2 and 110,3; Massimo Moretti in Dal Poggetto 2004, p. 367, no. IX.7.
6. Massimo Moretti in Dal Poggetto 2004, p. 367, no. IX.7.
7. In the symbolic language of the time, which would have been familiar to many people, six pearls would bespeak "effort" and "achievement" and also half of the zodiac, or six months of the year.
8. Hall 1979, p. 249.
9. Impelluso 2005, p. 145. The seventeenth-century iconologist Cesare Ripa was reminded by the pomegranate's myriad seeds of the unity of many people under one authority, such as the Church or a secular ruler, and related values, such as alliance and friendship.
10. Compare an amber casket in *Schatzkästchen und Kabinettschrank* 1989, pp. 100–101, no. 7.
11. Once it was made, the cabinet must have caught the attention of other artists and influenced the next generation of craftsmen. The putto may have served as a model for Giovanni Battista Foggini's "dancing putti" compositions in the side compartments of the elector Palatine's cabinet; see cat. no. 59 and González-Palacios 1983, ill. p. 16. For a similar collector's cabinet made by the independent Florentine cabinetmaker Amman for the grand duchess, see Bohr 1993, pp. 67–68, no. V.4.4, pp. 168–72, no. I.24.1, figs. 56–59; Giusti 1992, pl. 40.
12. For the terms, see Giusti 2006b, p. 95; for carved hardstone fruit, see Jervis 2007, figs. 1, 6.
13. Sigrid Sangl in Langer and Württemberg 1996, pp. 261–62, no. 73. The cabinet is described in the 1778 palace inventory: "No. 11 . . . On this chest is a cabinet with twelve fire-gilded brass balls, the cabinet of ebony inlaid with various stones; above, a basket with stone fruits, along with a child, and gilded-brass monkey. 250 fl[orins]." ("Nro.11 . . . Auf diesem Kasten befündet sich ein aufsatz mit zwölf in Feuer vergoldet messingen Kugeln, der aufsatz von Ebenholz mit verschiedener Stein Füllung, in der höhe ein Korb mit Früchten von Stein, nebst einem Kind, und Affen von vergoldeten Messing. 250 fl.") This information was kindly provided by Sigrid Sangl in a fax communication of January 8, 2008.
14. Ibid.

48. Collector's cabinet

Galleria dei Lavori, Florence, ca. 1690
Design attributed to Giovanni Battista Foggini
Ebony and other exotic woods on a poplar, pine, and walnut carcass, gilded bronze and silver (?) mounts; 52⅜ × 39¼ × 22⅝ in. (133 × 99.5 × 57.5 cm)
Plaques: Probably by the Pandolfini workshop and a successor, Florence, 1620s–1630s and later
Hardstones and marble
Bayerisches Nationalmuseum, Munich R2130

PROVENANCE: Maximilian II Emanuel, elector of Bavaria (1662–1726), Residenz, Munich (first recorded there in 1800); Bayerische Akademie der Wissenschaften, Munich, and later the Königliches Münzkabinett [medal cabinet], Munich; transferred to the Bayerisches Nationalmuseum, ca. 1855

REFERENCES: Himmelheber in Glaser 1976, no. 245, pl. XI; Himmelheber 1977, pp. 59–60, 74, no. 65; González-Palacios 1982a, p. 62, ill. p. 63; Bohr 1993, pp. 182–85, I.29, figs. 77–81; Eikelmann 2000, p. 191

In the third story of this grandiose cabinet, two stylized Nereids made of gilded metal hold a cartouche crowned by an elector's bonnet and the mirrored monogram *MEC* (for Maximilian Emanuel Curfürst). These designations document that the piece once belonged to Maximilian II Emanuel, elector (*Kurfürst*) of Bavaria (r. 1679–1726). Generally, it is assumed that the elector commissioned the cabinet sometime after 1680;[1] however, scholars have suggested alternatively that he may have received it as a diplomatic gift from the Medici family.[2] Indeed, in 1689 his youngest sister, Violante Beatrix, married Grand Prince Ferdinand de' Medici (1663–1713). The occasion would have offered an excellent reason for the gift. The cabinet's form, which is distantly reminiscent of ancient triumphal architecture, and the depiction in pietre dure of a triumphal arch in the front center are appropriate choices for a princely present.[3] Triumphal arches were a symbol of rule and worldly power, following the imperial Roman tradition.[4] Not unexpectedly, the front also recalls Florentine Baroque church facades, such as that of the Ognissanti, by Matteo Nigetti. That architect was a student of the court artist Bernardo Buontalenti (see cat. no. 22), who created never-realized designs for the facade of the Duomo.[5]

While the sides display simple hardstone inlays and the back is entirely of wood veneer, the cabinet's front dazzles the eye with an intricately designed and masterfully assembled arrangement incorporating colorful *commesso di pietre dure*

plaques that contrast pleasingly with dark ebony and palisander woods and gilded ripple moldings. The landscape panels in the Prague style—to the left and right of the arch and door—and the two panels in the base, each decorated with a spiked polygon, were likely made in the workshop of Giuliano di Piero Pandolfini in Florence in the late 1620s or 1630s. The polygons were inspired by geometrical inventions of the goldsmith Wenzel Jamnitzer, illustrated in his *Perspectiva Corporum Regularium* of 1568, and appear in similar form in *commessi* decorations on several cabinets made in Florence and Augsburg.[6] Among them are a Florentine cabinet in the Kunsthistorisches Museum in Vienna and two Augsburg cabinets with inserted Florentine pietre dure panels in the Royal Collection at Windsor Castle and at Rosenborg Palace in Copenhagen.[7]

The hardstone plaque affixed to the fall-front door in the center of the facade and the one at the top are of later date and represent the work of an immediate successor to the Pandolfini atelier. Under the influence of and economic pressure from the Galleria dei Lavori, the shop gradually stopped producing landscape *commessi* (see "The Castrucci and the Miseroni" by Rudolf Distelberger in this publication). As for the cabinet as a whole, its decoration differs from that of other cabinets that are considered typical of Florence in the last third of the seventeenth century.[8] If it was a diplomatic gift, Giovanni Battista Foggini (1652–1725), to whom the design can be attributed as an

early work, may have been catering specifically to the taste of a northern European prince. The cabinet's middle section can be compared with the middle section of a large cabinet acquired by the Medici grand duchess Vittoria della Rovere in 1677 and still in the Palazzo Pitti, Florence, which is documented as having been made in Florence in an independent workshop by the German cabinet-maker Amman. That artisan added decorative ornaments popular north of the Alps to a cabinet of typical Florentine structure.[9] Since Foggini worked for the Medici court, he was surely familiar with this prominent piece, which could have been his inspiration when he was designing a cabinet so that its individual appearance would be appreciated by the Bavarian elector.

WK

Sigrid Sangl, Curator, Bayerisches Nationalmuseum, Munich, kindly provided archival information about this piece, and Rudolf Distelberger, Vienna, helped me with many invaluable comments. I am most grateful for their advice.

1. Himmelheber in Glaser 1976, no. 245, pl. XI; Himmelheber 1977, pp. 59–60, 74, no. 65; Eikelmann 2000, p. 191.
2. Bohr 1993, p. 182; Bohr suggests a date of 1690–1700.
3. Ibid., p. 183.
4. See L'Entrée de Henri II à Rouen 1551 (1974 ed.); Prater 1988.
5. Heikamp 1963, pp. 215–21, and figs. 29, 34.
6. Various pietre dure works created for the Liechtenstein family were inspired by the same publication (see fig. 34 and also Vincent 1987, pp. 175–77.)
7. For the Florentine cabinet, see Giusti 2006b, ill. no. 98, and p. 121 (there described as "produced in Prague"); compare Rudolf Distelberger's essay in this publication. The other two cabinets are in González-Palacios 1982a, p. 60 (Windsor Castle), and Alfter 1986, p. 99, no. 28, fig. 74 (Rosenborg Palace).
8. Bohr 1993, p. 184.
9. Ibid., pp. 171, 395–98, figs. 56–61.

49. Bust of Vittoria della Rovere

Galleria dei Lavori, Florence, ca. 1697
By Giuseppe Antonio Torricelli
Chalcedony, jasper, and Egyptian chalcedony; H. 27⅝ in. (70 cm)
Museo degli Argenti, Palazzo Pitti, Florence

PROVENANCE: Medici collections; Conservatorio delle Suore Montalve, Florence, 1780; Villa La Quiete, near Florence; Museo degli Argenti, from 1991

REFERENCES: Giulanelli 1753, p. 86; Zobi 1853, pp. 270–71; Bartoli and Maser 1953, pp. 13, 31, ill. 61; Lankheit 1962, p. 209, n. 30, pp. 317, 324, doc. nos. 548, 553, 618; Aschengreen Piacenti in Twilight of the Medici 1974, p. 368, no. 208; Giusti in Baldini, Giusti, and Pampaloni Martelli 1979, pp. 298–99, no. 120; Langedijk 1979; Langedijk 1981–87, vol. 1, p. 201, vol. 2, pp. 1505–6, no. 59; Giusti in Giusti 1988, p. 174, no. 44; Giusti 1992, p. 259, n. 90; Casazza 2004b, p. 95, fig. 16

At the Medici workshops, the manufacture of hardstone sculptures—both in relief and in the round—dates from the reign of Ferdinand I de' Medici (r. 1587–1609; see cat. no. 24); during the reign of Cosimo III (r. 1670–1723) there was a resurgence of interest in both types of objects. These were made from separately carved pieces of stone that were assembled to make a single work. The particular demand for them in Cosimo's time reflects the Baroque taste for sculpture in general and, in particular, the presence in the workshops of Giuseppe Antonio Torricelli (1659–1719), a virtuoso craftsman with extraordinary technical ability.

The bust of Grand Duchess Vittoria della Rovere is unique in Torricelli's extensive oeuvre because of its dimensions—it is almost lifesize. Such a large-scale sculpture had not been made before at the workshops and would not be attempted again. In a few passages by the master published posthumously in 1753, he described his achievement with understandable pride: "I created . . . a lifesize portrait in which the face was made from a stone that came from our own Maremma, from Volterra."[1] This stone, which was used to fashion a likeness of the grand duchess's plump countenance, is a single piece of Volterran chalcedony. Lacunae were left in the face, into which Torricelli fitted jasper for the lips and

Egyptian cailloux, a type of chalcedony, for the eyebrows. The eyes were inserted by working from inside the block that forms the face. With their translucent chalcedony corneas and sardonyx pupils, they give the portrait a vaguely disquieting realism.

Vittoria della Rovere died in 1694. Cosimo commissioned the bust to honor his beloved mother shortly thereafter and chose to have it made in the most perdurable of materials, pietre dure. It depicts Vittoria as a young woman, dressed in the austere but magnificent habit of the Oblates of Montalve, whose patronness she was. The costume may support Karla Langedijk's hypothesis that the bust was originally intended for Vittoria's tomb, which was under construction at the time the sculpture was created, in the chapel of the Conservatorio delle Suore Montalve at the Villa La Quiete, in the hills just outside Florence.[2] The project was overseen by Giovanni Battista Foggini (1652–1725) and executed by the grand-ducal workshops. We can say with some certainty that Torricelli's likeness is based on Foggini's marble bust of the young Vittoria, now at the Galleria degli Uffizi.

AG

1. This passage was published for the first time in Giulanelli 1753, p. 86.
2. Langedijk 1979.

50. Cameo depicting Cosimo III de' Medici and Tuscany before the Temple of Peace

Galleria dei Lavori, Florence,
early 18th century
By Giuseppe Antonio Torricelli
Chalcedony; 6¾ × 4⅜ in. (17 × 11 cm)
Museo dell'Opificio delle Pietre
Dure, Florence OA 1911:580

PROVENANCE: Galleria dei Lavori,
Florence, workshop of Gaetano
Torricelli, until 1748; Galleria dei
Lavori (subsequently Opificio delle
Pietre Dure); Museo dell'Opificio,
from 1953

REFERENCES: Pampaloni Martelli
in Giusti, Mazzoni, and Pampaloni
Martelli 1978, p. 306, no. 312, pl. 275;
Maria Sframeli in Giusti 1988,
p. 176, no. 45 (with bibliography);
Giusti 1995, p. 43, ill. no. 15; Giusti
1997a, pp. 193, 195, n. 37; Giusti in
Giusti et al. 2004, p. 209; Giusti in
Giusti 2006a, p. 68, no. 8

This large cameo was carved from a single piece of chalcedony found at Graubünden, Switzerland. It shows Cosimo III de' Medici with the allegorical figure of Tuscany, represented as a woman wearing a crown, in front of the Roman Temple of Peace. This composition derives with a few variations from a bronze medal by Massimiliano Soldani-Benzi, a sculptor who also worked as an engraver in the Medici mint. In 1684 he had designed a silver coin with Cosimo's portrait, on which he based the medal; it in turn inspired the image on this cameo.

Cameos were not produced at the grand-ducal workshops under the first Medici rulers. During the reign of Cosimo III (r. 1670–1723), however, master carvers called *maestri di intaglio* did carve cameos, which for the most part were either religious images or portraits of members of the Medici family. The Museo dell'Opificio delle Pietre

Dure and the Museo degli Argenti in Florence have several examples of both types in their collections. This chalcedony cameo is one of the most remarkable. Its theme and large size make it likely that the gem was inspired by Roman imperial cameos, although it differs in being shaped like a shield. The inference is that it was intended to be mounted in some splendid context, perhaps on a large cabinet to be dedicated to Cosimo III but never finished. The existence in the Opificio of an unfinished chalcedony figure of Cosimo suggests that such a cabinet may well have been planned. The pose of this unfinished figure is much like that of the chalcedony and bronze statuette of the elector Palatine on the monumental cabinet that Cosimo sent the elector as a gift in 1709 (cat. no. 59; fig. 88).

The present cameo, which probably dates to about the same time, can in my opinion be attributed to Giuseppe Antonio Torricelli (1659–1719), who worked as a lapidary for the Medici grand dukes. The fact that Giuseppe's son Gaetano, who became an expert gem carver in the workshops under the grand dukes of Habsburg-Lorraine, still had the cameo in his shop in 1748 supports an attribution to his father. Giuseppe was an extraordinarily gifted carver of semiprecious stones, and he used the same techniques when he carved cameos. Unlike classical cameos, which were cut in layers and played on the contrasting colors of the figure and the ground, Torricelli's are delicately modeled bas-reliefs made vibrant by the luminous and changing colors of a single stone.

AG

51. Night clock

Galleria dei Lavori, Florence,
early 18th century
By Giovanni Battista Foggini,
Leonardo van der Vinne, and per-
haps Massimiliano Soldani-Benzi;
mechanism by Francesco Papillion
Inscribed on clockwork: *Francesco
Papillion in Firenze*
Ebony, hardstones, and gilded
bronze; 37⅜ × 24¾ × 11 in. (95 ×
62.9 × 28 cm)
The J. Paul Getty Museum,
Los Angeles 97.DB37

PROVENANCE: Private collection,
Lugano; acquired by the Getty
Museum, 1997

REFERENCES: J. Paul Getty
Museum 2001, p. 262; Wilson and
Hess 2001, p. 194, no. 387

From 1694 to 1725, during the tenure of Giovanni Battista Foggini (1652–1725) as artistic director of the grand-ducal workshop in Florence, the atelier moved in new directions in terms of both the quality and the variety of the furniture and furnishings made there. Table clocks, for example, became more fashionable. Most had ebony cases embellished with panels of pietre dure reliefs or mosaics and gilded bronze appliqués. Although archival documents suggest a fair number of such clocks were produced, especially in the first two decades of the eighteenth century, surviving

examples are rather limited in number.[1] These clocks tend to be similar in that they are generally set in an architectural structure of some sort, but they are differentiated by design details or ornamentation.

Like most products of the grand-ducal workshops, they were the result of a collaboration among various artists. This is certainly the case with the Getty night clock, a type found throughout Europe in the seventeenth century. These clocks were designed with a small oil lamp behind the face that made it possible to read the dial even in the dark. The mechanism of this one was made by Francesco Papillion, who matriculated in the clockmaker's guild in Florence in 1705 and is known to have made other surviving clocks.[2]

Leonardo van der Vinne (active 1659–1713), the Flemish craftsman and ebony specialist, made the case, which is richly decorated with hardstone mosaics. The multicolor parrot on the clockface is especially striking, as are the various and unusual stylized flowers. A seahorse spirals across the center of the clock's base, flanked by two small dragons on the column plinths. There is a third dragon puffing on the cornice, just below the clockface. These amusing small monsters reveal Foggini's taste for the bizarre, a mark of the late Florentine Mannerism that inspired his own artistic fantasies on more than one occasion.

The decorative elements cast in gilded bronze are less fanciful, but graceful nonetheless. They consist of two dynamic putti resting on flanking volutes and, atop the clock's crowning element, a running wild boar. That animal is a faithful copy in miniature of Pietro Tacca's famous bronze of about 1630, one of the most famous symbols of Florence. Called "Il Porcellino"—the piglet—it is copied from a Hellenistic marble at the Uffizi.

Cosimo III was an extremely generous ruler, so it seems likely that this clock was intended as a gift or souvenir for some illustrious foreign visitor. Massimiliano Soldani-Benzi (1656–1740), one of the sculptors and bronze workers active in the grand-ducal workshop at this time, made bronze miniatures of famous sculptures on more than one occasion. He may have been responsible for the bronze elements on this clock, including the putti, all of which reveal an inventive formal quality typical of Soldani-Benzi's output.

AG

1. The most complete source is in González-Palacios 1986, "Cassette e orologi," pp. 41–47.
2. Ibid., p. 47, n. 22. Papillion's name suggests he was French; a second clockmaker at the court of Cosimo III de' Medici, Ignazio Hugford, came from England and was active there from the end of the seventeenth century.

52. Casket or wig box

Galleria dei Lavori, Florence, ca. 1690–95
Design by Giovanni Battista Foggini; cabinetwork attributed to Leonardo van der Vinne
Ebony with olive, apple, maple, walnut, boxwood, padouk, and citron wood marquetry on a poplar carcass, agates, amethyst, chalcedony, lapis lazuli, bloodstone, and other hardstones, marble, gilded bronze mounts;
11½ × 22 × 16⅝ in. (29 × 56 × 42 cm)
Staatliche Museen zu Berlin, Stiftung Preussischer Kulturbesitz, Kunstgewerbemuseum 97,9

PROVENANCE: Mr. Hochbrunn, London; acquired from him by the Kunstgewerbemuseum, Berlin, 1897

REFERENCES: González-Palacios 1969, pp. 63–64, figs. 4–8; Petra Krutisch in Schatzkästchen und Kabinettschrank 1989, pp. 134–35, no. 24, pl. IV (with bibliography); Jervis 2007, p. 251, no. 23, fig. 14

The captivating beauty of this casket is fully revealed only after the lid is raised and a flat slab in the base is pulled out. Then begins a visual interplay of colors, textures, and patterns that bespeaks the artistic virtuosity of the designer, Giovanni Battista Foggini (1652–1725), and all the other craftsmen involved. On the outside, the ebony veneer and gilded mounts set off the hardstone mosaic relief decorations, which feature birds, butterflies, and other tiny insects surrounded by fruits, flowers, and floral scrolls. These mosaics are of considerable quality and create the illusion of reality, evoking—most improbably, considering the hardness of the material—the colored wax reliefs that were very much en vogue for art objects in this period. An abundance of motifs is also found in the wood marquetry that lines the casket's interior and covers the slab. The inside of the lid presents a basket filled with dozens of different kinds of flowers framed by floral sprays and acanthus-leaf scrolls. The illusionistic marquetry work can be attributed to Leonardo van der Vinne (active 1659–1713), who was a master at combining different woods of various colors, either natural or enhanced by stains and shading with hot sand.[1]

The purpose of this luxurious portable receptacle is not totally clear. The round compartments in the four corners may have held small containers for cosmetic implements. The large compartment may have been for jewels or other collectibles, which, piece after piece, could have been lifted up and placed on the slide-out surface for examination. Similar boxes, however, were used as repositories for wigs, those essential items of a gentleman's formal attire. The embellishments of a wig box were carefully chosen to reflect the owner's taste and social status.[2] Related caskets are in the Corsini collection, Florence; the Museumslandschaft Hessen Kassel; Charlecote Park, Warwickshire, England; and the Kunsthistorisches Museum, Vienna.[3]

WK

1. Petra Krutisch in *Schatzkästchen und Kabinettschrank* 1989, pp. 134–35, no. 24; Michaelsen and Buchholz 2006, fig. 127.

2. See Koeppe in Kisluk-Grosheide, Koeppe, and Rieder 2006, pp. 53–56, no. 18.

3. For the examples in: Florence, see González-Palacios 1969, fig. 9, and Giusti in Giusti 2006a, pp. 73–74, no. 13; Kassel, see Schmidberger and T. Richter 2001, pp. 270–71, no. 118; and Charlecote Park, see Jervis 2007, pp. 249–50, no. 11, fig. 11.

53. Casket

Eger, Bohemia (now Chêb, Czech Republic), ca. 1650
Attributed to Adam Eck
Partly stained and ebonized soft woods and fruitwoods, marbleized paper lining, iron mounts; 8¾ × 16⅜ × 13 in. (22 × 41.5 × 33 cm)
Georg Laue, Munich

PROVENANCE: Private collection, Germany; the present owner

REFERENCES: Voigt 1999, p. 11, fig. 3, p. 326, no. III.3; Laue 2008, pp. 263–65, no. 34

Four crouching lions of carved and gilded wood support this rectangular casket decorated with relief wood marquetry panels, meant to create an effect similar to that of relief pietre dure, such as that on the previous casket (cat. no. 52). The panels depict allegories of the four Elements.[1] The subject of each panel can be identified not only by the characteristic attributes of each element but also by the names inscribed in Latin on small scrolls: AQUA (water), TERRA (earth), AER (air), and IGNIS (fire). The scenes are based on engravings by the Italian artist Antonio Tempesta (1555–1630) of about 1600—as is the relief marquetry on a large collector's cabinet also made in the Bohemian town of Eger, which long enjoyed imperial privileges.[2] The border on the slanted lid of the present casket features fourteen flower motifs, dominated by the then extremely fashionable tulip.[3] The large panel in the center of the lid shows a scene with Saint George and is inscribed on a scroll S.GEORGIVS. This patron of soldiers was popular during the seventeenth century in all southern European Catholic regions, but especially in Bavaria (see fig. 58). Surrounding the panels and running along the lid and base are ripple moldings that reflect light and enliven the straight lines of the casket, indulging the Baroque passion for movement.

This celebrated casket was one of the centerpieces of the first exhibition devoted to the subject of Eger marquetry, held in Leipzig in 1999.[4] The present author has pointed out that proximity to Prague, where the memory of Rudolf II's court workshop and splendid Kunstkammer lingered on through decades of economic decline during the Thirty Years' War, inspired the gifted cabinetmakers of Eger to imitate the techniques of hardstone mosaic in locally available, affordable materials.[5]

In Eger marquetry, shaped pieces of relief veneer of different woods are fitted together on a support panel to create decorative or narrative compositions, producing an effect not unlike that of a relief commesso di pietre dure. And, as is also the case with stone, the use of diverse woods to form an artistic work has the appeal of combining ars and natura.[6]

Adolf Feuler had pointed out in 1927 that the marquetry technique was practiced in isolated instances as early as the fifteenth century at the monastery of Sacra Monte sopra Varese, Milan,[7] but his observation was not taken into account by other scholars until 1992.[8]

Adam Eck (1604–1664) was the most prominent member of a dynasty of Bohemian cabinetmakers who practiced the Eger marquetry technique. They produced for the most part magnificent collector's cabinets and precious objects that were often given by the town council of Eger as gifts to visiting dignitaries.[9] Stylistically, this casket is close to other works created by Eck.

WK

1. Similar feet are found on a cabinet in the Museum Schloss Burgk an der Saale, Germany (Voigt 1999, p. 175, fig. 159, pp. 294–95, no. I.48) and another at Schloss Neuenstein in Hohenlohe, Germany (ibid., p. 148, fig. 127, pp. 261–62, no. I.9).
2. Nagler 1835–52, vol. 18 (1848), p. 181.
3. Goes 2004.
4. Voigt 1999, p. 11, fig. 3, p. 326, no. III.3.
5. Koeppe 1992, pp. 235–37, no. M139 (the Hearst Cabinet).
6. Ibid., p. 236.
7. Feulner 1927, p. 390.
8. Sturm 1961, pp. 31ff., does not mention it; Jochen Voigt (1999) does not refer to the theory of the present author about the evolution of the technique but does mention entries M139 and M140 in Koeppe 1992, in which the theory is discussed in a different context.
9. Voigt 1999, pp. 105–22 (diplomatic gifts and patrons).

54. Jewelry box

Galleria dei Lavori, Florence, ca. 1720–30
Design by Giovanni Battista Foggini
Lapis lazuli, jasper, agate, chalcedony and other hardstones, marble, and slate, oak and ebony frame, gilded bronze mounts with semiprecious stones; 13¾ × 20¾ × 17 in. (34.9 × 52.7 × 43.2 cm)
Minneapolis Institute of Arts, Gift of funds from Bruce B. Dayton 86.85

PROVENANCE: Possibly Prince Marc de Beauvau Craon, governor of Tuscany (d. 1754); acquired by the Minneapolis Institute of Arts, 1986

REFERENCES: Minneapolis Institute of Arts 1998, p. 58, ill.; González-Palacios 2004b, p. 44, fig. 6 (as "present whereabouts unknown"); Minneapolis Institute of Arts forthcoming

Boxes of this type were made by the Florentine grand-ducal workshops either as luxurious display items for the use of the Medici themselves or as diplomatic gifts to the kings and courtiers of Europe. The simple form offered rather large, flat surfaces on which to display the superior skill of the Florentine pietre dure masters and, by extension, suggest the grandeur of Florence's ruling dynasty. Drawings of related caskets and bronze mounts by the designer of this box, Giovanni Battista Foggini (1652–1725), in the Gabinetto Disegni e Stampe degli Uffizi in Florence,[1] together with a drawing by Foggini in the Minneapolis Institute of Arts[2] that shows a mask stylistically related to the ones in hardstone inserted into the corner decorations here, demonstrate that the design for the present object was Foggini's, although perhaps executed after his death. The use of flesh-colored chalcedony (calcedonio di Volterra) instead of the usual bronze for the faces at the corners of the box (compare cat. no. 52)[3] may have been intended to convey a special message. If, for example, the box was to be a bridal gift, these hardstone faces that never age and never wrinkle would remind the mortal recipient that human beauty is fleeting. Similar chalcedony masks appear on Foggini's cabinet for the elector Palatine (see cat. no. 59) and on the Badminton Cabinet (fig. 87).[4]

The selection of hardstones on this box appears very carefully considered, with each piece chosen not only for its intense color but also for its purity or its unusual natural markings and veins. These refined colorations and their interplay on the box are enhanced by the bold bands of Sicilian red jasper and the dark ebony frame, an arresting combination. The corners of the otherwise rectangular wooden body are angled, evoking the floor plan of a Baroque fortress, and the architectural look of the piece is intensified by the projecting moldings of the lid and base. The gilded bronze scrolling feet that seem playfully to grasp and lift the canted base give a sophisticated Baroque movement to the object.

Because the casket is a veritable sampler of techniques, it gives a good idea of the number of different specialties practiced in the grand-ducal workshops and about the division of labor there. As artistic director and principal designer, Foggini would have coordinated and supervised the team of specialists on this project—from the stonecutters and stone carvers who produced the three-dimensional corner masks and flat floral inlay to the cabinetmakers, metalworkers, chasers, and gilders. The back is slightly less elaborate than the front, giving the piece a clear orientation and indicating that it was intended to be displayed against a backdrop. It may originally have been placed on its own carved stand. Similarities in the detailing and use of materials on this box and on the Badminton Cabinet, as well as the striking juxtapositions of colors in both pieces, suggest a date of about 1720–30 or later, toward the end of the Medici era. The catalogue of the most recent auction of the Badminton Cabinet (2004) illustrates this jewelry box and includes a caption to the effect that it was presumably made for Prince Marc de Beauvau Craon (1679–1754), governor of Tuscany after the death of the last Medici ruler, Gian Gastone, in 1737.[5]

W K

1. González-Palacios 1969, figs. 10, 11.
2. Acc. no. 64.54.2, Gift of Mr. Anthony M. Clark.
3. For the use of bronze masks as corner ornaments on other boxes, see González-Palacios 1969, figs. 5, 9; Christie's: Review 1990, p. 273.
4. Christie's 2004, ill. pp. 74–75; González-Palacios 2004b, ill. p. 40.
5. González-Palacios 2004b, p. 44, fig. 6; the caption indicates that the whereabouts of the box were unknown at that time. The photograph shows the object with parts of the molding and hardstone decoration missing. The present box has been restored; nevertheless, it is certainly the one seen in the photograph because the veining of the stones is the same on both pieces.

55. Prie-dieu made for the electress Palatine

Galleria dei Lavori, Florence, 1706
Design by Giovanni Battista
Foggini; lapidary work by
Giuseppe Antonio Torricelli;
cabinetry by Adam Suster
Ebony and hardstones, gilded
bronze mounts; 36¼ × 26⅞ ×
20½ in. (92 × 68 × 52 cm)
Palazzo Pitti, Florence,
Appartamenti Reali
OA 1911:386

PROVENANCE: Galleria dei Lavori,
Florence; Residenz, Düsseldorf,
1706; Palazzo Pitti, Florence,
from 1717

REFERENCES: Zobi 1853, pp. 275–
76; Lankheit 1962, pp. 64, 322,
doc. nos. 608, 609, fig. 246;
Aschengreen Piacenti and
González-Palacios in *Twilight
of the Medici* 1974, p. 348, no. 194;
González-Palacios 1977e, p. 58,
fig. 14; Giusti in Baldini, Giusti,
and Pampaloni Martelli 1979,
p. 279, no. 81, pl. 102; González-
Palacios 1986, vol. 1, pp. 50–51,
vol. 2, fig. 134; Colle in Giusti
1988, p. 182, no. 48; Giusti 1992,
pp. 109–10, pl. 45; Massinelli 1993,
fig. 128; Colle in Colle 1997,
pp. 233–34, no. 73; Colle in Colle,
Griseri, and Valeriani 2001,
p. 80, no. 25; Giusti 2003, p. 254,
fig. 24; Giusti in Casciu 2006, p. 276,
no. 143; Giusti 2006b, pp. 98–99

This extraordinary prie-dieu, or prayer stool, was one of the magnificent furnishings Cosimo III de' Medici sent to his daughter Anna Maria Luisa, who in 1691 had married Johann Wilhelm, the elector Palatine, and moved to his court in Düsseldorf. The grand duke of Tuscany generously gave precious objects created in his famous Florentine workshops to courts across Europe, but he saved the best for his cherished daughter. The most superb pieces were made in the early eighteenth century, when the workshops were directed by Giovanni Battista Foggini (1652–1725), an artist of inexhaustible inventiveness. The craftsmen he oversaw were also consummate masters in their own specialties.

In 1705 Cosimo sent two clocks to Düsseldorf, and a year later he dispatched this prie-dieu designed by Foggini and intended for Anna Maria Luisa's private devotions. Austerity is banished from this magnificent piece of furniture in favor of the Baroque taste for the theatrical and the luxurious exaltation of precious materials.

As in much of Foggini's furniture, ebony, gilded bronze, and semiprecious stones are combined with a sensuality that invites the viewer to touch the silky surface of the wood—worked by Foggini's contemporary, Adam Suster—or to caress the heads of the cherubs, whose soft-looking hair is in reality carved from rock-hard chalcedony. Made by Giuseppe Antonio Torricelli (1659–1719), the greatest master of Florentine mosaic employed in the workshops at the time the piece was manufactured, these cherubs' heads were cut from a single piece of Volterran chalcedony. They are among the finest examples of Torricelli's skilled manipulation of nuances in the stone to achieve a chromatic effect, which moves from the flesh tones of the faces to the cherubs' blond hair. Hardstones were also used in the exuberant and naturalistic swags laden with colorful fruit, recurring devices in Foggini's work. Here they are enlarged to a monumental scale without losing any of their gracefulness.

The prie-dieu's hinged top can be flipped up to provide access to a small storage space, perhaps for a prayer book. The top of the kneeling board also lifts, revealing a perfect place in which to store a cushion.   AG

56. Reliquary of Saint Ambrose

Galleria dei Lavori, Florence, 1705
By Giuseppe Antonio Torricelli,
Cosimo Merlini, Cristofano
Vincler, Pietro Motti, and Giovanni
Battista Foggini, after a design by
Giovanni Battista Foggini
Ebony, hardstones, silver, and
gilded bronze; H. 26¾ in. (68 cm)
Museo delle Cappelle Medicee,
Florence, Tesoro di San Lorenzo 39

PROVENANCE: Cappella Reale,
Palazzo Pitti, Florence; Basilica
di San Lorenzo, Florence, 1785;
Museo delle Cappelle Medicee,
from 1945

REFERENCES: Zobi 1853, p. 263;
Lankheit 1962, pp. 61–62, 322,
doc. nos. 601, 604; Aschengreen
Piacenti and González-Palacios in
Twilight of the Medici 1974, p. 346,
no. 193; Monaci 1977, p. 122, no. 6;
Giusti in Baldini, Giusti, and
Pampaloni Martelli 1979, pp. 297–
98, no. 117, pl. 173; Siponta De
Salvia 1984, ill. p. 338; Nardinocchi
in *San Lorenzo* 1993, pp. 176–77,
no. 3.21; Nardinocchi in Bertani
and Nardinocchi 1995, p. 66, no. 21

This reliquary was part of a series of such works that Cosimo III de' Medici commissioned from the grand-ducal workshops for various court chapels (see cat. no. 57). Now named for Saint Ambrose, it originally contained the relics of Daniel, the Old Testament prophet represented in relief on the pietre dure plaque at the center.

The Giornale dei Lavori della Galleria Medicea, the workshops' ledger, records that the reliquary was finished on October 13, 1705, and lists the names of the craftsmen who made it.[1] Giovanni Battista Foggini, artistic director of the workshop and himself a sculptor, designed and executed the bronze ornaments, combining sculptural elements and naturalistic details, such as the massive garlands of fruit and the springy cartouche-shaped legs, as he often did in the furniture he designed for the workshop. A good example of Foggini's

exuberant decorative style, this reliquary must have been intended as a pendant for that of Saint Mary of Egypt, finished the year before and in almost exactly the same form—from the vibrant figures of angels supporting the rock crystal container to the acanthus leaves and fruit garlands framing the central medallion.[2]

The other expert craftsmen who collaborated on the piece included Pietro Motti, who was responsible for the fire-gilding of the bronzes modeled and cast by Foggini; the goldsmith Cosimo Merlini, who made the silver supports for the urn; and Cristofano Vincler, carver of the fruit that seems to erupt from the swollen garlands. Giuseppe Antonio Torricelli made the marvelous pietre dure mosaic relief of *Daniel in the Lions' Den*, demonstrating his virtuosity by shaping the hardstone into seeming soft forms and deftly using translucent stones for lions' manes and the rocks in the background. Torricelli also carved the rock crystal container for

the relics, a material that had been used for sacred objects since medieval times because it was seen as a symbol of divine light and purity. Documents mention that the woodworker Sabatino Franchini made the reliquary's now-lost walnut case; perhaps he was also responsible for its elegantly shaped ebony base.

This reliquary and the others in the series held little appeal for Grand Duke Peter Leopold, a man of Neoclassical tastes; in 1785 he gave them to San Lorenzo in return for the fourteenth- and fifteenth-century vases that had belonged to Lorenzo the Magnificent (see cat. no. 7), which he then transferred to the Palazzo degli Uffizi.

A G

1. Published in Lankheit 1962, p. 322, doc. no. 604.
2. See Giusti in Baldini, Giusti, and Pampaloni Martelli 1979, p. 297, no. 116, pl. 172. This reliquary, too, is now in the Museo delle Cappelle Medicee.

57. Reliquary of Saint Emeric

Galleria dei Lavori, Florence, 1698 and 1717
By Giuseppe Antonio Torricelli
Ebony, diamonds, rubies, amethysts, and other hardstones, gold, gilded bronze, and gilded copper; H. 29½ in. (75 cm)
Museo delle Cappelle Medicee, Florence, Tesoro di San Lorenzo 137

PROVENANCE: Cappella delle Reliquie, Palazzo Pitti, Florence, 1753; transferred to the Basilica di San Lorenzo, Florence, 1785; Museo delle Cappelle Medicee, from 1945

REFERENCES: Zobi 1853, pp. 260–61; Lankheit 1962, pp. 60–61, 325, doc. no. 627, fig. 241; Aschengreen Piacenti and González-Palacios in *Twilight of the Medici* 1974, p. 370, no. 209; Giusti in Baldini, Giusti, and Pampaloni Martelli 1979, p. 298, no. 119, pl. 177; Siponta De Salvia 1984, ill. p. 339; Maria Sframeli in Giusti 1988, p. 180, no. 47; Tuena 1992a, p. 202; Nardinocchi in Bertani and Nardinocchi 1995, p. 70, no. 23; Monica Bietti in Giusti 2006a, p. 72, no. 12

Although this reliquary was finished in 1717 and is generally dated to that time, recently it has been suggested that it was designed earlier.[1] In 1698 the famous ebony worker Leonardo van der Vinne was paid for a wood model in the form of an altar: "a design for the reliquary of Saint Emeric to be made in pietre dure by Giuseppe Antonio Torricelli."[2] Torricelli, the greatest gem carver of his day, was then given colors with which to paint the model, since it was common practice in the workshop for color to be indicated on the wood or wax model of a pietre dure object as an aid in choosing the stones. Then, for some unknown reason, work on the piece either proceeded very slowly or, more likely, was suspended, and it was not finished until about twenty years after the model was made, spurred on, perhaps, because of pressure exerted on the workshop by Cosimo III.

Compared to other works that can be dated to Giovanni Battista Foggini's tenure as director of the grand-ducal workshops (beginning in 1694), this reliquary is one in which the gilded bronze elements play a relatively subdued role, forming rays of light that surround and enhance the swirl

of clouds, angels, and the figures of Mary and Christ, all of which are carved from hardstone. The scene represents the vision of Saint Emeric, the son of Saint Stephen, first king of Hungary (in the workshop documents he is sometimes referred to as Ermenegildo). Dressed in royal regalia, Emeric kneels in front of an altar above which he sees a vision of the Pietà.

It is likely that Torricelli, who was also a sculptor, was responsible for both the marvelously carved pietre dure elements and the overall composition of the piece, which is remarkable for the harmonious and rhythmic group of angels who carry the symbols of Christ's Passion; for the effective handling of the dead Christ, who seems almost to fall from his mother's outstretched arms; and, finally, for the refined execution of the saint, carved in the round, whose eloquent pose recalls the figure of Cosimo II in prayer in the ex-voto of 1624 (see cat. no. 35). Emeric is dressed in Bohemian red agate and has a mantle of yellow Sicilian jasper lined with purple amethyst. His garments are edged with a delicate border of gold set with small diamonds and rubies; his legs are clad in red Gururate agate and his boots made from

57

Casentino flint. The cuffs of his boots, the upper part of his robe, and the sword imbedded in the ground in front of him are studded with diamonds and rubies set in delicate gold fretwork. Although no artist's name is recorded in any of the documents, these exquisite appliqués were surely the work of one of the goldsmiths active in the workshop.

The design of the work has been attributed to Foggini.[3] Although the reliquary is rather simple compared to his more complex creations, the bril-liant, Bernini-esque rays certainly recall his oeuvre, contributing, as they do in other contemporary objects, to the theatrical effect of the whole.[4]

AG

1. Nardinocchi in Bertani and Nardinocchi 1995, p. 70, no. 23; this opinion was affirmed by Monica Bietti in Giusti 2006a, p. 72, no. 12.
2. Document quoted in ibid.
3. Lankheit 1962, pp. 60–61.
4. An example is the holy-water stoup made for the electress Palatine that is now in the Palazzo Pitti (see entry for cat. no. 58).

58. Holy-water stoup

Galleria dei Lavori, Florence,
early 18th century
Design by Giovanni Battista
Foggini; lapidary work by
Giuseppe Antonio Torricelli
Hardstones and gilded bronze;
30¾ × 18⅛ × 4¾ in. (78 × 46 × 12 cm)
Museo dell'Opificio delle Pietre
Dure, Florence 1905:1615

PROVENANCE: Palazzo Pitti,
Florence; Museo dell'Opificio,
from 1905

Stoups for holy water of this type, fairly common bedroom furnishings at the court of Cosimo III de' Medici, were used during private prayers. One identical to this is in the collection of the Palazzo Pitti in Florence.[1] In 1704 Cosimo sent a larger font of a different design as a gift to his daughter, Anna Maria Luisa, the electress Palatine, at the court in Düsseldorf.[2] While a small basin is the functional element of such objects, an Annunciation decorates all of these stoups, as it does other devotional objects made for Cosimo III.[3] The composition was inspired by a famous fourteenth-century fresco in the Church of Santissima Annunziata in Florence, a work that had long been the object of a devotional cult and one that was especially important to the grand duke.

The sumptuously exuberant taste of Giovanni Battista Foggini (1652–1725), who directed the grand-ducal workshops from 1694 until his death, is immediately evident in these three fonts. Foggini made designs for various projects undertaken by the grand-ducal workshops as well as three-dimensional models for objects to be carved from hardstone and embellished with elements fashioned in gilded bronze. He had been deeply impressed by the decorative taste of the Roman

REFERENCES: Zobi 1853, p. 276; Bartoli and Maser 1953, pp. 13–14, 31–32; Giusti in Giusti, Mazzoni, and Pampaloni Martelli 1978, p. 314, no. 440, pl. 363; Giusti in Giusti 1988, p. 170, no. 42; Giusti in Giusti et al. 2004, p. 218; Giusti in Giusti 2006a, p. 69, no. 9

High Baroque when he visited Rome as a student; that influence is evident here in the Bernini-esque rays that unify this holy-water font and are its most characteristic feature. Rays occur in some of Foggini's other works (see the reliquary of Saint Emeric, cat. no. 57) but are especially prominent here because they form a backdrop for the diaphanous mass of chalcedony clouds from which the dove of the Holy Spirit emerges.

The design and execution of the bronze elements on this piece are extraordinary, and the lapidary work is no less magisterial. The heads of the angel and the Virgin, for example, are each adroitly carved from a single piece of Volterran chalcedony. The lighter parts of the stone were used to evoke the delicate hues of the faces and the blond hair, each represented by a different tone in the stone. The various colors of the chalcedony were used with the same skill in the head of the cherub between the garlands of fruit. The latter are very similar to, although much smaller and of lesser quality than, those on the electress Palatine's prie-dieu (cat. no. 55). No surviving documents make reference to this holy-water container, but the evidence of the object itself suggests that the hardstones were carved by Giuseppe Antonio Torricelli (1659–1719) and should be dated to about the same time as the objects made for the electress.   AG

1. OA no. 805.
2. Giusti in Casciu 2006, p. 274, no. 141 (with bibliography).
3. Among them are a plaque, sent to Pope Innocent XII in 1700 (see Massinelli in Giusti 1988, p. 178, no. 46), and a wall plaque made later and sent to the margravine of Baden in the same year, now in the Rijksmuseum, Amsterdam (see Giusti in Giusti 2006a, pp. 70–71, no. 10).

59. Cabinet made for the elector Palatine

Galleria dei Lavori, Florence, 1709
Design by Giovanni Battista Foggini; original lapidary work probably by Giuseppe Antonio Torricelli (some panels replaced in 1836); cabinetry by Adam Suster
Ebony, hardstones, gilded bronze, mother-of-pearl, rock crystal; 9 ft. 2¼ × 63¾ × 21¼ in. (280 × 162 × 54 cm)
Museo degli Argenti, Palazzo Pitti, Florence OA 1911:909

PROVENANCE: Galleria dei Lavori, Florence; Residenz, Düsseldorf, 1710; Palazzo Pitti, Florence, from 1717; Museo degli Argenti, Palazzo Pitti, by 1911

REFERENCES: Zobi 1853, pp. 273–74; Lankheit 1962, pp. 65–66, 323–24, doc. nos. 614–17, figs. 248–50; Jörg Gamer in Europäische Barockplastik 1971, pp. 399–401, no. 369, pls. 230, 231; Aschengreen Piacenti and González-Palacios in Twilight of the Medici 1974, p. 348, no. 195; Giusti in Baldini, Giusti, and Pampaloni Martelli 1979, pp. 260–62, no. 14, pls. 29–35; Colle in Giusti 1988, p. 184, no. 49; Giusti 1992, pp. 111–12, pls. 48, 49; Bohr 1993, pp. 188–90, no. 1.31, figs. 84–87; Massinelli 1993, fig. 129; Colle in Colle 1997, pp. 222–27, no. 70; Giusti 1997a, p. 193; Colle 2000, pp. 182–84, no. 43; Mosco 2004a, pp. 159–60, fig. 9; Giusti in Casciu 2006, pp. 277–78, no. 144; Giusti 2006b, p. 102, ill. no. 84

Even among the extraordinary gifts Cosimo III de' Medici sent at the turn of the eighteenth century to his daughter Anna Maria Luisa in Düsseldorf, this cabinet is remarkable. It was intended for her husband, Johann Wilhelm, the elector Palatine, who is portrayed in the cabinet's central niche, sculpted in chalcedony and gilded bronze and seated on military trophies symbolic of the martial virtues (see fig. 88). The complementary virtues of magnanimity and strength are represented by the two bronze figures of women reclining on the pediment above the niche.

Crowning the cabinet is an attic story where the elector's heraldic symbols and motto, "Dominus virtutum nobiscum" (The Lord of hosts is with us),[1] appear. The triumphal and purely decorative motifs used in this work—to produce, on the one hand, a sense of theatrical grandeur and, on the other, an exquisite perfection of detail—are in absolute balance, making the cabinet one of the masterpieces of the European Baroque. This remains true despite some damage suffered in the nineteenth century. Seven mosaic panels on the front of the cabinet and an eighth on its base were removed in 1826, and only some of them were replaced in 1836. The three narrow mosaic panels at the bottom of the facade are original; the others either are copies or, in an already historicizing attempt to honor the cabinet's original style, were cannibalized from other pieces of furniture dating from the end of the Medici dynasty.

The concealed features that characterize the interior of the cabinet are still intact. Reflecting the Baroque desire to amaze, the two upper doors hide six drawers, the fronts of which are inlaid with mother-of-pearl that gleams on an ebony ground. There is another trio of hidden drawers in the lower fascia of the cabinet, behind the three original mosaic panels, and four with rosewood veneer behind the door in the base. The most magnificent surprise awaits the viewer behind the two largest doors, which flank the central niche. They open to reveal two symmetrical spaces decorated with mirrors and hardstone columns, and each contains a circle of five dancing putti beneath a tiny but perfect crystal chandelier in a miniature room.

The vivid imagination of Giovanni Battista Foggini (1652–1725) was given full rein in this work, which was begun in 1707 and completed two years later. It was made according to his design, and he himself modeled the sculptural elements in bronze. The whole is a graceful combination balancing the design's architectonic sensibility—deeply rooted in the Florentine tradition—with Baroque exuberance evident in the sculptural and decorative elements. Although no documents have been found to prove it, the gem carver Giuseppe Antonio Torricelli (1659–1719) probably also worked on this cabinet. Framed by the translucent curls of his chalcedony wig, the elector's face demonstrates the same power of observation as that marking Torricelli's monumental bust of Vittoria della Rovere of about 1697 (cat. no. 49).   AG

1. Psalms, 46:7.

60. Table with top depicting flowers, fruit, and birds

Tabletop: Galleria dei Lavori, Florence, ca. 1710–20
Hardstones
Base: By George Bullock, London, 19th century
Wood
H. 28 ½ in. (72.4 cm), Diam. 52 ¼ in. (132.7 cm)
Private collection

PROVENANCE: Probably Sir George Byng (ca. 1720–d. 1733); by family descent, until 2005 (sale, Christie's, London, June 9, 2005, lot 50); acquired at that sale by a private collector

REFERENCES: González-Palacios 2005; Giusti in Giusti 2006a, pp. 65–66, no. 6

This octagonal tabletop recently appeared on the art market.[1] It was previously unknown and represents an important addition to the group of surviving objects produced in the grand-ducal workshops in Florence at the end of the Medici era. An oral tradition attaches it to Sir George Byng, who held the office of British Plenipotentiary to the Princes and States of Italy from 1718 to 1720. Byng was in Florence in 1720 for Cosimo III de' Medici's birthday celebrations, and perhaps on that occasion he came into possession of this work. The piece is of such splendor that it seems unlikely it was a gift from the grand duke to the English gentleman, who had not yet been made first Viscount Torrington and thus was not yet of the first rank. Instead, Byng might have ordered it directly from the grand-ducal workshops, which were struggling financially under the last of the Medici grand dukes;[2] however, the lapidary work is so richly decorative and complex that the tabletop certainly took a number of years to create and therefore likely predates Byng's brief sojourn in Italy. Perhaps he purchased it from a previous owner.

The compositional and formal qualities of the table's naturalistic decoration appear to support a date between 1710 and 1720. The resplendent floral garland recalls the style of some Florentine painters at the end of the seventeenth century and the beginning of the eighteenth who specialized in painting flowers, such as Bartolomeo Bimbi and Andrea Scacciati. Scacciati (1642–1710) collaborated with the masters of hardstone mosaic during the time Giovanni Battista Foggini directed the Florentine workshops. Documents record that in 1698 the painter "colored" a drawing by Foggini for a chest "with hardstone mosaics of flowers" and in 1700 did another drawing "for a clockface . . . with grotesques, flowers, and birds . . . an invention of Sig. Foggini."[3] Certainly a painted *modello* for this tabletop could have been made at about that time by an accomplished flower painter such as Scacciati, for the work reveals a consummate knowledge of natural forms and an imagination inventive enough to produce a design with thirty-three different types of flowers and twenty-one different fruits as well as sixteen kinds of birds and eight insects. An astonishingly large selection of semiprecious stones was used to make this ensemble—at first glance, it seems to contain the whole vast assortment of stones so feverishly collected by the Medici. We can assume that, as was so often the case, an artist worked with the skilled masters of pietre dure. He, and perhaps Foggini himself, would have guided them in the choice of colors, so that the stone palette would imbue with a perennial freshness the myriad natural forms represented in this masterpiece.

The fact that an elaborate wooden base was made for the table in the nineteenth century is evidence that pietre dure was highly appreciated in the Britain of George IV.   AG

1. Christie's, London, June 9, 2005, sale cat., lot 50.
2. In the 1720s the duke of Beaufort commissioned the *Badminton Cabinet* (fig. 87) for his own collection, from the Galleria dei Lavori in Florence; see Kräftner 2007.
3. Lankheit 1962, p. 318, doc. nos. 567, 568.

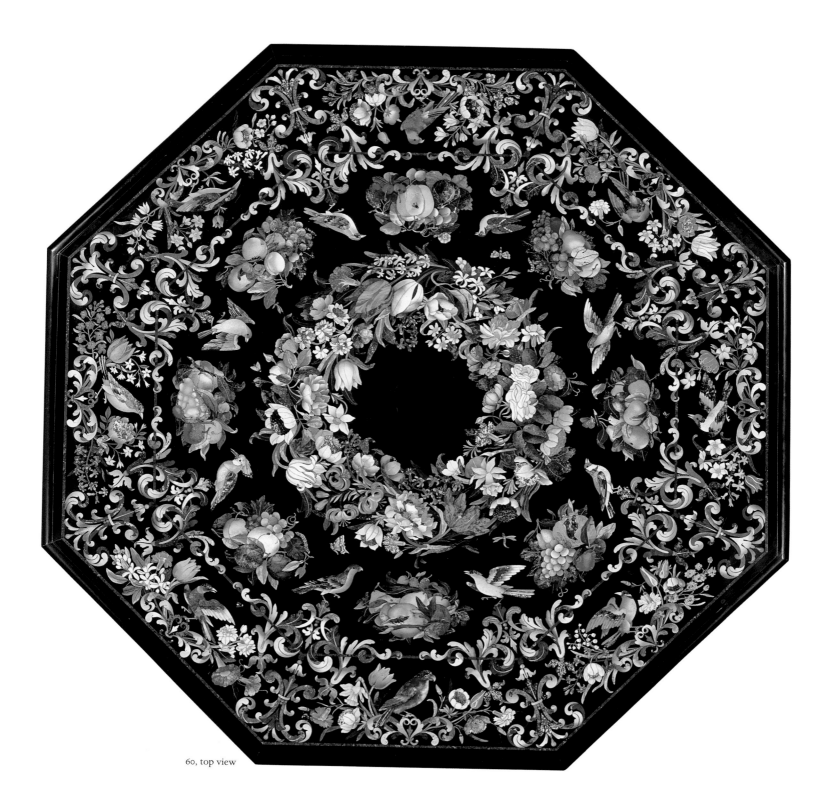

60, top view

61. Panel depicting flowers in an urn

By Gennaro Mannelli, Salerno,
1726
Scagliola on slate; 37⅜ × 20½ in.
(95 × 52 cm)
Signed and dated: *Januarius
Mannelli / Salernitanus / excudendo
pingebat / Anno Dom^{ni}: 1726*
Helen Costantino Fioratti,
New York

REFERENCE: Fioratti 2004,
ill. no. 449

Scagliola, a term derived from *scaglia* (Italian for "scales" or "chips"), is a technique by which a surface of finely crushed and polished gypsum is made to simulate marble and hardstone decorations.[1] In the sixteenth century scagliola was perfected as a less expensive and, if properly mastered, supposedly time-saving alternative to pietre dure. To make it, pulverized selenite and alabaster are diluted with glue and applied to a wet gesso or stone ground, creating a surface of intense colors that can be polished to a high gloss, similar to that of hardstone mosaic.

In the early seventeenth century Blasius Fistulator and his circle in Munich achieved a very high level of refinement using this unusual technique (see p. 61 and fig. 64). Whereas in Italy scagliola was seen mainly as an affordable substitute for hardstone, breccia, or colored marble, north of the Alps it was celebrated as an art form in its own right, and it was held in high esteem in England during the seventeenth and eighteenth centuries.[2] About 1740 the English writer and statesman Horace Walpole ordered a scagliola tabletop from the Florentine friar Ferdinando Henrico Hugford. Pleased with his purchase, Walpole asked his friend Sir Horace Mann, British envoy to Florence, for help in acquiring more scagliola works. Mann advised Walpole to "make the greater account of them [the ones he already had], as it is impossible to get any more of the same man [Hugford], nor indeed of his disciple here [Belloni], who is a priest too, and has been four years about a pair I bespoke of him. . . . They work for diversion and won't be hurried."[3]

The flowers on the present panel are arranged in a playful, somewhat unorthodox composition that can be compared to the compositions on the wooden inlaid panels and pietre dure inlays on a Florentine cabinet now in the Palazzo Vecchio.[4] As with pietre dure, each of the various centers of scagliola production had its own stylistic characteristics. The master who made this piece, Gennaro Mannelli, was part of the Neapolitan school, known for its airy, decorative creations, which extended to neighboring cities such as Salerno.[5] His knowledge of the tradition of floral still lifes and of the vogue across western Europe for all kinds of floral decor is evident.[6] Pietre dure and scagliola works are rarely fully signed and dated, as is the present panel. Mannelli is recorded as working for the d'Alvalos and Cito families of Naples and the Grimaldi family of Genoa.[7]

W K

1. Fleming and Honour 1989, "Scagliola," pp. 727–28;
   Prudon 1989.
2. Klein 1969.
3. Mann to Walpole, October 10, 1749, in Walpole 1960,
   p. 93. See also Fleming 1955, p. 109.
4. Bohr 1993, pp. 179–82, no. I.28, pp. 405, 406, fig. 73.
5. For other panels in the same airy Neapolitan style, see
   Fioratti 2004, p. 289, ill. nos. 447, 448.
6. Koeppe 1992, pp. 204–6, no. M106; Koeppe in *Liselotte von
   der Pfalz* 1996, p. 182, no. 297.
7. Information supplied by Helen Costantino Fioratti,
   New York.

62. Basilisk-shaped table ornament

Saracchi workshop, Milan,
ca. 1575–80
Rock crystal; 8¾ × 7¼ in. (22.2 ×
18.4 cm)
Mounts: ca. late 19th century
Attributed to Alfred André
Gold and enamel set with rubies,
diamonds, and other hardstones
The Metropolitan Museum of Art,
New York, Gift of J. Pierpont
Morgan, 1917 17.190.538

PROVENANCE: Lord Hastings;
J. Pierpont Morgan (1837–1913);
his gift to the Metropolitan
Museum, 1917

REFERENCES: Williamson 1910,
pp. 92–93, no. 61, pls. XXXIV, XL;
Hackenbroch 1984–85, p. 209, fig. 90

This rock crystal ornament in the shape of a legendary monster called a basilisk reflects the taste of the late sixteenth century for the grotesque.[1] Such virtuoso creations were made for display, not use. On special occasions, however, they might become part of a table arrangement that included other zoomorphic inventions executed in less valuable, often more ephemeral, but equally decorative materials, such as glass, puff pastry, brown sugar, or even ice.

This basilisk is in the form of a cockerel with a curly snakelike tail. The entire surface of the body is decorated with scales, arranged in such a way as to conceal small flaws in the rock crystal. If the transparent body were filled with a colored liquid—such as a gleaming gold white wine or a sumptuous red, or a colorful fruit liqueur—the object would be decorative indeed.

Although the circumstances of its making and its early history are not known, the presence of signs that in its original state the work had mounts shows that from the beginning it was meant for a princely collection. Collecting such marvels of virtuosity required enormous financial means and during the Renaissance became a distinctive mark of princely power. Especially north of the Alps, the demand for such luxury items was inexhaustible. The dukes of Bavaria built a multistory *Kunstkammer* to house their collection of nearly 3,500 precious objects, and an inventory of 1586–87 at the electoral treasury in Dresden turned up no less than forty-two vessels of rock crystal alone.[2]

The more-than-competent craftsmanship of this work cannot compare with the extraordinary finish and design of some of the inventions of Gasparo Miseroni, who dominated the art of rock crystal carving in Milan during the mid-sixteenth century.[3] Nevertheless, the basilisk's cabochon-cut ruby eyes are distinctively Milanese, and the object may well be a product of the Saracchi workshop, as seems likely from comparison with many Saracchi carvings in the Kunsthistorisches Museum in Vienna.[4] The present, much later gold mounts partly disguise broken areas, especially around the neck. They have been attributed by Clare Vincent to the French goldsmith and restorer Alfred André (1839–1919).[5]

WK

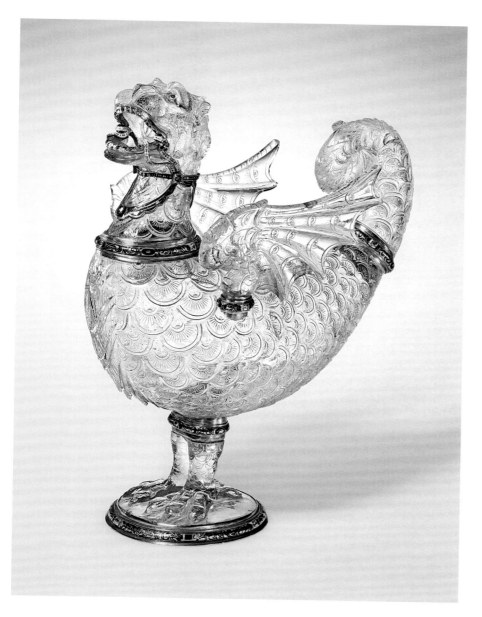

I am most grateful to Clare Vincent for discussing this item with me.

1. *Rabisch* 1998; see also Koeppe 2004, ill. pp. 83, 86, and p. 84, n. 26. The piece has stylistical and technical similarities to the rock crystal "fish-dragons" made at the Milanese Miseroni and Saracchi workshops during the late sixteenth century; see Distelberger 2002, p. 183, no. 98, p. 207, no. 120. The carving points to a member of the Saracchi workshop, but the carver has not yet been convincingly identified.
2. *Treasury in the Residenz Munich* 1988. See also Koeppe 2002a.
3. Distelberger 2002, pp. 173–87, nos. 90–101.
4. Ibid., pp. 201–7, nos. 115–21.
5. On André, see Distelberger 1993; Distelberger 2000.

63. Two plaques depicting scenes from the life of Hercules

Milan, before 1584
By Annibale Fontana
Rock crystal; gold and champlevé
enamel frame; each 3¹⁄₁₆ × 4¹⁄₁₆ in.
(7.8 × 10.3 cm)
The Metropolitan Museum of Art,
New York, The Friedsam
Collection, Bequest of Michael
Friedsam, 1931 32.100.237, 238

PROVENANCE: Probably part of a
casket in the collection of Duke
Vincenzo I Gonzaga (r. 1587–1612),
Mantua; Gonzaga collection, until
at least the late 1620s; Daniel Nys,
Venice; Agostino Correggio, in
1667; Spitzer collection; Juritzky
von Warberg; Michael Friedsam,
New York; his bequest to the
Metropolitan Museum, 1931

REFERENCES: Kris 1929, vol. 1,
pp. 109, 181, nos. 484, 485; Kris 1930,
p. 552, figs. 7, 8; Raggio 1952,
pp. 199–200, ill. pp. 196, 197; Raggio
1971, pp. 12–13, pl. 19a; Venturelli in
Rabisch 1998, pp. 269–70, nos. 64, 65;
Morselli 2002, pp. 290–91, no. 81, b, c;
Venturelli 2005, p. 125, figs. 53, 54

It is astonishing that the detailed pictorial compositions seen here were undertaken at all in the intransigent medium of rock crystal cutting and engraving. And why did the artist choose to disregard the one obvious advantage presented by the medium—its durability—by cutting the stone into thin plaques that are as fragile as glass? Projects of this sort, however, were part of the Mannerists' interest in breaking the barriers between art forms and then combining them in extraordinary displays of intellectual and technical accomplishment.

These two oval plaques were not conceived as individual treasures to be admired and handled; rather, they formed part of a series of intaglio engravings that once embellished an octagonal ebony casket.[1] They depict events in the life of Hercules, hero of Greek and Roman mythology: Hercules slaying the centaur Nessus (seen above) and Hercules overcoming the river god Acheloüs (below). These episodes are not among the Twelve Labors of Hercules, a popular theme for illustration in classical and Renaissance art. Paola Venturelli has suggested that the casket was one listed in the 1626–27 Gonzaga inventory and described there as "an ebony cassetta with twelve pieces of crystal engraved with scenes from the life of Hercules, with four Harpies as bases, studded with gold and pearls."[2] The fact that the inventory notes the scenes as from the life of Hercules rather than the Twelve Labors makes her suggestion very plausible. Alessandro Algardi had seen the precious casket in the Palazzo Ducale in Mantua in 1620, and in 1627 the German architect Fürrtenbach described it as one of the palazzo's chief "marvels."[3] Related caskets are known: Raffaello Borghini, in his 1584 treatise on art, mentioned a casket (perhaps the same as the one discussed here) for which the artist cut twelve plaques illustrating the Twelve Labors.[4] There is a casket with plaques by Fontana in the Schatzkammer in the Residenz, Munich, and another in the Palacio Real, Madrid. Why the Gonzaga casket was dismantled is not known. It may have been the victim of a change in fashion, or the last owner may have needed the precious metal mounts and gems for another purpose.

The Metropolitan Museum's plaques are fascinating for their subtle balance between matte areas of the intaglio and the clear, luminous background, and for the powerful modeling of the bodies. Hercules' overwhelming physical strength is conveyed by the violent swinging motion of the pelt of the Nemean lion flung over his shoulders. The beast's legs and curly tail billow in the air like the sail of a ship breasting a stormy ocean.

Annibale Fontana (1540–1587), a trained medal engraver and sculptor, was a specialist in delicate intaglios such as these. His imaginative compositions and magnificent anatomical renderings had a great influence on following generations.[5] In these plaques, he has captured the male human body in full action and immortalized it in one of the purest and hardest of materials, using just two surface treatments, engraving and polishing. The plaques represent the Milanese art of rock crystal carving at the highest level (for later developments, see "The Castrucci and the Miseroni" by Rudolf Distelberger in this publication). We can assume that in the case of an important commission such as this one, the head of the workshop and his assistants chose the raw material with the utmost care. The plaques were created in two steps by at least two artisans. The *arte grossa* master was responsible for grinding, cutting, and polishing the surface of the tablets. The execution of the intaglio engraving was done by Annibale Fontana, the *arte minuta* master, whose abilities were more highly valued. He had to transfer and adapt his composition to the stone. If he discovered any flaws in the crystal, he was the one who covered them up by changing the placement of elements of the design. Ultimately, he had to take responsibility for a perfect outcome, and there was never much room for mistakes.[6]

W K

I am most grateful to Olga Raggio, Distinguished Research Curator, and Clare Vincent, Associate Curator, Department of European Sculpture and Decorative Arts, Metropolitan Museum, for discussing this entry with me.
1. Distelberger 2002, pp. 130–31, no. 48, discusses the casket and lists the other plaques that once decorated it.
2. Venturelli 2001, pp. 141–44.
3. Schizzerotto 1981, pp. 140, 156.
4. Borghini 1584 (1967 ed.), p. 565; see also Distelberger 2002, p. 130.
5. Dante Isella, "Annibale Fontana," in Lomazzo 1589 (1993 ed.), pp. 342–44.
6. Rudolf Distelberger (2002, p. 130) observed some small slips in one plaque from the series, which the artist skillfully concealed by incorporating them into the overall design.

64. Flask with a cameo

Saracchi workshop, Milan,
mid-16th century
Jasper and sardonyx, enamel and
gold mounts set with pearls and
rubies; 10⅞ × 9⅝ in. (27.6 × 24.3 cm)
Museo degli Argenti, Palazzo Pitti,
Florence Gemme 1921:705

PROVENANCE: Catherine
de' Medici (d. 1589); her bequest to
her granddaughter Christina of
Lorraine (1565–1637), grand duchess
of Tuscany; entered the Palazzo
degli Uffizi, Florence, in 1609 and
the Museo degli Argenti in 1921

REFERENCES: Zobi 1853, pp. 52–53;
Rossi (Filippo) 1956, p. 50, pl. LXXIV;
Aschengreen Piacenti 1967, p. 139,
no. 203, pl. 20; Hayward 1976, p. 369,
pl. 335; Fock in *Palazzo Vecchio* 1980,
p. 232, no. 445; Barocchi and Gaeta
Bertelà 1990, p. 555, n. 9; Massinelli
1992, pp. 110, 111; Mario Scalini in
Magnificenza alla corte dei Medici
1997, p. 157, no. 118; Aschengreen
Piacenti 2003, p. 38, fig. 5; Maria
Sframeli in Giusti et al. 2004, p. 120;
Mosco 2004c, p. 78, fig. 21

The body of this flask, one of the preeminent pieces in the Medici collection of vases, was carved from a type of Sicilian jasper referred to in the archival documents as *corallino* because of the vivid red veins that stand out against the stone's yellow ground. The shape of the flask derives from that of a cockleshell. The band of gold that runs around the body is studded with four rubies and four pearls on each side. A sardonyx cameo has been set in the center of one side of the flask. It represents the head of a Saracen woman; the craftsman who carved it made exquisite use of the layers of color in the stone so that the brown head stands out against the milky ground of the oval. The cameo has an enameled frame set with four rubies.

There was originally a second cameo in the center of the other side of the flask, carved with the head of a Moor. It was lost about 1768, when the keeper of the Galleria degli Uffizi, Giuseppe Bianchi, stole pieces from some of the most precious vases in the collection.[1] At the same time, the flask was also stripped of its gold chain, twenty pearls (the 1609 Uffizi inventory describes it as having twenty-eight pearls, and at present only eight remain), and several emeralds.[2]

Although no longer as valuable as it was originally, this flask remains an exceptional example of the work produced in the Milanese workshop of the Saracchi family, the gem carvers to whom the work is attributed. In the sixteenth century their shop was one of the most famous in Milan, and it received commissions from a number of European courts. This flask was ordered for the French royal family. By tradition, it was made for Catherine de' Medici, who then bequeathed it to her granddaughter Christina of Lorraine. Possibly, however, the flask was commissioned by King Henry II Valois, king of France, Catherine's husband.[3] The shell that inspired its shape is a heraldic symbol of the French royal house and also appears in the collar worn by the group of loyal nobles who constituted the Order of Saint-Michel, founded by King Louis XI and of special importance to Francis I and his son Henry II.

This flask must have been among the precious objects Christina of Lorraine brought with her to Florence when she married Grand Duke Ferdinand I in 1589. It was first mentioned in the inventory of 1609 and apparently remained for some time among her personal possessions. She finally gave it to her grandson Ferdinando II de' Medici in 1635.

By the time the flask came to Florence, the craftsmen of the grand-ducal workshops were expert in executing pietre dure vases and sculptures (see, for example, cat. no. 24), but when it was made, in the middle of the previous century, Milan was considered the more important center of gem carving, for reasons that the flask's very refined cameo makes evident. Its exotic subject matter, much in vogue for cameos at the time, was handled with an exquisite softness in the modeling and an extraordinary skill in exploiting the layers of color in the stone.

A G

1. See entry for cat. no. 22 for the theft of pieces of Bernardo Buontalenti's lapis lazuli flask. The documents concerning Giuseppe Bianchi's trial for theft in 1768–69 are published in Barocchi and Gaeta Bertelà 1990.
2. The inventory was quoted by Mario Scalini in *Magnificenza alla corte dei Medici* 1997, p. 157, no. 118.
3. Scalini in ibid.; Mosco 2004c, p. 78.

detail

Northern Europe, Seventeenth and
Eighteenth Centuries

65. Shell-shaped cup carved with a monster's head

Miseroni workshop, Milan,
ca. 1556
By Gasparo Miseroni
Bloodstone; 3⅜ × 7⅞ × 4¾ in.
(8.5 × 20 × 12 cm)
Museo degli Argenti, Palazzo
Pitti, Florence Gemme 1921:764

PROVENANCE: Cosimo I de' Medici
(mentioned in 1560 and 1570 inventories of the Medici collection);
Gabinetto delle Gemme, Palazzo
degli Uffizi, Florence; entered
the Museo degli Argenti, 1921

REFERENCES: Vasari 1568 (1878–85
ed.), vol. 5, p. 389; Kris 1929, vol. 1,
p. 188, no. 593; *Le Triomphe du
maniérisme européen* 1955, p. 216,
no. 475; Aschengreen Piacenti 1967,
p. 140, no. 235; Heikamp 1971,
pp. 198–99, fig. 11; Fock 1976, pp. 123–
24, fig. 4; Distelberger 1978, p. 83,
fig. 51; Fock in *Palazzo Vecchio*
1980, pp. 220–21, no. 415; Venturelli
in *Rabisch* 1998, p. 275, no. 80;
Distelberger 2002, pp. 134–35,
no. 52; Aschengreen Piacenti 2003,
p. 39; Distelberger 2003, p. 88, fig. 1

In the second edition of his *Lives*, Georgio Vasari wrote of a piece that was "marvelous for its size and amazing for its carving." In 1976 C. W. Fock recognized the present cup, thought to have been executed in Florence, as the work of the Milanese gem carver Gasparo Miseroni (1518–ca. 1573), who made it for Cosimo I de' Medici.[1] Fock was able to associate it with a payment of 200 scudi sent to Miseroni on January 14, 1557, as part of the 300 scudi he was to be paid for "making a large, bloodstone vase." This same object was also described in the grand-ducal inventory of 1560 as "a bloodstone cup half a braccia long with a satyr carved into it."

Later inventories that list the cup mention a serpent rather than a satyr, but this discrepancy can be seen as confirming the fantastical nature of this monster, whose coils constitute the rim of the cup and at the same time define its form. Once the cup had been identified as Gasparo Miseroni's work, it was possible to attribute to him a lapis lazuli cup that is similar both in its design and in the quality of its carving.[2] It was among the objects Catherine de' Medici left to her grand-daughter Christina of Lorraine, who brought it to Florence in 1589 when she married Ferdinand I.

Milan was the recognized center for the pro-duction of vases carved from rock crystal and col-ored stone until Francesco de' Medici brought the Caroni and Gaffurri workshops, both Milanese, to Florence in the early 1570s. Until then the Medici went to Milan when they wanted such objects. Gasparo Miseroni came from a family of gemstone carvers and engravers, and he and then his descen-dants counted the imperial court in Vienna and the papal court in Rome among their clients, who also consistently included Cosimo I de' Medici

and his wife, Eleonora of Toledo. Forward-looking vessels like the present one would soon form the basis of a style admired by northern clients. Miseroni came to Florence on several occasions to bring the grand duchess rock crystal vases as well as jewels and gold objects—although in this case his role may well have been that of a dealer in pre-cious objects rather than a craftsman.

Miseroni also made the first lapis lazuli cup to enter Cosimo I's collection. It was finished a few years after this bloodstone cup and also has a shell-shaped form with a sea monster carved into it. Cosimo I commissioned it from Miseroni in 1563 after he saw and approved a wax model for it.[3]

The shell-shaped cup with carved, zoomorphic decoration was Miseroni's own, successful inven-tion, and he made several versions of it.[4] This blood-stone cup stands out among them for its dynamic form and the vigorous plasticity of its carving. Its skilled execution is set off by the splendid green stone accented with small red veins. Bloodstone comes from India, and it was well known and sought after even in antiquity for the intrinsic beauty of its emerald green color as well as for the magical properties attributed to it.[5]

AG

1. Vasari 1568 (1878–85 ed.), vol. 5, p. 389; Fock 1976, pp. 123–24.
2. This piece is also in the Museo degli Argenti (inv. 766). See Massinelli 1992, ill. p. 76.
3. Fock 1976, pp. 120ff. This cup is now in the Museo di Mineralogia e Litologia, Florence (inv. 1947 13683/647).
4. For a systematic discussion of this type, see Distelberger 2003.
5. There is a scoffing reference to this in Boccaccio's mid-fourteenth century *Decameron* (8:3), in the famous story of Calandrino, who believes that bloodstone will make the person carrying it invisible.

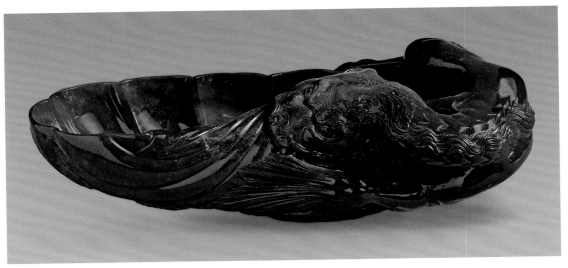

66. Landscape with a Chapel and a Bridge

Castrucci workshop, Prague, 1596
By Cosimo Castrucci
Agates and jaspers; 7¼ × 9¾ in.
(18.3 × 24.5 cm)
Signed and dated on back: *Cosimo Castruccj Flor*[en]*tino FE*[ligature]*citt Anno 1596*
Kunsthistorisches Museum, Vienna, Kunstkammer KK 3037

PROVENANCE: Schatzkammer (imperial treasury), Vienna (not identified in the 1750 inventory); transferred to the Kunsthistorisches Museum, Vienna, 1890

REFERENCES: Neumann 1957, pp. 184, 194–96, 199, no. 1, figs. 197, 198 (illustration of signature of Cosimo Castrucci on verso); Giusti in *Palazzo Vecchio* 1980, p. 244, no. 471; Vincent 1987, pp. 163, 165,

This panel is the earliest known pure landscape in the Florentine mosaic technique. The similarity in composition to Flemish landscape paintings is obvious, and here, for the first time, we identify the work after which it was patterned, *Hunters in the Snow*, of 1565, by Pieter Bruegel the Elder (Kunsthistorisches Museum, Vienna). A chapel takes the place of the inn in Bruegel's painting, and the line of trees has been reduced to two, one of them only a stump. On the right, as in the Bruegel, a bridge spans a river and beyond the bridge stands a house. In the background the river flows past three villages, the second of which (far right, and see fig. 32) closely resembles the one in the painting. To set off the foreground more effectively, the artist, Cosimo Castrucci (d. 1602), also leads the river along the descending diagonal of the hill; he even reproduces Bruegel's figure of a

hunter wearing a hat and carrying a stick across his shoulders on the left. So many similarities can hardly be coincidental. Although Castrucci adopted important elements of the composition, his landscape differs from the original, especially in its colors. Additionally, the extreme reduction in size and the execution in slices of stone made simplifications inevitable.

Bruegel's series of pictures of the four Seasons was shipped to Vienna from Brussels as part of the collection of Archduke Ernst of Austria, who died in February 1595. His estate inventory is dated July 17 of that year. The series must have been forwarded immediately to Emperor Rudolf II in Prague, where Castrucci was able to admire the painting of Winter. Only in Prague (not in Vienna) was there a supply of stones in sufficient variety to make possible the creation of a *commesso di pietre*

fig. 5; Fock 1988, p. 52, fig. 1; Bukovinská in *Prag um 1600* 1988, vol. 1, p. 513, no. 384; Giusti 1992, pp. 138–40, fig. 40; Distelberger in Fučíková et al. 1997, p. 485, no. 11.62; Distelberger 2002, pp. 287–88, no. 172 (with illustration of signature of Castrucci on verso); Bukovinská 2003, p. 120, fig. 4; Giusti 2006b, p. 117, ill. no. 92

dure. Therefore Cosimo's panel must have been produced in the city where he had worked in the emperor's service since at least 1592.

The mosaic is signed on the back—the only piece to bear a signature—and dated 1596. The signature was first published by Erwin Neumann, who thought the date was 1576, although he did not exclude the possibility of reading it as 1596.[1] Subsequently Clare Vincent, Beket Bukovinská, and I debated the question and advanced reasons for the latter reading.[2] With the relationship between the mosaic and the Bruegel painting now perceived, the 1596 date is confirmed.

The panel, which is made up of speckled and striated agates and jaspers from Bohemia, provides a clear idea of Cosimo Castrucci's *macchia*—that is, his unique way of reproducing a scene with the help of the natural markings in the varicolored stones. For the foreground he used large, darker slices, saving lighter ones for the depiction of the distant view with its delicate shading, which gives the impression of atmospheric perspective; meanwhile, the composition's diagonals create additional depth. At that time the Galleria dei Lavori

in Florence was not interested in landscape. In the early seventeenth century it was still constructing vistas and background views composed of planes stacked parallel to the picture surface. Accordingly, the creation of a landscape *commesso* utilizing linear and aerial perspective must be credited to Cosimo Castrucci and to his Prague workshop.

Although it is relatively small, Cosimo Castrucci's panel was not meant to be part of a tabletop or to form some other piece of furniture but rather to be displayed as an independent picture. Otherwise, the signature and the strengthening of the back by means of a copper frame would make no sense. This was a distinct novelty at the time, another indication of the panel's historic significance. *Landscape with a Chapel and a Bridge* manifests in united form the artistry of nature and the mastery of the artist—a highly desirable achievement in the Prague of Rudolf II.

RD

1. Neumann 1957, pp. 184, 194–96, fig. 198.
2. Vincent 1987, p. 165; Bukovinská in *Prague um 1600* 1988, vol. 1, p. 513, no. 384; Distelberger in Fučíková et al. 1977, p. 485, no. 11.62; Distelberger 2002, pp. 287–88, no. 172.

67. *Landscape with the Sacrifice of Isaac*

Castrucci workshop, Prague, before 1603
By Cosimo Castrucci
Agates and jaspers; 17⅛ × 22¾ in. (43.4 × 57.7 cm)
Kunsthistorisches Museum, Vienna, Kunstkammer KK 3411

PROVENANCE: Schatzkammer (imperial treasury), Vienna, by 1750 (1750 inventory: outside the cases, next to the window, no. 2, p. 611); Kunsthistorisches Museum, Vienna

REFERENCES: Neumann 1957, pp. 188, 200, no. 21, fig. 213; Przyborowski 1982, pp. 257–58, no. 8.3; Bukovinská in *Prag um 1600* 1988, vol. 1, pp. 515–16, no. 390; Distelberger in *Prague um 1600* 1988, vol. 2, p. 244, under no. 726; Distelberger in Fučíková et al. 1997, p. 485, no. 11.63; Distelberger 2002, pp. 288–90, no. 173; Giusti 2006b, p. 120, ill. no. 95

This hardstone mosaic represents a refinement of the artistic ideas explored in Cosimo Castrucci's small signed panel *Landscape with a Chapel and a Bridge* (cat. no. 66). The composition follows the same pattern. A diagonal separates the foreground, made up of large slices of stone in strong colors, from the distant view, rendered in smaller, light-colored pieces of agate. Once again, a large tree joins the two areas. The ostensible subject of the picture is embedded in a dramatically dark tumble of rocks at left and linked, by the figures' gaze, to the angel appearing in the clouds at the upper right. Abraham stands facing the viewer, and Isaac kneels beside his father in strict profile. On line with Abraham's right arm is the ram that God has sent as a sacrifice to substitute for Isaac. At Abraham's feet lies his multicolored turban, and on the rock in front of it stands a vessel holding fire.

To date, no model for this scene has been identified. Much as in Pieter Bruegel the Elder's etchings, here the human activity serves as a mere

pretext for depicting a magnificent world landscape—the finest ever executed in hardstone mosaic. The right half of the picture provides a view into the far distance. Rushing water in the foreground, tranquil riverbanks farther back, a mill and village, a city, a castle, and mountains draw one's gaze into the receding space beyond the bridge. In the very front, far below the standpoint of the viewer, a man in a boat is struggling against the waves. A remarkable effort was put into the creation of this landscape. It reveals the typical style and practice of Cosimo Castrucci; no one else can reasonably be assumed to have produced it. Cosimo's son Giovanni certainly executed several mosaic landscapes (see cat. no. 68), but none of them approaches this panel in quality.

Claudia Przyborowski saw this panel as an imitation of the hardstone *commesso* on the same subject in the high altar at San Lorenzo in Florence, which was originally planned for the pedestal of the retable and ciborium of the Cappella dei Principi.[1] But aside from their subject matter, the

detail

two works have nothing in common. Przyborowski dates the Florentine panel to 1603–5; thus, it cannot have served as a model for the present work, which must have been created between 1596 (the date of the signed *Landscape with a Chapel and a Bridge*) and 1602 (when Cosimo died). The Old Testament scene, depicted in the Florentine panel with relatively more complex movement, plays only a marginal role in Castrucci's picture. At the turn of the seventeenth century there was nothing being made at the grand-ducal workshops in Florence remotely comparable in quality to this landscape.

Emperor Rudolf II was particularly interested in landscape. In 1594 he summoned to his court the Flemish painter Pieter Stevens, who worked in the style of Paul Bril. In fashion at the time were views from a height of a remote, idealized landscape, precisely the formula used here by Cosimo Castrucci. It was only with the arrival in Prague of Roelant Savery and Paulus van Vianen, both in 1603, that the style shifted to more realistic depictions of more intimate landscapes.[2] In *Landscape with the Sacrifice of Isaac* there is not yet any sign of such a change. Given the lively exchange of ideas within Prague's artist colony, this would also indicate a date before 1603.

RD

1. Przyborowski 1982, p. 257, no. 8.3.
2. Fučíková 1988, pp. 188–90.

68. *Landscape with an Obelisk*

Castrucci workshop, Prague,
before 1611
By Giovanni Castrucci
Agates and jaspers; 13½ × 19½ in.
(34.2 × 49.3 cm)
Kunsthistorisches Museum,
Vienna, Kunstkammer KK 3397

PROVENANCE: Collection of Emperor Rudolf II, Prague, by 1611 (inventory of 1607–11, no. 2813); Schatzkammer (imperial treasury), Vienna (1750 inventory: outside the cases, p. 614); Kunsthistorisches Museum, Vienna

REFERENCES: Neumann 1957, pp. 185, 188, 199, no. 3, fig. 201; Bauer and Haupt 1976, pp. 140, 143, fig. 35; Giusti in *Palazzo Vecchio* 1980, p. 244, no. 471; Vincent 1987, pp. 163, 165, fig. 6; Bukovinská in *Prag um 1600* 1988, vol. 1, pp. 514–15, no. 388; Giusti 1992, pp. 140–41, fig. 44; Distelberger in Fučíková et al. 1997, p. 485, no. II.65; Distelberger 2002, pp. 290–91, no. 174; Bukovinská 2003, p. 120, fig. 5; Giusti 2006b, p. 119, ill. no. 93

Giovanni Castrucci's approach to the challenges of his art differs considerably from that of his father, Cosimo (see entry for cat. no. 66). In this panel, for example, the landscape unfolds in successive zones parallel to the picture plane; the artist made no attempt to create the illusion of spatial depth. As Erwin Neumann recognized, the composition is based on *River Landscape with a Scene from Aesop*, a 1599 engraving by Johann Sadeler I after a drawing by Lodewijk Toeput, who worked in Italy under the name Lodovico Pozzoserrato.[1] Giovanni altered Toeput's composition—which provided a sense of depth—instead moving from one spatial zone to another with no transitions. He borrowed the motif of the well and the woman bending over it with her water vessel from a large octagonal hardstone mosaic, executed by Cosimo Castrucci, which was set in an elegant table now in the Schatzkammer of the Residenz in Munich.[2] There the well appears at lower right, and here it was placed in the left-hand corner, but shown from the same perspective. The picture as a whole does not reflect a unified point of view. The trees at the right edge stand close to the viewer, yet one can see down into the well at left. Giovanni shows the top edge of the base of the obelisk in perspective but then forgets the angled side in the area of the coat of arms. His inability to visualize space is evident throughout the tableau. What he produces instead is surface pattern. For the hill topped by a castle in the background he chose colors that are just as strong as those in the foreground, thereby undercutting any effect of aerial perspective. Especially in the left half of the picture, he used a number of stones with indistinct markings, failing to create realistic forms with them and deliberately leaving the relationships of space and volume unclear. As an artist, he was more concerned with the decorative effect of his mosaic than with producing an illusionistic picture. Once one has become familiar with these features of Giovanni's style in this assured major work, one can recognize his hand in other panels and would never consider him a finer artist than his father.

Giovanni Castrucci's authorship of this piece is attested by the following entry in the 1607–11 inventory of Emperor Rudolf II's Schatzkammer: "A large hardstone picture by the hand of Johann Castrucci in which [one sees] a wagoner with a loaded cart and an obelisk with the Roman emperor's coat of arms with eagle, crown, and [Golden] Fleece."[3] This entry stands between the descriptions of two objects said to have found their way into the imperial collection in 1611, thus providing a terminus ante quem for the panel. Cosimo's son from his first marriage, Giovanni had come to Prague about 1598. In 1599, when he was identified as "jeweler to His Majesty the Emperor in Prague," he delivered amethysts, garnets, and smoky quartz to the deputy director of the Florentine court workshops, Jacques Bijlivert, for a ciborium that was being created at that time.[4] Giovanni often made such entrepreneurial trips, leaving his

lapidary work to assistants. The results were of very uneven quality. The 1607–11 inventory lists seven panels attributed to Giovanni; however, the man who compiled it, Daniel Fröschl, was only familiar with the name of the son, not with that of his father, Cosimo.   RD

1. Neumann 1957. For the engraving, see Neumann 1957, fig. 200; Distelberger 2002, p. 291, fig. 1.
2. Giusti 2006b, ill. no. 103.
3. Neumann 1957, p. 199, no. 3; Bauer and Haupt 1976, p. 140, no. 2813.
4. Przyborowski 1982, p. 528, doc. no. XVIII.3.

69. Landscape with a Flaming Sky

Castrucci workshop, Prague, between ca. 1615 and 1622
Agates, jaspers, and cherts, frame (not shown) of ebony on oak; without frame 8½ × 11⅞ in. (21.5 × 30 cm), with frame 12¼ × 15⅝ in. (31 × 39.5 cm)
Kunsthistorisches Museum, Vienna, Kunstkammer KK 3039

PROVENANCE: Ambras Castle, Innsbruck, by 1788 (1788 inventory, vol. 2, no. 11, p. 258); Vienna, 1806; Ambras Collection, Vienna, by 1821 (1821 inventory, p. 374, no. 49); Kunsthistorisches Museum, Vienna

REFERENCES: Neumann 1957, pp. 188, 200, no. 26, fig. 210; Distelberger in *Prag um 1600* 1988, vol. 2, pp. 247–48, no. 731; Distelberger in Fučíková et al. 1997, p. 538, no. II.327; Distelberger 2002, p. 296, no. 179

This hardstone mosaic depicting a landscape under a dramatic sky—the 1788 inventory of Ambras Castle colorfully describes it as a "conflagration"—presents a variant of the Castrucci workshop style that combines Cosimo's atmospheric perspective and Giovanni's stacked picture planes. The artist recognized that distance tends to blur objects and that forms in the foreground are more distinct than those in the background. The variety and coloring of the stones and the strong chiaroscuro give the picture an agitated quality. Rocks, trees, and dense foliage in dark tones create a foreground frame for the view into the distance. On the left, a road leads across a waterfall to a middle distance that is only suggested. In the background lies a city flanked by two fortified promontories. This city, the center of which features a tall tower, a shorter one, and a broad arch, was based on a city in an engraving by an artist named Sadeler (perhaps Justus Sadeler) after the Flemish artist Paul Bril.[1] The composition would become a virtual set piece for the late Castrucci workshop.

The city type appears again in a mosaic in the Kunsthistorisches Museum, Vienna, with the penitent Saint Mary Magdalen, which was conceived as a pendant to the present one.[2] More interesting is the fact that the same engraving was also used as the basis for details in the large central mosaic of the pietre dure table in the Museo degli Argenti, Florence.[3] There the city lies somewhat hidden in the background on the right, next to a larger city in the center. Farther to the right, in front of the bluff, the artist has quoted from the engraving the fortress with a round tower. These repetitions suggest that one of the ways the Castrucci workshop managed to produce as much as it did was by using simple images in different configurations.[4] As Clare Vincent was able to show,[5] Sadeler's engravings play a major role in the late work of the Castrucci atelier—the period after the death of Giovanni Castrucci in 1615, in which it was administrated by Ottavio Miseroni. During this time it produced, between 1621 and 1623, the well-known tabletop and chest for Karl von Liechtenstein (figs. 34, 35). *Landscape with a Flaming Sky* must also date from this period.

The appearance of new masters at the workshop explains this variant of the Prague style. In 1615, Cosimo the younger, son of Giovanni, took the place of his father. One of the pieces begun by Giovanni that the younger artist worked on was the famous hardstone mosaic depicting Abraham and the Three Angels, after an original composition by Bernardino Poccetti.[6] The younger Cosimo is no longer mentioned after 1619 and presumably died that year. The Abraham panel was finally finished by Giovanni Castrucci's son-in-law, Giuliano di Piero Pandolfini, who delivered it to Florence in 1622.[7] The two younger masters were sufficiently self-assured to develop a style of their own, of which this mosaic is a beautiful example, and under Pandolfini, from 1619 onward, the Prague atelier enjoyed a major resurgence. The works that Pandolfini later produced in Florence confirm that he was an artist of no small ability. The reasons for the demise of the Prague mosaic workshop were doubtless of a political nature; its disappearance was not the result of a gradual artistic decline. It is hoped that the inclusion of four Prague landscape mosaics in the present exhibition (cat. nos. 66–69) will bring about a greater appreciation for the achievements of this workshop and its masters.   RD

1. Vincent 1987, fig. 23.
2. Kunstkammer, inv. 3006; Distelberger 2002, pp. 294–96, no. 178; Giusti 2006b, ill. no. 94.
3. Giusti 2006b, ill. nos. 104, 105.
4. Neumann 1957, p. 188.
5. Vincent 1987, pp. 165, 173–74.
6. Giusti 2006b, ill. no. 100.
7. Przyborowski 1982, pp. 276–77.

70. Collector's cabinet

Castrucci workshop and court workshop in the Hradschin Palace, Prague, ca. 1610
Macassar ebony and ebonized and gilded wood, hardstones; 19⅛ × 18⅜ × 10 in. (48.6 × 46.7 × 25.4 cm)
The Rosalinde and Arthur Gilbert Collection on loan to the Victoria and Albert Museum, London 1996.210 (MM 39)

PROVENANCE: Le Beau, New York; Gilbert Collection, 1966; on loan to the Los Angeles County Museum of Art; displayed at Somerset House, London, from 1996; transferred to the Victoria and Albert Museum, 2008

REFERENCES: Sherman 1971, pp. 58–59, pl. XXXI; González-Palacios 1977a, p. 26, no. 1; Distelberger 1980, p. 54; González-Palacios and Röttgen in González-Palacios, Röttgen, and Przyborowski 1982, pp. 83–84, no. 1; Vincent in *Liechtenstein* 1985, p. 45, under no. 25; Giusti 1992, p.173, pl. 88; Massinelli 2000, pp. 29–31, no. 1

Elaborate collector's cabinets, such as Philipp Hainhofer's monumental Augsburg display cabinet (cat. no. 78), frequently were sold already furnished with rare natural specimens, art objects, and items from faraway countries and were usually crafted and assembled by several cooperating workshops over a period of months or even years.[1] The present example belongs to a category that in documents of the period was called *Trüchlein* (small cabinet). These jewel-like objects were portable and could be used to store valuables, potions and pills, and toilette implements.[2] The design of the present example was possibly inspired by ancient temple forms: the slightly pyramidal stepped roof with four inserted hardstone "windows" suggests a rectangular version of a pantheon. At the center of the facade is an arched *commesso di pietre dure* panel (see detail) depicting a canal with a palace in extreme perspective at left and a gondola with two passengers and a gondolier below; a fisherman sits in the background at quayside in front of a large pot containing a bluish green agave, an exotic plant that had been brought to Europe from the Americas only about fifty years earlier.[3]

This attractive scene, found on other objects from the Castrucci workshop—for example, on the front of Karl von Liechtenstein's well-known chest (fig. 35)—is set within a framelike aedicula with a broken pediment in ebony and pilaster strips of mauve-colored veined agate. This whole central section is a door that when opened allows the flanking panels on the right and left to slide, giving access to six drawers behind them. Compositions

on other panels—for example, the one with cut corners on the right side of the cabinet showing a view of Krumay Castle in Bohemia—were repeated several times by the Castrucci workshop.[4]

Together, the colorful plaques on this cabinet conjure up a world where nature and ceaseless human activity coexist in harmony. The season is almost always spring, and the buildings nestle as snugly into the landscape as the hardstones of the *commessi* fit together. Magnificently conceived and executed, this *Trüchlein* may have been one of Emperor Rudolf II's diplomatic gifts. It epitomizes the splendor of his court.   WK

1. Alfter 1986, p. 97, nos. 12–14, figs. 33, 37–40.
2. Ibid., pp. 57–59; Koeppe 1992, pp. 238–40, 266–67, nos. M141, M142, M144, ill. pp. 256, 257.
3. Krausch 2007, pp. 40–41.
4. It appears on the lid of the Liechtenstein casket; see Kräftner 2007a, p. 51. The *commessi* on that casket are framed by what seems to be the same mauve-colored Bohemian agate as is seen here, on the front of the Gilbert Collection cabinet.

detail showing
center panel

71. Fame

Castrucci workshop, Prague, before 1620
By Cosimo di Giovanni Castrucci
Hardstones; 10¼ × 15¾ in.
(26 × 40 cm)
Museo dell'Opificio delle Pietre Dure, Florence OA 1911:465

PROVENANCE: The artist's heirs; Ferdinand II de' Medici, grand duke of Tuscany, in 1659; Medici collections, in 1669; deposited at an unknown date in the Galleria dei Lavori (subsequently Opificio delle Pietre Dure), Florence; Museo dell'Opificio, by 1911

REFERENCES: Marchionni 1891, p. 129; Bartoli and Maser 1953, pp. 9, 27; Rossi (Ferdinando) 1967, p. 94, pl. XI; Pampaloni Martelli 1975, p. 42, no. 19; Giusti in Giusti, Mazzoni, and Pampaloni Martelli 1978, pp. 290–91, no. 81, pl. 67; Giusti in *Palazzo Vecchio* 1980, pp. 242–43, no. 466; Giusti in Giusti 1988, p. 142, no. 28; Giusti 1992, p. 170, pl. 82; Giusti 1995, p. 39, ill. no. 13; Distelberger 2002, pp. 251, 257, n. 43; Giusti 2006b, p. 128, ill. no. 97

This small panel is a masterpiece of invention and craftsmanship. It represents the allegorical figure of Fame as she flies above the world blowing her two trumpets. The entire figure, the background (made with Grishun chalcedony), and the terrestrial orb (of Bohemian jasper) were all executed in pietre dure. Vivid Sicilian jaspers act as highlights on Fame's drapery as it blows in the wind, and her flesh tones seem variegated, thanks to the delicate rosy hues of the translucent chalcedony.

Archival documents reveal that Cosimo di Giovanni Castrucci's heirs sold this panel to Grand Duke Ferdinand II de' Medici in 1659.[1] The document recording the sale, drawn up by the artist's nephews, makes reference to the younger Cosimo and describes the panel as "made by the hand of our uncle, Cosimo Castrucci." By 1659 the imperial workshops in Prague had long since stopped producing hardstone mosaics, and the last craftsman related to Castrucci—his brother-in-law, Giuliano di Piero Pandolfini—had returned to Florence, where he was employed in the grand-ducal workshop.[2] The panel depicting Fame had remained the property of Castrucci's heirs, but it was certainly made long before it was sold to Ferdinand II.

It seems that the history of this piece parallels that of the *Abraham and the Three Angels*, part of a series of panels with biblical subjects intended for the Cappella dei Principi in Florence.[3] The painted model for that mosaic was made by the painter Bernardino Poccetti in Florence between 1606 and 1610. It was then sent to Prague, where it was the basis for a work executed in pietre dure and finished in 1620. The sophisticated Mannerism of this figure of Fame recalls the style of the Florentine painters at Ferdinand I de' Medici's court and of Poccetti in particular; however, the relationship between the workshops in Prague and Florence was particularly close in the first two decades of the seventeenth century, the period when the Castrucci shop was at its peak. The waning of the imperial workshop is suggested by Pandolfini's transfer from Prague to Florence.[4]

In 1636 Pandolfini made a sumptuous table-top for Prince Karl Eusebius von Liechtenstein (r. 1627–84). It is decorated with naturalistic motifs, and at its center there is a stylized quatrefoil almost identical to that of *Fame*. This device does not appear in any other known mosaics made in Florence.[5] It seems likely, therefore, that *Fame* was intended to be the central motif in a tabletop that was ultimately never finished at the declining workshop in Prague.

A G

1. See Krčálová and Aschengreen Piacenti 1979, p. 251; Giusti 1992, p. 262, n. 46.
2. See "The Castrucci and the Miseroni" by Rudolf Distelberger in this publication.
3. This mosaic is now in the Museo dell'Opificio delle Pietre Dure, inv. 460. For the documents regarding this work, see Przyborowski in Giusti 1988, p. 118, no. 18.
4. The closeness of the relationship is further underscored by the fact that an ebony and silver cabinet with pietre dure landscapes that was made in Prague was delivered to the Medici villa at Poggio Imperiale, near Florence, in 1624. It is now in the Museo dell'Opificio delle Pietre Dure (inv. 567). See Giusti in Giusti 1988, p. 240, no. 72; Giusti 1992, pls. 84, 85; Bohr 1993, p. 221, no. XI, fig. 107. For the furnishings of the Villa del Poggio Imperiale, see Bohr 1994.
5. Giusti 2006b, p. 135, and ill. no. 108.

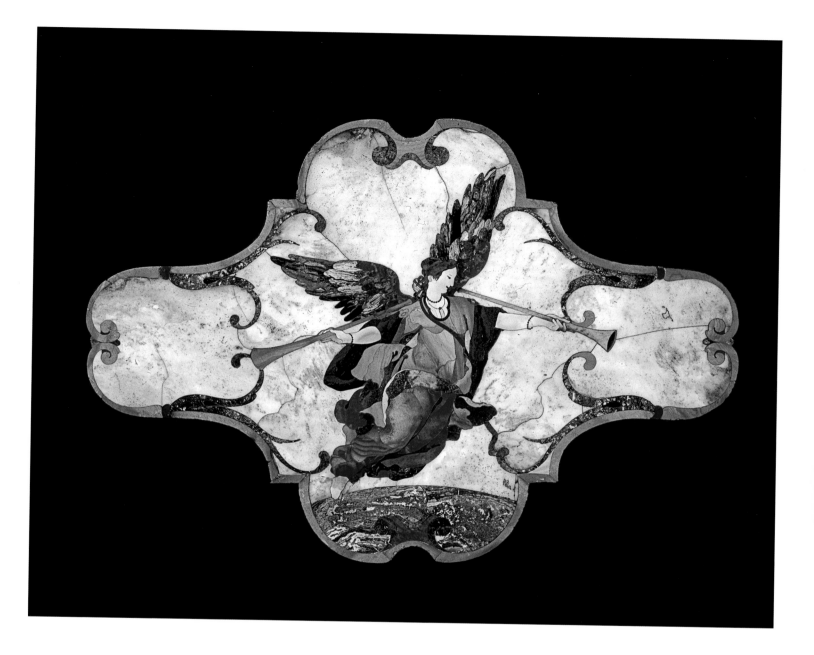

Earlier, Ernst Kris had recognized a close similarity in style between this medallion and the oval mosaics, also signed, on two reliquary monstrances in the Geistliche Schatzkammer (Ecclesiastical Treasury) in Vienna, one depicting the Madonna and Child and the other Saint Anne.[2] He therefore dated it to the time of the small monstrances, about 1620. The delicate relief and the richer execution of such details as the hair, the drapery, and the hands nevertheless place *Saint Mary Magdalen* closer to *Lady with a Feather Fan*, another hardstone relief mosaic in the Kunsthistorisches Museum, Vienna, which has a gold backplate with deeply incised enamel decoration (ca. 1610).[3]

RD

1. Inv. 5109 (2070); Zimmer 1971, p. 146, no. C1, fig. 117.
2. Kris in Eichler and Kris 1927, p. 143, no. 302. The inventory numbers of the monstrances are Kap. 219 and Kap. 220; see Distelberger 2002, pp. 284–86, nos. 169, 170. Giusti 2006b, p. 111, erroneously identifies the two medallions as cameos.
3. Kunstkammer, inv. XII 140; Distelberger 2002, pp. 277–78, no. 160.

74. Six-lobed bowl

Miseroni workshop, Prague, 1590–1600
Mounts attributed to Anton Schweinberger
Jasper, gold mounts; 3¾ × 8⅝ × 8⅜ in. (9.3 × 21.7 × 21.3 cm)
Kunsthistorisches Museum, Vienna, Kunstkammer KK 1900

PROVENANCE: Schatzkammer (imperial treasury), Vienna, by 1750 (1750 inventory: case 4, no. 144, p. 234); Kunsthistorisches Museum, Vienna

REFERENCES: Distelberger in *Prag um 1600* 1988, vol. 2, p. 229, no. 696; Distelberger in Fučíková et al. 1997, p. 473, no. II.2; Distelberger 2002, p. 258, no. 142

The most exceptional feature of this bowl is the extraordinary beauty of the stone, which the precision of the grinding and the high polish perfectly display. The stone's source has not as yet been identified, and no other vessel made from this special type of jasper is known. There are several reasons for attributing the object to the Prague workshop of Ottavio Miseroni during its first period. Obvious general similarities to vessels made in the Miseroni workshop in Milan are apparent but are combined with a feature that would be seen again in Prague. The overall shape of the oval, six-lobed bowl is in the Milan tradition, although in silhouette it appears rather heavier than usual, owing to the massive foot and deep body. But by contrast with the practice in Milan, the narrow bands with a concave spine in the indentation were not extended all the way to the rim, which is delicately rounded on the inside—a characteristic Ottavio Miseroni touch. The form of the foot also points to him; its profile, both outside and underneath, is repeated in an oval bowl of variegated jasper in Vienna, there with a mounting of enameled gold (fig. 37). In both examples the foot is deeply indented. One has the impression that the present piece is monolithic; however, the foot has been almost seamlessly attached to the bowl above the round molding. Such solutions were uncommon in the Milan shop, where individual pieces were joined by a mount—generally of gold. Apparently during their first years in Prague, the Miseroni were unwilling to entrust their work to a goldsmith.

The delicate, symmetrical vine engraved on the outside of the shorter sides forms a clear link with Milan. Intaglio decoration is rather uncommon in opaque stone, as it can hardly be seen. One finds it on several agate vessels in the Schatzkammer at the Residenz in Munich, for example, all of which were made at the Miseroni workshop in Milan,[1] and on an eight-lobed chalcedony bowl in the collection of the Prado, Madrid.[2] A shop specialist in so-called *arte minuta* (fine work) was responsible for such intaglios.

Ottavio Miseroni (ca. 1568–1624) entered the imperial service in Prague in January 1588, when he was only twenty years old. His younger brothers Aurelio and Alessandro accompanied him, and his stepbrother Giovanni Ambrogio (ca. 1551/52–1616), seventeen years older and a child of his father Girolamo's first marriage, stayed in Prague for a time to help out. It was important for the workshop to convince the emperor of its abilities during its first years. The bowl was a collaborative effort.

The choice of gold for the handles indicates how highly the stone and the bowl's perfect workmanship were valued. The handles can be attributed to the Augsburg goldsmith Anton Schweinberger (d. 1603), who was active in Prague beginning in 1587. The same kind of scrollwork is found on the famous pitcher made from half of a Seychelles nut and mounted in gilded silver, now in Vienna's Kunsthistorisches Museum.[3] Before the arrival in Prague of Jan Vermeyen—that is to say, before 1597—there was no goldsmith in Prague who could make mounts of enameled gold.

RD

1. Brunner 1970, no. 377, fig. 44, nos. 402–7, and no. 480, fig. 47.
2. Alhajas del Delfin; Arbeteta Mira 2001, pp. 191–92, no. 51.
3. Kunstkammer, inv. 6874; Distelberger in *Prag um 1600* 1988, vol. 1, p. 470, no. 340.

75. Dish in the form of a shell

Dish: Miseroni workshop, Prague,
ca. 1610–22
By Ottavio Miseroni
Nephrite; 12¾ × 14⅝ × 13⅜ in.
(32.3 × 37 × 34 cm)
Mounts: By Master HC, Vienna,
1630s
Gilded silver
Kunsthistorisches Museum,
Vienna, Kunstkammer KK 6828

PROVENANCE: Delivered to the
Schatzkammer (imperial treasury),
Vienna, in 1622; imperial collection;
Kunsthistorisches Museum, Vienna,
Kunstkammer

REFERENCES: Distelberger 1978,
p. 142, figs. 120, 121; Distelberger
in *Prag um 1600* 1988, vol. 2,
pp. 233–34, no. 704; Distelberger
2002, pp. 281–82, no. 166

The great value of the large block of nephrite (jade) from which this object was carved called for some kind of elaborate treatment, but its shape posed considerable difficulties. The only thing that could be made from the thick slab was a very wide vessel with a flat bottom. The viewer sees mainly the large smooth surfaces of the bowl's interior; the rich exterior decor is difficult to appreciate. The edge rises slightly toward the back, widening, then turning into a gently convex, broad band that is deeply undercut on the inside and on the outside is set off from the profile of the wall. At the back of the shell the band twists into a spiral. Out of this protuberance emerge acanthus leaves, which cling to the band on the inside but cover the entire back and base on the exterior, extending as a broad, richly articulated leaf to the beginning of the foot. Delicately curving, flat bands lead out from the leaf, across the floor and wall, and up to the rim. The stone is relatively coarse-grained and so could not be brought to a high polish.

The piece appears at the top of a list drawn up by the imperial treasurer Nikolaus von Kurland of the vessels that Ottavio Miseroni delivered to Vienna himself on September 5, 1622. It was noted there that it had no foot and also that handles would have to be made for it.[1] Ottavio's authorship of the bowl is thus confirmed. The piece had already been included in Ottavio's list, dated September 18, 1621, of "drinking and other vessels" that he had made and placed out of the reach of the rebels (doubtless these were the Bohemians, who rose against Ferdinand II in 1619), some already finished and some still incomplete.[2] There the master mentions "a very beautiful large vessel of jade," for which a foot still needed to be made.

The ornamentation is that of the Miseroni workshop in Milan from the period before and just after 1600. Ottavio had already employed this style on a lidded bowl of pink agate to which a gold enamel mount was added by the Vermeyen workshop between 1603 and 1608.[3] Thus, the concept for this large nephrite bowl was presumably set in the first decade of the seventeenth century, yet the piece lay in the workshop for some years. This is by no means surprising. Emperor Matthias had moved his residence back from Prague to Vienna, and Ferdinand II was preoccupied with the religious and military conflicts of the Thirty Years' War. In 1622 Ottavio Miseroni was thus able to take to Vienna some twenty-nine objects that had piled up in his atelier. He apparently considered this bowl alone unfinished, and was hoping for a goldsmith who would know how to set off his work. His hope was not realized, for the successors of Rudolf II showed little interest. On this bowl there is no trace of the sharp-edged cutting of Ottavio's late period. It is the second-largest surviving vessel by Ottavio Miseroni, after the Paris jasper bowl of 1608.[4]

The gilded silver mounts were created in Vienna in the 1630s by an unknown craftsman whose mark was *HC*. As one can see in the case of other vessels by Ottavio, the goldsmith did not understand the idiom of stonecutting, and with Neptune and the leafy swirl on which he stands, he covered up crucial parts of the carved decor.

R D

1. Bodenstein 1916, pp. CXVI, doc. no. 20608, app. 5.
2. Bodenstein 1913–14, p. IV, doc. no. 20316.
3. Distelberger 2002, pp. 268–69, no. 150.
4. Musée du Louvre, Paris, MR 143; Alcouffe 2001, pp. 343–44, no. 168; Distelberger 2002, pp. 272–74, no. 155.

76. Cup

Miseroni workshop, Prague,
ca. 1600
By Ottavio Miseroni; mounts by
Jan Vermeyen
Moss agate, gold and enamel
mounts; 3½ × 5 × 4 in. (8.8 ×
12.7 × 10 cm)
Museumslandschaft Hessen
Kassel, Sammlung für
Kunsthandwerk und Plastik
B II.154

PROVENANCE: Probably commis-
sioned by Emperor Rudolf II,
Prague; his gift to Landgrave
Moritz the Learned of Hesse
(r. 1592–1627); documented in the
Museum Fridericianum, Kassel,
in 1779; entered the Staatliche
Museen (now Museumslandschaft
Hessen Kassel)

REFERENCE: Schütte in
Schmidberger and T. Richter 2001,
p. 156, no. 61

The lip of this cup is decorated in three places with a gentle indentation terminating on the inside in two small volutes that spiral in opposite directions. Their slight bulge makes even more astonishing the narrowing of the lip on the front, where the wall is only a few millimeters thick. It is easy to imagine that their curling movement is still in progress and that the hardstone itself is in a state of transformation. Perhaps Ottavio Miseroni's greatest gift was the ability to bestow on some his hardstone creations the appearance of a malleable material that could easily be shaped into the desired form with a small push of his creative fingers.

Ottavio Miseroni (ca. 1568–1624) was one of the master stonecutters in the service of Emperor Rudolf II beginning in 1588.[1] He was ennobled for his service in 1608. In an era when talented craftsmen were often shackled by local guild regulations and treated like lackeys by rich city patricians, Emperor Rudolf's expression of gratitude was extraordinary, reflecting his high regard for outstanding ability.

The shape of the lip and its almost fleshy softness suggest that Miseroni planned no mounts to highlight the bowl.[2] The detailed and elegant gold mounts on the stem and foot may be attributed to the equally gifted court goldsmith Jan Vermeyen (before 1559–1608), who was entrusted by Rudolf II with the creation of the new imperial crown. The artist evaluated the color nuances of this hardstone cup and designed his fashionable gold and enamel mounts to set off the beauty of the stone, not to compete with it. It is remarkable how the dominant colors in the hardstone are complemented by the translucent enamel mounts in green and blue and by the white opaque enamel and the sparkling gold. The desire and ability to strike a balance between *ars* and *natura*—art and nature—distinguished the Prague court workshops from all others in northern Europe at this time.

W K

1. See Distelberger 1988, pp. 457–62; Distelberger in *Prag um 1600* 1988, vol. 1, pp. 484–86, 487, 505–6, nos. 365, 366, 368, 372; and in this publication "The Castrucci and the Miseroni" by Rudolf Distelberger and cat. nos. 74, 75.
2. For examples of cups by Miseroni with no mounts, see Sybille Ebert-Schifferer in *Faszination Edelstein* 1992, pp. 181–83, nos. 86, 87.

77. Oblong bowl

Miseroni workshop, Prague, 1650
By Dionysio Miseroni
Citrine; 3¼ × 7⅜ × 4⅜ in. (8 × 18.5 × 10.9 cm)
Kunsthistorisches Museum, Vienna, Kunstkammer KK 1367

PROVENANCE: Purchased from the artist for the Schatzkammer (imperial treasury), Vienna, in 1651 (not in 1750 inventory, although certainly there); transferred to Kunsthistorisches Museum, Vienna, 1890

REFERENCES: Distelberger 1979, pp. 120–21, 136, fig. 98; Distelberger in Fučíková et al. 1997, p. 540, no. II.336; Distelberger 2002, pp. 305–6, no. 188

When Ottavio Miseroni died in 1624, his son Dionysio (1607?–1661) was still too young to have completed his artistic training, yet in the previous year the emperor had already transferred to him his father's stonecutter's stipend. The Viennese court had to wait ten years for the completion of the vessels Ottavio left unfinished at his death. Dionysio must have learned a great deal while working on that material. In the earliest object documented as his own, a large quartz vase completed in 1639 for Prince Karl Eusebius von Liechtenstein, he exhibits a new decorative style. The entire surface of the crystal is carved with fluting, swirls, and branch-like motifs in relief, giving it a shimmering quality. Ottavio had provided the impetus toward this new type of surface treatment in his late period with a few small pieces made of smoky quartz. The present bowl, of citrine, also a quartz, displays the new style in its perfected form.

The bowl's shape refers back to an oval basin of variegated jasper from Ottavio's middle period (fig. 37), although here the shape has become markedly stiffer. Dionysio's elongated bowl is perfectly symmetrical. The ends are almost semicircles, but in the middle the rim describes parallel straight lines. Decorating the outside of this middle section is an ornamental mask with a heart-shaped mouth. Soft volutes form the eyes, while the nose—much as in the Liechtenstein vase—is an almost regular horizontal oval quatrefoil. Ottavio had first employed a mask motif composed of abstract shapes on the central axis of the oblong bowl of variegated jasper—there, to be sure, wholly under the spell of the incipient Auricular style. The deep shells on either side of the wide mouth can be understood as handles or grips. Along the flanks are swirls of concave grooves that coalesce into abstract masks on the bowl's narrow ends. It is clear that some time separates the style of soft forms, which characterize Ottavio's major works, and the turn toward cruder and heavier Baroque forms as seen in this bowl.

The bowl appears at the top of a delivery list submitted by Dionysio in February 1651 and itemizing works completed in the previous year. He had purchased the raw stone himself and asked 400 thalers for it, a particularly large sum.

The Baroque mentality permeated Dionysio's late work from the 1650s. It was now a matter of making an impression more with the size or weight of a vessel than with the subtlety of its details. At this time Dionysio employed fourteen workers in his atelier. His most famous piece was the so-called "Pyramid" made of rock crystal, just under six feet high, in which four cylindrical vessels stand atop a heavy vase from which they themselves were cut (fig. 39).[1]

After 1661, Dionysio's son Ferdinand Eusebio presided over the Prague workshop, its quality clearly declining, until his death in 1684. In the meantime, other Italian stonecutters had established themselves at the court in Vienna, creating strong competition for the workshop in Prague.

RD

1. This monumental piece is in the Kunstkammer of the Kunsthistorisches Museum, Vienna, inv. 2251–54. See Distelberger 2002, pp. 310–13, no. 194.

Augsburg, ca. 1625/26–31
Design and project oversight by
Philipp Hainhofer; cabinetry
by Ulrich Baumgartner and his
workshop; silver engraving by
Lucas Kilian, among others;
paintings by Johann König
Ebony and other tropical and
exotic woods on an oak and fir
carcass, hardstones, reused antique
marble and other marbles, silver,
enamel, cast and gilded bronze,
mother-of-pearl, coral, Seychelles
nut, shells, oil paint, wax, and collected objects; overall 94½ × 38⅝ ×
33⅞ in. (240 × 98 × 86 cm), door
23¼ × 17⅞ in. (59.2 × 45.4 cm), pull-
out panel 17⅜ × 16 in. (44 × 40.5 cm)
Stamped: *EBEN* [guarantee of real
ebony] and a pine cone
Museum Gustavianum, Uppsala
University, Sweden UUK 0112
(door), UUK 0079 (pull-out panel)

*In exhibition: a door and a pull-out
panel*

door on left side

In April 1632 the Augsburg art agent, diplomat,
and connoisseur Philipp Hainhofer (1578–1647),
who designed and supervised the construction
of this extraordinary cabinet, noted in his diary:
"After the meal [in Augsburg], his Maj[esty, King
Gustavus II Adolphus of Sweden] went with the
princes to the writing desk [the present cabi-
net], . . . I showed [them] the front part for an hour
[and] they discussed the contents of one drawer
after the other . . . and identified many things
through their knowledge."[1] Some days later he
wrote, "After lunch his Maj[esty] looked at the third
part of the writing desk and the summit with a coco
d'India [Seychelles nut] (which I had to lift down)
for one hour . . . and [I] was assured [that it] is a
magister omnium artium [teacher of all the arts]."[2]

Gustavus Adolphus was killed in battle in the
late autumn of the same year and never had an
opportunity to enjoy this gift bought for him by
the Lutheran city fathers of Augsburg, who were
grateful to him for liberating their city from
Catholic rule. The cabinet was dismantled, packed

up, and delivered from Augsburg to the widowed
queen, Maria Eleonora, at Svartslö Castle, Uppland.
It has remained safely in Sweden ever since, with
most of its decorations and contents intact, unlike
three similar cabinets that Hainhofer commissioned, one of which, the *Pomeranian Cabinet,* was
destroyed in World War II. (On Hainhofer, his
own *Kunstkammer,* and his team of craftsmen, see
also cat. no. 79 and "Pietre Dure North of the Alps"
by Wolfram Koeppe in this publication.) So delicate,
complex, and sophisticated were these monumental collector's cabinets that they required continual
maintenance to function properly. Shipment of this
example with all its parts and contents—there are
about one thousand diverse items in the drawers
alone, and many more adorn the various surfaces—took a full year. The cabinet was escorted by
the "cabinetmaker Martin Behm," a craftsman possibly of Augsburg, who reassembled it in Sweden.[3]
His intimate familiarity with this "wondrous" object
prompted his appointment as its "caretaker," a post
he filled until his death in 1651—possibly shortly
after he supervised its transport once again, to
Uppsala,[4] at the order of the king's successor,
Queen Christina. Because of the history and age of
this monument of human accomplishment, its
curators have decided that it should never be moved
from Sweden again. Nevertheless, two key elements
of the cabinet, a lateral door depicting Solomon's
Temple (shown at left) and a pull-out panel in
the lower part of the main section, have—for the
first time in centuries—been removed from the
structure and sent abroad, for this exhibition at
the Metropolitan Museum.

The cabinet was intended to represent everything in the world, and not only the natural world
but the intellectual achievements of humans, including those in the fields of science, art, and religion.
Many pages could be devoted to describing its
drawers, compartments, concealed spaces, mechanical devices, toilette objects, games, Florentine mosaic
panels, and more than two hundred miniature paintings on hardstone. Its wooden walls enclose an enormous body of knowledge, suggesting a comparison
with the city walls of Augsburg, where artisans and
craftsmen from all over Europe and beyond came to
ply their trades.[5] We do not know the exact number
of artisans involved in making this cabinet, but a
painting by Anton Mozart of the presentation of
Hainhofer's first large collector's cabinet to the duke
of Pomerania-Stettin depicts the team that worked

PROVENANCE: Commissioned and produced by Philipp Hainhofer, Augsburg, ca. 1625/26–31; Lutheran town councillors of Augsburg, 1632; presented by them to King Gustavus II Adolphus of Sweden (d. 1632); his widow, Queen Maria Eleonora, Svartslö Castle, Uppland; their daughter, Queen Christina of Sweden (r. 1632–54); descended in her family and kept at Uppsala Castle; presented by King Charles XI of Sweden to the University of Uppsala, 1694; Museum Gustavianum

REFERENCES: Alfter 1986, p. 97, no. 14, figs. 39–42; Rey 2000 (with numerous photographs); Boström 2001; Mauriès 2002, pp. 59–63

on it, which seems to number about twenty-seven in all (see fig. 126). Ulrich Baumgartner (1580–1652), the head of one of the leading Augsburg cabinet-making workshops, was responsible for the woodwork of most of Hainhofer's famous creations.

Despite its intricacy and ambitious purpose, this *Gesamtkunstwerk* has only three main parts. The bulkiness of the massive base is relieved by light-colored veneers, while its carved ebony decoration emphasizes the architectural nature of its design, which is also underscored by ripple moldings that catch and reflect light. This base contains a folding trestle table with an ebony-veneered top decorated with tablets of curiously veined stone (*pietra paesina*) and *commessi di pietre dure* depicting birds. Objects contained within the cabinet could be removed and set on this table to be admired individually.[6] Also stored in the base is a folding ladder. Having climbed this ladder to the summit of the cabinet, one can closely examine the assemblage of natural objects gathered there on a recessed rectangular socle that conceals an octave virginal (a small harpsichord). When the instrument is connected to a table clock (hidden by the natural objects) it will play three tunes automatically. On top of the socle there appears a profusion of exotic shells and corals that symbolize the deeps of far-away oceans and varicolored minerals that bespeak the riches buried in the land.[7] Crowning this composition is a partially gilded silver figure of Venus seated on a boat-shaped ewer cut from a Seychelles nut and supported by a figure of Neptune. Seychelles nuts, called *cocos-de-mer*, were believed to come from palm trees that grew beneath the waves of tropical oceans. Venus, the goddess of love, presides from the apex of the cabinet over everything below—especially the small enamels, carvings, and miniatures with scenes from the Old Testament that allude to love in its many variations. Is the theme of the cabinet, then, Virgil's aphorism "Love conquers all"?[8] While love seems to dominate it physically, the cabinet nevertheless represents the sum of everything in the world, and that necessarily includes hate. In the central niche on the front, set against a background dark as night, is an ivory statuette that illustrates the brutal story of Cain and Abel, the first children of Love after the expulsion from Paradise. (All of these instructive compositions can be viewed with ease because a revolving mechanism in the bulging section just above the base allows the upper part of the cabinet to be turned.)

The pull-out panel (see illustrations on p. 241) is often called a writing or reading board, but it probably had an intellectual and moral purpose rather than a utilitarian one. On the underside is a large painting on *pietra paesina* of the Old Testament story of Jonah, who was punished by God for disobeying His command. In the midst of a storm, the prophet is being thrown from the ship by the crew as a whale approaches to swallow him up. The heaving swells of water are indicated, with amazing realism, by the veins in the carefully selected stone. Because Jonah repented and was disgorged by the great fish after three days, his story is thought to prefigure Christ's death and resurrection; perhaps for that reason, the four Evangelists, authors of the New Testament, are depicted in minutely engraved silver rectangles around the painting. The large painting on the front of the panel, attributed to Johann König (1586–1642),[9] is a mythological river landscape, representing a piece of ideal nature.[10] Shown at left is the centaur Nessus carrying off Hercules' wife, Deianeira, in an attempt to ravish her. Hercules draws his bow and will slay Nessus.[11] The scene exemplifies human courage and virtue in conflict with the animal instinct-driven, amoral powers of nature. Eight cartouches around the painting display finely engraved silver figures by Lucas Kilian (1579–1637)[12] representing the sciences, arts, and crafts. Clockwise from the lower right, they are: study, painting, arithmetic, music, perspective (geometry), goldsmithing (the noblest craft), weaving (Hainhofer was the scion of a textile-producing family, and the craft was among Augsburg's most lucrative), and printing.[13]

The pull-out panel offers a summary of the cabinet's overall theme of the interplay of art and nature, which is present even in small details like the natural "oceans" of the *pietra paesina* panels enriched with man-made painting. The silver cartouches suggest that one of the cabinet's tasks may be to serve as a princely educational tool, inspiring contemplation and meditation.[14] This surely reflects Hainhofer's interest in the writings of the theologian Johann Valentin Andreae (1586–1654), with whom he corresponded. In 1619 Andreae published a description of a utopian state called Christianopolis, whose citizens seek both spiritual fulfillment and knowledge. Scientific pursuits, judged the most important, always have a practical side; that is, like Hainhofer, the scientists of Christianopolis are craftsmen as well as theoreticians. Andreae was influenced by the philosophical writings of Tommaso Campanella, especially his utopian treatise *La Città del Sole* (*The City of the Sun*), published in 1602. Campanella believed that "human knowledge had become ever more obscure and confused because it had distanced

pull-out panel, top

itself progressively from the direct experience of nature" through the senses. In the *City of the Sun*, therefore—and just as in Hainhofer's cabinet—the walls are painted with images drawn from all the arts and sciences, including ingenious inventions. The author believed, as Hainhofer must have done, that knowledge absorbed visually and continually in this way would be retained more easily.[15]

The cabinet's exterior and pull-out board are decorated with ovals filled with green, reddish, and yellow stones and marble in a black frame. This type of colorful rosettelike design element was already being used in the sixteenth century, for example on a Florentine tabletop made by Domenico del Tasso about 1590 and now in the Residenz, Munich.[16] Hainhofer must have seen a similar hardstone decoration on one of his trips to Munich or Italy. The same motif is noticeable in the hardstone inlay of a later cabinet made about 1642–46 for Ferdinand II de' Medici after a design of Matteo Nigetti and Jacopo Autelli (called Monnicca) which was in the Tribuna in Florence.[17] The continued appearance of this sophisticated detail demonstrates once again the long-lasting appreciation of hardstone mosaic throughout Europe.   W K

pull-out panel, bottom

1. Böttiger 1909–10, vol. 1, p. 68; Alfter 1986, pp. 55, 59.
2. Böttiger 1909–10, vol. 1, pp. 68, 69; Alfter 1986, p. 55.
3. Cederlund and Norrby 2003, pp. 4–5. Behm is not mentioned in Alfter 1986 nor in Boström 2001, and the name has not been found in Augsburg documents; possibly it was misspelled in the Swedish inventories.
4. Cederlund and Norrby 2003, p. 5.
5. Böttiger 1909–10 and Boström 2001 offer the most comprehensive descriptions of the cabinet.
6. Boström 2001, p. 296, fig. 31.
7. See Koeppe 2004.
8. *Eclogues* 10:69. See Hall 1979, p. 88.
9. See the entry on König by Hana Seifertova in *Dictionary of Art* 1996, vol. 18, p. 225.
10. Alfter 1986, p. 53.
11. Hall 1979, p. 152. The story is recounted by Ovid (*Metamorphoses* 9:101–33).
12. On Kilian, see Langer in Langer and Württemberg 1996, pp. 62–67, no. 5.
13. The subjects of these eight scenes were misinterpreted in Alfter 1986, p. 44; but if they are compared with the four similar scenes inlaid in a pull-out board in the *Pomeranian Cabinet*, together with Hainhofer's own description of the same cabinet, a correct identification can be made.
14. Boström 2001, p. 317.
15. See Alfter 1986, p. 55; Boström 2001. On Andreae, see http://www.enotes.com/literary-criticism/andreae-johann-valentin/introduction. On Campanella, and for the quotation, see the entry by Germana Ernst in Stanford Encyclopedia of Philosophy online (http://plato.stanford.edu/entries/campanella/).
16. Sigrid Sangl in Langer and Württemberg 1996, pp. 261–62, no. 73.
17. Giusti 1992, pl. 41; Bohr 1993, pp. 153–56, no. 1.18.3, figs. 40–43.

79. Display cabinet

Augsburg, ca. 1630
Ebony and other tropical and
European woods, red Egyptian
porphyry, semiprecious stones,
marble and other Italian stones,
pewter, ivory, tortoiseshell,
enamel, mother-of-pearl, mirror
glass, and painted stone; 28¾ ×
22⅞ × 23¼ in. (73 × 58 × 59 cm)
The J. Paul Getty Museum,
Los Angeles 89.DA.28

PROVENANCE: Private collection,
Sweden; [Galerie J. Kugel, Paris,
mid-1970s–1989]; acquired by the
J. Paul Getty Museum, 1989

REFERENCES: Alfter 1986, pp. 69–
70, 98, no. 23, figs. 56–58;
"Acquisitions" 1990, pp. 196–97,
no. 58; Bremer-David 1993,
p. 226, no. 393; Stafford 2001,
p. 15; Terpak 2001, figs. 27–30;
Mauriès 2002, ill. p. 58

Architectural in its form, this ebony cabinet is embellished with many kinds of decoration in wood and in stone, including semiprecious gems. Surmounted by a projecting cornice whose flat top is inlaid with a panel of red porphyry, the cabinet proper—a rectangular box that opens on every side—stands on a stepped socle inlaid on all four sides with panels of jasper and porphyry. In the front, a drawer is set into the top step of the socle on the front, above that are double doors, and over those a cartouche rests on a broken gable that pulls out, offering a surface on which the precious items contained within the cabinet could have been displayed. The cartouche-and-gable element also appears on the sides and back of the cabinet, but there it is not movable.

On each side of the cabinet, the hinged element swings open to reveal a small door surrounded by rows of drawers. On the front of the cabinet, these drawers are inlaid with black ebonized wood, snakewood, and hardstone medallions painted with miniature scenes of the life of Christ and symbols of the Passion. The small door at the center conceals a miniature compartment decorated with lapis lazuli and other semiprecious stones, orange and yellow tortoiseshell, ivory, and gilded or gold-colored details. Below the small door is a covered drawer that pulls out of the cabinet and must have served as a small writing desk in which writing implements could be stored. The two large doors on this main side of the cabinet display, on their inner sides, carved ebony arches framed by symbols of death executed in fruitwood, including skulls, torches, and blighted trees; in medallions below are, on one side, a basilisk (a mythical serpent hatched from a cock's egg and

front, doors closed

front, doors open

symbolizing alchemy), and on the other, an armillary sphere (symbolizing astronomy).

On the opposite side of the cabinet, a single door opens to show another group of small drawers; here they are veneered with tortoiseshell, inlaid with lapis lazuli, carnelian, and other semiprecious stones, and painted with images of the four Seasons and the four Elements. The small central door conceals a silk-lined compartment, and on the back of the door is the image of Fortune carved in imitation of an antique intaglio. Medallions that imitate antique carved gems, made of carnelian, agate, and onyx, also embellish the inside of the large door on this side, and they depict the contest between Apollo and Marsyas and other classical subjects. These medallions border, above and below, a large panel decorated with an arch, partly covered with carved-ebony drapery, that frames a fruitwood cross standing on Golgotha. Four small holes on this cross indicate that a corpus Christi, now lost, was once attached to it. Below the cross, Christ's orb is depicted, together with skulls, representing death, and a dolphin, representing life.

On the left side of the cabinet a large mirror hinged to the interior of the door swings out to reveal a velvet-lined panel. The small drawers behind the door are embellished with hardstone panels painted with biblical subjects, including what is likely a martyrdom scene in the center and a depiction of Judith with the head of Holofernes below. A single Limoges enamel plaque carrying a profile bust of Juno appears above. Around these drawers, architectural decoration—a cupola above and stairs below—is rendered in inlaid ebony, fruitwood, mother-of-pearl, and palm wood. The small central door opens to reveal a silk-lined compartment that extends through the cabinet to the opposite side.

The door on the right facade of the cabinet is hinged at the bottom and opens downward. It also functions as a shallow glass-covered vitrine, the interior of which is lined in red velvet. The small drawers behind it are embellished with fruitwood medallions, four of which are illusionistically attached to the cabinet with carved-wood ribbons. Four of the small medallions, carved in the sixteenth century, illustrate stories about women: Phyllis riding on Aristotle's back (after a print by Georg Pencz);[1] Jupiter in the form of Diana seducing Callisto, who has been turned into a bear; Delilah cutting Samson's hair (after a print by Pencz);[2] and David and Abigail. The two large oval medallions, both signed by the Netherlandish sculptor Albert Jansz Vinckenbrinck (1604/5–1664/5),

show landscapes with scenes of the death of Cleopatra and the death of Lucretia. The square center panel, also signed by Vinckenbrinck, depicts Christ and the Woman of Samaria. There are also two portrait medallions, inscribed and dated "Conrat Schieser 1526" and "Hans Christof Bach 1527," respectively. Carved wood depictions of the four Winds, the four Seasons, and the four Elements surround the series of drawers.

The large number of decorations with subjects in which women figure prominently suggests that the cabinet was made for a woman. These motifs and the many symbols of Christ's Passion reflect a concern for Christian virtue—they were intended, perhaps, as a moral counterbalance to the worldly function of the cabinet, the storage and display of precious objects.

We must now introduce a fascinating and complex personality, Philipp Hainhofer (1578–1647),[3] who, directly or indirectly, probably had a hand in the creation of the Getty cabinet. A native of the imperial free city of Augsburg, he studied jurisprudence for more than two years in Padua, Bologna, and Siena and afterward traveled through Italy. Back in Augsburg, he became a merchant of luxury goods and an adviser to princes about politics and the customs and styles at the most fashionable European courts. Evidently Hainhofer had acquired a very complete knowledge of the Florentine grand-ducal workshops, where highly specialized artisans in many fields created sophisticated furnishings, for in Augsburg he organized the craftsmen of the various guilds along the lines of the Galleria dei Lavori in Florence. He must have been deeply impressed by the ebony cabinets in the Tribuna of the Uffizi, for he created—with a passion that went far beyond his commercial interests—similar showpieces whose rich iconography reflects his erudition in theology, history, and the natural sciences. His own famous *Wunderkammer*-collection, which was in a constant state of revision, supplied him with gems, carved reliefs and semiprecious stones, and medals with which to embellish his furniture. Certain *objets de vertu* on the Getty cabinet—the enamel portrait of Juno, the fruitwood medallions, and other ornaments—do not fit seamlessly into the iconographic program of the cabinet; probably Hainhofer selected them from his *Kunstkammer*, judging them aesthetically suitable for the new piece.[4] Allusions to virtuous women appear often in the decorations on furniture made under Hainhofer's direction for highborn female patrons, who must have received a remarkably thorough humanistic education to be able to appreciate them.[5]

right side, with bottom-hinged door open

Many craftsmen contributed to these lavish pieces. At the solemn consignment of the *Pomeranian Cabinet* made about 1615 for Duke Philip II of Pomerania (destroyed 1945; fragments in Kunstgewerbemuseum, Berlin), all the artisans involved were present; at least twenty-seven of them can be counted in a picture that commemorates the event (fig. 126). Certain parts of the Getty cabinet seem to have been made by the same artisans who worked on the Hainhofer cabinet presented to Gustavus Adolphus, king of Sweden, and now at Uppsala University (cat. no 78).[6]

On a first glance at the exterior, the Getty cabinet appears quite different in style from the usual Hainhofer furniture, which is more Baroque in its shapes and more lavishly decorated with hardstone mosaic panels and medallions, carvings, and silver ornaments. Most Hainhofer pieces also have

an artisanal spirit and do not adhere in a highly disciplined way to canons of architectural form and proportion. In a wooden intarsia picture of cabinetmakers in a workshop, set within the Uppsala cabinet,[7] for example, one senses the pride of the privileged guild members of an imperial free city—a kind of Meistersinger mentality quite foreign to the values of courtly society that emanate so clearly from products of the Galleria dei Lavori.

On the other hand, the Getty cabinet, when closed, has the strict proportions and simple appearance of a piece of Renaissance furniture, looking not at all like the model of an existing or projected building, as do its Tuscan counterparts.[9] More specifically, it resembles furniture of the Cinquecento, the period of Giorgio Vasari and Bartolomeo Ammanati. As a matter of fact, we know that Hainhofer planned furniture of this very kind, which he rightly called "all'antica." In the years 1627–29 he designed a "table," which, to judge from the drawings, was a chest in the Vasarian taste. Its Renaissance look is similar in spirit to that of the Getty cabinet's exterior.[9]

The white-veined jasper slabs on the doors of the Getty cabinet bring to mind the solemn Florentine sarcophagi of the Cinquecento. When the doors are opened, the contrast between the exterior and the interior is dramatic. Inside, bright colors and rich ornament prevail; nevertheless, they are displayed in rational geometric patterns that harmonize with the anti-Baroque exterior. The brightness of the color is always handled with the utmost delicacy—as on the Italian *stipos* (cabinets) manufactured in Rome and Naples.[10] The artisan responsible for the decoration of this cabinet must have had experience in the court workshops of Italy.

The Getty cabinet is not the most magnificent furniture created under Hainhofer's aegis, nor is it the most flawless in execution; certainly, however, it is one of the most elegant pieces to leave the Augsburg workshops in the first decades of the seventeenth century.   D H

1. R. A. Koch 1980, p. 120, no. 97.
2. Ibid., p. 95, no. 28.
3. See Alfter 1986, pp. 46–49.
4. Peter Fusco, Catherine Hess et al., typescript, curatorial files, Department of Sculpture and Decorative Arts, The J. Paul Getty Museum, Los Angeles.
5. Hainhofer pieces lend themselves well to gender studies. See Alfter 1986, p. 53, and fig. 1.
6. See Boström 2001.
7. Alfter 1986, pl. 1.
8. Bohr 1993, pp. 127–33, nos. I.6, I.8, I.10, figs. 12, 14, 16.
9. Heikamp 1966.
10. See Riccardi-Cubitt 1992, pp. 59, 175, pls. 24, 25.

80. Cup with cover

Freiburg im Breisgau (southwest Germany), ca. 1560–70
Rock crystal, partly gilded silver mounts; H. 9¾ in. (24.5 cm)
The Metropolitan Museum of Art, New York, Gift of J. Pierpont Morgan, 1917 17.190.532

PROVENANCE: Baron Albert Oppenheim, Cologne, by 1904; acquired from him by J. Pierpont Morgan (1837–1913), by 1910; his gift to the Metropolitan Museum, 1917

REFERENCES: Molinier 1904, p. 64, no. 149; Williamson 1910, pp. 97–98, no. 66, pl. XLV; Irmscher 1997, p. 115, no. 35

The gilded silver mounts of this splendid covered cup hold its various pieces of shaped rock crystal together and at the same time echo their curves. At least five specimens of virtually the same high degree of purity were assembled to make the precious cup, stem, and lid. During the Renaissance such objects were collected by princes because they symbolized worldly power. Elector August of Saxony had forty-two rock-crystal vessels, which he kept not in his *Kunstkammer* but in the specially secured treasury of his Dresden palace, so valuable and significant were they in his estimation.[1]

Rock crystal is a type of quartz composed of large hexagonal crystals. Because the finest pieces have no metallic impurities, it is extremely difficult to pinpoint their place of origin. Nevertheless, for stylistic reasons, this object can be attributed to the Freiburg region—in the late sixteenth century part of Austria—where rich deposits were located. The stonecutters of Freiburg could not compete with their counterparts in Milan, who from flawless rock crystal tablets created paper-thin intaglio-decorated masterworks, but they developed their own style, faceting and gadrooning rock crystal in a very pleasing way. The ovoid bowl of this cup and the surface treatment of the acorn knop point strongly to a Freiburg manufactory. The cup should be compared to an example with Freiburg silver mounts originally in the Residenz, Munich (now in the Bayerisches Nationalmuseum, Munich, no. 2205), and the knop to that on another cup, in the Grünes Gewölbe, Dresden.[2]

The initial purpose of the cup and cover was surely to display a wonder of nature, the "petrified tears of the ancient gods," as rock crystal was sometimes described in ancient times, and perhaps also to hold healing liquids, as the transparent stone was associated with miracles and good health. In Christian symbolism, rock crystal was compared to divine purity and strong faith.[3] Later, this covered cup probably served as a reliquary. The finial in the form of an acorn suggests its new purpose, since a fallen oak tree symbolizes the conversion of the pagans.[4] Furthermore, the addition of a hook and eye on the lip mount meant that the vessel could be closed and sealed, as required by the Catholic Church in order to preserve holy relics without fear of tampering.

WK

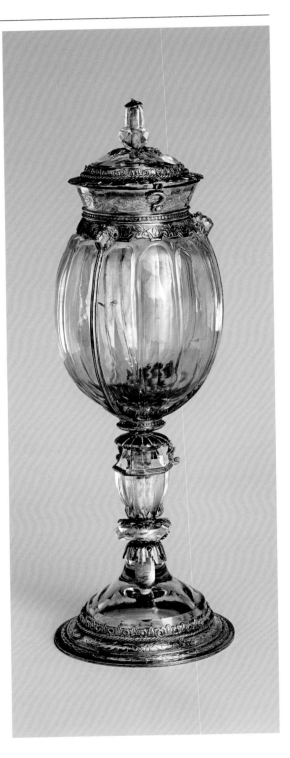

1. Kappel 2004, p. 250.
2. Irmscher 1997, pp. 85–88, nos. 1, 2.
3. Hahnloser and Brugger-Koch 1985, p. 10.
4. Hall 1979, p. 227.

81. Bust of a young woman

Kassel, ca. 1690
By Christoph Labhardt
Hardstones; H. 7½ in. (18.9 cm)
Museumslandschaft Hessen
Kassel, Sammlung für
Kunsthandwerk und Plastik
B VI.22

PROVENANCE: Landgrave Karl I of
Hesse-Kassel (before 1695 until
d. 1730); Kassel collections; entered
the Staatliche Museen, Kassel, now
Museumslandschaft Hessen Kassel

REFERENCES: Schmidberger 1986,
p. 46, fig. 16; Schnackenburg-Praël
1999, p. 897, fig. 4

The discovery of deposits of agate, jasper, and other semiprecious stones in the Hesse region of Germany, offering the hope of diversifying the predominantly agricultural economy, encouraged the local lord, Landgrave Karl I of Hesse-Kassel (1654–1730), to invest in a stonecutting mill, which was erected at the moat in the fortifications around Kassel Castle in 1680. In his description of the Hesse territories in 1697, Johann-Just Winkelmann stressed the great success of the water-driven machinery of the mill, located only a short walking distance from the Kassel *Kunstkammer*.[1] That house of curiosities would become the home of many precious items made close by.

In fact, hardstone cutting already had a long tradition in the region, although earlier works were probably small jewels, paving stones, and miscellaneous objects without much decoration. This situation changed dramatically with the arrival of a very gifted artisan at Karl's court. In his publication of 1697 Winkelmann mentions the production of "cups of *crystal de Montagne* [rock crystal] with carved figures, scenes, and portraits, which were not seen before" made by the "famous artist Christoph Labhardt."[2] The present object, a relatively small bust of a young woman by Labhardt, is carved from a carefully selected variety of veined stones with which the artist tested his ability to evoke on a small scale the monumentality of ancient female busts. Labhardt (1644–1695) achieved similar results in a superb bust of a woman (fig. 85) made of two different kinds of amber, a substance that during the Baroque period was still counted among the semiprecious stones. The coiffure of the present bust, the hair parted in the center and gathered in thick strands in the back, echoes in its restrained order the regular folds of the stolelike garment that is knotted just below the young woman's décolleté. Her head is turned slightly down and to her left, and she is obviously lost in thought. The bust is mounted on a stepped base and a pedestal in the shape of confronted scrolls. The facial features and sculptural characteristics find close parallels in the various female figures on Labhardt's chef d'oeuvre, a monumental relief (31 × 56 inches) that the artist created at the court of Count Johannes of Nassau in Idstein between 1671 and 1679 (today in the Grünes Gewölbe, Dresden).[3]

Whether this delicate display object was part of a larger group or was intended for a special purpose is not known. A very similar bust is recognizable in the tympanum of a miniature facade that was obviously meant to be decorated with various hardstones (see fig. 70). This design, by Johann Albrecht Lavilette, a student of Labhardt's, may document an ambitious project for a cabinetlike structure that was never realized.[4] Just before the printing of this catalogue, it was learned that a miniature facade of this type survives in part; uncovering its history will require further study.[5]   WK

1. Winkelmann 1697, pt. 3, chap. 8, p. 389, cited in Schmidberger 1986, p. 41. See also K.-H. Meyer 1973; Meinolf Siemer in Schmidberger and T. Richter 2001, pp. 298–99, no. 133.
2. Winkelmann 1697, pt. 3, chap. 8, p. 389, cited in Schmidberger 1986, p. 42.
3. Schnackenburg-Praël 1999; Kappel in Syndram, Kappel, and Weinhold 2006, pp. 118–19 (figures at left).
4. Schnackenburg-Praël 1999, p. 897.
5. E-mail communication from Antje Scherner, Museumslandschaft Hessen Kassel, January 11, 2008.

82. Dish on stand, box, and footed bowl

Kassel, early 18th century
Mounts by Johann Melchior
Lennep and Johann Christoph
Homagius
Jasper, gilded silver mounts; dish
on stand 4¾ × 4⅛ in. (11.9 ×
10.3 cm), box 3¼ × 4¾ in. (8 ×
12 cm), footed bowl 4¼ × 7½ in.
(10.7 × 19.1 cm)
Museumslandschaft Hessen
Kassel, Sammlung für
Kunsthandwerk und Plastik
B II.167, B II.131, B II.125

PROVENANCE: Landgrave Karl I
of Hesse-Kassel (until d. 1730);
Hesse-Kassel Kunsthaus, 1763;
Museum Fridericianum, Kassel,
1779; Museumslandschaft Hessen
Kassel, 1913

REFERENCES: Schmidberger 1986,
pp. 41–42, fig. 1; Schmidberger in
Schmidberger and T. Richter 2001,
p. 295, no. 131

These three vessels were made for Landgrave Karl I of Hesse-Kassel (1654–1730) from a white-speckled red jasper (called Frankenberg agate) locally quarried in Frankenberg and Schmalkalden and decorated with gilded silver mounts by Johann Melchior Lennep (1683–1767) and Johann Christoph Homagius (1684/85–1735), goldsmiths at the Kassel court.[1] A water-powered stone-grinding mill was operated at the moat surrounding Kassel Castle from about 1680 to 1693, when the lapidary workshop was moved to the Agathof in Bettenhausen, outside the city. In 1699 it was transferred to Frankenberg, in immediate proximity to the stone quarries.

For mercantilist purposes Karl I invested in local industries and supported craftsmen of extraordinary artistic talent. Although before modern times lapidaries and gem cutters generally remained anonymous, two artisans of Karl's court, Christoph Labhardt (see cat. no. 81) and his pupil Johann Albrecht Lavilette, achieved wide renown.[2] Among the goldsmiths, who mounted the stones as well as producing sumptuous metal objects for the court such as gold boxes, D. Corstens, Johann Balthasar Jehner, Johann Melchior Lennep, and Johann Christoph Homagius (who also worked as a lapidary) are the best known. Together these artists produced numerous vessels in which the beauty of the local jasper is brought out by the fine quality of the carving and the intricately fashioned mounts. Some pieces served as diplomatic gifts, advertising the superior products of the Kassel workshop abroad; others remained at Kassel Castle; and the finest were kept in the Kunsthaus, Karl's treasury, established in a separate building near his residence in 1696.[3]   F K

1. Schmidberger in Schmidberger and T. Richter 2001, p. 295,
   no. 131.
2. Schmidberger 1986.
3. Leopold 1995, p. 154.

83. Game board

Germany, possibly a workshop in Kassel, before 1683
Boxwood and walnut on a core of linden wood, agates, honestone, gilded metal, and enamel; 3 × 12½ × 12½ in. (7.5 × 31.5 × 31.5 cm)
Museumslandschaft Hessen Kassel, Sammlung für Kunsthandwerk und Plastik B II.409

PROVENANCE: Landgravine Hedwig Sophie von Hessen-Kassel (1649–1683); Museumslandschaft Hessen Kassel

Game boards that could be used for a variety of tête-à-tête games were often made with fancifully carved chess pieces and elaborately embellished counters for other pastimes. The board itself—usually with sixty-four squares in two alternating colors—offered artisans the opportunity to show off their marquetry or stonecutting skills. Boards made for the amusements of the princely European courts were decorated in the most lavish way.

Hardstone chessmen were made in Europe by about the year one thousand, as is documented by a set of rock-crystal pieces at the monastery of San Rosendo de Celanova in northwestern Spain.[1] The artisans of the Renaissance and Baroque periods created sumptuously ornamented courtly game boards. Most are of great artistic merit and value, befitting their owner's princely status. One example is a board of 1550–60 covered with engraved metalwork and glass with delicate ornamentation gilded and painted on the reverse (*verre églomisé*) that is now in the Kunstgewerbemuseum in Berlin.[2] A seventeenth-century game set with Eger relief marquetry (see entry for cat. no. 53) is one of the attractions of the Grünes Gewölbe in Dresden.[3] An early inventory of the *Kunstkammer* of the dukes of Württemberg lists "a chessboard of agate stone," perhaps similar to the one seen here, which has survived in the Landesmuseum in Stuttgart.[4]

When closed, the present example offers the player, on one side, a chess- and checkerboard of hardstone, and on the other, a game field of inlaid wood for the games Dame and Mühle. Opened, it reveals two fields for backgammon or a variant called trictrac, in stone and gilded and enameled metal. On the outside, the gilded metal repoussé frame with fluted and leaf scrolls is decorated with applied enamel cartouches bearing the monogram *HSLH*, for Hedwig Sophie, landgravine of Hessen-Kassel (daughter of Georg Wilhelm, elector of Brandenburg), under a princely crown that indicates her high rank. The other fields have emblems with scenes and inscriptions such as "Sans ombre" (without shadow), "Constant et fidel" (steadfast and loyal), and "Rienne me change que la mort" (Nothing changes me but death) and memento mori motifs.[5]

It is difficult to decide where this board was made. The use of local agates (from Hesse quarries) points to Kassel, which would make this object one of the first true showpieces made in a Kassel manufactory. It would also confirm the presence there of a fair number of highly qualified specialists in carving, enameling, and goldsmithing.   W K

1. Cazaux 2000; see also Himmelheber 1972.
2. Ryser in Ryser and Salmen 1995, pp. 112–14, no. 17.
3. Voigt 1999, pp. 222–23.
4. "ein Schachspiel von Agatstein"; inv. WLM KK82. See Fleischhauer 1976, p. 30.
5. I am most grateful to Antje Scherner, Museumslandschaft Hessen Kassel, for this information.

84. Tea service

Lapidary work: Court workshop, Kassel, ca. 1690–95
Agate
Mounts: Baur workshop, Augsburg, ca. 1695–1700
Gilded silver and cold-painted enamel
Teapot 6⅜ × 9⅛ in. (16 × 23 cm); candlesticks 6⅝ and 6⅞ × 4⅞ in. (16.5 and 17.5 × 12.2 cm); footed tray 3½ × 8⅞ × 7¾ in. (8.7 × 22.5 × 19.5 cm); cups H. 1⅝ in. (4 cm), Diam. 2¾ in. (7 cm); saucers H. 1¼ in. (3 cm), Diam. 5 in. (12.5 cm); spoons L. 4½–4⅝ in. (11.3–11.6 cm)

This twenty-one-piece tea service is one of the earliest sets of its kind with gilded silver mounts that survives. It is mentioned in the 1740 estate inventory of Duchess Marie Amalie von Sachsen-Zeitz together with an agate toilette set that also included many pieces, which has since been lost. The duchess's toilette set may have looked like a gilded silver example with polished agate decoration in the Germanisches National-museum in Nuremberg.[1] The elaborate form and size of this tea set belonging to her, not to men-tion its costly gilding, point to a princely patron. Services mounted with precious metals were exclusively made for royalty or members of ruling dynasties. Frequently they were wedding gifts that

remained the personal property of the bride. The fact that Duchess Marie Amalie left the present set to her daughter may reflect this custom.

At the end of the seventeenth century, tea leaves imported from China were expensive and used primarily for medicinal purposes. Gradually, well-to-do Europeans discovered the delicious and refreshing aspect of various sorts of tea. Much attention was paid to the equipment used for all aspects of tea drinking;[2] additionally, the costli-ness of the tea leaves and of the sugar for sweeten-ing the drink demanded containers with airtight lids, in this instance a vase-shaped tea caddy and an oval sugar box. The design of other pieces, such as the small cups and the teapot with a bizarre

Museumslandschaft Hessen
Kassel, Sammlung für
Kunsthandwerk und Plastik
B II.126, 173, 174, 198a,b, 199–210

PROVENANCE: Duchess Marie
Amalie von Sachsen-Zeitz (1670–
1739); her daughter Princess
Dorothea Wilhelmine (1691–
1743), who married Landgrave
Wilhelm VIII von Hessen-Kassel
in 1717; entered the Museum
Fridericianum, Kassel, in 1779
(1780, 1827 inventories); transferred
to the Staatliche Museen, Kassel
(now Museumslandschaft Hessen
Kassel)

REFERENCES: Hannelore Müller
in *Augsburger Barock* 1968, pp. 293–94,
no. 425; Ulla Krempel in *Bayern*
1972, pp. 450–51, no. 1390;
Hernmarck 1977, vol. 1, p. 146,
vol. 2, p. 115, pl. 308; Heitmann
1979, pp. 38, 58, 76–77, 82–83, 157–58,
no. 17; Seling 1980, vol. 1, pp. 127,
293, no. 562, vol. 2, pl. 562, vol. 3,
p. 247, no. 1776, g, and p. 256,
no. 1809, e; Blair 1987, ill. p. 106;
Schmidberger in Baumstark and
Seling 1994, vol. 2, pp. 441–43,
no. 118; Ottomeyer 1999, fig. 5;
Weinhold 2000, pp. 68–69; Meinolf
Siemer in Schmidberger and
T. Richter 2001, p. 296, no. 132;
Schütte 2003, pp. 332–37, no. 21

zoomorphic spout, was adapted from exotic porcelain forms imported from China and Japan.

The elegant look of this ensemble results in large part from the contrast between the polished agate, filled with reddish nuances, and the gilded mounts, with their restrained gadrooning and refined scroll decoration. Quite extraordinary accessories are the two triple-dish stands (see below), which may have been used to serve sweets. They could also have served as spice dishes and are perhaps survivors of the lost toilette set, which likely included table-service equipment.

The imperial city of Augsburg, in southern Germany, was the most important center of goldsmithing in central Europe from the late sixteenth until the early nineteenth century.[3] Tobias Baur and his brother Matthäus II probably executed this set. With Elias Adam they were the city's chief specialists in mounting hardstone vessels, but they

could also produce services of ruby-colored glass, lacquer, and enamel mounted in their trademark settings of gilded silver.[4]

The red Kellerwald agate and other agates used in this tea set were possibly mined in northern Hesse and then were shaped at the stonecutting mill built in 1680 in the fortifications at Kassel Castle (see entry for cat. no. 82) before being sent to Augsburg to be assembled and mounted.[5]

WK

1. Pechstein 1987, pp. 168–76, no. 83.
2. Schiedlausky 1961; Adriaensens 1993.
3. See Baumstark and Seling 1994; for the Kassel set, see Schmidberger in vol. 2, pp. 441–43, no. 118. For a gilded silver toilette set at the Metropolitan Museum, made in Augsburg, see Koeppe in "Recent Acquisitions" 2006, pp. 40–41.
4. Baumstark and Seling 1994, vol. 2, pp. 409–49.
5. Schütte 2003, p. 336.

triple-dish stand

85. Bowl crowned with the figure of Mercury

Stuttgart, 1610–23
Lapidary work probably by
Hans Kobenhaupt; mounts prob-
ably by Hans Kobenhaupt and/or
François Guichard
Jasper, enameled gold mounts;
H. with figure 4⅞ in. (12.3 cm);
H. without figure 3 in. (7.5 cm)
Staatliche Kunstsammlungen
Dresden, Grünes Gewölbe V15

PROVENANCE: First mentioned in
the inventory of precious objects
in the Grünes Gewölbe, Dresden,
1725 (fol. 155v, no. 17)

REFERENCES: J. Erbstein and
A. Erbstein 1884, p. 110, no. 15;
Sponsel 1921, p. 155; Sponsel 1929,
p. 220, pl. 27; Menzhausen 1977,
p. 187, fig. 117; Syndram, Arnold,
and Kappel 1997, p. 150, no. 9;
Kappel in Kappel and Weinhold
2007, p. 111

This bowl in the shape of a shell was first listed among the precious objects in Dresden's Grünes Gewölbe (Green Vault) in 1725.[1] The inventory presents an overview of the treasury's holdings of carved stone vessels in nephrite, jasper, onyx and sardonyx, chalcedony, agate, alabaster, carnelian, garnet, lapis lazuli, serpentine, and of course rock crystal.[2] The dating and attribution of these bowls have varied considerably. Julius and Albert Erbstein (1884) dated this one to 1600. In 1921 Jean-Louis Sponsel thought that the gold rim of its foot, which is decorated with hunting scenes, suggested the work of the Dresden goldsmith Gabriel Gipfel (d. 1617). A few years later Sponsel reconsidered, judging the bowl to be Italian work. Finally in 1977 Joachim Menzhausen attributed the piece to Hans Kobenhaupt in Stuttgart (d. 1623). This last assessment has held in the years since then, with slight refinements.[3]

In stonecutting style the bowl differs from other vessels in various European collections attributed to Hans Kobenhaupt. Most are furnished with lids that provide a base on which to place the crowning figures. Their walls were either left smooth or decorated with delicate engraving.[4] Kobenhaupt only rarely chose the stylized shell shape. On the edge of a similarly cut bowl of about 1620 in the Louvre, small gilded enamel figures of Neptune and Venus stand atop a volute[5]—a composition similar to that of the present work from the Grünes Gewölbe. To be sure, this one lacks the foliate cuffs with curving dolphins of enameled gold between the shaft and the body of the bowl, which are characteristic of Kobenhaupt's work.[6] Mounts with these dolphins and also with tiny, extremely delicately enameled gold figures, most frequently representing Victory, Fortuna, Minerva, Venus Marina, or Mercury (as in the present case), are among the distinguishing characteristics of Kobenhaupt's vessels. As yet it is uncertain who was responsible for these exquisite enameled works. Werner Fleischhauer suggested that their maker was the goldsmith and medalist François Guichard, who began working at the court in Stuttgart in 1610, shortly after the arrival of Kobenhaupt in 1609.[7] It seems perfectly conceivable that this piece represents a collaboration between the stonecutter Kobenhaupt and the superbly trained goldsmith Guichard. Such a collaboration of equals would fully accord with contemporary workshop traditions as they are known from Milan and Prague.[8]

The bowl shown here and its pendant in the Grünes Gewölbe are made of jasper from the Baumholder deposit in the Idar and Oberstein regions of the Rhineland-Palatinate, a native raw material that is extremely attractive both in color and in texture.[9]

JK

1. Mentioned in the same inventory is a pendant bowl (no. 18), on the edge of which stands a small enameled gold figure of Venus with a dolphin (Venus Marina). Its present inventory number is V32.
2. The Historisches Grünes Gewölbe (Historic Green Vault) was opened to the public in the Dresden Royal Palace in 2006. Its holdings of hardstone carvings are impressively displayed in the hall of precious objects, with mirrored walls. See Syndram, Kappel, and Weinhold 2006, pp. 100–123.
3. In the 1994/97 guide to the Grünes Gewölbe, the attribution was "probably by Hans Kobenhaupt," but in the 2007 guide, the bowl (and its pendant) were firmly grouped by the present author with two other altogether typical Kobenhaupt bowls in the Dresden collection (inv. V6 and V214). See Syndram, Arnold, and Kappel 1997, p. 150, no. 9; Kappel in Kappel and Weinhold 2007, p. 111.
4. For works by Kobenhaupt in other collections, see Reinhard Sänger in *Die Renaissance im deutschen Südwesten* 1986, pp. 621–23, nos. LII–LI3: Alcouffe 2001, pp. 345–51, nos. 169–72.

5. Alcouffe 2001, pp. 348–49, no. 171, and fig. 171a (which illustrates another shell-shaped bowl, in the Kunsthistorisches Museum, Vienna).
6. There are bowls with such dolphin ornaments in the Grünes Gewölbe (inv. V6, V214) and others in Copenhagen, among them the only dated (1620) and signed Kobenhaupt bowl (Rosenborg Palace, inv. 1–121).
7. Fleischhauer 1972, p. 30. See also Irmscher 1997, p. 32.

8. Rudolf Distelberger suspected that either Kobenhaupt produced the settings himself or an apprentice in his workshop was entrusted with them. See Distelberger 2002, pp. 239–42, no. 140.
9. For the location of the deposit, see R. Schmidt 1995, pp. 112–13. I am also indebted to the mineralogists Professor Klaus Thalheim, Dresden, and Dr. Gerhard Holzhey, Erfurt, for information about this variety of jasper.

86. Two bowls

Workshop of Johann Friedrich Böttger, Dresden, 1714
Coral agate
Mounts: Early 19th century
Gilded brass
a. H. 3¾ in. (9.5 cm), b. H. 4¼ in. (10.7 cm)
Staatliche Kunstsammlungen Dresden, Grünes Gewölbe
a. V507 (polishing unfinished), b. V520 (finished)

PROVENANCE: Delivered from the Böttger workshop on October 1, 1714; first mentioned in the inventory of precious objects in the Grünes Gewölbe, Dresden, 1733 (p. 913, nos. 205, 206)

REFERENCES: *Johann Friedrich Böttger* 1982, p. 218, illus. p. 216; Kappel in *Königliches Dresden* 1990, p. 79, nos. 75, 76; Kappel in *Unter einer Krone* 1997, p. 152, no. 183; Kappel 1998, p. 167, nos. 65, 66; Kappel in Kappel and Weinhold 2007, p. 256

After silver, colored gemstones were Saxony's most valuable mineral resource. As early as 1575 Elector Augustus (r. 1553–86) commissioned the multitalented architect and sculptor Giovanni Maria Nosseni to undertake a systematic search for new deposits.

The type of stone used for these two bowls was given the name "coral agate" at the time of its discovery in reference to its splendid color. In February 1697 the German scientist and mathematician Ehrenfried Walther von Tschirnhaus (see entry for cat. no. 87) informed the reigning elector of Saxony, Frederick Augustus I (Augustus the Strong), that this agate variety had been found in the village of Halsbach, near Freiberg in the Saxon Erzgebirge, and submitted samples of it.[1]

The elector suggested setting up a new factory in which to work the stone, and in fact Tschirnhaus did briefly operate a grinding and polishing mill he built himself outside the Dresden city gates. Nevertheless, the venture never prospered. Only polished samples, displaying the "Güthe und Schönheit" (quality and beauty) of the stone, were produced.[2] In 1708, after Tschirnhaus's death, Frederick King Augustus I, who also ruled Poland-Lithuania under the name King Augustus II, engaged Johann Friedrich Böttger (1682–1719), the inventor of the process for manufacturing Meissen's famous white porcelain, to oversee a grinding and polishing mill for Saxon gemstones; it was in operation from 1713 to 1715.[3] The two bowls displayed here, both decorated with acanthus-and-scale ornaments and one never

a, b

finished, are known to have been part of a delivery from the Böttger factory on October 1, 1714.[4] The archival document relates that eight of a total of nine coral agate bowls had been "aussgemuschelt und polirt" (hollowed out in the form of shells and polished). These two bowls show that the Böttger grinding and polishing mill was capable of highly refined work and also made use of the skills of glass cutters to carry out the decoration. Nevertheless, many of the projects Böttger planned

must not have been realized, for the king found the grinding mill insufficiently profitable.[5]   J K

1. Tschirnhaus to Frederick Augustus I, February 21, 1697, Sächsisches Hauptstaatsarchiv Dresden, Loc. 36179, no. 2926, fol. 4. See also Quellmalz 1990, pp. 35, 75.
2. Quoted in Steinbrück 1717 (1982 ed.), [vol. 1], p. 32, [vol. 2], p. 57.
3. Böttger's job description was "Manufactur-Administrator." See Steinbrück 1717 (1982 ed.), [vol. 1], p. 40, [vol. 2], p. 61.
4. Sächsisches Hauptstaatsarchiv Dresden, Loc. 1340, fol. 332. See also Menzhausen 1982.
5. For the Tschirnhaus and Böttger grinding mills, see Kappel 1998, pp. 64–66.

87. Bust of a woman

Dresden, 1725–30
Attributed to Paul Heermann
and Johann Christoph Hübner
Amethyst, tufa, serpentine breccia, and gilded bronze; H. 21⅞ in. (55.5 cm)
Staatliche Kunstsammlungen Dresden, Grünes Gewölbe V592

PROVENANCE: First mentioned in the inventory of precious objects in the Grünes Gewölbe, Dresden, 1733 (p. 361)

REFERENCES: Menzhausen in *Königliches Dresden* 1990, pp. 80–81, no. 91; Kappel 1998, pp. 172–73, no. 71; Kappel in *Glory of Baroque Dresden* 2004, pp. 170–72, no. 4.28; Kappel in *Splendeurs de la cour de Saxe* 2006, pp. 198–99, no. 103; Kappel in Syndram, Kappel, and Weinhold 2006, p. 120

In 1696 Elector Frederick Augustus I commissioned Ehrenfried Walther von Tschirnhaus to find and develop deposits of gemstones in Saxon territory (see entry for cat. no. 86). He wished to discover how such finds "might be exploited commercially."[1] Geological expeditions such as this, not to mention pure chance, which is not to be discounted, led in 1721 to the first written mention of an amethyst deposit in the village of Schlottwitz, near Glashütte, not far from Dresden.[2] Precise mineralogical analysis has determined that the rich violet amethyst used in the bust under discussion came from that deposit. In 1733 this sculptural masterwork was prominently displayed on a table in one of the window niches of the Grünes Gewölbe in the Dresden Royal Palace.[3]

The design for the bust in the antique style is certainly the work of Paul Heermann (1673–1732). After arriving from Rome, he took up his position as court sculptor in Dresden in 1705 at the latest.[4] The pose, the facial features, and the hairdo are reminiscent of early Hellenistic precedents, like those on which Heermann based his marble *Recumbent Venus* of about 1720, for example.[5] The complex stonecutting must have been entrusted to Johann Christoph Hübner (1665–1739), who collaborated on treasury art pieces created by the Dresden court jeweler Johann Melchior Dinglinger and was considered the best of Dresden's gem cutters.[6]

In terms of technique, the execution of the bust is fascinating; the proper right side of the face is made up of fragments of amethyst fitted together, whereas the left side was cut from a single piece.

The neck, shoulders, and breast section, above the garment of gilded bronze, was carved from tufa, to which carefully cut and polished pieces of amethyst were cemented.[7] The modeling is exquisite, especially the animated folds of the drapery, which skillfully reflect the shape of the breasts.[8] The casting must have been executed in Dresden as well. Michael Johann Weinhold (1662–1732), from Danzig, a craftsman highly esteemed at court, operated a bronze-casting workshop in the city.

J K

1. "Ins Commercium zubringen sein möchten." Quoted in Quellmalz 1990, p. 35.
2. Thalheim 1998, p. 20; Thalheim in Kappel 1998, p. 185, no. 78.
3. With the opening of the Baroque Historisches Grünes Gewölbe in September 2006, the bust was returned to its former location, which is precisely indicated in the inventory of precious objects in the Grünes Gewölbe, 1733. See Kappel in Syndram, Kappel, and Weinhold 2006, p. 120.
4. For details of Heermann's biography, see E. D. Schmidt 2005, pp. 21, 65–66.
5. Staatliche Kunstsammlungen Dresden, Skulpturensammlung, inv. no. ZV 3607. As early as 1726 this work was displayed in the picture gallery of the Dresden Royal Palace, not in the Kunstkammer. See Martin Raumschüssel in *Verborgene Schätze der Skulpturensammlung* 1992, pp. 52–53, no. 37; E. D. Schmidt 2005, p. 30, fig. 22, and pp. 67–68, n. 44, which relates that Heermann restored six antique sculptures in Dresden (four of them busts), as mentioned in the inventory made in 1728 of the sculpture gallery.
6. For Hübner, see Watzdorf 1972, esp. pp. 17ff.
7. When the bust was dismantled during restoration work in 1990, conservators discovered that the head was affixed to the neck by two iron pins implanted in the tufa.
8. Busts with drapery by Heermann are mentioned in E. D. Schmidt 2005, pp. 22–28, figs. 15–19, pp. 66–67, and see also figs. 11–14 (busts of the four Seasons, Paul Heermann [?], Rome, ca. 1720, Národní Galerie, Prague).

88. Ceremonial cup

Frankfurt am Main, ca. 1700–1705
Jade (nephrite), alabaster
(aragonite), chalcedony, banded
agate, diamonds, rubies, garnets,
gold, gilded silver, and enamel;
H. 16 in. (40.6 cm)
The Metropolitan Museum of
Art, New York, Robert Lehman
Collection, 1975 1975.1.1508

PROVENANCE: Robert Lehman,
New York; his gift to the
Metropolitan Museum in 1975

REFERENCE: Draper 2008, p. 32,
no. 63

The oval jade cup and cover of this piece are supported by the figure of a bearded Turk carved out of alabaster, who kneels on a jade base.[1] The enchained Ottoman is doomed to hold the position forever and thus is prevented from using the weapons that are teasingly placed at his feet. This finely cut statuette is a reminder of the defeat of the Ottoman army by a European one at the Battle of Vienna (1683) and of the Treaty of Karlovci in 1699,[2] which established the Habsburg dynasty as one of the main European military powers.

The finial on the lid consists of the crowned bust of a Roman emperor and below that an alabaster medallion decorated on the front with the double-headed eagle of the Holy Roman Empire, which carries on its breast the enameled arms of the Habsburgs. The arms are "backed up" on the reverse by enameled arms of the three ecclesiastical electors of the empire, the archbishops of Mainz, Trier, and Cologne. The arms of their six secular counterparts are placed within two cartouches on the cup below. (On the electors of the empire, see cat. no. 93).

The jade cup, cover, and foot are decorated with moldings cut into the jade. They separate triangular fields filled with pierced, lace-inspired gold ornaments representing aristocratic interests and amusements: amid garlands and blossoms are huntsmen, trophies, classical statues, and exotic beasts and birds (most central European rulers had private menageries, as did Prince Eugene of Savoy, the general who won the Battle of Zenta for the Habsburgs). Eight chalcedony male and female busts in the antique style and an abundance of cameos testify to the period's passion for lapidary work. The inclusion of the arms of the electoral council suggests that this cup was made as an official gift to be presented on the occasion of an imperial election in Frankfurt am Main at the turn of the eighteenth century. This free city was the place where the Holy Roman emperors were elected and crowned.[3] However, the cup's shape, which has close parallels in works in ivory,[4] and the style of its decoration are obviously rooted in the ornamental vocabulary of the last third of the seventeenth century. While the long-held assumption

that it was executed and held in readiness for the crowning of Charles VI as Holy Roman emperor in 1711 could be correct, there is also no clear reason why the object could not have been sent years earlier to the emperor-elect Joseph I, who ascended the throne in 1705, after the death of his father, Emperor Leopold I.[5] There was a long tradition in imperial cities of sending gifts to the emperor and of being prepared for a visit from royalty or a strong candidate in an upcoming election. For example, the Nuremberg town council always kept on hand some precious objects to bestow at any moment; a valuable gift would serve to express the city's loyalty and at the same time to demonstrate the high artistic standards and technical ability of local craftsmen.[6]

The stones cut for the present piece could have originated in the quarries of Idar and Oberstein near Frankfurt.[7] That city had a prosperous art market and was the location of important trade fairs that were regularly visited by court art agents from all over Europe. The local goldsmiths' guild contained very talented and skillful artists, who would have been capable of manufacturing an ambitious item such as this cup.[8] Nevertheless, the absence from the cup of the coat of arms of the city of Frankfurt leaves open the question of its patronage.

W K

1. I am grateful to James H. Frantz, Research Scientist, Department of Scientific Research, Metropolitan Museum, for his examination report of January 21, 2005, on the materials used for this cup, and to James David Draper, Henry R. Kravis Curator of European Sculpture and Decorative Arts, Metropolitan Museum, for his advice regarding this entry.
2. For the motif of the "supporting Turk," see Koeppe 1996, p. 61. The constant fear of Ottoman incursions into Europe would persist until Prince Eugene of Savoy won the Battle of Belgrade in 1717, ending the Austro-Turkish War and the serious threat from the east once and for all.
3. See the discussion of this cup in the Metropolitan Museum's Timeline of Art History (www.metmuseum.org/toah).
4. On works in ivory, see Haag 2007, pp. 94–97, nos. 29, 30, especially the pieces by the Maucher family and their circle. See also Kenseth 1991, pp. 259–60, no. 33. An Augsburg cup in ivory of about 1675 was on the art market in 2002; see *Axel Vervoordt: Catalogue II* (Antwerp, 2002), pp. 38–39.
5. For a history of this period, see Crankshaw 1971.
6. *Wenzel Jamnitzer* 1985; Pechstein 1992.
7. Schnackenburg-Prael 1999.
8. See entry for cat. no. 89. See also Ketelsen 1996; Ketelsen 1998.

89. Two statuettes of Roman emperors

Frankfurt am Main
By Johann Bernhard
Schwarze(n)burger

Titus
Shortly before 1730
Hardstones, gold, black enamel,
and precious stones; H. with
pedestal 10½ in. (26.6 cm)
Staatliche Kunstsammlungen
Dresden, Grünes Gewölbe V151

Vespasian
Shortly before 1731
Hardstones, gold, and precious
stones; H. with pedestal 10⅝ in.
(26.8 cm)
Staatliche Kunstsammlungen
Dresden, Grünes Gewölbe V148

PROVENANCES: *Titus*: Purchased
by Augustus the Strong, elector
of Saxony and king of Poland-
Lithuania, 1730; first mentioned in
the inventory of precious objects
in the Grünes Gewölbe, Dresden,
1725–33 (supplement).[1] *Vespasian*:
Purchased from the lapidary by
Augustus the Strong, April 20, 1731;
first mentioned in the inventory of
precious objects in the Grünes
Gewölbe, 1725–33 (supplement)[2]

REFERENCES: Heres 1982,
pp. 209–10 (with references to
additional emperor series in the
Grünes Gewölbe); Kappel 1998,
pp. 159–60, no. 59 (*Titus*), no. 60
(*Vespasian*); Kappel in Syndram
2006, no. 37 (*Titus*)

In the years 1729–31, Frederick Augustus I of Saxony, elected king of Poland-Lithuania in 1697 as Augustus II and known to history as Augustus the Strong, purchased four statuettes of Roman emperors that are preserved in the collection of the Grünes Gewölbe in Dresden.[3] Two of them are included in this exhibition. The first one Augustus acquired, of Emperor Domitian,[4] was brought back to Dresden from the Leipzig fair in 1729 by Raymond Leplat, the king's art agent. Augustus was obviously delighted with the statuette, for he purchased the matching one of Emperor Titus a year later, just at the time of an event of great military and political importance: in June 1730 he demonstrated the strength of his army to various European rulers and guests, most notably King Frederick William I of Prussia, with maneuvers and festivities near Zeithain and Radewitz on the Elbe.[5] An accounting issued on June 3, 1730, shows that the king authorized payment to the sculptor "Bernhardt Schwartzenburg" immediately after taking possession of the *Titus* statuette and while the huge encampment was still in progress.[6] Count Heinrich von Brühl, one of the most influential figures at the Saxon-Polish court, negotiated the business. According to an inventory entry, the king purchased the statuette of Emperor Vespasian on April 20, 1731, and as early as October of that same year acquired the figure of Emperor Julius Caesar by "Schwarzeburger Von Franckfurth."[7]

Little is known about the lapidary, Johann Bernhard Schwarzenburger (1672–1741). He was active in Frankfurt am Main, and his connection to the Dresden court was probably related to the fact that as early as 1712 his son Valentin was engaged in Dresden in the workshop of the court sculptor Balthasar Permoser.[8] Schwarzenburger created the figures and pedestals of the statuettes out of variously colored semiprecious gems, mainly from the Idar and Oberstein region, among them chalcedony, agate, and jasper. The pieces of clothing, limbs, and faces were all carved sepa-

rately and then assembled with the use of strong adhesives. Restoration work in 1996–97 revealed that these were extremely stable. The swords, sword belts, and other ornamentation are of gold with inset gems.

Schwarzenburger was by no means the "inventor" of such stone figures. There are precedents in the work of Orazio Mochi and Giuseppe Antonio Torricelli.[9] Like Schwarzenburger, Christoph Labhardt, who worked for the court in Kassel between 1680 and 1695, had also mastered the art of combining select varieties of semiprecious stones. Archival documents attest that he produced his most important work, a panel adorned with numerous polychrome stone figures as allegories of the Virtues, Sciences, and Arts, for the court at Idstein between 1671 and 1679.[10] That panel was added to the collection of precious objects in Dresden's Grünes Gewölbe in 1729.[11]

JK

1. Supplement, fols. 75–76: "von dem Bildhauer Schwarzenburger verfertiget" (executed by the sculptor Schwarzenburger).
2. Supplement, fols. 74–76: "Ist von dem Bildhauer Schwarzenburger zu Franckfurt am Mayn verfertiget, und am 20. April 1731 von Ihro Königl. Maj. erkaufft und zur Verwahrung gegeben worden" (Executed by the sculptor Schwarzenburger in Frankfurt am Main and purchased by Your Royal Majesty on April 20, 1731, and turned over for safekeeping).
3. Kappel 1998, pp. 158–61, nos. 58–61; see also Kappel in Syndram 2006, no. 37 (*Titus*), no. 38 (*Domitian*). For the popularity of emperor series in princely collections, see Lessmann in Lessmann and König-Lein 2002, pp. 38–45, nos. 11–20.
4. Staatliche Kunstsammlungen Dresden, Grünes Gewölbe, inv. V149; Kappel in Syndram 2006, no. 38.
5. Czok 1987, pp. 260–61 (on the encampments in Zeithain and Radewitz).
6. Sächsisches Hauptstaatsarchiv Dresden, documents for the years 1637–1747, Loc. 354, vol. 4, no. 184.
7. Staatliche Kunstsammlungen Dresden, Grünes Gewölbe, inv. V150. For the acquisition, see Syndram and Weinhold 2007, p. 87, n. 1 (quotation from the accounting).
8. Asche 1978, p. 80.
9. See Tuena 1992a, pp. 198–206.
10. Staatliche Kunstsammlungen Dresden, Grünes Gewölbe, inv. V146; see Lentz 2000.
11. Kappel in Syndram, Kappel, and Weinhold 2006, pp. 118–19.

Titus

Vespasian

90. Snuffbox

Berlin, ca. 1765
Possibly designed by Jean
Guillaume George Krüger
Chrysoprase, diamonds, and other
hardstones, gold, and metal foil,
gold mounts; 2 × 4 × 3⅛ in. (4.9 ×
10 × 7.8 cm)
The Rosalinde and Arthur Gilbert
Collection on loan to the Victoria
and Albert Museum, London
1996.469 (GB 120)

PROVENANCE: Frederick II, king
of Prussia (according to tradition,
his gift to his brother Prince
Augustus William [d. 1758]);
Frederick William II, king of
Prussia (d. 1797); by descent in the
Hohenzollern family; Empress
Augusta Victoria, wife of Emperor
William II (d. 1921); their son
Prince Oskar of Prussia (1888–
1958); thence by descent (sale,
Christie's, Geneva, November 11,
1986, lot 444); acquired by the
Rosalinde and Arthur Gilbert
Collection

REFERENCES: Sarre 1895, fig. 5;
Seidel 1901, p. 82, no. 14; Truman
1991, pp. 208–11, no. 71; Baer 1993,
pp. 54–55, no. 36; Massinelli 2000,
p. 141, no. 52

Throughout the history of the decorative arts, rarely has there been a type of collectible so various in shape and decoration as the precious box. Particularly popular as luxury items during the eighteenth century, boxes made of valuable materials were used to store sugar, candies, cosmetic implements and beauty patches, and even the owner's jottings on paper (see cat. no. 92). The type on which the most attention was lavished was the snuffbox, or *tabatière*. One royal aficionado of the snuffbox was King Frederick the Great of Prussia (1712–1786). Always concerned with the state of his country's exchequer, Frederick tried from the early years of his reign to develop a luxury-goods industry on a par with that in France. In 1740, the year of his accession to the throne, he ordered this protectionist measure: "For the good of the Berlin gold workers . . . [we] totally forbade the import of all French gold boxes, *étuis,* and *objets de bijou*."[1] When the king's chamberlain, Michael Gabriel Fredersdorff, visited Paris in 1751 he received a letter from Frederick asking him to bring back a box, "the best that can be found there, so that we can find out how they are made."[2] Frederick's mercantilist efforts eventually led to the establishment of successful manufactories of gold objects and jewelry in Berlin, and, after Augsburg and Dresden (see "Pietre Dure North of the Alps" by Wolfram Koeppe in this publication), Berlin became one of central Europe's most important centers for such artistic creations.

After the king's death, on August 17, 1786, two hundred sumptuous boxes were inventoried at Sanssouci, his chief residence, at Potsdam. Only one was made of gold alone; the others were decorated in his favorite style, with diamonds.[3] During his last illness, when the king could hardly write or even read any longer, he passed the time enjoying his little treasures, his "jewels, boxes, and finger rings, and [pieces of] cut and raw chrysoprase," together with the daily portfolio of state papers.[4]

The present box was carved from a single block of chrysoprase, as was the slightly domed lid. The hardstone was mined at Ząbkowice (formerly Frankenstein in Schlesien), in Silesia, which Frederick largely occupied in 1741, during the first Silesian War. In the king's later years, between 1780 and 1786, he commissioned David Wend(t),

glass- and stonecutter to the Berlin court, to deliver at least one chrysoprase box every month. So fond was he of the apple green stone that he had the tops of two console tables veneered with it and placed in the Neues Palais at Sanssouci.[5] Part of the gem's appeal may have been its reputation for healing powers: in ancient and medieval times, it was believed to protect against gout,[6] from which Frederick suffered almost all his life.

The box's blossom-shaped incrustations of diamonds are among the most beautiful decorations on Frederick's surviving snuffboxes. There is an enchanting, almost mesmerizing, appeal to this example. It displays all of Frederick's favorite Rococo ornaments. The elegant diamond rosettes, set in gold over foil in delicate pastel colors, and the golden trellis that playfully scrolls in rocaille formation around the center of the lid produce a magical light when the box is turned to the sun or a flickering candle by admirers. The subtle curves of the box and lid are characteristic of the highly individual Berlin style and reject the restrained canon that underlies the smooth elliptical or rectangular lines of contemporary Parisian examples.

Winfried Baer proposed a date of 1765 for this box, which is in conflict with the life dates of the purported second owner, Prince Augustus William (1722–1758). Nevertheless, the close resemblance of the decoration to that on snuffboxes designed for the king about that time by Jean Guillaume George Krüger (1728–1791) strongly supports Baer's dating in the mid-1760s.[7]   WK

1. That is, cases and jeweled objects. Quoted in Baer 1993, p. 2.
2. Baer 1980, p. 96.
3. Baer 1993, p. 2.
4. Thiébault 1901, p. 138.
5. Both tabletops were lost during World War II; see Seidel 1901, p. 80.
6. Friess 1980, p. 116; Termolen 1990, p. 80.
7. Frederick's gift of this box to his brother is undocumented. It was mentioned in the catalogue of the 1986 sale at Christie's, Geneva. On the dating of the box, see Baer 1993, pp. 8–9, 18–23, nos. 1–17; and Massinelli 2000, p. 141, no. 52. Massinelli follows Truman 1991 (p. 211) in dating the box to about 1755, stating that its "style . . . [is] markedly rococo," overlooking the fully mature rocaille on the top, a decoration that was at its peak in the mid-1760s. For the Rococo in Berlin, see Hohenzollern 1992; Eggeling 2003.

91. Snuff box

Berlin, ca. 1775–80
Black marble (or onyx?), hardstones, glass paste, and gold, gold
mounts; 2 × 3⅞ × 3⅛ in. (4.9 × 9.8 ×
7.7 cm)
Marked: *VB* between two pellets
[initials unidentified, but associated
with the widow of the Parisian
jeweler Louis Buyrette]; warranty
mark for gold, France, from May
10, 1838, onward; import mark, the
Netherlands, 1906–53
The Rosalinde and Arthur Gilbert
Collection on loan to the Victoria
and Albert Museum, London
1996.488 (GB 140)

PROVENANCE: Frederick II, king
of Prussia; sale, Christie's, Geneva,
May 11, 1982, lot 194; acquired by
Arthur Gilbert

REFERENCES: Truman 1991,
pp. 222–25, no. 75 (marks depicted
p. 223); Baer 1993, pp. 76–77, no. 50;
Massinelli 2000, p. 147, no. 56 (mistakenly dated "c. 1865"), ill. p. 136

In addition to diamond-studded hardstone snuff-boxes and golden examples decorated with enamel,[1] Frederick the Great had a particular liking for *tabatières* cut out of hardstones and embellished with an ornamental polychrome arrangement of hardstones in relief. The technique can be compared to Florentine relief mosaic (see cat. no. 52) or the wooden relief marquetry of the town of Eger (see cat. no. 53). Sometimes hardstones in the desired colors were unobtainable, and then colored glass paste was substituted (see p. 87).

The flat C-scrolls and engraved leaf decoration on the gold mounts attached to this box are still rooted in the Rococo, but their movement is restrained, and the nearly symmetrical carnelian bow that clasps the stems of the floral bouquet establishes an element of quietness, a breath of the Neoclassical style that the lapidary decided to introduce. This was a daring step, since Frederick despised the bold forms of the new *goût grec* and continued to live in palaces decorated in the naturalistic Rococo style that would later bear his name (see p. 66 and entry for cat. no. 90).

The box's color scheme and sophisticated look are not achieved by a lavish display of gold, diamonds, and semiprecious stones; rather, they reflect the artisan's advanced technical skills and his desire to utilize the natural beauty of the hardstones by cutting them in an artistic manner to form an imaginative creation. Gold is sparingly applied, serving only to accent the still-Rococo outlines of the box. The unexpected juxtaposition of the strong red carnelian bow with the black marble or onyx ground and the shimmering gold mounts are touches that make this example of Prussian stonecutting a masterpiece.[2]

Including the two hundred boxes that his nephew and successor Frederick William II brought from Potsdam to the palace in Berlin after the king's death, the number of Frederick the Great's *tabatières* can be estimated at about three to four hundred in all.[3] The majority were decorated with diamonds or gold. The divergent type discussed here may belong to a group of objects that were made to be used as royal diplomatic or personal gifts and were frequently filled with other valuables before being presented.[4]   WK

1. Baer 1993, pp. 34–75, nos. 23–49. On pp. 32–33, no. 22,
   an exceptional example with the portrait of the king
   (Metropolitan Museum, 17.190.1242) is discussed.
2. On the marks on this box, see Carré 1971, p. 213; Voet 1974,
   no. 46.
3. Baer 1993, p. 2.
4. Baer 1992; Baer in Hohenzollern 1992, pp. 220–83,
   nos. 87–139.

92. Notebook

Workshop of Johann Christian
Neuber, Dresden, ca. 1780–90
Hardstones, gold, and miniature
paintings on ivory, silk lining; each
cover 4⅝ × 3¼ × ½ in. (11.7 × 8.3 ×
1.27 cm)
The Rosalinde and Arthur Gilbert
Collection on loan to the Victoria
and Albert Museum, London
1996.319 (MM 218)

PROVENANCE: King Farouk I of
Egypt and of Sudan (1920–1965),
Koubbeh Palace, Cairo (sale,
Sotheby's, Cairo, March 18, 1954,
lot 703); Baron Alexis de Redé
(1922–2004), Hôtel Lambert, Paris
(sale, Sotheby's, Monaco, May
25–26, 1975, lot 41); acquired by the
Rosalinde and Arthur Gilbert
Collection

REFERENCES: *Princely Taste* 1995,
p. 75; Massinelli 2000, p. 200, no. 86

The frame of this delightful object consists of two gold plates hinged together on one side by a strip of gold to create a miniature bookbinding. Loops on the right-hand side accommodate a gold pencil that fastens the booklet. The covers are embellished with colorful hardstone lozenges in diamond-shaped compartments formed by a network of thin gold bands. The decoration is an example of *Zellenmosaik* (cell mosaic), although the stone pieces are smaller than usual.[1] The technique was developed by the Dresden goldsmith Heinrich Taddel, director of the Grünes Gewölbe (see entry for cat. no. 146) and father-in-law of Johann Christian Neuber (1736–1808), in whose workshop this little notebook was made.[2] In the center of each cover is a gold-framed portrait: on the front, Louis XVI of France appears, and on the back is his queen, Marie Antoinette.

The distinctive effects that Neuber achieved by using a wide variety of techniques and surprising juxtapositions of materials to enhance the sumptuous look of his bijouteries made them greatly sought after. Neuber's best-known cell mosaic pieces are boxes inlaid with choice hardstone specimens, each numbered on the gold band that forms its cell. Inside the box is a pamphlet giving a key to the stones and the origin of each.[3]

The notebook from the Gilbert Collection is usually dated about 1800,[4] but an earlier date seems more probable. Neuber became a guild master in 1762 and was appointed court jeweler about 1775. One of his masterworks, several hardstone-decorated stands for groups of white Meissen porcelain statuettes, was delivered in 1766. The miniatures of Louis XVI and Marie Antoinette are more likely to celebrate the famous couple as reigning king and queen than to commemorate them after the fall of the French monarchy. Both are presented as rulers of France. Louis proudly wears the insignia of the most illustrious orders of Austria and France: the Cordon rouge and the Golden Fleece (*Toison d'or*) and the star of the French Order of the Holy Ghost (Ordre du Saint-Esprit). Given the fact that in 1779 Louis's mother-in-law, Empress Maria Theresa, commissioned from Neuber the so-called *Teschen Table* (fig. 71), embellished with 128 different stones, as a diplomatic gift for Louis-Auguste, baron de Breteuil, the miniature portraits on this notebook should probably be dated to the 1780s, a decade of ostentatious luxury and conspicuous consumption in France. The hardstone notebook was either commissioned or made to be sold to a high-ranking aristocrat at one of the trade fairs in Leipzig or Frankfurt am Main.

WK

1. Massinelli 2000, pp. 149–50, nos. 58, 59.
2. See Kappel 1998, p. 174.
3. Ibid., p. 68.
4. Sotheby's, Monaco, May 25–26, 1975, sale cat., lot 41.

93. Ring ensemble

Germany (Palatinate?), ca. 1730–40
Hardstones and gilded silver, silk-lined leather case
Each hardstone insert ca. 1 × ¾ in. (2.5 × 1.8 cm)
Schatzkammer, Burg Eltz, Rhineland-Palatinate, Germany

PROVENANCE: By tradition, made for Philipp Karl, Reichsgraf von Eltz zu Kempenich (1665–1743); by descent in the Eltz family after the elector's death

REFERENCE: Rogasch 2004, p. 94, pl. 53, and p. 253

Ordained a priest on June 3, 1731, Philipp Karl von Eltz was unanimously elected by the cathedral's chapter only twelve months later to be the archbishop of Mainz and archchancellor of the Holy Roman Empire. As a consequence, the nearly seventy-year-old cleric became one of the great territorial lords in Germany and the highest-ranking ecclesiastical prince-elector as well. The process of choosing the Holy Roman emperor had been regulated by the Golden Bull of 1366. There were to be seven electors, who as members of the emperor's "ceremonial household" were considered the pillars of the empire. Three were prelates, the archbishops of Mainz, Trier, and Cologne. With their secular counterparts, the electors of the Palatinate, Bohemia, Saxony, and Brandenburg (and later of Bavaria and Brunswick-Lüneburg), they all were free to vote for whomever they wished, including themselves.[1] Substantial monetary contributions to "secure" the electors' loyalty (usually to the house of Habsburg), and even bribes, were often part of the "election."

Philipp Karl's two gilded silver ring settings and the forty-nine simply shaped yet technically refined stones cut to fill them make the Eltz ring ensemble a rare example of its type. Recent scholarship has dated similar ensembles to the last quarter of the eighteenth century and attributed some of them to Johann Christian Neuber (1736–1808) in Dresden (see cat. no. 92),[2] but inventories indicate that this example was made in the 1730s. Therefore it should be understood as heralding a fashion that would satisfy in an attractive way both the need for personal adornment and the growing interest in geology and mineralogy.

It is fruitless to look for the distinctive style of a specific workshop in such simply designed objects. In the nearby imperial city of Frankfurt am Main, the stonecutter and jeweler Johann Bernhard Schwarzeburger, or Schwarzenburger (see entry for cat. no. 89), was certainly capable of assembling such a wide variety of semiprecious stones, as were lesser-known masters in the hardstone-cutting manufactories of Idar and Oberstein in the Rhineland-Palatinate (see entry for cat. no. 81). By the late seventeenth century those manufactories had a fully developed infrastructure and a staff of specialized artisans who could practice all aspects of hardstone cutting for jewelry, display objects, and sculptural works of art.[3]

This ring ensemble may have been acquired by Elector Philipp Karl himself or one of his agents at the trade fair in Frankfurt am Main, where artisans from all over the empire and neighboring states offered their luxury goods and artworks for sale (see entry for cat. no. 88).[4] Alternatively, he may have received it as a diplomatic gift during the decade when he held the highest imperial state office as archchancellor.

Several quite similar—but probably later—ensembles of this type have survived. The number of stones varies. An example in the Grünes Gewölbe in Dresden contains no fewer than eighty-six.[5] The grandest example may be the "mineral casket" attributed to the workshop of Gottlob Heinrich Lang in Augsburg, which is today part of the mineralogical collection of the Observatory at Kremsmünster Monastery in Austria. That mahogany casket encloses twelve drawers filled with 365 same-size cabochon inserts of precious stone, hardstone, or glass paste, thus enabling the owner to change the look of the ring on each day of the year. Although it is wearable, as is this ensemble of Elector Philipp Karl von Eltz, both sets may have been considered virtuoso display objects.[6]

WK

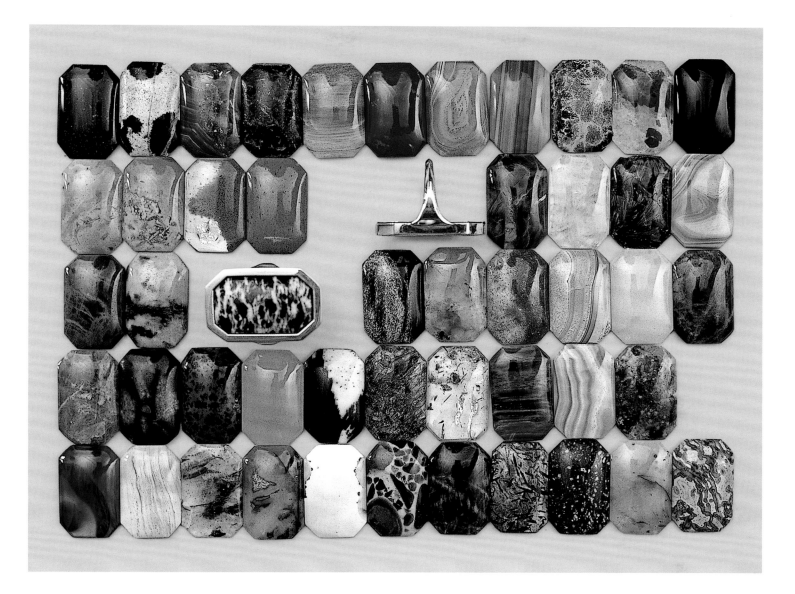

1. The number of the secular electors varied over the centuries, but the domain and number of the three ecclesiastical ones remained the same.
2. Kappel 1998, pp. 176–77, nos. 73, 74; Ottomeyer, Schröder, and Winters 2006, p. 172, pl. 114, p. 350, no. V-21.
3. Fischer 1979; Schnackenburg-Praël 1999, pp. 896–97.
4. For the luxury-object and painting trade in Frankfurt am Main, see Ketelsen 1998, pp. 143–46, 149–50.
5. Inv. 1924/1; Kappel 1998, p. 177, no. 74.
6. E. J. Zirkel in *Die lasterhafte Panazee* 1992, pp. 100–101, no. II.51.

94. Vase

France, mid-16th century
By Bénédict Ramel
Breccia decorated with silver, gilded silver, and gold
Lid and mount: Paris, mid-17th century
Partly gilded silver
H. 8¼ in. (20.8 cm), Diam. 5¾ in. (14.5 cm)
Marked: 74 [inventory of the French royal collection, 1791]
Musée du Louvre, Paris MR 220

PROVENANCE: Probably Jeanne d'Albret, queen of Navarre, by 1561–62; her son Henry IV, king of France, from 1601 (Château de Pau until 1602, then Château de Fontainebleau); his wife, Maria de' Medici, 1610 (1613 inventory, fol. 6); Cardinal Jules Mazarin, 1642 (1661 inventory, no. 370); French royal collection, Louvre, Paris, 1661–1791 (1681 inventory, no. 42; 1775, no. 32; 1791, no. 74); transferred to the Muséum National d'Histoire Naturelle, Paris, on 16 Fructidor, year IV (September 2, 1796); returned to the Louvre, 1802 (1802 inventory, no. 377; 1857, N 364, today MR 220)

REFERENCES: Alcouffe 1974, pp. 514, 517; Alcouffe 2001, pp. 166–69, no. 57; Bimbenet-Privat and Crépin-Leblond 2004, pp. 113, 117, fig. 2

Probably first mentioned in a 1561–62 inventory of the collection of Queen Jeanne d'Albret of Navarre, this vase found a place in the Cabinet de Navarrenx of her son Henry IV at the Château de Pau, in southwestern France, in 1601, and then at Fontainebleau from 1602.[1] It was among the 164 objects personally selected by Maria de' Medici after her husband's assassination in 1610, and after her own death it became a prominent piece in the collection of Cardinal Jules Mazarin. There it was one of only two vases to be decorated with his coat of arms.[2] After Mazarin's death, in 1661, the vase reentered the French royal collection and—after a brief period of exile in the Muséum National d'Histoire Naturelle in the years immediately following the Revolution—was reinstated at the Louvre, where it remains today.

The early inventory at Pau names Bénédict Ramel as the maker of a vase believed to be this one, and an entry in the queen's account lists a payment to Ramel of 225 livres, representing his annual salary as a lapidary in the year 1557.[3] Ramel, from Ferrara, was a medalist and worker in damascene (precious metal applied into iron or steel to produce decorative designs) who was first recorded as employed in France in 1530.[4] If this vase is indeed the one mentioned in these two archival sources, it testifies to Ramel's extraordinary talent as a stonecutter and a metal engraver who was able to combine the two media in a skillfully executed chef d'oeuvre. Strongly veined breccia has been carved into a hollow vessel with thin (7 mm) walls and decorated with maritime scenes of men and animals engraved both in the stone and in finely inlaid applications in silver, gilded silver, and gold. The silver lid and mount were made in Paris and were added to personalize the object for Mazarin's collection in the 1640s or 1650s.[5]

FK

1. Daniel Alcouffe suggests that this vase and its case be identified with a "vaze d'une pierre du gaure mys en oeuvre par Benedic; avec son estuy" listed in an inventory made at the Château de Pau in 1561–62. See Alcouffe 2001, p. 168.
2. Ministère des Affaires Étrangères, Paris, Archives, Mémoires et documents, France 769, pièce 7, fol. 6 (May 5, 1613), cited in Bimbenet-Privat and Crépin-Leblond 2004, pp. 113, 117; Alcouffe 1974, pp. 514, 517.
3. Raymond 1867, p. 44.
4. Rondot 1904, pp. 85, 189.
5. The lid is mentioned in Mazarin's probate inventory (1661, no. 370), where the vase (with its *étui*) is assigned a value of 1,000 livres; see Alcouffe 2001, p. 166.

reverse

95. Glove tray

France, probably Paris, ca. 1630–35
Attributed to François Roberday
Sardonyx, gilded silver mounts;
3⅛ × 12 × 9¼ in. (7.7 × 30.5 × 23.4 cm)
Marked: *338* [inventory of the
French royal collection, 1791]
Musée du Louvre, Paris MR 250

PROVENANCE: Entered the collection of Cardinal Jules Mazarin
between 1653 and 1661 (1661 inventory, no. 410); transferred under
Louis XIV to the French royal
collection, Louvre, Paris (1681
inventory, no. 73; 1775, no. 56; 1791,
no. 338); transferred to the Muséum
National d'Histoire Naturelle,
Paris, on 9 Fructidor, year IV
(August 26, 1796); returned to
the Louvre, 1802 (1802 inventory,
no. 129; 1857, no. N 391; today
MR 250)

REFERENCES: Bion, Christin, and
Delattre 1791, vol. 2, p. 179, no. 338;
Guiffrey 1885–86, vol. 1, p. 182,
no. 73; Alcouffe 1974, pp. 518, 520;
Alcouffe 2001, pp. 380–81, no. 183;
Bimbenet-Privat 2002, vol. 2,
pp. 440–41; Alcouffe in *Un Temps
d'exubérance* 2002, p. 278, no. 168;
Bimbenet-Privat 2003, pp. 150–51,
figs. 11, 12

This elegant glove tray can be attributed to the silversmith François Roberday (active 1621–51), who maintained workshops in the Palais de Tuileries in Paris where he produced luxury goods for King Louis XIII and his brother until 1643, and from 1643 to 1651 for Anne of Austria and her chief minister, Cardinal Jules Mazarin. Although it is first recorded as part of Cardinal Mazarin's collection, the small tray may in fact have been made for a member of the royal family, since gloves on a tray were customarily presented to an aristocratic lady on her engagement.[1] Its gilded silver oval frame held twenty-seven thin panels of sardonyx (one is now missing). Two are engraved with allegorical scenes of Abundance and Love.[2] The rim of the tray is decorated with a band of gilded silver pearls. An octagonal foot of gilded silver is imbedded with sixteen sardonyx plaques.

Whereas the mounting of engraved translucent panels into an encasing frame depends on sixteenth-century techniques, the floral designs of the repoussé decoration on top of the tray and

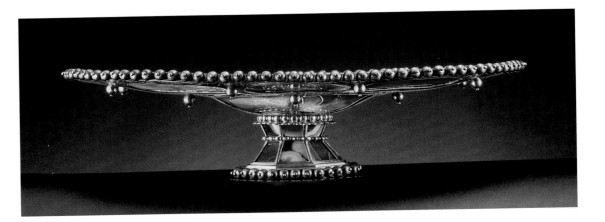

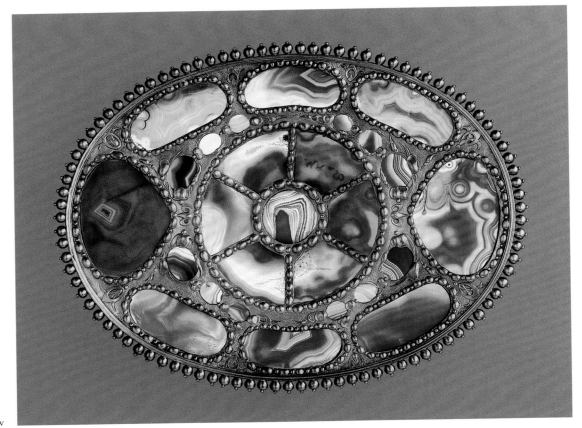

top view

of its engraving on the reverse show the stylistic influence of Pierre Delabarre, Roberday's colleague and neighbor in the privileged royal workshops at the Louvre from 1625 to 1638.[3] Roberday made a number of composite objects, and, according to his wife's probate inventory (1640), he stocked in his Tuileries workshops semiprecious stones such as agate, lapis lazuli, and rock crystal for the manufacture of exuberantly decorated *objets de luxe*, some of which were registered in the French royal treasury and form part of the Musée du Louvre's collection today.[4]

FK

1. Bimbenet-Privat 2003, pp. 149–51.
2. Alcouffe in *Un Temps d'exubérance* 2002, p. 278, no. 168.
3. Alcouffe 2001, p. 381, under no. 183; Alcouffe in *Un Temps d'exubérance* 2002, p. 278, under no. 168; Bimbenet-Privat 2002, vol. 1, p. 300.
4. Archives Nationales, Paris, Minutier Central, LXI-194; Guiffrey 1885–86, vol. 1, pp. 42, 46, nos. 67, 68, 139–42. See also Bimbenet-Privat 2002, vol. 2, p. 441.

96. Cup

Byzantine, 900–1100
Sardonyx
Stem, base, and mounts: Paris, 1655–60
Sardonyx, gold and enamel
Overall 4⅞ × 5⅛ × 2⅞ in. (12.4 × 13 × 7.3 cm)
Marked: 427 [inventory of the French royal collection, 1791]
The Metropolitan Museum of Art, New York, Gift of J. Pierpont Morgan, 1917 17.190.594

PROVENANCE: Entered the French royal collection, Louvre, Paris, between 1684 and 1701 (1701 inventory, no. 268; 1775, no. 190; 1791, no. 427); transferred to the Muséum National d'Histoire Naturelle, Paris, on 6 Fructidor, year IV (August 23, 1796); returned to the Louvre, 1802 (inventory no. 117, 1810 and 1824, no. MR 122); stolen from the Louvre, July 29, 1830; Charles Mannheim (1833–1910); J. Pierpont Morgan; his gift to the Metropolitan Museum, 1917

REFERENCES: Alcouffe 1977, pp. 121–22, figs. 12, 12 *bis*; Alcouffe 2001, pp. 88–89, no. 23

In its present state this medieval Byzantine cup has all the characteristic qualities of a seventeenth-century collector's item.[1] The early history of the finely carved, exquisitely thin (5.5 mm) oval sardonyx bowl is unknown. It was modernized and made more fashionable when the sardonyx stem and base and the meticulously chased gold and enamel mounts were added in Paris in 1655–60.[2] The piece entered the French royal collection, where it was last inventoried in 1791.[3] When the cup became unfashionable for social and political reasons after the Revolution, it was transferred, together with numerous other royal objects, to the museum of natural history in Paris.[4] In the nineteenth and twentieth centuries it regained its cachet with private collectors.

In France, Cardinals Richelieu and Mazarin were the first connoisseurs to develop a serious interest in hardstone carvings, which they popularized at the French court, initiating a campaign to establish local workshops of hardstone objects.[5] In 1668 Louis XIV brought pietre dure craftsmen from Florence and set them up at the Royal Gobelins workshops in Paris, with French assistants. By the

time this cup was registered by the bureau in charge of furnishing the court residences (the Garde-Meuble), the lapidaries at the Gobelins had achieved an outstanding reputation, but because these artisans specialized exclusively in mosaic panels, three-dimensional carved hardstone objects such as this cup remained prized rarities in Louis XIV's Galerie d'Apollon at the Louvre and his state apartments at Versailles.

FK

1. As Rudolf Distelberger has shown for a very similar bowl and other hardstone vessels in the Kunsthistorisches Museum, Vienna, that have only lately been recognized as of Byzantine origin, both the early history and later modifications often remain obscure, and rare medieval treasures become erroneously classified as seventeenth-century objects. See Distelberger 2004.

2. Four small holes in the upper rim indicate the fixture of an earlier mount.

3. In that inventory the cup was listed as no. 427—the figure engraved in its base—and valued at 12,000 livres. See Alcouffe 1977, pp. 121–22. For an almost identical cup formerly in the collection of Cardinal Mazarin (1661 inventory, no. 384), then in the French royal collection (1673 inventory, no. 55), and today in the Louvre (MR 118), see Alcouffe 1974, p. 518, and fig. 19.

4. Among the objects transferred with this one to the Muséum National d'Histoire Naturelle in 1796 were some similar vessels, including another oval Byzantine bowl, an oval cup of unknown date, a fifteenth-century cup, and two Milanese sixteenth-century cups. See Alcouffe 2001, pp. 87–88, 137, 198–99, 276–77, 519, nos. 22, 41, 72, 123, 273. The marble vase by Bénédict Ramel in this catalogue (cat. no. 94) has a similar history.

5. Mazarin had introduced to France two ebony tables decorated with Florentine pietre dure panels even prior to his move to Paris in 1640 and continued to import directly from Florence once he was settled in France. See Laurain-Portemer 1975, pp. 67–68; and "Pierres fines" by Florian Knothe in this publication.

97. Cup with cover

Paris, mid-17th century
Agates, mounts of gilded silver, gold, and enamel
Finial: 19th or early 20th century
Gilded silver, gold, enamel, rubies, and a diamond
Overall 7 × 5 × 3⅜ in. (17.8 × 12.5 × 8.5 cm)
Marked: I–IV; *318* [inventory of the French royal collection, 1791]
The Metropolitan Museum of Art, New York, The Friedsam Collection, Bequest of Michael Friedsam, 1931 32.100.241 a, b

PROVENANCE: Entered the French royal collection, Louvre, Paris, mid-1680s (1701 inventory, no. 273; 1775, no. 193; 1791, no. 318); Pierre van Recum, on 25 Thermidor, year IV (August 12, 1796); Baron Carl Meyer de Rothschild (d. 1855); his grand-daughter Princesse Jacques de Broglie, née Marguerite de Wagram (sale, Galerie Georges Petit, Paris, June 12–13, 1911); François Guérault; Michael Friedsam; his bequest to the Metropolitan Museum, 1931

REFERENCES: Bion, Christin, and Delattre 1791, vol. 2, p. 76, no. 318; Guiffrey 1885–86, vol. 1, p. 221, no. 273; Alcouffe 1977, pp. 114–15, fig. 5; Hackenbrock 1984–85, p. 201, fig. 80; Alcouffe 2001, pp. 446–47, no. 217

Described in the first post-Revolutionary inventory of the French royal collection as an "oval cup with cover of whitish yellow Oriental agate on a baluster foot enriched with gilded bronze mounts and colored enamel," this precious object had been acquired for the treasury of Louis XIV in the mid-1680s.[1] Like a number of other hardstone objects originally displayed in the Galerie d'Apollon at the Louvre and in other princely collections (see also cat. no. 96), it incorporates earlier elements. The cup and its base were cut from one kind of agate and the lid from another, all in France in the decades between 1640 and 1660. The finely chased, partly enameled gold and gilded-silver mounts were made in the same period by a French silversmith influenced by the Milanese style of the late sixteenth century. Their dense scroll design can also be found in engravings by Jacques Caillart and Jean Lepautre; though most typical of French goldsmithing under Louis XIII, it remained widespread and popular throughout the seventeenth century.[2] The partially enameled stag on a base set with a diamond and rubies, mounted on the cup's cover as a finial that serves as a handle, dates from the nineteenth or early twentieth century.[3] Thus, in this single object several virtuoso artistic techniques of different genres and times are displayed, something considered desirable in a *Kunstkammer* piece, as was the use of rare and sumptuous materials.[4]

FK

1. For entries in the royal inventory describing this cup, see Bion, Christin, and Delattre 1791, vol. 2, p. 76, no. 318; Guiffrey 1885–86, vol. 1, p. 221, no. 273.

2. Bimbenet-Privat 2002, vol. 1, pp. 157–74.

3. Alcouffe 1977, p. 115; Alcouffe 2001, pp. 446–47, no. 217.

4. T. Richter 2005.

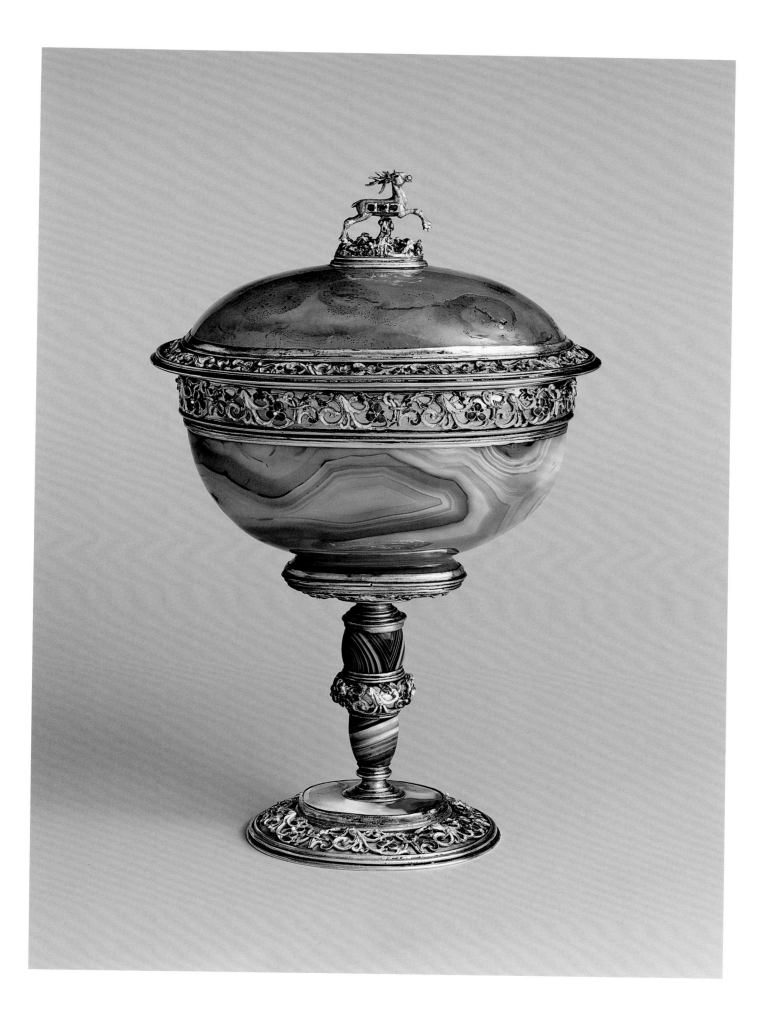

98. Tabletop depicting landscapes, birds, and the goddess Diana

Manufacture Royale des Gobelins, Paris, ca. 1670–80
Design by Charles Le Brun and his workshop; lapidary work by Horace and Ferdinand Megliorini, Philippe Branchi, or Jean Ambrosio Gachetti
Agate, amethyst, jasper, lapis lazuli, sardonyx, serpentine, smaragdite, and marble; 68⅛ × 52⅜ in. (173 × 133 cm)
Musée National du Château de Compiègne, France C464C

PROVENANCE: French royal collection, Louvre, Paris; transferred to the Château de Compiègne, mid-18th century

REFERENCE: Moulin 1992, pp. 67–68, ill.

This hardstone tabletop was made for the royal collection of Louis XIV about 1670–80 in the lapidary workshop of either Horace and Ferdinand Megliorini, Philippe Branchi, or Jean Ambrosio Gachetti at the Manufacture Royale des Gobelins in Paris.[1] It displays individually framed panels of different sizes and shapes arranged in one larger pictorial composition. Four panels depicting flowers, six showing birds, and six featuring landscapes are set around an oval medallion representing Diana, goddess of the hunt, suggesting that the iconographic scheme refers to the royal hunt of the Bourbon kings. The four corner panels showing stylized exotic birds and the four smaller landscape scenes in the central field are reminiscent of Florentine mosaics in their designs and manufacture, but the larger ornithological depictions and the overall layout of the tabletop are not. Instead they reflect the influence of Charles Le Brun (1619–1690) on the artistic production at the royal manufactory in Paris. All the works of art from the Gobelins were made for the king's household or for its use as diplomatic gifts, and the absence here of a royal cipher and emblems is unusual. Unusual too are the representations of four large fruiting branches—grape, pear, plum, and pomegranate—that, interspersed with butterflies of different sizes and colors, decorate the slab of black marble into which the smaller landscapes and central medallion are set.

The design of the tabletop—which could be called a trademark of the Gobelins *pierres fines* mosaic style—corresponds to one of four surviving gouache drawings (fig. 47).[2] The close match between the drawing and the finished tabletop in motifs, layout, and color scheme shows that, as in the tapestry-weaving workshop at the Gobelins, Le Brun and his assistants closely supervised the execution of the costly and propagandistic artifacts. These four gouache drawings for tabletops, two of which are in public collections today,[3] and entries in the royal inventory for no fewer than seventeen mosaic tables (some of an earlier period) suggest that the Gobelins workshops specialized in pietre dure panels, rather than hardstone sculpture; they seem to have produced a range of very similar tables as well as smaller panels made to decorate wooden cabinets.[4] This table would have been produced for one of Louis XIV's major residences, but during the reign of Louis XV it was moved, together with three now-lost companion pieces, to the Château de Compiègne, where it remains today.[5]

FK

1. See *"Pierres fines"* by Florian Knothe in this publication.
2. Bibliothèque Nationale de France, Paris, Fonds Robert de Cotte, F000282.
3. The other one is in the Musée du Louvre, Paris, OA 5508.
4. See Guiffrey 1885–86, vol. 2, pp. 131–132, 136–40, 147, 151, 155, 159, nos. 12, 13, 53–56, 60, 62–65, 69, 164, 234, 279, 339, 340.
5. Moulin 1992, p. 68.

99. Tabletop with a map of France

Probably Manufacture Royale des Gobelins, Paris, 1684
Design by Claude-Antoine Couplet; lapidary work probably by Horace and Ferdinand Megliorini, Philippe Branchi, and Jean Ambrosio Gachetti
Hardstones, marble, and alabaster; 43³⁄₈ × 30³⁄₄ × 1⁵⁄₈ in. (110 × 78 × 4 cm)
Musée du Louvre, Paris (6632), on long-term loan to the Musée National des Châteaux de Versailles et de Trianon (V 3537)

PROVENANCE: French royal collection, Château de Versailles, in or after 1684; transferred to the Grand Trianon, Versailles, before 1787; French national collection, at the Palais des Tuileries, then the

Unique in its iconography and composition, this hardstone mosaic tabletop was probably made at the Manufacture Royale des Gobelins, Paris.[1] Inlaid in the white marble ground and framed in slate blue marble is a polychrome map of France in the year 1684, with the departments, including those newly annexed to the north and east of the country, depicted in hardstones of different colors. The political message of the piece is emphasized by the quotation from Virgil, "HÆ TIBI ERVNT ARTES" (These are your arts), inlaid in a laurel-framed medallion at the lower left corner of the panel, which is intended to glorify Louis XIV for his successful military campaigns. The inscription further states that this table was presented to the king by Claude-Antoine Couplet (1642–1722), a founding member of and professor

of mathematics at the Académie des Sciences in Paris. The gift honored the king not only as military commander but also as head of the academy, and possibly also served to advance Couplet in his career. If it was made at the royal manufactory, the panel represents one of a very few private commissions—or rather, semiprivate, given the patron's position in the service of the king—executed by the highly talented royal artisans who, much like Couplet himself, received an annual stipend from the Crown.[2]

A spectacular work of political propaganda, this table has always occupied a public place—first at Versailles, in the château and then in the Grand Trianon. After the Revolution it was moved to Paris to decorate the Palais des Tuileries and, later, the Palais de l'Élysée, residence of the French

Palais de l'Élysée, then the Musée du Louvre, Paris

REFERENCES: Dreyfus 1922, p. 21, no. 27; Dimier 1925; D. Meyer 2002, vol. 1, pp. 194–95

president and political center of the country.[3] In the wake of the Franco-Prussian War (1870–71)—which was disastrous for France and in which some regions annexed under Louis XIV were occupied by Prussia—militarism lost its appeal, and the table was removed to the realm of art, in the Musée du Louvre.

FK

1. See "Pierres fines" by Florian Knothe in this publication, pp. 44–45.
2. The lapidaries at the Gobelins received the comparatively large annual salary of 1,920 livres and were paid additionally for individual works of art. See the entries for Horace and Ferdinand Megliorini, Philippe Branchi, and Jean Ambrosio Gachetti in the royal account book, quoted in Guiffrey 1881–1901.
3. D. Meyer 2002, vol. 1, p. 194.

100. Pair of vases

Italy, early 17th century
Golden alabaster, black marble bases; each 14 × 16⅞ in. (35.5 × 42.7 cm)
The J. Paul Getty Museum, Los Angeles 92.DJ.68.1–.2

PROVENANCE: Private collection, France (sale, Sotheby's, Monaco, March 3, 1990, lot 70); [Didier Aaron, Paris]; [Same Art Ltd., Zurich]; acquired by the Getty Museum, 1992

REFERENCES: "Acquisitions" 1993, p. 144; Bremer-David 1993, p. 223, no. 390; Wilson and Hess 2001, p. 243, no. 504

Of classical design, these vases are in the tradition of carved alabaster objects originally produced during Roman times, from the first century B.C. through the first century A.D., in the southern Italian town of Tarantum.[1] Their boat shape became popular in the Late Mannerist period, when there was also a renewed interest in alabaster (stalagmitic limestone), a development that would have enhanced the value and appeal of decorative artifacts such as these. Princely European collectors were also becoming fascinated by objects that survived from earlier times (see cat. nos. 2, 3, 96) and commissioned from contemporary artists works inspired by the past, to complement the ancient ones in their collections (see cat. no. 10).[2]

Alabastro dorato, called golden or Oriental alabaster, was particularly prized in the seventeenth

and eighteenth centuries, and contemporary paintings and engravings document how pairs of vases of this type and size were displayed in sumptuous buffet settings (see cat. no. 101).[3] Few deposits of stalagmitic limestone had been discovered in Europe in that era, so sculptors and lapidaries regularly salvaged alabaster, as well as marble and porphyry, from ancient buildings and monuments for the manufacture of contemporary pieces.[4]

FK

1. Bühler 1973, pp. 30–31.
2. T. Richter 2005.
3. "Acquisitions" 1993, p. 144.
4. In the Middle Ages a different type of alabaster (alabastrine gypsum) was found in Volterra and the surrounding Tuscan countryside, and a center for the carving of decorative objects developed there that is still important to the local economy. See Luperini 1999; Orlandi 2005.

101. Still life with silver and hardstone objects

Alexandre-François Desportes,
Paris, ca. 1726
Oil on canvas; 103 × 73¾ in. (261.6 ×
187.3 cm)
Signed at lower right: *Desportes*
The Metropolitan Museum of Art,
New York, Purchase, Mary
Wetmore Shively Bequest, in
memory of her husband, Henry L.
Shively, M.D., 1964 64.315

PROVENANCE: Possibly Jean-
Baptiste Machault d'Arnouville,
Château d'Arnouville, until d. 1794;
Yvon, Paris, until 1881 (anonymous
sale, Hôtel Drouot, Paris, January
27–28, 1881, no. 14, as "Fruits");
private collection, until 1903 (sale,
Hôtel Drouot, Paris, May 30, 1903,
no. 18, as "Un Dressoir," to Lévy);
[Lévy, Paris, from 1903]; private
collection, until 1938 (sale, Galerie
Charpentier, Paris, March 31, 1938,
no. 28, as "Le Buffet"); [Jacques
Helft, Paris and Buenos Aires,
1938–64]; [Société Matteo, Paris,
1964]; purchased by the
Metropolitan Museum

REFERENCES: *Versailles et les tables
royales* 1993, p. 266, no. 38; Baetjer
1995, p. 366

This painting is a luscious celebration of life. What appear to be the entire contents of a princely cupboard—vases, bowls, platters, bottles, and jars of various shapes and costly materials—have been placed in a pyramidal, tiered arrangement on a greenish marble buffet supported by a gilded wood stand. In the center of the lowest tier is a silver centerpiece upheld by silver satyrs and loaded with ripe fruits ready to burst with juice. At either side of this confection a silver ewer stands guard. The relief decoration on the ewer at left represents water and on the one at right, wine—indicating that at the time, two objects did not need to be identical in order to be considered a pair.[1] The tier above is draped with lush blue silk velvet and displays in the center a massive silver tureen with a cartouche on the bowl showing Venus and Amor. The exotic dragon handles stand out like heraldic devices against two gilded platters with a scalloped border. East Asian porcelain, flowers, and polychrome marble vases are supported by canted brackets, and at the far ends of the shelf, hardstone vessels, perhaps made of agate, lend a smoldering touch of dark red. A satyr's mask with a collar of flowers and a large scallop shell for a crown smiles down from above. It is evident that the dishes and flowers have been brought out for a banquet, where any amount of delicious food and wine will be consumed and any excess on the part of the guests will be sanctioned by this ambassador of Bacchus, the god of wine, presiding at the top. The painting may illustrate a line from *The Eunuch*, written in 161 B.C. by the Roman dramatist Terence, "Sine Cerere et Libero friget Venus" (Without Ceres and Bacchus, Venus will freeze), meaning that without food and wine, love grows cold.[2] Ceres is represented by the harvested fruits and Bacchus by the satyrs and ram's heads, while Venus appears on the tureen.

The display of metal, marble, porcelain, and hardstones is intended to please the eye and possibly to suggest the beauty, variety, and dazzling transformations that nature, with the help of the human hand, is able to achieve. The French artist Alexandre-François Desportes (1661–1743) painted many such elaborately staged buffets.[3] They were immensely popular, not only in France but also in England; indeed, as one scholar observed, "By the late 1720s, nearly every prince and princess of the blood and many important private collectors had acquired works by Desportes."[4] This particular painting documents forms of silverware of the late seventeenth and early eighteenth centuries that have not survived in real examples.

WK

1. About 1767 the Parisian bronze worker Pierre Gouthière created two different figures mounted as handles on a pair of porphyry ewers, one a mermaid (water) and the other a satyr (wine), that are in the Qizilbash collection. Probably while traveling in France in 1782, Grand Duke Paul of Russia acquired them as a pair for the Winter Palace (see Christie's, Paris, December 19, 2007, sale cat., lot 802, with bibliography and many stylistic comparisons).
2. On this subject, see Koeppe in Kisluk-Grosheide, Koeppe, and Rieder 2006, pp. 42–43, nn. 11, 12.
3. For a similar decorative buffet arrangement by Desportes, see *Versailles et les tables royales* 1993, pp. 131, 265–66, no. 36; Malgouyres 2003, p. 148, fig. 71.
4. Laurie G. Winters, "Desportes," in *Dictionary of Art* 1996, vol. 8, pp. 811–14 (the quotation is on p. 813); on Desportes, see also Lastic Saint-Jal 1961.

102. Vase on a column stand

Lapidary workshop, Hôtel des
Menus-Plaisirs, Versailles, after
1771–72
Design by François-Joseph
Bélanger; lapidary work probably
by Augustin Bocciardi
Egyptian porphyry
Mounts: Paris, ca. 1780
Attributed to Pierre-Philippe
Thomire
Gilded bronze
H. without mounts 39⅞ in.
(100.3 cm), H. with mounts 41¼ in.
(104.8 cm), H. of stand 35⅝ in.
(90.5 cm), Diam. 16⅜ in. (41.6 cm)
The Metropolitan Museum of Art,
New York, Gift of Mr. and Mrs.
Charles Wrightsman, 1971
1971.206.44

PROVENANCE: Possibly Louis
Marie Augustin, duc d'Aumont
(d. 1782); Mr. and Mrs. Charles
Wrightsman, New York, until 1971;
their gift to the Metropolitan
Museum

REFERENCES: *France in the
Eighteenth Century* 1968, p. 148,
no. 887; Watson 1969, p. 188, pl. IV;
Watson in Watson and Dauterman
1970, pp. 70–74, no. 306

The diameter of this Egyptian porphyry vase and its stand are the same, suggesting that they were cut from the same stone, probably an ancient column. The discovery of an impurity that runs up through the stand and continues into the vase at the same position clinches the argument.[1] The column was probably taken from an ancient Roman structure, either an extant monument or an excavated ruin, and shipped to France. It was refashioned when Neoclassicism was in full spate and transformed into a collector's item; the vase was never meant to be used, as it was not hollowed out. The craftsmanship can be attributed to the stonecutting workshop at the Hôtel des Menus-Plaisirs in Versailles, which had been established by the order of Louis Marie Augustin, duc d'Aumont, in 1771 or 1772. D'Aumont had appointed François-Joseph Bélanger (1744–1818), one of France's foremost architects and designers, as artistic inspector to ensure the manufactory's success. Bélanger's education included a grounding in physics, and he had a practical approach to realizing his ideas. His early fame was based on previous commissions executed for important clients and on collaborations with principal artisans. As a member of the prestigious Académie Royale d'Architecture, he became a protégé of the antiquarian Grecophile comte de Caylus. In 1767 he was appointed designer for the Menus-Plaisirs, the organization responsible for entertainments at the court of Versailles; later he was named *premier architecte* to the comte d'Artois, brother of Louis XVI and one of the great connoisseurs of his time.[2]

The duc d'Aumont had been taken with the idea of setting up his own lapidary workshop after he acquired from the collection of the duc de Richelieu two monumental vases also cut from ancient Roman porphyry columns.[3] A lecture by "Le sieur Radel" on March 4, 1776, at the Académie Royale d'Architecture "on establishing a manufactory of works in granite, porphyry, jasper, and other French stones" offers details on the infrastructure and working methods of d'Aumont's lapidary workshop.[4] Vases by the sculptor Augustin Bocciardi (ca. 1729–1797), who probably cut the present vase and stand, are mentioned among the ostentatious furnishings of the Château de Menars, a residence of the marquis de Marigny, brother of Madame de Pompadour.[5]

The bronze mounts, on the theme of Bacchus, Roman god of wine, are attributed to Pierre-Philippe Thomire (1751–1843), who became a master metal finisher to the king. They are of superb quality and a tour de force of casting and chasing. Thomire had to cast the right horn of each ram's-head handle separately and use dowels to secure them.[6]

WK

1. First observed by Francis Watson in Watson and Dauterman 1970, p. 73; for the importance of ancient columns, see Binding 2002.
2. See the entry on Bélanger by Susan B. Taylor in *Dictionary of Art* 1996, vol. 3, pp. 523–24.
3. Watson in Watson and Dauterman 1970, p. 70. The catalogue of the sale of d'Aumont's collection, on December 12, 1782, mentions several such vases and includes a description of the duke's wide-ranging knowledge of hardstones (p. 8; for the catalogue, see Lugt 1930–87, vol. 1, no. 3488). See also Malgouyres 2003, pp. 172, 173–77, nos. 65–68 on the duc d'Aumont and porphyry objects in his collection, and p. 67 and fig. 29 for Early Christian use of porphyry columns.
4. Académie Royale d'Architecture 1911–29, vol. 8 (1924), pp. 252–53.
5. Gordon 2003; Hughes 2004. For a pair of gilded bronze wall lights by Bélanger, see Bremer-David 1993, pp. 105–6, no. 173.
6. For Thomire, see Cohen 1986.

Italy and Spain, Eighteenth and
Early Nineteenth Centuries

103. Lithotheque (stone sampler)

Rome (?), ca. 1763
Wood, bronze, and polychrome
stones; 19¼ × 38⅛ × 8¼ in. (49 × 97 ×
21 cm)
Inscribed: *LITHOTECA-M/
PICTURAE ET ARCHITECTURAE /
COMMODO ET INCREMENTO /
JOANNES MARIA RIMINALDUS
FERRARIENSIS / SAL.PALATII ST.
LITIBUS IUDICANDIS XII VIR /
MUSEO PATRIO / D D D / ANNO
DOMINI MDCCLXIII*
Musei Civici di Arte Antica,
Ferrara OA 922

PROVENANCE: Cardinal Gian
Maria Riminaldi; Museo Patrio
(later Musei Civici di Arte Antica),
Ferrara, from 1763

REFERENCES: Giusti 1985; Visser
Travagli 1991, p. 486; Giusti 1992,
p. 33, pl. 11; Maria Teresa Gulinelli
in De Nuccio and Ungaro 2002,
p. 575, no. 342; Carmela Vaccaro in
Bonatti and Gulinelli 2006,
pp. 174–76, no. 20

This unusual object is an early example of a portable stone sampler—a *litoteca*, or lithotheque, a genre that started to become fashionable in the second half of the eighteenth century. This version is distinguished by its ingenious and elegant structure, which hides the sampler's contents within what at first appears to be a small, handy piece of furniture. The sampler could be set down on a tabletop and opened to reveal, to the wonderment of a connoisseur, its fascinating array: 146 samples of marble and other stones taken from ancient sources and cut into small square slabs. The samples are framed in a wood grid and set within two wood tablets, each bordered by a molding like those found around the perimeter of console tabletops of the period, and joined by metal hinges. When opened, the lithotheque stands on four gilded-bronze lion's paws; when closed, its dedicatory inscription from "Joannes Maria Riminaldus Ferrariensis," painted in trompe l'oeil porphyry, can be seen on the top surface.

The lithotheque was donated to Ferrara's Museo Patrio in 1763[1] by the Ferrarese cardinal Gian Maria Riminaldi, who enjoyed a brilliant career in Rome and who was also named president of the Collegio dei Riformatori dello Studio (the University of Ferrara) by Pope Clement XIV. Initially part of the university, the Museo Patrio was the nucleus of what later became Ferrara's Musei Civici di Arte Antica. At that time the museum was built around a collection of Roman-era epigraphs and ancient coins and medals, to which the cardinal contributed by donating works he acquired on the Roman antiquarian market. The lithotheque, too, very likely came from Rome, then considered the most important center for the production of such samplers, which wedded the scientific interests of Enlightenment culture with the classicist passion for stones of the ancient world. We know from the travel writings of Jérôme de Lalande[2] that the stonecutter Antonio Minelli, who specialized in sampler table groupings of as many as 170 types of marble, was working in Rome about 1765–66. The cardinal's lithotheque thus may well have come out of Minelli's atelier or a similar workshop, no doubt produced in collaboration with a cabinetmaker and a bronze worker.

AG

1. In the first inventory taken by the Museo Patrio, published in 1771–72, the lithotheque is described as a "collection of ancient and rare marble arranged in a precious furnishing."
2. Lalande 1769, vol. 5, p. 224.

104. Console tabletop with *Allegory of Water*

Galleria dei Lavori, Florence, 1761
Design by Giuseppe Zocchi; lapi-
dary work by Rubini; frame by
Bombicci
Hardstones in a lapis lazuli
ground, bronze frame; 26 × 41¾ in.
(66 × 106 cm)
Hofburg, Vienna, Kaiserliches
Hofmobiliendepot MD 036355

PROVENANCE: Francis Stephen,
grand duke of Habsburg-Lorraine
(Emperor Francis I), Vienna, from
1761; imperial collection, Vienna;
Hofburg

REFERENCES: Zobi 1853, p. 296;
González-Palacios 1979, pp. 80–81;
Giusti in Giusti, Mazzoni, and
Pampaloni Martelli 1978, p. 324,
under no. 517; González-Palacios
1986, vol. 1, pp. 82–83, vol. 2,
fig. 232; Valeriani in Giusti 1988,
p. 192, no. 52; Giusti 1992, p. 115;
Giusti 2006b, p. 181

This astonishing and exquisitely worked tabletop was executed in little more than a year, a
surprisingly brief period. Giuseppe Zocchi (1711 or
1717–1767) delivered his painted design in January
1760, and within a few weeks the lapis lazuli for
the background had been purchased. By April 1761
the tabletop was completed and on its way to the
Viennese residence of Grand Duke Francis Stephen
of Habsburg-Lorraine (Emperor Francis I), along
with its wooden base. That base is now lost and
has been replaced. Contemporary documents
describe a mermaid and shell that decorated the
original base, in keeping with the theme of the
top,[1] and also mention the names of the craftsmen
who worked on the project, all of them active in
the grand-ducal workshops: the sculptor Rubini
carved the stone, Gaetano Corsani gilded the lost
wooden base, and the metalworker Bombicci made
the still-extant bronze frame around the tabletop.

This still life in stone—in which precious shells,
coral, and pearls seem magically imbued with an
icy but sensuous beauty—was so widely admired
that in 1766 the new grand duke of Tuscany,
Peter Leopold, commissioned a replica of it for his
Florentine residence and had it mounted on a gilded
wood base carved with shell motifs (cat. no. 105).
The replica top was made to be paired with a tabletop decorated with an Allegory of Air (cat. no. 106),
which had been finished the same year. Thirty years
later, Napoleon's agents took both tabletops from
the Palazzo Pitti and sent them to Paris.[2]

The replica tabletop decorated with marine
motifs was considered fine enough for the residence
of Empress Joséphine at the Château de Malmaison.
It was modified, however, by the famous furniture
maker François Jacob-Desmalter. He regularized the
top's by then out-of-date curvilinear Rococo shape,
transforming it into a rectangle and giving it a new,
Empire-style base. That table came to Russia in 1809
and is now in the State Hermitage Museum in Saint
Petersburg.[3]

The existence of yet another tabletop with the
same decorative theme confirms the enduring
admiration for Zocchi's sophisticated design. It is a
rectangular version, made in Florence between
1801 and 1806 for María Luisa, queen of Etruria,
and today is in the Palacio Real, Madrid.[4]

A G

1. González-Palacios 1986, vol. 1, pp. 82–83.
2. Among the objects looted by Napoleon's troops were nineteen tabletops from Florence; they were recorded in an inventory, "Inventaire descriptif des tableaux et autres objets d'arts, extraits du Palais Pitti et déposés au Musée le 21

Termidor," MS, August 9, 1801, Archives, Galleria degli Uffizi, Florence; cited in González-Palacios 1986, vol. 1, pp. 94–95.
3. Colle in Giusti 2006a, p. 142, no. 70.
4. González-Palacios 1993, vol. 1, pp. 438–41, vol. 2, fig. 785.

105. Console table base decorated with shell motifs

Galleria dei Lavori, Florence, 1767
Carving by Giovanni Battista
Dolci; gilding by Francesco Ristori
Gilded wood; 35½ × 42⅛ × 26⅜ in.
(90 × 107 × 67 cm)
Palazzo Pitti, Florence,
Appartamento della Regina,
Gabinetto Ovale MPP 1911 12504

PROVENANCE: Commissioned by
Peter Leopold, grand duke of
Tuscany, Florence; Habsburg-
Lorraine collection, Palazzo Pitti,
Florence (1771, 1791 inventories),
1767 until the present

REFERENCES: González-Palacios
1986, vol. 1, p. 83, vol. 2, fig. 240;
Valeriani in Giusti 1988, p. 192,
under no. 52; Colle 1991, p. 66;
Colle 1992, pp. 109–10, no. 39;
Chiarini and Padovani 1993, p. 275,
no. IX.12; Colle 2003, p. 214, no. 48;
Colle in Giusti 2006a, p. 139, no. 68

This base for a console table was made to support a tabletop with pietre dure decorations depicting shells, corals, and pearls, now in the State Hermitage Museum in Saint Petersburg. That top is an exact copy of one in this exhibition depicting an Allegory of Water (cat. no. 104). Peter Leopold, the new grand duke of Tuscany (r. 1765–90), admired the original and decided to order a replica and the present base; the new table would serve as a pendant for a console table with an Allegory of Air (cat. nos. 106, 107) that was already being built for him at the Galleria dei Lavori. The two table bases made for the grand duke were inspired by the fully developed Italianate version of Rococo taste. The four legs on each are curved and terminate in foliated volutes. They are supported by crosspieces also formed by curving volutes decorated with small, curling leaves. The only real differences between the two bases are in the carving of the apron above the legs and the intersection of the crosspieces below. In this table, the decoration is composed of drapery and coral and shell compositions; the other console base displays short garlands and bunches of flowers. Thus each base alludes to the theme of its top.

Carved by Giovanni Battista Dolci, the two tabletops were completed in 1766, and this table base was finished in June 1767, having been gilded by Francesco Ristori. The tabletops and bases were listed in an inventory of the Palazzo Pitti in 1771 and another in 1791. The tops left the palace in 1799, when Napoleon's troops occupied Florence. Today they are in the Musée du Louvre and the State Hermitage Museum. The bases, probably judged too old-fashioned in style, were left behind in Tuscany.   AG

106. Console tabletop with *Allegory of Air*

Galleria dei Lavori, Florence, 1766
Design by Giuseppe Zocchi
Hardstones in an alabaster ground,
gilded bronze frame; 26⅜ × 41¾ in.
(67 × 106 cm)
Musée du Louvre, Paris MR 407

PROVENANCE: Peter Leopold,
grand duke of Tuscany; Habsburg-
Lorraine collection, Palazzo Pitti,
Florence (1771, 1790 inventories),
from 1766; brought by Napoleon's
army to Paris, ca. 1800; entered the
Musée du Louvre by 1801

REFERENCES: Zobi 1853, p. 296;
González-Palacios 1986, vol. 1,
p. 86, vol. 2, fig. 234; Giusti 1992,
p. 115, pl. 55; Alcouffe, Dion-
Tenenbaum, and Lefébure 1993,
p. 342, no. 118; Colle in Giusti
2006a, pp. 138–39, no. 67, and p. 139,
under no. 68; Giusti 2006b, p. 181,
ill. no. 149

Begun as soon as Giuseppe Zocchi (1711 or 1717–1767) finished his painted design for it (cat. no. 109) at the end of 1764, this tabletop was completed sometime in 1766. Its exuberant composition of butterflies and flowers on an airy sky-blue ground presents a convincing Allegory of Air. The wood-carver Giovanni Battista Dolci was paid for its base (cat. no. 107) in October 1766. The table had been envisioned as a pendant to the console table with an Allegory of Water (cat. no. 104), which was sent in 1761 to the Viennese residence of Francis Stephen of Habsburg-Lorraine, grand duke of Tuscany and Holy Roman emperor. But Francis Stephen died in Innsbruck in August 1765 and was succeeded as grand duke by his younger son, Peter Leopold. The new ruler decided, understandably, to keep this splendid table at the Palazzo Pitti, Florence, his official residence.

Napoleon's army arrived in Florence in 1799, having forced Leopold's son, Grand Duke Ferdinand III, to abandon the city. Much of the furniture and many objects decorated with hardstone mosaic in the Palazzo Pitti were sent to Paris, including this tabletop.[1] It never returned to Florence, although after the Congress of Vienna the French government sent back some of the other stolen works of art. The table's base remained in Florence and is still in the collection of the Palazzo Pitti.

A G

1. Among the objects looted by Napoleon's troops were nineteen tabletops from Florence; they were recorded in an inventory, "Inventaire descriptif des tableaux et autres objets d'arts, extraits du Palais Pitti et déposés au Musée le 21 Termidor," MS, August 9, 1801, Archives, Galleria degli Uffizi, Florence; cited in González-Palacios 1986, vol. 1, pp. 94–95.

107. Console table base decorated with flowers and butterflies

Galleria dei Lavori, Florence, 1766
Carving by Giovanni Battista
Dolci; gilding by Francesco Ristori
Gilded wood; 35½ × 42⅛ × 26⅜ in.
(90 × 107 × 67 cm)
Palazzo Pitti, Florence,
Appartamento della Regina,
Gabinetto Ovale MPP 1911 12503

PROVENANCE: Commissioned
by Peter Leopold, grand duke of
Tuscany, Florence; Habsburg-
Lorraine collection, Palazzo Pitti,
Florence (1771, 1791 inventories),
1766 until the present

REFERENCES: González-Palacios
1986, vol. 1, p. 83, vol. 2, fig. 239;
Valeriani in Giusti 1988, p. 192,
under no. 52; Colle 1991, p. 66,
fig. 5; Colle 1992, pp. 109–10, no. 39;
Colle 2003, p. 214, under no. 48;
Chiarini and Padovani 1993, p. 275,
no. IX.12, ill.; Colle in Giusti 2006a,
p. 139, under no. 68

The mate to a table base decorated with marine motifs (cat. no. 105), this graceful Rococo stand was made to support a top decorated in pietre dure with an Allegory of Air (cat. no. 106). Both bases were executed in the Galleria dei Lavori in Florence by the wood-carver Giovanni Battista Dolci for Grand Duke Peter Leopold of the Habsburg-Lorraine dynasty. The tops were finished early in 1766, and in October of the same year Dolci was paid for making this console base, "with four legs in the French style,"[1] and appropriately decorated with flowers and butterflies, emblematic of the air. It was gilded, like its companion, by Francesco Ristori.

Like its companion, too, it was left in the Palazzo Pitti, Florence, by Napoleon's agents in 1799, when they carried away both tops to Paris. The top with an Allegory of Water is now in the State Hermitage Museum, Saint Petersburg.[2] The top with an Allegory of Air remained in Paris and is now in the Musée du Louvre; but for the present exhibition, it has been reunited with this, its original base, allowing us to see what an enchanting impression the original ensemble made.

AG

1. Quoted by Colle in Giusti 2006a, p. 139, no. 68.
2. Colle in ibid., p. 142, no. 70.

108. *Allegory of Air*, preliminary sketch for a tabletop

Galleria dei Lavori, Florence, 1764
By Giuseppe Zocchi
Watercolor on paper; 24⅜ × 40⅜ in.
(61.7 × 102.3 cm)
Museo dell'Opificio delle Pietre
Dure, Florence IDO 3058

PROVENANCE: Galleria dei Lavori
(subsequently Opificio delle Pietre
Dure), Florence, from 1764; later
Museo dell'Opificio

REFERENCES: González-Palacios
1986, vol. 1, p. 83, vol. 2, fig. 233;
Colle in Giusti 2006a, p. 138, no. 65

The painter Giuseppe Zocchi's long collaboration with the grand-ducal workshops began in the middle of the eighteenth century. Toward the end of his life, Zocchi (1711 or 1717–1767) started to expand his subject matter, which had been mostly centered on the human figure. His two designs for console tabletops made in the 1760s, one with butterfly and flower motifs (cat. no. 106) and the other with shells, coral, and pearls (cat. no. 104), reveal an unexpected flair for decoration. In both designs he brought freshness to the kind of naturalistic image that had dominated Florentine mosaics from the beginning of the seventeenth century until the recent past. The subject of this one, *Allegory of Air*, offered Zocchi an opportunity to paint an enchanting floral garland stirring in a light breeze. The flowers have attracted a flight of butterflies, each differentiated from the others with the precision of a lepidopterist.

It was normal practice at this time for a painter to provide the grand-ducal workshops with preliminary ideas for a design in the form of a watercolor drawing of this sort. Once it had been approved by the director (in this period he was Cosimo Siriès), the design was reworked to its definitive form in oil on canvas (cat. no. 109).

This watercolor sketch represents a moment in the creative process when variations on an idea for the final design were put forward. Thus, Zocchi offers, for example, two alternatives for the background color—white on the left and white and light green on the right. Also, the floral garlands are rendered differently on each side of the sketch. On the left they are more delicate and seem to show more branches, while on the right the flowers and foliage are denser and seen from a closer vantage point. Because the oil painting Zocchi made from this drawing was paid for on January 1, 1765, we can assume that this watercolor dates from a slightly earlier moment in 1764.   A G

109. *Allegory of Air,* design for a tabletop

Galleria dei Lavori, Florence, 1764
By Giuseppe Zocchi
Oil on canvas; 26 × 41¾ in. (66 × 106 cm)
Museo dell'Opificio delle Pietre Dure, Florence OA 1911:788

PROVENANCE: Galleria dei Lavori (subsequently Opificio delle Pietre Dure), Florence; Museo dell'Opificio, from 1953

REFERENCES: Marchionni 1891, p. 105; Bartoli and Maser 1953, pp. 12, 30; Giusti in Giusti, Mazzoni, and Pampaloni Martelli 1978, p. 324, no. 518, pl. 458; Giusti 1995, p. 59, ill. no. 26; Colle in Giusti 2006a, p. 138, no. 66

This final design in oil on canvas for the decoration of the top of a console table destined for Vienna (cat. nos. 106, 107) is based on a preparatory drawing (cat. no. 108). Some of the design ideas offered on the right side of the drawing have been reworked, and there are several other changes as well. The leafy vine has been transformed into a full-fledged festoon of foliage supported by a capriciously curling ribbon that seems to be ruffled by the same breeze that stirs the flowers. They, too, are denser and more varied than in the preliminary study, and there are more butterflies—their brilliant colors match those of the blossoms.

The definitive design for a hardstone mosaic was usually arrived at by degrees, shaped by a series of alternative proposals that led to the final choice. This common practice in the Florentine workshops was followed especially under the grand dukes of Habsburg-Lorraine. For the present design the process involved the collaboration between Giuseppe Zocchi (1711 or 1717–1767), the painter, and Cosimo Siriès, director of the workshops, who earlier in his career had been a silversmith and a bronze worker.[1]

The console table was intended as a pendant to one with an Allegory of Water that had already been sent to Vienna (cat. no. 104). Zocchi was paid for his oil *modello* for this second tabletop on January 1, 1765; thus, it probably was finished in the last months of 1764. While the motif of naturalistically rendered flowers had been dominant in the mosaics produced at the grand-ducal workshops from the beginning of the seventeenth century, Zocchi's concept offers fresh ideas, such as the festoon draped with ribbons and the subtle juxtapositions of color. The design's light, luminous polychromy accorded well with the contemporary Rococo taste. Zocchi's deft, inventive *modello* was transformed into a hardstone mosaic in 1766, and the table base was made the same year.

A G

1. Giusti 2006c, pp. 20–21.

110. *Allegory of Sculpture*

Galleria dei Lavori, Florence,
ca. 1775–80
Design by Giuseppe Zocchi; frame
designed by Gesualdo Ferri
Hardstones, soft stones, gilded
bronze; 24 × 31½ in. (61 × 80 cm)
Museo dell'Opificio delle Pietre
Dure, Florence OA 1911:1528

PROVENANCE: Habsburg-Lorraine
collection, Palazzo Pitti, Florence;
Museo degli Argenti, Palazzo
Pitti (1911 inventory); Museo
dell'Opificio delle Pietre Dure,
Florence, from 1952

REFERENCES: Zobi 1853, p. 299;
Bartoli and Maser 1953, pp. 11, 29,
ill. p. 53; Honour 1958, ill. no. 5;
Rossi (Ferdinando) 1967, p. 112;
Giusti in Giusti, Mazzoni, and

Four panels dedicated to the Fine Arts—Music, Painting, Sculpture, and Architecture—were among the group of mosaic pictures made in the Florentine workshops for Francis Stephen of Habsburg-Lorraine, grand duke of Tuscany. More than sixty in all, they were finished in 1754 and sent to his residence in Vienna. The oil-on-canvas *modelli* painted by Giuseppe Zocchi for these mosaics in 1752–53 (see cat. no. 111) stayed in Florence, however. Some twenty years later a second set of mosaics in hardstones was made from these graceful scenes for Grand Duke Peter Leopold, who had succeeded his father in 1765 and established his own court in Florence. The subject of the Arts had remained popular at European courts, as is attested by the intarsia representations of them on the large cabinet that the German furniture maker David Roentgen

executed in the late 1770s for Frederick William of Prussia (Kunstgewerbemuseum, Berlin).

It is likely that the theme of this panel and its three companions particularly appealed to Peter Leopold, who was a great patron of the arts. His set of mosaics was begun in 1775. Drawings were made of Zocchi's designs and then divided into sections for transfer to the stone. When creating the first set of mosaics for Vienna, the Florentine craftsmen had mastered the difficulties of representing the human figure in hardstone. The second series, based on Zocchi's original designs, is no less magisterial, and shows the craftsmen's extraordinary skill in capturing the nuances of color. They used especially tiny chips to create the effect of paint applied fluidly to canvas and then magically transformed into pietre dure.

Pampaloni Martelli 1978, p. 284, no. 55, pl. 61; González-Palacios 1979; González-Palacios 1986, vol. 1, p. 85, vol.2, fig. 230; Giusti in Giusti 1988, p. 198, no. 55; Giusti 1992, p. 115, pl. 53; González-Palacios 1993, vol. 1, pp. 433–34; Tosi 1997, p. 158, ill. p. 154; Giusti 2006b, pp. 176, 181

The traditional bronze frames used for the first set of mosaics were rejected in favor of inlaid panels of colored marble in metal settings. The painter Gesualdo Ferri (1728–documented until 1797), who collaborated from time to time with the Florentine lapidary workshops, was commissioned to paint frame designs—still preserved in the Museo dell'Opificio delle Pietre Dure, Florence—in the contemporary Neoclassical style. The four depictions of the Fine Arts are framed in fascicled panels ornamented with spiraling ribbons. Roundels at the four corners display the attributes of the Fine Arts in exquisite, minuscule passages of mosaic.

AG

III. *Allegory of Sculpture*, design for a mosaic panel

Galleria dei Lavori, Florence, 1752
By Giuseppe Zocchi
Oil on canvas; 20½ × 27⅝ in.
(52 × 70 cm)
Museo dell'Opificio delle Pietre Dure, Florence OA 1911:961

PROVENANCE: Galleria dei Lavori (subsequently Opificio delle Pietre Dure), Florence, by 1911; later Museo dell'Opificio

REFERENCES: Bartoli and Maser 1953, pp. 11, 29, ill. p. 53; Maser 1967, p. 53, under no. 18; Giusti in Giusti, Mazzoni, and Pampaloni Martelli 1978, pp. 321–22, no. 485, pl. 414; González-Palacios 1979; González-Palacios 1986, vol. 1, pp. 84–85, 97–99; Giusti 1992, p. 115, pl. 52; Tosi 1997, p. 158; Giusti in Dolcini and Zanettin 1999, pp. 60–63; Giusti 2006b, pp. 176, 181

In 1750 Louis Siriès, a French goldsmith who had become director of the grand-ducal workshops in Florence two years earlier, engaged the painter Giuseppe Zocchi (1711 or 1717–1767) to create models for the mosaics produced at the manufactory.[1] Zocchi was already well known for his *Selection of 24 Views of the City of Florence*, a series of etchings made from his drawings of Florence and published in 1744.

During the seventeen years he was employed at the workshops, Zocchi expanded and refreshed its repertoire of subject matter. He moved away from the naturalistically rendered motifs set against a black marble ground that were still being produced there under the new dynasty of Habsburg-Lorraine and instead devised figural subjects that he judiciously selected from fashionable pictorial sources. Between 1750 and 1762 the painter made more than sixty oil sketches, grouped in thematic series of two to six images. They included views of classical ruins in the style of Giovanni Paolo Panini, the leading exponent of that genre, as well as landscapes and scenes of aristocratic life based on the work of Claude-Joseph Vernet, a painter in whose Roman studio Zocchi had spent time as a young man. Also among the studies were ones on allegorical subjects, which especially appealed to the scholarly taste of the time.

The series representing the Fine Arts consists of four pictures, including this *Allegory of Sculpture*. Each work combines an allegorical representation of an artistic activity meant to delight the eye and the spirit with an elegant slice of contemporary life. Zocchi was paid for the first two paintings in this series, on Painting and Sculpture, in November 1752. The designs for Music (cat. nos. 112, 113, 114) and Architecture followed soon after, in January 1753. All of the designs were used to create an unusual gallery of mosaic pictures for the Viennese residence of Francis Stephen of Habsburg-Lorraine, grand duke of Tuscany.

The Fine Arts panels were finished in 1754 and dispatched to Vienna. A quarter century later the painted designs, which had remained in Florence, were used to make a second set of hardstone mosaics (see cat. no. 110) for the new grand duke, Peter Leopold.

AG

1. For Siriès and those of his descendants who were also directors of the workshops, see Giusti in Giusti 2006c.

112. *Allegory of Music*

Galleria dei Lavori, Florence,
1775–80
Design by Giuseppe Zocchi; frame
designed by Gesualdo Ferri
Hardstones, soft stones, gilded
bronze; 24 × 31½ in. (61 × 80 cm)
Museo dell'Opificio delle Pietre
Dure, Florence OA 1911:1530

PROVENANCE: Habsburg-Lorraine
collection, Palazzo Pitti, Florence;
Museo degli Argenti, Palazzo
Pitti (1911 inventory); Museo
dell'Opificio delle Pietre Dure,
Florence, from 1952

REFERENCES: Zobi 1853, p. 299;
Bartoli and Maser 1953, pp. 11, 29;
Rossi (Ferdinando) 1967, pp. 94,
112, pl. XXXVII; Giusti in Giusti,
Mazzoni, and Pampaloni Martelli
1978, p. 284, no. 57, pl. 57; Rossi
(Ferdinando) 1984, ill. p. 116;
González-Palacios 1986, vol. I,

Of the series of pietre dure pictures made for the Viennese residence of Francis Stephen of Habsburg-Lorraine, those representing the Fine Arts after oil sketches made by Giuseppe Zocchi in 1752–53 were among the most admired. About twenty years later, a second set of mosaics was made from Zocchi's designs; these were destined for the Florentine palace of Grand Duke Peter Leopold of Tuscany.[1] Line drawings were made of the original paintings, still being kept in the workshop, from which the craftsmen then made the tracings used to divide the composition into sections and re-create it in hardstone mosaic. This painstaking process was further complicated by the fact that the image included human figures, which had reappeared in the repertory of pietre dure subjects in the mid-eighteenth century. The revival of populated scenes had been the result of a collaboration between the workshop's then-new director, Louis Siriès (ca. 1686–1762)—who moved

from France to Florence and became the first in his family to head the grand-ducal workshop— and Zocchi himself, who had been brought in to revise the style of Florentine mosaics.[2]

The craftsmen in the grand-ducal workshop, having made more than sixty mosaic pictures for the Vienna palace, demonstrated their perfect mastery of medium and palette in executing the second version of the Fine Arts panels. In the *Allegory of Music,* the scene seems to be bathed in afternoon light, the figures as remote and enchanting as a Mozart aria. And yet despite their success in accomplishing such complicated scenes, the Galleria dei Lavori's pietre dure artists, always looking for fresh challenges, were about to abandon figural subject matter yet again and turn instead to still lifes of antique vases and shells. Antonio Cioci, the painter in charge of making designs for mosaics in the early 1770s, would be largely responsible for this shift in subject matter as well as style. In his paintings, Cioci,

p. 85; Giusti in Giusti 1988, p. 198, no. 55; Tosi 1997, pp. 158–60, ill.; Giusti in Giusti 2006a, p. 170, no. 90; Giusti 2007, pp. 185–86

more sympathetic to Neoclassical taste than to the painterly qualities of the Rococo, tended to exploit pietre dure's potential for abstract renderings and a cool luminosity.

There is some hint of this shift in taste in the second series of Fine Arts panels. For the first time in the history of the Florentine workshop, for example, the mosaics were given frames of pietre dure and gilded bronze, which are embellished with a Neoclassical motif of Roman fasces. The corners of the frames are decorated with emblems of the individual Arts, each a small but exquisite passage of still life rendered with the same cold lucidity Cioci shortly thereafter employed in his more complex compositions for several tables made for the Palazzo Pitti.[3] The painter Gesualdo Ferri's designs for these emblems, as Alvar

González-Palacios has noted, were later reused in small mosaics produced in great quantities in the Florentine workshop in the last quarter of the eighteenth century.[4] For example, a snuffbox that dates from 1822, after the French occupation of Florence (1799–1815), is decorated on its lid with a close variant of the emblem represented in the lower left corner of this frame.[5]   AG

1. For a discussion of the characteristics of this second group, see the entry for the *Allegory of Sculpture* (cat. no. 110).
2. For Zocchi's activity as a painter in general, see Tosi 1997. For his work for the grand-ducal workshop, see Giusti 2006a, nos. 48, 51, 53, 54, 57–59.
3. Published in Baldini, Giusti, and Pampaloni Martelli 1979, pp. 272–74, nos. 66–71, pls. 72–84, p. 283, nos. 90, 91, pls. 115–17.
4. González-Palacios 1986, vol. 1, p. 85.
5. For the snuffbox, see Massinelli 2000, p. 154, no. 63.

113. *Allegory of Music*, preparatory sketch

Galleria dei Lavori, Florence, 1752
By Giuseppe Zocchi
Ink and watercolor on paper;
6½ × 9 in. (16.5 × 23 cm)
Galleria degli Uffizi, Florence, Gabinetto Disegni e Stampe 6502 S

PROVENANCE: Santarelli collection; Galleria degli Uffizi, Florence

REFERENCES: Maser 1967, p. 53, no. 23, pl. 43; Giusti in Giusti, Mazzoni, and Pampaloni Martelli 1978, p. 328, under nos. 484–87; González-Palacios 1986, vol. 1, p. 85, vol. 2, fig. 203; Tosi 1997, pp. 158–60, ill. p. 157

From 1750 to 1767 Giuseppe Zocchi (1711 or 1717–1767), a painter in the grand-ducal workshop of Florence, made oil sketches (*modelli*) for a series of hardstone mosaics destined for the Austrian emperor (see cat. nos. 109, 111). Before executing the final painting of a given work, however, Zocchi was expected to submit several sketches of his ideas to the workshop's director, Louis Siriès. There are a good number of these preliminary drawings in the Galleria degli Uffizi, Florence. They are generally characterized by the freshness and spontaneity of an idea quickly tossed off on paper. They are also appealing documents of the artist's creative process—especially since in many instances the ideas expressed in the sketches were modified in the final painting in a way that makes the finished scene more academic. It is tempting to wonder if Siriès reined in the livelier aspects of Zocchi's compositions, which as the artist originally envisioned them were not without humor. For example, one painting from a series of the Hours of the day, showing a lady at her morning toilette, is set in an orderly room that includes a gallant gracefully offering her a rose.[1] In the preliminary drawing, by contrast, we glimpse a shadowy corner complete with an unmade bed and several gentlemen who have the air of some shared intimacy with the lady.[2]

This drawing is one of four preparatory sketches for the *Allegory of Music* (cat. no. 112); they seem to reflect not a restraint imposed on the artist but rather a progressive development of the subject.[3]

Indeed, there is a marked improvement from drawing to drawing as the artist settles on a final composition, which seems to depict an orchestra rehearsal. In what is perhaps the earliest of the drawings, the technique is almost summary and the line renderings virtual caricatures. Yet here again we glimpse the artist's sense of humor in the sketch of a singer shown in profile with mouth open wide, while agitation is evident among the musicians.[4] In the other three drawings the scene becomes less boisterous and emerges as almost solemn in the sketch that sets the concert in a large hall illuminated by a chandelier.[5] A related drawing, which shows figures reading, is perhaps, as Alessandro Tosi has posited, an unfinished project for an *Allegory of Poetry*.[6] The present drawing is set outdoors in a loggia, like the one in the painting. It is the closest to Zocchi's painting for the mosaic (cat. no. 114), although there are several important differences, including the fact that the groupings and poses of the figures are more animated in the sketch than they are on canvas.

AG

1. See Giusti in Giusti 2006a, pp. 120–21, no. 53.
2. Ibid.
3. All are in the Galleria degli Uffizi, Gabinetto Disegni e Stampe (Sant. 6502, 6503, 6504, and 6513). See Maser 1967, p. 53, nos. 20–23, pls. 40–43; Tosi 1997, ill. pp. 155, 157, 158.
4. Tosi 1997, ill. p. 158.
5. Ibid., ill. p. 157.
6. Ibid., ill. p. 161.

115. Tabletop with an image of porcelain vessels

Galleria dei Lavori, Florence,
ca. 1797
Design by Antonio Cioci
Nephrite and other hardstones,
gilded bronze frame (not shown);
32¾ × 58¾ in. (83 × 149 cm)
Palazzo Pitti, Florence,
Appartamenti Reali OA 1911:934

PROVENANCE: Grand Duke
Ferdinand III, Palazzo Pitti,
Florence, by 1797; brought by
Napoleon's army to Paris, ca. 1800;
returned to the Palazzo Pitti, 1816

REFERENCES: Zobi 1853, p. 302;
Gregori in *La natura morta italiana*
1964, p. 122, under no. 294;
Aschengreen Piacenti 1967, p. 174,
no. 809; Rossi (Ferdinando) 1967,
p. 114, pls. XXXIX, XL; Giusti in
Baldini, Giusti, and Pampaloni
Martelli 1979, p. 283, no. 90, pls. 115,
116; Rossi (Ferdinando) 1984, ill.
pp. 119, 120; González-Palacios
1986, vol. 1, pp. 87–88, vol. 2,
fig. 249; Colle in Giusti 1988, p. 206,
no. 58; Colle 2005, p. 74, fig. 29;
Colle in Giusti 2006a, p. 186, no. 105

This tabletop and its pendant, which is also in the Palazzo Pitti, Florence, are among the most admired and imitated of the works made in the Galleria dei Lavori for the grand dukes of the Habsburg-Lorraine dynasty. Their mosaic decoration is based on designs furnished in 1785–86 by the painter Antonio Cioci (d. 1792). Work on the mosaics did not begin until 1792, however. In a letter dated August 20 of that year, Luigi Siriès, director of the workshops, wrote to Grand Duke Ferdinand III and proposed using porphyry as a background for the nephrite and other hardstones. But the duke did not like the idea, perhaps because two pairs of pietre dure tables that had been delivered to the Palazzo Pitti in 1784 and 1790–91—one decorated with depictions of shells and the other with images of antique vases—were of porphyry.[1] Ten days later, in a second letter to Ferdinand, Siriès said he had made a thorough inventory of the stones available in the workshop and that he had found "an Egyptian nephrite that is valued for its rarity and well suited to set the work off to great advantage."[2]

The silicate known as nephrite, so called because of the ancient tradition that it could cure kidney ailments (*nephros* means kidney in Greek), was not among the stones used in ancient Roman mosaics. That is probably the reason for a reluctance to use it in intarsia during the Renaissance and again in the Neoclassical period, when there was a renewed interest in the stones used by the ancient Romans. Siriès's choice, however, was an innovative and felicitous one. The dark tones of the Egyptian nephrite set off the mosaic images inlaid in it, while at the same time the vividness of its mottled, velvety green surface makes the whole work vibrant, as Siriès noted. The success of these two tabletops was so great that nephrite became a commonly used background for a variety of subjects pictured in hardstone mosaic in the nineteenth century.

The tabletops must have been fairly well along in 1795, because work was begun then on their gilded bronze frames and the bases that were to support them. Only this table, however, was listed among the furniture in the Palazzo Pitti on January 5, 1797; its pendant remained in the Galleria dei Lavori for several more years, which saved it from being plundered by the French in 1799. The table exhibited here did go to Paris but was returned to the Palazzo Pitti in 1816, a year after the fall of the Napoleonic empire. It was reunited with its mate in 1868, when the latter was returned from Parma, where it had been taken by the Bourbon royalty who ruled Florence briefly in the early years of the nineteenth century. It is not surprising that kings and emperors were impressed with these two marvelous tables, in which Cioci's graceful designs were enhanced by their transformation into precise, brilliantly colored hardstone mosaic. Especially notable are the virtuoso rendering of the decorations on the porcelain and the skillful handling of the lights and darks.

AG

1. Two other tables whose tops show antique vases, now in the Sala di Apollo of the Galleria Palatina in the Palazzo Pitti, were also based on designs by Cioci. The artist also designed the two tabletops depicting shells in pietre dure that were exhibited in the Sala di Giove. See Giusti in Baldini, Giusti, and Pampaloni Martelli 1979, pp. 272–73, nos. 66–69, pls. 72–78.
2. Giusti in ibid., p. 283, under nos. 90, 91.

116. *Table with Porcelain Vessels,* design for a tabletop

Galleria dei Lavori, Florence, 1786
By Antonio Cioci
Oil on canvas; 30⅜ × 66⅝ in.
(77 × 169 cm)
Museo dell'Opificio delle Pietre
Dure, Florence OA 1911:929

PROVENANCE: Galleria dei Lavori
(subsequently Opificio delle Pietre
Dure), Florence, by 1911; Museo
dell'Opificio, from 1953

REFERENCES: Marchionni 1891,
p. 106; Bartoli and Maser 1953,
pp. 9, 27; Ginori Lisci 1963, fig. 68;
Gregori in *La natura morta italiana*
1964, p. 122, no. 294; Giusti in
Giusti, Mazzoni, and Pampaloni
Martelli 1978, pp. 327–38, no. 544,
pl. 474; González-Palacios 1986,
vol. 1, pp. 87–88, vol. 2, fig. 248;
Colle in Giusti 1988, p. 206, under
no. 58; Colle in Giusti 2006a, p. 186,
no. 104

Antonio Cioci (d. 1792) became official painter of the Galleria dei Lavori in 1771, replacing Giuseppe Zocchi, who had died a few years earlier. In 1780 Cioci introduced a new repertory of subject matter for the Galleria's works in pietre dure—still lifes depicting arrangements of vases, pitchers, bowls, and other containers[1]—abandoning the figural designs that had dominated the workshops' production since the middle of the eighteenth century and that he himself had produced for nine years at the Galleria dei Lavori. As they had at other moments in their long history, Florentine mosaics moved away from the imitation of figure painting, in this case toward a Neoclassical aesthetic.

Beginning in the late 1770s, Cioci's own works—that is, his paintings not associated with the Galleria dei Lavori—revealed an interest in still lifes that were domestic and intimate in nature.[2] His designs for hardstone mosaics in the 1780s, however, show a refinement of composition and light that seems to derive from several different sources. The influences come from contemporary French painting but are also from some Italian work of earlier in the 1700s, such as still lifes by Cristoforo Munari or, in a particularly Florentine context, Bartolomeo Bimbi. The latter's work was well represented in the grand-ducal collections.

This design for a tabletop, which Cioci painted in 1786, and its pendant, painted a year earlier, were for a pair of console tables intended for the Palazzo Pitti, Florence.[3] The ancient vases Cioci so often represented have been replaced here with modern porcelain pieces made by the manufactory Ginori da Doccia and Japanese porcelains that were then in the grand-ducal collections.[4] Although Cioci probably painted the work from life, as he did for his still lifes of the shells he studied at the Museo della Specola, his quiet compositions seem to border on the surreal. The porcelain containers are bathed in a quiet light that has mysteriously penetrated the atmospheric vacuum in which the stone shelf supporting the still life seems to exist, although without conveying any real sense of gravity. The tendrils of flowering vines are the only references to the natural world. They seem to foreshadow the passion for flowers that would mark the Romantic style of the nineteenth century and have its own impact on Florentine mosaics.   AG

1. Cioci prepared designs depicting antique vases for two large porphyry tabletops completed in 1784 and now in the Galleria Palatina at the Palazzo Pitti, Florence.
2. Cioci's painting of a corner of his studio, dated 1789, is just such a domestic picture (Galleria degli Uffizi, Florence: 1890, no. 9459).
3. The design executed in 1785 is also preserved in the Museo dell'Opificio delle Pietre Dure (inv. 927).
4. The porcelain manufacturing shop was founded in 1737 at Doccia, near Florence, by Marchese Carlo Ginori. It enjoyed immediate and lasting success at home and abroad.

117. View of the Pantheon

Galleria dei Lavori, Florence,
1795–97
Design by Ferdinando Partini
Hardstones and petrified wood;
21¼ × 30 in. (54 × 76 cm)
Museo dell'Opificio delle Pietre
Dure, Florence OA 1911:1931

PROVENANCE: Grand Duke
Ferdinand III, Palazzo Pitti,
Florence; brought by Napoleon's
army to Paris, ca. 1800; returned to
the Palazzo Pitti in 1815; transferred to the Museo dell'Opificio
delle Pietre Dure, 1953

REFERENCES: Zobi 1853, pp. 298–
99; Bartoli and Maser 1953, pp. 12,
30, ill. p. 55; Rossi (Ferdinando)
1967, p. 113, pl. XXXVIII; Pampaloni
Martelli 1975, p. 91, no. 48;
González-Palacios 1977a, p. 47;
Giusti in Giusti, Mazzoni, and
Pampaloni Martelli 1978,
pp. 284–85, no. 58, pl. 58; Rossi
(Ferdinando) 1984, ill. p. 118;
González-Palacios 1986, vol. 1,
p. 90; González-Palacios 1993,
vol. 1, p. 436; Giusti 1995, p. 64;
Giusti in Calbi 2000, p. 191, no. 123;
Colle in *Il Neoclassicismo in Italia*
2002, p. 412, no. I.20; Colle in Giusti
2006a, p. 228, no. 146

This mosaic picture is based on a design by the Roman painter Ferdinando Partini (see also cat. no. 118) and was part of a larger project for six views of ancient Roman monuments that the director of the Florentine workshops proposed to Grand Duke Ferdinand III in the 1790s. The enterprising director was Luigi Siriès, and his idea was to create a series of mosaic pictures for the Palazzo Pitti, the grand duke's residence, based on a similar but more grandiose project executed several decades earlier by the Florentine workshop for Francis Stephen of Habsburg-Lorraine. That series included more than sixty hardstone mosaic pictures based on designs by the painter Giuseppe Zocchi.

We do not know if Siriès intended to expand this series of six views with other subjects because the project was interrupted by the arrival of Napoleonic troops in Florence in 1799. *View of the Pantheon* was the first image to be executed, and it was begun shortly after the painted model had been delivered, in November 1794. It was finished in the autumn of 1797, along with a second pietre dure image, *The Tomb of Cecilia Metella.*[1] Both pictures were in the Palazzo Pitti in 1799, when French Commissioner Jolly removed them, together with many other works of art and valuable objects, and sent them to Paris. They were returned to Florence after Napoleon's empire fell, in 1815.

The Florentine workshop largely abandoned landscape vistas and figures as subject matter after the completion of the pietre dure pictures derived from Zocchi's models. This image and the three others in the same series that were completed demonstrate, however, that the craftsmen had lost nothing of their old mastery. The buildings are represented with a refined play of light and shadow that gives the piazza a sense of space and atmosphere, all under an alabaster sky that was shaded on the reverse with a brush. The mosaic differs in several small ways from the painted model, especially in the figures on the right. Most especially, however, Partini's slightly pale, almost monotone painting is much more vivid and luminous in its stone incarnation, whose harmonious color scheme is an arrangement of chalcedony, jaspers, and petrified wood.

AG

1. In 1857 Grand Duke Leopold II gave that work (which had been returned to the Palazzo Pitti along with *View of the Pantheon* after the Restoration began in 1815) to Pope Pius IX, to mark a papal visit there. It is now in the Gilbert Collection at the Victoria and Albert Museum, London. The Museo dell'Opificio delle Pietre Dure has a second version of the subject, a faithful copy of the eighteenth-century image, which the grand duke commissioned in 1857 from the Galleria dei Lavori to replace the one he had given the pope.

Florence, 1794
By Ferdinando Partini; figures by
Giovanni Battista dell'Era
Oil on canvas; 20⅞ × 29½ in.
(53 × 75 cm)
Museo dell'Opificio delle Pietre
Dure, Florence OA 1911:931

PROVENANCE: Galleria dei Lavori
(subsequently Opificio delle Pietre
Dure), Florence, by 1911; Museo
dell'Opificio delle Pietre Dure

REFERENCES: Zobi 1853, pp. 298–99;
Marchionni 1891, p. 105; Bartoli and
Maser 1953, pp. 12, 30; Pampaloni
Martelli 1975, p. 90, no. 47; Giusti in
Giusti, Mazzoni, and Pampaloni
Martelli 1978, pp. 328–29, no. 549,
pl. 480, and p. 329, under
nos. 551–55; González-Palacios
1986, vol. 1, p. 90, vol. 2, fig. 260;
González-Palacios 1993, vol. 1,
pp. 435–38; Giusti in Calbi 2000,
p. 191, no. 122, and pp. 194–97,
under nos. 124–27; Colle in *Il
Neoclassicismo in Italia* 2002, p. 412,
under no. I.20; Colle in Giusti
2006a, p. 228, no. 147

This painting was the first in a series of six views of ancient Rome that were intended as designs for hardstone mosaics to "decorate a study"[1] in the grand duke's official residence at the Palazzo Pitti. The series was the idea of the director of the Galleria dei Lavori, Luigi Siriès. Siriès had written to Ferdinand III in 1794 to suggest that his gallery of hardstone mosaics should include depictions of "a number of ancient buildings, given that Architecture is that genre which can be represented with the most perfection."[2]

After a period of about thirty years during which sophisticated still lifes with vases or shells, mostly designed by the Galleria dei Lavori's official painter, Antonio Cioci, had dominated mosaic production in the Florentine workshop, the series of views of ancient Roman buildings was part of a brief return to figural and landscape subjects. These Roman views followed in the wake of the resounding success of the engravings of similar subjects made by Giovanni Battista Piranesi between 1748 and 1778. Because the position of "official" painter at the Galleria dei Lavori remained vacant in 1792, after Cioci died, Siriès turned to Ferdinando Partini (active from the 1790s), an obscure Roman artist, giving him his only known commission.

The first two pictures Partini delivered were *View of the Pantheon* and *The Tomb of Cecilia Metella*, for which he was paid, respectively, in November 1794 and February 1795. Partini finished two more pairs of landscapes in 1796 and 1798, although at Siriès's request they were painted without figures.[3] Recognizing the modesty of Partini's abilities, Siriès elected to entrust to Giovanni Battista dell'Era (1765–1798), a young but already well-known Lombard artist, the task of adding figures to Partini's pictures. Ultimately only four of Partini's six paintings were made into hardstone mosaics.[4] Napoleon's army arrived in Florence in 1799, forcing the grand duke to flee and interrupting for a time the activity of the Florentine workshops.

AG

1. Published by Giusti, Mazzoni, and Pampaloni Martelli 1978, p. 328, under no. 549.
2. Ibid.
3. The other four are *View of the Temple of Peace* and *The Temple of Janus*, which date to 1796, and *View of the Ponte Molle* and *View of the Forum of Nerva*, which date to 1798. All six are now housed at the Museo dell'Opificio delle Pietre Dure.
4. *View of the Ponte Molle* and *View of the Forum of Nerva* were never executed in pietre dure.

119. Frame for a miniature portrait of Grand Duke Peter Leopold and his family

Galleria dei Lavori, Florence, 1776
By Antonio Graziani; gilding by
Cosimo Siriès
Hardstones, gilded bronze; 20⅞ ×
19¾ in. (53 × 50 cm)
Painting: Copy of a portrait by
Johann Zoffany, 1776
Gouache on metal
Hofburg, Vienna, Kaiserliches
Hofmobiliendepot AB 21

Not in exhibition

PROVENANCE: Maria Christina
of Austria, Vienna; Habsburg
collection; Hofburg, Vienna

REFERENCES: González-Palacios
1986, vol. 1, pp. 111–12, vol. 2,
fig. 288; Valeriani in Giusti 1988,
p. 202, no. 56; Ilsebill Barta in
Marie-Antoinette 2008, p. 161, no. 103

Once Grand Duke Peter Leopold of Habsburg-Lorraine had arrived in Florence in 1765, the lapidary workshop there enjoyed a new burst of energy. The renewed presence of a sovereign and his court in the city created consumers for the precious furniture that had always been the Florentine workshop's specialty and pride. This exquisite frame was among the works Peter Leopold commissioned; it was made to enclose a portrait of the grand duke and his family and was intended as a gift to his beloved sister Archduchess Maria Christina of Austria.

The miniature is a copy by an unknown artist of a painting made by the German artist Johann Zoffany, in Florence, in 1775–76. It portrayed Peter Leopold; his wife, Maria Ludovica of Spain, whom he married in 1765; and the eight children they had then (they would have sixteen in all), with the courtyard of the Palazzo Pitti in the background. Zoffany presented that portrait to Peter Leopold's mother, Empress Maria Theresa of Austria, on December 4, 1776, and in exchange was made a baron. In the same year, documents from the Galleria dei Lavori mention payments to an otherwise unknown Antonio Graziani "for making the decorations for the picture sent to Vienna for the Archduchess Christina," and to the director of the workshop, Cosimo Siriès, for the four days he spent gilding "the bronze frame of the royal family."[1]

Cosimo was the son of the French goldsmith Louis (Luigi) Siriès, who had been director of the Florentine workshops before him. Cosimo also had a separate career as a silversmith and bronze worker, and it is certainly possible that in addition to gilding the frame he was also responsible for casting the lovely Neoclassical drapery that forms the frame's pediment.[2] Especially notable is the hardstone mosaic strip, a graceful garland of flowers set against a luminous ground of yellow jasper, that runs around the four sides and identifies the frame as an original work of the Florentine Galleria dei Lavori. That workshop often produced mosaic frames in the Medici period, and some of them were important works in their own right (see cat. no. 46). Those mosaics, however, decorated wooden frames; here, the frame itself is made of pietre dure.

There is an anonymous watercolor design for this frame in the archives at the Opificio delle Pietre Dure in Florence. Only two sides are shown, but that must have been enough to guide the artist, given that the flowers in the garlands repeat themselves with a confident elegance. Antonio Cioci may have made the watercolor, since he was responsible for making designs for the mosaics produced by the Florentine workshop from 1771 until he died, in 1792. Furthermore, the simplicity of the flowers is reminiscent of his work before 1780, when he began to create sophisticated still-life compositions of vases for translation into mosaic. The "pearls" on the frame, made from Oriental chalcedony, have a special splendor; such pearls of stone were the invention of the painter Giuseppe Zocchi (see cat. no. 104) and were often repeated by Cioci.

In its graceful delicacy, the mosaic frame foreshadows the minute and subtly elegant items—jewelry, snuffboxes, cases, and similar trinkets—that became popular and were produced by the Florentine workshops, alongside their larger and more important works, beginning in the last quarter of the eighteenth century.　　AG

1. Published by González-Palacios 1986, vol. 1, p. 111.
2. For Cosimo Siriès, see Giusti 2006a.

120. Inkstand in the form of the Quirinal Monument, with leather case

Rome, 1792
By Vincenzo Coaci
Lapis lazuli, *rosso antico* marble,
silver, and gilded silver; 28½ ×
20½ × 14¾ in. (72.4 × 52.1 × 37.5 cm)
Inscribed: *Vincentis Coacius fecit
Roma 1792; Vincenco Coaci Argentiere*
Case: Gilded leather
Minneapolis Institute of Arts, Gift
of the Morse Foundation
69.80a, b

PROVENANCE: Possibly presented
to Pope Pius VI in 1792; acquired
by the Minneapolis Institute, 1969

REFERENCES: Parsons 1969;
William Rieder in *Age of Neo-
Classicism* 1972, pp. 835–36, no. 1753,
pl. 159a, b; Minneapolis Institute
of Arts 1998, p. 57, ill.; González-
Palacios in Bowron and Rishel
2000, pp. 191–94, no. 82

This inkstand by the Roman silversmith Vincenzo Coaci (1756–1794) is a marvel of ingenuity and refined craftsmanship. At the apex a silver obelisk is raised high above a platform covered in lapis lazuli, where four sphinxes crouch with baskets on their heads that lift out to disclose candleholders. On either side of the obelisk are groups of horses and men standing on lids that slide out, giving access to an inkwell and a box for sand. Pushing a lever causes the two turtledoves hovering over the basin below the obelisk to move together. A hidden drawer contains engravings, the silversmith's business card, a musical score, and other images. The base is decorated with *rosso antico* marble, strings of silver and gilded silver pearls, and bracket feet. The goldsmith's selective use of gilding in combination with the royal blue of lapis lazuli and the royal red of the marble achieves an effect of noble serenity and Neoclassical elegance, testimony to his superior abilities.

The object is a decorative interpretation of the monument that was erected between 1783 and 1786, after designs by the architect Giovanni Antinori, opposite the Palazzo del Quirinale in Rome, the pope's summer residence. The Egyptian obelisk that rises in the center of the piazza had recently been found near the Mausoleum of Augustus and transferred to the Quirinal Hill by the order of Pope Pius VI. Two ancient colossal marble statues of Castor and Pollux with their horses, which had been standing on the hill for centuries, were restored and placed on either side of the obelisk. These twin gods were known as horse tamers, and with their presence here the monument becomes—like an equestrian statue—a symbol of dominating power.[1]

This small-scale reproduction in precious materials of the mighty Roman monument is out of the ordinary. Contemporary miniature reproductions of ancient buildings or monuments such as triumphal arches[2] were usually made of much more colorful hardstones, gilded bronze, or even cork, which was then very fashionable.[3] We know that by 1785 the pope had in his antechamber a model of the Quirinal Monument made of scagliola and that late the same year a second version in scagliola was shown by the architect Antinori to a group of high officials.[4] Alvar González-Palacios has observed that in 1787 an inkstand very similar to this one was given to Pope Pius VI by an anonymous donor, possibly to replace the scagliola model with a truly regal work of art. (He adds that the present object may not be the one given to the pope, since neither the piece itself nor the original leather case bears an inscription to that effect.)[5]

The large basin in gray Oriental granite that completes the Quirinal Monument was originally in the Campo Vaccino in the Forum and was not moved from there before 1818. This notable event may have inspired a patron who perhaps admired the present inkstand to order a simplified version from a goldsmith named Scheggi in Pistoia sometime between 1818 and 1824.[6]

The inkstand's elegant tooled leather case evokes an entirely different period and culture. The tall central tower and flanking shallow domes have a distinctly Ottoman flavor. The wall—its stone blocks picked out in gold—suggests a heavy, fortified structure, as inward-looking in its appearance as the inkstand is extroverted and exuberant. Original cases are rare, and the imaginative design and fine execution of the present example give it special interest and importance.

W K

1. Haskell and Penny 1981, pp. 136–41, no. 3, figs. 71, 72.
2. González-Palacios in González-Palacios 1997, pp. 215–20, no. 93, ill. p. 217 and pl. XXXI; Prater 1988.
3. Helmberger and Kockel 1993.
4. González-Palacios in Bowron and Rishel 2000, p. 192.
5. Ibid., pp. 191–92.
6. Donald Garstang in González-Palacios 1983, pp. 76–77, no. 37.

122. Table with hardstone inlays and a herm base

Rome and Milan, 1804
Tabletop: By Giacomo Raffaelli
Marble, hardstones, and metal foil
Base: By Francesco Righetti
Gilded bronze
34¾ × 30¼ × 22⅞ in. (88.3 × 77 × 58 cm)
Mr. and Mrs. Peter Pritchard

PROVENANCE: Purchased in Paris by the present owners

This superb piece of furniture, published here for the first time, consists of a white marble tabletop with hardstone inlays and a gilded bronze base composed of four male herms. Most of the stones used for the tabletop are of regular geometric shape, but at the center is a large piece of German agate that retains the irregular contours of the section as originally cut from the stone. A red-violet metallic foil inserted beneath the agate can be seen through the transparent area at its heart. The medallions and oval forms arranged around it are made of a dazzling array of stones, from amethysts to carnelians, jaspers, Egyptian chalcedony, lapis lazuli, variegated agates, and a sardonyx that allows us a glimpse of the golden foil beneath it.

The tall sides of the base are set with panels of red, green, and pink jasper; the panels at each of the corners are concave, allowing room for the heads of the herms. There are two types of herms, matched diagonally across from one another: a bearded adult with short curly hair, and a youth whose beardless face is surrounded by wavy ringlets. Each herm figure holds a pair of nude female figures, one in each arm, just below their waists. The eight women reach their arms along the sides of the table, and the two on the long sides seem to be trying to pick fruit out of two bronze cornucopias hanging between them. The base is fire-gilded, although its surfaces are treated differently. The decorative parts are polished and brilliant, while the figures have a satin finish that permits light to fall softly across their nude forms.

This table, with its harmoniously integrated top and base, is one of the outstanding works of pietre dure made in a Roman style in the early nineteenth century. I believe it was made in the shop of the famous mosaicist Giacomo Raffaelli (1753–1836) (see cat. no. 123), an attribution based first on the close similarities between this tabletop and other inlay work that can be associated with Raffaelli, and second on documentary evidence that points to him. There is, for example, another white marble tabletop with hardstone inlays that is almost identical to this one and that is documented as coming from Raffaelli's shop.[1] That table is now in the State Hermitage Museum, Saint Petersburg, which also has two console tables with hardstone and micromosaics (made from tiny tesserae) that can be associated with works Raffaelli exhibited at the Accademia di Belle Arti di Brera, Milan, in 1814.[2]

The artist had been living in Milan for about ten years by then, having moved there from Rome at the invitation of the viceroy, Eugène de Beauharnais, who founded a school of mosaics in what was then the capital of the recently established Kingdom of Italy. Although Raffaelli's first specialty was micromosaics, over time his furniture became enriched with ornaments and appliqués in a variety of materials, including hardstones, which were becoming more important in his work by the time of his arrival in Milan about 1803–4. Raffaelli's shop employed a craftsman referred to as "Vincenzo marmoraro," or Vincenzo the marble worker, but the master must have been directly involved in the execution of the pietre dure, since we can recognize in these inlays a style analogous to that of the two tables in the Hermitage as well as to one in the Palacio Real, Madrid, which dates to before 1803. Alvar González-Palacios has correctly attributed the latter to Raffaelli based on its similarity to the two console tables in Saint Petersburg.[3] The two smaller tabletops—this one and the one in the Hermitage—are the more beautiful of Raffaelli's creations, perhaps because of their size. In each work the bright palette of stones is the sole, dazzling protagonist, whereas in the Madrid table the hardstones compete with the ancient marble, and in the two consoles in Saint Petersburg the hardstones are used to frame the micromosaics. In the smaller tabletops, by contrast, the white, statuary-grade marble ground both connects and sets off the geometry of the elegant composition.

Although we do not know the exact date of the Saint Petersburg tabletop, I believe we can suggest one for its "kin" based on previously published documents,[4] notably correspondence between Raffaelli and his Roman associates, who, even though the artist had a shop in Milan, continued to send him materials or even finished works from Rome. On August 8, 1804, Raffaelli received a group of bronze objects, including two pairs of caryatids and two pairs of cornucopias, from two men referred to only as Roccheggiani and Domenico (the former can be identified as Lorenzo Roccheggiani, who made several popular series of prints of furniture and ornament).[5] I believe these bronze elements were for the base of the present table, whose hardstone top can thus be dated to about the same period the bronzes arrived from Rome.

There is a pendant to the base, which González-Palacios published as being in the Invernizzi collection and attributed to an anonymous Roman bronze master; he dates it to about 1770–75.[6] I think it likely that the Invernizzi table originally had a top similar to the present example. Its porphyry top is surely an addition or a replacement, since it is too thick for the base and its border does not match it harmoniously. The quality of both bronze bases is high in terms of both the modeling and the surface finishing. They may have been made by Francesco Righetti (1749–1819),[7] whose growing fame both in and beyond Rome helped popularize Roman bronze work. Indeed, in the Neoclassical and Empire periods, Roman bronze work was noted for its sculptural quality and for the sense of grandiosity with which it interpreted antique models. In this bronze base, the poses and delicate torsion of the female figures, as they stretch away sinuously from the grasp of the herms, are comparable to qualities of the corner figures in a gilded bronze lectern made by Righetti in 1801–3, now in the Church of San Giorgio Maggiore in Venice.[8] Other examples of mythological bronzes made by Righetti—such as the head of Juno of 1797 (formerly Galerie J. Kugel), or the Bacchus and Ariadne for the royal residence at Caserta—also bear a certain resemblance to the herms on this table, particularly in their slightly long noses, square ears, and low brows.

In the burnished areas of the base, the gilding conveys the density and splendor of gold. This is particularly true of the finishing of the figures, cornucopias, and other details, where an extremely fine granularity creates a satinlike surface quality that contrasts with the areas of smooth, brilliant gilding. Although this differentiation of the gilded bronze surfaces was not unique to Righetti's shop—it can be found in the work of other contemporary bronze masters, especially those from Rome—here the distinction seems more significant. We can compare the work to two hardstone plaques with gilded bronze reliefs of Saint

Francesco di Paola and Saint Ferdinando that Righetti made in 1819 (Palazzo Reale, Naples).[9] There the contrast between the polished and satin finishes is equally refined, but the effects of the two are reversed: the brilliant surfaces are reserved for areas of flesh and the satin finish for the draperies.

AG

1. Efimova 1968, p. 101, no. 60.
2. Ibid., nos. 57, 59.
3. González-Palacios 2001, pp. 240–43, no. 43.
4. Alfieri 2000.
5. Ibid., p. 266.
6. González-Palacios 1984, vol. 1, p. 67, vol. 2, fig. 146.
7. Righetti's career and artistic skill have been amply explored by Alvar González-Palacios. See ibid., vol. 1, pp. 139–47.
8. This and the works discussed below were published in González-Palacios 1984.
9. Valeriani in Colle, Griseri, and Valeriani 2001, p. 238, no. 67.

123. Clock

Rome, 1804
By Giacomo Raffaelli
Marble, hardstones, micromosaic made from enamel, and gilded bronze; 35½ × 20⅛ × 8⅛ in. (90.2 × 51.1 × 20.6 cm)
Clockwork: By Abraham-Louis Breguet
Signed and dated on back: *Giacomo Raffaelli/fece anno 1804*
Inscribed on clock face: *Breguet/ a Paris*
The Rosalinde and Arthur Gilbert Collection on loan to the Victoria and Albert Museum, London 1996.624 (MM 243)

PROVENANCE: Gift from Pope Pius VII to Napoleon; Empress Joséphine, Château de Malmaison; probably Eugène de Beauharnais, first duke of Leuchtenberg; probably Joséphine Beauharnais, queen of Sweden, and her descendants; Sir Alexander Kleinwort, London; H. Burton Jones; A. Gifford-Scott (sale, Sotheby's, London, lot 33, June 15, 1973); [John Partridge, London, 1976]; Arthur Gilbert, from 1982

REFERENCES: Grandjean 1964, pp. 197–98, no. 1539; González-Palacios 1976a, pp. 42–43, fig. 34b; González-Palacios 1977a, p. 58, no. 29, pl. 29; González-Palacios 1982b, p. 20; González-Palacios and Röttgen in González-Palacios, Röttgen, and Przyborowski 1982,

This clock, made in the form of a triumphal arch and decorated with gilded bronze sculptures, hardstones, and micromosaics, should be counted among the masterpieces of Empire furniture, particularly in light of its long list of illustrious former owners. The brilliant white marble from which it was built is a reference to classical antiquity, but marble is also the ideal ground for showcasing the pietre dure and micromosaic decoration. The latter consists of eight panels depicting military trophies that are applied to the sides of the main piers. Amethyst, agate, jasper, lapis lazuli, garnet, and Labrador stone (labradorite) were used to make the architectural elements and revetments of this courtly monument in miniature, which is dedicated to the god of war, Mars; he is present as a small gilded bronze figure standing on a colored stone pedestal in the arch's center bay. Other gilded bronze sculptures crown the attic story, at the ends of which are an eagle and a rooster, animals sacred to Mars. A trophy of ancient Roman arms is placed above the curved clock face at the center, flanked by figures of Victory (left) and Fame (right). The structure is signed and dated on the back; the clock face is inscribed "Breguet/a Paris."

The sculptor Antonio Canova was charged by Pope Pius VII with finding appropriate gifts to mark the coronation of Napoleon as emperor, an event that was to take place shortly in Paris and that the pope would attend. Canova selected this exquisite object, whose triumphal arch form would be understood as a tribute to Napoleon,

and also a mantelpiece, from the Roman studio of the famous mosaicist Giacomo Raffaelli (1753–1836). The presentation of these pieces to such a prestigious recipient doubtless confirms Raffaelli's international reputation in the field of micromosaics, which came into vogue in Rome in the last decade of the eighteenth century and was practiced by a number of artists working for a vast Italian and foreign clientele. These tiny mosaics were executed using the technique of *smalti filati*, in which opaque enamel is heated, pulled into long strands, and then broken into small tesserae or tiles. Unlike contemporary Roman ateliers, which largely confined themselves to making micromosaics, Raffaelli's studio produced furnishings made from a variety of materials, often combining marble, bronze fittings, and hardstones to great decorative effect (see cat. no. 122).

To guarantee that the works made in his shop met a high standard of formal and technical excellence, Raffaelli made use of multiple collaborators both within and outside his atelier: specialists in a variety of crafts whose names sometimes appear in the registers and documents of the time. It seems likely that the refined bronze elements on this clock came from one of the many Roman workshops that worked with this material. The pietre dure elements, on the other hand, were probably made in Raffaelli's own shop, since a few years earlier, in 1801, it had produced a similar triumphal arch (State Hermitage Museum, Saint Petersburg), although that work is less elaborate and has no bronze elements.[1]

p. 116, no. 29, pl. 29; González-
Palacios 1984, vol. 1, p. 143, pl. XXIV,
vol. 2, fig. 296; Massinelli 2000,
pp. 62–64, no. 13

Despite the fact that this clock celebrates Mars, god of war, and thus must have seemed an especially appropriate gift for the triumphant emperor-warrior, the object itself expresses the delicate sensibility of the Neoclassical style: an almost feminine grace, rather than the solemnity of the Empire period. This, perhaps, helps explain the clock's presence in Empress Joséphine's private residence (it is mentioned in the inventory of the furniture at the Château de Malmaison drawn up at her death in 1814). The French clockwork must have been added in Paris or, perhaps, replaced the original. It is the work of Abraham-Louis Breguet (1747–1823), an ingenious and famous clockmaker who had many clients at the court at Versailles, and among high society in the Napoleonic period.

AG

1. Efimova 1968, p. 100, no. 52.

124. Snuffbox with military trophies

Galleria dei Lavori, Florence, 1822
Design attributed to Giovan
Battista Giorgi
Lapis lazuli, other hardstones,
and gold; ⅞ × 3⅜ × 2 in. (2.2 × 8.5 ×
5.2 cm)
The Rosalinde and Arthur Gilbert
Collection on loan to the Victoria
and Albert Museum, London
1996.531 (GB 183)

PROVENANCE: [Galerie J. Kugel,
Paris, 1994]; Gilbert Collection,
London, from 1996

REFERENCES: Giusti 1992, pp. 120,
260, n. 133, pl. 66; Massinelli 2000,
p. 155, no. 64

The lid of this snuffbox is decorated with a pietre dure panel depicting military implements, including a Roman helmet, a round shield, and a spear placed against a laurel branch. Finely worked motifs of military trophies alternate with leafy vines on the granulated gold bands framing the lid. The side panels are likewise set into gold frames, these engraved with geometric designs. The interior of the snuffbox is lined with smooth, brightly polished gold.

This small but precious and refined box, whose lapis lazuli panels are attractively uniform in color, is likely the one mentioned briefly in the registers of the Galleria dei Lavori, Florence, as a lapis lazuli snuffbox with a helmet and shield. That work was finished on December 11, 1822.[1] Beginning in 1815 the painter in charge of preparing designs for hardstone mosaics in the workshop was Giovan Battista Giorgi, an artist with academic training. It seems likely, then, that he was responsible for designing the motif on the lid of this box, which is almost identical to that in two watercolors now preserved in the archives of the Opificio delle Pietre Dure, Florence.[2] They may have been intended as designs for similar mosaics (Giorgi was a capable decorator with a limited repertoire) or, perhaps, they were alternate designs that were to be presented to the workshop director so that he could choose between them. This practice had

been followed by Carlo Siriès when he became head of the workshop in 1811, in keeping with a tradition initiated by three generations of his family who had preceded him in that position.[3]

Military trophies were an enormously popular decorative motif during the Empire period, thanks, in part, to Charles Percier and Pierre-François-Léonard Fontaine's 1801 publication the *Recueil de décorations intérieures*, which helped define and then spread the Empire decorative vocabulary in the Napoleonic period. Even makers of Florentine mosaics, always careful to match their own tradition to new trends, used military trophies for a time. For example, a sophisticated trophy motif was placed at the center of a lapis lazuli and chalcedony table commissioned by María Luisa, queen of Napoleon's Kingdom of Etruria, in 1807 (Palazzo Pitti, Florence).[4] The soft but brilliant combination of colors in that work—created by lapis lazuli, translucent and opalescent chalcedony, and luminous, golden chalcedony—is also present in this snuffbox. Similar effects are seen in the majority of mosaics produced in the Florentine workshops during the Bourbon Restoration, when craftsmen continued to draw inspiration from the brilliant production of the period of French rule. This box, if not remarkable for its inventiveness, is nonetheless characterized by a certain gracefulness and by exquisite craftsmanship.   AG

1. Cited in Giusti 1992, p. 260, n. 133, and quoted in Massinelli 2000, p. 155, no. 64.
2. Published by Massinelli 2000, figs. 16, 17.
3. For the four generations of the Siriès family who directed the grand-ducal workshops under the Habsburg-Lorraine dynasty, see Giusti 2006c. As early as the middle of the eighteenth century, Louis Siriès asked the painter Giuseppe Zocchi to furnish several variations for both floral and decorative designs for mosaics (see, for example, cat. no. 108).
4. The center of the table, or *surtout*, one of the masterpieces of the decorative arts of the Napoleonic period, was admired and sought after by several monarchs. It was left unfinished when María Luisa left Florence for the Duchy of Lucca, but work continued on it during the reign of Élisa Bonaparte, who intended to give it to Napoleon as a gift and then tried to keep it for herself after his defeat. When Grand Duke Ferdinand III was restored to power in Tuscany, he saw that the table was returned and finished it with a gilded bronze frame. See Colle in Giusti 2006a, p. 254, no. 173.

125. Set of jewelry made for Caroline Bonaparte Murat

Plaques: Galleria dei Lavori, Florence, ca. 1810
Design by Carlo Carlieri
Hardstones
Settings: Paris
Gold
Comb, H. 4⅝ in. (11.7 cm); diadem, Diam. 5¾ in. (14.6 cm); necklace, L. 17⅝ in. (44.8 cm); earrings, L. 2⅛ in. (5.4 cm)
Marked on clasp and earrings: *ET* in a rectangle
Case: Gilded leather
The Rosalinde and Arthur Gilbert Collection on loan to the Victoria and Albert Museum, London 1996.850–853 (MMI 86)

PROVENANCE: Caroline Bonaparte Murat, queen of Naples; Delessert family; Marthe Bocher; [Galerie J. Kugel, Paris, 1975]; Gilbert Collection

REFERENCES: González-Palacios 1977a, p. 60, no. 30; González-Palacios 1982b, p. 70, ill. p. 69;

In the three centuries of their activity, the Florentine grand-ducal workshops only briefly, during the last two decades of the 1700s and first few decades of the 1800s, produced jewelry, snuffboxes, buttons, and other small items for aristocrats who wanted beautiful baubles to display their exquisite taste. This period at the Galleria dei Lavori saw a happy marriage of jewelry and hardstone mosaic, two kinds of objects that had always been produced at the workshops, but separately.

There are only a few surviving examples of this production. This suite of jewelry is remarkable among them for its illustrious provenance and its superb quality. It was made to be a gift from Napoleon's sister Élisa Bonaparte, who became grand duchess of Tuscany in 1809, to her sister Caroline Bonaparte Murat, queen of Naples. A document of 1894 attests to Caroline Murat's ownership of the set and then traces its passage from collection to collection. The original case, of red leather with a stamped and gilded border of

sphinxes and amphorae surrounding a gold crown and the initial *C*, confirms that the jewelry first belonged to Caroline.[1]

At the Museo dell'Opificio delle Pietre Dure is a watercolor sketch for the diadem probably done by Carlo Carlieri (d. 1816), who was then the head designer at the workshops.[2] Recognizable in the sketch are the two triangular plaques in the comb, and the shell and strung "pearls," although their placement is different in the object itself. The alteration may have been made by the firm of Parisian goldsmiths that Élisa Bonaparte continued to patronize even after she moved to Florence. The firm probably also made the sober but refined gold setting for this jewelry.

The decoration of the hardstone mosaic plaques, on the other hand, is exquisitely Florentine. The clear blue of the lapis lazuli ground intensifies the cool luminosity of the chalcedony from which the pearls and shells are carved. This type of marine theme came into fashion in the middle of the

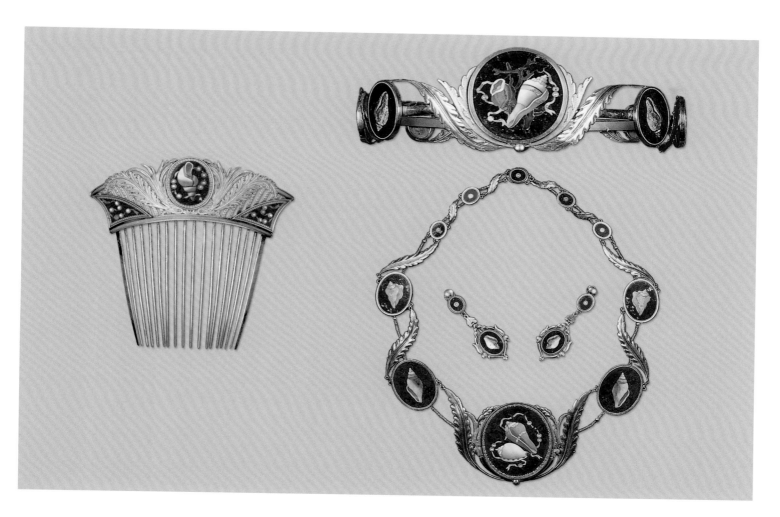

González-Palacios, Röttgen, and Przyborowski 1982, pp. 60, 122–23, no. 32; Giusti 1992, pp. 245–46, pl. 122; Massinelli 2000, pp. 201–2, no. 87; Giusti in Giusti 2006a, pp. 252–53, no. 170; Giusti 2006b, p. 216, ill. no. 173

previous century after Giuseppe Zocchi designed a tabletop with hardstone shells, coral, and pearls for the emperor in Vienna (cat. no. 104). By the Napoleonic period it had become a favorite subject in Florentine mosaics and was as much appreci-

ated by the grand dukes of the Habsburg-Lorraine dynasty as it was by the French "usurpers" in Italy.

AG

1. Massinelli 2000, p. 202.
2. Giusti in Giusti 2006a, pp. 252–53, no. 70.

126. Monumental vase

Lapidary work: Probably Florence, early 19th century
Russian malachite and composite core
Pedestal and mounts: Paris, 1819
By Pierre-Philippe Thomire
Bronze and gilded bronze
H. without pedestal 5 ft. 7½ in. (1.72 m), H. with pedestal 9 ft. 2 in. (2.79 m)
Incised on pedestal: *THOMIRE A PARIS 1819*
The Metropolitan Museum of Art, New York, Purchase, Admiral Frederic R. Harris Gift, 1944
44.152a, b

PROVENANCE: Count Nikolai Demidov, San Donato, near Florence (until d. 1828); his heir, Prince Anatole Demidov (until d. 1870); bought from the Demidov estate by William Henry Vanderbilt, New York, 1880; entered the Metropolitan Museum, 1944

REFERENCE: Koeppe in Kisluk-Grosheide, Koeppe, and Rieder 2006, pp. 224–26, no. 94 (with bibliography)

Malachite is a carbonate mineral often associated with copper ores. As explained by Jeffrey Post, it "grows in layers of tiny crystals, and its colors correlate with different crystal sizes: smaller crystals form light green bands and larger crystals make darker ones."[1] In the late eighteenth and nineteenth centuries, most malachite came from mines in Russia owned by the noble Demidov family, who exploited hardstone quarries and metal deposits on their estates in the remote Ural Mountains. One of the great discoveries in the history of semiprecious stones occurred in the 1820s, when an enormous boulder of malachite weighing about five hundred tons was unearthed in the Urals.[2] A schistose material, malachite is extremely brittle, and only small display objects can be cut from single blocks of this rock. Large objects require a core structure, to which the malachite can be attached in thin pieces. Russian craftsmen perfected a way of utilizing the stone's natural pattern and a precision cutting technique to form a continuing or, on the round body of a vase, an "endless" ornament. This type of veneer, called "Russian mosaic," looks almost seamless.[3]

The Demidovs used the showy appearance of malachite to increase their social status. They filled their palaces and decorated a whole room in one of them with the green stone, inspiring Czar Nicholas I to commission the famous Malachite Room in the Winter Palace in Saint Petersburg.[4]

The Metropolitan Museum's vase is modeled on one type of ancient Roman bell-shaped krater, the most famous example of which is the first-century *Medici Vase*, now in the Galleria degli Uffizi, Florence. The form was much admired in the early nineteenth century.[5] Count Nikolai Demidov commissioned this monumental example for his villa at San Donato, near Florence. From a distance, the malachite veneer seems to be of the Russian mosaic type. Closer inspection reveals an uneven use of the stone that differs considerably from Russian work; moreover, large areas of the surface are composed of small

malachite particles mixed with a filling substance in the manner of modern terrazzo. Demidov probably had the raw malachite transported from one of his mines to Florence. There it would have been shaped and finished by local artists, who were not trained in the specialized Russian technique, and afterward sent on to Paris to be fitted with its mounts and pedestal. In an essay on the vase by this author published in 2006, the Italian, perhaps Florentine, origin of the lapidary work was suggested for the first time.[6] Although it initiated a spirited discussion, this new attribution has not—to the author's knowledge—been questioned in a written review. The presence in this exhibition of an undisputed masterwork of Russian mosaic in malachite, the *Stroganov Tazza* (cat. no. 144), offers an opportunity to compare the veneer on these two closely related objects and, it is hoped, to resolve any lingering questions about their manufacture.

The winged female figures in gilded bronze mounted on the body of the vase represent Fame. Their trumpets are shaped like handles—something of a paradox, since the object is far too heavy to be lifted like a loving cup. A gilded bronze garland of laurel runs under the lip mount. This evergreen plant, *Laurus nobilis*, had been adopted by Lorenzo de' Medici, who was also a lavish patron of the arts,[7] as an emblem of his house, together with the motto "Ita ut virtus," or "Thus is virtue"—that is to say, virtue is evergreen. Evergreen too, is the precious stone that embellishes this vase. It seems that Count Demidov wished for his own family both virtue and an "evergreen" fortune.

Pierre-Philippe Thomire (1751–1843), who made the mounts and bronze pedestal and signed the latter, was known throughout Europe for his bronze decorations and ornamental sculpture. Before the French Revolution, he established a reputation with his beautiful mounts for Sèvres porcelain vases. In 1804 he founded a workshop that produced furniture as well as luxury bronzes.[8]

WK

1. Post 1997, pp. 132–33.
2. Guseva 1990, p. 90.
3. Ibid.; see also Kennett 1973, p. 41.
4. Kennett 1973, p. 41.
5. Héricart de Thury 1819, p. 80, no. 1; Ottomeyer 2004, p. 16.
6. Koeppe in Kisluk-Grosheide, Koeppe, and Rieder 2006, pp. 224–26, no. 94.

7. Hall 1979, p. 190.
8. This entry is largely based on Koeppe in Kisluk-Grosheide, Koeppe, and Rieder 2006, pp. 224–26, no. 94. As always, I am grateful to Marina Nudel, Senior Research Associate, Department of European Sculpture and Decorative Arts, Metropolitan Museum, for her advice.

127. Table with top depicting birds, vegetables, and a string of pearls

Real Laboratorio, Naples, 1738–49
Tabletop: Hardstones
Base: By Giacomo Ceci
Ebony, gilded bronze, and hardstones
33½ × 43¾ × 30¾ in. (85 × 111 × 78 cm)
Museo Nacional del Prado, Madrid
O-512

PROVENANCE: Real Laboratorio, San Carlo alle Mortella, Naples; Charles II of Spain, 1794; Spanish royal collection, until 1834; Museo Real (subsequently Museo Nacional del Prado), Madrid

REFERENCES: González-Palacios in *Golden Age of Naples* 1981, vol. 2, pp. 356–57, no. 115; González-Palacios 1982b, p. 57, ill. p. 52; González-Palacios in *El arte de la corte de Nápoles* 1990, pp. 225–27, no. 2; González-Palacios 1993, vol. 1, p. 148, pls. XXII, XXIII, vol. 2, fig. 222; González-Palacios 2001, pp. 142–45, no. 24

This table and its pendant were two of the first objects produced by the Neapolitan pietre dure workshop founded by Charles of Bourbon, king of Naples and Sicily, in 1737.[1] The two tables have similar decorative motifs, made of hardstone inlays set against a black marble ground, and their ebony legs, embellished with bronze appliqués, are identical. Having spent time in Florence as a young man, Charles (or Don Carlos de Borbón) came to know and admire the extraordinary Medici pietre dure workshop. Thus when Gian Gastone de' Medici died in 1737, extinguishing the Medici line, at least ten craftsmen from the Florentine workshop, fearing for the future of an institution that had been so closely tied to the family, accepted Charles's invitation and moved to Naples, where they established a new pietre dure workshop modeled on that in Florence.

The Neapolitan royal workshop, headquartered in the complex at San Carlo alle Mortella, survived until the end of the Kingdom of the Two Sicilies, in 1861. It reached its apogee early on, however, thanks to a small but experienced group of Florentine craftsmen working under the direction of

Francesco Ghinghi (1689–1766), a specialist in carving hardstone. In their creations for the Neapolitan court, Ghinghi and his team of masters made expert use of the precious materials that in the span of a few short years had begun to flow into Naples from a variety of places, including Florence. Indeed, the Neapolitan workshop continued to depend on the "mother house" in Florence, which despite the earlier worries had flourished under the new Habsburg-Lorraine dynasty. Moreover, the style of the works made in Naples relied heavily on Florentine models from the late Medici period.

That is certainly the case with these two tables, whose decoration centers on a string of pearls. This motif enjoyed a long history in the Florentine workshop, appearing first, perhaps, in a tabletop made for Cardinal Antonio Barberini in 1658.[2] The luxuriant jumble of flowers and fruits on which multicolored birds perch elegantly recalls the exuberant naturalism of Late Baroque Florentine mosaics. The latter were also the source for the stylized acanthus leaves, which establish a rhythm across the colorful composition, and the chalcedony, used to create luminous accents.

top view

The leaves and yellow chalcedony were a signature motif of Giovanni Battista Foggini, director of the Florentine workshops from 1694 to 1725. It is worth noting that at the time these two tabletops were being made in Naples, the Florentine workshop, too, was being influenced by antiquated though apparently still alluring motifs dating back to the revolutionary work of Louis Siriès and Giuseppe Zocchi (see cat. nos. 104, 106, 112, 114).

Several Neapolitan documents from 1739 record progress being made on a "tabletop of flowers and birds."[3] Five craftsmen labored on it, and "the design used to make it was made by the same masters"—that is, the design and the stonecutting were executed by the same artist. This went against the ironclad rules of the Florentine workshop, in which the painted models for mosaics were always made by fine artists, meaning painters or sculptors—never by the craftsmen, who were responsible solely for selecting and cutting the stones. Other documents from 1748–49 record the completion of the two tables and note payments made to Giacomo Ceci for fabricating and

gilding the bronze bases.[4] These, too, were inspired by Florentine prototypes, in particular a table Foggini designed in 1716 that was famous for the cartouches at its corners and for its legs, which were shaped like truncated pyramids and decorated with inset lapis lazuli and bronze garlands studded with hardstones in the shape of fruit.[5] The slimmer bases of the Neapolitan tables, the dynamism of the cartouches, and the lively scroll ornament on their fronts suggest that they were updated to reflect a more Rococo taste. It is likely that both tables accompanied Charles to Madrid, where in 1759 he acceded to the throne as Charles III of Spain.[6]   A G

1. The pendant is also in the Museo Nacional del Prado, O-511; see González-Palacios 2001, pp. 142–45, no. 24.
2. González-Palacios 1993, vol. 2, fig. 719.
3. See González-Palacios 2001, pp. 142–45.
4. Ibid., p. 316, doc. no. 4.
5. Giusti in Baldini, Giusti, and Pampaloni Martelli 1979, p. 270, no. 59, pls. 63, 64.
6. Suggested by González-Palacios 2001, p. 245, based on a 1759 document that mentions "two marble buffets that had to be sent to Spain."

128. Table with chessboard

Real Laboratorio, Naples, 1811
and 1835
Marble, reused ancient marble
sculptures, petrified wood, hardstones, and gilded bronze; 33⅞ ×
37 × 27½ in. (86 × 94 × 70 cm)
Museo Nazionale di Capodimonte,
Naples I.C. 4167

PROVENANCE: Ferdinand II, king
of Naples; Museo Nazionale di
Capodimonte

REFERENCES: González-Palacios
1982b, pp. 73–74, figs. 1, 2; Valeriani
in Giusti 1988, p. 256, no. 76; Giusti
1992, p. 245, pl. 121

The royal pietre dure workshop at San Carlo alle Mortella, founded in 1737, continued to operate throughout the Napoleonic period, when the Kingdom of Naples was ruled by Joachim Murat and his wife, Caroline Bonaparte, Napoleon's sister. The registers of the workshop from that time record the production of several stone-inlaid chessboards, a type that had become common fare for pietre dure workshops, since the gameboard's distinctive two-color scheme could be made using contrasting colors of stone. Small tables with chessboards are also recorded in the registers of the grand-ducal workshop in Florence as early as the reign of Ferdinand I.[1]

Four chessboards were produced in Naples during the imperial occupation (1809–11). Although the chessboards themselves seem to have been relatively sober in concept and design, they were inserted into beautiful, elegant pieces of furniture, as seen, for example, in a gilded bronze gueridon recorded in 1809 that was made to be a gift from the Murats for Napoleon himself (Musée National du Château de Malmaison, Paris).[2]

A document of 1811 that makes reference to the present tabletop mentions the chessboard and also describes "an oval-shaped table made from a piece of Oriental petrified wood."[3] It is this very cross section of fossilized wood that makes the table so spectacular and unusual. The top comprises the entire diameter of the trunk, and the chessboard, made from pieces of white and black chalcedony outlined with lapis lazuli and red jasper, is inserted at its center.

In its transformation from an organic material to stone, petrified wood acquires characteristics very similar to those of pietre dure: it becomes hard, often has a pattern, and can be highly polished. Admired in Florence from the end of the sixteenth century, it was often used in the mosaics manufactured in the grand-ducal workshop. Interest in the wood's curious geologic characteristics was revived during the Enlightenment, a period when scientific inquiry was in vogue. This is probably why petrified wood was used in this tabletop, and, specifically, why the cross section retains the natural shape and size of the tree trunk. The block from which it was cut must have been among the stock of stones in the Bourbon workshop in Naples. When that workshop closed in 1861, some of its supply was sent to the Opificio delle Pietre Dure in Florence, including the large block of petrified wood now in the workshop's museum.

The table and chessboard were not finished until more than twenty years after they had been started. Work began in 1834 on the restoration of two ancient, winged genii that would serve as supports for the tabletop; a central support designed in an *all'antica* mode was added to help them bear the weight. The final touches included a thick band of marble and lapis lazuli on the side of the tabletop as well as a thin bronze rim decorated with foliage. The table was eventually completed on January 17, 1835, in time for Ferdinand II's birthday celebrations.   AG

1. One of the most famous pieces in the Florentine collections was a chessboard that was made in 1619 after a design by Jacopo Ligozzi and embellished with a border of flowers and butterflies. See Colle in Giusti 1988, p. 154, no. 34.
2. Noted by González-Palacios 1982b, p. 70.
3. González-Palacios identified this table and the relevant documents; see González-Palacios 1982b, pp. 73–74.

top view

129. Console table with a trompe l'oeil top

Buen Retiro workshop, Madrid, 1784
Top: Design by Charles-Joseph Flipart; lapidary work by Domenico Stecchi and Francesco Poggetti
Hardstones
Base: By Giovanni Battista Ferroni, 1786
Gilded bronze
38 × 70½ × 28¾ in. (96.5 × 179 × 73 cm)
Inscribed on underside of tabletop: *Se empezò esta obra el 27 de Enero del 83 y se acabò a 30 Dice.de otro ano*
Museo Nacional del Prado, Madrid O-214

PROVENANCE: Charles III, king of Spain (r. 1759–88); Museo Real (subsequently Museo Nacional del Prado), Madrid, 1827

REFERENCES: Pérez-Villamil 1904, p. III; "Des Tableaux de marbre" 1957, ill. p. 104; Zambelli 1962, p. 191, pl. 68, c; Rossi (Ferdinando) 1967, p. 122, pl. LIV; Battersby 1974, pl. V; González-Palacios 1982a, p. 73, ill. p. 71, fig. 9; González-Palacios 1988b; Giusti 1992, p. 248, fig. 96; González-Palacios 1992, ill. pp. 88–89, 91; González-Palacios 2001, pp. 177–79, no. 29

The widespread fame of the grand-ducal workshops in Florence and an appreciation of their production led many European rulers to establish similar pietre dure mosaic shops. Rudolf II and Louis XIV both founded such manufactories in the seventeenth century, in Prague and at the Gobelins, Paris, respectively. Charles of Bourbon followed suit in Naples in 1737, and when he became King Charles III of Spain in 1759 he established the Buen Retiro workshop in Madrid, which was active from 1762 until 1808.

The central figures at the Buen Retiro in its early years were two specialists in Florentine hardstone mosaic, Domenico Stecchi and Francesco Poggetti, who arrived in Spain in 1761. Working with many local assistants, these Italian craftsmen were responsible for one of the largest commissions in the shop's brief but productive history: nine tabletops of similar shape and size and with like decorative motifs. They were made between 1779 and 1788. Their splendid gilded bronze bases, which took longer to create, were fabricated with the assistance of another Florentine craftsman, Giovanni Battista Ferroni.

The artist commissioned to paint the designs for the tabletops, Charles-Joseph Flipart (1721–1797), was French.[1] Although his compositions are varied, they all depend on trompe l'oeil effects, and such carefully manipulated illusionism is the only subject of four of the tabletops, including this one. These show realistically rendered paintings, prints, playing cards, musical instruments, and a variety of other objects scattered across them with a studied casualness. The designs demonstrate an extraordinary originality, and there are no precedents, in Florence or elsewhere, for such a clear and precise treatment of this kind of subject matter.[2] Their translation into hardstone mosaic is doubly intriguing because the illusionism

of the subject plays on that of the stone, which is meant to imitate painting.

The first pair of trompe l'oeil tabletops designed by Flipart was made in the late 1770s.[3] The table exhibited here comes from the second pair (its mate is shown in fig. 118), completed, as the inscription on the underside of the mosaic states, in about two years' time, between January 1783 and December 1784. The second set of designs is more complex than the first, and its execution in stone more splendid. (Flipart's painted model for the present work appeared recently on the antiquarian market.) The mosaic version suggests a unity and exquisiteness of detail that makes this piece one of the most successful creations of the Madrid workshops.

The gilded bronze bases for the second pair of tables have the same figural and decorative ornaments as the others in the series. They differ, however, in the use of rare striped jasper as the background for the royal monogram. The table bases were begun in 1783 and finished in 1786.

A G

1. Very little is known about Flipart, except that he moved to Madrid after a long sojourn in Venice from 1739 to 1753. In Spain he became court painter (*pintor de cámara*), first to Ferdinand VI (r. 1746–59) and then to his successor. It seems likely that Flipart's skill as an illusionistic painter was rooted in his early training; there was an established tradition of fantastical trompe l'oeil painting in France throughout the eighteenth century.
2. The painter who made designs for the Florentine workshops in the same period was Antonio Cioci. Although he used trompe l'oeil in his own work, it was never included in his sophisticated designs for pietre dure tabletops. It should be noted, however, that his compositions of antique and modern vases (see cat. no. 115) take on somewhat surreal and sometimes illusionistic effects when rendered in hardstone.
3. Museo Nacional del Prado, Madrid, O-474, O-475. See González-Palacios 2001, pp. 172–74, no. 27.

129

Fig. 118. Console table with a trompe l'oeil top (mate of cat. no. 129), Buen Retiro workshop, Madrid, 1784–86. Design by Charles-Joseph Flipart, top by Domenico Stecchi and Francesco Poggetti, base by Giovanni Battista Ferroni. Hardstones and gilded bronze, 38 × 70½ × 28¾ in. Museo Nacional del Prado, Madrid O-476

The Reclaiming of Pietre Dure

130. Roman scene with an owl and other birds

Marcello Provenzale, Rome, 1616
Stone mosaic; 13¼ × 21¼ in. (33.5 ×
54 cm)
Signed and dated in the mosaic:
Provenzale 1616
Museo degli Argenti, Palazzo Pitti,
Florence 1890:872

PROVENANCE: Cardinal Scipione
Borghese, Rome; gift to
Ferdinand II de' Medici, Florence;
Museo degli Argenti, Palazzo Pitti,
from 1631

REFERENCES: González-Palacios
1976b, pp. 26–28, fig. 3; González-
Palacios 1982b, pp. 11–12, ill. p. 10;
Giusti 1992, p. 218

Originally from Cento in Emilia, Marcello Provenzale (1575–1639) was one of the most important figures in Rome's late sixteenth-century revival of the art of true mosaic—made of small square pieces, or tesserae. In fact, the ancient mosaic tradition had never entirely disappeared in Rome (as it had in Florence, where it vanished with the passing of the last generation of such great fifteenth-century mosaicists as Alesso Baldovinetti and Domenico and David Ghirlandaio). Especially because an antiquarian passion gripped the city in the sixteenth century, Rome was the perfect milieu for the revival of this noble but also most common art form of antiquity. Mosaics reappeared in their traditional role as architectural revetment but also were made into small, portable works prized by collectors. Provenzale, who worked in both formats, was responsible for some of the mosaics at Saint Peter's and in other Roman churches. The pictorial quality of his style comes across best in the smaller mosaics, however, for which he received commissions from a number of illustrious patrons, including Pope Paul V (r. 1605–21) and his nephew Cardinal Scipione Borghese.[1]

Although Provenzale was admired in his own time and is mentioned in eighteenth-century texts, subsequently he was almost completely forgotten. Even today his work still awaits monographic treatment. Alvar González-Palacios has done some pioneering work on Provenzale, including identifying the present work in the storerooms of the Palazzo Pitti and recognizing its importance. The subject of the mosaic is rather unusual; in the foreground is an owl surrounded by other birds, and in the extreme background there is a view of Rome, wherein we can recognize the fountain of the Acqua Paola on the left and the facade of Old

Saint Peter's, demolished shortly afterward, on the right. A small mosaic cartouche just below the owl's talons contains Provenzale's signature and the date 1616. The owl is a symbol of wisdom, and it is likely that the mosaic has some allegorical meaning that has yet to be clarified. Perhaps the scene relates to the Aesop fable in which the owl counsels the other birds to prudent actions but instead is dismissed by them as insane. Mosaic artists of the time did not design their own compositions, so Provenzale would have used some pictorial source, perhaps, as González-Palacios suggested in the same work, that by an artist in the circle of landscape painters around Paul Bril (ca. 1554–1626), a Flemish artist working in Rome.[2]

A document dated June 3, 1631, records the arrival of this mosaic in the Medici collection and describes "the engraved coat of arms of Cardinal Borghese" on the reverse of the then-extant brass casing.[3] The cardinal, one of the greatest patrons and collectors in Rome in the early seventeenth century, commissioned works from Provenzale on several occasions. The gift of this mosaic to Grand Duke Ferdinand II de' Medici some fifteen years after it was finished may have been part of an exchange of "courtesies," or perhaps it had a diplomatic purpose. The mosaic was so widely admired in Florence that it was copied by the grand-ducal workshop as a Florentine-style mosaic, using inlaid pieces of carefully cut hardstones (see cat. no. 131).

A G

1. For more on Provenzale's portable mosaics, see González-
   Palacios 1976b.
2. Ibid., p. 28.
3. Ibid., pp. 27, 31, n. 10. Another mention is in the 1642 *Vite* of
   Giovanni Baglione, who cites a mosaic of an owl surrounded by "a variety of birds so lovely they appear to be
   alive" among the works Provenzale made for Cardinal
   Borghese. See Baglione 1642, p. 350.

131. Center table

Table: Paris, ca. 1780
By Martin Carlin
Ebony and copper on an oak carcass, gilded bronze mounts;
30⅜ × 30⅞ × 23⅛ in. (77.3 × 78.4 × 58.6 cm)
Plaques: Galleria dei Lavori, Florence, 17th century
Hardstone
Musée National des Châteaux de Versailles et de Trianon, Versailles
Vmb 13753

PROVENANCE: Possibly the duc de Brissac, Paris; French national collection, Château de Saint-Cloud, near Paris, from the early 19th century; transferred to the Musée du Louvre, Paris, 1870 ; transferred to the Château de Versailles, 1888

REFERENCES: Giusti 1992, p. 218, figs. 77, 78; D. Meyer 2002, vol. 2, pp. 107–9, no. 32

This small center table, designed to be seen from all sides, was made about 1780. The cabinetmaker, or *ébéniste*, was Martin Carlin (ca. 1730–1785), a German-born craftsman who became a master in Paris in 1766 and thereafter maintained his own workshop on the rue du Faubourg Saint Antoine. Like other contemporary Parisian cabinetmakers, Carlin seems to have made furniture for the entrepreneur, or *marchand-mercier*, Simon-Philippe Poirier. Their association began in the mid-1760s, and after Poirier retired in 1776, Carlin continued to work with Poirier's partner and successor, Dominique Daguerre, becoming his principal *ébéniste*. Carlin is perhaps best known for his sophisticated furniture mounted with plaques of porcelain, hardstones, or lacquer, which were commissioned or purchased for that purpose by his employer. The *marchands-merciers* also hired draftsmen to design the extravagant pieces, bronze workers to produce their gilded mounts, and cabinetmakers like Carlin to construct and mount the wooden carcasses.[1]

This piece is unusual in Carlin's production, for it incorporates hardstone panels of seventeenth-century Florentine origin. Presumably cut at the grand-ducal workshop a century earlier, the thirteen plaques were chosen and assembled according to their size rather than their iconography. The large scene mounted as the top illustrates Aesop's fable "The Owl and the Birds"—a celebration of wisdom, since the fable reveals the owl to be the wisest bird. Two seascapes, six depictions of birds, and four of flowers decorate the frieze beneath. Such a composite piece reflects a revival of the fashion for hardstone mosaics. The pictorial panels exemplify those produced in the 1600s for

detail of tabletop plaque

collectors and as souvenirs for visitors to Florence, and the stones, and thus also the colors, used in the plaques are typical of the manufacture at the Medici workshop in that period. However, the three genres represented—fables, marines or landscapes, and depictions of flora and fauna—are timeless.[2]

Furniture of this kind is collaborative work, demonstrating the great skill of the *ébénistes*, bronze casters, chasers, and lapidaries, as well as the marketing and managerial abilities of the *marchands-merciers*. The latter also influenced taste and fashion in the world of the urban aristocracy and haute bourgeoisie. Among these wealthy patrons, Louis-Hercule Timoléon de Cossé (1734–1792), duc de

Brissac, the governor of Paris from 1760 and colonel of the royal and then the constitutional guard, may have been the original owner of this piece.[3] It was probably confiscated from its owner during the French Revolution.

FK

1. Pradère 1989, pp. 30–40.
2. The popularity of fables as a theme in Florentine mosaics is further documented by a panel of the same Aesop episode executed in micromosaic by the Italian painter and lapidary Marcello Provenzale (see cat. no. 130).
3. Also at the Château de Versailles are two marquetry-veneered bookcases (RF 5511, 5512) that may have belonged to the duc de Brissac as well. See D. Meyer 2002, vol. 2, p. 107.

132. Commode

Paris, ca. 1778
Cabinetry by Martin Carlin
Ebony on an oak carcass, marble
top, gilded bronze mounts; 37⅜ ×
59⅞ × 23 in. (94.8 × 152.2 × 58.4 cm)
Front mosaic panels: Manufacture
Royale des Gobelins, Paris, 17th
century
Hardstone
Side mosaic panels: Galleria dei
Lavori, Florence, early 18th
century (?)
Hardstone
Stamped: *CARLIN*; signed on two
fruit plaques: *Gachetti*
The Royal Collection, London
RCIN 2588

PROVENANCE: Claude François
Julliot; Marie-Joséphine Laguerre
(her sale, 1782); Pierre Victor
Besenval de Bronstatt, until d. 1794
(his sale, 1795); purchased, possibly
by Dominique Daguerre, for the
Prince of Wales (later George IV,
d. 1830), Carlton House, London;
The Royal Collection

REFERENCES: Setterwall 1959,
p. 430, figs. 12, 15, 16; De Bellaigue
in J. Harris, De Bellaigue, and
Millar 1968, p. 146, ill.; Lemonnier
1984, p. 14, ill.; Pradère 1989,
ill. no. 415

The Paris-based *ébéniste* Martin Carlin (ca. 1730–1785) is best known for inventive small-scale furniture of various types that were mounted with plaques usually of Sèvres porcelain or Japanese lacquer.[1] Born in Germany, he settled in 1759 in Paris, where he trained as cabinetmaker. Later he would become one of the most celebrated artisans of his time and the principal provider of luxury furnishings to the dealer Dominique Daguerre, who catered especially to members of the French royal entourage (see cat. no. 131). This commode, however, was commissioned by the dealer Claude François Julliot, who probably sold it to the opera singer Marie-Joséphine Laguerre. It is described in the catalogue of her estate sale in 1782 as "one of the prettiest pieces known in this genre."[2] The present exhibition offers a thrilling opportunity to see together what are generally regarded as the three finest examples of French furniture of the eighteenth century featuring pietre dure decoration: this commode by Carlin, a commode that bears the stamps of both Carlin and Adam Weisweiler, and a cabinet by Weisweiler (cat. nos. 133, 134). The group is discussed further in "An Enduring Seductiveness" by Wolfram Koeppe and Florian Knothe in this publication.

The Carlin commode was conceived at the height of a Neoclassical fashion in French furniture design favoring rectangular shapes, an architectural look, and tapering feet.[3] Three-dimensionality is emphasized by the sculptural and sumptuously gilded mounts and the hardstone panels on the front, which has a central bay whose protrusion is echoed in the shaped marble top. This bay is decorated with a tall hardstone relief panel made at the Manufacture Royale des Gobelins in Paris in the late seventeenth century that depicts a vase resembling an antique urn filled with flowers. The bouquet reflects the passion at the time for floral arrangements; they were depicted in sculpture, in painting, in lacquer, and above all in color-stained marquetry that covered the walls of entire rooms.[4] The two lateral doors are each decorated with three Gobelins-made mosaic panels, all displaying dishes filled with fruit. The panels at the same level in the three rows are similar, but not identical, in the color and arrangement of the hardstones. The individual fruits are exceptionally realistic in their three-dimensionality. The flat Florentine mosaic panels on the sides of the commode make a pleasant contrast with the light-catching clusters of fruit on the front. Two of them are incised with the name "Gachetti."[5] All the colorful panels are set off to fine effect by the dark ebony veneer.   WK

1. For examples of Carlin furniture with Sèvres plaques, see Pradère 1989, ill. nos. 401–30; Kisluk-Grosheide in Kisluk-Grosheide, Koeppe, and Rieder 2006, pp. 156–58, no. 63, pp. 162–64, no. 67.
2. Setterwall 1959, p. 430; see also Dauterman and Parker 1960, p. 276.
3. The commode is shown here after recent conservation, in which corner blocks between the legs and the carcass were removed in order to lower the piece to its original height.
4. For a bureau covered with floral marquetry, see Koeppe 1992, pp. 204–6, M106, ill. p. 248.
5. Watson 1960.

133. Commode

By Martin Carlin and Adam
Weisweiler, Paris, ca. 1786
Ebony, walnut, and marquetry
of brass, copper, and pewter on an
oak carcass, *vert d'Egypte* marble,
gilded bronze mounts; 38 × 65¾ ×
19¼ in. (96.5 × 167 × 49 cm)
Stamped: twice *M.CARLIN JME,*
once *M.CARLIN,* and once *A.
WEISWEILER JME,* the last accom-
panied by the inscriptions *B612* (?)
in red and *X/249*
Fruit garland panels: Manufacture
Royale des Gobelins, Paris, late
17th century
Hardstone
Pictorial panels: Galleria dei Lavori,
Florence, early 18th century
Hardstone
Private collection

PROVENANCE: Possibly Dominique
Daguerre; Rothschild collection,
Paris; Akram Ojjeh, 1983
(sale, Christie's, Monte Carlo,
December 12, 1999, lot 30); the
present owner

REFERENCES: Cooper 1963, p. 172;
González-Palacios 1982b, ill. p. 48;
Lemonnier 1983, p. 177, no. 41,
ill. pp. 33, 50–51 (image reversed)

Extreme luxury and lavish expenditure characterized upper-class life in France early in the
reign of Louis XVI (r. 1774–92). Louis-Sébastien
Mercier noted then that "six hundred mansions
were built that on the inside looked like a fairy-
land; because [human] imagination does not go
beyond a luxury so exquisite."[1] Those were the
glory years of the Parisian *marchands-merciers*, men
like Dominique Daguerre, who ordered, sold, and
sometimes designed ornate furniture. They dominated European taste far beyond the political fron-
tiers of France. The demands of a spoiled clientele
that was accustomed to spend lavishly on what it
wanted led the premier cabinetmakers of the
period to rapidly invent a variety of new furniture
types, including various kinds of commodes, or

chests of drawers. Martin Carlin (ca. 1730–1785)
and Adam Weisweiler (1744–1820) belonged to a
small group of outstanding artisans who were
preeminent in this circle. In their workshops they
produced pieces with imaginative designs and
creative decorations under the inspired guidance
of the *marchants-merciers* (see "An Enduring
Seductiveness" by Wolfram Koeppe and Florian
Knothe in this publication).

This commode with compartments at the sides
is a type called *commode à encoignures.*[2] It is made
with open corners, here fitted at the bottom with
a shelflike green marble floors and recalling the
commode à l'anglais, which usually had at least two
shelves.[3] The open-corner solution offered not
only a space in which to display precious items but

center panel

an opportunity for the cabinetmaker to create his own contemporary version of Boulle-style metal marquetry, as seen here in the two concave panels that form the back of each corner compartment.[4]

On the front, five Florentine *commesso di pietre dure* seascapes are seductively combined with the seventeenth-century Gobelins garlands of hardstone-relief fruit that frame the central panel. Related seascape mosaic panels of the same date are included in a writing desk at the Musée du Louvre, Paris, in the *Kimbolton Cabinet*, dated 1709 (cat. no. 136), and in the wall decoration of the Florentine chamber at Schloss Favorite, near Rastatt, Germany (fig. 91).[5] Unusually, only four rather slender, tapering legs support the heavy body of this commode, an ingenious way to create a graceful appearance. The designer also achieved a sense of lightness by enclosing the seascapes in windowlike frames, within which an ormolu border subtly enhances the deep perspective views.

Two cabinetmakers' names are stamped on the commode.[6] This raises the possibility of collaboration, but more likely the piece was begun by Martin Carlin and left unfinished at the time of his death. Adam Weisweiler worked for the same *marchands-merciers*, and probably his atelier finished and refined the work. It is widely thought

that Dominique Daguerre commissioned the commode.

The festoons and bow-tie mounts on the back corners are typical features of Carlin's furniture and found especially on examples he made for the French court.[7] The frieze on the concave entablature beneath the marble top, with alternating acanthus leaves of two different sizes, is a trademark of the Weisweiler manufactory. A similar example ornaments a cabinet in the English royal collection (cat. no. 134), a writing desk from the palace at Pavlovsk, near Saint Petersburg, and other important pieces.[8]

WK

1. Mercier 1782–83, vol. 1, p. 283, vol. 4, p. 121, quoted in translation in Stürmer 1979, p. 497.
2. Fleming and Honour 1989, p. 210; Pradère 1989, p. 433.
3. Pradère 1989, p. 433.
4. André-Charles Boulle (1642–1732), cabinetmaker to Louis XIV, perfected an intricate brass and tortoiseshell marquetry that bears his name. See Fleming and Honour 1989, pp. 114–16.
5. For the writing desk in the Louvre, see Alcouffe, Dion-Tenenbaum, and Lefébure 1993, p. 244, no. 77; for the Schloss Favorite examples, see Przyborowski 1998, figs. 10, 11, 15, 16.
6. The monogram *JME* following the names is a quality guarantee made by the inspectors of the Parisian cabinetmakers' guild (the Menuisiers-Ébénistes).
7. Pradère 1989, ill. no. 416; for additional examples with these features, see ill. nos. 402, 407, 408, 419.
8. Ibid., ill. nos. 485, 496.

134. Commode

By Adam Weisweiler, Paris,
ca. 1785–90
Ebony, boxwood, purplewood,
mahogany, and marquetry of
brass, pewter, and tortoiseshell
veneer on an oak carcass, broca-
telle marble top, gilded bronze
and gilded brass mounts; 39⅜ ×
59⅛ × 19⅜ in. (100 × 150 × 49 cm)
Stamped on top of carcass:
A.WEISWEILER
Side and front flanking mosaic panels:
Galleria dei Lavori, Florence, 17th
century
Hardstones
Center mosaic panel and relief panel:
Manufacture Royale des Gobelins,
Paris, late 17th century
Hardstones, including lapis lazuli
The Royal Collection, London
RCIN 2593

PROVENANCE: Dominique
Daguerre, by 1791 (sold Christie's,
London, March 25, 1791, lot 59);
purchased probably at that sale by
the Prince of Wales (later King
George IV, d. 1830), Carlton House,
London; The Royal Collection

REFERENCES: De Bellaigue in
J. Harris, De Bellaigue, and Millar
1968, p. 175, ill. p. 174; González-
Palacios 1982b, ill. p. 46; Lemonnier
1983, p. 175, no. 19, ill. p. 45; Pradère
1989, ill. no. 498; *Carlton House* 1991,
pp. 76–77, no. 28, pl. XI

The cryptic notation "bt. GW" on a copy of a Christie's, London, 1791 auction catalogue[1] has convinced many scholars that it was the Prince of Wales, heir to the British throne, who acquired this ravishing commode at a sale of luxury goods that the French *marchand-mercier* Dominique Daguerre had assembled and shipped to England in the second year of the French Revolution.[2] During this turbulent period, an abundance of beautiful and valuable objects came on the market. The French luxury trade in furnishings and art had begun to deteriorate by 1790, as had the monetary value of its products, and this slump lasted through the period of Napoleon's empire and until the restoration of the Bourbon dynasty in 1814. All over Europe connoisseurs and art collectors took advantage of astonishing bargains being offered. In Scotland, the tenth duke of Hamilton amassed a collection second in value only to that of the British Crown. Empress Catherine the Great of Russia also profited from the fall of the French monarchy, enriching her legendary collection, as did other Russian grandees in their palaces built in the new Neoclassical style in booming Saint Petersburg.[3] Eastern European aristocrats like Prince Aleksandr Andreyevich Bezborodko, Count Aleksandr Sergeievich Stroganov, and other members of Russia's cosmopolitan elite also bought "only the best" from desperate French merchants and aristocrats.[4]

The design of this commode depends for its success on the surprising harmony achieved between a sober Neoclassical furniture form and showy Florentine and Parisian hardstone works of the seventeenth century. By the 1780s pietre dure panels of earlier times had become precious collector's items and were handed over only to well-known cabinetmakers, who would mount them tastefully in an almost reliquary-like setting, elevating the art of furniture making to the highest level (see "An Enduring Seductiveness" by Wolfram Koeppe and Florian Knothe in this publication).

Six pietre dure panels embellish this commode executed in the shop of Adam Weisweiler (1744–1820), who worked almost exclusively for Daguerre and became his principal supplier after the death in 1785 of another genius of French cabinetmaking, Martin Carlin.[5] Each side is decorated with a panel showing a bird sitting on a branch. On the front the two side doors bear a still-life panel of great serenity, each depicting one single flower, a tulip on the left and an imposing crown imperial on the right. Similar large panels capturing the beauty of one blossoming plant were made in the Galleria dei Lavori in Florence in the second half of the seventeenth century.[6] The present upright panels are framed by marquetry in the manner of the earlier cabinetmaker André Boulle, but its geometric, lacelike look and ornamental density show that it was made at the time of the carcass's construction, about 1785–90.

The central door is testimony to the art of combining very different materials in a homogeneous painterly composition. In the square central panel, a polychrome basket with an exotic bird as well as flowers, fruits, and butterflies harmonizes with a relief mosaic below. Both were probably made at the Gobelins in Paris at the end of the seventeenth century or later. The whole decoration—a flamboyant evocation of nature's bounty—is framed on three sides by a late seventeenth- or early eighteenth-century example of Boulle marquetry: engraved brass and pewter scrolls and leaves set into a tortoiseshell ground.

The entire commode is enhanced by the gilded bronze moldings and the gilded brass fluting inlaid into the corner columns. The six short legs were given spiraled flutes, probably to reduce, through their upward motion, the heavy look of the superstructure. The color of the hardstones has changed little over the centuries, whereas furniture of the same period decorated with pictorial marquetry usually began to fade within a few decades of its manufacture.

Behind the central door of the commode are shelves, and concealed in the flanking compartments are drawers. Strictly speaking, then, the piece is a cross between a *commode à vantaux*—which has drawers hidden behind its three doors—and a variation called *commode en bas d'armoire*.[7]

W K

1. See *Carlton House* 1991, pp. 76–77, no. 28. The notation may be deciphered as "bought [by] George Wales."
2. Sargentson 1996.
3. Koeppe forthcoming.
4. For example, Prince Bezborodko purchased items from the collections of the duc d'Orléans and the duc du Choiseuil. See Asvarishch 1993, p. 3. For Count Stroganov, see entries for cat. nos. 141, 144.
5. Pradère 1989, p. 390.
6. For an example, see the sale catalogue of the Keck collection, Sotheby's, New York, December 5 and 6, 1991, lot 50.
7. Havard 1887–90, vol. 1, col. 937, pl. 54; Fleming and Honour 1989, p. 210.

136. *Kimbolton Cabinet*

London, 1771–74
Design by Robert Adam; cabinetry
by William Ince and John Mayhew
Satinwood and rosewood
marquetry on a mahogany and oak
carcass; 74½ × 71¾ × 14⅜ in. (189 ×
182 × 36.5 cm)
Mounts: Soho Manufactory, near
Birmingham
By Matthew Boulton and John
Fothergill
Gilded bronze
Plaques: Galleria dei Lavori,
Florence, 1709
By Baccio Cappelli
Hardstone
Victoria and Albert Museum,
London, Purchase funded by the
Vallentin Bequest W.43-1949

PROVENANCE: Elizabeth Montagu,
Duchess of Manchester, Kimbolton
Castle (1774 inventory; sale,
Knight, Frank & Rutley, July 19,
1949, lot 314); John Bly, London;
purchased by the Victoria and
Albert Museum, 1949

REFERENCES: Honour 1958,
ill. no. 9; Setterwall 1959, p. 435;
Boynton 1966; Goodison 1974,
pp. 133–35, pls. 52–62; Przyborowski
1998, p. 407, fig. 12; E. Harris 2001,
p. 195, pl. 285; Goodison 2002,
pp. 249–54, pls. 200, 203–7

This cabinet on stand was designed in the Neoclassical style by the famous British architect Robert Adam (1728–1792) for Elizabeth Montagu, née Dashwood, Duchess of Manchester, in 1771. It was executed by the London firm of William Ince and John Mayhew, with which Adam collaborated repeatedly, and its gilded bronze mounts were supplied by Matthew Boulton (1728–1809) and John Fothergill (d. 1782) from their Soho Manufactory, near Birmingham.[1] English in its construction and style, the piece is mounted with eleven early eighteenth-century hardstone mosaic plaques depicting landscape scenes, all of which were made, and one signed and dated (1709), by Baccio Cappelli, one of the foremost lapidaries at the Galleria dei Lavori, the Medici mosaic workshop in Florence.[2] Trained in the long-established techniques and conversant with the repertoire of compositions (most typically, landscapes and ornithological depictions) upon which the Florentine lapidaries had built their reputation since 1588, Cappelli continued this tradition into the eighteenth century and produced some of the most superbly cut and carefully assembled pietre dure panels ever made. His works were treasured throughout Europe, as the panels of the large cabinet he made for Henry Scudamore, third duke of Beaufort, now in the Liechtenstein Museum in Vienna (fig. 87), and a related set of plaques sent to the elector of Saxony Frederick Augustus II and displayed in Dresden's Grünes Gewölbe (Green Vault) demonstrate.[3]

This piece, known as the *Kimbolton Cabinet*—it remained at Kimbolton Castle until 1949, when the family collection of the dukes of Manchester was dispersed—documents the revived interest in hardstone mosaics in England.[4] In quality it equals the best contemporary hardstone-mounted furniture of Parisian origin, which was very popular with English collectors.[5] Elizabeth Dashwood, who commissioned this work, was herself born into a family of prominent collectors. The cabinet's designer, Robert Adam, had contributed to the vogue for pietre dure when he traveled abroad with young noblemen, such as Charles Hope-Weir, and influenced their taste; later he would accept their commissions for buildings, decorative interiors, and furniture that reflected the styles they had studied abroad and that incorporated works of art—such as hardstone panels—purchased there, especially in Italy.[6] Adam's specific involvement with the *Kimbolton Cabinet* is documented in two preliminary drawings preserved in Sir John Soane's Museum in London. Although they were not followed exactly in the execution, the drawings show the Italianate facade that Adam envisioned for the piece and the placement of individual plaques that were presumably already in his possession.[7] However decorative it is as a showpiece, the cabinet is easily unbalanced because of the heavy weight of the stone panels, a limitation unforeseen by Adam and unanticipated by Ince and Mayhew, who had little experience in mounting pietre dure.   FK

1. Goodison 1974, pp. 133–35, pls. 52–62; Goodison 2002, p. 249.
2. Przyborowski 1998, p. 407.
3. González-Palacios 1993, vol. 1, pp. 419–32; González-Palacios 2007a, pp. 88–90.
4. In the 1949 sale, the object was described as "an antique Italian satinwood and rosewood marqueterie cabinet." See Knight, Frank & Rutley, London, July 19, 1949, sale cat., lot 314.
5. See Setterwall 1959, p. 435; see also "An Enduring Seductiveness" by Wolfram Koeppe and Florian Knothe in this publication.
6. L. A. Smith 1996; Coleridge 1997.
7. Soane Manuscripts, vol. 17, no. 218, vol. 27, no. 51, illustrated in Goodison 1974, pls. 53, 54.

137. Miniature secretary with clock

London, 1766–72
Design by James Cox
Agate, gold, gilded bronze, glass,
and paste jewels; 12½ × 5⅝ × 4¼ in.
(31.8 × 14.3 × 10.8 cm)
The Metropolitan Museum of
Art, New York, Gift of Admiral
Frederic R. Harris, in memory of
his wife, Dena Sperry Harris, 1946
46.184 a–c

PROVENANCE: Sold in London by
lottery in 1773; Peter Carl Fabergé;
Princess Z. M. Youssoupof, before
1904–after 1905; Count Gregor
Stroganov, before 1931; [Wartski
and Co., London, after 1931–after
1937]; Edward Bradshaw; [Á la
Vieille Russie, New York, before
1944–46]; Admiral Frederic R.
Harris; his gift to the Metropolitan
Museum, 1946

This clock in the shape of a miniature secretary was made by an anonymous goldsmith in London after a design by James Cox (ca. 1723–1800), who has been described as a "creative entrepreneur" rather than the trained goldsmith he called himself. Much like the *marchands-merciers* of Paris (see cat. nos. 131–135), Cox relied on a network of highly talented jewelers, clockmakers, and lapidaries, including the noted inventor John Joseph Merlin (1735–1803), to manufacture his jewel-mounted clocks, *nécessaires*, and mechanical toys.[1] The Rococo carcass of this hybrid object, whose frame is constructed from gold set with agates, houses a musical movement and a clock, exemplifying the exuberance of Cox's style as well as his clients' extravagant tastes in mechanical devices.[2] Exhibited among a variety of similar, richly decorated works in Cox's London museum

of automata in 1773, it typifies the kind of finely executed clocks and jeweler's works that from the mid-1760s Cox exported en masse to merchants in India and China, where his curiosities and novelties garnered him a reputation he otherwise achieved only with Russian collectors beginning in 1775.[3] Although this piece was originally designed and made for the Chinese court, initially it remained unsold. After being exhibited in London and sold by lottery in 1773, however, it enjoyed a long provenance with distinguished Russian collectors such as Princess Z. M. Youssoupof.[4] Indeed, princely Russian patrons, like members of the Chinese court, greatly favored such clocks, whose prestige among the Russian elite was later rivaled only by the jeweled confections of Peter Carl Fabergé (1846–1920).[5]

FK

detail

REFERENCES: Cox 1773, p. 17, no. 9;
Le Corbeiller 1960, p. 320, ill. p. 323;
Le Corbeiller 1970, p. 352, fig. 1;
Young 1996, pp. 402–3, fig. 69

1. Le Corbeiller 1960, p. 318; Le Corbeiller 1970, p. 352; R. Smith 2000, p. 353.
2. A preliminary drawing, attributed to Charles Magniac, survives at the Victoria and Albert Museum, London. See Young 1996.
3. Significant numbers of Cox's toys were exported to China beginning in 1766, long before he and his son John Henry ran a shop in Canton in 1781–88 and 1790–91. Le Corbeiller 1960, pp. 320–21, 323; Le Corbeiller 1970, pp. 355–56; Pagani 1995, pp. 18–21; R. Smith 2000, pp. 356–61.
4. Cox 1773, p. 17, no. 9.
5. Dukelskaya 1979, pls. 207–9.

138. Pair of perfume burners

Soho Manufactory, near
Birmingham, 1770–72
By Matthew Boulton and John
Fothergill
Derbyshire spar, tortoiseshell, and
wood, Carrara marble base, gilded
brass mounts, gilded copper liner;
each 13 × 5⅝ × 5⅝ in. (33 × 14.3 ×
14.3 cm)
The Metropolitan Museum of Art,
New York, Gift of Irwin
Untermyer, 1964 64.101.1633, 1634

PROVENANCE: Irwin Untermyer,
New York; his gift to the
Metropolitan Museum, 1964

REFERENCES: Hackenbroch 1962,
p. lxiv, pl. 192, fig. 216; Goodison
1974, p. 205, n. 513; Vincent in
Metropolitan Museum 1977,
pp. 183–84, no. 339; Goodison 2002,
pp. 351, 401, n. 671; Jessica Lanier
in McCormick and Ottomeyer
2004, pp. 102–3, no. 45

This pair of perfume burners was made in Matthew Boulton and John Fothergill's Soho Manufactory, two miles north of Birmingham, in 1770–72.[1] Each burner consists of a vase carved from Derbyshire spar and decorated with gilded brass mounts on a base of white Carrara marble, supported on each of its four sides by a gilded brass sphinx resting on a wooden plinth veneered with tortoiseshell and embellished with filigree gilded brass moldings.[2] Inside is a gilded copper liner, and atop the burner is a perforated cover also made of spar. The shape of the container is that of the classic Greek (Attic) vase known as a calyx krater. It was repeatedly employed by Boulton, the artistic genius of the workshop, for perfume burners and vases.[3]

Boulton, who may have worked up this design after drawings by King George III's architect Sir William Chambers, developed an extensive line of cast and finely chiseled gilded brass mounts, many of which were combined with porcelain, lacquer, and hardstone—such as Derbyshire marble and spar—and assembled into vases and candelabra.[4] His particular predilection was for the colorful,

locally mined fluorspar commonly known as "blue john." Fluorspar was discovered in the East Midlands in the early 1700s, was quarried professionally from about 1760, and became a popular medium, especially for English Neoclassical hardstone works.[5] Boulton is documented as having purchased fourteen tons of it beginning in 1769.[6] The English aristocracy appreciated its decorative quality and Boulton's excellent and artistic workmanship, and used his elaborate perfume burners, as well as his vases for freshly cut flowers and fragranced rose petals, to sweeten the air in their apartments. Charcoal was ignited in the lower section of the perfume burners, and its heat burned scented pastilles in the liner above.[7]

F K

1. Goodison 1974, pp. 163–64; Goodison 2002, pp. 350–51.
2. A very similar pair of perfume burners was ordered by King George III's wife, Queen Charlotte, in 1770 and survives in the English royal collection at Windsor Castle. See *Treasures from the Royal Collection* 1988, p. 104, no. 99; Roberts 2004, pp. 269–70, no. 275. Other examples of the same model have appeared on the art market in recent decades (Sotheby's, London, February 12–15, 1988, lot 7, and July 7, 1995, lot 74; Christie's, Paris, December 19, 2007, lot 382).
3. McCormick and Ottomeyer 2004, pp. 30, 102–3, no. 45 (entry by Jessica Lanier).
4. Goodison 1972; Goodison 2002, pp. 319–23, pls. 313, 314.
5. Goodison 1974, pp. 29–32.
6. In that year, Boulton, who has never been recorded as the owner of any quarries, signed a contract with the Derbyshire miners and became their principal client. Ibid., p. 30.
7. The fact that Boulton's perfume burners, candelabra, and vases exist in pairs suggests that they were displayed symmetrically as ornamental objets d'art on mantelpieces.

139. Side table with a marble and hardstone top

Top: by John Wildsmith, London, 1759

Marbles, including *rosso* and *nero antico*, orange Veronese, yellow Siena, brown, gray, and white *fleur de pêcher*, black and gold Portor, orange and violet Spanish *brocatello*, and white Carrara, and hardstones, including gray and red granite, red and white jasper, pink quartz, porphyry, bloodstone,

This pietre dure tabletop framed in black marble was made by the London mason and sculptor John Wildsmith (recorded 1757–69) for Croome Court, residence of the sixth earl of Coventry, in 1759. Wildsmith inlaid 176 squares of differently colored hardstone specimens in a diagonal checkerboard pattern in order to display "all the curious sorts." The stand was probably designed and made by John Mayhew (1736–1811) of the London firm of William Ince and John Mayhew in 1794, and like the marble top it is described in a bill to Coventry.[1] The discrepancy in the dates suggests that the valuable mosaic top represents the treasured collectible item, that it was displayed differently at first, and that it was later fitted onto an equally splendid "large Frame . . . on turned legs, neatly carved and the whole gilt in burnished gold."

top view

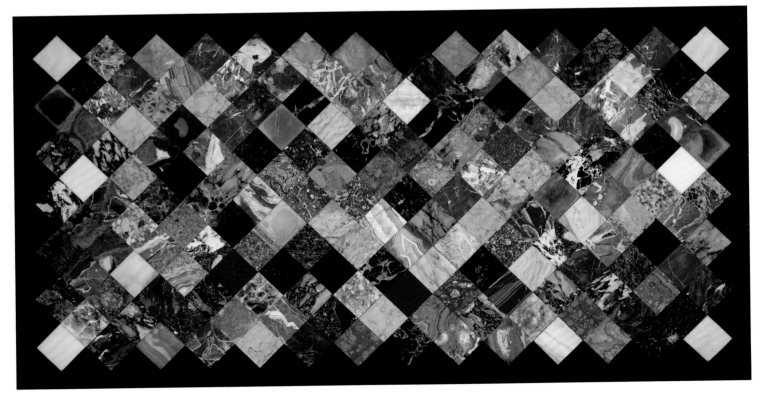

serpentine, golden and brown
agate and onyx, and lapis lazuli;
$1\frac{1}{2} \times 61\frac{5}{8} \times 33$ in. (3.7 × 156.5 ×
83.8 cm)
Stand: By John Mayhew, London,
1794
Gilded pine; 37 × 60¼ × 31⅛ in.
(94 × 153 × 79.1 cm)
The Metropolitan Museum of Art,
New York, Gift of Samuel H. Kress
Foundation, 1958 58.75.13a, b

The fashion for decorative inlaid and specimen panels originated in Florence and also flourished in other prosperous European cities, including Rome and Paris (the painting in fig. 119 shows a table-top similar to the present example).[2] Wealthy Englishmen are known to have collected works of art, among them pietre dure objects, on their educa-tional grand tours. Coventry's tabletop is, however, a rare example of London manufacture—documented by the payment to Wildsmith—and testifies to the spread of lapidary skill as well as the fashion for

lapidary work across the English Channel. Robert Adam, the architect responsible for some of the outer buildings and for decorating the principal rooms at Croome Court, had traveled in Italy him-self, and it was his practice to employ and direct experienced artisans, including Ince and Mayhew, with whom he collaborated repeatedly, to execute his designs. Among these craftsmen was John Wildsmith, who received payments also for marble chimneypieces he supplied to Croome and who is likely to have inlaid this tabletop to specific orders.[3]

Provenance: Earls of Coventry, Croome Court, Worcestershire, until 1948 (sale, Sotheby's, June 25, 1948, lot. 141); Samuel H. Kress Foundation, 1948; its gift to the Metropolitan Museum, 1958

References: Parker 1959, pp. 89–90, ill.; Parker 1960; Parker 1961, p. 113, ill. p. 112; Metropolitan Museum 1964, pp. 40–42, no. 4, fig. 16

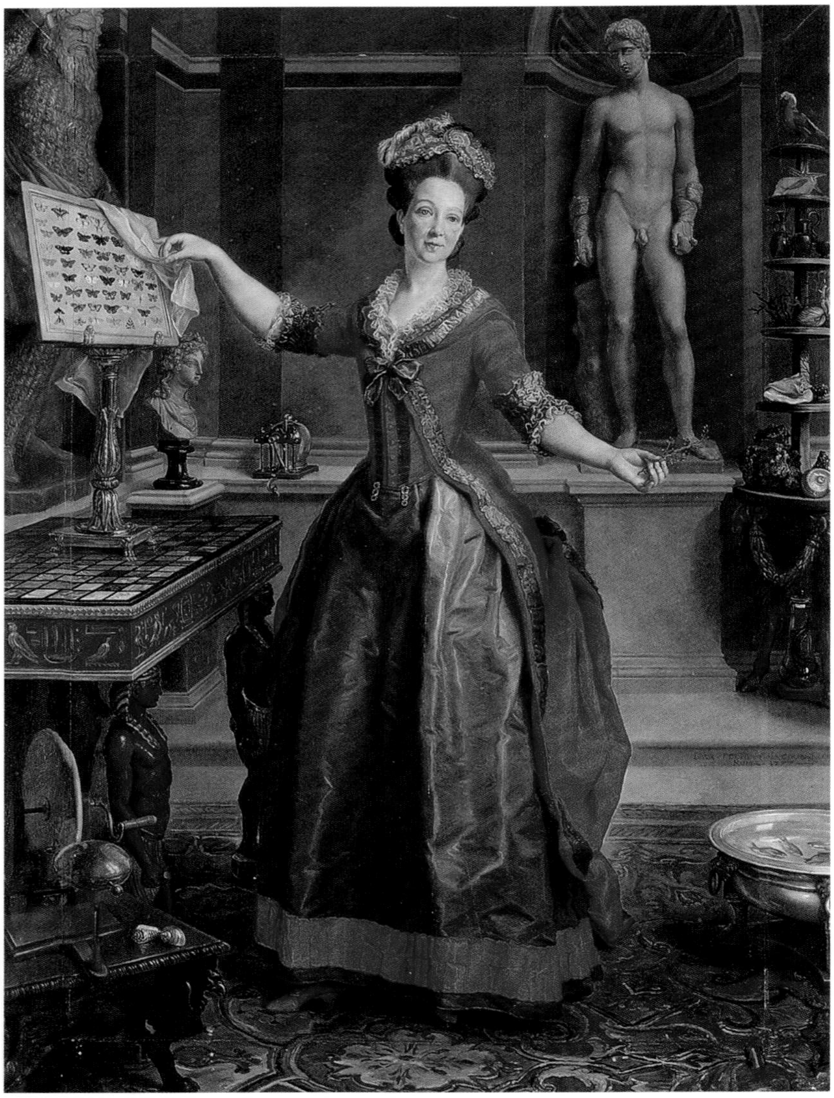

Fig. 119. Laurent Pécheux, *The Marchesa Margherita Gentili Boccapaduli*, 1777. Oil on canvas, 42 ⅛ × 31 ½ in. Private collection, Rome

Adam and Coventry were following the latest fashion when they displayed in the reception room at Croome this collectible item that alludes so obviously to the "obligatory" grand tour and includes, among its large range of stones, varieties used for the carved objects alongside which it was displayed in the same setting.

FK

1. The tabletop cost £42 10s (July 28, 1759) and its stand £17 10s (May 17, 1794). The bills for these commissions survive in the account book of the sixth earl of Coventry (pages 11, 119). See the object file, Department of European Sculpture and Decorative Arts, Metropolitan Museum.
2. A similar specimen table, thought to have been made for Thomas Rumbold by Ince and Mayhew about 1775, is now in the English royal collection. See *Treasures from the Royal Collection* 1988, pp. 102–3, no. 97. Another piece of comparable design was offered at the sale of Bailli de Breteuil in Paris on January 16, 1786 (lot 233), and two tabletop panels, each measuring 29⅝ × 63 inches and with 104 marble squares, are today at the Galleria Borghese in Rome. See Metropolitan Museum 1964, p. 41; *Opere in mosaico* 1971, pp. 44–45.
3. The bills for the three chimneypieces date to June 13, 1760, and May 21, 1763. See Metropolitan Museum 1964, p. 40.

Sweden and Russia, Eighteenth and
Early Nineteenth Centuries

140. Set of vases

Probably the Älvdalen workshop, Sweden, early 19th century Porphyry, gilded bronze mounts; shortest H. 13 in. (33 cm), tallest H. 22⅛ in. (56 cm) Ambassador Paul and Trudy Cejas

PROVENANCE: [Ariane Dandois, Paris; sale, Christie's, New York, May 18, 2005, lot 530]; the present owners

These five porphyry vases exemplify the hardstone carving in the western European lapidary tradition that was produced at independent Swedish workshops beginning in the 1780s.[1] The vases cannot be ascribed to a particular master carver, but their forms relate closely to those in drawings of about 1788–90 by the Swedish architect Carl Fredrik Sundvall. His compositions for decorative objects remained popular into the nineteenth century and are reflected in an illustrated price list of the Älvdalen manufactory in central Sweden of about 1805 (fig. 120).[2] The present set of vases was probably produced there.

Porphyry was discovered in the valley of Älvdalen (Elfdal) in 1731, but serious mining there was only begun some fifty years later, after Count Nils Adam Bielke showed samples of the stone to King Gustav III (r. 1771–92) and the Bergskollegium, or Mines Authority, established a privately run workshop in 1788 with the aim of producing porphyry objects.[3] With Bielke's support, the workshop's first master, Eric Hagström, introduced a new mining campaign and within a few years was operating three grinding mills in Näset with the latest water-powered machinery. Despite the high quality of its designs and production, the business suffered financial difficulties, and it was acquired in 1818 by Charles XIV, founder of Sweden's present royal house, whose intention was to introduce the grand French Empire style into Sweden.[4]

Typically of elegant, slender design, porphyry objects from Älvdalen were often left unadorned, possibly reflecting the style of the modest Neoclassical interiors at the Swedish court. However, other vases and urns—similar to the ones seen here—were turned at the workshop in Älvdalen and then sent to Paris to be decorated with fine gilded bronze mounts;[5] they were destined for distribution as diplomatic gifts to courts in neighboring western Europe and Russia. Distinguished by its speckled appearance, the porphyry at Älvdalen has been sorted into more than twenty different types. An inventory compiled by the Mining Intendance in Stockholm in the early nineteenth century called two of them "granitelle"—that is, resembling granite, while the others were named after the Älvdalen locales that were their sources.[6]

In 1857 Charles XIV's son Oskar I sold the Älvdalen manufactory to a local businessman, who operated the workshop until it burned down a decade later; thereafter, with only one of the mills surviving, the production of porphyry objects was continued on a limited scale until the mid-1890s. Because of its rarity, Swedish porphyry was treasured throughout Europe during the nineteenth century, and as a national export and symbol of pride in Sweden, it enjoyed high status at home as well.[7]

FK

1. See Malgouyres 2003; González-Palacios 2004a, pp. 114–15.

Fig. 120. "Prix-courant des differentes pièces de la manufacture des Porphyres d'Elfdal en Suède, qui se vendent à Stockholm"; a price list for vases made at the Älvaden manufactory, Sweden, ca. 1805

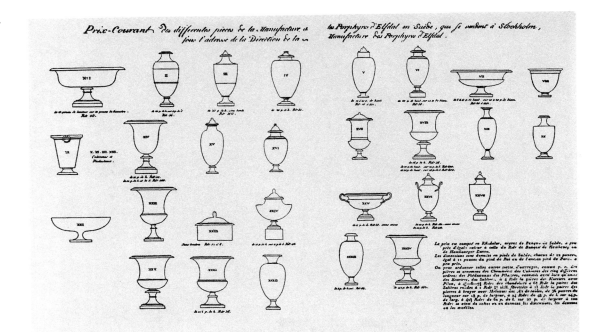

2. On the Älvdalen manufactory, see Bruun-Neergaard 1806; Sandqvist and Tunander 1989 (where the price list is illustrated on p. 36).
3. Sundblom, Tunander, and Uggla 1985, pp. 16–19.
4. Ibid., pp. 20–24.
5. Abraham Niklas Edelcrantz (1754–1821) traveled to Europe to study art and in 1790–91 in Paris initiated an artistic exchange between France and his native Sweden and arranged for Parisian bronziers to be employed in mounting Älvdalen porphyry vases. (In the early nineteenth century

these French craftsmen sometimes preferred to be paid in Swedish porphyry rather than money; this information was kindly provided to Wolfram Koeppe by Lars Ljungström.) See Sundblom, Tunander, and Uggla 1985, pp. 40–48. In his actions Edelcrantz resembled his countryman Nikodemus Tessin a century before; see Knothe 2007b.
6. *Porphyre* 1990, p. 2.
7. In the nineteenth century, sarcophagi and tombstones of Swedish porphyry were made throughout Europe. See Malgouyres 2003, pp. 185–90.

141. Drinking set

Peterhof Lapidary Works, near Saint Petersburg, 1754
Kalkan jasper; each cup 1⅛ × 1½ × 1½ in. (2.7 × 3.7 × 3.7 cm), tray ½ × 6⅞ × 5¾ in. (1.3 × 17.3 × 14.5 cm)
Inscribed on label on tray (in Russian): . . . *grayish green jasper with black speckles and with it six charki*
The State Hermitage Museum, Saint Petersburg WI 9104–9110

PROVENANCE: Stroganov collection, Saint Petersburg; transferred to the State Hermitage Museum, 1925

REFERENCES: Mavrodina in *Stroganoff* 2000, pp. 210–11, no. 62, ill. p. 165; Mavrodina 2007, p. 47, no. II, I

By the middle of the eighteenth century, Russian interest in geological exploration and mineralogy had developed into "a common disease," in the words of Empress Catherine the Great (r. 1762–96), who had become an enthusiast and who took pride in the ever-increasing number of hardstone deposits newly discovered in one corner or another of her far-flung realm.[1] The story had begun earlier with one of her predecessors on the throne of Russia, Peter the Great, who in 1721 founded, by imperial edict, the first Russian lapidary manufactory and hardstone grinding mill, in Peterhof, near Saint Petersburg. The czar encouraged mercantilists' interest in the workshop, which quickly developed into a very successful enterprise, producing widely admired objects of great beauty and variety. Under the monarchs who ruled Russia from the 1730s to the 1750s, the factory established itself as one of the leading creators of luxury goods in eastern Europe. Semiprecious stones and rare marbles were brought to Saint Petersburg from all over the empire as well as from foreign countries and were transformed at the manufactory into lavish works of art.[2] Most of the stone originated in the Ural Mountains, more than six hundred miles away.

The form of the present cups was clearly influenced by East Asian porcelains; they are shaped in the fashionable chinoiserie style that had conquered all of Europe in the eighteenth century.[3] It has been suggested that Chinese gold cups, some examples of which are preserved in the State Hermitage Museum's collection, may have served as an inspiration.[4] A label on one side of the delicate tray referring to the astonishingly thin-walled cups as *charki* is evidence that they were made to be used in drinking ceremonies. The *charka*, a shot cup usually used for serving vodka, most often has a single handle and is frequently made of metal and decorated with enamel.[5] Given the sometimes rough exuberance of guests at Russian drinking parties, where breaking glasses was part of the entertainment, the perfect condition of the present set strongly suggests that it was never used but

rather kept as a treasured display object. An archival document mentions the dispatch "to the Cabinet of His Imperial Majesty on August 3, 1754, of a box with finished works. Among them were two trays of grayish jasper with black veins, six large *charki*, and six small *charki* of the same stone." One tray and the small cups probably made up the present set. The document is testimony that fine hardstone objects of this sort from the imperial lapidary were used at court.[6]

It is not known when this tray and the cups— which so clearly bespeak the ingenuity and mastery of Russian stonecutters as well as the progressive nature of Russian design—entered the fabled Stroganov collection. They must have been among the prized items that the discerning Count Aleksandr Sergeievich Stroganov gathered in a special mineral cabinet during the renovation of his palace on the Nevsky Prospect, Saint Petersburg, in 1791. One scholar commented at the time, "Now Stroganoff can brilliantly accommodate his extremely rich collection of ores and minerals, and also his rare collection of books on geology and mineralogy, in no way inferior in its completeness to similar ones belonging to European collectors."[7] As the director of the Imperial Lapidary Works, Aleksandr Stroganov dominated the development of Russian stone carving from 1800 until his death, in 1811 (see entry for cat. no. 142).[8]   WK

1. See Mavrodina 2000, p. 163.
2. Tarasova 1990b. Guseva (1990, p. 89) mentions a foundation date of 1723 for the manufactory.
3. For similar local Russian interpretations of "chinoiserie," see Koeppe 1997.
4. Mavrodina in *Stroganoff* 2000, pp. 210–11, no. 62.
5. Solodkoff 1981, figs. 33–35, 64, 65.
6. For the contents of the archival document, see Mavrodina in *Stroganoff* 2000, p. 210. The document mentions that the boxed set was sent to the czar ("His Imperial Majesty"), but in 1754 the ruler of Russia was Elizabeth Petrovna I (r. 1741–62), the unmarried daughter of Peter the Great. The error may be one of transcription.
7. Quoted in translation from Trubinov 1996, p. 74, in Mavrodina 2000, p. 163.
8. Mavrodina 2000, p. 163.

142. Vase

Peterhof Lapidary Works, near
Saint Petersburg, 1800–1806
Design by Andrei N. Voronikhin
Smoky rock crystal
Mounts: Imperial Bronze Foundry,
Saint Petersburg
Gilded silver
H. 18⅛ in. (46 cm), W. 12 in. (30.5 cm)
Inscribed on plinth, in Cyrillic,
abbreviated: *Made in Peterhof
factory*
The State Hermitage Museum,
Saint Petersburg WI 862

PROVENANCE: Commissioned
by Count Aleksandr Sergeievich
Stroganov; Russian imperial collection; The State Hermitage
Museum

REFERENCES: Mavrodina in
Ice For Ever 2006, p. 147, no. 116;
Mavrodina 2007, pp. 90–91, no. 11,
83 (with bibliography)

The imperial Russian lapidary founded in 1721 at Peterhof, near Saint Petersburg, and the other state stone manufactories, in Yekaterinburg (founded 1726) and Kolyvan in the remote Altai Mountains (founded 1786), came under the administration of Count Aleksandr Sergeievich Stroganov in 1800. In little more than a decade and until his death, in 1811, this sophisticated aristocrat revolutionized the Russian lapidary industry. An art connoisseur of international reputation, he lived from 1771 to 1778 in Paris, absorbing its Enlightenment culture, and was a leading European collector. Among his principal goals were to raise the quality of Russian lapidary products by modernizing the grinding mills and to perfect the quality and designs of the bronze mounts that complemented the stone objects. On aesthetic matters, he turned to the prolific architect and designer Andrei N. Voronikhin (1759–1814), whose Kazan Cathedral (1801–11), in the Neoclassical style, quickly became the architectural and spiritual center of Saint Petersburg. Modeled on Saint Peter's in Rome, it was adorned on the inside and in the semicircular colonnades in front with monolithic granite columns, each weighing more than thirty tons. Both Stroganov and Voronikhin were forward-looking, and the artistic training of the next generation of lapidary masters was another priority of theirs.[1]

Six years into his administration, in 1806, Count Stroganov showed to Czar Alexander I (r. 1801–25) this exceptional vase carved out of rare smoky rock crystal, a quartzite that in the eighteenth century was also known as topaz. Greatly prized, the stone may then still have been associated with healing powers, such as the ability to strengthen the human body's nervous system.[2] The block from which this vase and perhaps one or two others were cut[3] was remarkable for its size and color and for its inclusions, which appeared as bizarre vein formations. It was discovered near Nerchinsk, in Siberia. The demanding task of transforming the crystal lump into a graceful vessel, reportedly all one piece, required skilled stoneworkers able to comprehend and execute the design that Stroganov commissioned from Voronikhin. Two years earlier, Pierre Agie, a metal sculptor and chaser who taught at the Academy of Fine Arts, had decided to move away from Saint Petersburg, leaving behind the workshop where he had executed private commissions. Count Stroganov, recognizing a unique chance to acquire for the

imperial workshops a fully equipped foundry with up-to-date machinery and working models, bought the workshop in 1804 and had the foundry installed near the academy, convenient to the court and to the master craftsmen who would supervise the work.[4] I propose here that the present vase's rather heavy gilded silver mounts originated in the new Imperial Bronze Foundry, an idea supported by the fact that the metal is not marked. This would only have occurred in a workshop with special court privileges and thus exempt from guild restrictions; otherwise, the precious metal used for decorative purposes would have to be assayed and marked with a guarantee of purity.

Bronze mounts—or as in this rare case, silver ones—were often used to conceal small flaws in a stone. Here almost nothing on the crystal's polished surface needed to be covered up, and the mounted figures—two maidens in Greek dress, resembling handles but too fragile to serve as such—seem barely attached to the vase. Their chitons, which cling to their bodies as though blown by an uplifting breeze, suggest rapid movement, making a fine contrast with the earthbound monumentality of the vase. It is difficult to decide whether the maidens are enacting an ancient ritual or spiritedly placing a gilded pine cone atop the lid. In any case, the viewer is enticed to walk around the vase or, if permitted, to hold, turn, and explore the object.

The disparity between the vase's palpable weight and the handles' apparent weightlessness is vaguely disturbing, as is the contrast between the reflective surface of the silver mounts and the mysterious nebula of veins inside the crystal. Seen by candlelight, these baffling formations seem to move. The powerful force of a genie pent up in a bottle comes to mind, but the vase's nameless genie is without force or escape—held in place forever by the incorruptible hardstone.[5]

The Russian taste for unconventional lapidary work initiated the creation of some of the most magnificent works of decorative art ever produced. This extraordinary ornamental vase must be counted as one of them. WK

1. Mavrodina 2000, pp. 163–64.
2. Graf 1999, p. 74.
3. Mavrodina 2007, p. 91.
4. Makarov 1938, pp. 22, 25.
5. I am most grateful to Natalya Guseva, Marina Lopato, Natalya Mavrodina, and Tamara Rappe, all of the State Hermitage Museum, Saint Petersburg, for giving me advice and help on several of my visits to the museum.

143. Pair of vases

Yekaterinburg Lapidary Works,
ca. 1801
Design by Andrei N. Voronikhin
Breccia
Mounts: Imperial Bronze Foundry,
Saint Petersburg
Gilded bronze
H. 23¼ in. (59 cm)
The State Hermitage Museum,
Saint Petersburg E 2688, 2689

PROVENANCE: Russian imperial
collection; The State Hermitage
Museum

Fig. 121. Aleksandr Grigorievich
Varnek, *Aleksandr Sergeievich
Stroganov,* 1814. Oil on canvas,
98⅞ × 72½ in. The State Russian
Museum, Saint Petersburg 5497

Egypt, the land of the pharaohs, is even farther from Russia than is western Europe, but at the end of the eighteenth century young members of the most important Russian aristocratic families were encouraged by Catherine the Great—who had a thirst for knowledge and was in correspondence with some of the sharpest minds of the age, such as Voltaire and Denis Diderot—to include that remote country on their grand tours. Soon exotic-looking Egyptian motifs began to appear in the rather conservative decorative vocabulary of Russian artists.

Despite their extremely elegant outline, these two turned and finely polished breccia vases (only one is illustrated) are solid enough to support the heavy Egyptianizing figures that are mounted on each vase facing each other as they kneel on the concave neck, holding the whole composition in place with their strong arms. Vladimir Makarov

observed that these human figures were actually "aquatic creatures with Triton's tails instead of human legs" and dated them about 1800.[1] The mermen wear a stylized version of the *nemes,* the headcloth of Egyptian kings, and pleated loincloths. To the Saint Petersburg aristocracy these sumptuous mounts must have looked as exotic as the brightly colored stone that they complement. The extreme muscularity of the Tritons represents a distinctly Russian interpretation of Neoclassicism that was highly unusual in Europe at that period.[2] It is interesting to compare the mounts with feminine counterparts, such as the slender ballerina-like Neoclassical maidens that decorate other Russian vases in this exhibition (see cat. no. 142).

The designer of these vases, Andrei N. Voronikhin (1759–1814), undoubtedly supervised the work of making and attaching the mounts.[3] Painstaking attention to even the smallest detail and a technically perfect execution cemented the Europe-wide reputation of Russian lapidary work during this period. Highly prized, pieces such as these were often chosen as diplomatic gifts. The mounts were made at the Imperial Bronze Foundry, located on Vasilievsky Island, across from the Winter Palace, in Saint Petersburg. The chief artistic figure there was the metal sculptor and chaser Pierre Agie (1752–1828), who arrived in Russia about 1781 and left in 1804 (see cat. no. 142). Soon after his arrival in Saint Petersburg he received the prestigious title Artistic Professor of Ornamental Sculpture from the Academy of Fine Arts.

The combination of sparkling gold and the warm red and brownish shades of breccia was very fashionable in the early 1800s. A posthumous portrait of Aleksandr Stroganov, director of the Imperial Lapidary Works, shows him seated in the shadow of a monumental bust of Zeus, next to an elaborately mounted table supported by Egyptian caryatids (fig. 121). On the table stands a lidded breccia vase mounted with Triton figures facing outward.

The Yekaterinburg Lapidary Works operated the second-oldest stone-grinding mill in the Russian Empire, built in 1726, five years after the mill at Peterhof, and only three years after the establishment of the town itself, on the threshold between Europe and Asia, in the Ural Mountains. The manufactory was able to process large hardstone blocks that would have been difficult to transport across the country.[4]   WK

REFERENCES: Makarov 1938, p. 76, no. 129; Mavrodina in *St. Petersburg um 1800* 1990, p. 409, no. 354; Mavrodina 2007, pp. 183–84, no. E, 13 (with bibliography)

1. Makarov 1938, p. 76, no. 129. The inspiration for the design possibly came from French bronze mounts on furnishings in the imperial Russian palaces. About 1767 the Parisian bronze worker Pierre Gouthière created two fine examples, a mermaid with a fish tail and a satyr with goat feet, that were mounted as handles on a pair of porphyry ewers (Qizilbash collection). Grand Duke Paul probably acquired them for the Winter Palace while in France on his grand tour in 1782 (see Christie's, Paris, December 19, 2007, sale cat., lot 802, with bibliography and stylistic comparisons).

2. Stylistically related Egyptianizing figures embellish other pairs of hardstone vases in the State Hermitage Museum.

See Makarov 1938, p. 22; for other examples, see p. 25, nos. 154, 155 (also Mavrodina 2007, pp. 195–97, no. E, 33, ill., and no. E, 34).

3. We know from documentary sources that Voronikhin was involved in the early 1800s in the manufacture of other Egyptianizing hardstone sculptures; see Albina Vasilyeva in *Stroganoff* 2000, p. 213, no. 73, ill. p. 182. See also Mavrodina in ibid., pp. 170, 212, no. 68, ill. p. 171, for a set of hardstone table ornaments with Egyptian figures, designed by Voronikhin between 1801 and 1806 for the Stroganov Palace in Saint Petersburg.

4. Tarasova 1990b, p. 408; see also Semenov and Shakinko 1982.

144. *Stroganov Tazza*

Peterhof Lapidary Works, near Saint Petersburg, possibly 1809–10
Design by Andrei N. Voronikhin
Malachite veneer on a supporting core
Mounts: Imperial Bronze Foundry, Academy of Fine Arts, Saint Petersburg
Gilded and patinated bronze
H. 52¾ in. (134 cm), bowl Diam. 42⅛ in. (107 cm)
The State Hermitage Museum, Saint Petersburg E 6721

PROVENANCE: Possibly commissioned by Aleksandr Sergeievich Stroganov, Stroganov Palace, Saint Petersburg; transferred to The State Hermitage Museum, 1925

The *Stroganov Tazza* is one of the most celebrated semiprecious stone objects in existence.[1] Considered a national treasure, it has seldom been allowed to leave its country of origin.

Among the many hardstones of which deposits were discovered in Russia in the eighteenth century and the first half of the nineteenth century—including aventurine, quartzite (see cat. no. 142), lapis lazuli, jasper, variously colored breccia, and rhodonite, to name just a few—malachite always commanded the most attention. The mineral's surface has color shades that run from emerald to a black green and can change dramatically in different lights. The mosaiclike Russian technique of veneering malachite (see entry for cat. no. 126) is impeccably executed in this display object, which in its breathtaking perfection has no equal.

The year in which this magnificent basin on a stand, or tazza, was made has been widely debated. The proposed dating ranges from the late eighteenth century to 1815 or later.[2] A painting made by Nikolai S. Nikitin in 1832 (fig. 122) shows the

Fig. 122. Nikolai Stepanovich Nikitin, *Picture Gallery of the Stroganov Palace*, 1832. Oil on canvas, 27⅝ × 38¼ in. The State Russian Museum, Saint Petersburg 5126

REFERENCES: Makarov 1938, p. 79, no. 135; Mavrodina in *Stroganoff* 2000, pp. 168, 212–13, no. 72, ill. pp. 162, 169; Mavrodina 2007, pp. 92–94, no. II, 86 (with bibliography)

picture gallery in the Stroganov Palace, with this monumental piece the focal point. (On the right, Nicolas Poussin's *The Rest on the Flight into Egypt*, another highlight of the Stroganov treasures, is easily recognized.)

Exhibiting the tazza among the Stroganov collection of paintings and sculptures may have been the idea of Andrei N. Voronikhin (1759–1814), who designed the picture gallery as well as the tazza and its gilded bronze tripod base. The latter takes the form of three winged genies, each supported on the leg of a goat, a creature associated with Bacchus. The ancient god of wine is alluded to again by the vine twisting around the metal pole that helps to support the heavy upper structure. The tripod form also has classical roots. It found a new use in the second half of the eighteenth century, when the *athénienne* was reinvented in France as a perfume burner or washstand.[3]

The distinguished mineralogist Alexander E. Fersman (1883–1945) observed of malachite and the Russian techniques for working it, "One has to visit the galleries of the Hermitage and look at the vases and bowls, one has to study the Malachite Room in the Winter Palace, to fully appreciate this stone of radiant power and *raffinesse*; one has to study the technical and artistic achievements [of the Russian lapidary craftsmen] to be able [to understand] what can be created out of this genuinely Russian stone."[4]

WK

1. It would exceed the limits of this entry to list all references to this important example of Russian decorative art, as almost all publications on ornamental hardstone objects, in every language, mention this key piece.
2. Mavrodina in *Stroganoff* 2000, pp. 212–13, no. 72.
3. See Rieder in Kisluk-Grosheide, Koeppe, and Rieder 2006, pp. 166–67, no. 69; Koeppe in ibid., pp. 216–18, no. 91.
4. Tarasova 1990a, p. 411.

Pietre Dure as an Artistic Medium

145. Strozzi stone collection

Rome, late 17th century
Leather, gilded bronze, parchment, and hardstones; two volumes, each 13 × 10⅞ in.
(33 × 27.5 cm)
Philip Hewat-Jaboor

PROVENANCE: Leone Strozzi, Rome; Palazzo Strozzi, Rome, until 1746; the present owner

REFERENCES: González-Palacios 1993, vol. 1, pp. 414–17, pl. LXX, vol. 2, figs. 746–50; González-Palacios in Bowron and Rishel 2000, p. 203, no. 91

This unusual collection of stones was designed to be displayed in two leather-bound volumes. Set into each cover is a piece of green porphyry surrounded by a gilded bronze laurel wreath and three gilded bronze crescent moons in the corners. The faux books are each composed of eight parchment pages backed with leather; holes have been cut into the parchment allowing for thinly sliced sections of various semiprecious stones, set into shallow cavities, to be displayed. The specimens are numbered in pen on the page and their names listed in Italian on the facing page. Drawn on the inside front cover of the first volume in pen and ink is a large cartouche containing the Strozzi family coat of arms, which contains the same crescent moons found on the cover. The inside front cover of the second volume has a drawing of a frame, draped with material, on brown-tinted paper. Written inside the frame are several lines from the sixteenth-century poet Ludovico Ariosto's *Orlando Furioso*: "Nor only marvellous the gems; the skill / Of the artificer and substance bright / So well contend for mastery."[1] The patron and owner of this collection, the prelate Leone Strozzi (1652–1722), no doubt requested the inclusion of this quotation from Ariosto, an especially appropriate one for a work that marries the intrinsic beauty of natural stones with a uniquely inventive manner of presentation.

Alvar González-Palacios has noted that the vogue for collecting hardstones began in Rome at the end of the seventeenth century.[2] The beauty of the Strozzi collection is extolled many times in eighteenth-century sources. The earliest mention of it is in Bernard de Montfaucon's 1702 *Diarium italicum*, which provides a terminus ante quem for its dating. Montfaucon describes the collection as "a book joining together marbles cut from the tablet with wonderful thinness, so that all the types of marbles to be looked at are presented in order to the person who opens it."[3] A quarter century later, the illustrious traveler and political philosopher Montesquieu visited the Palazzo Strozzi, on Rome's Largo Argentina, a frequent destination for erudite travelers because it is where Monsignor Strozzi kept his important collection of ancient sculpture and, especially, his cameos and medallions. Montesquieu paused over the "lovely book" whose pages presented every type of marble.[4] In 1739 the French scholar Charles de Brosses likewise stated his frank admiration for the books, but he mistakenly believed the stones had been painted on the parchment.[5] Such an error seems less strange if we remember that at the time there were catalogues of stones that were presented as elaborate books and in which the different qualities of the stones were carefully rendered in watercolor.

The Strozzi cameos and medallions were looted in 1746. Another devastating theft the same year likely claimed these two volumes, which vanished without a trace until they recently reemerged.

AG

facing page

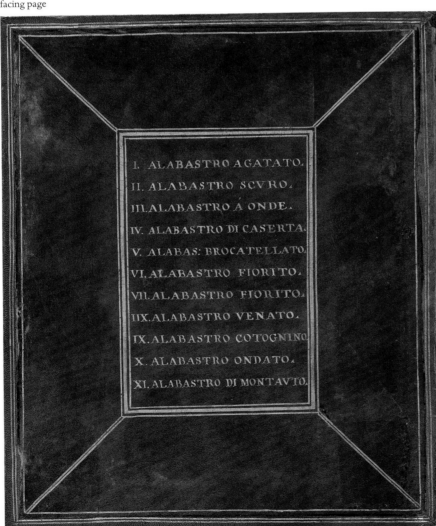

I. ALABASTRO AGATATO.
II. ALABASTRO SCVRO.
III. ALABASTRO A ONDE.
IV. ALABASTRO DI CASERTA.
V. ALABAS: BROCATELLATO.
VI. ALABASTRO FIORITO.
VII. ALABASTRO FIORITO.
IIX. ALABASTRO VENATO.
IX. ALABASTRO COTOGNINO.
X. ALABASTRO ONDATO.
XI. ALABASTRO DI MONTAVTO.

1. "Ne mirabil vi son le pietre sole, / ma la material e l'artificio adorno / contendon." English translation from Ariosto, *Orlando Furioso* (1905 ed.), p. 165 (canto 10, verse 60).
2. González-Palacios 1993, vol. 1, pp. 414–17.
3. "Liber item marmoreis ex tabulis mira tenuitate exsectis, concinnitus, ut evolventi omnia marmorum genera ordine expectanda offrantur." Montfaucon 1702, p. 48.
4. *Voyage en Italie*; see Montesquieu 1894–96, vol. 1, pp. 205–6.
5. Brosses 1885, vol. 2, pp. 110–11.

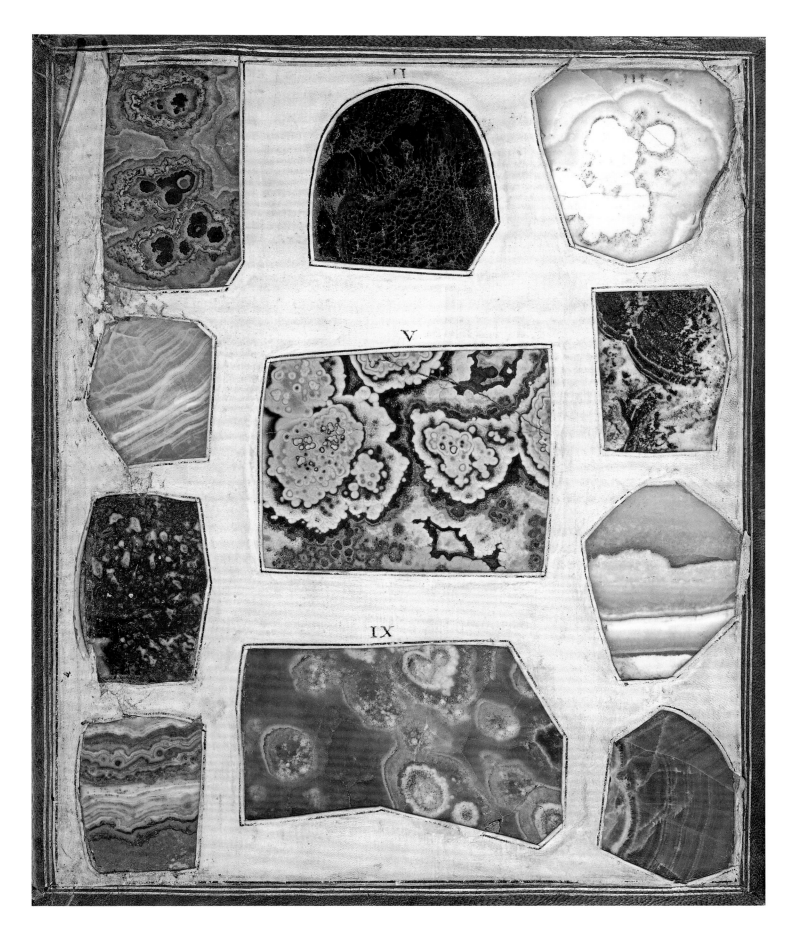

a   b   e   f

c   d   g   h

146. Eight polished samples from Heinrich Taddel's stone collection

Assembled 1764–75
Hardstones, paper labels
Left-hand group: a. jasper from
Zwickau; b. agate from
Cunnersdorf; c. agate from
Rochlitz; d. amethyst from
Cunnersdorf
Right-hand group: e. petrified wood
from the Chemnitz region; f. jasper
from Waldheim; g. jasper from
Bohemia; h. jasper from Bohemia
Each approx. 1½ × 1¼ in. (3.9 ×
3.3 cm)
Staatliche Kunstsammlungen
Dresden, Grünes Gewölbe 1937/2

PROVENANCE: Acquired by the
Grünes Gewölbe, 1937

REFERENCES: Quellmalz 1990,
p. 180, fig. 34; Kappel 1998, p. 174,
no. 72 and no. 72.1 (listed in inventory); Kappel in Kappel and
Weinhold 2007, pp. 299–300

The Seven Years' War (1756–63), which involved the major European powers and their colonial possessions, was devastating for Saxony. After it ended, ways were sought to shore up the country's finances. The discovery of new deposits of semiprecious stones and the rediscovery of those already known were an important aspect of such efforts. They involved some rather unconventional measures. In 1764, for example, an electoral decree authorized the Dresden goldsmith Heinrich Taddel (1715–1794)—who between 1748 and 1767 served as privy chamberlain and inspector of the castle museum known as the Grünes Gewölbe (Green Vault)—to search for semiprecious stones, freely and unhindered, in the electorate of Saxony, "in all corners of this country,"[1] and also to mine them. The fruit of these mineralogical investigations, which must have been carried out for more than a decade,[2] is the collection of polished stone samples Taddel put together, which originally numbered 214 pieces and of which 182 survive. The samples are identified, together with the places they were found, by handwritten labels on small strips of paper. In addition, a handwritten list signed by Taddel himself, unfortunately undated, contains all the relevant information about each sample. Included in the present exhibition are eight samples from this *Lithothek*, or lithotheque, a collection of various types of stones arranged by source (see also cat. no. 103).[3]

JK

1. "in hiesigen Landen aller Orten." Sächsisches Hauptstaatsarchiv Dresden, Loc. 36179, vol. 1, fols. 3, 33, 88; quoted in Quellmalz 1990, p. 79, n. 240.
2. In 1775 the concession passed to Taddel's son-in-law, the Dresden court jeweler Johann Christian Neuber, who achieved fame with his gold boxes adorned with samples of Saxon stones. For Taddel and Neuber, see Kappel in Kappel and Weinhold 2007, pp. 299–300. For examples of Neuber's work, see fig. 71 and cat. no. 92 in this publication.
3. The present selection of stone samples corresponds, in sequence, to nos. 6, 24, 40, 60, 132, and 160 (native stones) and nos. 24 and 23 (foreign stones) in the handwritten list signed by Taddel: "Catalogus Einer Sammlung von Orientalischen und andern Aus- und Innländischen Steinen"; paper, bound in pink silk, 12⅝ × 8¼ in., Staatliche Kunstsammlungen Dresden, Grünes Gewölbe. See S. Huber and P. Huber 2006.

147. Workbench for the production of cameos and intaglios

Tuscany, late 18th or early
19th century
Walnut wood, iron, and brass;
overall 33⅛ × 36¼ × 44⅞ in. (84 ×
92 × 114 cm)
Figurine: bronze; H. 10½ in. (26 cm)
Museo dell'Opificio delle Pietre
Dure, Florence OA 1911:1511

PROVENANCE: Probably
Accademia di Belle Arti, Florence;
Opificio delle Pietre Dure, from
1860; later Museo dell'Opificio

REFERENCES: Mazzoni in Giusti,
Mazzoni, and Pampaloni Martelli
1978, pp. 357–58, no. 681, pls. 610,
612; Giusti 1992, p. 274; Giusti in
Giusti 2006a, p. 244, no. 161

The Museo dell'Opificio delle Pietre Dure—the direct successor of the Galleria dei Lavori in Florence, where hardstone mosaics were made for the grand dukes—has a rare collection of workbenches and tools that date to the eighteenth and nineteenth centuries. They were used, for the most part, to produce three-dimensional objects such as vases, reliefs, small sculptures, cameos, and carved gemstones.

The furniture is practically designed and without decorative elements; this workbench for carving cameos and gemstones is the single exception. Affixed to the upper shelf is a bronze figurine of Atlas, the Titan of classical mythology who carried the Earth on his bent back. The globe contains a pulley connected to a pedal below. Pressure on the pedal causes the spindles that protrude from the globe to rotate, and drills inserted into the spindles are used to cut hardstones. Thus the bench is functional as well as decorative. The figure of Atlas also has a double meaning. It symbolizes the effort exerted by the craftsman plying his trade at the bench below, and it recalls the antiquity of the tradition that the master carvers of gems in the Neoclassical period strove to revive and continue.

The bronze figurine is not the workbench's only refinement. The stand on the lower shelf has been shaped ergonomically to facilitate the performing of tasks by the craftsman seated at the bench. The nineteen small drawers can be locked or unlocked at the same time with a single key, and one of the drawers contains a wooden case for storing the 105 drills of various sizes and types used during different phases of work. The Museo dell'Opificio's collection of furniture includes two benches similarly outfitted. It is possible that all three were given to the museum workshop in 1860 by the nearby Accademia di Belle Arti, where, in 1808, a school for carving gemstones opened under the direction of the famous engraver Antonio Santarelli.[1]

AG

1. An inventory of 1860 records the transfer of various workbenches with *castelletti* (the *castelletto* is the fixed vertical arm supporting the drill mechanism—on the present example, the Atlas figure) from the Accademia to the Opificio.

A note on the traditional process of creating hardstone mosaics

REFERENCES: Rossi (Ferdinando) 1967, pp. 71–80; Pampaloni Martelli 1978; Rossi (Ferdinando) 1984, pp. 78–83; Rossi (Ferdinando) 1988; Giusti 1992, pp. 273–93; Giusti 1999

Every pietre dure mosaic produced in the grand-ducal workshop in Florence was based on a full-scale, painted design commissioned from an artist.[1] Beginning in the sixteenth century these models were executed either in oil on canvas as finished paintings or, more often, in watercolor on paper (see cat. nos. 108, 109). When choosing his colors, the artist had to consider the natural palette of the stones available and set forth general, rather than precise, chromatic instructions.

Once finished, the design was given to the master responsible for executing the mosaic. The artist/designer could trust in the skill of the craftsmen who executed the pietre dure work to interpret the guidelines in his design, using the wide range of colored stones at his disposal. Designs for large pieces were entrusted to several craftsmen so as to shorten the length of time required to produce them. The master craftsman, using a pencil or pen and ink, would mark out its divisions and the stone he would use for each part (see fig. 123). This stage was crucial because the choice of the individual

stone pieces had an enormous impact on the quality of the final work. The next stage, however, even more important and laborious, involved the final choice of colors and the final determination of the correct pieces of stone to be used in the mosaic. The master examined the many available slices of stone that had been selected and cut by less experienced craftsmen. He had to work with extraordinary patience and self-assuredness as he looked for appropriate material for the background as well as the colors that would best suit the composition and clearly suggest the effects of light, shadow, and three-dimensionality sought by the Florentine mosaicists. The consummate skill of the master craftsmen was what made it possible for the grand dukes to refer to the pieces produced in their workshop as "paintings in stone."

The tracings of the original model allowed the

flaw, the whole slice of stone was backed with a thin layer of slate to prevent it from breaking as it was being cut. This backing was left in place when the pieces of stone were assembled into the whole composition. Then the entire mosaic was backed with a single piece of slate that acted as a support.

To make pietre dure relief elements, the craftsman also used a drawn design, which in this case had to be translated into three dimensions (see fig. 125). Here too the choice of an appropriate stone was crucial for achieving a satisfactory result. The task was given to a highly specialized artisan able to judge how color changes or veins within the raw material could best be utilized.

The same kinds of tools used to cut pieces of stone inlay in the Renaissance are utilized today. Because they are very simple tools, the process of cutting and shaping stones depends largely on the craftsman's profound skill. The slice of stone is held in a vertical position by a vice attached to the wooden workbench, which prevents the stone from moving while it is being cut. That cutting is done with a small saw, called an *archetto*, made from a piece of bent chestnut wood and an iron wire (fig. 124). With each stroke of the saw the

Fig. 124. A master of Florentine mosaic work cutting stones in the traditional fashion, using a chestnut bow-saw, or *archetto*, whose iron wire is spread with dampened abrasive powders. Museo dell'Opificio delle Pietre Dure, Florence

Fig. 125. Stages in the making of a pietre dure relief of a lion mask. Left: model, a drawing on paper, surrounded by various stages of cutting of the lion mask. Center: metal drill bits and cutting heads that are used with a tool for working hardstone, stored in a wooden board; plaster casts of cameos to be used as models. Right: non-hardstone materials including mother-of-pearl, shells, and coral. Museo dell'Opificio delle Pietre Dure, Florence

craftsman applies damp emery—an abrasive grit—over the cut he is making, spreading it with a tool he holds in his free hand. The combined action of the wire and grit enables the master to cut the stone with precision along the outline pasted to it. The work proceeds slowly, especially if the stone is particularly hard. The pieces of stone for the background that frames the mosaic's motif are cut in the same laborious way.

To make the seams between the stones, in what are essentially maniacal puzzles, as invisible as possible, the cut stones must be perfect. This perfection is ensured when the pieces of stone that were cut with the *archetto* are rubbed with metal files and abrasive grit to adjust their thickness. At this point assembling of the pieces begins. The cut stones are turned upside down and glued together, being held in place temporarily with small wooden dowels or pieces of slate that work as clamps. To make sure the finished mosaic will be absolutely smooth, a stone slab is mortared to its front side. The back of the mosaic is smoothed with a coarse abrasive. Spacers are applied to ensure that the two sides of the mosaic remain perfectly parallel. The mosaic is now ready to be backed. A natural glue, made of rosin and beeswax, which was also used to hold the individual pieces of stone together, is heated until it liquefies and is applied to the back of the mosaic. A slab of slate is attached to the back of the work to become its support. Once this support is in place, the mosaic is turned over, and the slate that was used to protect its surface is removed. The surface emerges perfectly assembled and smooth, although it is opaque. The luminous splendor of the stone, which accounts for much of its appeal, is created with the final polishing. For this, the surface of the mosaic is rubbed with an increasingly fine, damp grit. A small block of stone is used in the first few passes, but as work progresses more elastic lead sheets are employed, allowing the grit to better adhere to the virtually imperceptible variations of the surface and cover it completely. Then the phantasmagorical colors of the stones appear, illuminated in the intangible, reflective brilliance sought by the Florentine craftsmen, a seductive luster that enthralled both those who made the mosaics and those for whom they were created.   A G

1. The tools and materials shown in this text were gathered by Giancarlo Raddi, longtime head of the pietre dure workshop at the present-day Opificio delle Pietre Dure in Florence.

GLOSSARY
BIBLIOGRAPHY
INDEX
PHOTOGRAPH AND COPYRIGHT CREDITS

Fig. 126. Anton Mozart, *Delivery of the Collector's Cabinet by Philipp Hainhofer to Duke Philipp II von Pommern-Stettin on August 30, 1617, at Schloss Stettin*, Augsburg, before 1617. Oil on wood, 15½ × 17⅞ in. Staatliche Museen zu Berlin, Stiftung Preussischer Kulturbesitz, Kunstgewerbemuseum P 183a. The monumental ebony cabinet, lavishly decorated with silver, hardstones, and paintings, had also been furnished with precious collector's items. The art merchant Philipp Hainhofer (see cat. nos. 78, 79) here presents to the duke and duchess for their examination a drawer of the cabinet filled with small treasures. Standing at the right and on the staircase are some twenty-seven artists and craftsmen who were involved in the making of the cabinet; numbers key them to identifications on the back of the painting giving their names and professions. The cabinet was destroyed during World War II, but many of its contents were saved—including this small painting, made before the cabinet's presentation and kept in a secret compartment.

Glossary

FLORIAN KNOTHE

SMALL CAPITALS indicate that a term is defined in this Glossary.

Albarese, or **alberese**: a white, marblelike limestone. Two varieties are PIETRA PAESINA and PIETRA D'ARNO, or LINEATO D'ARNO.

amber: a fossil resin that was long considered a SEMIPRECIOUS STONE. It occurs in a range of translucent, opaque, and milky orange-yellow colors.

arteficialia: precious man-made objects, both ornamental and scientific, collected and displayed together with NATURALIA in princely KUNSTKAMMERN.

arte grossa: the lapidary's art of cutting, grinding, and polishing HARDSTONES.

arte minuta: the lapidary's art of finely engraving HARDSTONES.

bardiglio: marble from the Apuan Alps that is found in different shades of gray.

bianco antico: type of white BRECCIA.

black Belgian marble: dense black marble found at several sites in southern Belgium. It was frequently used as the background stone in PIETRE DURE panels, often as an alternative to the more expensive PARAGONE.

bleu turquin: bluish gray marble quarried in Italy (near Genoa) and in France and frequently used in Neoclassical works of the late eighteenth and early nineteenth centuries.

blue john: see **fluorspar**.

Boulle marquetry: type of MARQUETRY popularized by the French court ÉBÉNISTE André-Charles Boulle (1642–1732) in which thin pieces of precious materials in contrasting colors, most typically tortoiseshell and brass, are glued together and then cut in a design, usually an arabesque or intricate foliage pattern. The cutout pieces are inlaid within each other—light within dark or dark within light— and are VENEERED onto the CARCASS of a piece of furniture.

breccia: limestone—often mistakenly referred to as marble—that is composed of large angular chunks, or clasts, of previously formed rock. During the eighteenth century it was widely used in plain sheets on the tops of COMMODES and for sculpture and inlay. Breccia is found in many regions of Europe; varieties often bear the name of their place of origin, for example, *breccia di Tivoli*.

brocatelle, brocatello, **or Siena marble**: cloudy white marble veined in gray, yellow, and red, in which the yellow usually prevails and which often includes fossiliferous streaks. It is quarried around Siena and also exists in large quantities in Spain and in the Altay Shan Mountains in Siberia.

cabochon: a GEMSTONE that has been smoothly shaped and polished rather than faceted. The top is usually convex (cut *en cabochon*) and the bottom flat.

cailloux: French word meaning small stones or pebbles. *Cailloux d'Égypte* is an Egyptian jasper with strong dark bands that often resemble landscapes.

calcedonia: Italian word for chalcedony, a variety of quartz.

cameo: small carving in raised relief on a piece of opaque SEMIPRECIOUS STONE, coral, or shell. Usually the material is stratified, having two or more unlike layers, and the carving is done so that the relief and the background are in different colors.

carcass: undecorated wooden framework of a piece of furniture.

cipolin: highly decorative whitish marble traversed by green veins and resembling the cross section of an onion (*cipollino* means "little onion" in Italian). It is mostly used for columns and other architectural elements.

commesso di pietre dure, or *commesso* (pl. *commessi*): an assemblage of thin slices of stone cut into diverse shapes, fitted seamlessly together, and secured to a stone backing, typically of slate, to form an ornamental or pictorial panel. In a relief *commesso di pietre dure*, the stone pieces are carved in relief rather than flat.

commode: a chest of drawers.

corallino: red coral; also the term for bright red Sicilian jasper, which was employed as a substitute for coral in FLORENTINE MOSAIC panels. True coral was commonly used by Milanese gem cutters.

damascene: metalworking technique, originally practiced in Damascus, in which one metal is inlaid within another—such as gold or silver in steel—in intricate ornamental patterns.

Derbyshire spar: see **fluorspar**.

ebanista: see *ébéniste*.

ébéniste: French word for a cabinetmaker specializing in furniture surfaced with VENEER. The Italian equivalent is *ebanista*.

Eger marquetry: type of MARQUETRY developed in the town of Eger in Bohemia (now the Czech Republic) in which pieces of wood carved in relief and stained are assembled on a support to make ornamental or pictorial images that somewhat resemble relief COMMESSI DI PIETRE DURE.

étui: French word meaning case.

fall front: a wooden panel hinged to the front of a piece of furniture so that it can be lowered to a horizontal position to serve as a surface for writing or displaying objects.

Florentine mosaic: a name given to COMMESSO DI PIETRE DURE because the art form was perfected in Florence in the sixteenth century before spreading across Europe.

fluorspar, also called Derbyshire spar or blue john: a banded purple-blue fluorite quarried in Derbyshire, England, among other places. It is most often made into vases and other ornamental objects.

fruttante, fruttista (pl. *fruttanti, fruttisti*): Italian terms for a lapidary who specialized in carving colorful hardstones into the three-dimensional fruits that sometimes play a part in PIETRE DURE decoration.

Galleria dei Lavori: a group of Florentine workshops specializing in different crafts, officially established in the Palazzo degli Uffizi in 1588 as court workshops for the Medici grand dukes. The Galleria dei Lavori outlasted the Medici and the Habsburg-Lorraine grand dukes who followed them. In the nineteenth century the lapidary workshops became the Opificio delle Pietre Dure, which now specializes in restoration.

Garde-Meuble de la Couronne: Royal warehouse of furniture and furnishings for the residence of the king of France and his courtiers.

gem or **gemstone**: cut and polished precious or SEMIPRECIOUS STONE, used in jewelry or to adorn objects.

giallo di Siena: a veined yellow marble quarried in the valley of the Elsa River, near Siena in Tuscany.

glyptic: ultimately derived from the Greek term for "carved," the word denotes the art of carving and engraving HARDSTONES in both the CAMEO and the INTAGLIO techniques, and also of carving SEMIPRECIOUS STONES into objects such as vessels.

golden alabaster, also called **Oriental alabaster**: a rare stalagmitic limestone imported from Egypt and the Far East into Europe, where it was cherished for its rich yellow color.

hardstone: a SEMIPRECIOUS STONE that has a hardness of at least 6 on the Mohs scale, such as rock crystal or jasper. The term is often broadened to include softer stones such as lapis lazuli.

intaglio: a negative image incised in HARDSTONE that forms a raised image when the stone is impressed into a soft substance; also a GEM so carved.

intarsia: an inlay of woods of varied colors, both natural and stained, into cavities carved in a solid wooden matrix, to make a pattern. Compare MARQUETRY.

Kunstkammer (pl. *Kunstkammern*): the chamber in which a collection of curiosities and wonders was kept. Renaissance and Baroque princes assembled ARTEFICIALIA and NATURALIA in these chambers, together with books, drawings, prints, and paintings, for humanist and scientific study.

lithotheque, *Lithotek* (German), *litoteca* (Italian): a collection of stones, organized by type and geologic area of origin.

marchand-mercier: French term for an eighteenth-century dealer in luxury furnishings who exerted influence over the design and manufacture of furniture.

marmo bigio or **bigio antico**: white marble quarried in Greece and used as a building material and in mosaic panels.

marquetry or **wooden marquetry**: decorative technique in which small, variously colored pieces of different wood VENEERS, and sometimes also of ivory and mother-of-pearl, are assembled to form a pattern or an image. Aesthetically related to PIETRE DURE and evolved from BOULLE MARQUETRY, wooden marquetry became extremely popular in the Rococo period for decorating the surfaces of furniture, especially works made in Paris from the 1730s to the 1770s. See also **Eger marquetry**.

menuisier: cabinetmaker; a woodworker who produces furniture and paneling in solid wood, before the application of any VENEER or other surface decoration. His work is called *menuiserie*.

micromosaic: type of MOSAIC composed of minute pieces of glass or stone assembled to form an ornamental or pictorial panel used to decorate surfaces such as tabletops, snuffboxes, and jewelry.

modello: model or preparatory design.

mosaic: although frequently referring to a composition made of small squares (TESSERAE) of stone or glass, when used with PIETRE DURE works the word means a COMMESSO.

naturalia: objects found in nature, such as pearls and shells, appreciated for their beauty and rarity, that were collected and often kept in *KUNSTKAMMERN* and displayed together with *ARTEFICIALIA*.

nero antico: a dark gray or black BRECCIA.

opus sectile: ancient Roman technique of creating an ornamental or pictorial design using flat, shaped pieces of marble and HARDSTONES; the ancestor of *COMMESSO*.

Oriental alabaster: see **golden alabaster**.

paragone: a black siliceous HARDSTONE that was both quarried in Italy (in Bergamo) and imported into Tuscany from Flanders. It was employed as a background in seventeenth- and eighteenth-century FLORENTINE MOSAIC panels. Compare **black Belgian marble**.

pelta (pl. **peltae**): an ancient arched shield shape that commonly appears in Roman MOSAICS.

pierre de rapport: French term for inlaid stonework or MOSAIC.

pietra paesina and **pietra d'Arno**, or **lineato d'Arno**: two varieties of ALBARESE often selected for PIETRE DURE work because of their markings suggestive of landscape; the latter is found in and near the bed of the Arno River in Tuscany.

pietre dure, **pierres fines** (**pierres dures**), **pietras duras**: Italian, French, and Spanish terms, respectively, meaning HARDSTONES; also used to signify artwork made with hardstones (and sometimes soft stones).

pietre tenere: soft stones; also used to signify artworks made of them. Soft stones—that is, stones graded at less than 6 on the Mohs scale of hardness, for example, marble, alabaster, and soapstone—are in fact often used in PIETRE DURE work.

pietrista: a lapidary.

Portor marble: a black marble quarried at the foot of the Apuan Alps, near Carrara. There are two varieties; the finer is veined in yellow, the other in white.

repoussé work: metalworking technique in which a design in relief is created by hammering and pressing a thin sheet of metal on the reverse side.

rosso antico: fine-grained, deep red marble, occasionally with thin black veins and white markings, quarried in Greece and used since early Greek and Roman times primarily for architectural elements.

scagliola: imitation stone prepared by mixing finely ground plaster with glue, pigments, and stone dust, allowing it to harden, and then giving the surface a shiny polish. It is used in interiors as a substitute for marble panels and columns. In wet, pastelike form, scagliola can be spread into cavities in a stone matrix; it can also be cut into pieces and assembled to make pictorial and ornamental wall panels and tabletops in the manner of FLORENTINE MOSAIC.

sectilia pavimenta: a patterned pavement assembled from small, usually square pieces of HARDSTONE or glass.

semiprecious stone: a natural stone mined from the earth and valued for its coloration or patterning, but not as rare as precious stone; HARDSTONE.

soft stone: see *pietre tenere*.

stipo: a large cupboard or cabinet.

studiolo: a study or private chamber; also, a small cabinet placed on a table.

tabatière: snuffbox.

tessera (pl. **tesserae**): small, squarish piece of HARDSTONE, ceramic, or glass, used in a traditional (not Florentine) MOSAIC.

veneer: thin layer of wood or MARQUETRY applied to the CARCASS of a piece of furniture as its surface layer.

verde antico: a type of banded green BRECCIA.

verre églomisé: glass decorated on the reverse with a painted or gilded design or metal foil and then backed with varnish or another sheet of glass.

Bibliography

Académie Royale d'Architecture 1911–29
Procès-Verbaux de l'Académie Royale d'Architecture, 1691–1793. 10 vols. Société de l'Histoire de l'Art Français. Paris, 1911–29.

Acidini 2003
Cristina Acidini Luchinat. "La missione dell'Opificio delle Pietre Dure: Appunti e riflessioni." *OPD restauro* 15 (2003; pub. 2004), pp. 7–14.

Acidini et al. 2002
Cristina Acidini Luchinat et al. *The Medici, Michelangelo, and the Art of Late Renaissance Florence.* Exh. cat., Art Institute of Chicago; Detroit Institute of Arts. Detroit, 2002. [Italian ed.: *L'ombra del genio: Michelangelo e l'arte a Firenze, 1537–1631.* Edited by Marco Chiarini, Alan P. Darr, and Cristina Giannini. Exh. cat., Palazzo Strozzi, Florence. Milan, 2002.]

"Acquisitions" 1990
"Acquisitions / 1989." *J. Paul Getty Museum Journal* 18 (1990), pp. 157–209.

"Acquisitions" 1993
"Acquisitions / 1992." *J. Paul Getty Museum Journal* 21 (1993), pp. 101–63.

Adriaensens 1993
Anne-Mie Adriaensens. *Driemaal exotisch drinken: Cacao, thee en koffie.* Provinciaal Museum Sterckshof-Zilvercentrum. Antwerp, 1993.

Age of Neo-Classicism **1972**
The Age of Neo-Classicism. Exh. cat., Royal Academy of Arts; Victoria and Albert Museum. London, 1972.

Alcouffe 1974
Daniel Alcouffe. "The Collection of Cardinal Mazarin's Gems." *Burlington Magazine* 116 (September 1974), pp. 514–26.

Alcouffe 1977
Daniel Alcouffe. "La Collection de gemmes de Louis XIV: Identification de quelques pièces aliénées." *Bulletin de la Société de l'Histoire de l'Art Français,* 1977 (pub. 1979), pp. 109–25.

Alcouffe 1999
Daniel Alcouffe. "Un Aspect du goût de Marie-Antoinette: Les Vases en pierres dures." *Versalia,* no. 2 (1999), pp. 6–15.

Alcouffe 2001
Daniel Alcouffe. *Les Gemmes de la Couronne.* Exh. cat., Musée du Louvre. Paris, 2001.

Alcouffe, Dion-Tenenbaum, and Lefébure 1993
Daniel Alcouffe, Anne Dion-Tenenbaum, and Amaury Lefébure. *Furniture Collections in the Louvre.* Vol. 1, *Middle Ages, Renaissance, Seventeenth–Eighteenth Centuries (Ébénisterie), Nineteenth Century.* 2 vols. Dijon, 1993.

Alfieri 2000
Massimo Alfieri. "New Notes on Giacomo Raffaelli and Michelangelo Barberi." In Jeanette Hanisee Gabriel, *Micromosaics,* pp. 263–80. Gilbert Collection. London, 2000.

Alfter 1986
Dieter Alfter. *Die Geschichte des Augsburger Kabinettschranks.* Schwäbische Geschichtsquellen und Forschungen 15. Augsburg, 1986. [Originally presented as the author's Ph.D. diss., Universität Hamburg, 1981.]

Angeli 1989
Wilhelm Angeli. *Die Venus von Willendorf.* Vienna, 1989.

Arbeteta Mira 2001
Letizia Arbeteta Mira. *El tesoro del Delfín: Alhajas de Felipe V recibidas por herencia de su padre Luis, gran delfín de Francia.* Museo Nacional del Prado. Madrid, 2001.

Ariosto, *Orlando Furioso* (1905 ed.)
Ludovico Ariosto. *Orlando Furioso.* [Ferrara], 1516/1532. English trans.: *The Orlando Furioso of Ludovico Ariosto.* Translated by William Stewart Rose. 2 vols. Bohn's Illustrated Library. London, 1905.

El arte de la corte de Nápoles **1990**
El arte de la corte de Nápoles en el siglo XVIII. Exh. cat., Museo Arqueológico Nacional. Madrid, 1990.

Artisti alla corte granducale **1969**
Artisti alla corte granducale. Exh. cat., Appartamenti Monumentali, Palazzo Pitti. Florence, 1969.

Arts in Latin America **2006**
The Arts in Latin America, 1492–1820. Exh. cat., Philadelphia Museum of Art; Antiguo Colegio de San Ildefonso, Mexico City; Los Angeles County Museum of Art. Philadelphia, Mexico City, Los Angeles, and New Haven, 2006.

Arts under Napoleon **1978**
The Arts under Napoleon. Exh. cat., The Metropolitan Museum of Art. New York, 1978.

Asche 1978
Sigfried Asche. *Balthasar Permoser: Leben und Werk.* Berlin, 1978.

Aschengreen Piacenti 1965
Cristina Aschengreen Piacenti. "Two Jewellers at the Grand Ducal Court of Florence around 1618."

Mitteilungen des Kunsthistorischen Institutes in Florenz 12 (December 1965), pp. 107–24.

Aschengreen Piacenti 1967
Cristina Aschengreen Piacenti, ed. *Il Museo degli Argenti a Firenze.* Gallerie e musei di Firenze. Milan, 1967.

Aschengreen Piacenti 1974
Cristina Aschengreen Piacenti. "Osservazioni intorno a un inginocchiatoio al Museo degli Argenti." *Antichità viva* 13, no. 3 (May–June 1974), pp. 44–47.

Aschengreen Piacenti 1981
Cristina Aschengreen Piacenti. "Ambre." In Cristina Aschengreen Piacenti, Hugh Honour, and Ronald Lightbown, *Ambre, avori, lacche, cere,* pp. 19–26. I quaderni dell'antiquariato. Collana di arti decorative 2, anno I. Milan, 1981.

Aschengreen Piacenti 2003
Cristina Aschengreen Piacenti. "La Collection des grands-ducs de Toscane." In *Les Vases en pierres dures: Actes du colloque organisé au Musée du Louvre par le Service Culturel le 9 juin 2001,* edited by Daniel Alcouffe, pp. 31–56. Paris, 2003.

Asvarishch 1993
Boris Asvarishch. *Kushelevskaia Gallery: Western European Painting of the Nineteenth Century.* [In Russian.] State Hermitage Museum. Saint Petersburg, 1993.

Augsburger Barock **1968**
Augsburger Barock. Exh. cat., Rathaus and Holbeinhaus. Augsburg, 1968.

Aumale 1861
Henri-Eugène-Philippe-Louis d'Orléans, duc d'Aumale, ed. *Inventaire de tous les meubles du Cardinal Mazarin, dressé en 1653, et publié d'après l'original.* London, 1861.

Avery 1997
Charles Avery. *Bernini: Genius of the Baroque.* London, 1997.

Babelon 1897
Ernest Babelon. *Catalogue des camées antiques et modernes de la Bibliothèque Nationale.* 2 vols. Paris, 1897.

Bacci 1963a
Mina Bacci. "Jacopo Ligozzi e la sua posizione nella pittura fiorentina." *Proporzioni* 4 (1963), pp. 46–84.

Bacci 1963b
Mina Bacci. "A Portable Altar by Ligozzi." *Bulletin* (Allen Memorial Art Museum, Oberlin College) 20, no. 2 (Winter 1963), pp. 47–55.

Bacci and Forlani Tempesti 1961
Mina Bacci and Anna Forlani [Tempesti], eds. *Mostra di disegni di Jacopo Ligozzi (1547–1626).* Gabinetto Disegni e Stampe degli Uffizi 12. Florence, 1961.

Baer 1980
Winfried Baer. "Gold and Precious Stone: The Boxes of Frederick the Great." *Connaissance des arts* (U.S. ed.), no. 11 (December 1980), pp. 92–97.

Baer 1992
Winfried Baer. "Berliner Golddosen für den König." In Hohenzollern 1992, pp. 210–19.

Baer 1993
Winfried Baer. *Prunk-Tabatièren Friedrichs des Grossen.* Exh. cat., Neue Kammern, Park Sanssouci. Organized by the Stiftung Schlösser und Gärten Potsdam-Sanssouci. Munich, 1993.

Baetjer 1995
Katharine Baetjer. *European Paintings in The Metropolitan Museum of Art by Artists Born before 1865: A Summary Catalogue.* New York, 1995.

Baetjer and Draper 1999
Katharine Baetjer and James David Draper, eds. *"Only the Best": Masterpieces of the Calouste Gulbenkian Museum, Lisbon.* Exh. cat., The Metropolitan Museum of Art. New York, 1999.

Baglione 1642
Giovanni Baglione. *Le vite de' pittori, scultori et architetti: Dal Pontificato di Gregorio XIII del 1572, in fino a' tempi di Papa Urbano Ottavo nel 1642.* Rome, 1642. [Repr.: Edited by Jacob Hess and Herwarth Röttgen. 3 vols. Studi e testi 367. Vatican City, 1995.]

Baldini 1978–81
Umberto Baldini. *Teoria del restauro e unità di metodologia.* 2 vols. Arte e restauro. Florence, 1978–81.

Baldini, Giusti, and Pampaloni Martelli 1979
Umberto Baldini, Annamaria Giusti, and Annapaula Pampaloni Martelli, eds. *La Cappella dei Principi e le pietre dure a Firenze.* Gallerie e musei di Firenze. Milan, 1979.

Baldinucci 1681–1728 (1845–47 ed.)
Filippo Baldinucci. *Notizie de' professori del disegno da Cimabue in qua . . . .* 6 vols. Florence, 1681–1728. 1845–47 ed.: Edited by Ferdinando Ranalli. 5 vols. Florence, 1845–47.

Barocchi and Gaeta Bertelà 1990
Paola Barocchi and Giovanna Gaeta Bertelà. "Danni e furti di Giuseppe Bianchi in galleria." *Annali della Scuola Normale Superiore di Pisa,* 3rd ser., 20, nos. 2–3 (1990), pp. 553–68.

Bartoli and Maser 1953
Lando Bartoli and Edward Andrew Maser. *Il Museo dell'Opificio delle Pietre Dure di Firenze.* [In Italian and English.] Prato, 1953.

Battersby 1974
Martin Battersby. *Trompe l'Oeil: The Eye Deceived.* New York, 1974.

Bauer and Haupt 1976
Rotraud Bauer and Herbert Haupt, eds. "Das Kunstkammerinventar Kaiser Rudolfs II., 1607–1611." *Jahrbuch der Kunsthistorischen Sammlungen in Wien* 72 (1976).

Baulez 2003
Christian Baulez. "Versailles: L'Appartement du Roi retrouve son éclat." *L'Estampille/L'Objet d'art,* no. 378 (March 2003), pp. 72–82.

Baulez 2007
Christian Baulez. "Versailles à l'encan." In Christian Baulez, *Versailles: Deux Siècles d'histoire de l'art; études et chroniques de Christian Baulez,* pp. 91–97. Versailles, 2007. [Originally published in *Connaissance des arts,* 1989 (special number).]

Baumgärtner 1995
Sabine Baumgärtner. "Der Gastwirt als Kunstagent: Augsburger Steinschnittarbeiten für den Württemberger Hof." *Weltkunst* 65, no. 13 (July 1, 1995), pp. 1809–11.

Baumstark and Seling 1994
Reinhold Baumstark and Helmut Seling, eds. *Silber und Gold: Augsburger Goldschmiedekunst für die Höfe Europas.* 2 vols. Exh. cat., Bayerisches Nationalmuseum. Munich, 1994.

Bayern 1972
Bayern: Kunst und Kultur. Exh. cat., Münchner Stadtmuseum. Munich, 1972.

Becherucci and Brunetti 1969
Luisa Becherucci and Giulia Brunetti, eds. *Il Museo dell'Opera del Duomo a Firenze.* 2 vols. Gallerie e musei di Firenze. Venice, 1969.

Belting 1984
Hans Belting. "Das Aachener Münster im 19. Jahrhundert: Zur ersten Krise des Denkmal-Konzepts." *Wallraf-Richartz-Jahrbuch* 45 (1984), pp. 257–89.

Bennett and Sargentson 2008
Shelley Bennett and Carolyn Sargentson. *French Eighteenth-Century Art at the Huntington.* New Haven, 2008.

Bertani and Nardinocchi 1995
Licia Bertani and Elisabetta Nardinocchi. *Treasures of San Lorenzo: 100 Masterpieces in Gold and Silver. The Medici Chapels, Firenze.* Florence and Livorno, 1995.

Berti 1951–52
Luciano Berti. "Matteo Nigetti." *Rivista d'arte,* 3rd ser., 2 (1951–52; pub. 1953), pp. 93–106.

Berti 1967
Luciano Berti. *Il principe dello studiolo: Francesco I dei Medici e la fine del Rinascimento fiorentino.* Grandangolare. Florence, 1967.

Bertolotti 1877
Antonino Bertolotti. "Esportazione di oggetti di belle arti da Roma nei secoli XVI, XVII, XVIII." *Archivio storico, artistico, archeologico e letterario della città e provincia di Roma* 2 (1877), pp. 21–46.

Bertolotti 1889
Antonino Bertolotti. *Le arti minori alla corte di Mantova nei secoli XV, XVI e XVII: Ricerche storiche negli archivi mantovani.* Milan, 1889.

Beschi 1983
Luigi Beschi. "Le antichità di Lorenzo il Magnifico: Caratteri e vicende." In *Gli Uffizi, quattro secoli di una galleria: Atti del Convegno Internazionale di Studi (Firenze 20–24 settembre 1982),* edited by Paola Barocchi and Giovanna Ragionieri, vol. 1, pp. 161–76. Florence, 1983.

Bimbenet-Privat 2002
Michèle Bimbenet-Privat. *Les Orfèvres et l'orfèvrerie de Paris au XVIIᵉ siècle.* 2 vols. Paris, 2002.

Bimbenet-Privat 2003
Michèle Bimbenet-Privat. "Vases en pierres dures de la collection de Louis XIV provenant des ateliers du Louvre et des Tuileries (1620–1650)." In *Les Vases en pierres dures: Actes du colloque organisé au Musée du Louvre par le Service Culturel le 9 juin 2001,* edited by Daniel Alcouffe, pp. 139–64. Paris, 2003.

Bimbenet-Privat and Crépin-Leblond 2004
Michèle Bimbenet-Privat and Thierry Crépin-Leblond. "Un Inventaire inédit d'objets d'orfèvrerie choisis au cabinet du Roi par Marie de Médicis." In *Objets d'art: Mélanges en l'honneur de Daniel Alcouffe,* pp. 110–23. Dijon, 2004.

Binding 1996
Günther Binding. *Deutsche Königspfalzen, von Karl dem Grossen bis Friedrich II. (765–1240).* Darmstadt, 1996.

Binding 2002
Günther Binding. *Vom dreifachen Wert der Säule im frühen und hohen Mittelalter.* Sitzungsberichte der Sächsischen Akademie der Wissenschaften zu Leipzig, Philologisch-Historische Klasse, vol. 138, no. 2. Leipzig, 2002.

Bion, Christin, and Delattre 1791
Jean-Marie Bion, Charles-Gabriel-Frédéric Christin, and François-Pascal Delattre. *Inventaire des diamans de la Couronne, perles, pierreries, tableaux, pierres gravées, et autres monumens des arts & des sciences existans au Garde-Meuble.* 2 vols. Paris, 1791.

Bischoff 1999
Franz Bischoff. *Burkhard Engelberg, "Der vilkunstreiche Architector und der Statt Augspurg Wercke Meister": Burkhard Engelberg und die süddeutsche Architektur um 1500. Anmerkungen der sozialen Stellung und Arbeitsweise spätgotischer Steinmetzen und Werkmeister.* Schwäbische Geschichtsquellen und Forschungen 18. Augsburg, 1999. [Originally presented as the author's Ph.D. diss., Universität Bamberg, 1987.]

Bissell 1997
Gerhard Bissell. *Pierre Le Gros, 1666–1719*. Reading, Berkshire, United Kingdom, 1997.

Blair 1987
Claude Blair, ed. *The History of Silver*. New York, 1987.

Blühm 1996
Andreas Blühm. "In Living Colour: A Short History of Colour in Sculpture in the Nineteenth Century." In Andreas Blühm et al., *The Colour of Sculpture, 1840–1910*, pp. 11–60. Exh. cat., Rijksmuseum Vincent Van Gogh, Amsterdam; Henry Moore Institute, Leeds. Zwolle, 1996.

Bodenstein 1913–14
Gustav Bodenstein. "Urkunden und Regesten aus dem K. und K. Reichsfinanz-Archiv in Wien." *Jahrbuch der Kunsthistorischen Sammlungen des Allerhöchsten Kaiserhauses* 31 (1913–14), pp. I–LVII.

Bodenstein 1916
Gustav Bodenstein. "Urkunden und Regesten aus dem K. und K. Reichsfinanz-Archiv in Wien." *Jahrbuch der Kunsthistorischen Sammlungen des Allerhöchsten Kaiserhauses* 33 (1916), pp. I–CXVIII.

Boeheim 1889
Wendelin Boeheim. "Urkunden und Regesten aus der K. K. Hofbibliothek." *Jahrbuch der Kunsthistorischen Sammlungen des Allerhöchsten Kaiserhauses* 10 (1889), pp. I–XIX.

Boehm and Fajt 2005
Barbara Drake Boehm and Jiří Fajt, eds. *Prague: The Crown of Bohemia, 1347–1437*. Exh. cat., The Metropolitan Museum of Art, New York; Prague Castle. New York, 2005.

Bohr 1993
Michael Bohr. *Die Entwicklung der Kabinettschränke in Florenz*. Europäische Hochschulschriften, ser. 28, Kunstgeschichte 182. Frankfurt am Main, 1993. [Originally presented as the author's Ph.D. diss., Universität Mainz, 1991.]

Bohr 1994
Michael Bohr. "Die Villa del Poggio Imperiale und die Skizzenbücher des Architekten Diacinto Maria Marmi: Zur Bautypologie und Innenraumgestaltung mediceischer Profanbauten um die Wende vom 17. zum 18. Jahrhundert." *Mitteilungen des Kunsthistorischen Institutes in Florenz* 38 (1994), pp. 337–418.

Bollea 1942
Luigi Cesare Bollea. *Lorenzo Pecheux: Maestro di pittura nella R. Accademia delle Belle Arti di Torino*. Collezione "La R. Accademia Albertina delle Belle Arti" 8. Turin, 1942.

Bonatti and Gulinelli 2006
Elena Bonatti and Maria Teresa Gulinelli, eds. *Museo Riminaldi*. Exh. cat., Palazzo Bonacossi, Ferrara. Rome, 2006.

De Boodt 1609
Anselmus Boetius de Boodt. *Gemmarum et Lapidum Historia*. Hanau, 1609.

Borea 1975
Evelina Borea. "Dipinti alla Petraia per Don Lorenzo de' Medici: Stefano della Bella, Vincenzo Mannozzi, il Volterrano, il Dandini e altri." *Prospettiva*, no. 2 (July 1975), pp. 24–39.

Borea 1977
Evelina Borea, ed., with Anna Maria Petrioli Tofani and Karla Langedijk. *La quadreria di Don Lorenzo de' Medici*. Exh. cat., Villa Medicea di Poggio a Caiano. Florence, 1977.

Borghini 1584 (1967 ed.)
Raffaello Borghini. *Il Riposo di Raffaello Borghini: In cui della pittura, e della scultura si favella, de' più illustri pittori, e scultori, e delle più famose opere loro si fa mentione; e le cose principali appartenenti à dette arti s'insegnano*. Florence, 1584. 1967 ed.: Edited by Mario Rosci. 2 vols. Gli storici della letteratura artistica italiana 13, 14. Milan, 1967.

Boström 2001
Hans-Olof Boström. *Det underbara skåpet: Philipp Hainhofer och Gustav II Adolfs konstskåp*. Uppsala and Stockholm, 2001.

Böttiger 1909–10
John Böttiger. *Philipp Hainhofer und der Kunstschrank Gustav Adolfs in Upsala*. 4 vols. Stockholm, 1909–10.

Botto 1968
Ida Maria Botto, ed. *Mostra dei disegni di Bernardo Buontalenti (1531–1608)*. Gabinetto Disegni e Stampe degli Uffizi 28. Florence, 1968.

Bowersox and and Chamberlin 1995
Gary W. Bowersox and Bonita E. Chamberlin. *Gemstones of Afghanistan*. Tucson, 1995.

Bowron 2002
Edgar Peters Bowron. "La *Madeleine en Méditation devant un Crucifix* de Benedetto Luti (1666–1724): L'Artiste et les mécènes et collectionneurs français dans la Rome du XVIIIᵉ siècle." *Revue du Louvre/La Revue des musées de France*, 2002, no. 1 (February), pp. 45–51.

Bowron and Rishel 2000
Edgar Peters Bowron and Joseph J. Rishel, eds. *Art in Rome in the Eighteenth Century*. Exh. cat., Philadelphia Museum of Art; Museum of Fine Arts, Houston. Philadelphia, 2000.

Boynton 1966
Lindsay Boynton. "Italian Craft in an English Cabinet." *Country Life* 140 (September 29, 1966), pp. 768–69.

Brandi 2005
Cesare Brandi. *Theory of Restoration*. Edited by Giuseppe Basile. Translated by Cynthia Rockwell. Arte e restauro. Rome and Florence, 2005.

Braun 1924
Joseph Braun. *Der christliche Altar in seiner geschichtlichen Entwicklung*. 2 vols. Munich, 1924.

Braunfels 1968
Wolfgang Braunfels. *Die Welt der Karolinger und ihre Kunst*. Kulturgeschichte in Einzeldarstellungen. Munich, 1968.

Bremer-David 1993
Charissa Bremer-David, with Peggy Fogelman, Peter Fusco, and Catherine Hess. *Decorative Arts: An Illustrated Summary Catalogue of the Collections of the J. Paul Getty Museum*. Malibu, 1993.

Briat 1973
René Briat. *Le Miracle de Breteuil*. Guide to the Château de Breteuil. Chevreuse, 1973.

Brice 1725
Germain Brice. *Nouvelle Description de la ville de Paris, et de tout ce qu'elle contient de plus remarquable*. 8th ed. 4 vols. Paris, 1725. [1st ed.: *Description nouvelle de ce qu'il y a de plus remarquable dans la ville de Paris*. 2 vols. Paris, 1684.]

Briggs 1991
Robin Briggs. "The Académie Royale des Sciences and the Pursuit of Utility." *Past and Present*, no. 131 (May 1991), pp. 38–88.

Brooke 1962
Humphrey Brooke. "The National Gallery Cleaning Controversy." *Burlington Magazine* 104 (April 1962), p. 165.

Brosses 1885
Charles de Brosses. *Le Président de Brosses en Italie: Lettres familières écrites d'Italie en 1739 et 1740*. Edited by Romain Colomb. 2 vols. 4th ed. Paris, 1885.

Brown 2004
Patricia Fortini Brown. *Private Lives in Renaissance Venice: Art, Architecture, and the Family*. New Haven, 2004.

Brugger-Koch 1985
Susanne Brugger-Koch. "Venedig und Paris: Die wichtigsten Zentren des hochmittelalterlichen Hartsteinschliffs im Spiegel der Quellen." *Zeitschrift des deutschen Vereins für Kulturwissenschaft* 39, nos. 1–4 (1985), pp. 3–39.

Brunner 1970
Herbert Brunner, ed. *Schatzkammer der Residenz München: Katalog*. 3rd ed. Munich, 1970.

Bruun-Neergaard 1806
Tønnes Christian Bruun-Neergaard. *Description de la manufacture de porphyre d'Elfredalen en Suède*. [Paris, ca. 1806].

Bühler 1973
Hans-Peter Bühler. *Antike Gefässe aus Edelsteinen*. Mainz, 1973.

Bukovinská 1988
Beket Bukovinská. "Kunsthandwerk." In *Die Kunst am Hofe Rudolfs II*, pp. 141–77. [Hanau] and Prague, 1988.

Bukovinská 2003
Beket Bukovinská. "Pierre dure, matière tendre: Quelques Remarques à propos du bassin en jaspe sanguin de Rodolphe II." In *Les Vases en pierres dures: Actes du colloque organisé au Musée du Louvre par le Service Culturel le 9 juin 2001*, edited by Daniel Alcouffe, pp. 115–38. Paris, 2003.

Bulgari 1958–59
Costantino G. Bulgari. *Argentieri, gemmari e orafi d'Italia: Notizie storiche e raccolta dei loro contrassegni con la riproduzione grafica dei punzoni individuali e dei punzoni di stato.* Vol. 1, *Roma*. 2 vols. Rome, 1958–59.

Butters 1996
Suzanne B. Butters. *The Triumph of Vulcan: Sculptors' Tools, Porphyry, and the Prince in Ducal Florence.* 2 vols. Villa I Tatti 14. Florence, 1996.

Byrne 1981
Janet S. Byrne. *Renaissance Ornament Prints and Drawings.* Exh. cat., The Metropolitan Museum of Art. New York, 1981.

Calbi 2000
Emilia Calbi, ed. *Giovan Battista Dell'Era (1765–1799): Un artista lombarda nella Roma neoclassica.* Exh. cat., Museo Civico Ernesto e Teresa Delle Torre, Treviglio. Milan and Treviglio, 2000.

Campbell 2007
Thomas P. Campbell, ed. *Tapestry in the Baroque: Threads of Splendor.* Exh. cat., The Metropolitan Museum of Art, New York; Palacio Real, Madrid. New York, 2007.

Cantelli 1996
Giuseppe Cantelli. *Storia dell'oreficeria dell'arte tessile in Toscana dal Medioevo all'età moderna.* Florence, 1996.

Carboni 2007
Stefano Carboni, ed. *Venice and the Islamic World, 828–1797.* Exh. cat., Institut du Monde Arabe, Paris; The Metropolitan Museum of Art, New York. New York, 2007.

Carlton House 1991
Carlton House: The Past Glories of George IV's Palace. Exh. cat., The Queen's Gallery, Buckingham Palace. London, 1991.

Carré 1971
Louis Carré. *A Guide to Old French Plate.* London, 1971.

Casarosa 1973
Mariarita Casarosa. "Ricerche negli archivi e nei musei: La collezione granducale delle gemme dal Settecento ad oggi." *Arte illustrata*, no. 54 (August 1973), pp. 286–97.

Casazza 2004a
Ornella Casazza. "Cameos and Intaglios: From Cosimo the Elder to the Electress Palatine.'" In Marilena Mosco and Ornella Casazza, *The Museo degli Argenti: Collections and Collectors*, pp. 16–29. Florence, 2004.

Casazza 2004b
Ornella Casazza. "Ferdinando I and Florentine 'Commesso.'" In Marilena Mosco and Ornella Casazza, *The Museo degli Argenti: Collections and Collectors*, pp. 82–95. Florence, 2004.

Casciu 2006
Stefano Casciu, ed. *La principessa saggia: L'eredità di Anna Maria Luisa de' Medici, Elettrice Palatina.* Exh. cat., Galleria Palatina, Palazzo Pitti. Florence, 2006.

Cassidy-Geiger 1999
Maureen Cassidy-Geiger. "Meissen and Saint-Cloud, Dresden and Paris: Royal and Lesser Connections and Parallels." In *Discovering the Secrets of Soft-Paste Porcelain at the Saint-Cloud Manufactory, ca. 1690–1766*, edited by Bertrand Rondot, pp. 97–111. Exh. cat., Bard Graduate Center for Studies in the Decorative Arts, Design, and Culture, New York. New Haven, 1999.

Cassidy-Geiger 2007a
Maureen Cassidy-Geiger, ed. *Fragile Diplomacy: Meissen Porcelain for European Courts, ca. 1710–63.* Exh. cat., Bard Graduate Center for Studies in the Decorative Arts, Design, and Culture, New York. New Haven, 2007.

Cassidy-Geiger 2007b
Maureen Cassidy-Geiger. "Princes and Porcelain on the Grand Tour of Italy." In Cassidy-Geiger 2007a, pp. 209–55.

Castelnuovo 1991
Enrico Castelnuovo, ed. *Ori e argenti dei santi: Il tesoro del Duomo di Trento.* Storia dell'arte e della cultura. Trent, 1991.

Castelnuovo 2007
Enrico Castelnuovo, ed. *La Reggia di Venaria e i Savoia: Arte, magnificenza e storia di una corte europea.* 2 vols. Exh. cat., Reggia di Venaria Reale. Turin, 2007.

Catalogue des marbres 1777
Catalogue des marbres, bronzes, agates, porcelaines anciennes, modernes . . . composant le magasin de Julliot, marchand, rue Saint Honoré . . . . Paris, 1777.

Catalogue des vases 1782
Catalogue des vases, colonnes, tables de marbres rares, figures de bronze . . . & autres effets importants qui composent le cabinet de feu M. le duc d'Aumont. Paris, 1782.

Caylus 1752–67
Anne-Claude-Philippe, comte de Caylus. *Recueil d'antiquités égyptiennes, étrusques, grecques et romaines.* 7 vols. Paris, 1752–67.

Cazaux 2000
Jean-Louis Cazaux. *L'Univers des échecs.* Univers du jeu. Paris, 2000.

Cecchi 1986
Alessandro Cecchi. "La Pêche des Perles aux Indes: Une Peinture d'Antonio Tempesta." *La Revue du Louvre et des musées de France*, 1986, no. 1, pp. 45–57.

Cederlund and Norrby 2003
Johan Cederlund and Mikael Norrby. *The Augsburg Art Cabinet.* Uppsala, 2003.

Chiarini 1970
Marco Chiarini. "Pittura su pietre." *Antichità viva* 9, no. 2 (March–April 1970), pp. 29–37.

Chiarini and Acidini 2000
Marco Chiarini and Cristina Acidini Luchinat, eds. *Bizzarrie di pietre dipinte dalle collezioni dei Medici.* Exh. cat., Galleria dell'Accademia and Museo dell'Opificio delle Pietre Dure, Florence. Cinisello Balsamo (Milan), 2000. Also published as *Pietre colorate: Capricci del XVII secolo dalle collezioni medicee.* Exh. cat., Palazzo Franchi Servanzi, San Severino Marche. Cinisello Balsamo (Milan), 2000.

Chiarini and Padovani 1993
Marco Chiarini and Serena Padovani, eds. *Gli Appartamenti Reali di Palazzo Pitti: Una reggia per tre dinastie, Medici, Lorena e Savoia, tra Granducato e Regno d'Italia.* Florence, 1993.

Chong, Pegazzano, and Zikos 2003
Alan Chong, Donatella Pegazzano, and Dimitrios Zikos, eds. *Raphael, Cellini, and a Renaissance Banker: The Patronage of Bindo Altoviti.* Exh. cat., Isabella Stewart Gardner Museum, Boston; Museo Nazionale del Bargello, Florence. Boston, 2003.

Christie's 1990
Christie, Manson & Woods, London. *The Badminton Cabinet.* Sale cat., July 5, 1990.

Christie's 2004
Christie's, London. *The Badminton Cabinet.* Sale cat., December 9, 2004.

Christie's: Review 1990
Christie's: Review of the Season, 1990. Edited by Mark Wrey and Anne Montefiore. London, 1990.

Ciatti, Giusti, and Innocenti 2004
Marco Ciatti, Annamaria Giusti, and Clarice Innocenti. "Le 'belle materie': Commesso lapideo e mosaico, arazzi, tessili, oreficerie." In *Lacuna: Riflessioni sulle esperienze dell'Opificio delle Pietre Dure; Atti dei Convegni del 7 aprile 2002 e del 5 aprile 2003 . . . Ferrara*, pp. 65–74. Florence, 2004.

Ciggaar 1995
Krijna Ciggaar. "Theophano: An Empress Reconsidered." In Davids 1995, pp. 49–63.

Claussen 1989
Peter Cornelius Claussen. "Marmi antichi nel medioevo romano: L'arte dei Cosmati." In *Marmi*

antichi, edited by Gabriele Borghini, pp. 65–80. Materiali della cultura artistica 1. Rome, 1989.

Cohen 1986
David Harris Cohen. "Pierre-Philippe Thomire: Unternehmer und Künstler." In Hans Ottomeyer and Peter Pröschel, with contributions by Jean-Dominique Augarde et al., *Vergoldete Bronzen: Bronzearbeiten des Spätbarock und Klassizismus*, vol. 2, pp. 657–65. Munich, 1986.

Coleridge 1997
Anthony Coleridge. "The Hope-Weir Cabinet." *Magazine Antiques* 151 (June 1997), pp. 852–59.

Collareta 1991
Marco Collareta. "Forma fidei: Il significato dello stile negli arredi liturgici." In Castelnuovo 1991, pp. 21–33.

Colle 1991
Enrico Colle. "Traccia per una storia del mobile in Toscana da Pietro Leopoldo a Ferdinando III." *Antichità viva* 30, nos. 4–5 (July–October 1991), pp. 65–74.

Colle 1992
Enrico Colle, ed. *I mobili di Palazzo Pitti.* [Vol. 2], *Il primo periodo lorenese, 1737–1799.* Florence, 1992.

Colle 1993
Enrico Colle. *Arredi dalle dimore medicee.* Medicea. Florence, 1993.

Colle 1997
Enrico Colle, ed. *I mobili di Palazzo Pitti.* [Vol. 1], *Il periodo dei Medici, 1537–1737.* Florence, 1997.

Colle 2000
Enrico Colle. *Il mobili barocco in Italia: Arredi e decorazioni d'interni dal 1600 al 1738.* Repertori d'arti decorative. Milan, 2000.

Colle 2003
Enrico Colle. *Il mobile rococò in Italia: Arredi e decorazioni d'interni dal 1738 al 1775.* Repertori d'arti decorative. Milan, 2003.

Colle 2005
Enrico Colle. *Il mobile di corte a Lucca, 1805–1847.* Lucca, 2005.

Colle and Livi Bacci 1997
Enrico Colle and Lorenzo Livi Bacci, eds. "Regesto degli artigiani attivi per la corte medicea." In Colle 1997, pp. 271–309.

Colle, Griseri, and Valeriani 2001
Enrico Colle, Angela Griseri, and Roberto Valeriani. *Bronzi decorativi in Italia: Bronzisti e fonditori italiani dal Seicento all'Ottocento.* Milan, 2001.

Collections de Louis XIV 1977
Collections de Louis XIV: Dessins, albums, manuscrits. Exh. cat., Orangerie des Tuileries. Paris, 1977.

Conihout and Michel 2006
Isabelle de Conihout and Patrick Michel, eds. *Mazarin: Les Lettres et les arts.* Paris and Saint-Rémy-en-l'Eau, 2006.

Contadini 1998
Anna Contadini. *Fatimid Art at the Victoria and Albert Museum.* London, 1998.

Conti 1893
Cosimo Conti. *La prima reggia di Cosimo I de' Medici nel Palazzo già della Signoria di Firenze.* Florence, 1893.

Cooper 1963
Douglas Cooper. "Baron Elie de Rothschild, Paris. European Paintings, Objets d'Art and Furniture." In *Great Private Collections*, edited by Douglas Cooper, pp. 168–79. New York, 1963.

Corsini 1993
Diletta Corsini. "Argenti del sedicesimo secolo: Fra officina granducale e botteghe di città, 1537–1600." In Liscia Bemporad 1993, vol. 1, pp. 57–99.

Cowen 2003
Pamela Cowen. *A Fanfare for the Sun King: Unfolding Fans for Louis XIV.* Exh. cat., Fan Museum, Greenwich. London, 2003.

Cox 1773
James Cox. *A Descriptive Inventory of the Several Exquisite and Magnificent Pieces of Mechanism and Jewellery, Comprised in the Schedule Annexed to an Act of Parliament, Made in the Thirteenth Year of His Present Majesty, George the Third, for Enabling Mr. James Cox, . . . Jeweller, to Dispose of His Museum by Way of Lottery.* London, 1773.

Crankshaw 1971
Edward Crankshaw. *The Habsburgs: Portrait of a Dynasty.* A Studio Book. New York, 1971.

Czok 1987
Karl Czok. *August der Starke und Kursachsen.* Leipzig, 1987.

Dal Poggetto 2004
Paolo Dal Poggetto, ed. *I Della Rovere: Piero della Francesca, Raffaello, Tiziano.* Exh. cat., Palazzo Ducale, Senigallia; Palazzo Ducale, Urbino; Palazzo Ducale, Pesaro; Palazzo Ducale, Urbania. Milan, 2004.

Dal Prà 1993
Laura Dal Prà, ed. *I Madruzzo e l'Europa, 1539–1658: I principi vescovi di Trento tra Papato e Impero.* Exh. cat., Castello del Buonconsiglio, Trent; Chiesa dell'Inviolato, Riva del Garda. Milan, 1993.

Dauterman and Parker 1960
Carl Christian Dauterman and James Parker. "The Kress Galleries of French Decorative Arts: The Porcelain Furniture." *The Metropolitan Museum of Art Bulletin*, n.s., 18, no. 9 (May 1960), pp. 274–84.

Davanzo Poli 1999
Doretta Davanzo Poli. *Arts and Crafts in Venice.* Cologne, 1999.

Davids 1995
Adelbert Davids, ed. *The Empress Theophano: Byzantium and the West at the Turn of the First Millennium.* Cambridge, 1995.

De Bellaigue 1968
Geoffrey De Bellaigue. "Martin-Eloy Lignereux and England." *Gazette des beaux-arts*, 6th ser., 71 (May–June 1968), pp. 283–94.

De Bellaigue 1974
Geoffrey De Bellaigue. *Furniture, Clocks, and Gilt Bronzes.* 2 vols. The James A. de Rothschild Collection at Waddesdon Manor. Fribourg, 1974.

De Bellaigue 1995
Geoffrey De Bellaigue. "Daguerre and England." In *Bernard Molitor, 1755–1833: Ébéniste parisien d'origine luxembourgeoise / Parisier Kunsttischler Luxemburger Herkunft*, edited by Ulrich Leben, pp. 157–79. Exh. cat., Villa Vauban. Luxembourg, 1995.

De Boodt. Listed under B.

De Caro 1996
Stefano De Caro. *The National Archaeological Museum of Naples.* Guide artistiche Electa Napoli. Naples, 1996.

De Nuccio and Ungaro 2002
Marilda De Nuccio and Lucrezia Ungaro, eds. *I marmi colorati della Roma imperiale.* Exh. cat., Mercati di Traiano, Rome. Venice, 2002.

Del Riccio 1597 (1996 ed.)
Agostino Del Riccio. *Istoria delle pietre.* [1597.] Edited by Raniero Gnoli and Attilia Sironi. Archivi di arti decorative. Turin, 1996. [Transcription of Cod. 230 in the Biblioteca Riccardiana, Florence.]

Del Tuppo 1485
Francesco del Tuppo, trans. *Aesopus: Vita et Fabulae.* Naples, 1485. [Repr., Milan, 1963.]

"Des Tableaux de marbre" 1957
"Des Tableaux de marbre sur des pieds de bronze." *Connaissance des arts*, no. 70 (December 1957), pp. 102–7.

"Description de la galerie" 1682
"Description de la galerie, du sallon, & du grand apartement de Versailles, & de tout ce qui s'y passe les jours de jeu." *Mercure galant*, December 1682, pp. 1–73.

"Description de la galerie de Versailles" 1686
"Description de la galerie de Versailles, du grand appartement, de petit appartement, cabinet appellé des curiositez, grand escalier." *Mercure galant*, November 1686, pt. 2 (suppl. titled "Voyage des ambassadeurs de Siam en France"), pp. 272–308.

Dictionary of Art 1996
The Dictionary of Art. Edited by Jane Turner.
34 vols. New York, 1996.

Dimier 1925
Louis Dimier. "Une Table du cabinet des curiosités
à Versailles." *Bulletin de la Société de l'Histoire de l'Art
Français*, 1925, p. 200.

Distelberger 1978
Rudolf Distelberger. "Beobachtungen zu den
Steinschneidewerkstätten der Miseroni in Mailand
und Prag." *Jahrbuch der Kunsthistorischen Sammlungen
in Wien* 74 (1978), pp. 79–152.

Distelberger 1979
Rudolf Distelberger. "Dionysio und Ferdinand
Eusebio Miseroni." *Jahrbuch der Kunsthistorischen
Sammlungen in Wien* 75 (1979), pp. 109–88.

Distelberger 1980
Rudolf Distelberger. "The Pietra Dura Works of
the Prince of Liechtenstein." *Connaissance des arts*
(U.S. edition), no. 8 (September 1980), pp. 52–57.
[French ed.: "Pierres précieuses du Liechtenstein."
Connaissance des arts, no. 343 (September 1980),
pp. 61–66.]

Distelberger 1988
Rudolf Distelberger. "Kunstkammerstücke." In
Prag um 1600 1988, vol. I, pp. 437–66.

Distelberger 1993
Rudolf Distelberger. "Alfred André, 1839–1919." In
Rudolf Distelberger et al., *Western Decorative Arts,
Part 1: Medieval, Renaissance, and Historicizing Styles,
including Metalwork, Enamels, and Ceramics*, pp. 282–
87. The Collections of the National Gallery of Art,
Systematic Catalogue. Washington, D.C., 1993.

Distelberger 1997
Rudolf Distelberger. "Thoughts on Rudolfine Art
in the 'Court Workshops' in Prague." In Fučíková
et al. 1997, pp. 189–98.

Distelberger 1998
Rudolf Distelberger. "Ein Florentiner Kabinett-
schrank mit Commessi im Prager Stil: Der Einfluss
der Prager Werkstatt auf das *Opificio delle Pietre
Dure* in Florenz." In *Rudolf II, Prague and the World:
Papers from the International Conference, Prague, 2–4
September 1997*, edited by Lubomír Konečný, with
Beket Bukovinská and Ivan Muchka, pp. 40–48.
Prague, 1998.

Distelberger 1999
Rudolf Distelberger. "Archivnotizen zur Familie
Miseroni in Mailand." *Jahrbuch des Kunsthistorischen
Museums Wien* I (1999), pp. 310–14.

Distelberger 2000
Rudolf Distelberger. "Les Moulages en plâtre et
modèles de bijoux de l'atelier du restaurateur
Alfred André (1839–1919)." In Alexis Kugel, with
Rudolf Distelberger and Michèle Bimbenet-Privat,
Joyaux Renaissance: Une Splendeur retrouvée, n.p.
Exh. cat., Galerie J. Kugel. Paris, 2000.

Distelberger 2002
Rudolf Distelberger. *Die Kunst des Steinschnitts:
Prunkgefässe, Kameen und Commessi aus der Kunst-
kammer.* Edited by Wilfried Seipel. Exh. cat.,
Kunsthistorisches Museum, Vienna. Vienna and
Milan, 2002.

Distelberger 2003
Rudolf Distelberger. "Milan ou Prague: L'Atelier
des Miseroni." In *Les Vases en pierres dures: Actes du
colloque organisé au Musée du Louvre par le Service
Culturel le 9 juin 2001*, edited by Daniel Alcouffe,
pp. 83–113. Paris, 2003.

Distelberger 2004
Rudolf Distelberger. "Eine unbekannte byzan-
tinische Schale aus Sardonyx." In *Objets d'art:
Mélanges en l'honneur de Daniel Alcouffe*, pp. 26–35.
Dijon, 2004.

Dodge 1988
Hazel Dodge. "Decorative Stones for Architec-
ture in the Roman Empire." *Oxford Journal of
Archaeology* 7, no. I (1988), pp. 65–80.

Doering 1894
Oscar Doering. *Des Augsburger Patriciers Philipp
Hainhofer Beziehungen zum Herzog Philipp II. von
Pommern-Stettin: Correspondenzen aus den Jahren
1610–1619.* Quellenschriften für Kunstgeschichte
und Kunsttechnik des Mittelalters und der
Neuzeit, n.s., 6. Vienna, 1894.

Dolcini and Zanettin 1999
Loretta Dolcini and Bruno Zanettin. *Cristalli e
gemme: Realtà fisica e immaginario, simbologia
tecniche e arte.* Exh. cat., Palazzo Loredan.
Venice, 1999.

Draper 2008
James David Draper. "Cameo Appearances." *The
Metropolitan Museum of Art Bulletin*, n.s., 65, no. 4
(Spring 2008).

Dreyfus 1922
Carle Dreyfus. *Catalogue sommaire du mobilier et des
objets d'art du XVIIᵉ et XVIIIᵉ siècle: Meubles, sièges,
tapisseries, bronzes d'ameublement, porcelaines, marbres et laques montés en bronzes, objets d'orfèvrerie.*
2nd ed. Musée du Louvre. Paris, 1922.

Dukelskaya 1979
Larissa Dukelskaya. *The Hermitage: English Art,
Sixteenth to Nineteenth Century, Paintings, Sculpture,
Prints and Drawings, Minor Arts.* Leningrad and
London, 1979.

Durand 1901–3
Georges Durand. *Monographie de l'église Notre-
Dame: Cathédrale d'Amiens.* 2 vols. Mémoires de la
Société des Antiquaires de Picardie. Amiens and
Paris, 1901–3.

Duvaux 1965
*Livre-Journal de Lazare Duvaux, marchand-bijoutier
ordinaire du Roy, 1748–1758.* Edited by Louis
Courajod. 2 vols. Paris, 1965. [Repr. of 1873 ed.]

Ebner 2002
Hemma Ebner. *Salzburger Bergkristall: Die hoch-
fürstliche Kristallmühle.* Exh. cat., Dommuseum.
Salzburg, 2002.

Efimova 1968
Evdokiia Mikhailovna Efimova. *West European
Mosaic of the Thirteenth–Nineteenth Centuries in
the Collection of the Hermitage.* [In Russian.] State
Hermitage Museum. Leningrad, 1968.

Egg 1959
Friedrich Egg. "Die Freiburger Kristallschleifer
und der Innsbrucker Hof." In *Schau-ins-Land* 77
(1959), pp. 55–61.

Eggeling 2003
Tilo Eggeling. *Raum und Ornament: Georg
Wenceslaus von Knobelsdorff und das friderizianische
Rokoko.* 2nd ed. Regensburg, 2003.

Egypt and the Ancient Near East 1987
Egypt and the Ancient Near East. Introduction by
Peter Dorman, Prudence Oliver Harper, and
Holly Pittman. The Metropolitan Museum of Art.
New York, 1987.

Eichler and Kris 1927
Fritz Eichler and Ernst Kris. *Die Kameen im
Kunsthistorischen Museum: Beschreibender Katalog.*
Publikationen aus den Kunsthistorischen
Sammlungen in Wien 2. Vienna, 1927.

Eikelmann 2000
Renate Eikelmann, ed. *Bayerisches Nationalmuseum:
Handbuch der kunst- und kulturgeschichtlichen
Sammlungen.* Munich, 2000.

L'Entrée de Henri II à Rouen 1551 **(1974 ed.)**
L'Entrée de Henri II à Rouen, 1550. [Rouen], 1551.
1974 ed.: Introduction by Margaret M. McGowan.
Amsterdam, 1974.

Epiphanius 1934
Epiphanius. *Epiphanius de Gemmis: The Old Georgian
Version and Fragments of the Armenian Version.*
Edited and translated by Robert P. Blake and Henri
de Vis. Studies and Documents 2. London, 1934.

Epstein 1998
Steven R. Epstein. "Craft Guilds, Apprenticeship,
and Technological Change in Preindustrial
Europe." *Journal of Economic History* 58, no. 3
(September 1998), pp. 684–713.

J. Erbstein and A. Erbstein 1884
Julius Erbstein and Albert Erbstein. *Das Königliche
Grüne Gewölbe zu Dresden.* Dresden, 1884.

El Escorial 1967
El Escorial: Eighth Marvel of the World. Madrid,
1967.

Europäische Barockplastik 1971
*Europäische Barockplastik am Niederrhein: Grupello
und seine Zeit.* Exh. cat., Kunstmuseum Düsseldorf.
Düsseldorf, 1971.

Evans and Marr 2006
Robert John Weston Evans and Alexander Marr, eds. *Curiosity and Wonder from the Renaissance to the Enlightenment*. Aldershot, 2006.

Fajt 2006
Jiří Fajt, ed., with Markus Hörsch, Andrea Langer, and Barbara Drake Boehm. *Karl IV., Kaiser von Gottes Gnaden: Kunst und Repräsentation des Hauses Luxemburg, 1310–1437*. Munich, 2006.

Faroqhi 1990
Suraiya Faroqhi. *Herrscher über Mekka: Die Geschichte der Pilgerfahrt*. Munich, 1990.

Faszination Edelstein 1992
Faszination Edelstein aus den Schatzkammern der Welt: Mythos, Kunst, Wissenschaft. Exh. cat., Hessisches Landesmuseum. Darmstadt, 1992.

Fenaille 1903–23
Maurice Fenaille. *État général des tapisseries de la Manufacture des Gobelins depuis son origine jusqu'à nos jours, 1600–1900*. 6 vols in 5. Paris, 1903–23.

Feulner 1927
Adolf Feulner. *Kunstgeschichte des Möbels*. 3rd ed. Berlin, 1927.

Feustel and Heunisch 1992
Hanns Feustel and Carmen Heunisch. "Organische oder biogene 'Edelsteine.'" In *Faszination Edelstein* 1992, pp. 41–51.

Fickler 2004
Johann Baptist Fickler. *Johann Baptist Fickler: Das Inventar der Münchner herzoglichen Kunstkammer von 1598*. Edited by Pieter Diemer, with Elke Bujok and Dorothea Diemer. Abhandlungen, Bayerische Akademie der Wissenschaften, Philosophisch-Historische Klasse, n.s., 125. Munich, 2004. [Transcription of MS Cgm 2133 in the Bayerische Staatsbibliothek, Munich.]

Field 1987
Leslie Field. *The Queen's Jewels: The Personal Collection of Elizabeth II*. New York, 1987.

Fioratti 2004
Helen Costantino Fioratti. *Il mobile italiano: Dall'antichità allo stile impero*. Edited by Gloria Fossi. Florence, 2004.

Fischer 1979
W. Fischer. "Zur Geschichte der Idar-Obersteiner Edelsteinindustrie." *Der Aufschluss* (Vereinigung der Freunde der Mineralogie und Geologie, Heidelberg), special number, 19 (1979), pp. 13–34.

Fleischhauer 1972
Werner Fleischhauer. "Ein Werk des Edelsteinschneiders Hans Kobenhaupt in der Sammlung Faesch." *Jahresberichte* (Historisches Museum Basel), 1972, pp. 27–32.

Fleischhauer 1976
Werner Fleischhauer. *Die Geschichte der Kunstkammer der Herzöge von Württemberg in Stuttgart*. Veröffentlichungen der Kommission für Geschichtliche Landeskunde in Baden-Württemberg, ser. B, Forschungen 8. Stuttgart, 1976.

Fleming 1955
John Fleming. "The Hugfords of Florence." Pt. 1. *Connoisseur* 136 (October 1955), pp. 106–10.

Fleming and Honour 1989
John Fleming and Hugh Honour. *The Penguin Dictionary of Decorative Arts*. New ed. London, 1989.

Fock 1974
C. Willemijn Fock. "Der Goldschmied Jaques Bylivelt aus Delft und sein Wirken in der Mediceischen Hofwerkstatt in Florenz." *Jahrbuch der Kunsthistorischen Sammlungen in Wien* 70 (1974), pp. 89–178.

Fock 1976
C. Willemijn Fock. "Vases en lapis-lazuli des collections médicéennes du seizième siècle." *Münchner Jahrbuch der bildenden Kunst*, 3rd ser., 27 (1976), pp. 119–54.

Fock 1980
C. Willemijn Fock. "Francesco I e Ferdinando I: Mecenati di orefici e intagliatori di pietre dure." In *Le arti del principato mediceo*, pp. 317–63. Specimen 6. Florence, 1980.

Fock 1988
C. Willemijn Fock. "Pietre Dure Work at the Court of Prague and Florence: Some Relations." In *Prag um 1600: Beiträge zur Kunst und Kultur am Hofe Rudolfs II*, pp. 51–58. Freren, 1988.

France in the Eighteenth Century 1968
France in the Eighteenth Century. Compiled by Denys Sutton. Exh. cat., Royal Academy of Arts. London, 1968.

Frerichs 1969
Wendell W. Frerichs. "Precious Stones as Biblical Symbols." Düsseldorf, 1969. [Originally presented as the author's Ph.D. diss., University of Basel.]

Friess 1980
Gerda Friess. *Edelsteine im Mittelalter: Wandel und Kontinuität in ihrer Bedeutung durch zwölf Jahrhunderte (in Aberglauben, Medizin, Theologie und Goldschmiedekunst)*. Hildesheim, 1980.

Fritz 1982
Johann Michael Fritz. *Goldschmiedekunst der Gotik in Mitteleuropa*. Munich, 1982.

Fučíková 1988
Eliška Fučíková. "Die Malerei am Hofe Rudolfs II." In *Prag um 1600* 1988, vol. 1, pp. 177–92.

Fučíková et al. 1997
Eliška Fučíková et al., eds. *Rudolf II and Prague: The Court and the City*. Exh. cat., Prague Castle; Wallenstein Palace, Prague. Prague, London, and Milan, 1997.

Fuhring 1989
Peter Fuhring. *Design into Art: Drawings for Architecture and Ornament. The Lodewijk Houthakker Collection*. 2 vols. London, 1989.

Fuhring 1999
Peter Fuhring. *Juste-Aurèle Meissonnier: Un Génie du Rococo, 1695–1750*. 2 vols. Archives d'arts décoratifs. Turin and London, 1999.

Fusco and Hess 1994
Peter Fusco and Catherine Hess. "A Rediscovered 'Commesso' Portrait." *Burlington Magazine* 136 (February 1994), pp. 68–72.

Galleria degli Uffizi 1979
Galleria degli Uffizi. *Gli Uffizi: Catalogo generale*. Florence, 1979.

Giansiracusa 1991
Paolo Giansiracusa, ed. *Vanitas vanitatum: Studi sulla ceroplastica di Gaetano Giulio Zumbo*. [Siracusa], 1991.

Ginori Lisci 1963
Leonardo Ginori Lisci. *La porcellana di Doccia*. Milan, 1963.

Giulanelli 1753
Andrea Pietro Giulanelli. *Memorie degli intagliatori moderni in pietre dure, cammei, e gioje dal secolo XV. fino al secolo XVIII*. Livorno, 1753.

Giusti 1985
Annamaria Giusti. "La litoteca donata dal cardinal Riminaldi." In *Il Museo Civico in Ferrara: Donazioni e restauri*, p. 139. Exh. cat., Chiesa di San Romano, Ferrara. Florence, 1985.

Giusti 1988
Annamaria Giusti, ed. *Splendori di pietre dure: L'arte di corte nella Firenze dei granduchi*. Exh. cat., Sala Bianca, Palazzo Pitti. Organized by the Centro Mostre di Firenze and the Opificio delle Pietre Dure. Florence, 1988.

Giusti 1988a
Annamaria Giusti. "Origine e sviluppi della manifattura granducale." In Giusti 1988, pp. 10–23.

Giusti 1989
Annamaria Giusti. *Masterpieces in Pietre Dure: Palazzo Pitti, the Uffizi and Other Museums and Monuments in Florence*. Artistic Guides Electa. Milan, 1989.

Giusti 1992
Annamaria Giusti. *Pietre Dure: Hardstone in Furniture and Decorations*. Translated by Jenny Condie and Mark Roberts. Foreword by Alvar González-Palacios. London, 1992. [Italian ed.: *Pietre dure: L'arte europea del mosaico negli arredi e nelle decorazioni dal 1500 al 1800*. Turin, 1992.]

Giusti 1995
Annamaria Giusti. *Guida al museo*. Museo dell'Opificio delle Pietre Dure. Florence, 1995.

Giusti 1997a
Annamaria Giusti. "Golden Twilight: The Reign
of Cosimo III." In *Treasures of Florence: The Medici
Collection, 1400–1700*, edited by Cristina Acidini
Luchinat, pp. 173–95. Munich and New York, 1997.
[Italian ed.: *Tesori dalle collezioni medicee*. Florence,
1997.]

Giusti 1997b
Annamaria Giusti. "The Grand Ducal Workshops
at the Time of Ferdinando I and Cosimo II." In
Treasures of Florence: The Medici Collection, 1400–1700,
edited by Cristina Acidini Luchinat, pp. 115–43.
Munich and New York, 1997. [Italian ed.: *Tesori
dalle collezioni medicee*. Florence, 1997.]

Giusti 1997c
Annamaria Giusti. "L''ingegnoso artificio' delle
pietre dure." In *Magnificenza alla corte dei Medici*
1997, pp. 380–84.

Giusti 1999
Annamaria Giusti. "Strumenti e materiali per la
realizzazione di un commesso di pietre dure." In
Dolcini and Zanettin 1999, pp. 71–76.

Giusti 2003a
Annamaria Giusti. "Da Firenze all'Europa: I fasti
delle pietre dure." In *Eternità e nobiltà di materia:
Itinerario artistico fra le pietre policrome*, edited by
Annamaria Giusti, pp. 231–70. Florence, 2003.

Giusti 2003b
Annamaria Giusti. "Da Roma a Firenze: Gli esordi
del commesso rinascimentale." In *Eternità e nobiltà
di materia: Itinerario artistico fra le pietre policrome*,
edited by Annamaria Giusti, pp. 197–230. Florence,
2003.

Giusti 2006a
Annamaria Giusti, ed. *Arte e manifattura di corte
a Firenze, dal tramonto dei Medici all'Impero (1732–
1815)*. Exh. cat., Palazzo Pitti, Florence. Livorno,
2006.

Giusti 2006b
Annamaria Giusti. *Pietre Dure and the Art of
Florentine Inlay*. London, 2006. Also published
as *Pietre Dure: The Art of Semiprecious Stonework*.
Los Angeles, 2006. [Italian ed.: *L'arte delle pietre
dure: Da Firenze all'Europa*. Florence, 2005.]

Giusti 2006c
Annamaria Giusti. "I Siries: Una dinastia di artisti
alla guida della manifattura granducale." In Giusti
2006a, pp. 16–27.

Giusti 2007
Annamaria Giusti. *Museo dell'Opificio delle Pietre
Dure: La guida ufficiale*. Livorno, 2007.

Giusti and Frizzi 1986
Annamaria Giusti and Piero Frizzi. "Stipo." *OPD
restauro*, no. 1 (1986), pp. 94–96.

Giusti, Mazzoni, and Pampaloni Martelli 1978
Annamaria Giusti, Paolo Mazzoni, and Annapaula

Pampaloni Martelli, eds. *Il Museo dell'Opificio delle
Pietre Dure a Firenze*. Milan, 1978.

Giusti et al. 1986
Annamaria Giusti, Piero Frizzi, Giancarlo Raddi,
and Lorenzo Lazzarini. "Piano di tavola." In
Restauro del marmo: Opere e problemi, pp. 194–204.
Florence, 1986. Special issue of *OPD restauro*.

Giusti et al. 2002
Annamaria Giusti, Giancarlo Raddi, Chiara
Martinelli, and Francesca Toso. "Piano di tavolo."
OPD restauro, no. 14 (2002), pp. 196, 207–11.

Giusti et al. 2004
Annamaria Giusti et al. *Masters of Florence: Glory
and Genius at the Court of the Medici*. Exh. cat.
Memphis, Tenn., 2004.

Glaser 1976
Hubert Glaser, ed. *Kurfürst Max Emanuel: Bayern
und Europa um 1700*. 2 vols. Vol. 2 published for an
exhibition at the Altes Schloss Schleissheim.
Munich, 1976.

Glory of Baroque Dresden 2004
*The Glory of Baroque Dresden: The State Art
Collections, Dresden*. Exh cat., Mississippi Arts
Pavilion. Jackson, 2004.

Goes 2004
André van der Goes. *Tulpomanie: Die Tulpe in der
Kunst des 16. und 17. Jahrhunderts*. Exh. cat., Schloss
Pillnitz. Organized by the Kunstgewerbemuseum
Dresden. Zwolle and Dresden, 2004.

Goldberg 1996
Edward L. Goldberg. "Artistic Relations between
the Medici and the Spanish Courts, 1587–1621."
Burlington Magazine 138 (February, August 1996),
pp. 105–14, 529–40.

Golden Age of Naples 1981
*The Golden Age of Naples: Art and Civilization under the
Bourbons, 1734–1805*. 2 vols. Exh. cat., Detroit Institute
of Arts; Art Institute of Chicago. Detroit, 1981.

Goldfarb 2002
Hilliard Todd Goldfarb, ed. *Richelieu, 1585–1642:
Kunst, Macht und Politik*. Exh. cat., Museum of
Fine Arts, Montreal; Wallraf-Richartz-Museum &
Fondation Corboud, Cologne. Montreal, 2002.

González-Palacios 1969
Alvar González-Palacios. "Ricerche sulla mobilia
italiana: Tre lavori della Galleria Medicea." *Arte
illustrata*, nos. 17–18 (May–June 1969), pp. 58–65.

González-Palacios 1971
Alvar González-Palacios. "La mobilia del Palazzo
Pallavicini." *Arte illustrata*, nos. 37–38 (January–
February 1971), pp. 64–73.

González-Palacios 1976a
Alvar González-Palacios. "I mani del Piranesi
(I Righetti, Boschi, Boschetti, Raffaelli)."
Paragone, no. 315 (May 1976), pp. 33–48.

González-Palacios 1976b
Alvar González-Palacios. "Provenzale e Moretti:
Indagini su due mosaici." *Antichità viva* 15, no. 4
(July–August 1976), pp. 26–33.

González-Palacios 1977a
Alvar González-Palacios. *The Art of Mosaics: Selections
from the Gilbert Collection*. Exh. cat., Los Angeles
County Museum of Art. Los Angeles, 1977.

González-Palacios 1977b
Alvar González-Palacios. "Un'autobiografia di
Francesco Ghinghi (1689–1762)." *Antologia di belle
arti*, no. 3 (September 1977), pp. 271–81.

González-Palacios 1977c
Alvar González-Palacios. "Limiti e contesto di
Leonardo van der Vinne." *Paragone*, no. 333
(November 1977), pp. 37–68.

González-Palacios 1977d
Alvar González-Palacios. "Un quadro e un mobile
di Don Lorenzo de' Medici." *Antologia di belle arti*,
no. 3 (September 1977), pp. 301–3.

González-Palacios 1977e
Alvar González-Palacios. "Taccuini delle pietre
dure: Attorno al Foggini." *Antologia di belle arti*,
no. 1 (March 1977), pp. 57–64.

González-Palacios 1979
Alvar González-Palacios. "Commessi granducali e
ambizioni galliche (e note sulle pietre dure ai
Gobelins e a Firenze nel Settecento)." In *Florence et
la France: "Rapports sous la Révolution et l'Empire,"
Florence 2–3–4 juin 1977*, pp. 51–113. Florence and
Paris, 1979.

González-Palacios 1982a
Alvar González-Palacios. *Mosaici e pietre dure:
Firenze, paesi germanici, Madrid*. I quaderni
dell'antiquariato. Collana di arti decorative 21,
anno II. Milan, 1982.

González-Palacios 1982b
Alvar González-Palacios. *Mosaici e pietre dure:
Mosaici a piccole tessere. Pietre dure a Parigi e a Napoli*.
I quaderni dell'antiquariato. Collana di arti decora-
tive 20, anno II. Milan, 1982.

González-Palacios 1983
Alvar González-Palacios, ed., with Donald
Garstang. *The Adjectives of History: Furniture and
Works of Art, 1550–1870*. Exh. cat., P & D Colnaghi &
Co. London, 1983.

González-Palacios 1984
Alvar González-Palacios. *Il tempio del gusto: Roma e
il Regno delle Due Sicilie. Le arti decorative in Italia fra
classicismi e barocco*. 2 vols. I marmi 126. Milan,
1984.

González-Palacios 1986
Alvar González-Palacios. *Il tempio del gusto:
Il Granducato di Toscana e gli stati settentrionali.
Le arti decorative in Italia fra classicismi e barocco*.
2 vols. I marmi 136. Milan, 1986.

González-Palacios 1988a
Alvar González-Palacios. "Itinerario da Roma a Firenze." In Giusti 1988, pp. 43–52.

González-Palacios 1988b
Alvar González-Palacios. "Il laboratorio delle pietre dure del 'Buen Retiro' a Madrid (1762–1808)." In Giusti 1988, pp. 260–63.

González-Palacios 1991
Alvar González-Palacios, ed. *Fasto romano: Dipinti, sculture, arredi dai palazzi di Roma.* Exh. cat., Palazzo Sacchetti. Rome, 1991.

González-Palacios 1992
Alvar González-Palacios. "Illusions in Stones: Pietre Dure; Tables of Buen Retiro." *FMR* (International/English ed.), no. 59 (1992), pp. 69–96.

González-Palacios 1993
Alvar González-Palacios. *Il gusto dei principi: Arte di corte del XVII e del XVIII secolo.* 2 vols. I marmi 162. Milan, 1993.

González-Palacios 1995a
Alvar González-Palacios. "Giovanni Giardini: New Works and New Documents." *Burlington Magazine* 137 (June 1995), pp. 367–76.

González-Palacios 1995b
Alvar González-Palacios. "Two Candelabra by Luigi Valadier from Palazzo Borghese." *Metropolitan Museum Journal* 30 (1995), pp. 97–102.

González-Palacios 1996a
Alvar González-Palacios, with Edi Baccheschi. *Il mobile in Liguria.* Genoa, 1996.

González-Palacios 1996b
Alvar González-Palacios, with Roberto Valeriani. *I mobili italiani.* Il patrimonio artistico del Quirinale. Milan, 1996.

González-Palacios 1997
Alvar González-Palacios, ed. *L'oro di Valadier: Un genio nella Roma del Settecento.* Exh. cat., Villa Medici. Rome, 1997.

González-Palacios 2001
Alvar González-Palacios. *Las colecciones reales españolas de mosaicos y piedras duras.* Madrid, 2001.

González-Palacios 2003a
Alvar González-Palacios. "Daguerre, Lignereux and the King of Naples's Cabinet at Caserta." *Burlington Magazine* 145 (June 2003), pp. 431–42.

González-Palacios 2003b
Alvar González-Palacios. "Francesco Mochi, Giuseppe Antonio Torricelli (attrib.): Ancona in ebano e pietre dure / Altarpiece in Ebony and Pietre Dure." In *Altomani & Sons*, n.p. (no. 15). Dealer's cat. Pesaro and Milan, 2003.

González-Palacios 2004a
Alvar González-Palacios. *Arredi e ornamenti alla corte di Roma, 1560–1795.* Milan, 2004.

González-Palacios 2004b
Alvar González-Palacios. "The Badminton Cabinet." In Christie's 2004, pp. 30–58.

González-Palacios 2005
Alvar González-Palacios. "An Octagonal Italian Pietra Dura Table Top from the Florentine Grand Ducal Workshops." In *Two Late Regency Collectors: Philip John Miles and George Byng, 1815–45,* pp. 118–27 (under lot 50). Christie's, London, sale cat., June 9, 2005.

González-Palacios 2007a
Alvar González-Palacios. "The Badminton Cabinet." In Kräftner 2007, pp. 69–107.

González-Palacios 2007b
Alvar González-Palacios. "Octagonal Tables: Rome and Florence." In *Important Italian and Continental Furniture,* pp. 48–54 (under lot 21). Sotheby's, London, sale cat., December 4, 2007.

González-Palacios, Röttgen, and Przyborowski 1982
Alvar González-Palacios, Steffi Röttgen, and Claudia Przyborowski. *The Art of Mosaics: Selections from the Gilbert Collection.* Rev. ed. Translated by Alla Theodora Hall. Los Angeles, 1982.

Goodison 1972
Nicholas Goodison. "The King's Vases." *Furniture History* 8 (1972), pp. 35–40.

Goodison 1974
Nicholas Goodison. *Ormolu: The Work of Matthew Boulton.* London, 1974.

Goodison 2002
Nicholas Goodison. *Matthew Boulton: Ormolu.* London, 2002.

Gordon 2003
Alden R. Gordon. *The Houses and Collections of the Marquis de Marigny.* Edited by Carolyne Ayçaguer-Ron, with Maria L. Gilbert, Elizabeth A. Spatz, and Patricia A. Teter. Documents for the History of Collecting, French Inventories 1. Los Angeles, 2003.

Gori 1748–53
Antonio Francesco Gori. *Symbolae Litterariae: Opuscula varia Philologica, Scientifica, Antiquaria, Signa, Lapides, Numismata, Gemmas et Monumenta Medii Aevi nunc Primum Edita Complectentes.* 10 vols. Florence, 1748–53.

Gori 1767
Antonio Francesco Gori. *Dactyliotheca Smithiana.* 2 vols. Venice, 1767.

Gotti 1872
Aurelio Gotti. *Le gallerie di Firenze: Relazione al Ministro della Pubblica Istruzione in Italia.* Florence, 1872.

Goyau 1911
Georges Goyau. "Mazarin, Jules." In *The Catholic Encyclopedia,* vol. 10, pp. 92–93. New York, 1911.

Grabski 1990
Józef Grabski. *Opus Sacrum: Catalogue of the Exhibition from the Collection of Barbara Piasecka Johnson.* Exh. cat., Royal Castle. Warsaw, 1990.

Graf 1999
Bernhard Graf. *Heilen mit Edelsteinen: Die wichtigsten Heilsteine und ihre Wirkungen; wie sie ihre persönlichen Steine auswählen; Heilenergie verstärken mit Wasser, Sonne & Mond.* Munich, 1999.

Graf 2001
Bernhard Graf. *Gems: The World's Greatest Treasures and Their Stories.* Munich, 2001.

Gramberg 1959
Werner Gramberg. "Die Hamburger Bronzebüste Paul III. Farnese von Guglielmo della Porta." In *Festschrift für Erich Meyer zum sechzigsten Geburtstag, 29. Oktober 1957: Studien zu Werken in den Sammlungen des Museums für Kunst und Gewerbe,* pp. 160–72. Hamburg, 1959.

Grandjean 1964
Serge Grandjean. *Inventaire après décès de l'impératrice Joséphine à Malmaison.* Paris, 1964.

Gregori and Hohenzollern 2002
Mina Gregori and Johann Georg Prinz von Hohenzollern, eds. *Natura morta italiana tra Cinquecento e Settecento.* Exh. cat., Kunsthalle, Hypo-Kulturstiftung, Munich. Milan and Munich, 2002.

Griffin 1979
Jasper Griffin. "The Fourth *Georgic*, Virgil, and Rome." *Greece and Rome,* 2nd ser., 26, no. 1 (April 1979), pp. 61–80.

Grube 2007
Ernst J. Grube. "Venetian Lacquer and Bookbindings of the Sixteenth Century." In Carboni 2007, pp. 230–43.

Guidobaldi 2003
Federico Guidobaldi. "Sectilia pavimenta e incrustationes: I rivestimenti policromi pavimentali e parietali in marmo o materiali litici e litoidi dell'antichità romana." In *Eternità e nobiltà di materia: Itinerario artistico fra le pietre policrome,* edited by Annamaria Giusti, pp. 15–75. Florence, 2003.

Guiffrey 1881–1901
Jules Guiffrey. *Comptes des Bâtiments du Roi sous le règne de Louis XIV.* 5 vols. Collection de documents inédits sur l'histoire de France, 3rd ser., Archéologie. Paris, 1881–1901.

Guiffrey 1885–86
Jules Guiffrey. *Inventaire général du mobilier de la Couronne sous Louis XIV (1663–1715).* 2 vols. Paris, 1885–86.

Guillemé-Brulon 1983
Dorothée Guillemé-Brulon. "Porcelaine: Les Plaques de Sèvres dans le mobilier." *L'Estampille,* no. 163 (November 1983), pp. 34–45.

Kenseth 1991
Joy Kenseth, ed. *The Age of the Marvelous.* Exh. cat., Hood Museum of Art, Dartmouth College, Hanover, New Hampshire; North Carolina Museum of Art, Raleigh; Museum of Fine Arts, Houston. Hanover, 1991.

Ketelsen 1996
Thomas Ketelsen. "Goethe weiss, was ein Bild vorstellt: Kenner ästimieren die Manier." *Frankfurter Allgemeine Zeitung,* February 3, 1996, pp. 37–38.

Ketelsen 1998
Thomas Ketelsen. "Art Auctions in Germany during the Eighteenth Century." In *Art Markets in Europe, 1400–1800,* edited by Michael North and David Ormrod, pp. 143–52. Aldershot, 1998.

Kisluk-Grosheide 2003
Daniëlle O. Kisluk-Grosheide. "Lack und Porzellan in *en-suite*-Dekorationen ostasiatisch inspirierter Raumensembles." In *Schwartz Porcelain: Die Leidenschaft für Lack und ihre Wirkung auf das europäische Porzellan,* pp. 77–95. Exh. cat., Museum für Lackkunst, Münster; Schloss Favorite bei Rastatt. Munich, Münster, and Karlsruhe, 2003.

Kisluk-Grosheide, Koeppe, and Rieder 2006
Daniëlle O. Kisluk-Grosheide, Wolfram Koeppe, and William Rieder. *European Furniture in The Metropolitan Museum of Art: Highlights of the Collection.* New York, 2006.

Klapsia 1944
Heinrich Klapsia. "Dionysio Miseroni." *Jahrbuch der Kunsthistorischen Sammlungen in Wien,* n.s., 13 (1944), pp. 301–58.

Klein 1969
Heinrich-Josef Klein. "Ornamentierte Antependien in Pietradura-, Scagliola- und Stuccolustro-Technik." In *Kunstgeschichtliche Aufsätze: Von seinen Schülern und Freunden des KhIK Heinz Ladendorf zum 29. Juni 1969 gewidmet,* edited by Joachim Gaus, pp. 276–308. Cologne, 1969.

Knothe 2006
Florian Knothe. "André-Charles Boulle's Early Production of *Bureaux Plats*: A Newly Attributed Writing Desk in the Huntington Collection." *Furniture History* 42 (2006), pp. 53–61.

Knothe 2007a
Florian Knothe. "French Furniture? German Artisans in Eighteenth-Century Paris and the Transfer of Knowledge by Traveling Journeymen." Paper presented at the symposium "At Home and Abroad: Geography and the Decorative Arts," held at the Bard Graduate Center for Studies in the Decorative Arts, Design, and Culture, New York, April 27, 2007.

Knothe 2007b
Florian Knothe. "L'Influence de la Manufacture Royale des Gobelins à l'étranger: Les Artisans de Louis XIV à Stockholm." In *L'Objet d'art en France du XVIᵉ au XVIIIᵉ siècle: De la création à l'imaginaire,* edited by Marc Favreau and Patrick Michel, pp. 75–88. Bordeaux, 2007.

Knothe 2008
Florian Knothe. "Ingenuity and Imitation: *Pietre Dure* and Its Colorful Progeny." *Magazine Antiques* 174 (July 2008).

Knothe forthcoming a
Florian Knothe. "The *Manufacture des Meubles de la Couronne aux Gobelins* under Louis XIV: A Social, Political and Cultural History." Ph.D. diss., University of London. Forthcoming.

Knothe forthcoming b
Florian Knothe. "Privileged Production: Furniture-Making by the *Artisans du Roi* in Seventeenth-Century Paris." To be published in a volume of papers presented at the Sir Francis Watson symposium held at the Wallace Collection, London, July 4, 2007. Forthcoming.

E. Koch 1987
Ebba Koch. "Pietre Dure and Other Artistic Contacts between the Court of the Mughals and That of the Medici." In *A Mirror of Princes: The Mughals and the Medici,* edited by Dalu Jones, pp. 29–56. Bombay, 1987.

E. Koch 1988
Ebba Koch. *Shah Jahan and Orpheus: The Pietre Dure Decoration and the Programme of the Throne in the Hall of Public Audiences at the Red Fort of Delhi.* Graz, 1988. [Reprinted in Ebba Koch, *Mughal Art and Imperial Ideology: Collected Essays,* pp. 61–129. New Delhi, 2001.]

R. A. Koch 1980
Robert A. Koch, ed. *Early German Masters: Jacob Bink, Georg Pencz, Heinrich Aldegrever.* The Illustrated Bartsch, vol. 16 (formerly vol. 8, pt. 3). New York, 1980.

Koeppe 1992
Wolfram Koeppe. *Die Lemmers-Danforth-Sammlung Wetzlar: Europäische Wohnkultur aus Renaissance und Barock.* Heidelberg, 1992.

Koeppe 1995
Wolfram Koeppe. "The Chest in the Italian and Central European Bedchamber from the Fifteenth to the Seventeenth Century." In *The Bedroom from the Renaissance to Art Deco,* compiled and edited by Meredith Chilton, pp. 13–24. Edited lectures of the Decorative Arts Institute, April 28–May 2, 1993. Toronto, 1995.

Koeppe 1996
Wolfram Koeppe. "The Swiss Room: Flims, Seventeenth Century." In Amelia Peck et al., *Period Rooms in The Metropolitan Museum of Art,* pp. 58–67. New York, 1996.

Koeppe 1997
Wolfram Koeppe. "Chinese Shells, French Prints, and Russian Goldsmithing: A Curious Group of Eighteenth-Century Russian Table Snuffboxes." *Metropolitan Museum Journal* 32 (1997), pp. 207–14.

Koeppe 2002a
Wolfram Koeppe. "Collecting for the Kunstkammer." [October 2002.] In The Metropolitan Museum of Art, New York, Timeline of Art History, 2000–. http://www.metmuseum.org/toah/hd/kuns/hd_kuns.htm

Koeppe 2002b
Wolfram Koeppe. "An Early Meissen Discovery: A *Shield Bearer* Designed by Hans Daucher for the Ducal Chapel in the Cathedral of Meissen." *Metropolitan Museum Journal* 37 (2002), pp. 41–62.

Koeppe 2004
Wolfram Koeppe. "Exotica and the Kunstkammer: 'Snake Stones, Iridescent Sea Snails, and Eggs of the Giant Iron-Devouring Bird.'" In *Princely Splendor: The Dresden Court, 1580–1620,* edited by Dirk Syndram and Antje Scherner, pp. 80–89. Exh. cat., Museum für Kunst und Gewerbe Hamburg; The Metropolitan Museum of Art, New York; Fondazione Memmo, Palazzo Ruspoli, Rome. Milan, Dresden, and New York, 2004.

Koeppe forthcoming
Wolfram Koeppe. "Gone with the Wind to the Western Hemisphere: Selling Off Furniture by David Roentgen and Decorative Arts of the Eighteenth Century." Special issue, edited by Anne Odom and Wendy Salmond, *Canadian American Slavic Studies* 43, nos. 1–4 (2009), pp. 247–74. Also to be published as a separate volume, *Treasures into Tractors: The Selling of Russia's Cultural Heritage, 1918–38* (Washington, D.C.: Hillwood Estate, Museum and Gardens, 2009).

Koeppe and Lupo 1991
Wolfram Koeppe and Michelangelo Lupo. "Lo *Heiltumsaltar* nella sacrestia della cattedrale di Trento." In Castelnuovo 1991, pp. 35–56.

***Königliches Dresden* 1990**
Königliches Dresden: Höfische Kunst im 18. Jahrhundert. Exh. cat., Kunsthalle, Hypo-Kulturstiftung. Munich, 1990.

Köpl 1911–12
Karl Köpl. "Urkunden und Regesten aus dem K. K. Statthalterei-Archiv in Prag." *Jahrbuch der Kunsthistorischen Sammlungen des Allerhöchsten Kaiserhauses* 30 (1911–12), pp. I–XXXIII.

Korzeniewski 2005
Uta Korzeniewski. *Karfunkelstein und Rosenquarz: Mythos und Symbolik edler Steine.* Ostfildern, 2005.

Kräftner 2007
Johann Kräftner, ed. *The Badminton Cabinet: Commessi di Pietre Dure in the Collections of the Prince of Liechtenstein.* Munich, 2007.

Kräftner 2007a
Johann Kräftner. "Stone-Cutting in Antiquity and

Its Renaissance in Central Italy." In Kräftner 2007, pp. 8–55.

Kramp 2000
Mario Kramp, ed. *Krönungen: Könige in Aachen—Geschichte und Mythos.* 2 vols. Exh. cat. Organized by the Verein Aachener Krönungsgeschichte. Mainz, 2000.

Krausch 2007
Heinz-Dieter Krausch. *"Kaiserkron und Päonien rot . . .": Von der Entdeckung und Einführung unserer Gartenblumen.* Munich and Hamburg, 2007.

Krčálová and Aschengreen Piacenti 1979
Jarmila Krčálová and Cristina Aschengreen Piacenti. "Castrucci." In *Dizionario biografico degli italiani,* vol. 22, pp. 251–53. Rome, 1979.

Kris 1929
Ernst Kris. *Meister und Meisterwerke der Steinschneidekunst in der italienischen Renaissance.* 2 vols. Vienna, 1929. [Repr., 1979.]

Kris 1930
Ernst Kris. "Zur Mailänder Glyptik der Renaissance." *Pantheon* 6 (December 1930), pp. 548–54.

Kubler 1978
George Kubler. "Drawings by G. A. Montorsoli in Madrid." In *Collaboration in Italian Renaissance Art,* edited by Wendy Stedman Sheard and John T. Paoletti, pp. 143–50. New Haven, 1978.

Kuchumov 1975
Anatolii Mikhailovich Kuchumov. *Pavlovsk Palace and Park.* Translated by V. Travlinsky and J. Hine. Leningrad, 1975.

Kuchumov 1981
Anatolii Mikhailovich Kuchumov. *Russian Decorative Art in the Collection of the Pavlovsk Palace Museum.* [In Russian.] State Hermitage Museum. Leningrad, 1981.

La Mare 1722
Nicolas de La Mare. *Traité de la police; ou, L'On trouvera l'histoire de son établissement, les fonctions et les prérogatives de ses magistrats, toutes les loix et tous les règlemens qui la concernent.* 2nd ed. 4 vols. Paris, 1722.

Lacuna 2004
Lacuna: Riflessioni sulle esperienze dell'Opificio delle Pietre Dure; Atti dei Convegni del 7 aprile 2002 e del 5 aprile 2003 . . . Ferrara. Florence, 2004.

Lafontaine-Dosogne 1995
Jacqueline Lafontaine-Dosogne. "The Art of Byzantium and Its Relation to Germany in the Time of the Empress Theophano." In Davids 1995, pp. 211–30.

Lalande 1769
Joseph-Jérôme Le Français de Lalande. *Voyage d'un François en Italie, fait dans les années 1765 & 1766.* 8 vols. Venice, 1769.

Lamm 1929–30
Carl Johan Lamm. *Mittelalterliche Gläser und Steinschnittarbeiten aus dem Nahen Osten.* 2 vols. Forschungen zur islamischen Kunst 5. Berlin, 1929–30.

Landman et al. 2001
Neil H. Landman, Paula M. Mikkelsen, Rüdiger Bieler, and Bennet Bronson. *Pearls: A Natural History.* Exh. cat., American Museum of Natural History, New York; Field Museum, Chicago. New York, 2001.

Langedijk 1978
Karla Langedijk. "A Lapis Lazuli Medallion of Cosimo I de' Medici." *Metropolitan Museum Journal* 13 (1978), pp. 75–78.

Langedijk 1979
Karla Langedijk. "Giovan Battista Foggini: The Monument to Vittoria delle Rovere at the Villa La Quiete and the Busts from Poggio Imperiale." *Mitteilungen des Kunsthistorischen Institutes in Florenz* 23 (1979), pp. 347–56.

Langedijk 1981–87
Karla Langedijk. *The Portraits of the Medici, Fifteenth–Eighteenth Centuries.* 3 vols. Florence, 1981–87.

Langer 1996
Brigitte Langer. "Frühe Prunkmöbel des 16. und 17. Jahrhunderts der Residenz München." In Langer and Württemberg 1996, pp. 18–30.

Langer and Württemberg 1996
Brigitte Langer and Alexander Herzog von Württemberg. *Die deutschen Möbel des 16. bis 18. Jahrhunderts.* Vol. 2 of *Die Möbel der Residenz München,* edited by Gerhard Hojer and Hans Ottomeyer. Bayerische Verwaltung der Staatlichen Schlösser, Gärten und Seen, Kataloge der Kunstsammlungen. Munich, 1996.

Lankheit 1962
Klaus Lankheit. *Florentinische Barockplastik: Die Kunst am Hofe der letzten Medici, 1670–1743.* Italienische Forschungen, 3rd ser., vol. 2. Munich, 1962.

Lanz and Seelig 1999
Hanspeter Lanz and Lorenz Seelig, eds. *Farbige Kostbarkeiten aus Glas: Kabinettstücke der Zürcher Hinterglasmalerei, 1600–1650.* Exh. cat., Bayerisches Nationalmuseum, Munich; Schweizerisches Landesmuseum, Zurich. Munich and Zurich, 1999.

Die lasterhafte Panazee 1992
Die lasterhafte Panazee: 500 Jahre Tabakkultur in Europa. Exh. cat., Österreichisches Tabakmuseum, Vienna. Schriftenreihe des Österreichischen Tabakmuseums 5. [Vienna], 1992.

Lastic Saint-Jal 1961
Georges de Lastic Saint-Jal. "Desportes." *Connaissance des arts,* no. 107 (January 1961), pp. 56–65.

Lastri 1799
Marco Lastri. *L'osservatore fiorentino sugli edifizi della sua patria per servire alla storia della medesima.* 2nd ed. Vol. 6. Florence, 1799.

Laue 2008
Georg Laue, ed. *Möbel für die Kunstkammern Europas: Kabinettschränke und Prunkkassetten / Furniture for European Kunstkammer: Collector's Cabinets and Caskets.* Munich, 2008.

Laurain-Portemer 1975
Madeleine Laurain-Portemer. "Mazarin militant de l'art baroque au temps de Richelieu (1634–1642)." *Bulletin de la Société de l'Histoire de l'Art Français,* 1975 (pub. 1976), pp. 65–100.

Lawrence 2007
Sarah E. Lawrence, ed. *Piranesi as Designer.* Exh. cat., Cooper Hewitt, National Design Museum, Smithsonian Institution. New York, 2007.

Le Corbeiller 1960
Clare Le Corbeiller. "James Cox and His Curious Toys." *The Metropolitan Museum of Art Bulletin,* n.s., 18, no. 10 (June 1960), pp. 318–24.

Le Corbeiller 1970
Clare Le Corbeiller. "James Cox: A Biographical Review." *Burlington Magazine* 112 (June 1970), pp. 351–58.

Leben 1992
Ulrich Leben. *Molitor: Ébéniste from the Ancien Régime to the Bourbon Restoration, with a Complete Catalogue of the Furniture.* London, 1992.

Legner 1978
Anton Legner. "Wände aus Edelstein und Gefässe aus Kristall." In *Die Parler und der schöne Stil, 1350–1400: Europäische Kunst unter den Luxemburgern,* vol. 3, pp. 169–82. Exh. cat., Museen der Stadt Köln. Cologne, 1978.

Legner 1985
Anton Legner, ed. *Ornamenta Ecclesiae: Kunst und Künstler der Romanik.* Exh. cat., Josef-Haubrich-Kunsthalle. Organized by the Schnütgen-Museum. Cologne, 1985.

Lemonnier 1983
Patricia Lemonnier. *Weisweiler.* Paris, 1983.

Lemonnier 1984
Patricia Lemonnier. "Les Commodes de Martin Carlin." *L'Estampille,* nos. 171–72 (July–August 1984), pp. 6–19.

Lentz 2000
Christel Lentz. "Ein Idsteiner Kunstwerk im Grünen Gewölbe zu Dresden." *Nassauische Annalen* 111 (2000), pp. 205–12.

Leopold 1995
John H. Leopold. "Collecting Instruments in Protestant Europe before 1800." *Journal of the History of Collections* 7, no. 2 (1995), pp. 151–57.

Leoshko 1989
Janice Leoshko. "Mausoleum for an Empress." In Pratapaditya Pal, Janice Leoshko, Joseph M. Dye III, and Stephen Markel, *Romance of the Taj Mahal*, pp. 53–87. Exh. cat., Los Angeles County Museum of Art; Asia Society, New York; and other venues. London and Los Angeles, 1989.

Lerner 1984
Martin Lerner. *The Flame and the Lotus: Indian and Southeast Asian Art from the Kronos Collections.* Exh. cat., The Metropolitan Museum of Art. New York, 1984.

Lessmann and König-Lein 2002
Johanna Lessmann and Susanne König-Lein. *Wachsarbeiten des 16. bis 20. Jahrhunderts.* Sammlungskataloge des Herzog Anton Ulrich-Museums Braunschweig 9. Braunschweig, 2002.

Lewis 1958
Bernard Lewis. *The Arabs in History.* Rev. ed. New York, 1958.

Liechtenstein 1985
Liechtenstein, the Princely Collections: The Collections of the Prince of Liechtenstein. Exh. cat., The Metropolitan Museum of Art. New York, 1985.

Lietzmann 1998
Hilda Lietzmann. *Valentin Drausch und Herzog Wilhelm V. von Bayern: Ein Edelsteinschneider der Spätrenaissance und sein Auftraggeber.* Kunstwissenschaftliche Studien 75. Munich, 1998.

Liscia Bemporad 1993
Dora Liscia Bemporad, ed. *Argenti fiorentini dal XV al XIX secolo: Tipologie e marchi.* 3 vols. Florence, 1993.

Liscia Bemporad 1996
Dora Liscia Bemporad. "Un gruppo di montature dei vasi del Tesoro di Lorenzo il Magnifico." In *La Toscana al tempo di Lorenzo il Magnifico: Politica, economia, cultura, arte*, vol. 1, pp. 261–75. Convegno Internazionale di Studi, Florence, Pisa, and Siena, November 5–8, 1992. Pisa, 1996.

Liselotte von der Pfalz 1996
Liselotte von der Pfalz: Madame am Hofe des Sonnenkönigs. Exh. cat., Heidelberger Schloss. Heidelberg, 1996.

Loats 1997
Carol L. Loats. "Gender, Guilds, and Work Identity: Perspectives from Sixteenth-Century Paris." *French Historical Studies* 20, no. 1 (Winter 1997), pp. 15–30.

Loewental, Harden, and Bromehead 1949
A. I. Loewental, D. B. Harden, and C. E. N. Bromehead. "Vasa Murrina." *Journal of Roman Studies* 39, nos. 1–2 (1949), pp. 31–37.

Lomazzo 1589 (1993 ed.)
Giovanni Paolo Lomazzo. *Rabisch.* Milan, 1589. 1993 ed.: Edited by Dante Isella. Turin, 1993.

Love 1996
Ronald S. Love. "Rituals of Majesty: France, Siam, and Court Spectacle in Royal Image-Building at Versailles in 1685 and 1686." *Canadian Journal of History* 31, no. 2 (August 1996), pp. 171–98.

Lugt 1938–87
Frits Lugt. *Répertoire des catalogues de ventes publiques, intéressant l'art ou la curiosité . . . .* 4 vols. The Hague, 1938–87.

Luperini 1999
Ilario Luperini, ed. *Disegnare l'alabastro.* Ospedaletto, 1999.

Magnificenza alla corte dei Medici 1997
Magnificenza alla corte dei Medici: Arte a Firenze alla fine del Cinquecento. Exh. cat., Museo degli Argenti, Palazzo Pitti, Florence. Milan, 1997.

Makarov 1938
Vladimir Kuz'mich Makarov. *Objects Made of Colored Stone in the Hermitage Collection.* [In Russian]. State Hermitage Museum. Leningrad, 1938.

Malgouyres 2003
Philippe Malgouyres. *Porphyre: La Pierre pourpre des Ptolémées aux Bonaparte.* Exh. cat., Musée du Louvre. Paris, 2003.

Marchionni 1891
Edoardo Marchionni. *Guida per il visatore delle R. R. Cappelle Medicee e R. Opificio delle Pietre Dure in Firenze.* Florence, 1891.

Margerie and Papet 2004
Laure de Margerie and Édouard Papet. *Facing the Other: Charles Cordier (1827–1905), Ethnographic Sculptor.* Translated by Lenora Ammon, Laurel Hirsch, and Clare Palmieri. Exh. cat., Musée d'Orsay, Paris; Musée National des Beaux-Arts du Québec; Dahesh Museum, New York. New York, 2004.

A. Marie and J. Marie 1976
Alfred Marie and Jeanne Marie. *Versailles au temps de Louis XIV.* Pt. 3, *Mansart et Robert de Cotte.* Paris, 1976.

Marie-Antoinette 2008
Marie-Antoinette. Exh. cat., Galeries Nationales du Grand Palais. Paris, 2008.

Martial 1993
Martial. *Epigrams.* Edited and translated by D. R. Shackleton Bailey. 3 vols. Loeb Classical Library. Cambridge, Mass., 1993.

Maser 1967
Edward Andrew Maser. "Drawings by Giuseppe Zocchi for Works in Florentine Mosaic." *Master Drawings* 5, no. 1 (1967), pp. 47–53.

Massinelli 1990
Anna Maria Massinelli. "Magnificenze medicee: Gli stipi della Tribuna." *Antologia di belle arti*, n.s.,
nos. 35–38 (1990), pp. 111–34. Volume titled *Il Neoclassicismo II.*

Massinelli 1992
Anna Maria Massinelli. "Cosimo I and His Sons: The Treasures of the Grand Dukes." In Anna Maria Massinelli and Filippo Tuena, *Treasures of the Medici*, pp. 57–143. New York, 1992.

Massinelli 1993
Anna Maria Massinelli. *Il mobile toscano.* Milan, 1993.

Massinelli 2000
Anna Maria Massinelli. *Hardstones.* Gilbert Collection. London, 2000.

Mauriès 2002
Patrick Mauriès. *Cabinets of Curiosities.* London, 2002.

Mavrodina 2000
Natalya Mavrodina. "Decorative Stonework." In *Stroganoff* 2000, pp. 163–65.

Mavrodina 2007
Natalya Mavrodina. *The Art of Russian Stone Carvers, Eighteenth–Nineteenth Centuries: The Catalogue of the Collection.* [In Russian.] State Hermitage Museum. Saint Petersburg, 2007.

McClees 1925
Helen McClees. *The Daily Life of the Greeks and Romans as Illustrated in the Classical Collections.* The Metropolitan Museum of Art. New York, 1925.

McClees 1933
Helen McClees. *The Daily Life of the Greeks and Romans as Illustrated in the Classical Collections.* With additions by C. Alexander. The Metropolitan Museum of Art. New York, 1933.

McCormick and Ottomeyer 2004
Heather Jane McCormick and Hans Ottomeyer, eds. *Vasemania: Neoclassical Form and Ornament in Europe. Selections from The Metropolitan Museum of Art.* Exh. cat., Bard Graduate Center for Studies in the Decorative Arts, Design, and Culture. New York, 2004.

McCrory 1979
Martha McCrory. "Some Gems from the Medici Cabinet of the Cinquecento." *Burlington Magazine* 121 (August 1979), pp. 511–14.

McCrory 1998
Martha McCrory. "Immutable Images: Glyptic Portraits at the Medici Court in Sixteenth-Century Florence." In *The Image of the Individual: Portraits in the Renaissance*, edited by Nicholas Mann and Luke Syson, pp. 40–54. London, 1998.

Meier-Staubach 1977
Christel Meier[-Staubach]. *Gemma Spiritalis: Methode und Gebrauch der Edelsteinallegorese vom frühen Christentum bis ins 18. Jahrhundert.* Vol. 1.

Münstersche Mittelalter-Schriften 34. Munich, 1977.

Menzhausen 1977
Joachim Menzhausen. *Dresdener Kunstkammer und Grünes Gewölbe*. Vienna, 1977.

Menzhausen 1982
Joachim Menzhausen. "Böttgers Schleif- und Poliermühle." In *Johann Friedrich Böttger 1982*, pp. 213–21.

Mercier 1782–83
Louis-Sébastien Mercier. *Tableau de Paris*. 4 vols. New ed. Amsterdam, 1782–83.

Metropolitan Museum 1964
The Metropolitan Museum of Art. *Decorative Art from the Samuel H. Kress Collection at The Metropolitan Museum of Art: The Tapestry Room from Croome Court, Furniture, Textiles, Sèvres Porcelains, and Other Objects*. London, 1964.

Metropolitan Museum 1977
The Metropolitan Museum of Art. *Highlights of the Untermyer Collection of English and Continental Decorative Arts*. New York, 1977.

Metropolitan Museum 1988
The Metropolitan Museum of Art. *Recent Acquisitions: A Selection, 1987–1988*. New York, 1988.

D. Meyer 1980
Daniel Meyer. *L'Histoire du Roy*. Paris, 1980.

D. Meyer 2002
Daniel Meyer. *Versailles: Furniture of the Royal Palace, Seventeenth and Eighteenth Centuries*. Translated by Ann Sautier-Greening. 2 vols. Volume 2 by Pierre Arizzoli-Clémentel. Dijon, 2002.

K.-H. Meyer 1973
Klaus-Heinrich Meyer. "Studien zum Steinschnitt des 17. und der ersten Hälfte des 18. Jahrhunderts: Unter besonderer Berücksichtigung der Werkstatt am Hofe von Hessen-Kassel in den Jahren 1680–1730." Ph.D. diss., Universität Hamburg, 1973.

Michaelsen and Buchholz 2006
Hans Michaelsen and Ralf Buchholz. *Vom Färben des Holzes, Holzbeizen von der Antike bis in die Gegenwart: Literatur, Geschichte, Technologie, Rekonstruktion, 2000 Rezepturen*. Petersberg, 2006.

Michel 1999
Patrick Michel. *Mazarin, prince des collectionneurs: Les Collections et l'ameublement du Cardinal Mazarin (1602–1661). Histoire et analyse*. Notes et documents des musées de France 34. Paris, 1999.

Mielsch 1985
Harald Mielsch. *Buntmarmore aus Rom im Antikenmuseum Berlin*. Staatliche Museen Preussischer Kulturbesitz. Berlin, 1985.

Minnaert 1998
Jean-Baptiste Minnaert, ed. *Le Faubourg Saint-*

Antoine: Architecture et métiers d'art. Collection Paris and son patrimoine. Paris, 1998.

Minneapolis Institute of Arts 1998
Minneapolis Institute of Arts. *Treasures from the Minneapolis Institute of Arts*. Minneapolis, 1998.

Minneapolis Institute of Arts forthcoming
Minneapolis Institute of Arts. *Minneapolis Institute of Arts Handbook of the Collection*. Forthcoming.

Molinier 1904
Émile Molinier. *Collection du baron A. Oppenheim: Tableaux et objets d'art*. Paris, 1904.

Monaci 1977
Lucia Monaci. *Disegni di Giovan Battista Foggini (1652–1725)*. Gabinetto Disegni e Stampe degli Uffizi 48. Florence, 1977.

Montagu 1985
Jennifer Montagu. *Alessandro Algardi*. 2 vols. New Haven, 1985.

Montagu 1989
Jennifer Montagu. *Roman Baroque Sculpture: The Industry of Art*. New Haven, 1989.

Montagu 1996
Jennifer Montagu. *Gold, Silver, and Bronze: Metal Sculpture of the Roman Baroque*. Bollingen Series 35, 39. A. W. Mellon Lectures in the Fine Arts, 1990. Princeton, 1996.

Montesquieu 1894–96
Charles de Secondat, baron de Montesquieu. *Voyage en Italie*. In *Voyages de Montesquieu*, vol. 1, pp. 17–296, vol. 2, pp. 1–126. Edited by Le baron Albert de Montesquieu. Collection bordelaise. Bordeaux, 1894–96.

Montevecchi and Vasco Rocca 1987
Benedetta Montevecchi and Sandra Vasco Rocca, eds. *Suppellettile ecclesiastica I*. Dizionari terminologici 4. Florence, 1987.

Montfaucon 1702
Bernard de Montfaucon. *Diarium Italicum*. Paris, 1702.

Morassi 1964
Antonio Morassi. *Art Treasures of the Medici: Jewellery, Silverware, Hard-Stone*. Translated by Paul Colacicchi. London, 1964. [Italian ed.: *Il tesoro dei Medici: Oreficerie, argenterie, pietre dure*. Milan, 1963.]

Morávek 1937
Jan Morávek. *Nově objevený inventář rudolfinských sbírek na hradě pražském*. Prague, 1937.

Morigia 1595
Paolo Morigia. *La nobiltà di Milano*. Milan, 1595.

Morley 1999
John Morley. *The History of Furniture: Twenty-five Centuries of Style and Design in the Western Tradition*. Boston, 1999.

Morselli 2002
Raffaella Morselli, ed. *Gonzaga: La Celeste Galeria*. Vol. 1, *Le raccolte*. Exh. cat., Palazzo Te and Palazzo Ducale, Mantua. Milan, 2002.

Mosco 2004a
Marilena Mosco. "Cosimo III and 'Gran Principe' Ferdinando: From Sacred to Profane." In Marilena Mosco and Ornella Casazza, *The Museo degli Argenti: Collections and Collectors*, pp. 152–67. Florence, 2004.

Mosco 2004b
Marilena Mosco. "Lorenzo the Magnificent: Vases." In Marilena Mosco and Ornella Casazza, *The Museo degli Argenti: Collections and Collectors*, pp. 30–45. Florence, 2004.

Mosco 2004c
Marilena Mosco. "Francesco I and the Casino di San Marco: Crystal and 'Pietre Dure.'" In Marilena Mosco and Ornella Casazza, *The Museo degli Argenti: Collections and Collectors*, pp. 64–81. Florence, 2004.

Mosco 2004d
Marilena Mosco. "The Medici and the Allure of the Exotic." In Marilena Mosco and Ornella Casazza, *The Museo degli Argenti: Collections and Collectors*, pp. 168–83. Florence, 2004.

Mosheim 1863
John Laurence von Mosheim. *Institutes of Ecclesiastical History, Ancient and Modern*. 3 vols. London, 1863.

Moulin 1992
Jean-Marie Moulin. *Guide du Musée National du Château de Compiègne*. Paris, 1992.

Naeve and Roberts 1986
Milo M. Naeve and Lynn Springer Roberts, with contributions by Ian Wardropper, Christian Witt-Dörring, and Joanne Berens. *A Decade of Decorative Arts: The Antiquarian Society of the Art Institute of Chicago*. Exh. cat., Art Institute of Chicago. Chicago, 1986.

Nagler 1835–52
Georg Kaspar Nagler. *Neues allgemeines Künstler-Lexicon: Oder Nachrichten von dem Leben und den Werken der Maler, Bildhauer, Baumeister, Kupferstecher etc*. 22 vols. Munich, 1835–52.

Napoleone 2003
Caterina Napoleone. "Cultura antiquaria nel collezionismo dei marmi colorati tra XVI e XVII secolo." In *Eternità e nobiltà di materia: Itinerario artistico fra le pietre policrome*, edited by Annamaria Giusti, pp. 169–83. Florence, 2003.

Napoleone 2006
Caterina Napoleone. *I marmi del trattato di Faustino Corsi: Catalogo descrittivo di una collezione delle pietre usate dagli antichi per costruzione e decorazione . . . .* Florence, 2006.

Nardinocchi 1993
Elisabetta Nardinocchi. "Laboratori in galleria e

botteghe sul Ponte Vecchio: Sviluppi e vicende dell'oreficeria nella Firenze del Seicento." In Liscia Bemporad 1993, vol. 1, pp. 101–67.

La natura morta italiana 1964
La natura morta italiana. Exh. cat., Zurich Art Gallery; Boymans Museum, Rotterdam; Palazzo Reale, Naples. Milan, 1964.

Il Neoclassicismo in Italia 2002
Il Neoclassicismo in Italia: Da Tiepolo a Canova. Exh. cat., Palazzo Reale, Milan. Milan and Florence, 2002.

Neugebauer-Maresch 1990
Christine Neugebauer-Maresch. "Zum Neufund einer 30 000 Jahre alten weiblichen Statuette bei Krems, Niederösterreich." *Antike Welt* 21, no. 1 (1990), pp. 3–13.

Neumann 1957
Erwin Neumann. "Florentiner Mosaik aus Prag." *Jahrbuch der Kunsthistorischen Sammlungen in Wien* 53 (1957), pp. 157–202.

Nicht 1980
Jutta Nicht. *Die Möbel im Neuen Palais.* Neues Palais in Sanssouci. Potsdam-Sanssouci, 1980.

Oesterreich 1773
Matthias Oesterreich. *Beschreibung aller Gemählde, Antiquitäten, und anderer kostbarer und merkwürdiger Sachen, so in denen beyden Schlössern von Sans-Souci, wie auch in dem Schlosse zu Potsdam und Charlottenburg enthalten sind.* Berlin, 1773.

Okada 2003
Amina Okada. *A Jewel of Mughal India: The Mausoleum of I'timad ud-Daulah.* Karakorum 1. Milan, 2003.

Oldershaw 2003
Cally Oldershaw. *Firefly Guide to Gems.* Toronto, 2003.

Olszewski 1999
Edward J. Olszewski. "Decorating the Palace: Cardinal Pietro Ottoboni (1667–1740) in the Cancelleria." In Walker and Hammond 1999, pp. 93–111.

Olszewski 2003
Edward J. Olszewski. "Liturgical Silver Commissioned by Cardinal Pietro Ottoboni (1667–1740)." *Cleveland Studies in the History of Art* 8 (2003), pp. 96–119.

Opere in mosaico 1971
Opere in mosaico: Intarsi e pietra paesina. Catalogo. Galleria Borghese. Rome, 1971.

Orlandi 2005
Paolo Orlandi. "Geositi minerari e mineralogici della provincia di Pisa." In *La geologia della provincia di Pisa: Cartografia, geositi e banche dati*, pp. 55–280. Pisa, 2005.

Ottomeyer 1999
Hans Ottomeyer. "Provenance and Use of Renaissance Drinking Vessels in the Kassel Collections." In *Mesas reais europeias / Encomendas e ofertas / Royal and Princely Tables of Europe: Commissions and Gifts / Tables royales en Europe: Commandes et cadeaux*, pp. 86–101. Acts of the International Colloquium, Lisbon, December 1996. [Lisbon], 1999.

Ottomeyer 2004
Hans Ottomeyer. "The Metamorphosis of the Neoclassical Vase." In McCormick and Ottomeyer 2004, pp. 15–29.

Ottomeyer, Schröder, and Winters 2006
Hans Ottomeyer, Klaus Albrecht Schröder, and Laurie Winters. *Biedermeier: The Invention of Simplicity.* Exh. cat., Milwaukee Art Museum and other venues. Milwaukee, 2006.

Pagani 1995
Catherine Pagani. "The Clocks of James Cox: Chinoiserie and the Clock Trade with China in the Late Eighteenth Century." *Apollo* 141 (January 1995), pp. 15–22.

Palazzo Vecchio 1980
Palazzo Vecchio: Committenza e collezionismo medicei. Published for the exhibition "Firenze e la Toscana dei Medici nell'Europa del Cinquecento," held at the Palazzo Vecchio and seven other locations in Florence. Florence, 1980.

Palma 1983
Beatrice Palma. *I marmi Ludovisi: Storia della collezione.* Vol. 1, pt. 4, of *Le sculture*, edited by Antonio Giuliano. Museo Nazionale Romano. Rome, 1983.

Pampaloni Martelli 1975
Annapaula Pampaloni Martelli. *Museo dell'Opificio delle Pietre Dure di Firenze.* Florence, 1975.

Pampaloni Martelli 1978
Annapaula Pampaloni Martelli. "Il commesso fiorentino." In Giusti, Mazzoni, and Pampaloni Martelli 1978, p. 275.

Parker 1959
James Parker. "Croome Court: The Architecture and Furniture." *The Metropolitan Museum of Art Bulletin*, n.s., 18, no. 3 (November 1959), pp. 79–95.

Parker 1960
James Parker. "The Metropolitan's Room from Croome Court: The Architecture and the Furniture." *Magazine Antiques* 77 (January 1960), pp. 81–82.

Parker 1961
James Parker. "The Tapestry Room from Croome Court." *Connoisseur* 147 (March 1961), pp. 109–13.

Parker 1966
James Parker. "French Eighteenth-Century Furniture Depicted on Canvas." *The Metropolitan Museum of Art Bulletin*, n.s., 24, no. 5 (January 1966), pp. 177–92.

Parsons 1969
Merribell Maddux Parsons. "A Monument of Rome." *Minneapolis Institute of Arts Bulletin* 58 (1969), pp. 46–53.

Parures d'or et de pourpre 2002
Parures d'or et de pourpre: Le Mobilier à la cour des Valois. Exh. cat., Château de Blois. Paris and Blois, 2002.

Pastor 1952
Ludwig Pastor. *The History of the Popes, from the Close of the Middle Ages.* Edited by Ralph Francis Kerr. Vol. 23, *Clement VIII (1592–1605).* London and St. Louis, 1952.

Patrologiae cursus completus 1844–65
Jacques-Paul Migne, ed. *Patrologiae cursus completus . . . [Series Latina].* 221 vols. Paris, 1844–65.

Pechstein 1987
Klaus Pechstein. *Deutsche Goldschmiedekunst vom 15. bis zum 20. Jahrhundert aus dem Germanischen Nationalmuseum.* Exh. cat., Germanisches Nationalmuseum Nürnberg and other venues. Nuremberg and Berlin, 1987.

Pechstein 1992
Klaus Pechstein, ed. *Schätze deutscher Goldschmiedekunst von 1500–1920 aus dem Germanischen Nationalmuseum.* Exh. cat., Germanisches Nationalmuseum Nürnberg. Nuremberg and Berlin, 1992.

Pedretti 1978
Carlo Pedretti. *Leonardo architetto.* Milan, 1978.

Pellant 1992
Chris Pellant. *Rocks and Minerals.* Dorling Kindersley Handbooks. London, 1992.

Penny 1993
Nicholas Penny. *The Materials of Sculpture.* New Haven, 1993.

Pérez-Villamil 1904
Manuel Pérez-Villamil. *Artes é industrias del Buen Retiro: La fábrica de la china, el laboratorio de piedras duras y mosaico, obradores de bronces y marfiles.* Madrid, 1904.

Philippovich 1961
Eugen von Philippovich. *Simon Troger und andere Elfenbeinkünstler aus Tirol.* Schlern-Schriften 216. Innsbruck, 1961.

"Piano di tavolo con fiori" 1993
"Piano di tavolo con fiori." *OPD restauro*, no. 5 (1993), pp. 169–73 and p. 168.

Picón et al. 2007
Carlos A. Picón et al. *Art of the Classical World in The Metropolitan Museum of Art: Greece, Cyprus, Etruria, Rome.* New York, 2007.

Pittura su pietra 1970
Pittura su pietra. Exh. cat., Galleria Palatina, Palazzo Pitti. Florence, 1970.

Pliny the Elder 1855–57
Pliny the Elder. *The Natural History of Pliny.*
Translated and edited by John Bostock and H. T.
Riley. 6 vols. Bohn's Classical Library. London,
1855–57.

Poggi 1916
Giovanni Poggi. "Di un cammeo di Giovan
Antonio De' Rossi nel R. Museo Nazionale di
Firenze." *Rivista d'arte* 9 (1916; pub. 1918),
pp. 41–48.

Poggi 1920
Giovanni Poggi. "Un vaso in lapislazzuli nel
gabinetto delle gemme agli Uffizi." *Dedalo* 1
(1920), pp. 5–7.

Porphyre 1990
*Porphyre, la pierre royale: La Vieille Taillerie de
Älvdalen—son histoire et sa production.* Exh. cat.,
Centre Culturel Suédois. Paris, 1990.

Post 1997
Jeffrey E. Post. *The National Gem Collection.* National
Museum of Natural History, Smithsonian Institution.
New York, 1997.

Die Pracht der Medici 1998
Die Pracht der Medici: Florenz und Europa. 2 vols.
Exh. cat., Kunsthalle, Hypo-Kulturstiftung,
Munich; Kunsthistorisches Museum, Vienna;
Château de Blois. Munich and Vienna, 1998.

Pradère 1988
Alexandre Pradère. "Boulle: Du Louis XIV, sous
Louis XVI." *L'Objet d'art,* no. 4 (February 1988),
pp. 28–43.

Pradère 1989
Alexandre Pradère. *French Furniture Makers: The
Art of the Ébéniste from Louis XIV to the Revolution.*
Translated by Perran Wood. London, 1989.

Pradère 2007
Alexandre Pradère. "Baron van Hoorn: An *Amateur*
of Boulle, Antiquity, and the Middle Ages under
the Empire." *Furniture History* 43 (2007), pp. 205–25.

Prag um 1600 1988
*Prag um 1600: Kunst und Kultur am Hofe Kaiser
Rudolfs II.* 2 vols. Exh. cat., Villa Hügel, Essen;
Kunsthistorisches Museum, Vienna. Freren, 1988.

Prat 1963
Jean-Honoré Prat. *Histoire du faubourg Saint-
Antoine: Vieux Chemin de Paris, faubourg artisanal,
quartier des grands ébénistes du XVIIIᵉ siècle, nerf des
révolutions, capitale du meuble.* 2nd ed. Paris, 1963.

Prater 1988
Andreas Prater. *Cellinis Salzfass für Franz I.: Ein
Tischgerät als Herrschaftszeichen.* Stuttgart, 1988.

Pratesi 1993
Giovanni Pratesi, ed. *Repertorio della scultura fiorentina del Seicento e Settecento.* 3 vols. Archivi di arte
antica. Turin, 1993.

"Presens qui sont partis pour Siam" 1687
"Liste des presens qui sont partis pour Siam."
Mercure galant, May 1687, pp. 51–106.

Pressouyre 1984
Sylvia Pressouyre. *Nicolas Cordier: Recherches sur la
sculpture à Rome autour de 1600.* 2 vols. Collection de
l'École Française de Rome 73. Rome, 1984.

Princely Taste 1995
Princely Taste: Treasures from Great Private Collections.
Exh. cat., Israel Museum. Jerusalem, 1995.

Prudon 1989
Theodore H. M. Prudon. "Simulating Stone, 1860–
1940: Artificial Marble, Artificial Stone, and Cast
Stone." *APT Bulletin* (Association for Preservation
Technology International) 21, nos. 3–4 (1989),
pp. 79–91.

Przyborowski 1982
Claudia Przyborowski. *Die Ausstattung der Fürsten-
kapelle an der Basilika von San Lorenzo in Florenz:
Versuch einer Rekonstruktion.* 2 vols. Würzburg,
1982. [Originally presented as the author's Ph.D.
diss., Technische Universität, Berlin, 1980.]

Przyborowski 1998
Claudia Przyborowski. "Commesso-Tafeln im
Florentiner Kabinett in Schloss Favorite bei Rastatt:
Studien zu Arbeiten der Galleria dei Lavori in Florenz
zu Beginn des 18. Jahrhunderts." *Mitteilungen des
Kunsthistorischen Institutes in Florenz* 42 (1998),
pp. 383–457.

Quellmalz 1990
Werner Quellmalz. *Die edlen Steine Sachsens.*
Leipzig, 1990.

Quiccheberg 1565
Samuel Quiccheberg. *Inscriptiones vel Tituli Theatri
amplissimi.* Munich, 1565.

Rabisch 1998
*Rabisch: Il grottesco nell'arte del Cinquecento.
L'Accademia della Val di Blenio, Lomazzo e l'ambiente
milanese.* Exh. cat., Museo Cantonale d'Arte,
Lugano. Milan, 1998.

Raggio 1952
Olga Raggio. "Light and Line in Renaissance
Crystal Engravings." *The Metropolitan Museum of
Art Bulletin,* n.s., 10, no. 7 (March 1952), pp. 193–202.

Raggio 1960
Olga Raggio. "The Farnese Table: A Rediscovered
Work by Vignola." *The Metropolitan Museum of Art
Bulletin,* n.s., 18, no. 7 (March 1960), pp. 213–31.

Raggio 1971
Olga Raggio. "Alessandro Algardi e gli stucchi di
Villa Pamphili." *Paragone,* no. 251 (January 1971),
pp. 3–38.

Raggio 1994
Olga Raggio. "Rethinking the Collections: New
Presentations of European Decorative Arts at The

Metropolitan Museum of Art." *Apollo* 139 (January
1994), pp. 3–19.

Ramond 1994
Pierre Ramond. *Chefs-d'oeuvre des marqueteurs.*
Vol. 1, *Des origines à Louis XIV.* Dourdan, 1994.

Raymond 1867
Paul Raymond. "Notes extraites des comptes de
Jeanne d'Albret et de ses enfants, 1556–1608." *Revue
d'Aquitaine et des Pyrénées* 11 (1867), pp. 43–49.

"Recent Acquisitions" 1995
"Recent Acquisitions: A Selection, 1994–1995."
The Metropolitan Museum of Art Bulletin, n.s., 53,
no. 2 (Fall 1995).

"Recent Acquisitions" 2001
"Recent Acquisitions: A Selection, 2000–2001."
The Metropolitan Museum of Art Bulletin, n.s., 59,
no. 2 (Fall 2001).

"Recent Acquisitions" 2006
"Recent Acquisitions: A Selection, 2005–2006."
The Metropolitan Museum of Art Bulletin, n.s., 64,
no. 2 (Fall 2006).

"Recent Acquisitions" 2007
"Recent Acquisitions: A Selection, 2006–2007."
The Metropolitan Museum of Art Bulletin, n.s., 65,
no. 2 (Fall 2007).

Die Renaissance im deutschen Südwesten 1986
*Die Renaissance im deutschen Südwesten: Die
Renaissance im deutschen Südwesten zwischen
Reformation und Dreissigjährigem Krieg.* 2 vols.
Exh. cat., Heidelberger Schloss. Karlsruhe, 1986.

"Il restauro di un tavolo in pietre dure" 2007
"Il restauro di un tavolo in pietre dure del
Kunsthistorisches Museum di Vienna." *Newsletter*
(Amici dell'Opificio), no. 6 (July 2007).

Rey 2000
Daniel Rey. "The Boundless Chest: The Uppsala
Cabinet." *FMR* (International ed.), no. 102
(February 2000), pp. 29–50.

Riccardi-Cubitt 1992
Monique Riccardi-Cubitt. *The Art of the Cabinet,
including a Chronological Guide to Styles.* London,
1992.

G. M. A. Richter 1915
Gisela M. A. Richter. "Department of Classical Art,
Accessions of 1914: Terracottas, Bronzes, Glass and
Gems." *Bulletin of The Metropolitan Museum of Art* 10,
no. 10 (October 1915), pp. 208–12.

T. Richter 2005
Thomas Richter. *Die Wunderkammer: Kunst,
Natur und Wissenschaft in Renaissance und Barock.*
Glanzlichter aus dem Bernischen Historischen
Museum 15. Zurich, 2005.

Il Rinascimento in Italia 2001
Itaria runesansu: Kyūtei to toshi no bunkaten /

Il Rinascimento in Italia: La civiltà delle corti. [In Japanese; preface and captions also in Italian.] Exh. cat., Kokuritsu Seiyō Bijutsukan. Tokyo, 2001.

Roberts 2004
Jane Roberts, ed. *George III and Queen Charlotte: Patronage, Collecting and Court Taste*. London, 2004.

Rogasch 2004
Wilfried Rogasch. *Schatzhäuser Deutschlands: Kunst in adligem Privatbesitz*. Exh. cat., Haus der Kunst. Munich, 2004.

Ronfort 1991–92
Jean-Nérée Ronfort. "Jean Ménard (c. 1525–1582): Marqueteur et sculpteur en marbre et sa famille." *Antologia di belle arti*, n.s., nos. 39–42 (1991–92), pp. 139–47. Volume titled *Il Neoclassicismo III.*

Rossi (Ferdinando) 1967
Ferdinando Rossi. *La pittura di pietra*. Florence, 1967.

Rossi (Ferdinando) 1984
Ferdinando Rossi. *La pittura di pietra*. Edited by Ugo Procacci. Florence, 1984.

Rossi (Ferdinando) 1988
Ferdinando Rossi. "Il commesso e la glittica all'Opificio delle Pietre Dure." In Giusti 1988, pp. 276–78.

Rossi (Ferdinando) 2002
Ferdinando Rossi. *La pittura di pietra: Dall'arte del mosaico allo splendore delle pietre dure*. Rev. ed. Florence, 2002.

Rossi (Filippo) 1956
Filippo Rossi. *Capolavori di oreficeria italiana dall'XI al XVIII secolo*. Milan, 1956.

Rotondo Briasco 1962
Paola Rotondo Briasco. *Filippo Parodi*. Quaderni (Istituto di Storia dell'Arte, Università di Genova) 3. Genoa, 1962.

Roubo 1769–72
André Jacob Roubo. *L'Art du menuisier en meubles: Reproduction de l'ouvrage de l'époque, 1770–72*. 4 vols. Paris, 1769–72.

Ryser and Salmen 1995
Frieder Ryser and Brigitte Salmen. *"Amalierte Stuck uff Glas / Hinter Glas gemalte Historien und Gemäld": Hinterglaskunst von der Antike bis zur Neuzeit*. Exh. cat., Schlossmuseum Murnau. Murnau and Diessen, 1995.

Salort and Kubersky-Piredda 2007
Salvador Salort and Susanne Kubersky-Piredda. "Art Collecting in Philip II's Spain: The Role of Gonzalo de Liaño, King's Dwarf and Gentleman of the Bedchamber." Pt. 2. *Burlington Magazine* 149 (April 2007), pp. 224–31.

Sammartini 2000
Tudy Sammartini. *Steinböden in Venedig*. Munich, 2000.

San Lorenzo 1993
San Lorenzo: I documenti e i tesori nascosti. Exh. cat., Basilica of San Lorenzo, Florence. Venice, 1993.

Sandqvist and Tunander 1989
Inga-Britta Sandqvist and Ingemar Tunander. *Porfyr från Älvdalen*. Porfyrmuseet i Älvdalen. Älvdalen, 1989.

Sargentson 1996
Carolyn Sargentson. *Merchants and Luxury Markets: The Marchands Merciers of Eighteenth Century Paris*. Victoria and Albert Museum Studies in the History of Art and Design. London, 1996.

Sarre 1895
Friedrich Sarre. *Die Berliner Goldschmiede-Zunft von ihrem Entstehen bis zum Jahre 1800: Ein Beitrag zur Kunst- und Gewerbe- Geschichte Berlins*. Berlin, 1895.

Sassoon and Wilson 1986
Adrian Sassoon and Gillian Wilson. *Decorative Arts: A Handbook of the Collections of the J. Paul Getty Museum*. Malibu, 1986.

Saule 1982
Béatrix Saule. "Précisions sur la grande table en marqueterie de pierres dures du Muséum d'Histoire Naturelle de Paris. *Revue de gemmologie*, no. 73 (December 1982), pp. 2–4.

Scarisbrick 1993
Diana Scarisbrick. *Rings: Symbols of Wealth, Power and Affection*. London, 1993.

Schatzkästchen und Kabinettschrank 1989
Schatzkästchen und Kabinettschrank: Möbel für Sammler. Exh. cat., Kunstgewerbemuseum, Staatliche Museen Preussischer Kulturbesitz. Bestandskatalog XIV des Kunstgewerbemuseums. Berlin, 1989.

Schiedlausky 1961
Günther Schiedlausky. *Tee, Kaffee, Schokolade: Ihr Eintritt in die europäische Gesellschaft*. Bibliothek des Germanischen National-Museums Nürnberg zur Deutschen Kunst- und Kulturgeschichte 17. Munich, 1961.

Schizzerotto 1981
Giancarlo Schizzerotto. *Mantova 2000: Anni di ritratti*. Mantua, 1981.

Schmidberger 1986
Ekkehard Schmidberger. "Edelsteinschnitt des Barock." *Kunst & Antiquitäten*, 1986, no. 6, pp. 40–51.

Schmidberger and T. Richter 2001
Ekkehard Schmidberger and Thomas Richter. *Schatzkunst 800 bis 1800: Kunsthandwerk und Plastik der Staatlichen Museen Kassel im Hessischen Landes-museum Kassel*. Exh. cat., Hessisches Landesmuseum Kassel. Kassel and Wolfratshausen, 2001.

E. D. Schmidt 2005
Eike D. Schmidt. *Paul Heermann (1673–1732): Meister der Barockskulptur in Böhmen und Sachsen. Neue*

Aspekte seines Schaffens. [In German and English.] Munich, 2005.

P. Schmidt 1948
Philipp Schmidt. *Edelsteine: Ihr Wesen und ihr Wert bei den Kulturvölkern*. Bonn, 1948.

R. Schmidt 1995
Ralf Schmidt. "Die Schmucksteinsammlung des Meininger Herzogs Anton Ulrich (1687–1763)." *Veröffentlichungen* (Naturhistorisches Museum, Schloss Bertholdsburg, Schleusingen) 10 (1995), pp. 87–120.

Schnackenburg-Praël 1999
Heidi Schnackenburg-Praël. "Die Edelsteintafel im Grünen Gewölbe." *Weltkunst* 69, no. 5 (May 1999), pp. 894–97.

Schramm and Mütherich 1962
Percy Ernst Schramm and Florentine Mütherich. *Denkmale der deutschen Könige und Kaiser*. [Vol. 1], *Ein Beitrag zur Herrschergeschichte von Karl dem Grossen bis Friedrich II., 768–1250*. Veröffentlichungen des Zentralinstituts für Kunstgeschichte in München 2. Munich, 1962.

Schubnel 1977
Henri-Jean Schubnel. "Pierres précieuses, gemmes & objets d'art de la galerie de minéralogie du muséum (Jardin des Plantes)." *Revue de gemmologie*, special number (June 1977).

Schumann 2006
Walter Schumann. *Gemstones of the World*. Translated by Annette Englander and Daniel Shea. 3rd ed. New York, 2006.

Schütte 2003
Rudolf-Alexander Schütte. *Die Silberkammer der Landgrafen von Hessen-Kassel: Bestandskatalog der Goldschmiedearbeiten des 15. bis 18. Jahrhunderts in den Staatlichen Museen Kassel*. Kataloge der Staatlichen Museen Kassel 30. Kassel and Wolfratshausen, 2003.

Schütze 2007
Sebastian Schütze. *Kardinal Maffeo Barberini, später Papst Urban VIII. und die Entstehung des römanischen Hochbarock*. Römische Forschungen der Bibliotheca Hertziana 32. Munich, 2007.

Schwarzacher 1984
Susanne Schwarzacher. "Studien zum barocken Gefässchnitt in Süddeutschland und Österreich, Schwerpunkt Salzburg." Ph.D. diss., Universität Wien, 1984.

Scott 1995
Katie Scott. *The Rococo Interior: Decoration and Social Spaces in Early Eighteenth-Century Paris*. New Haven, 1995.

Seelig 1985a
Lorenz Seelig. "Farbige Einlegearbeiten aus Stein und Stuck in Münchner Schlössern." In *Schöndruck, Widerdruck: Schriften-Fest für Michael Meier zum 20. Dezember 1985*, pp. 28–45. Munich, 1985.

Seelig 1985b
Lorenz Seelig. "The Munich *Kunstkammer*, 1565–1807." In *The Origins of Museums: The Cabinet of Curiosities in Sixteenth- and Seventeenth-Century Europe*, edited by Oliver Impey and Arthur MacGregor, pp. 76–89. Oxford, 1985.

Seelig 1987
Lorenz Seelig. "Scagliola und Pietra Dura: Farbige Stein- und Stuckintarsien in Münchner Schlössern und Museen." *Kunst & Antiquitäten*, 1987, no. 1, pp. 26–39.

Seidel 1901
Paul Seidel. "Zur Geschichte der Kunst unter Friedrich dem Grossen." Pt. 2, "Die Prunkdosen Friedrich des Grossen." *Hohenzollern-Jahrbuch* 5 (1901), pp. 74–86.

Seipel 2005
Wilfried Seipel, ed. *Bernstein für Thron und Altar: Das Gold des Meeres in fürstlichen Kunst- und Schatzkammern.* Exh. cat., Kunsthistorisches Museum, Vienna. Vienna and Milan, 2005.

Seling 1980
Helmut Seling. *Die Kunst der Augsburger Goldschmiede, 1529–1868: Meister, Marken, Werke.* 3 vols. Munich, 1980.

Semenov and Shakinko 1982
Vladislav Borisovich Semenov and I. M. Shakinko. *Semiprecious Stones from the Ural Mountains: The History of Stone Carving and Grinding in the Urals.* [In Russian.] Sverdlovsk, 1982.

Setterwall 1959
Åke Setterwall. "Some Louis XVI Furniture Decorated with *Pietre Dure* Reliefs." *Burlington Magazine* 101 (December 1959), pp. 425–35.

Sherman 1971
Anthony C. Sherman. *The Gilbert Mosaic Collection.* Edited by M. Barbara Scheibel. West Haven, Conn., 1971.

Siponta De Salvia 1984
Maria Siponta De Salvia. "Gli arredi sacri." In *Il complesso monumentale di San Lorenzo: La basilica, le sagrestie, le cappelle, la biblioteca*, edited by Umberto Baldini and Bruno Nardini, pp. 321–39. Florence, 1984.

L. A. Smith 1996
Lucy Abel Smith. "The Duke of Beaufort's Marble Room." *Burlington Magazine* 138 (January 1996), pp. 25–30.

R. Smith 2000
Roger Smith. "James Cox (c. 1723–1800): A Revised Biography." *Burlington Magazine* 142 (June 2000), pp. 353–61.

Solodkoff 1981
Alexander von Solodkoff. *Russische Goldschmiede-kunst, 17.–19. Jahrhundert: Silber, Email, Niello, Golddosen, Schmuck.* Munich, 1981. [English ed.: *Russian Gold and Silverwork, Seventeenth–Nineteenth Century.* Translated by Christopher Holme. New York, 1981.]

Speer and Binding 2000
Andreas Speer and Günther Binding, eds. *Abt Suger von Saint-Denis, ausgewählte Schriften: Ordinatio, De Consecratione, De Administratione.* Darmstadt, 2000.

Spini 1976
Giorgio Spini, ed. *Architettura e politica da Cosimo I a Ferdinando I.* Studi sulla Toscana medicea 1. Florence, 1976.

Splendeurs de la cour de Saxe 2006
Splendeurs de la cour de Saxe: Dresde à Versailles. Exh. cat., Musée National des Châteaux de Versailles et de Trianon. Paris, 2006.

Splendour of the Medici 2008
The Splendour of the Medici: Art and Life in Renaissance Florence. Exh. cat., Museum of Fine Arts. Budapest, 2008.

Sponsel 1921
Jean-Louis Sponsel. *Führer durch das Grüne Gewölbe zu Dresden.* 2nd ed. Dresden, 1921.

Sponsel 1929
Jean-Louis Sponsel. *Das Grüne Gewölbe zu Dresden: Eine Auswahl an Meisterwerken der Goldschmiede-kunst in vier Bänden.* Vol. 3, *Kleinodien der Gold-schmiedekunst verziert mit Email und Juwelen, Erzeugnisse der Steinschneidekunst in Bergkristall und farbigen Steinarten in kostbarsten Fassungen, Galanterie-waren und Nippesfiguren, Kabinettstücke.* Leipzig, 1929.

St. Petersburg um 1800 1990
St. Petersburg um 1800: Ein goldenes Zeitalter des rus-sischen Zarenreichs. Meisterwerke und authentische Zeugnisse der Zeit aus der Staatlichen Ermitage, Leningrad. Exh. cat., Villa Hügel, Essen. Recklinghausen, 1990.

Stafford 2001
Barbara Maria Stafford. "Revealing Technologies / Magical Domains." In Barbara Maria Stafford and Frances Terpak, *Devices of Wonder: From the World in a Box to Images on a Screen*, pp. 1–142. Exh. cat., J. Paul Getty Museum. Los Angeles, 2001.

Staudinger 1995
Manfred Staudinger. "Hans Vermeyen: Kammer-goldschmied Kaiser Rudolfs II. in Prag." *Jahrbuch der Kunsthistorischen Sammlungen in Wien* 91 (1995), pp. 263–71.

Steinberg 1932
Sigfrid H. Steinberg. "Abendländische Darstel-lungen der Maria Playtytera." In *Zeitschrift für Kirchengeschichte* 51 (1932), pp. 512–16.

Steinberg 1938
Sigfrid H. Steinberg. "A Portable Altar in the British Museum." *Journal of the Warburg Institute* 2, no. 1 (July 1938), pp. 71–72.

Steinbrück 1717 (1982 ed.)
Johann Melchior Steinbrück. *Bericht über die Porzellanmanufaktur Meissen von den Anfängen bis zum Jahre 1717.* Commentary by Ingelore Menzhausen. 2 vols. [Vol. 1], facsimile reprint of 1717 manuscript in the archives of the Dresdener Porzellansammlung. Gütersloh, 1982.

Steingräber 1955
Erich Steingräber. "Studien zur Florentiner Goldschmiedekunst." Pt. 1. *Mitteilungen des Kunsthistorischen Institutes in Florenz* 7 (August 1955), pp. 87–110.

Stiegemann and Wemhoff 2006
Christoph Stiegemann and Matthias Wemhoff, eds. *Canossa 1077: Erschütterung der Welt. Geschichte, Kunst und Kultur am Aufgang der Romanik.* 2 vols. Exh. cat., Museum in der Kaiserpfalz, Erzbischöf-liches Diözesanmuseum, and Städtische Galerie am Abdinghof, Paderborn. Munich, 2006.

Streidt and Frahm 1996
Gert Streidt and Klaus Frahm. *Potsdam: Die Schlösser und Gärten der Hohenzollern / Palaces and Gardens of the Hohenzollern / Châteaux et jardins des Hohenzollern.* Cologne, 1996.

Stroganoff 2000
Stroganoff: The Palace and Collections of a Russian Noble Family. Exh. cat., Portland Art Museum, Oregon; Kimbell Art Museum, Fort Worth. New York, 2000.

Sturm 1961
Heribert Sturm. *Egerer Reliefintarsien.* Veröffent-lichungen des Collegium Carolium 13. Munich, 1961.

Stürmer 1979
Michael Stürmer. "An Economy of Delight: Court Artisans of the Eighteenth Century." *Business History Review* 53, no. 4 (Winter 1979), pp. 496–528.

Suger 1979
Abbot Suger. *Abbot Suger on the Abbey Church of St.-Denis and Its Art Treasures.* Edited and translated by Erwin Panofsky. 2nd ed. by Gerda Panofsky-Soergel. Princeton, 1979.

Sundblom, Tunander, and Uggla 1985
Hans Sundblom, Ingemar Tunander, and Gabriel Uggla. *Porfyr: En utställning kring föremål från Älvdalens Gamla Porfyrverk.* Exh. cat., Bukowskis. Stockholm, 1985.

"Sur la beauté des apartemens du Roy à Versailles" 1682
"Sur la beauté des apartemens du Roy à Versailles, & les divertissemens que sa Majesté y donne à toute sa cour." *Mercure galant*, November 1682, pp. 359–71.

Syndram 1998
Dirk Syndram. "Ein Denkmal für die Kunst: Der Obeliscus Augustalis im Grünen Gewölbe." In Kappel 1998, pp. 73–87.

Syndram 2004a
Dirk Syndram. "Princely Diversion and Courtly Display: The Kunstkammer and Dresden's Renaissance Collections." In *Princely Splendor: The Dresden Court, 1580–1620*, edited by Dirk Syndram and Antje Scherner, pp. 54–69. Exh. cat., Museum für Kunst und Gewerbe Hamburg; The Metropolitan Museum of Art, New York; Fondazione Memmo, Palazzo Ruspoli, Rome. Milan, Dresden, and New York, 2004.

Syndram 2004b
Dirk Syndram. *Renaissance and Baroque Treasury Art: The Green Vault in Dresden.* Translated by Daniel Kletke. Munich, 2004.

Syndram 2006
Dirk Syndram. *Cabinet of Treasures of August the Strong from the Collection of the Green Vault, Dresden.* [In Russian.] Exh. cat., Kremlin Museum. Moscow, 2006.

Syndram and Weinhold 2007
Dirk Syndram and Ulrike Weinhold. ". . . und ein Leib von Perl": Die Sammlung der barocken Perlfiguren im Grünen Gewölbe. 2nd ed. Wolfratshausen, 2007. [1st ed., 2000.]

Syndram, Arnold, and Kappel 1997
Dirk Syndram, Ulli Arnold, and Jutta Kappel. *Das Grüne Gewölbe zu Dresden: Führer durch seine Geschichte und seine Sammlungen.* 2nd ed. Munich, 1997. [1st ed., 1994.]

Syndram, Kappel, and Weinhold 2006
Dirk Syndram, Jutta Kappel, and Ulrike Weinhold. *The Baroque Treasury at the Grünes Gewölbe Dresden.* Dresden and Munich, 2006.

Synge 1999
Lanto Synge. *Mallett Millennium: Fine Antique Furniture and Works of Art.* London, 1999.

Tarasova 1990a
Lina Tarasova. "Arbeiten aus Malachit." In *St. Petersburg um 1800* 1990, pp. 410–11.

Tarasova 1990b
Lina Tarasova. "Gefässe aus Stein." In *St. Petersburg um 1800* 1990, pp. 407–8.

Un Temps d'exubérance 2002
Un Temps d'exubérance: Les Arts décoratifs sous Louis XIII et Anne d'Autriche. Exh. cat., Galeries Nationales du Grand Palais. Paris, 2002.

Termolen 1990
Rosel Termolen, ed. *Heilkraft der Edelsteine: Heilige Hildegard.* Augsburg, 1990.

Terpak 2001
Frances Terpak. "Display Cabinet with Assemblage." In Barbara Maria Stafford and Frances Terpak, *Devices of Wonder: From the World in a Box to Images on a Screen,* pp. 158–65. Exh. cat., J. Paul Getty Museum. Los Angeles, 2001.

Thalheim 1998
Klaus Thalheim. "Die Suche nach 'edlen Steinen' in Sachsen vom 16. bis zum 18. Jahrhundert." In Kappel 1998, pp. 11–25.

Theuerkauff 1986
Christian Theuerkauff. *Die Bildwerke in Elfenbein des 16.–19. Jahrhunderts: Skulpturengalerie, Staatliche Museen Preussischer Kulturbesitz.* Die Bildwerke der Skulpturengalerie Berlin 2. Berlin, 1986.

Thiébault 1901
Dieudonné Thiébault. *Friedrich der Grosse und sein Hof: Persönliche Erinnerungen an einen 20 jährigen Aufenthalt in Berlin.* 2 vols. Memoirenbibliothek. Stuttgart, 1901.

Thillay 2002
Alain Thillay. *Le Faubourg Saint-Antoine et ses "faux ouvriers": La Liberté du travail à Paris aux XVIIe et XVIIIe siècles.* Paris, 2002.

Tinagli 2001
Paola Tinagli. "Claiming a Place in History: Giorgio Vasari's *Ragionamenti* and the Primacy of the Medici." In *The Cultural Politics of Duke Cosimo I de' Medici,* edited by Konrad Eisenbichler, pp. 63–76. Aldershot, 2001.

Tiziano 2006
Tiziano e il ritratto di corte da Raffaello ai Carracci. Exh. cat., Museo di Capodimonte. Naples, 2006.

Toderi 1993
Giuseppe Toderi. *Ritratti medicei in cera: Modelli di medaglie di Antonio Selvi, MDCCXXXIX.* Florence, 1993.

Tongiorgi Tomasi 1993
Lucia Tongiorgi Tomasi. *I ritratti di piante di Iacopo Ligozzi.* Ospedaletto, 1993.

Tongiorgi Tomasi and Hirschauer 2002
Lucia Tongiorgi Tomasi and Gretchen A. Hirschauer. *The Flowering of Florence: Botanical Art for the Medici.* Exh. cat., Nationl Gallery of Art. Washington, D.C., 2002.

Tosi 1997
Alessandro Tosi. *Inventare la realtà: Giuseppe Zocchi e la Toscana del Settecento.* Le stanze toscane. Florence, 1997.

Treasures from the Royal Collection 1988
Treasures from the Royal Collection: The Queen's Gallery, Buckingham Palace. Exh. cat. London, 1988.

Treasury in the Residenz Munich 1988
The Treasury in the Residenz Munich: Official Guide. 5th ed. Munich, 1988.

Le Triomphe du maniérisme européen 1955
Le Triomphe du maniérisme européen de Michel-Ange au Gréco. Exh. cat., Rijksmuseum. Amsterdam, 1955.

Trubinov 1996
Iu. V. Trubinov. *Stroganov Palace.* [In Russian.] Saint Petersburg, 1996.

Truman 1991
Charles Truman. *The Gilbert Collection of Goldboxes.* Los Angeles, 1991.

Tuena 1988
Filippo Tuena. "Appunti per la storia del commesso romano: Il 'franciosino' maestro di tavole e il cardinale Giovanni Ricci." *Antologia di belle arti,* n.s., nos. 33–34 (1988), pp. 54–69. Volume titled *Il Neoclassicismo I.*

Tuena 1992a
Filippo Tuena. "Cosimo III and Gian Gastone: The End of the Dynasty." In Anna Maria Massinelli and Filippo Tuena, *Treasures of the Medici,* pp. 175–229. London, 1992.

Tuena 1992b
Filippo Tuena. "The First Medici: Humanist Collecting." In Anna Maria Massinelli and Filippo Tuena, *Treasures of the Medici,* pp. 17–55. New York, 1992.

Turchia 2006
Turchia: 7000 anni di storia. Exh. cat., Palazzo Quirinale. Rome, 2006.

Turpin 2001
Adriana Turpin. "Filling the Void: The Development of Beckford's Taste and the Market in Furniture." In *William Beckford, 1760–1844: An Eye for the Magnificent,* edited by Derek E. Ostergard, pp. 177–201. Exh. cat., Bard Graduate Center for Studies in the Decorative Arts, Design, and Culture, New York. New Haven, 2001.

Turpin 2006
Adriana Turpin. "The New World Collections of Duke Cosimo I de' Medici and Their Role in the Creation of a *Kunst-* and *Wunderkammer* in the Palazzo Vecchio." In Evans and Marr 2006, pp. 63–85.

Twilight of the Medici 1974
The Twilight of the Medici: Late Baroque Art in Florence, 1670–1743. Exh. cat., Detroit Institute of Arts; Palazzo Pitti, Florence. Detroit and Florence, 1974. [Italian ed.: *Gli ultimi Medici: Il tardo barocco a Firenze, 1670–1743.* Florence, 1974.]

Unter einer Krone 1997
Unter einer Krone: Kunst und Kultur der sächsisch-polnischen Union. Exh. cat., Dresdner Schloss. Leipzig, 1997.

Untermann 2003
Matthias Untermann. "'Primus lapis fundamentum deponitur': Kunsthistorische Überlegungen zur Funktion der Grundsteinlegung im Mittelalter." In *Cistercienser: Brandenburgische Zeitschrift rund um das cisterciensische Erbe* 6, no. 23 (2003), pp. 5–18.

Valeriani 1988
Roberto Valeriani. "Il Real Laboratorio delle pietre dure di Napoli (1737–1861)." In Giusti 1988, pp. 250–53.

Vasari 1568 (1878–85 ed.)
Giorgio Vasari. *Le vite de' più eccellenti pittori,*

scultori ed architettori. Florence, 1568. 1878–85 ed.: Edited by Gaetano Milanese. 9 vols. Florence, 1878–85.

Vasari 1568 (1962–66 ed.)
Giorgio Vasari. *Le vite de' più eccellenti pittori, scultori ed architettori.* Florence, 1568. 1962–66 ed.: Edited by Giovanni Previtali. 8 vols. Milan, 1962–66.

Vasari 1588 (1906 ed.)
Giorgio Vasari. *Ragionamenti del sig. cavaliere Giorgio Vasari, pittore et architetto aretino, sopra le invenzioni da lui dipinte in Firenze nel palazzo di loro Altezze Serenissime.* Florence, 1588. Reprinted in Giorgio Vasari, *Le vite de' più eccellenti pittori, scultori ed architettori,* edited by Gaetano Milanese, vol. 8, pp. 5–225. Florence, 1906.

Vasari 1762
Giorgio Vasari. *Ragionamenti del signor cavaliere Giorgio Vasari, pittore e architetto aretino, sopra le invenzioni da lui dipinte in Firenze nel palazzo di loro Altezze Serenissime.* 2nd ed. Arezzo, 1762.

Venturelli 2001
Paola Venturelli. "A proposito di un recente articolo sugli 'Scala e altri cristallai milanesi.' Con notizie circa un'opera di Annibale Fontana." *Nuova rivista storica* 85, no. 1 (January–April 2001), pp. 135–44.

Venturelli 2005
Paola Venturelli. *Le collezioni Gonzaga.* [Vol. 12], *Cammei, cristalli, pietre dure, oreficerie, cassettine, stipetti: Intorno all'elenco dei beni del 1626–1627 da Guglielmo a Vincenzo II Gonzaga.* Cinisello Balsamo (Milan), 2005.

Verborgene Schätze der Skulpturensammlung **1992**
Verborgene Schätze der Skulpturensammlung. Exh. cat., Albertinum. Dresden, 1992.

Verlet 1990
Pierre Verlet. *Le Mobilier royal français.* Vol. 4, *Meubles de la Couronne conservés en Europe et aux États-Unis.* Paris, 1990.

Versailles et les tables royales **1993**
Versailles et les tables royales en Europe, XVIIème–XIXème siècles. Exh. cat., Musée National des Châteaux de Versailles et de Trianon. Paris, 1993.

Vincent 1987
Clare Vincent. "Prince Karl I of Liechtenstein's Pietre Dure Tabletop." *Metropolitan Museum Journal* 22 (1987), pp. 157–78.

Visser Travagli 1991
Anna Maria Visser Travagli. "Gian Maria Riminaldi e il museo universitario." In *La rinascita del sapere: Libri e maestri dello studio ferrarese,* edited by Patrizia Castelli, pp. 486–92. Venice, 1991.

Voet 1974
Elias Voet Jr. *Nederlandse gould- en zilvermerken.* 7th ed. The Hague, 1974.

Voigt 1999
Jochen Voigt. *Reliefintarsien aus Eger für die Kunstkammern Europas.* Exh. cat., Grassimuseum, Leipzig. Halle an der Saale, 1999.

"Voyage des ambassadeurs de Siam en France" 1686
"Voyage des ambassadeurs de Siam en France." *Mercure galant,* September 1686, pt. 2 (suppl.).

Waddy 1990
Patricia Waddy. *Seventeenth-Century Roman Palaces: Use and the Art of the Plan.* New York and Cambridge, Mass., 1990.

Walker and Hammond 1999
Stefanie Walker and Frederick Hammond, eds. *Life and the Arts in the Baroque Palaces of Rome: Ambiente Barocco.* Exh. cat., Bard Graduate Center for Studies in the Decorative Arts, Design, and Culture. New York, 1999.

Walpole 1960
Horace Walpole. *Horace Walpole's Correspondence with Sir Horace Mann.* Edited by W. S. Lewis, Warren Hunting Smith, and George L. Lam. Vol. 4. The Yale Edition of Horace Walpole's Correspondence 20. New Haven, 1960.

Wardropper 2001
Ian Wardropper. "Collecting European Sculpture at the Art Institute of Chicago." *Apollo* 154 (September 2001), pp. 3–12.

Warren 2005
Jeremy Warren. Review of *Johann Baptist Fickler: Das Inventar der Münchner herzoglichen Kunstkammer von 1598,* edited by Pieter Diemer, with Elke Bujok and Dorothea Diemer. *Journal of the History of Collections* 17, no. 2 (2005), pp. 241–42.

Watson 1960
F. J. B. Watson. "G. A. Giachetti and the Decoration of French Furniture with Pietri Commessi." *Burlington Magazine* 102 (June 1960), p. 265.

Watson 1969
F. J. B. Watson. "The Craftsmanship of the Ancien Régime." *Apollo* 90 (September 1969), pp. 180–89.

Watson and Dauterman 1970
F. J. B. Watson and Carl Christian Dauterman. *The Wrightsman Collection.* Vol. 3. The Metropolitan Museum of Art. New York, 1970.

Watzdorf 1962
Erna von Watzdorf. *Johann Melchior Dinglinger: Der Goldschmied des deutschen Barock.* 2 vols. Berlin, 1962.

Watzdorf 1972
Erna von Watzdorf. "Der Dresdner Edelstein-schneider Johann Christoph Hübner um 1665 bis 1739." *Zeitschrift des deutschen Vereins für Kunstwissenschaft* 26, nos. 1–4 (1972), pp. 15–42.

Weigelt 1931
Hilde Weigelt. "Florentiner Mosaik in Halbedelsteinen." *Belvedere* 10 (January–June 1931), pp. 166–77.

Weinhold 2000
Ulrike Weinhold. *Emailmalerei an Augsburger Goldschmiedearbeiten von 1650 bis 1750.* Forschungshefte, Bayerisches Nationalmuseum 16. Munich, 2000.

Welch 1985
Stuart Cary Welch. *India: Art and Culture, 1300–1900.* Exh. cat., The Metropolitan Museum of Art. New York, 1985.

Wells 2004
Colin Michael Wells. *The Roman Empire.* 2nd ed. Cambridge, Mass., 2004.

Wentzel 1972
Hans Wentzel. "Das byzantinische Erbe der ottonischen Kaiser: Hypothesen über den Brautschatz der Theophano." *Aachener Kunstblätter* 43 (1972), pp. 11–96.

Wenzel Jamnitzer **1985**
Wenzel Jamnitzer und die Nürnberger Goldschmiedekunst, 1500–1700: Goldschmiedearbeiten—Entwürfe, Modelle, Medaillen, Ornamentstiche, Schmuck, Porträts. Exh. cat., Germanisches Nationalmuseum Nürnberg. Munich, 1985.

Westermann-Angerhausen 1995
Hiltrud Westermann-Angerhausen. "Did Theophano Leave Her Mark on the Ottonian Sumptuary Arts?" In Davids 1995, pp. 244–64.

Westminster Abbey **1972**
Westminster Abbey. Radnor, Pa., 1972.

Williamson 1910
George Charles Williamson, comp. *Catalogue of the Collection of Jewels and Precious Works of Art: The Property of J. Pierpont Morgan.* London, 1910.

Wilson 1983
Gillian Wilson. *Selections from the Decorative Arts in the J. Paul Getty Museum.* Malibu, 1983.

Wilson 1985
Gillian Wilson. "A Pair of Cabinets for Louis XVI's Bedroom at Saint-Cloud: Their Present Appearance." *Furniture History* 21 (1985), pp. 39–47.

Wilson 2007
Gillian Wilson. "A Clock, a Coffer, and Their Covers." *Furniture History* 43 (2007), pp. 237–43.

Wilson and Hess 2001
Gillian Wilson and Catherine Hess. *Summary Catalogue of European Decorative Arts in the J. Paul Getty Museum.* Los Angeles, 2001.

Windisch-Graetz 1983
Franz Windisch-Graetz. *Möbel Europas.* Vol. 2,

Renaissance und Manierismus, vom 15. Jahrhundert bis in die erste Hälfte des 17. Jahrhunderts. Munich, 1983.

Winkelmann 1697
Johann-Just Winkelmann. *Gründliche und wahrhafte Beschreibung der Fürstenthümer Hessen und Hersfeld.* Bremen, 1697.

Wittkower 1966
Rudolf Wittkower. *Gian Lorenzo Bernini: The Sculptor of the Roman Baroque.* 2nd ed. London, 1966.

Wixom 1997
William D. Wixom. "Byzantine Art and the Latin West." In *The Glory of Byzantium: Art and Culture of the Middle Byzantine Era, A.D. 843–1261,* edited by Helen C. Evans and William D. Wixom, pp. 434–49. Exh. cat., The Metropolitan Museum of Art. New York, 1997.

Wolf 1991
Gunther Wolf, ed. *Kaiserin Theophanu, Prinzessin aus der Fremde: Des Westreichs Grosse Kaiserin.* Weimar, 1991.

Wolvesperges 2000
Thibaut Wolvesperges. *Le Meuble français en laque au XVIIIᵉ siècle.* Paris and Brussels, 2000.

Young 1996
Hilary Young. "A Drawing from the Circle of James Cox, Possibly by Charles Magniac." *Burlington Magazine* 138 (June 1996), pp. 402–4.

Zahn 1933
Robert Zahn. *Das Fürstengrab von Hassleben.* Pt. 2, *Die Silberteller von Hassleben und Augst.* Römisch-Germanische Forschungen 7. Berlin, 1933.

Zambelli 1962
D'Alma Folco Zambelli. "Contributo a Carlo Giuseppe Flipart." *Arte antica e moderna,* no. 18 (April–June 1962), pp. 186–99.

Zehnder 1982
Frank Günter Zehnder, ed. *Die Heiligen drei Könige: Darstellung und Verehrung.* Exh. cat., Wallraf-Richartz-Museum. Cologne, 1982.

Zimmer 1971
Jürgen Zimmer. *Joseph Heintz der Ältere als Maler.* Weissenhorn, 1971.

Zimmermann 1905
Heinrich Zimmermann. "Das Inventar der Prager Schatz- und Kunstkammer vom 6. Dezember 1621." *Jahrbuch der Kunsthistorischen Sammlungen des Allerhöchsten Kaiserhauses* 25 (1905), pp. XIII–LXXV.

Zobi 1853
Antonio Zobi. *Notizie storiche sull'origine e progressi dei lavori di commesso in pietre dure che si eseguiscono nell'I. e R. stabilimento di Firenze.* 2nd ed. Florence, 1853.

Index

Page numbers in **boldface** are those of the main catalogue entry and illustration; page numbers in *italics* are those of figure illustrations. Catalogued objects are indexed under the exact name used in the catalogue entry heading (e.g., "cup with cover"); all page references to the object are gathered at this main index entry. Where an object is listed as a subentry, only the page numbers of the catalogue entry are provided. While provenance lists are not indexed, some information taken from them is included here and is noted with an asterisk.

393

Domenico di Polo, 26–27n26

Domitian (by Johann Bernhard Schwarzenburger), 260

Donatello
Habakkuk, Florence Campanile, 148
Pazzi Madonna, 72

Donnini, Gaspare, 23

Doria, Agostino, doge of Genoa, miniature of, 124

Doria, Andrea, cameo of, 83n11

Dosio, Giovanni Antonio (1533–1609), 14, 166; design for a tabletop [fig. 16], 14, *14*, 172

dove motif, 184

Drausch, Valentin, 61, 69n27

drawing for a hardstone tabletop [fig. 45], 43, 44

drawing for a hardstone tabletop [fig. 47], 44, *44*, 274

drawing for a hardstone tabletop [fig. 48], 44, *44*

drawing for a hardstone tabletop [fig. 49], 44, *44*

drawing from a design book of an octagonal table with stand [fig. 113], 125, *125*

drawings of a cabinet (by Claude François Julliot) [fig. 97], 89, *89*, 90, 93n30

Dresden, 58, 66, 68, 80, 260, 262; (1725–30) bust of a woman [cat. no. 87], 73, **256–57**

Dresden *Kunstkammer*, 59

drinking set (Peterhof Lapidary Works) [cat. no. 141], **350–51**

Dubois, André, 42

Dubois, Jacques (master 1742), 88

Dubois, Jean, 42

Duke Cosimo I de' Medici (cameo) [fig. 75], 72, *73*

Duke Cosimo I de' Medici (by Romolo di Francesco Ferrucci del Tadda), 150, 173n2; model for (by Domenico Passignano), 150, 172, 173n2

Duomo, Florence, facade, 188

Dürer, Albrecht, 142

Duvaux, Lazard (ca. 1703–1758), 89

Eagle Cameo (Roman, ca. 27 B.C.), 55

ebony, 80

ecclesiastical and devotional objects, 10, 56. *See also* episcopal throne [fig. 9]; Eucharistic throne of exposition [cat. no. 16]; ex-voto of Cosimo II de' Medici [cat. no. 35]; prie-dieu made for the electress Palatine [cat. no. 55]; *and entries at* holy-water stoup [cat. nos. 18, 58]; *and at* reliquary [cat. nos. 8, 36, 56, 57; figs. 58, 89]

ecclesiastical rings, 5

Eck, Adam (1604–1664), 196; attributed to, casket [cat. no. 53], **196–97**

Edelcrantz, Abraham Niklas (1754–1821), 350n5

Eger, Bohemia (now Chêb, Czech Republic), 80, 196: casket [cat. no. 53], **196–97**

Eger marquetry, 87, 196, 250, 260, 264, 369

Egypt, 3, 5, 354
(2nd millenium B.C.), sphinx of Senwosret III [cat. no. 1], **104**
(Fatimid period, late 10th century), vase [fig. 12], *9*, 10

Egyptian alabaster. See *Farnese Table* [cat no. 10]

Egyptian motifs, 354

eight polished samples from Heinrich Taddel's stone collection [cat. no. 146], **362**

Elector Johann Wilhelm. See cabinet made for the elector Palatine [cat. no. 59]

Eleonora de Toledo, 218; in cameo depicting Cosimo I de' Medici and his family [cat. no. 13], 71, **128–29**

Elijah and the Angel (Galleria dei Lavori) [cat. no. 29], 20, 152, **154–55**, 156, 166

Élisa Bonaparte, grand duchess of Tuscany (1777–1820), 24, 316n4, 317

Elizabeth Petrovna I, empress of Russia (r. 1741–62), 350n6

Eltz zu Kempenich, Philipp Karl, Reichsgraf von (1665–1743), 266; cat. no. 93

Emanuele Tedesco, 153, 156, 156n4
design by, *Jonah after Escaping from the Whale* [cat. no. 30], 153, **156–57**
design by, *Samson and the Lion*, 154, 156

Emeric, Saint, reliquary. *See* reliquary of Saint Emeric [cat. no. 57]

emperor series, 260. *See also* two statuettes of Roman emperors [cat. no. 89]

Empire style, 90

England, 90–91, 92, 340

Enlightenment, 4, 23, 322

Epiphanius, Bishop, 10

episcopal throne, Santa Balbina, Rome [fig. 9], *8*, 10

Era, Giovanni Battista dell' (1765–1798), 304; figures by, in *View of the Pantheon* [cat. no. 118], **304–5**

Ernst, archduke of Austria (d. 1595), 219

Ernst of Wittelsbach, archbishop and elector of Cologne, 61

Erzgebirge Mountains, 29, 73, 255

Escorial Palace
chapel, 61
Virgin and Child (Romolo di Francesco Ferrucci del Tadda after Donatello), 72

Estrées, Gabrielle d', 62

Eucharistic symbols. *See* tabletop depicting Eucharistic symbols [cat. no. 37]

Eucharistic throne of exposition (Rome, ca. 1690; by Domenico Trionfi after a design by Antonio Maria Ricci) [cat. no. 16], 93n9, **134–35**

Eugene of Savoy, Prince, 258, 258n2

Evangelists series, 78, 80, 147–48, 148n1. See also *Saint Matthew* and *Saint Mark* [cat. no. 24]

ewer (France? 14th century; with mounts after a design by Juste-Aurèle Meissonnier) [fig. 96], 88, 89

ex-voto of Cosimo II de' Medici (Galleria dei Lavori; design by Giulio Parigi and perhaps Giovanni Bilivert; mosaic inlay and relief by Michele Castrucci and Gualtieri Cecchi; gem setting and enamel reliefs by Jonas Falk) [cat. no. 35], 20, 73, **164–65**, 203

Fabergé, Peter Carl (1846–1920), 342; cat. no. 137

Fabiano Tedesco, 156; after a design by Emanuele Tedesco, *Jonah after Escaping from the Whale* [cat. no. 30], **156–57**

Falk, Jonas, gem setting and enamel reliefs by, ex-voto of Cosimo II de' Medici [cat. no. 35], **164–65**

Fame (Castrucci workshop, Prague; by Cosimo di Giovanni Castrucci) [cat. no. 71], 32, **228–29**

Farnese, Alessandro, Cardinal, table for, 51n32, 120; cat. no. 10

Farnese Cup, 71

Farnese Palace workshop, Rome, table. See *Farnese Table* [cat. no. 10]

Farnese Table (Farnese Palace workshop; design by Jacopo Barozzi da Vignola; piers by Guglielmo della Porta; top attributed to

Giovanni Mynardo [Jean Ménard]) [cat. no. 10], 14, 15, 29, 51n3, 71, **120–22**, 124, 126, 133, 134, 277

Fatimid dynasty (A.D. 909–1171), 10; vase [fig. 12], 9, 10

Ferdinand I de' Medici (by Pietro Tacca) [fig. 103], 95, *95*

Ferdinand II, Holy Roman emperor (r. 1619–37), 68n21, 234

Ferdinand II, king of the Two Sicilies (r. 1830–59), 322

Ferdinand II of Tirol, archduke of Austria (r. 1564–95), 65, 142n4; coin cabinet of [fig. 95], 87, *87*

Ferdinand III, grand duke of Tuscany (r. 1790–1801, 1814–24), 287, 298, 302, 304, 316n4; cat. nos. 115, 117

Ferdinand IV, king of Naples (r. 1759–1806, 1815–25), 93n38

Ferdinand VI, king of Spain (r. 1746–59), 324n1

Ferri, Gesualdo (1728–documented until 1797), 292; frames designed by, for second Fine Arts series, 292, 294; *Allegory of Music* [cat. no. 112], **293–94**; *Allegory of Sculpture* [cat. no. 110], **291–92**

Ferroni, Giovanni Battista, 324
base by, console table with a trompe l'oeil top [cat. no. 129], **324–25**
base by, console table with a trompe l'oeil top [fig. 118], 324, *325*

Ferrucci, Francesco (Romolo di Francesco Ferrucci del Tadda) (d. 1621), 148, 179, 182, 184n3
Clement VIII [cat. no. 25], **148–50**, 182
Duke Cosimo I de' Medici (after model by Dominic Passignano), 150, 172, 173n2
Henry IV of France (after model by Santi di Tito), 148, 173n2, 182
panel depicting a vase of flowers [cat. no. 44], **179**, **181**
tabletop attributed to, table celebrating the sea victory at Lepanto [cat. no. 45], 148, **182–84**
Virgin and Child (copy after Donatello, *Pazzi Madonna*), 72
workshop of, 179, 182

Ferrucci, Francesco del Tadda (father of Romolo di Francesco), 184n3

Ferrucci, Matthias, 72; porphyry bust of Cosimo II de' Medici, 72

Fiammingo, Ermanno, portable altar, 140

Fiedler, Johann Gottlob, 93n44

Fig Branch with a Bird of Paradise and Exotic Finches (by Jacopo Ligozzi) [fig. 116], 168, *170*

Fine Arts series (design by Giuseppi Zocchi), 291, 292, 293, 296
designs for (1752–53), 291, 292, 296. See also *Allegory of Sculpture* [cat. no. 111]; *and entries at Allegory of Music* [cat. nos. 113, 114]
first hardstone series (by 1754; for imperial residence, Vienna), 291, 292, 293, 296
second hardstone series (1775–80; for Palazzo Pitti, Florence), 291–92, 293–94, 296. See also *Allegory of Music* [cat. no. 112]; *Allegory of Sculpture* [cat. no. 110]

finials. See pair of bedpost finials [cat. no. 26]

"fish-dragons," 211n2

Fistulator, Blasius (d. 1622), 61, 210

Flagellation of Christ (bronze) [fig. 79], 75, 76, 83n21

Flagellation of Christ (hardstones) [fig. 80], 75–76, *76*, 83n21

flagon (Prague, 3rd quarter of the 14th century) [cat. no. 6]. 29, **110–11**

Photograph and Copyright Credits

Photographs were in most cases provided by the institutions or individuals owning the works and are published with their permission; their courtesy is gratefully acknowledged. Additional information on photograph sources follows.

© Allen Memorial Art Museum, Oberlin College, Oberlin, Ohio: cat. no. 20

© Amministrazione Maria Camilla Pallavicini, Rome, photograph by Giuseppe Schiavinotto: cat. no. 19

© The Art Institute of Chicago: fig. 86

Art Resource, NY, photographs by Erich Lessing: figs. 2, 7

© Bayerisches Nationalmuseum, Munich: cat. nos. 47, 48

Bildarchiv Preussischer Kulturbesitz / Art Resource, NY: cat. no. 52, figs. 66, 122, 126

© Radovan Boček, Prague: fig. 63

© British Museum / Art Resource, NY: fig. 5

© The Trustees of the British Museum: fig. 3

© Christie's Images: fig. 114

© The Cleveland Museum of Art: cat. no. 17

Comune di Roma, Sovraintendenza ai Beni Culturali: fig. 6

DeAgostini Picture Library, photographs by Alfredo Dagli Orti: cat. nos. 36, 64

Gabinetto Fotografico, Soprintendenza Speciale per il Patrimonio Storico Artistico ed Etno-antropologico e per il Polo Museale della città di Firenze, su concessione del Ministero per i Beni e le Attività Culturali: cat. nos. 115, 130, figs. 14, 16, 22, 24, 74, 88, 116

© The J. Paul Getty Museum, Los Angeles: cat. nos. 25, 51, 79, 100, 135

© Stefano Giraldi, Pistoia: fig. 10

© Grünes Gewölbe, Staatliche Kunstsammlungen Dresden: cat. nos. 85–87, 89, 146, fig. 25

Herzog Anton Ulrich-Museum, Kunstmuseum des Landes Niedersachsen, Braunschweig: fig. 23

© Historisches Museum, Basel, photograph by HMB P. Portner: fig. 8

The Huntington Library, Art Collections, and Botanical Gardens, San Marino, California: fig. 99

© Ebba Koch, University of Vienna: fig. 117

© Kunsthistorisches Museum, Vienna: cat. nos. 66–68, 72, 74, 75, 77, figs. 1, 4, 31–33, 36–39, 62, 92, 95

Landesmedienzentrum, Stuttgart: fig. 91

© Lobkowicz Collections, Prague: fig. 115

© Lukas—Art in Flanders VZW: fig. 13

The Metropolitan Museum of Art, New York, The Photograph Studio: cat. nos. 1–6, 18, 41, 63, 80, 88, 101, 121, 126, 137, 138, figs. 75, 79, 94, 113; photographs by Bruce Schwarz, cat. nos. 10, 14, 15, 21; photographs by Peter Zeray, cat. nos. 62, 96, 97, 102, 139

Ministero per i Beni e le Attività Culturali
    Archivio dell'Opificio delle Pietre Dure di Firenze: cat. nos. 44, 116
    Direzione Generale per il Patrimonio Storico Artistico ed Etnoantropologico, Soprintendenza Speciale per il Polo Museale Romano: fig. 10
    Soprintendenza Speciale per il Polo Museale Napoletano: cat. no. 128, fig. 76

Musée des Arts Décoratifs, Paris, photograph by Jean Tholance: fig. 97

© Museo Nacional del Prado, Madrid: cat. nos. 127, 129, figs. 18, 30, 118

© Museumslandschaft Hessen Kassel, Kassel: cat. nos. 76, 81–84, fig. 85

© Národní Galerie, Prague, 2007: fig. 40

© Opera di Santa Maria del Fiore, Florence, photograph by Nicolò Orsi Bataglini: cat. no. 8

© Palazzo Quirinale, Rome, photographs by Mauro Coen: cat. no. 11

© Patrimonio Nacional, Madrid: fig. 26

Procuratoria di San Marco, Venice: fig. 12

Réunion des Musées Nationaux / Art Resource, NY: cat. nos. 94, 99, 131, fig. 43; photographs by Daniel Arnaudet, cat. nos. 98, 106, fig. 41; photographs by Jean-Gilles Berizzi, figs. 44, 57; photographs by Gérard Blot/Jean Schormans, cat. nos. 40, 95, fig. 42

Dieter Ritzenhofen: cat. no. 93

The Royal Collection, London © Her Majesty Queen Elizabeth II: cat. nos. 132, 134

© Royal Collections, Stockholm, photograph by Alexis Daflos: fig. 98

Scala / Art Resource, NY: figs. 15, 60, 102, 103

Soprintendenza per i Beni Architettonici e per il Paesaggio, per il Patrimonio Storico, Artistico ed Etnoantropologico per le provincie di Firenze, Prato e Pistoia: cat. nos. 26–32, 50, 58, 71, 108–12, 114, 117, 118, 147, figs. 27, 73

© The State Hermitage Museum, Saint Petersburg: cat. nos. 141–43

© 2008 State Russian Museum, Saint Petersburg: fig. 121

From Hans Sundblom, Ingemar Tunander, and Gabriel Uggla, *Porfyr: En utställning kring föremål från Älvdalens Gamla Porfyrverk* (Stockholm, 1985): fig. 120

Uppsala University Art Collections, Sweden: cat. no. 78

V&A Images / Victoria and Albert Museum, London: fig. 56

Victoria and Albert Museum, London / Art Resource, NY: cat. nos. 43, 136